SOTHIS PRESS

Sothis Press aims to completely reimagine the public domain book with an emphasis on universal access to captivatingly designed print editions. We believe that technology will enable every single book ever published to be perpetually accessible in beautiful print form. Sothis is beauty in ubiquity.

www.sothis.press
1 Waterhouse Square, London, ECIN 2ST

South African Legal Dictionary

Containing Most of the English, Latin and Dutch Terms, Phrases and Maxims Used in Roman-Dutch Law and South African Legal Practice; Together With Definitions Occurring in the Statutes of the South African Colonies

William Henry Somerset Bell

SOTHIS PRESS

ISBN 978-1-0365-0209-6

This edition is published by
Sothis Press © 2023. The company
is registered in England and Wales.
The Company Number is 14900389.

SOUTH AFRICAN LEGAL DICTIONARY,

CONTAINING MOST OF THE ENGLISH, LATIN AND DUTCH TERMS, PHRASES AND MAXIMS USED IN ROMAN-DUTCH LAW AND SOUTH AFRICAN LEGAL PRACTICE,

TOGETHER WITH

DEFINITIONS OCCURRING IN THE STATUTES OF THE SOUTH AFRICAN COLONIES.

BY

W. H. SOMERSET BELL,

ATTORNEY OF THE SUPREME COURTS OF THE TRANSVAAL AND CAPE COLONY.

AFRICAN BOOK COMPANY, LIMITED,
GRAHAMSTOWN, CAPE COLONY.
1910.

PREFACE.

It is with some diffidence that I venture to place this work before the public; but for many years I have been convinced that a dictionary of South African legal terms and phrases was much needed. When a student I frequently found myself hopelessly at sea in my reading for want of some book in which I could find a definition of legal expressions of which I did not know and could not ascertain the meaning. A reference to legal dictionaries published in England, though of much benefit, did not help me in any way in regard to our Roman-Dutch legal terms. I have since very often observed the same difficulty existing with other students and lawyers. A little more than three years ago I commenced this book, and have since devoted most of my spare time to its compilation, in the hope that it may supply the want above referred to. As the work proceeded it occurred to me that its value might be enhanced by the addition of definitions occurring in the statutes of the South African colonies, and this I have done. Some of them may be unimportant, but I think it can be claimed that they are fairly complete.

In many instances I have taken over definitions

from text-book writers in preference to framing a definition of my own, for obviously the definition of a specialist will be found more accurate than any I could frame. In such case, where definitions are taken over they are printed within inverted commas and the reference is given. I desire to express my indebtedness to the authors of the text-books quoted, and especially to Sir Andries Maasdorp, whose work, the *Institutes of Cape Law*, has been most helpful. Should the student desire to pursue any subject further, he cannot do better than refer to the text-books cited.

Such words and phrases as have received judicial interpretation in South Africa have also been inserted.

Probably the most laborious part of the work has been the finding of the words and phrases; this has necessitated reading nearly all the South African reports, statutes and text-books, besides a number of those published in England.

I am grateful to Mr. Justice J. G. Kotzé, Judge-President of the Eastern Districts' Court, who has checked the Dutch words, many of which he has suggested and some of which he has written. He has also very kindly read over the whole of the proofs of this book. It is partly due to his encouragement that the Dictionary has been completed.

I avail myself, too, of this opportunity to thank Mr. W. Boyd Berry, LL.B., of Johannesburg, who has given me great assistance. He has written the larger portion of the Latin words and phrases, besides reading and checking proofs. Dr. P. C. Anders, LL.D., has also contributed a number of Latin words and phrases, and to him likewise I desire to record my gratitude.

W. H. S. BELL.

JOHANNESBURG, *May*, 1910.

TABLE OF CASES.

TABLE OF CASES.

ERRATA.

P. 4, *sub voce* ABOLITIE, 2nd line, for *violate* read *annul.*
P. 35, *sub voce* ALLEGANS SUAM, &c., for *turpitudinam* read *turpitudinem.*

SOUTH AFRICAN LEGAL DICTIONARY.

A contrario sensu, in the opposite sense; on the other hand.

A fortiori, for the stronger reason; so much the more.

A mensa, thoro et communione bonorum, from board, bed and community of goods. When the conduct of a spouse is such as to make further cohabitation with him or her wholly insupportable, the other spouse is entitled to the benefit of a decree of judicial separation (*Poggenpoel* v. *Poggenpoel*, 15 S.C. 38). The effect of a decree of separation *à mensa et thoro* is that, though the marriage remains in force, neither party can compel the other to live with him or her; but if no order has been made regarding the property each party retains his or her rights of property unimpaired (*Wessels* v. *Wessels*, 12 S.C. 465). Attempts at reconciliation may always continue to be made (Grotius, 1, 5, 20).

A morte testatoris, from the death of the testator. A legacy does not vest until the death of the testator, and, therefore, if the legatee predeceases the testator the legacy lapses and will not go to the legatee's heir. The phrase is used to distinguish between rights under a will which vest upon the testator's death and rights of which the vesting is postponed to a later time.

A pari, equally; in like manner.

A priori, from what goes before, as distinguished from *à posteriori*, from what follows.

A tempore morae. *See* MORA.

A verbis legis non est recedendum, to depart from the words of a statute is not permitted. Where the language of a statute is clear and unambiguous, it must be read according to its necessary meaning. In such a case the statute is not open to construction, and the fact that the court might consider something else to have been the intention of the legislature will not justify an interpretation different from the meaning of the words actually employed (*De Villiers* v. *Cape Divisional Council*, Buch. 1875, p. 64; 2 App. Cas. 567; *Hess* v. *The State*, 2 Off. Rep. at pp. 117 *et seq.*; *Robinson* v. *Roper, N.O.*, 3 H.C.G. at p. 205; *Beedle & Co., in liquidation*, v. *Bowley*, 12 S.C. 401; *Moss* v. *Sissons and McKenzie*, [1907] E.D.C. 157). *See* ARGUMENTUM AB INCONVENIENTI, &c., and UT RES MAGIS VALEAT QUAM PEREAT.

A vinculo matrimonii, from the bonds of matrimony; divorce. The effect of a decree of divorce is to rescind the marriage contract altogether. The only grounds for such a decree are adultery and malicious desertion (*Wessels* v. *Wessels*, 12 S.C. 470).

Aafga (D.), *See* AZIG.

Aanbooedt (D.), appropriation, retraction (*retractus*).

Aandeel (D.), a share or portion. The term *aandeel* (pl. *aandeelen*) is usually, in South Africa, applied to shares in joint-stock companies. *Aandeelen aan toonder* are bearer shares; *volopbetaalde aandeelen* are fully paid up shares; *aandeel-certificaten* are share certificates; *aandeelhouders* are shareholders; *aandeelschuldige* is a contributory or a person who is liable in respect of shares that have not been fully paid up.

Aanlegger (D.), the plaintiff in an action. *See* EISCHER.

Aanmaning (D.), demand. *See* MINNELIJKE AANMANING.

Aanvrouwe (D.), great-grandmother.

Aanwas (1) (D.), the equivalent of the *jus accrescendi* of the Roman law. See Van Leeuwen's *Comm.* 3, 6, 7 and 8.

(2) (D.), Alluvion. Decker in a note to Van Leeuwen's *Comm.* (Kotzé's trans. vol. 1, p. 175) says: "Alluvion is of two kinds, *aanwas* and *aanwerp*. The former is termed *discretae, i.e.* those separated from the land by a portion of the water; and the latter *alluviones continuae, i.e.* those which are attached to the land."

Aanwerp (D.), a form of alluvion. *See* AANWAS.

Aasdoms, Aasdomsregt (D.), a term derived from *aesgadoem*, which in old Frisian law meant a decision of the *Aesge* or *Baljuw* (Bailiff or Sheriff) (Van Leeuwen's *Comm.* 1, 2, 23). *Aasdomsregt* denotes the Frisian law of succession *ab intestato*, having for its principle that "the nearest blood succeeds to the property" (*het naaste bloed erft het goed*). Distinguished from the *Schependoms* law of succession (the law of Zeeland), according to which "the property must return from whence it came" (*goed moet gaan van waar het gekomen is:* Van Leeuwen's *Comm.* 3, 12, 8).

"The principle of Frisian law is that *the nearest blood succeeds to the property*, it being well understood that descendants are preferred to ascendants (for there is an old proverb that *property does not readily climb*), and ascendants to collaterals, for the relationship of collaterals is derived from ascendants. The term *nearest* was interpreted strictly, so that no representation was allowed, and the children of a deceased child could not inherit as long as there were any children in the first degree to be found. This law, also, took no account of the source from whence the property came; but if a child who had inherited from his father died before his mother, the property so inherited went to the mother, and remained thenceforth on that side" (Grotius' *Introduction*, Maasdorp's trans. 2, 28, 3; see also Kersteman's *Woordenboek*, vol. 1, p. 10).

Ab initio, from the beginning.

Ab intestato, from a person dying intestate. If a person dies without leaving a valid will his property devolves according to a certain line of succession fixed by law. Those of this line who acquire the property, called in Roman law *heredes legitimi*, or legal heirs, as distinguished from heirs appointed such by will, are said to succeed *ab intestato*.

Ab irae impetu, under the impulse of anger. *See* IN RIXA.

Ab origine, from the origin or beginning.

Abakweta Dance, a dance common among natives throughout South Africa to celebrate the circumcision of the young men. The ceremony commences by the young men being removed from the kraal to a neighbouring kloof or other convenient and secluded spot, in charge of a selected man, who performs the rite of circumcision; there a hut is built for their accommodation during the continuance of the ceremony, which extends over three or four months, and sometimes even longer. The dance is held at the kraal in celebration of the occasion; it is also a feast, and friends of the parties concerned attend it from long distances. The dance is more pronounced and lively on the days of the commencement and the termination of the ceremony. After the young circumcised men have remained in seclusion for the appointed period they emerge from their retreat, but without any clothing or blankets; the hut and all it contained, including clothing, and blankets, is burnt; they are then regarded as men. The *abakweta dance* has ceased to be a custom among the Zulus, but among other native tribes it is a confirmed custom and an important occasion. In the Cape Colony the *abakweta dance* is prohibited in certain districts proclaimed and to be proclaimed by the Governor under Act 16 of 1891 (C.C.); this Act is extended to the district of Elliott by Proclamation 396 of 1896.

Abandon, to relinquish one's interest in some person, thing or right; to give up. In the Natal Mines and Collieries Act (43 of 1899, sec. 4), the term *abandon,* "when used in reference to a claim or holding, shall mean to summarily determine the right to and interest in such claim or holding."

Abatement, mitigation; removal; allowance. *See* WITHOUT ANY DEDUCTION OR ABATEMENT WHATEVER.

"By common law [in England] where one of two joint contractors was sued alone, the defendant had the right to compel the joinder of the other by means of a plea in *abatement*" (*per* Lord ESHER, M.R., in *Wilson, Sons & Co.* v. *Balcarres Brook S.S. Co.*, [1893] 1 Q.B. at p. 426); but "under the Judicature Act pleas in *abatement* are abolished" (*ibid.* at p. 427).

Abatement of a nuisance means the removal of the nuisance.

Abattoir, a public slaughter-house. *See* SLAUGHTER-HOUSE.

Abbreviation, a shortened form; a contraction.

Abduction, the taking away of a girl under the age of twenty-one years without the consent of her parents or guardians; such taking is a crime (*Queen* v. *Schut,* 1 A.C. 37). See Native Territories' Penal Code (Act 24 of 1886 (C.C.)), sec. 169; *Queen* v. *Buchenroeder* (13 S.C. 175); *Queen* v. *Wilderman* (6 S.C. 295); *Rex* v. *Njova* ([1906] E.D.C. 71); *Barnard* v. *Rex* ([1907] T.S. at p. 271).

The common law crime of *abduction* "consists in the taking away of any female under the age of twenty-one years from the custody of her parents, guardians or those having charge of her against their will. The object of the taking away need not necessarily be unlawful carnal connection; but of course it may be—and as a matter of fact it generally is. But under the common law, to take a girl away for the purpose of marrying her would be *abduction*" (*per* INNES, C.J., in *Rex* v. *Roberts,* [1908] T.S. at p. 283).

Abolitie (D.) is a technical term in old Roman-Dutch practice, derived from the Latin word *abolitio,* and signifies to violate; to destroy; to make completely void. It was understood by lawyers to be a means of pardon whereby a criminal sentence, though already pronounced, could be cancelled, with the result that the condemned person by virtue thereof was rehabilitated and restored to his former state (see Kersteman's *Woordenboek,* vols. 1 and 2). Van der Linden in his *Institutes* (Juta's trans. 3rd ed. p. 242), speaking of the different kinds of pardon granted in criminal cases, says: "*Abolition* . . . takes place in all sorts of crimes, and operates as a complete acquittal by reason of a concurrence of very favourable circumstances either in respect of the person committing the act or of the act committed." See also Van Leeuwen's *Comm.* 4, 43, 2.

"About." "The word *about* must be reasonably construed. The construction of the word must largely depend upon the circumstances.

One might be entitled to construe the word *about* much more liberally in one case than in others" (*per* BALE, C.J., in *Bergl & Co.* v. *Trott Bros.*, 24 N.L.R. at p. 510).

As to use of *about* in commercial transactions, see Benjamin on *Sales*, 4th ed. pp. 699 *et seq.*, where a number of cases are referred to. See also *Société Anonyme l'Industrielle Russo-Belge* v. *Scholefield* (7 Com. Cas. 114); *Frangopulo & Co.* v. *Lomas & Co.* (18 T.L.R. 461).

As to use of *about* in Workmen's Compensation Acts, see *Pattison* v. *White & Co., Ltd.* (20 T.L.R. 775): *Fenn* v. *Miller* ([1900] 1 Q.B. 788; 69 L.J. Q.B. 439; 82 L.T. 284; 16 T.L.R. 265); *Owens* v. *Campbell, Ltd.* ([1904] 2 K.B. 60; 73 L.J. K.B. 634; 90 L.T. 811; 20 T.L.R. 459).

Abrogate, to repeal; to annul by competent authority; to become obsolete by disuse. "Any Dutch law which is inconsistent with such well-established and reasonable custom [referring to South African usages], and has not, although relating to matters of frequent occurrence, been distinctly recognised and acted upon by the Supreme Court, may fairly be held to have been *abrogated* by disuse" (*per* DE VILLIERS, C.J., in *Seaville* v. *Colley*, 9 S.C. at p. 44). See also *Salisbury Reef G. M. Co.* v. *British South Africa Co.* (15 S.C. 375); *Parker* v. *Reed* (21 S.C. 496).

Absent, not present in a given place at a given time. See *Garlicke & Holdcroft* v. *Currie* (27 N.L.R. 154).

In the Transvaal Payment of Members of Parliament Act (12 of 1907, sec. 2) "*absent* in respect of a member shall mean *absent* from the House of Parliament, or a committee of which he is a member, during the whole of a working day for any cause other than his own sickness or injury." For the same definition see Act 21 of 1908 (O.R.C.), sec. 2.

"**Absent himself.**" Although there is a difference between the act of "absenting oneself," which is purely voluntary, and the fact of "being absent," which is voluntary or involuntary as the case may be, yet the fact that a person is absent under some strong compulsion, which does not amount to physical necessity, does not necessarily negative the voluntary aspect of his act, or show that he has not "absented himself" (*London and Northern Bank, Ltd.*; *McConnell's* Case, 84 L.T. 557; [1901] 1 Ch. 728; 9 Manson, 91).

Absolutie van de instantie (D.), absolution from the instance. See Van der Linden's *Institutes*, 3, 1, 2, 15. A form of judgment granted, where the plaintiff has not established his claim to the satisfaction of the court, enabling him, on obtaining better evidence, to institute proceedings *de novo*. *See* ABSOLUTION FROM THE INSTANCE.

Absolution from the instance. "By long practice in the courts of South Africa *absolution from the instance* has acquired a wider range than it possessed in the Dutch courts. The latter courts confined this form of judgment to those cases in which a plea in abatement would be successfully pleaded according to the practice of the English courts. In this [Cape] Colony, however, and I believe in the neighbouring States, it has been a constant practice to grant absolution in cases where the plaintiff has not established the facts in support of his case to the satisfaction of the court. At first it was treated as equivalent to a nonsuit, and confined to cases in which evidence had been given for the plaintiff only. In course of time, however, it was extended to cases in which evidence for the defendant had also been given. It was found convenient to have a form of judgment which would enable the plaintiff to take fresh proceedings without exposing himself to a plea of *lis finita*. But it has never been understood that a defendant is bound to accept *absolution from the instance* if the evidence given at the trial is of such a nature as to entitle him to judgment in his favour. In such a case he would, in my opinion, be quite entitled to object to absolution. But the objection should be taken at the time of judgment. In most cases a defendant is perfectly satisfied with absolution, and the judge who grants it would reasonably conclude that the defendant is satisfied if no objection is taken" (*per* De Villiers, C.J., in *Corbridge* v. *Welch*, 9 S.C. at p. 279). See Act 39 of 1896 (N.), sec. 53.

Acceptance means an *acceptance* completed by delivery or notification (sec. 1 of the English Bills of Exchange Act, 1882). The *acceptance* of a bill is the signification by the drawee of his assent to the order of the drawer. An *acceptance* is invalid unless it complies with the following conditions, namely: (*a*) It must be written on the bill and be signed by the drawee (the mere signature of the drawee without additional words is sufficient); (*b*) it must not express that the drawee will perform his promise by any other means than the payment of money (sec. 17 of English Bills of Exchange Act, 1882). Both sections above quoted have been taken over in the Bills of Exchange Acts of the South African colonies; see Act 19 of 1893 (C.C.), secs. 1 and 15; Law 8 of 1887 (N.), secs. 1 and 16: Proclamation 11 of 1902 (T.), secs. 1 and 15; Ordinance 28 of 1902 (O.R.C.), secs. 1 and 15.

Acceptilatio, the release of the debtor from the debt by the creditor without any consideration (Grotius' *Introduction*, 3, 41). An agreement to release a debt, when clearly established, is a good defence to an action brought by the executors of the creditor against the debtor for the recovery of the debt (*Van der Poel's Executors* v. *Malan*, 15 S.C. 70; see also *Duncker* v. *Paddon & Brock, Ltd.*, [1903] T.S. 463).

Acceptor. Under the Bills of Exchange Acts an *acceptor* is a person who accepts a bill (*see* Bill of Exchange), and by accepting it (*a*) engages that he will pay according to the tenor of his acceptance; and (*b*) is precluded from denying to a holder in due course: (1) the existence of the drawer, the genuineness of his signature, and his capacity and authority to draw the bill; (2) in the case of a bill payable to drawer's order, the then capacity of the drawer to indorse, but not the genuineness or validity of his indorsement; (3) in the case of a bill payable to the order of a third person, the existence of the payee and his then capacity to indorse, but not the genuineness or validity of his indorsement. See Act 19 of 1893 (C.C.), sec. 51; Law 8 of 1887 (N.), sec. 53; Proclamation 11 of 1902 (T.), sec. 52; Ordinance 28 of 1902 (O.R.C.), sec. 52; Bills of Exchange Regulations, 23 of 1895 (R.), sec. 52.

Access, approach, or means of approach or admission. Where in granting a decree of judicial separation, the custody of the minor children being given to the mother and the father to have reasonable *access* to the children, the Supreme Court of the Transvaal, on appeal, intimated its opinion that the right of reasonable *access* included the right to take the children for drives under reasonable conditions (*Mitchell* v. *Mitchell*, [1904] T.S. 128).

Accession, Accessio, or **Accessie** (D.), takes place when the more valuable of two things which are joined together takes to itself the less valuable (Grotius' *Introduction*, 2, 9, 1; see also Van Leeuwen's *Comm.* Kotzé's trans. vol. 1, p. 175). "*Accession* is the process by which one thing accedes or becomes added to or incorporated with another in such a way that it is regarded as forming part and parcel of the latter, and becomes by such process the property of the owner of the same" (Maasdorp's *Institutes*, vol. 1, p. 41). It takes place either by the action of nature or by the act of man. As examples of the former class may be mentioned the offspring of animals, alluvion, and formation of islands in rivers. Examples of the latter class are *specificatio*, confusion, building, planting, sowing, writing, painting.

Accessory. (1) The lesser object or thing which accedes to a principal object or thing; when these are joined together they cause what is called "accession." *See* ACCESSION.

(2) In criminal law the expression *accessory* signifies some person who was not present at the commission of a crime, but who in some way aided, or was concerned in its perpetration, either before or after the act.

No one can be found guilty as an *accessory* to a crime unless it is first proved that such crime has actually been committed either by a known or an unknown person as principal wrong-doer (*State* v. *Verkouteren*, 1 Off. Rep. Webber's trans. p. 192).

Accident, a fortuitous and unexpected happening. But an effect, although fortuitous and unexpected as regards one person, may as regards another be the result of negligence. For, "suppose a man were to go blindfold along the street and to run against something, could any one say he met with an *accident?* He would do an act that would be very likely to lead to a mischief. It is different with the person who might suffer by such act; *he* might fairly say that he met with an *accident*—a peril which is liable to every man who goes out in the road and meets with negligent people" (*per* BRAMWELL, B., in *Lloyd* v. *Gen. Iron Screw Collier Co.*, 33 L.J. Ex. 269).

It is not an *accident* within the meaning of sec. 1 of the Workmen's Compensation Act, 1897 (E.), if injury or death results from the rupturing of a blood-vessel through internal weakness (*Henry* v. *White*, [1900] 1 Q.B. 481; 81 L.T.R. 767; 69 L.J. Q.B. 188); or from a strain caused by unusual exertion (*Roper* v. *Greenwood*, 83 L.T.R. 471); but it is an *accident* where a miner dies from blood-poisoning brought about by a piece of coal working into his knee while he was hewing coal (*Thompson* v. *Ashington Coal Co., Ltd.*, 84 L.T.R. 412).

Accident Insurance "is a branch of life assurance by which persons are enabled to provide against loss to themselves or their families in case they are injured or disabled for a time or permanently, or killed by some one or other cause operating on them from without. . . A policy of insurance against accidents as usually drawn is not a contract of indemnity" (Porter's *Law of Insurance*, 5th ed. p. 496).

Accomplice, an associate or participator in a crime. But such persons as are admittedly employed by the public prosecutor for the detection of crime are not to be treated in law as accomplices of the prisoner (*per* DE VILLIERS, C.J., in *Queen* v. *Mary Pound*, 2 S.C. at p. 4). *See* PARTICEPS CRIMINIS.

Accord, an agreement or settlement.

Account stated. "What shall constitute, in the sense of a court of equity, a stated account, is in some measure dependent upon the particular circumstances of the case. An account in writing, examined and signed by the parties, will be deemed a stated account, notwithstanding it contains the ordinary preliminary clause that errors are excepted. But in order to make an account a stated account, it is not necessary that it should be signed by the parties. It is sufficient if it has been examined and accepted by both parties. And this acceptance need not be express; but may be implied from circumstances. Between merchants at home, an account which has been presented, and no objection made thereto, after the lapse of several posts, is treated, under ordinary circumstances, as being, by acquiescence, a stated account. Between merchants in different countries, a rule founded on similar considerations prevailed. If an account has been transmitted from the one to the other, and no objection is made after several opportunities of writing have occurred, it is treated as an acquiescence in the correctness of the account transmitted; and, therefore, it is deemed a stated account. In truth, in each case, the rule admits, or rather requires, the same general exposition. It is, that an account rendered shall be deemed an account stated, from the presumed approbation or acquiescence of the parties, unless an objection is made thereto within a reasonable time. That reasonable time is to be judged of, in ordinary cases, by the habits of business at home and abroad; and the usual course is required to be followed, unless there are special circumstances to vary it, or to excuse a departure from it" (Story's *Equity Jurisprudence*, sec. 526).

Accusatie (D.), a term employed in criminal practice in the Netherlands, signifying a complaint or charge.

Accusatio suspecti tutoris, the accusation of a suspected tutor. This was the name given in the Roman law to the action for the removal of a tutor, arising out of certain circumstances. According to Voet, the action also lies in the Roman-Dutch law, and, quoting Montanus, he reduces the grounds upon which it may be brought to the following heads: if the tutor bears or has borne enmity to the ward's father; if after the death of the testator the tutor shows an evil character which was previously unsuspected; if the tutor through prodigality begins to waste his own goods and to make away with his own property, so that he himself stands in need of a guardian; if inconsiderately or fraudulently he causes his ward to abstain from an inheritance; if he procured the guardianship by bribery or schemed to obtain it in any other way or forced himself into it; if he does not frame an inventory; if he robs or embezzles the estate or acts meanly or injuriously towards his ward; if he fraudulently sells the ward's property without an order of court; if he fails to present himself in order to have a certain amount of maintenance fixed for the ward; if he refuses to share the administration conjointly with a co-guardian; if, when he is appointed tutor, he does not appear, and upon being publicly summoned by edict he does not present himself (Voet's *Comm.* 26, 10, 2). Negligence, dilatoriness, rusticity, laziness, stupidity and folly are also grounds of removal (Voet's *Comm.* 26, 10, 7).

In addition to those common law grounds for the removal of a tutor, several others have been introduced by statute. In Cape Colony, Transvaal and the Orange River Colony a tutor whose estate has been placed under sequestration as insolvent is *ipso facto* removed from office (Ordinance 105 (C.C.), sec. 17; Administration of Estates Proclamation, 1902 (T.), sec. 87; Administration of Estates Ordinance, 1905 (O.R.C.), sec. 81). In the Transvaal and the Orange River Colony it is in addition provided that an executor, tutor or curator is liable to be removed from office where the court is of opinion that by reason of his absence from the colony, other avocations, failing health or other sufficient reason the interests of the estate would be furthered by his removal (Administration of Estates Proclamation, 1902 (T.), sec. 88; Administration of Estates Ordinance, 1905 (O.R.C.), sec. 82). By sec. 19 of Ordinance 105 (C.C.) failure of a guardian to frame an inventory is a ground for his removal, and as in the Transvaal and the Orange River Colony such conduct renders the guardian liable to a fine (Administration of Estates Proclamation, 1902 (T.), sec. 96; Administration of Estates Ordinance, 1905 (O.R.C.), sec. 83), it would probably be held a sufficient ground for his removal there also. Failure of a guardian to pay over to the Master of the Supreme Court moneys belonging to the person or estate under guardianship is also another statutory ground of removal (Ordinance 105 (C.C.), sec. 25; Administration of Estates Proclamation, 1902 (T.), sec. 95; Administration of Estates Ordinance, 1905 (O.R.C.), sec. 87).

The effect of the accusation of a suspected guardian is that while the case is pending he is removed from the administration and another is appointed temporarily in his place (Voet's *Comm.* 26, 10, 7). The application for removal may be made by the Master of the Supreme Court, or by any relative of the ward, or any person interested in his welfare (Voet's *Comm.* 26, 10, 4).

Achte (D.), a royal sentence; a considered judgment.

Achterborg (D.), rear surety; surety for an indemnity, a person who gives security for the deficiency after the excussion of the debtor or other surety (*Muller* v. *Meyer*, 1 Menz. 302).

Acqueste (D.—Lat. *acquisitum*, from *quaero*), a gain or acquisition. Hence *acquesteren*, in Roman-Dutch law, means to acquire or obtain something (see Meyer's *Woordenschat, sub voce*).

Acquests, (1) property acquired by purchase or donation; (2) property acquired by a spouse during marriage by virtue of community of property.

Acquiescence. "If a party, having a right, stands by and sees another dealing with the property in a manner inconsistent with that right, and makes no objection while the act is in progress, he cannot afterwards complain. That is the proper sense of the word *acquiescence*" (*per* COTTENHAM, L.C., in *Duke of Leeds* v. *Earl of Amherst*, 2 Phillips, at p. 123).

"There can be no *acquiescence* without knowledge of the facts" (*per* SOLOMON, J., in *Buck* v. *Palmer*, [1908] T.S. at p. 1106).

As to *acquiescence* of a servant in notice of dismissal, see *Bowling* v. *Kingwilliamstown Borough Council* (19 S.C. at p. 327).

Acquittance, a release or discharge from a liability.

Act, (1) As to whether the term *Acts* includes Ordinances see *Fitzpatrick* v. *Dawes* ([1907] E.D.C. at p. 323).
(2) *See* EVENT.

Act of Deliberation (*beneficium deliberandi*), a privilege granted by the praetorian law, by which an heir was allowed a certain time to deliberate whether he would undertake the representation of the deceased (Mackenzie's *Roman Law*, 7th ed. p. 286; *see* also BENEFIT OF INVENTORY). This privilege was also introduced into Dutch law. "Before the heir determined to accept or repudiate the inheritance he obtained a judicial *act of deliberation*, which enabled him to do certain necessary acts of administration without being on that account deemed to have accepted the inheritance. If after obtaining the *act of deliberation* and inquiring into the solvency of the estate, the heir still remained in uncertainty, he might apply to the Court of Holland for the writ of benefit of inventory" (*per* DE VILLIERS, C.J., in *Fischer v. Liquidators of Union Bank*, 8 S.C. at p. 51).

In considering the extent to which the Dutch law has been modified by the Cape legislature, and in more particularly referring to Ordinance 104 of 1833 (C.C.), DE VILLIERS, C.J., said: "The *act of deliberation* is wholly in disuse, and there is not a recorded case, at all events after the passing of the Ordinance, of any application to the Court for the writ of benefit of inventory."

Act of Superscription, the written statement indorsed by a notary on the envelope containing a closed will, to the effect that the testator declared the cover to contain his last will; this act of superscription is signed by the testator, the witnesses and the notary. See Van Leeuwen's *Comm.* 3, 2, 5; Maasdorp's *Institutes*, vol. 1. p. 121.

Acten (D.), a public document or writing which is made use of in the administration of justice. It was also understood in the Netherlands to mean all kinds of instruments employed in the judicial and notarial practice. In South Africa *acten* generally means deeds or formal documents.

Actie (D.), a judicial proceeding in a court of law.

Actio ad exhibendum, action for production of property. "Where the thing or property claimed is hidden or detained by a third party, or is joined to some other thing or property (in such a way that a separation can be legally demanded), [a plaintiff] may have recourse to an action for production of the property which is the subject of the vindicatory or possessory suit, this subsidiary action being known as the *actio ad exhibendum*. It is a personal action, and only movables can be the subject thereof. . It lies in favour not only of those who assert a right of ownership, but of those who claim a right of possession, or who claim a right of pledge, or a right of usufruct" (Nathan's *Common Law*, sec. 638). *See* ACTIO DE TIGNO JUNCTO.

Actio aestimatoria, *see* ACTIO QUANTI MINORIS.

Actio aquae pluviae arcendae, the action of obstructing the course of rain-water. The law against the diversion of rain-water by artificial means is of ancient origin. The remedy was the *actio aquae pluviae arcendae* for removal of the obstruction, or caution, for possible damage. In arid districts, such as those of Africa, this remedy lay against the defendant, not for directing the rain-water on the property of another, but for diverting in his own favour, which is looked upon as an injury (Colq. sec. 2180). In *Ludolph and Others* v. *Wegner and Others* (6 S.C. 197) DE VILLIERS, C.J., refers to this *actio*: "The action *aquae pluviae arcendae* is as old as the laws of the Twelve Tables, and rests upon the broad principle that no one has a right to do any acts for the improvement or benefit of his own land to the prejudice of his neighbour, unless there is an obligation in the nature of a servitude upon his neighbour's land to submit to such acts."

Actio calumniae, action for damages for malicious prosecution. Under the civil law a person against whom a false accusation had been maliciously laid could sue the *calumniator*, as the false accuser was called, either in the action *calumniae* or in the action *injuriarum*. The *actio calumniae* "seems to have fallen into disuse in the Netherlands. The *actio injuriarum*, however, remained in full vigour" (*per* DE VILLIERS, C.J., in *Lemue* v. *Zwartbooi*, 13 S.C. 406).

Actio commodati, action upon loan for use. The direct action (*actio commodati directa*) is employed by the lender to recover his property and compensation for damages done to the property, or damages sustained by reason of the non-delivery thereof at the agreed time. The *actio commodati contraria* lies in favour of the borrower for the recovery of damages for being obstructed by the lender in the use of the property, for a refund of extraordinary expenses to which he has been put, and for compensation if the property had some defect known to the lender which has occasioned damage.

Actio communi dividundo, the action for division of joint property. A person who holds property jointly with others in undivided shares may ask for a division and the performance of obligations due by the others in respect of his share. It is by this action that a partner can claim a division of the partnership property, and not by the *actio pro socio*.

Actio conducti, action of hiring: the lessee's action against the lessor upon the contract of letting. By this action the lessee claims that the lessor shall give proper and undisturbed use of the property hired from him.

Actio confessoria, the declaratory action instituted by the owner of the dominant tenement. The object of this action is that the defendant shall be compelled to respect the servitude, and give security against disturbing the right for the future.

Actio de constituta pecunia, an action brought against any one who has engaged to pay money, either for himself or for another, without any stipulation coming in. If promised by stipulation the promisor's liability was determined by the *jus civile*. This procedure is obsolete in Roman-Dutch law.

Actio de recepto, the action open to a person against an innkeeper. The reception of the person, or goods, or animal suffices to create an implied contract on the part of the hotel-keeper to answer for safe custody.

Actio de tigno juncto (or injuncto). If a person builds on his own ground with materials belonging to another, he is liable to the owner of the materials in the action known in the Roman law as the *actio de tigno juncto*. Under the term *tignum* (beam) are included all materials used for building purposes. Although the owner of the materials does not cease to be owner, the Twelve Tables, which introduced the action, in forbidding the needless destruction of property, suspended his right to reclaim them by the real action *ad exhibendum* so long as the building stood. When the building was destroyed and the materials were separated such an action could be brought. In the meantime the owner of the materials might, if he preferred, recover double their value by the *actio de tigno juncto*, in which case he lost his right of eventually reclaiming them. That was the law if the builder had used the materials in good faith. If he had acted in bad faith, the owner of the materials was in addition permitted to bring an action *ad exhibendum*. The effect of that action in Roman law was that the defendant was condemned in such a sum as the judge thought fit as a punishment for his having put it out of his power to produce the materials; but according to Voet the action lies for the value of the materials (*ad aestimationem tigni*). In addition, when the building was pulled or fell down the owner of the materials could reclaim them (Sandars' *Institutes of Justinian*, 10th ed. p. 105; Voet's *Comm.* 47, 3, 1).

Actio depositi, action upon deposit. It is either direct or indirect. The *actio depositi directa* is open to the person who makes the deposit against the person who has accepted the same for the redelivery of the property deposited, and for damages occasioned by his fault. The *actio depositi contraria* lies in favour of the depositary against the depositor for a refund of money expended in preserving the property and for damages sustained by him without any fault on his own part.

Actio directa, direct action (also called *legitima*)—an action which flows from the words and intention of a statute, or from direct, manifest and established law (Sande's *Cession of Actions*, 8, 1; Justinian's *Institutes*, 4, 6). The direct actions were those remedies which the civil law prescribed (Colq. sec. 2022). *See* ACTIO UTILIS.

Actio empti. *See* ACTIO EX EMPTO.

Actio ex empto or **actio empti,** the vendee's action upon the purchase. "Under the Roman-Dutch law a purchaser of goods is entitled, in an *actio ex empto*, to recover damages where there has been no delivery at all of the goods" (*per* DE VILLIERS, C.J., in

Irvine & Co. v. *Berg*, Buch. 1879, p. 188). In the action *ex empto* the delivery of the thing sold is sued for, if the thing is corporeal; and cession or other quasi-delivery if the thing is incorporeal; together with the fruits gathered subsequently to the sale and all accessions (Voet, 19, 1, 3). If the seller has knowingly deceived the buyer, by selling him an article of which he was not the owner, or an article possessing a latent defect, the purchaser is allowed to bring an action *ex empto* against the seller to make good all damages whatsoever (Benjamin on *Sales*, 3rd ed. p. 360; *Theron and Du Plessis* v. *Schoombie*, 14 S.C. 198; and *O'Brien* v. *Palmer*, 2 E.D.C. 350).

Actio ex stipulatu, action arising from a stipulation. By Roman-Dutch law the wife was allowed to sue upon the dissolution of the marriage for restitution of her dotal property by the *actio ex stipulatu*. The names of a host of the Roman actions have fallen into desuetude (Groenewegen, *ad Inst.* 4, 6, 2).

Actio exercitoria, the exercitorial action. The *exercitor* in Roman law was the owner or person appointing the master of a vessel. He took upon himself all the expenses and risks attaching to the vessel. The master of the vessel has implied authority to bind the *exercitor* in reference to matters affecting the ship. This was one of the original forms of agency.

Actio familiae erciscundae, the action for the division of an inheritance. When certain property has been bequeathed to several heirs, and it is uncertain what fraction each heir is to receive, the court will decree a division of the inheritance upon an action being brought for that purpose.

Actio finium regundorum, action for declaration of boundaries. Whenever the boundaries of adjoining properties have become confused, either owner may bring the action for regulation or declaration of the correct boundaries.

Actio furti, action for theft. In Roman law this action looked only to the recovery of the penalty, whether brought for twofold or fourfold the loss. It was open to any one that had an interest in the safety of the stolen property, even though he was not the owner. The *condictio furtiva* looked to the recovery of the stolen goods, and could only be brought by the owner. Where one person manufactures an article out of the materials of another, and has acted in bad faith, an action will lie in favour of the latter for the value of the materials and for damages (*actio furti et condictio furtiva*) for wrongful conversion.

Actio in factum ex lege aquilia, action on the Aquilian law upon the (special) facts. Damage done *nec corpore nec corpori* (neither with the body nor to the body) could be recovered by the *actio in factum* (Justinian's *Institutes*, 4, 3, 16). This action was likewise open to the owner of materials which have been *bonâ fide* used by another person in manufacturing an article.

Actio injuriarum, *see* INJURIA.

Actio institoria, the action in Roman law which was given against a person (*praeponens*) who had appointed another (*institor*) to manage a shop, business or undertaking on his behalf in order to enforce liabilities incurred by the *institor* to third parties in connection with the business. *See* INSTITOR.

Actio locati, the lessor's action against the lessee, upon the contract of hire, for rent, and damages for the breach of the express or implied conditions or obligations incidental to the contract.

Actio negatoria, the negatory action in servitudes, sometimes called *contraria.* It is open to the owner of property over which a servitude is claimed to have it declared that the property is free from the servitude; or, where a servitude does exist, that it is not the one which is sought to be exercised, or is not due to the tenement for which it is claimed. The action also applies where the owner of the *praedium dominans* wishes to exercise the servitude in a different manner from that to which he is entitled, as where he wishes to insert more beams in the wall of the *praedium serviens* than its owner allowed from the beginning, or to put them in in a different manner. It lies, too, where the servitude is due from one property, and its exercise causes damage to another tenement which is not subject to the servitude, as where one owner has pipes on the public way or on the property of another for the purpose of leading water and the pipes break and the water inundates a neighbour's wall; also, if an owner constructs a dung-pit or a bath against or near to his neighbour's wall and the wall is thereby moistened, or if the wall of one owner becomes bent and overhangs his neighbour's property by half of a foot or more, for although in such cases (Voet explains) the act complained of has been done not on the property which suffers injury, but on the doer's own property, and any one can lawfully do on his own property that which may cause injury to his neighbour if it is to his own advantage; yet this freedom of action is limited in so far as he cannot let anything go from his property on to that of his neighbour, whereas in the above cases he lets water and dampness reach his neighbour's wall and allows his wall to project over his neighbour's property. In the case of encroachment the action may contain a claim for its removal. The *actio negatoria* may also include a claim for damages and an interdict against future disturbance (Voet's *Comm.* 8, 5, 5).

Actio personalis moritur cum persona, a personal action dies with the person. This maxim has a much more limited application in the Roman-Dutch law than that which it receives in English law (see Morice's *English and Roman-Dutch Law,* 2nd ed. p. 238). In Roman-Dutch law the death of a person in no case affects his contractual rights and obligations, which transmit to and against his estate (Voet's *Comm.* 47, 1, 3). As regards torts or delicts, the maxim applies only to actions for *injuria* and actions for homicide. In its special sense, as it is used here, the term *injuriae* denotes wrongs to a man in his person, dignity or reputation, involving an element of insult, and includes such cases as assault, malicious arrest, and defamation. Here the right of action ceases with the death of either party and does not transmit to or against heirs, unless the death has taken place after *litis contestatio, i.e.* after the close of the pleadings (Voet's *Comm.* 47, 10, 22; *Meyer's Executors* v. *Gerricke*, Foord, 14). In the case of homicide the heirs of the deceased have no claim against the person who caused the death, except for funeral expenses and any other special expenses caused by the crime. The widow and children, however, and any others who were dependent upon the deceased for their support, have an action for damages against the wrong-doer (Voet's *Comm.* 9, 2, 11: Grotius' *Introduction*, 3, 33, 2; Van Leeuwen's *Comm.* 4, 34, 14).

Actio pignoratitia, action upon a pledge. It is either direct (*directa*) or indirect (*contraria*). The direct lies in favour of the debtor, who has discharged his debt, against the creditor for the redelivery of the property pledged, for damages caused thereto by his negligence, and for an account of the fruits which have sprung therefrom. The *actio pignoratitia contraria* lies in favour of the creditor against the debtor for an indemnity in cases where the latter has pledged a stranger's property as his own, or where a latent defect is discovered reducing the value of the security, or where the creditor has incurred expenses in the preservation of the property.

Actio praescriptis verbis. In Roman law the forms of action originally provided only for contracts falling under the well-known heads, such as sale, hiring, mandate and partnership. Thus, in the case of a sale the *demonstratio*, or first part of the *formula*, which set forth the facts, ran, *Quod Aulus Agerius Numerio Negidio hominem vendidit, i.e.* that Aulus Agerius (states he) sold a slave to Numerius Negidius. (For an example of a full formula, see Sandars' *Institutes*, Introduction, p. 68.) Where an agreement did not come under the known forms, *i.e.* was innominate, but nevertheless contained definite obligations, the praetor, to enforce performance, granted an action, the *demonstratio* of which set forth, instead of the short title appropriate to nominate contracts, the facts or circumstances upon which the plaintiff relied. The action was accordingly termed an *actio praescriptis verbis*, or *in factum*, sometimes (both expressions being combined) *in factum praescriptis verbis, i.e.* an action to meet the case, the words being set forth at the beginning.

Actio pro socio, action at suit of a partner. It lies in favour of one partner against the other, and the main ground of this action is the securing of compensation for losses sustained, or payment of profits withheld, or generally the rendering of an account by the administering partner.

Actio publiciana, the name given in Roman law to the action which lies in favour of a person for the recovery of property of which he has lost possession, where he is not yet the legal owner, but is in the way of becoming so through prescription (Voet's *Comm.* 6, 2).

Actio quanti minoris, action for a return of part of the purchase money proportionate to the defects discovered in the thing purchased. By this action a purchaser claims back the amount above what he would have paid if he had been aware of the defect. This action is also termed *actio aestimatoria* (action for a fair valuation of the article purchased). If the defect is such that the purchaser would not have bought at all had he known of it, he may avail himself of the *actio redhibitoria* (*q.v.*): but if the defect is such that he would notwithstanding have bought the thing, the purchase will be binding, and he can within a year claim a refund of the difference between the amount he would have paid and the amount he actually paid (Van Leeuwen's *Comm.* Kotzé's trans. vol. 2, p. **145**, and *O'Brien* v. *Palmer*, 2 E.D.C. **344**; see also *Irvine & Co.* v. *Berg*, Buch. 1879, p. 183).

Actio quod jussu "is a personal action given to a creditor who has contracted with the son on the authority of the father, whether such authority be general or special; and lies against the father, claiming the amount for which the father gave his authority to the contracting of the debt" (Nathan's *Common Law*, sec. 221).

Actio redhibitoria, the action which lies in favour of a purchaser for the purpose of enforcing rescission of the sale on the ground of latent defect in the thing sold. The remedy applies whether the seller knew of the defect or not, provided the defect is such as would have deterred the purchaser from buying if he had been aware of it before the sale was completed (*O'Brien* v. *Palmer*, 2 E.D.C. 344). If the purchaser would have bought notwithstanding the defect, his remedy is the *actio quanti minoris*, by which he claims back the excess of the price paid over the real value of the thing after allowing for the defect. According to the authorities the redhibitory action should be brought within six months after the sale, although the time may be extended by the court upon good cause being shown (*Christie* v. *Etheridge*, 19 S.C. at p. 370). In the Transvaal by Act 26 of 1908, sec. 3, one year is now fixed as the period of prescription in respect of both the *actio redhibitoria* and the *actio quanti minoris*.

Actio tributoria. "If the father have permitted the son to trade with such wares as are included in his *peculium profectitium*, he is obligated by the contracts of his son, and what are equivalent thereto, without any preference for his own claims, and must submit to the son's *peculium profectitium* being distributed *pro ratâ*, and to taking his share according to the relative goodness of the wares, and extent of the claims. Should any oversight have occurred, the person damnified must seek his indemnity from him who received a surplus. If, however, the plaintiff charge the father with a fraudulent favouritism, he can take his remedy by the *actio tributoria* for the damage caused him: the action will also lie for a fraudulent refusal to make a dividend" (Colq. sec. 2191; see also Voet, 14, 4, 1–8).

Actio tutelae directa and **Actio tutelae contraria**, the direct and indirect actions arising from guardianship. The direct action lies in favour of the ward to obtain an account of the guardian's administration, while the indirect action is open to the guardian to indemnify him for his losses or expenditure during the term of the tutelage. These actions are available upon the termination of the guardianship.

Actio utilis, an action given by the Roman praetor in cases where no direct action was applicable by the *jus civile*. A case wherein the praetor gave an action was often analogous to a case where an action had been given by the *jus civile*. Hence the right of action given by the praetor was given by way of analogy, and hence also the action was styled *utilis*, derived in this sense from *uti* the adverb, and not *uti* the verb. The praetor gave the action, *as* he would have given it *if* the case submitted by the applicant had fallen within the provision of the *jus civile* (Austin on *Jurisprudence*, sec. 35, p. 621). When the civil law prescribed an action and the praetor found it necessary to extend it to persons or cases not within its sphere, he granted the *utilis actio* (equitable action), after the pattern of the direct action (Sande's *Cession of Actions*, 8, 1; Justinian's *Institutes*, 4, 6). For example, in early Roman law an obligation could never be ceded; later on, however, the praetor gave the assignee the assignor's right of action, and modified the *intentio* in such a way as to instruct the *judex* to treat the assignee as the real creditor, and to decide accordingly. The assignor had the *actio directa*, while the assignee was allowed the *actio utilis* (*cf.* Anders' *Cession of Actions*, pp. 147 and 167).

Actio venditi or **Ex vendito**, the name given in the Roman law to the action to which a vendor is entitled for the recovery of the purchase-price of the thing sold (Voet's *Comm.* 19, 1, 16).

Action. (1) *Action* is the legal remedy which a person institutes by means of a summons against another in order to assert or maintain his rights, or redress a wrong committed against him. The person instituting the *action* is called the plaintiff, in Dutch *klager* or *aanlegger*, and the person against whom the *action* is brought, the defendant, in Dutch *verweerder* or *gedaagde*.

There are two main classes of *action*, viz., actions *in personam* or personal actions, and actions *in rem* or real actions (see Maasdorp's *Institutes*, vol. 2, p. 4). In the Cape Bills of Exchange Act (19 of

1893), sec. 1, the term *action* is defined to include "a counter-claim, claim in reconvention and set-off"; see also Law 8 of 1887 (N.), sec. 1; Proclamation 11 of 1902 (T.), sec. 1; Ordinance 28 of 1902 (O.R.C.), sec. 1.

(2) *See* EVENT.

Action of reclame. "This action is of a real nature, and lies for the recovery of the plaintiff's property in the possession of the defendant. It is either *direct* or *utilis.* In the former case it is given to those to whom the actual strict ownership belongs, and in the latter to those who have the beneficiary ownership or right of possession" (Decker's note to Van Leeuwen's *Comm.* Kotzé's trans. vol. 1, p. 187).

Active service. In the Cape Colony: "Any portion of the colonial forces shall be deemed to be on *active service* when (*a*) it has been called out under this Act for service against an enemy, or for service in a country or place wholly or partly occupied by an enemy: (*b*) it is in military occupation of any place outside this [Cape] Colony; (*c*) a proclamation has been issued by the Governor, under the powers conferred upon him by the 85th section of this Act, declaring that the whole of such portion of the colonial forces shall be deemed to be on active service for the period mentioned in such proclamation" (Act 32 of 1902 (C.C.), sec. 2). See Ordinance 37 of 1904 (T.), sec. 1; Ordinance 35 of 1905 (O.R.C.), sec. 1. *See* also MILITARY SERVICE.

Actor, plaintiff; antithetical to *reus*, defendant.

Actor or **Adjutor tutelae,** a joint guardian appointed by the judge or by the head of the State when the guardian is prevented from administering the tutelage (Voet's *Comm.* 26, 1, 1).

Actor rei forum sequitur, the plaintiff follows (*i.e.* must institute proceedings in) the defendant's court (*Code,* 3, 13, 2; Voet's *Comm.* 5, 1, 64). "The general rule is *actor sequitur forum rei,* although it is sometimes relaxed, as, for example, when the defendant or property belonging to him is found in this country" (*per* DE VILLIERS, C.J., in *Barkhuysen* v. *Van Huysten,* 1 S.C. 27). An arrest or attachment *ad fundandam jurisdictionem* is then essential, and the court issuing the arrest, although previously not the proper *forum rei,* becomes a *forum* in which the defendant can be sued by virtue of such arrest (*Hornblow* v. *Fotheringham,* 1 Menz. 365). But to entitle the plaintiff to arrest *ad fundandam jurisdictionem,* it is necessary that he should be domiciled within the jurisdiction of the court: a *peregrinus* cannot make such an arrest (*Einwald* v. *German West African Co.,* 5 S.C. 86; *Springle* v. *Mercantile Association of Swaziland,* [1904] T.S. 163).

Actore non probante, qui convenitur, etsi nihil ipse praestat, obtinebit, if the plaintiff fails in his proof, he who is sued, although he adduces no evidence, will prevail. *See* ACTORI INCUMBIT ONUS PROBANDI.

Actore non probante, reus absolvitur, if the plaintiff fails in his proof, the defendant is absolved. *See* ACTORI INCUMBIT ONUS PROBANDI.

Actori incumbit onus probandi, the burden of proof lies upon the plaintiff. He who invokes the aid of the law against another must advance sufficient proof to establish clearly his own right, and, until he does so, his adversary cannot be required to refute it. The same principle is variously expressed in the maxims, *Actore non probante, reus absolvitur* (if the plaintiff fails in his proof, the defendant is absolved): *Semper necessitas probandi incumbit illi qui agit* (the necessity of proof always lies upon him who takes action); *Actore non probante, qui convenitur, etsi nihil ipse praestat, obtinebit* (if the plaintiff fails in his proofs, he who is sued, although he adduces no evidence, will prevail); *Deficiente probante remanet reus ut erat antequam conveniretur* (when the proof fails the defendant remains as he was before he was sued). Of this the maxim *In obscuris minimum est sequendum* is a corollary, the application of which is illustrated by the case of *Channes* v. *Pezzey* (1 Camp. 8), referred to by Best on *Evidence* (10th ed. p. 243). In that case a liquor merchant sued for the price of goods sold and delivered, and the only evidence being that several bottles of liquor, of what kind did not appear, were delivered at the defendant's house, the jury were directed to presume that they were filled with the cheapest liquor in which the plaintiff dealt. It may, however, happen that the burden of proof is shifted to the defendant, for if, instead of denying the case of the plaintiff, he relies on some new matter as an answer to it, he is bound to show at least a *primâ facie* case. Here the maxim is, *Agere is videtur, qui exceptione utitur: nam reus in exceptione actor est,* he who avails himself of an exception is considered a plaintiff; for in respect of his exception a defendant is a plaintiff (Best on *Evidence*, 10th ed. sec. 267).

"**Actual cost**" does not include interest on capital during period of construction; see *Hills* v. *Colonial Government* (21 S.C. at p. 69); confirmed on appeal to the Judicial Committee of the Privy Council, see *Commissioner of Public Works* v. *Hills* (94 L.T. 833; [1906] A.C. 368; 22 T.L.R. 589: 75 L.J. P.C. 69).

In an action by contractors for railway construction against the Government, *actual cost* was held to mean "the cost actually incurred by the contractors in constructing the work, so far as the Government has had the benefit of it," and does not "include interest or goodwill or wasted expenditure, or material of which the Government has not had the benefit. As an illustration of what I mean by 'wasted expenditure' I may repeat the case of a culvert condemned by the engineers. If in consequence of faulty construction of such a culvert it is broken up and a new culvert is constructed, such new culvert alone forms part of the work taken over, and has to be paid for" (*per* DE VILLIERS, C.J., in *Hills* v. *Colonial Government*, 20 S.C. at pp. 133 and 135; also at p. 416). In *Bulawayo Municipality* v. *Bulawayo Waterworks Co., Ltd.* (16 C.T.R. 941; [1908] A.C. 241;

77 L.J. P.C. 70; 98 L.T. 600) B W had agreed to supply electric light in B to the inhabitants, streets, public places and private property. To carry out the work they were to do certain specified things and to provide everything necessary, although not specified, to supply the light to the street lamps, and the B M undertook to pay them such sum as would yield a return of 10 per cent. over the "actual cost of generating the light." *Held,* that *actual cost* did not include interest on capital, but did include depreciation of plant and machinery as well as rates, rents, taxes and insurance, and that *generating the light* included the whole process leading up to the production of the light in the street lamps. See also *Distributing Cold Storage Syndicate* v. *Imperial Cold Storage Co.* (17 C.T.R. 1085).

"Actual occupation." Where *actual occupation* is required by a statute relating to registration for voting purposes, it would seem that the personal presence of the occupier is necessary, and that constructive occupation will not suffice. "His personal presence may not be required for every day of the year, but he must have been in personal occupation of the premises for a sufficient time during the requisite period immediately preceding the registration as to satisfy the registering or revising officer as to his actual and *bonâ fide* occupation. If during the qualifying period there is a break not only in his *actual occupation*, but also in his right of occupation, the 3rd section of Act 48 of 1898 (C.C.) is not complied with, and registration cannot be allowed" (*per* DE VILLIERS, C.J., in *Alheit's Case,* 20 S.C. at p. 234).

"It would be difficult to lay down any general rule as to the number of days during which the personal presence of the occupier is required to establish his actual and *bonâ fide* occupation. An occasional presence merely for the purpose of giving colour to the claim for registration would not be enough, but there should be a personal occupation for such a period as would fairly entitle the occupier to be regarded as one of the inhabitants of the electoral division" (*per* DE VILLIERS, C.J., in *Michau's Case,* 20 S.C. at p. 235).

"Actual possession," discussed in *Israelson's Insolvent Estate* v. *Harris & Black and Others* (22 S.C. at p. 139).

Actuary, a person skilled in matters connected with complex calculations relating to life insurance, annuities, and the like.

Actus, a real servitude, consisting in the right of driving vehicles or animals over another's land.

Actus Dei, act of God.

Actus non facit reum, nisi mens sit rea, the act does not make (the performer) a criminal, unless there be a criminal intention. The essence of all crime, in other words, is the criminal intention with which the act has been committed. The maxim, however, does not mean that it is always necessary to establish clearly a criminal intention, for there are cases in which *mens rea* is presumed by the law, and in which the defence of want of intention would be of no avail. Thus if one assaults another with a weapon likely to cause death, and death ensues, the crime is murder, even though the accused should seek to prove that at the time of the assault he had no intention to kill, as the law will presume such intention from the fact that death was the natural and probable result of the means of attack employed, and that either such result was at the time present to the mind of the assailant or he was utterly regardless of the consequences of his act. Again, crime may consist not in any intention to do wrong, but in an omission to do what is right, where such neglect results in bodily injury to others; for example, culpable neglect of duty on the part of a pointsman in allowing a train to pass at a wrong time, whereby an accident is caused and persons are killed or injured. Here the crime is of a negative character, consisting not in doing that which is wrong, but in omitting to do what is right, accompanied by injury to others. In the case of statutes which expressly prohibit certain acts, for example, statutes regulating public health, such as Food and Drugs Acts, the commission of the prohibited act may infer punishment, although the doer acted in ignorance and without wrongful intention. Thus in *Dickson* v. *Pretoria Municipal Council* ([1906] T.S. 878), where a municipality in pursuance of its statutory powers made a bye-law prohibiting any person, being the owner or in possession of diseased meat from selling the same for human consumption, and the accused, a clerk in a butchery, sold on behalf of his employer diseased meat intended for human consumption, but without knowledge of its condition, it was held that knowledge on the part of the seller was not necessary to constitute a contravention, that the bye-law was not *ultra vires* and the accused was liable. So where accused were charged with selling hop-beer to coloured persons in contravention of sec. 46 of Ordinance 32 of 1902 (T.), hop-beer being included in intoxicating liquor as defined by that statute, the accused alleged that although they knew what they were selling, they did not know that it contained alcohol: but it was held that they had knowingly sold what the law prohibited, and that the absence of *mens rea* was no defence (*Wing Way and Ho Kam* v. *Rex*, [1907] T.S. 8).

In the case of civil actions to recover damages for negligence or misconduct, it is not the intention, but the result, of the act that is looked to. Whether an act was done knowingly or not is, however, very often an important consideration in civil actions (see *May* v. *Burdett*, (1846) 9 L.R. Q.B. 101; *Jackson* v. *Smithson*, (1846) 15 M. & W. 565; 15 L.J. Ex. 311; and *Hudson* v. *Roberts*, (1851) 6 Ex. 697).

Ad arbitrium, at will or pleasure.

Ad arbitrium judicis, at the discretion of the judge.

Ad factum praestandum, to perform an act. Provisional sentence cannot be granted on an obligation *ad factum praestandum* (for specific performance). See *Christie* v. *Kinnear* (2 Searle, 272), overruling *Borradailes & Co.* v. *Maynier* (1 Menz. 35).

Ad fundandam jurisdictionem, to found jurisdiction. "Where a defendant is domiciled outside this colony and the Court has [not]* otherwise jurisdiction, the invariable practice has been to attach the person or property of the defendant to found jurisdiction" (*per* De Villiers, C.J., in *McLeod* v. *Benjamin*, 9 S.C. 184). "The grounds upon which the jurisdiction of the Court can be exercised are threefold, viz., by virtue of the defendant's domicile being here, by virtue of the contract either having been entered into here or having to be performed here, and by virtue of the subject-matter in an action *in rem* being situated in the colony. If the defendant is domiciled here the process of attachment is wholly unnecessary" (*per* De Villiers, C.J., in *Einwald* v. *German West African Co.*, 5 S.C. at p. 91).

Ad medium filum, to the middle line. In English law, where a grant of land is made with a road or a river as the boundary, there is a presumption that the grant extends to the middle of the road or river, although the presumption may be rebutted by evidence to the contrary. As regards at least public rivers there is no such rule in the Roman-Dutch law, it being held that the right of a proprietor to the half of the bed of the river bounding his land must clearly appear from the terms of his grant (*Beaufort West Municipality* v. *Wernich*, 2 S.C. 36). As the interdict of Roman law which lay against any one who interfered with the navigation of a public river does not apply to private rivers, which are to be treated in the same way as other kinds of private property (Pothier on the *Pandects*, 43, 12, 1, secs. 1 and 3; Voet's *Comm.* 43, 12), there may be some ground for holding that the right of a proprietor of land bounded by a private river extends to the middle of the bed of the river. In Scots law, which also follows the Roman law, there is such a presumption (Bell's *Principles of the Law of Scotland*, sec. 738).

Ad valorem, according to the value. An expression used in statutes relating to customs, stamps and licenses, signifying that the duty charged or the stamp imposed is payable according to the value of the goods, or according to the amount in respect of which the stamp or license is payable.

Ad vitam aut culpam, for life or till fault. This phrase is used of an office the tenure of which is determinable by the death or delinquency of the holder. The equivalent phrase generally used in

---

* The word "not" has been evidently omitted from the report, for it is plain that if the Court *has otherwise* jurisdiction over the defendant there is no necessity for the arrest; this is borne out by reference to the report of the same case in 2 C.T.R. at p. 120, and to *Einwald* v. *German West African Co.* (5 S.C. at p. 91).

England is, *Dum se bene gesserit* (so long as he conducts himself properly; during good behaviour).

Judges of the Supreme Court hold their offices upon this tenure (Charter of Justice (C.C.), sec. 5; Supreme Court Act, 1896 (N.), sec. 26; Administration of Justice Proclamation, 1902 (T.), sec. 4; Administration of Justice Ordinance, 1902 (O.R.C.), sec. 6).

As a rule, however, a servant of the Crown holds his office during pleasure, and his dismissal gives no right of action, whatever may have been the terms of his original appointment (*Malcolm* v. *Commissioner of Railways*, [1904] T.S. 947; *Sheard* v. *Attorney-General*, [1909] T.S. 659). The only exceptions are statutory, such as the above (*In re Tufnell*, 3 Ch. D. 164; *Grant* v. *Secretary of State for India*, 2 C.P.D. 445).

Addictio in diem. This was the name given in the Roman law to a condition added to a contract of sale to the effect, either that the sale was to become binding only if the seller did not meet with a better offer within a certain time, or that the sale was to be immediately binding, but should be dissolved if better terms were offered by another person within a certain time. In the former case the *addictio* is suspensive, and until the condition fails through no better offer being received within the time fixed, the sale does not take effect. But where the *addictio* is resolutive, as in the latter case, the sale becomes at once binding, and although it will be dissolved should the resolutive condition be fulfilled, the risk, and by delivery the ownership also, will in the meantime pass to the purchaser (Voet's *Comm.* 18, 2, 1).

Addieeren or **adieeren** (D.), to adiate or enter upon or accept an inheritance. *See* ADIATION.

Adduce, to cite or bring forward some authority or evidence in support of some proposition.

Adelbroeder (D.), a brother on the mother's side.

Adhesive stamp, a gummed stamp capable of being affixed to letters, parcels, documents and the like. Adhesive stamps used for revenue purposes require to be cancelled within certain prescribed periods, and usually in a specific manner.

Adiation, a term adopted from the Roman law signifying the acceptance of an inheritance by the heir. The instituted heir was not bound to accept the inheritance; he might repudiate it, or take time to deliberate, or adiate it. The *adiation* "consists in the intention which may be indicated, not only by words, but by actions; for if the instituted heir, well knowing whether he has acquired a right to the inheritance by last will or *ab intestato*, disposes of any part of the inheritance, he is considered as adiating, unless he declares that he does so merely out of kindness, or unless he has received judicial permission to do so" (Grotius' *Introduction*, 2, 21, 5). The person adiating became liable for all the debts, even though they should exceed the assets of the estate, unless such person had availed himself of the right or benefit of inventory. *Adiation* as understood in Roman and Roman-Dutch law is now obsolete in South Africa. At the present time it means nothing more than the acceptance of the inheritance under a will by the heir. See *Denyssen* v. *Mostert* (Buch. 1873, p. 31).

Adjacent. According to the most modern decisions this term is not synonymous with "adjoining." In the judgment of the Judicial Committee of the Privy Council in *City of Wellington* v. *Borough of Lower Hutt* ([1904] A.C. 773; 91 L.T. 539; 20 T.L.R. 712) it was said that *adjacent* is "not confined to places adjoining, and it includes places close to or near. . . . What degree of proximity would justify the application of the word is entirely a question of circumstances." Cf. *Kimberley Waterworks Co., Ltd.*, v. *De Beers Consolidated Mines, Ltd.* ([1897] A.C. 515; 77 L.T. 117), where it was held that a mine situate four miles distant from another was not *adjacent* thereto. It would seem from the above that *adjacent* is confined to objects lying near to, but not necessarily in actual contact with, each other. *See* ADJOINING.

Adjoining. This term is generally used of objects which lie near to each other so as to touch in some part. Whether, however, the term connotes actual contiguity is a question of interpretation depending on the context in the document in each case. From the context a wider meaning is to be extracted in some cases than in others. Thus in *Re Bateman (Baroness) and Parker's Contract* ([1899] 1 Ch. 599, 80 L.T. 469) a plot of ground immediately opposite to, but separated by a highway 25 ft. wide from, an existing churchyard, was proposed to be added to the churchyard under the Consecration of Churchyards Act, 1867, which contains provisions for the conveyance and consecration "of portions of ground *adjoining* and added to existing churchyards;" it was held that the plot of ground was *adjoining* land within the meaning of the Act. See also *Coventry* v. *London, Brighton and South Coast Railway Co.* (L.R. 5 Eq. 104; 17 L.T. 368), where in the construction of sec. 128 of the Lands Clauses Consolidation Act, 1845, it was held that land separated by a private road was immediately *adjoining* certain superfluous lands; and *London and South Western Railway Co.* v. *Blackmoor* (L.R. 4 E. & I. App. 610; 23 L.T. 504), where lands divided by a wall were also held to be *adjoining*. See also *Haynes* v. *King* ([1893] 3 Ch. 439; 69 L.T. 855).

A contrary view was adopted in *Vale & Sons* v. *Moorgate Street and Broad Street Buildings, Ltd., and Albert Baker & Co., Ltd.* (80 L.T. 487), which dealt with a covenant by a lessor not to allow a certain trade to be carried on in the *adjoining* premises. Mr. Justice COZENS-HARDY held that the word *adjoining* was confined to the two houses on either side of the leased premises, although the lessor was, at the time of the lease, the owner of a block of buildings of which the two houses formed part only. To the same effect was the decision by the Court of Appeal in *Ind, Coope & Co., Ltd.*, v. *Hamblin* (84 L.T.

168). In that case the defendant in a conveyance to him of a portion of the plaintiffs' land covenanted that he would not "in the erection of any buildings *adjoining* the hereditaments of the vendors" insert or permit to be inserted any lights overlooking such hereditaments. The defendant constructed a number of houses, the backs of which were 20 ft. from the boundary fence separating the two properties; their yards or gardens stretched to this fence, and there were windows in the houses which overlooked the plaintiffs' property. The Court of Appeal, reversing the decision of Mr. Justice BUCKLEY (81 L.T. 779), who was of opinion that premises might be *adjoining* though they were not contiguous, held that the words must be construed in their ordinary sense, and that the houses not being actually contiguous to the plaintiffs' land, did not adjoin it within the meaning of the covenant. See also *White* v. *Harrow; Harrow* v. *Marylebone District Co., Ltd.* (86 L.T. 4; 18 T.L.R. 228) for another decision of the Court of Appeal to the same effect.

From the above two decisions of the Court of Appeal it would appear that *adjoining* in a legal writing is not to be read as equivalent to *adjacent* in the absence of some special reason to the contrary. *See* ADJACENT.

Adjunctio, the joining of one thing to another in such a way that they can either not be separated at all or at least not without detriment. In such a case the owner of the principal thing will be the owner of the accessory. Thus, where new wheels were made and attached to another person's wagon, which was then returned to the owner of the wagon, the latter became owner of the wheels (*Cooper* v. *Jordan*, 4 E.D.C. 181).

Adjutor tutelae. *See* ACTOR or ADJUTOR TUTELAE.

Administering poison with intent to do grievous bodily harm is a crime known to the law of the Cape Colony (see *Queen* v. *Kelaman*, 14 S.C. 329).

Administrator. "Our *administrator* to some extent corresponds to the English 'trustee'" (*per* DE VILLIERS, C.J., in *Hiddingh* v. *Denyssen and Others*, 3 S.C. at p. 441). An *administrator* is appointed by a testator where it is necessary in accordance with the will to manage the estate after the testator's death and to apply the income thereof as directed by the will. He is generally the same person as the executor, but the two offices are distinct, the office of the executor ceasing and that of the *administrator* commencing when the estate has been liquidated clear of debts and legacies (*In re Best*, 9 S.C. 488).

Admissible, capable of being used in evidence in a judicial proceeding; capable of being admitted.

Admissible evidence. *See* COMPETENT EVIDENCE.

Admission. (1) An acknowledgment that something is true or untrue.

(2) In the case of attorneys, notaries and conveyancers, *admission* signifies the order or authority permitting them to practise as such.

Admitted agent, a title by which a law agent is known in the Orange River Colony since the promulgation of Ordinance 7 of 1902. *See* LAW AGENT.

Adoption under Roman law was of two forms, being effected either by rescript of the Emperor (by which independent persons were adopted), or by the judicial authority of a magistrate (by which persons subject to the power of an ascendant were adopted). When a child in power was given in *adoption* to a stranger by his natural father, the power of the latter was not extinguished; no right passed to the adoptive father, nor was the person adopted in his power, though Justinian gave a right of succession in case of the adoptive father dying intestate. But if the person to whom the child was given in *adoption* by his natural father was not a stranger, but the child's own maternal grandfather, or, supposing the father to have been emancipated, its paternal grandfather, or its great-grandfather, paternal or maternal, in such case, because the rights given by nature and those given by *adoption* were vested in one and the same person, the old power of the adoptive father was left unimpaired, the strength of the natural bond of blood being augmented by the civil one of *adoption*, so that the child was in the family and power of an adoptive father, between whom and himself there existed antecedently the relationship described (Justinian's *Institutes*, 1, 11, 1 and 2). Roby in his *Roman Private Law* (vol. 1, p. 58) says that persons by *adoption* came into the family of a Roman, and were under his power just as if they were his lawful natural children. Grotius tells us (*Introduction*, 1, 6, 1) that "*adoption* is unknown in this country [Holland]." On the other hand, Van der Keessel (*Thes.* 102) says: "Although the *adoption* of children has not been practised in Holland, yet there is nothing to prevent not only arrogation, but even *adoption*, properly so called."

"The law of this colony [Cape Colony] does not recognise *adoption* as a means of creating the legal relationship of parent and child. Under the Roman law this relationship was created, but the Dutch law did not, in this respect, follow the Roman law" (*per* DE VILLIERS, C.J., in *Robb* v. *Mealey's Executor*, 16 S.C. 136; 9 C.T.R. 94).

Van Leeuwen in his *Comm.* (Kotzé's trans. vol. 1, p. 87) says: "The *adoption* of children as it existed among the ancients is unknown and not practised among us, although children adopted, *i.e.* taken into our family and educated by us may, like other persons, be instituted our heirs, without, however, our being obliged to do so; but, unlike children or blood relations, they cannot inherit *ab intestato*."

It is interesting, however, to note that there are several old Dutch plakaten, which, it is submitted, are still law in the Cape Colony, regulating the method of *adoption* (see Roos's article on "The Statute Law of the Cape in Pre-British Days, and some Judicial Decisions in relation thereto," 23 S.A.L.J. at p. 243).

Adrogation (*adrogatio*), one of the two procedures for adoption under Roman law. "*Adrogation* was effected only at Rome, and *per populum, i.e.* it required the solemnity of a bill (*rogatio*) passed by the *comitia curiata* under the authority of the pontifices. . . . The consents of the intended father and son are also formally demanded" (Roby's *Roman Private Law,* vol. 1, p. 60). Justinian speaks of *adrogation* being effected by rescript of the Emperor (*Institutes,* 1, 11, 1).

Adult, a person who has arrived at mature years and full strength. In Ordinance 19 of 1906 (T.), sec. 2, *adult* is defined to mean "every person of the age of sixteen years and upwards;" this corresponds with the English definition (Summary Jurisdiction Act, 1879, sec. 49). But see Ordinance 20 of 1906 (T.), sec. 1, where "*adult* male *native*" means an "aboriginal native apparently of the age of *eighteen* years or over," &c.

Adventitious property, certain property of minor children. "*Adventitious property* is such as is not derived from the parents or from third parties on their account" (Maasdorp's *Institutes,* vol. 1, p. 235). *See* PROFECTITIOUS PROPERTY.

Adverse user, the use and enjoyment of a thing without molestation by, and in conflict with the rights of, the owner thereof; such use and enjoyment may by prescription become an absolute right. For an instance of *adverse user* in respect of water in a perennial stream, see *Kohler and Others* v. *Baartman* (12 S.C. at p. 214): "It is clearly understood that in a servitude by prescription there must be *adverse user* for the full period of the prescription" (*per* DE VILLIERS, C.J., in *Lind* v. *Gibbs and Cooper,* 12 S.C. at p. 291).

Advocate. In Van der Linden's time no one was admitted as an *advocate* who had not taken the degree of Doctor of Laws at a recognised university, and who had not been sworn in as an advocate before the High Court of Holland. He tells us (*Institutes,* 3. 2, 4): "The profession of an advocate consists in general in advising upon all legal questions; in settling and signing all petitions; in drawing the pleadings which must be filed of record by the attorney; in drawing and signing all documents; in pleading orally in court; and, moreover, in using all legal means by which the case of the client may best be furthered." In the main these are the duties of an advocate of the present day. When the Supreme Court of the Cape of Good Hope was established by the Royal Charter of Justice in 1832, authority was given to that Court to admit and enrol "such persons as shall have been admitted as barristers in England or Ireland, or advocates in the Court of Session of Scotland, or to the degree of Doctor of Laws at our universities of Oxford, Cambridge or Dublin, to act as barristers or advocates of our said Supreme Court"; provision was also made for the admission as barristers or advocates of the Court of any persons who, previously to the promulgation of the Charter of Justice, had been actually admitted to practise as advocates in the Supreme Court of Justice—the highest tribunal at the Cape of Good Hope prior to the establishment of the present Supreme Court in 1832. The authority to admit and enrol has since been extended by various Acts: see sec. 2 of Act 12 of 1858, which is now replaced by sec. 20 of Act 16 of 1873, which authorised the admission of persons who had obtained the degree of Bachelor of Laws in the University of the Cape of Good Hope; see also Act 30 of 1892 (C.C.), sec. 1, which provides for the admission of advocates of Natal, the Transvaal and the Orange Free State. As regards Natal, by the rules of 14th July, 1904, applicants for admission as advocates must satisfy the following requirements: (1) Admission as a Natal attorney, and practice as such for a period of three years; (2) passing the Natal advocates' preliminary and Natal advocates' final examinations; and (3) payment of £50 to the Natal Law Society. The Court may also admit as advocates (1) English or Irish barristers; (2) Scotch advocates; (3) Transvaal advocates; or (4) advocates or barristers of the Supreme Court of any British colony who (*a*) have passed an examination in such colony approved by the Natal Supreme Court, or (*b*) have for seven years successively practised as advocates or barristers in the Supreme Court of such colony. Such persons must also pay a fee of £50 to the Natal Law Society. As regards the Transvaal, see sec. 10 of the Administration of Justice Proclamation (14 of 1902); and Orange River Colony, see sec. 11 of the Administration of Justice Ordinance (4 of 1902).

Advyzen or **Consultatien** (D.), verbal or written legal opinions. There are several collections of such *Advyzen* and *Consultatiën*, given by Dutch jurists of repute, dealing with the multifarious points of Roman-Dutch law and legal questions, in existence. The most widely known of these are *De Hollandsche Consultatiën*, in six vols. (see Wessels' *History*, pp. 241 *et seq.*).

Aedificium solo cedit, or **Omne quod inaedificatur solo cedit** (Justinian's *Institutes*, 2, 1, 29). The building accedes to the soil, or everything built on the soil accedes to it. The ground is the principal subject and the building follows it as accessory (*Henwood & Co.* v. *Westlake and Coles*, 5 S.C. 347).

A *bonâ fide* possessor of land retains his ownership in materials affixed by him to the land until he has parted with the possession. Even after the owner has demanded possession such *bonâ fide* possessor may retain possession until he is compensated for his improvements to the extent of the enhanced value of the land, and, failing payment of such compensation, he may remove the materials if he can do so without serious injury to the land, or he may surrender occupation and recover the compensation by action. A *malâ fide* possessor who has affixed materials to the land, and, before demand made by the owner, has disannexed and removed them, is not deemed to have parted with his ownership in the materials. After demand he no longer has the right to retain the land or remove the materials from the land, nor is he entitled to compensation except for such expenditure as he may have necessarily incurred for the protection or preservation of the land. If, however, the rightful owner has stood by and allowed the erection to proceed without notice of his claim, the possessor will have the same rights to retention and compensation as a *bonâ fide* possessor. "In the absence of special agreement, a lessee annexing materials, not being growing trees, to the soil is presumed to do so for the sake of temporary and not perpetual use, and, as between himself and the owner of the land, does not, during his tenancy, lose his ownership in the materials. He may, therefore, before the expiration of his term, disannex the materials and remove them from the land, subject to the rights of the owner to be secured against any injury to the land and to prevent any depreciation of his hypothecary rights for unpaid rent. At the expiration of the lease, however, the owner of the land becomes the owner of all materials then remaining annexed, and even of materials which, having been annexed without his consent, have been disannexed, but not removed by the lessee. The lessee has no right of retention after the expiration of his term, but may by action recover the value of the bare materials annexed by him with the landlord's consent, and the land becomes subject to a legal hypothec for such compensation when duly assessed" (*per* DE VILLIERS, C.J., in *De Beers Consolidated Mines, Ltd.*, v. *London and South African Exploration Co.*, 10 S.C. 359). In order that the maxim may apply it is necessary that the building should adhere to the soil as an immovable.

In deciding the question whether a structure is immovable or not, the main points to be considered are the nature of the structure, the manner in which it is fixed to the soil and the intention of the builder. Thus a wood and iron house which was fastened to wooden poles driven into the soil and projecting six inches above it, by nails six inches long, and which was erected as a permanent building, has been held to be immovable (*Olivier and Others* v. *Haarhof & Co.*, [1906] T.S. 497). On the other hand, where a tenant had placed iron piping underground, and had connected it with a bath in the bathroom, with the intention of removing the piping at the end of the lease, and it was possible to do this without injury to the premises, the court held that he possessed the right of removal (*McIntyre* v. *Johnston*, 2 Off. Rep. (1895), 202).

Aerarium. The early Roman emperors drew a distinction between *fiscus* and *aerarium*, the former belonging to the emperor and the latter to the people. Afterwards the rights of the two departments of the Treasury became intermixed, but a distinction still remained between the private patrimony of the princeps and the fiscal moneys or goods, the ownership of the latter vesting in the Treasury as representing the people, although the princeps had the administration of it.

Aestimatorius contractus, "an innominate contract of the class styled *bonae fidei,* whereby a thing on which a valuation has been placed is delivered to another to be sold, on the terms that he shall restore either the price or the thing itself intact" (Voet's *Comm.* 19, 3, 1).

Affidavit, a statement in writing sworn to before some one who has authority to administer an oath. Affidavits were not used in practice in the courts of Holland; their introduction is from the English practice (Van Zyl's *Judicial Practice,* 2nd ed. p. 354, *q.v.*). In the Cape Interpretation of Statutes Act (5 of 1883, sec. 3) it is provided that "*affidavit,* oath and swear shall include affirmation, declaration, affirming and declaring in the case of persons by any law, now or hereafter to be in force, allowed to declare or affirm instead of swearing." In Natal, under Act 14 of 1904, sec. 9, *affidavit* includes "affirmation, statutory or other declaration, acknowledgment, examination and attestation or protestation of honour." As to Transvaal, see Proclamation 15 of 1902, sec. 2.

Affiliation. (1) The assignment of a bastard child to its father, coupled with the obligation of the latter to maintain such child. The man's oath is entitled to preference over the woman's in an action of *affiliation*, if there is no *aliunde* evidence to support her evidence (*Gleeson* v. *Durrheim*, Buch. 1868, p. 244). "If the woman swears positively that the man is the father, and if the evidence of the alleged father is shaken on cross-examination, or any other evidence is produced in corroboration of the woman's story, I think her oath should be believed" (*per* SMITH, J., in *Van der Berg* v. *Elzbeth,* 3 S.C. at p. 37).

(2) In the Natal Code of Native Law (19 of 1891, sec. 22 of sch.) the word *affiliation* is used to signify "the attachment of a junior house to a senior or superior house for the purpose of providing against the failure of an heir in the senior or superior house. More than one house may be so affiliated. The senior or superior houses in a kraal to which *affiliation* may be made are, first, the *indhlunkulu*; secondly, the *iqadi*; thirdly, the *ikohlo*."

Affinity is the legal relationship which exists between each of the spouses and the blood relatives of the other; but not also between the relatives of the one spouse and the relatives of the other. Thus the brothers, sisters, uncles and aunts of the husband are *affines* of the wife, and *vice versâ* those of the wife are *affines* of the husband; but the brothers, sisters, uncles and aunts of the husband are not *affines* of those of the wife, and *vice versâ* those of the wife are not *affines* of those of the husband. They are only connections by marriage.

Affirmative servitude. "An affirmative or positive servitude is one which authorises the commission of some act on the property of another, *e.g.* a *jus itineris, actus, viae,*" &c. (Van Leeuwen's *Comm.* Kotzé's trans. vol 1, Decker's *note* on p. 306).

Affray. "An *affray* is the fighting of two or more persons in a public place to the terror of her Majesty's subjects" (Stephen's *Digest of the Criminal Law*, 5th ed. p. 54). See Native Territories' Penal Code (Act 24 of 1886 (C.C.)), secs. 94 and 95; Ordinance 18 of 1845 (N.), sec. 26.

Afperssing (D.), extortion. *See* KNEVELARIJ. The Latin equivalent is *concussio;* see *Notaris* v. *Rex* ([1903] T.S. 484).

Afschaffing (D), repeal—such as the repeal of a statute.

Agent. "An *agent* is a person who has authority, express or implied, to act on behalf of another person (the 'principal'), and to bind that other person by his acts and defaults" (*Digest of the English Civil Law*, book 1, sec. 121). A fuller definition is given by Manfred Nathan in his *Common Law of South Africa* (sec. 939) as follows: "When one person, whether authorised or not by another, represents that other in a transaction in such a manner as to create a legally binding obligation upon the person for whom he acts, the relationship between the parties is known as agency, and the person on whose behalf the act is done, and the person by whom the act is done, are known respectively as the principal and *agent*." See Ordinance 23 of 1905 (T.), sec. 2; and *Dely & De Kock* v. *Civil Commissioner* ([1906] T.S. 94).

As to good faith required, see *Transvaal Cold Storage Co., Ltd.,* v. *Palmer* ([1903] T.S. 4), and cases there quoted.

Agent of a foreign firm. *Agent of a foreign firm* means "any person other than an importer, who sells or offers for sale, by sample or otherwise, goods of a firm whose place of business is not in this [Cape] Colony; but shall not include a person who sells or offers for sale goods consigned to him by a foreign firm" (Act 38 of 1887 (C.C.), sec. 3). See also Act 28 of 1898 (C.C.), sec. 10.

In the Transvaal the corresponding term in the Revenue Licenses Ordinance (23 of 1905, sec. 2) is "agent or representative of a manufacturing or trading establishment carrying on business outside this colony," which means "any person who in any way advertises or holds himself out as the authorised representative or agent of such manufacturing or trading establishment outside this [Transvaal] Colony, and who solicits, receives or takes orders for the sale or supply of goods by such manufacturing or trading establishment to persons in this [Transvaal] Colony; but shall not include a person liable to take out a license as a general dealer under this Ordinance, by whom such goods are resold out of stock."

In the Orange River Colony *agent of a foreign firm* means "any person who sells or offers for sale, by sample or otherwise, goods of a firm whose place of business is not in this [Orange River] Colony; but shall not include a person who sells or offers for sale goods consigned to him by a foreign firm" (Ordinance 10 of 1903, sec. 2). See also Ordinance 10 of 1905 (O.R.C.), sec. 3.

Ager publicus, State lands. The Romans held that State lands were *res nullius* (no man's property), and regarded the same as lying outside the scope of private law altogether. The revenue, however, derived from the *ager publicus,* flowing into the public exchequer, became the national common property, though the State lands were not actually enjoyed by the nation at large.

Agere is videtur, qui exceptione utitur: nam reus in exceptione actor est, he who avails himself of an exception is considered a plaintiff; for in respect of his exception a defendant is a plaintiff. *See* ACTORI INCUMBIT ONUS PROBANDI.

Agio (D.), rate of exchange.

Agist, to feed or graze cattle or horses belonging to others for reward.

Agistment, the feeding or grazing of cattle or horses belonging to others for reward.

Agistor (also **agister**), one who feeds or grazes cattle or horses belonging to others for reward. See *Momsen* v. *Mostert* (1 S.C. 185).

Agri fiscalini. *See* HOFLANDEN.

Agriculturae promovendae causa, for the purpose of promoting agriculture. This phrase is used of an *emphyteuta* or quit-rent holder. As his right extends only to the surface of the ground *agriculturae promovendae causâ,* he cannot impoverish the ground itself, for example, by extracting minerals. For the same reason, if he has had absolutely no benefit from the land by reason of tempests, inundation or the like, he may claim exemption from payment of his nominal rent or canon (Van Leeuwen's *Comm.* 2, 10, 5; Decker, *ibid. in notis;* Voet's *Comm.* 6, 3, 16; *Neebe* v. *Registrar of Mining Rights,* [1902] T.S. at p. 81).

Agricultural distiller, an expression defined in the Cape Additional Taxation Act (36 of 1904), sec. 2, to mean "any owner or occupier of land who shall distil spirits exclusively from wine the produce of the land so owned or occupied by him."

Agricultural land, in the Transvaal Local Authorities Rating Further Amendment Act (35 of 1909), sec. 1, "shall mean arable, meadow or pasture land, market gardens, poultry farms, nursery gardens, plantations and orchards, but shall not include (*a*) land occupied as a park together with a house thereon; (*b*) land used as a garden other than as aforesaid; or (*c*) land kept or reserved for the purposes of sport, athletics, or recreation, or used as a racecourse."

Agriculture. This term is defined in the Cape Workman's Compensation Act (40 of 1905), sec. 4, to mean "horticulture, forestry and any work upon a farm or connected with farming," and in the Transvaal Workmen's Compensation Act (36 of 1907), sec. 2, to mean "any work connected with or incidental to the tilling of the soil, stock rearing or farming operations."

Aided farm school. In the Transvaal Education Act (25 of 1907), sec. 2, *aided farm school* means "a school at which instruction in accordance with regulation is given, and in aid of which capitation grants are made under the conditions prescribed in section seventeen [of the Act]."

"**Aided school,**" in the Orange River Colony School Act (35 of 1908), sec. 2, means "a private school in aid of which capitation grants are made subject to the conditions of this Act." *See* AIDED FARM SCHOOL.

Aleatory contract, a French term, signifying a contract "in which the equivalent consists in the chances for gain or loss, to the respective parties, depending upon an uncertain event. . . From *alea*, a die, dice, or throw of the dice; a word for which our adjectives 'gaming' and 'hazardous' are not exact equivalents" (May on *Insurance*, 4th ed. sec. 5, *et in notis*; see also Holland's *Jurisprudence*, 10th ed. p. 296).

Alibi, elsewhere. When in a criminal prosecution the accused puts forward the defence that at the time laid in the charge or indictment as the time when the offence was committed he was not at the place specified, but at some other place, he is said to set up the special defence known as an *alibi*. In the Cape Criminal Procedure Act (3 of 1861), secs. 13 and 14, it is provided that except where time is of the essence of the offence, if any day is laid in an indictment as the day upon which the offence was committed, proof that such offence was committed not more than three months before or after the day averred is taken to support the indictment. If, however, the defence is an *alibi*, such proof of the offence having been committed at any other time than that laid in the indictment may be rejected by the court if it considers that the accused would be prejudiced thereby. (See also Ordinance 1 of 1903 (T.), secs. 147 and 148; Law 6 of 1861 (N.), sec. 17; Ordinance 12 of 1902 (O.R.C.), sec. 82.)

Alienable things "are those which by their nature may belong to one person as well as to another, and which may be acquired by every one with the consent of the owner, and may be disposed of" (Van Leeuwen's *Comm.*, Kotzé's trans. vol. 1, p. 153).

Alienate, to transfer, make over, or convey some right, property or title from one person to another.

Alienatie (D.), an alienation or transfer. *See* ALIENATION.

Alienation, the act of alienating; the transfer or conveyance of some right, property, or title from one person to another. As to the rights and obligations of guardians in connection with the alienation of the property of their wards, see Nathan's *Common Law*, secs. 329 *et seq.*

Aliens, "(*uit-heymen*) are *outlanders* (*aliens*) who are born in some other country" (Van Leeuwen's *Comm.*, Kotzé's trans. vol. 1, p. 69). "The burden of proving that the respondent is an *alien* lies upon those who assert it" (*per* DE VILLIERS, C.J., in *Blignaut* v. *De Villiers,* 17 S.C. at p. 380).

Aliment or **Alimony (Alimentatie** (D)), money paid for the support of any one entitled to claim it; maintenance. "The obligation of parents to provide *aliment* for their children until the latter are able to maintain themselves has frequently been recognised by this [Supreme] Court. The obligation to protect a child against want may revive even after such child has reached an age at which he can maintain himself, if he is in distress and unable to work through bad health, and if the parents are possessed of the requisite means. . . . But if parents owe this duty to their children, the latter owe a reciprocal duty to their parents. If a father or mother is in distress and unable to work, his or her children who have the means can be compelled to contribute towards their parents' support. It would make no difference that the children are minors, for the obligation does not arise out of any implied contract, but out of the sense of dutifulness which every child is presumed to entertain towards his parents" (*per* DE VILLIERS, C.J., *In re Knoop,* 10 S.C. at p. 199). The duty to maintain children extends also to illegitimate children, and even children procreated in adultery or incest (*Davies* v. *Rex*, [1909] E.D.C. 149).

See Maasdorp's *Institutes,* vol. 1, pp. 78 and 232; Nathan's *Common Law,* secs. 144 *et seq.*; Van Leeuwen's *Comm.*, 1, 13, 7.

Under Roman-Dutch law *alimentatie* could not be made over to third parties except with the approval of the domiciliary judge. See Kersteman's *Woordenboek,* vol. 1, p. 11; see also Van der Linden's *Institutes*, 1, 14, 4.

Allegans contraria non est audiendus, he is not to be heard who alleges things contradictory to each other. The maxim, of which the law of estoppel is in great measure a development, applies when in consequence of a previous act or statement to which he has been a party, a person is precluded from showing the existence of a state of facts inconsistent with such act or statement (Broom's *Legal Maxims*, 2nd ed. pp. 132 and 238; Best on *Evidence,* 10th ed. sec. 533).

Allegans suam turpitudinam non est audiendus, he who alleges his own misconduct is not to be heard (Best on *Evidence*, 10th ed. sec. 545).

Allegation, a statement made by a party to a legal proceeding, and which such party asserts to be a fact. An *allegation* may also be made by a witness in a legal proceeding.

Allodial property, any property held under freehold tenure. *Odal* or *Alod* denotes entirely free property.

Alloy. *See* GOLD COINS.

Alluvial claim, a certain area of land, properly demarcated, and held under license for the purpose of working alluvial deposits of minerals or precious stones. In Natal an alluvial claim is of a size not exceeding 100 feet by 100 feet (0·229 acre)—(Act 43 of 1899, sec. 8).

In the Transvaal under the Gold Law, see Law 15 of 1898, secs. 62 *et seq.* (now repealed); also Precious Stones Ordinance (66 of 1903), sec. 50.

In the Orange River Colony, see Ordinance 3 of 1904, sec. 5.

Alluvial digging. In the Mining of Precious Stones Ordinance (4 of 1904 (O.R.C.)), sec. 5, *alluvial digging* means "such an area as may from time to time be proclaimed by the Lieutenant-Governor as such, and any area that has heretofore been so proclaimed under any previous Law and is at the date of the promulgation of this Ordinance being worked as such."

Alluvio, Alluvion, alluvial land; a deposit of earth upon the bank of a river so gradually that no one can perceive how much is added at any one moment of time; such deposit is inseparable from the native soil of the bank; and the owner of the latter acquires the former by right of accession. Land reclaimed from the sea intentionally and by artificial means belongs to the Crown, and cannot be claimed as an accession by *alluvion* by the owner of land adjoining that portion of the sea which has been so reclaimed (*Colonial Government* v. *Capetown Town Council*, 19 S.C. 97).

"Alluvion is of two kinds, *aanwas* and *aanwerp*. The former is termed *discretae, i.e.* those separated from the land by a portion of the water; and the latter *alluviones continuae, i.e.* those which are attached to the land" (Van Leeuwen's *Comm.*, Kotzé's trans. vol. 1, p. 175, Decker's *Note*).

Alluviones continuae, that form of alluvion which was known in Roman-Dutch law as *aanwerp*. *See* ALLUVIO.

Alterum non laedere, not to hurt another. This is one of the three maxims laid down by Justinian (*Institutes*, 1, 1, 3) as the foundation of all rules of law. The other two are *honeste vivere*, to live honourably, and *suum cuique tribuere*, to give to every man his due.

Altius non tollendi, *lit.* of not building higher: said of the servitude so called. *See* SERVITUS ALTIUS NON TOLLENDI.

Altius tollendi, of building higher. *See* SERVITUS ALTIUS TOLLENDI.

Amalgamation is not a legal, but a commercial expression, and bears no exact definite meaning. It involves the blending of two concerns into one; "substantially" the whole of the two undertakings must pass, and "substantially" all the corporators must be parties; and it may take place by the transfer of two undertakings to a new corporation, or by the continuance of both undertakings on the terms that the shareholders of one shall become shareholders of the other (*South African Supply and Cold Storage Co.; In re Wild* v. *South African Supply and Cold Storage Co.*, [1904] 2 Ch. 268; 73 L.J. Ch. 657; 91 L.T. 447).

Ambacht (D.), duty, office, jurisdiction. Hence in some places, where a considerable number of people form a body and have chosen a head or superior over them, the term *ambacht* is applied to them, and the head or superior is called the *ambachtsheer*. *Ambacht* also means a manor, and the *ambachtsheer* would be the lord of the manor.

Ambachtsbewaarder (D.), a bailiff; a steward of a manor.

Ambachtsheer (D.), *see* AMBACHT.

Ambiguitas latens et ambiguitas patens, latent and patent ambiguity. A latent ambiguity is that which is not apparent on the face of the deed, but which is introduced by extrinsic and collateral matter; while a patent ambiguity is that which appears *ex facie* the deed. In the former case, as the doubt arises from circumstances outside of the deed, extrinsic evidence is admissible to explain it; but in the latter case no explanation of the ambiguity is allowed which cannot be found in the deed itself (*In re Herold*, 1 S.C. 159).

Ameliorations, improvements. *See* IMPROVEMENTS. In referring to the expression "amount of any *ameliorations*" appearing in sec. 104 of Ordinance 6 of 1843 (C.C.), DE VILLIERS, C.J., said: "The amount of *ameliorations* in my opinion means no more or less than the amount representing the enhanced value of the land by reason of such *ameliorations*" (*Parkin* v. *Lippert*, 12 S.C. at 191).

Amendable, that which is capable of being altered or added to. *See* AMENDMENT.

Amendment, an alteration or addition to some proposed law, bill, resolution, indictment or pleading; an alteration or addition to an existing law, indictment or pleading; an alteration or addition to any document or writing.

Amends, compensation or reparation for some injury or loss.

Amicus curiae, a friend of the court; the name given to a member of the bar, or other bystander, who advises the court regarding a point of law or fact upon which information is required.

Amman (D.), a judge, leader or captain. A term also applied to the Schout.

Ammunition is defined in the Cape Firearms and Ammunition Act (17 of 1892) to mean "any explosive capable of being used in the explosion of firearms, and includes cartridges, cartridge cases, shot, bullets, lead and percussion caps."

For Natal, see Act 1 of 1906, sec. 3.

For Transvaal, see Act 10 of 1907, sec. 2.

For Orange River Colony, see Act 23 of 1908, sec. 2.

Anatocismus, accumulation of interest with capital—compound interest. In the absence of a special agreement compound interest cannot be charged (*Heinemann* v. *Barnes,* 6 C.T.R. 107).

Ancient customs, in Holland, "which were recognised during the sixteenth century as part of the common law of the land, were such as had from time immemorial been recognised as law. They were derived from various sources, from the *Lex Ripuaria*, the *Lex Salica*, the *Jus Saxonicum*, the *Jus Frisicum*, the *Lex Romana*, the *Capitularia* and other ancient bodies of law" (Wessels' *History*, p. 210). Customs were either general or particular, affecting only some district or town. As to the force of custom in Roman-Dutch law, see Voet, 1, 3, 27 *et seq.*; Kersteman, *sub voce* "*Costume*"; and Van der Linden, 1, 1. sec. 7. "By the civil law and the Roman-Dutch law a general custom may abrogate a written law. Such custom must, however, be reasonable, ancient and properly proved by acts and deeds" (*per* KOTZÉ, J., in *Zeiler* v. *Weeber*, 1 K. p. 18).

Anderling, Anderzweer (D.), a relation by blood in the second degree. *Anderzweeren, i.e.* the grandchildren of brothers and sisters (Meyer's *Woordenschat*).

Anderzweer (D.), *see* ANDERLING.

Animo remanendi, with the intention of remaining. "Every independent person can acquire a domicile of choice, by the combination of residence (*factum*), and intention of permanent or indefinite residence (*animus manendi*), but not otherwise" (Dicey's *Conflict of Laws*, p. 104). "The law of the domicile of marriage will prevail to regulate the rights of the spouses in regard to property acquired in this colony by persons married elsewhere, but who have subsequently removed to this colony *animo remanendi*" (*per* DE VILLIERS, C.J., in *Black* v. *Black's Executors*, 3 S.C. 202). This rule applies even to immovable property (*Chiwell* v. *Carlyon and Others*, 14 S.C. 61).

Animo revertendi, with the intention of returning. This is said of a person who leaves the country of his domicile merely for a temporary purpose or without the intention of settling in the country in which he has become resident. See *Weatherley* v. *Weatherley* (1 K. 66).

Animus contrahendi, an intention of entering into an agreement. The basis of a contract is the intention of producing an engagement by virtue of promises and of giving the party to whom they are made a right of demanding their performance (*Spiegel* v. *Eilenberg*, 20 S.C. 250).

Animus domini, the intention of owner. This was in Roman law the element which distinguished legal possession from mere physical possession or *detentio*. Legal possession exists where the possessor has both *detentio* and *animus domini*, or, as it is sometimes called, *animus possidendi*, *i.e.* where he not only holds the thing physically, but does so with the intention of keeping it for himself and not for another. Thus true owners and *boná fide*, and even *malá fide*, possessors who intend to hold as owners, have legal possession in this sense; while usufructuaries, borrowers or lessees, who hold subject to a recognition of the rights of others, have mere *detentio*. It was only legal possession that received the protection of the possessory interdicts (see Holland's *Jurisprudence*, 10th ed. pp. 190 *et seq.*).

Animus furandi, the intention of stealing. To constitute the crime of theft there must be proof of *animus furandi*. Thus in *Rex* v. *Murphy and Another* ([1906] E.D.C. 62), where two persons while under the influence of liquor took each a horse, and after riding some distance left the horses in a paddock, it was held that in the absence of proof of *animus furandi* this did not constitute theft. So where a person whose dog had been caught in a jackal trap, took the trap and hid it in a hole with the intention not of depriving the owner of his property, but of putting him to some trouble in finding it, a conviction for the theft of the trap was quashed on appeal (*Lessing* v. *Rex*, [1907] E.D.C. 220). See also *Rex* v. *Rossouw*, 20 S.C. 409 and *Rex* v. *Sumango*, 18 E.D.C. 173.

Animus injuriandi, intention to injure. The existence or absence of the *animus injuriandi* must be gathered from the circumstances of each particular case (*Mackay* v. *Philip*, 1 Menz. 463). "The ground upon which the action for defamation rests is the *injuria*, the personal insult or contumely to which the plaintiff has been exposed. No action lies for such injury, as such, unless the defendant was actuated by the *animus injuriandi*" (*per* De Villiers, C.J., in *Bennett* v. *Morris*, 10 S.C. 226). The mere use of defamatory words affords presumptive proof of malice, but the presumption may be rebutted by the fact that the communication was privileged or by such other circumstances as satisfy the court that the *animus injuriandi* did not exist (*Botha* v. *Brink*, Buch. 1878, at p. 130). See De Villiers' *Roman and*

Roman-Dutch Law of Injuries, p. 27, where the subject of *animus injuriandi* is ably and fully discussed; also article by the same author in 26 S.A.L.J., p. 512, on "Malice in the English and Roman Law of Defamation."

Animus possidendi, intention to possess. The requisites of legal possession are (1) detention, the physical element; and (2) intention, the mental element. *See* ANIMUS DOMINI.

Anni continui, continuous or successive years. *See* ANNI UTILES.

Anni utiles, years that can be used. As the principle underlying prescription is, that those who have been negligent or careless of their rights should be penalised by their forfeiture, it does not hold good of those who are under some legal or physical incapacity to exercise them, as, *e.g.* minors or married women under the marital control of their husbands, and persons of unsound mind or absent from the country. While the incapacity remains the period of prescription does not consist of *anni utiles* to such persons, and the time in their case is accordingly reckoned without counting the period during which they were unable to exercise their rights. On the other hand, to those who are fully able to assert their claims, the years of prescription are said to be *anni continui, i.e.* continuous or uninterrupted years. This is the sense in which these terms are used in the Roman law (*Digest*, 38, 15, fr. 2 pr.).

In the Roman-Dutch law an *annus utilis* sometimes means a year and a day with the addition of six weeks. An *annus utilis* in this sense, *e.g.* was fixed by the statutes of some places in Holland as the period within which the right of retraction (*jus retractus*) had to be exercised (Voet's *Comm.* 18, 3, 25).

Annuity, the payment of a yearly sum of money of fixed amount. The person who is entitled to receive the *annuity* is called the "annuitant."

Annus luctus. The year of mourning. "For fear of mixing the blood, a woman may not enter upon a new marriage within the year of her widow's grief under pain of infamy. . . . She will also enjoy no benefit out of the goods of her first husband by whatsoever title they may have been left to her" (Schorer's *Notes* to Grotius, 10). A widow may not marry within the period of probable pregnancy by her deceased husband (Grotius' *Introduction*, 1, 5, 3).

Van der Keessel says that the Roman definition of the *annus luctus* has been abrogated, but the duration of it is left to the just discretion of an honest judge. The Colonial Ordinance of De Mist declared it to be the law that a widower shall not marry within three months, and a widow not within five months, after the death of the other spouse. This Ordinance was enacted *om der eerbaarheid wille* (for decency's sake). No penalty, however, is prescribed for the breach of this law, and there is presumably nothing to prevent a widower or widow from remarrying within the aforesaid period. *Multa prohiberi in jure fieri quae tamen facta tenent* (many things, the performance whereof is prohibited in law, nevertheless are valid when done). Ward, in his *Marriage Laws* (pp. 5, 6) points out that the De Mist proclamation has not been incorporated in the statute book of the Cape Colony, and contends that the provisions of that proclamation are therefore inapplicable in that colony.

In the Transvaal, by sec. 9 of Law 3 of 1871, a widower may not marry within three months of his wife's death, and a widow not within 300 days of her husband's death, unless dispensation is granted her by the head of the State.

In the Orange River Colony, by Law 26 of 1899, sec. 13, a widower must wait three months and a widow 280 days before they may respectively remarry.

Anonymous partnership is a partnership "where several persons agree to participate in the profits of a certain business which is to be carried on by one or a certain number of the partners in his or their own name" (Nathan's *Common Law,* sec. 928). See also *Guardian Insurance and Trust Co.* v. *Lovemore's Executors,* 5 S.C. 205; *Davison's Estate* v. *Auret,* 22 S.C. at p. 19; *Shapiro* v. *Shapiro and Ketz's Trustee,* [1907] T.S. at p. 474.

Antenuptial contract is an agreement made by two intending spouses regarding the rules by which their future marriage is to be governed, and regulating the disposal of the property acquired by them before marriage, or of that which they may subsequently acquire (De Bruyn's *Opinions of Grotius,* p. 141). As a rule an *antenuptial contract* excludes community of property and profit and loss, as also the marital power. The contract must be executed before marriage in the presence of a notary (except in Natal), and must be duly registered in the office of the Registrar of Deeds of the colony or territory in which it is executed. The intending husband frequently avails himself of this opportunity to make a settlement upon his future wife and the children of the marriage; such settlement is then incorporated in the *antenuptial contract.* On good cause shown the court will decree the registration of an antenuptial contract after the marriage has been solemnised, saving, however, the rights of creditors during the interim.

Antichresis (ἄντι-χρῆσις,), in consideration of use. The pledgee is obliged to return to the pledgor the fruits or profits of the property pledged, or carry them to account in reduction of the debt, unless otherwise stipulated. It is often stipulated that the creditor shall have the fruits or profits of the article pledged in lieu of interest, and this is called a *pactum antichreseos* (Grotius' *Introduction,* 3, 9, 5).

Anticipatie (D.), anticipation. A *mandament van anticipatie* (writ of anticipation) was, in Holland, granted upon the request of the defendant to enable him to anticipate the return day of a penal interdict when such return day would otherwise have been too far off; or, in the case of a trial, the action became in a manner privileged as though its hearing could brook no delay, and by the *mandament van anticipatie* an early date was fixed for the hearing.

Antwoord (D.), a plea or answer of a defendant in an action. Formerly also called *conclusie van antwoord.*

"**Any cause whatever,**" for a discussion as to the effect of these words in a bill of lading, see *Clan Line of Steamers* v. *Alcock & Co.*, 13 S.C. at pp. 113 and 115.

"**Any debt.**" The words *any debt* appearing in sec. 71 of Ordinance 6 of 1843 (C.C.) must be restricted to debts provable against the insolvent's estate, for "a debt not provable in his insolvency has no connection with the estate under administration, and a person who has contracted such a debt, even without reasonable expectation of being able to pay it, cannot be convicted of culpable insolvency" (*per* DE VILLIERS, C.J., in *Queen* v. *Louis Klein*, 8 S.C. at p. 42).

Apocha, a receipt or acquittance. In one respect a receipt is more effectual than a written acknowledgment of debt, for while the exception *non numeratae pecuniae* can be pleaded against a receipt only within thirty days from its date, it may be taken to a document of debt at any time within two years. The creditor upon receiving payment of his debt is bound to give a receipt to the debtor, and it is not enough that he should return to him the instrument of obligation cancelled or erased or torn, as the production of the bond torn or cancelled is not sufficient proof of payment unless the debtor shows that the bond was given back to him by the creditor in this cancelled condition, a fact which circumstances may often render it difficult or impossible to prove (Voet's *Comm.* 46, 3, 15).

Apocha trium annorum, receipt or acquittance for three years. If in the case of payments which are made annually the debtor can produce receipts for three consecutive years he will be presumed to have paid the sums due for previous years, and the burden of proving otherwise will be upon the creditor unless the debtor has acknowledged the contrary in writing or unless the creditor has in his receipt reserved his right to payment of the sums previously due. The same applies to half-yearly, and probably also to any other termly or periodical, payments (Voet's *Comm.* 46, 3, 14).

Apparent servitude, "is one the existence of which is shown by external works, such as a door, a window, watercourse and the like" (Van Leeuwen's *Comm.*, Kotzé's trans. vol. 1, translator's note on p. 306).

Appearance, the coming before the court by a defendant in response to a summons issued against him. This is usually done in the superior courts by the defendant or his attorney noting appearance with the registrar in the prescribed manner, and serving notice of such *appearance* on the plaintiff's attorney. This is termed "entering appearance." In inferior courts the defendant or his attorney appears personally on the return day.

Speaking of the *appearance* of an attorney in the magistrate's court in terms of sec. 14 of schedule B of the Magistrates' Court Proclamation (T.), WESSELS, J., said: "By an *appearance* is not meant that the attorney should exhibit his face in court, or that he should put a piece of paper before the magistrate to the effect that he is appearing before the court. It means that the attorney who represents his client shall in person conduct the case entrusted to him. He cannot conduct the case by his clerk or by his office boy" (*Coomans* v. *Nelson*, [1907] T.S. at p. 625).

Appel (D.), appeal to a superior court. Also termed *Hooger* (or *hoger*) *beroep*.

Appraisers (sworn appraisers), persons appointed by the Master of the Supreme Court for the valuation of all estates and property, the appraisement of which shall become necessary, or shall be had for the better ascertaining the amount of the shares thereof which may belong or be due to any persons who, or to any estates which, shall at the time be under the guardianship of the Master, or of any tutor, either testamentary or dative, or curator nominate or dative or *bonis*. These *appraisers*, who are commonly known as sworn *appraisers*, may charge a reasonable fee; they are duly sworn on appointment; and their valuations are generally received by the Master in connection with all matters relating to the valuation of property in estates.

Apprehend, to arrest and take into custody, under a legal warrant, a person charged with the commission of a crime, or the commission or omission of some act or thing which has rendered him liable to apprehension.

Apprehensio, the laying hold or taking of a thing. Possession is acquired by the taking of a thing with the intention of retaining it to the exclusion of all others. Actual physical contact with the thing is not necessarily required as long as the person acquiring it places himself in a position to deal with it freely. See Maasdorp's *Institutes*, vol. 2, p. 19.

Apprentice, one who is bound under contract to serve some person, known as the master, for a fixed period for the purpose of learning some trade or occupation carried on or conducted by the master; and which trade or occupation the master is bound under the contract to teach or instruct the apprentice. In the Masters and Servants Act (15 of 1856, sec. 2) of the Cape Colony an *apprentice* is defined as being "any person indentured or bound by any contract of apprenticeship, made according to law, as *apprentice* to any other person." A similar definition is found in Ordinance 2 of 1850 (N.), sec. 2. See also Law 13 of 1880 (T.), sec. 2.

"**Approach to the river,**" *see* "RIGHT OF FREE APPROACH TO THE RIVER."

Approach to water (*watergang*), a form of servitude, "is the right of going over another's land to draw water from some public water, or from another's well, and this includes the right-of-way" Van Leeuwen's *Comm.* Kotzé's trans. vol. 1, p. 297).

Appropriation Act. In the Transvaal Audit and Exchequer Act (14 of 1907) *Appropriation Act* means "any law appropriating public moneys for services as in such law specified."

Appropriation of payments. "It is for the debtor, and failing him for the creditor, to indicate at the time of payment to which of more items than one such payment shall be imputed, and it is only on failure of both that the law steps in to make the appropriation. The debtor, and failing him the creditor, must declare his intention before or at the time of payment, in order that it may still be open to the creditor not to accept it upon the debtor's terms, and to the debtor not to make it upon the creditor's terms (Voet, 46, 3, 16). If the debtor's intention had been declared before payment and not withdrawn, the creditor would be quite justified in acting upon it, and if he did so act upon it there would be no necessity for any declaration of his intention. If the course of dealing between the parties has been such that the creditor has been reasonably led to believe that any payment was intended to be imputed to a particular item, and has acted upon that belief, the debtor cannot afterwards claim that the law shall step in to make the appropriation" (*per* DE VILLIERS, C.J., in *Stiglingh* v. *French*, 9 S.C. at p. 411).

Approval, *see* SALE ON APPROVAL. See also *Thompson* v. *Seale* (19 S.C. 294).

Approved diagram, a term used in the Transvaal Mining Rights Amendment Ordinance (6 of 1902, since repealed), where it means "a diagram approved by the Surveyor-General without publication." On the other hand a "confirmed diagram" requires confirmation by the Surveyor-General and publication in the *Gazette*. (*See* CONFIRMED DIAGRAM.

Appulsio, appulsion. This term equally with *avulsio* is applied to the case of a quantity of earth being torn from an estate by the force of a stream or river and carried to another estate situate along the banks of such stream or river. The ownership of such ground remains with the owner of the former estate until the ground has become firmly attached to the latter estate. *See* AVULSIO.

Aquaeductus, the servitude of water-leading. It is the right of leading water through or out of another man's landed property either from the fountain head or any other place according to agreement (Voet's *Comm.* 8, 3, 6). A servitude of *aquaeductus* acquired by prescription by a lower farm over an upper property on a perennial stream, by which the right is obtained to take all the water which collected in a dam situated on the upper farm for the use of the lower property, does not of itself deprive the upper proprietor of his riparian rights to the use of water out of the stream above the dam (*De Klerk* v. *Niehaus*, 14 S.C. 302). A servitude of *aquaeductus* does not give the owner of the dominant tenement the right to take materials from the servient tenement for the purposes of repairing and maintaining the aqueduct and of enabling him to better enjoy his servitude (*Steyn* v. *Zeeman*, 20 S.C. 221).

Aquaehaustus, a rural servitude entitling the owner of the dominant tenement to draw water from a well, pond or stream on the servient tenement. In the Roman law, which required a *causa perpetua* for all praedial servitudes, the servitude *aquaehaustus* could exist only with regard to a running body of water, but by the Roman-Dutch law it has been extended to water in a tank or cistern (Voet's *Comm.* 8, 3, 7; Van Leeuwen's *Comm.* 2, 21, 13; Grotius' *Introduction*, 2, 35, 13). The servitude includes a right-of-way to the water in favour of the dominant owner, and where the dominant and servient tenements are on different sides of a river forming the boundary between them it also includes a right to a footbridge over the river (*Hawkins* v. *Munnik*, 1 Menz. 465).

Arbiter (D.), arbitrator. A person chosen by parties to settle or decide a dispute between them. An *arbiter* must be a person of full age and capable of managing his own affairs (Kersteman's *Woordenboek*, vol. 1, p. 22).

Arbitrage (D.), arbitration. *See* ARBITRATION.

Arbitrage operations. "This is the name given to the transactions of certain bankers and mercantile houses who can draw upon, or be drawn upon by, a foreign house or agent. Profits can be made by buying bills in one centre and selling them in another, if there is sufficient difference in the rates ruling at these centres. It is a form of speculation in differences. There are *arbitrage* transactions in bills, in bullion, in stocks and shares, but in each case the operations are similar and the profits are made through the differences in price which may exist in various centres" (Sykes' *Banking and Currency*, p. 200).

"**Arbitrarily.**" "The word *arbitrarily* does not necessarily imply all want of restraint, for it has been defined to be a discretion to act at pleasure, only to a certain extent" (*per* BARRY, J.P., in *Donian* v. *Kingwilliamstown Borough Council*, 2 E.D.C. at p. 29).

Arbitrateur (D.), an arbitrator.

Arbitration, the reference, by agreement, of a matter in dispute to one or more impartial persons for their decision. The agreement under which the reference is made is called a "submission" or "deed of submission"; the persons chosen to decide the dispute, if one or two only, are called "arbitrators"; if a third is chosen, for the purpose of deciding in case the two arbitrators cannot agree, he is called an "umpire"; the decision of the arbitrators or umpire, as the case may be, is called an "award." See Act 29 of 1898 (C.C.); Act 24 of 1898 (N.); Ordinance 24 of 1904 (T.).

Arbitrium boni viri, the decision of a good man; a reasonable decision. Where anything is left to a person to decide he must make a reasonable decision (*Digest*, 50, 17, 22, 1). Thus where a wife's father undertakes to give a dowry, and the amount to be given is left to his discretion, he must exercise a reasonable discretion (*Digest*, 31, 1, 1).

Arglist (D.), deceit, fraud; equivalent to the Roman law *dolus malus*. *See* DOLUS MALUS.

Argumentum ab inconvenienti plurimum valet in lege, an argument drawn from inconvenience is of much force in law. This maxim has an important application in the construction both of private deeds and of Acts of Parliament. Although no departure can be permitted from the strict letter of a deed or statute, where the words are plain and admit of no ambiguity, yet where these are doubtful and have not a necessary meaning, the construction may be decided by considerations of convenience. Thus if in a will there be expressions of doubtful meaning and great inconvenience will result from the adoption of one construction, it will go far to show that such a construction was not according to the true intention of the testator, and will justify another construction which will not be followed by such inconvenience. If, however, the words are not equivocal, but can have only one meaning, arguments of inconvenience will not be allowed to induce a construction opposed to such meaning. So in the construction of an Act of Parliament, if the language is of doubtful meaning that construction will not be adopted which would result in great inconvenience, but another construction not attended with such inconvenience will be considered as more in accordance with the true intention of the legislature, and will be preferred (*Venter* v. *Rex*, [1907] T.S. 910).

Arms. In Act 10 of 1907 (T.), sec. 1, the term *arm* or *arms* includes "any gun, rifle, revolver, pistol or other firearm not being a cannon, or any material part of any *arm* as herein [in the Act] defined, but shall not include any *arm bonâ fide* kept as a curio." See also Act 23 of 1908 (O.R.C.), sec. 2.

Arraignment. "In its usual and ordinary acceptation the *arraignment* of an accused person means putting him on his trial" (*per* KOTZÉ, J.P., in *Kerr* v. *Rex*, [1907] E.D.C. at p. 332, and see authorities there quoted; also judgment of GRAHAM, J., at p. 348).

Arrha, earnest. *Arrhae* may consist either of money or other things. An *arrha* is often given as a token of a purchase and to knit the bargain; but sometimes it is given as a proof of an inchoate purchase to be further perfected in writing or otherwise in terms of an agreement of the parties. In the latter case the inchoate purchase may be receded from at the loss to the one party of the earnest given, or on restitution by the other of double the amount which he has received. In the former case all *poenitentia* is disallowed (see Voet's *Comm.* 18, 1, 25; *Brest and Ladon* v. *Heydenrych*, 13 S.C. 21; and *Joseph* v. *Halkett*, 19 S.C. 293).

Arrhae sponsalitiae, the earnest or present in Roman law which was given by the *sponsus* to the *sponsa* or her father, or by the *sponsa* to the *sponsus*, at the time of making the betrothal. If the marriage were for a good reason broken off the *arrhae* had to be returned; if without good reason it was forfeited to the innocent party. If the *sponsa* were to blame she had to restore the gift along with a penalty of fourfold its value, afterwards, however, reduced to a penalty of the value of the gift (Hunter's *Roman Law*, 4th ed. p. 696).

Arson. "This crime is committed when a person, with the wilful intent of injuring others, has set fire to buildings or other immovable property, whereby such property has caught fire and damage has been occasioned" (Van der Linden's *Institutes*, Juta's trans. 3rd. ed. p. 207). But where a man married in community of property set fire to a house which originally belonged to his wife, and thus burnt a house forming portion of the joint estate of himself and his wife, it was held that, as the sole administrator and part owner of such joint estate, he could not properly be convicted of the crime of *arson* (*Regina* v. *Van Vliet*, 9 S.C. 273). See the Native Territories' Penal Code (Act 24 of 1886 (C.C.)), secs. 236 *et seq.* See also INCENDIUM.

Art unions, voluntary associations established for the purpose of encouraging the arts, and for the purchase of paintings, drawings or other works of art to be afterwards allotted and distributed by chance among the members, subscribers or contributors, forming part of such association; or for raising money by subscription or contribution to be allotted or distributed by chance or otherwise as prizes among such members, subscribers or contributors on condition that such moneys so distributed be expended solely in the purchase of paintings, drawings or other works of art. *Art unions* were legalised in the Cape Colony by Act 28 of 1860.

"**As one with,**" the phrase "to be read *as one with*" discussed in *Rex* v. *Mason*, ([1907] E.D.C. at p. 21), where KOTZÉ, J.P., said, "The expression *as one with* is an objectionable phrase; it has not, so far as I am aware, received any authoritative judicial interpretation."

"As they stood." As to sale of bricks in kilns *as they stood*, see *Elliott* v. *McKillop* (19 S.C. 350).

Ascendants, ancestors; persons related to one another in the ascending line; opposed to "descendants."

Asiatic. The term *Asiatic* is defined in the East London Municipality Amendment Act (12 of 1895 (C.C.), sec. 25) to mean "any member of any aboriginal race of the continent or islands of Asia, and any person descended from any such race." In Act 1 of 1899 (N.), sec. 5, it is defined to "include all aboriginal natives of Asia and their descendants." See also Act 1 of 1906 (N.), sec. 3.

For the Transvaal, see Ordinance 29 of 1906, sec. 2, and Act 36 of 1908, sec. 1.

Assault, "an assault is (*a*) an attempt unlawfully to apply any the least actual force to the person of another directly or indirectly; (*b*) the act of using a gesture towards another giving him reasonable grounds to believe that the person using that gesture meant to apply such actual force to his person as aforesaid; (*c*) the act of depriving another of his liberty; in either case without the consent of the person assaulted, or with such consent if it is obtained by fraud" (Stephen's *Digest of the Criminal Law*, 5th ed. p. 202).

In the Native Territories' Penal Code (Act 24 of 1886 (C.C.), sec. 155) *assault* is thus defined: "An *assault* is the act of intentionally applying force to the person of another, directly or indirectly, or attempting or threatening by any act or gesture to apply such force to the person of another, if the person making the threat has or causes the other to believe upon reasonable grounds that he has the present ability to effect his purpose."

Assessment, the estimate of the value of property upon which a tax or charge is payable to a Government or local authority; also the tax or charge so payable; an estimate of the amount payable as damages, or by way of compensation by one person to another. Defined in the Cape Additional Taxation Act (36 of 1904), sec. 42, to mean "an estimate of the value of the amount of any income liable to taxation under this Act as well as the amount of tax imposed thereon respectively, and includes all matters comprised in any return required by or under this Act."

Assets, the property owned by a person.

Assign. (1) To make over or transfer a right or thing from one person to another.

(2) The person to whom some right or thing is made over or transferred.

Under the Cape Copyright Act (2 of 1873, sec. 9) the word *assigns* is construed to mean and include every person in whom the interest of an author in copyright shall be vested, whether derived from such author before or after the publication of any book, and whether acquired by sale, donation, legacy, or by operation of law or otherwise; see also Act 46 of 1905 (C.C.), sec. 1. A similar definition is to be found in the Natal Copyright Act (17 of 1897), sec. 3. For definition in Natal Play Rights Act, 1898, see Act 44 of 1898, sec. 2.

Assignatie (D.), an assignation whereby some person in writing requests his correspondent, or his debtor in matters of trade, to pay a certain sum of money on his account to the holder of the *assignatie*. An *assignatie* resembled a bill of exchange in some respects, while it differed in others; for instance, Van der Keessel tells us that in Roman-Dutch law there was no real exchange unless the bill was drawn at one place and was to be paid at another, which in an assignation was not necessary. Moreover, in exchange there was a sale and a purchase between the remittent and the drawer, whilst in an assignation there was only a simple mandate to pay money to the assignee (see Van der Keessel, *Thes.* 837–52).

Assignatus utitur jure auctoris, a cessionary exercises the right of his author or cedent. On the one hand, the cessionary is entitled to all the privileges of his cedent where these are not merely personal, as, for example, the privileges of the Treasury and of minors, but are real, attaching to the debt, such as the preference for funeral expenses and medical fees (Voet's *Comm.* 11, 4, 12; Matthaeus, *De Auctionibus*, 1, 21, 7). So also where security has been given for the payment of the debt, the cedent's right to sue the sureties or to realise the pledges will pass to the cessionary. On the other hand, the cessionary has no greater rights than his cedent, and is liable to all exceptions and defences which may be pleaded against the latter. An exception to this principle, however, lies in the case of bills of exchange, payment of which may be enforced by a holder in due course notwithstanding defects of title of prior parties and of personal defences which may be available to prior parties amongst themselves. If, however, a bill is negotiated after it is overdue, the indorsee acquires no better title than the person had from whom he took it. The same applies where a bill, which is not overdue, has been dishonoured and a person takes it with notice of dishonour: he takes the bill subject to any defect of title attaching to it at the time of dishonour.

Assignment. (1) The transference of a right or interest. In speaking of the word *assignment* as applied to leases INNES, C.J., in *Rolfes, Nebel & Co.* v. *Zweigenhaft* ([1903] T.S. at p. 189) said: "I have used the word *assignment* because it is used in the plea, though no such term with respect to leases is known to the Roman or Roman-Dutch law. It belongs purely to the terminology of English and Scotch law. The word *assignment* is derived from *assignare*, to point out, to mark out, and there is no derivative of that word used by the Dutch lawyers in connection with lease or cession. . . The technical distinctions of the English law regarding the *assignment* of leases are nowhere to be found in the Roman or Roman-Dutch law."

There must be strict proof that an absolute *assignment* has been made, and that notice of such *assignment* has been given to the lessor (*Parkins* v. *Lippert*, 12 S.C. at p. 187).

(2) The transference of the assets of an estate by the debtor to an assignee or trustee in trust for his creditors. Such *assignments* in favour of creditors are recognised by statute law in Natal (see secs. 158–164 of Law 47 of 1887) and in the Orange River Colony (see Ordinance 3 of 1906).

Assist at a crime. "Everybody who, in the opinion of the judge, does something to further the purpose of a criminal is a person who assists or helps at the crime. Even the person who keeps a look-out to see that the police do not interrupt the perpetrator of a crime is punishable according to our law" (*per* WESSELS, J., in *Rex* v. *Peerkhan and Lalloo*, [1906] T.S. at p. 804). "Our law differs considerably from the English law in that respect. Our law is void of any technicality. It says that a person who *assists at a crime* is himself guilty of the offence" (*per* WESSELS, J., *ibid.* at p. 803).

Assize. (1) A judicial assembly or court in England held under the King's Commission in every county to take criminal prosecutions and to hear cases at *nisi prius*.

(2) To regulate weights and measures in accordance with statute law.

Assizer, a person duly appointed to assize and mark weights and measures; one to whom the standards of weights and measure are entrusted. See Act 15 of 1876 (C.C.); Law 19 of 1872 (N.), secs. 66 *et seq.*

Association, an organised body of persons who have joined together under some contract, statute, regulations or rules, for the purpose of carrying out some common object. See Law 4 of 1892 (O.R.C.), sec. 1 (*b*); Act 3 of 1873 (C.C.), sec. 1.

"The word *association* in the sense in which it is now commonly used is etymologically inaccurate, for *association* does not properly describe the thing formed, but properly and etymologically describes the act of associating together, from which act of *association* there is formed a company or partnership. But I believe that according to the vernacular we use on these subjects the difference which the Act [Companies Act, 1862 (Eng.)] intended to draw between a company or *association* and an ordinary partnership is this: An ordinary partnership is a partnership composed of definite individuals bound together by contract between themselves to continue combined for some joint object, either during pleasure or during a limited time, and is essentially composed of the persons originally entering into the contract with one another. A company or *association* (which I take to be synonymous terms) is the result of an arrangement by which parties intend to form a partnership which is constantly changing, a partnership to-day consisting of certain members and to-morrow consisting of some only of those members along with others who have come in, so that there will be a constant shifting of the partnership, a determination of the old and the creation of a new partnership, and with the intention that, so far as the partners can by agreement between themselves bring about such a result, the new partnership shall succeed to the assets and liabilities of the old partnership. This object as regards liabilities could not in point of law be attained by any arrangement between the persons themselves, unless the persons contracting with them authorised the change by a novation, or unless by special provisions in Acts of Parliament sanction was given to such arrangements" (*per* JAMES, L.J., in *Smith* v. *Anderson*, 15 Ch. D. at p. 273).

Assumed curator, a person assumed or appointed by a curator nominate by virtue of a special authority contained in the will or other deed by which the curator nominate was himself appointed. Such *assumed curator*, when duly appointed and confirmed by letters of confirmation granted by the Master of the Supreme Court, occupies the same position in law as a curator dative.

Assumed executor, a person nominated or assumed by the executor testamentary in the estate of a deceased person by virtue of a special authority contained in the will; the assumption takes place by means of a written deed, which is filed with the Master of the Supreme Court (or, in Natal, with the Registrar of Deeds), who, on being satisfied that it is in order, and that it is authorised by the will, grants letters of administration to the *assumed executor* on his giving the required security. The law relating to executors dative is applicable to *assumed executors* (see sec. 24 of Ordinance 104 of 1833 (C.C.); sec. 8 of Act 19 of 1894 (N.); sec. 30 of Proclamation 28 of 1902 (T.); sec. 27 of Ordinance 18 of 1905 (O.R.C.). The Cape Ordinance is also operative in Rhodesia). See *Re Titterton's Estate*, 12 S.C. 1; 5 C.T.R. 17; Maasdorp's *Institutes*, 2nd ed. vol. 1, p. 217; Tennant's *Notary's Manual*, 6th ed. pp. 141, 196; Van Zyl's *Notarial Practice*, p. 299.

Assumed tutor, a person assumed or appointed by a tutor testamentary by virtue of a special authority contained in the will or other deed by which the tutor testamentary was himself appointed. Such *assumed tutor*, when duly appointed and confirmed by letters of confirmation granted by the Master of the Supreme Court, occupies the same position in law as a tutor dative.

Assumptie (D.), assumption. In Roman-Dutch law *assumptie* was a right which was given by a testamentary disposition to an administrator or guardian, authorising him during his administration or guardianship, as the case may be, to assume and appoint another person as co-administrator or co-guardian.

Assurance. *See* INSURANCE.

Assurantie (D.), assurance or insurance. *See* INSURANCE.

Assured. *See* INSURED.

Asylum, a place specially set apart for the reception and treatment or detention of persons suffering from mental or bodily infirmities or other misfortunes. In the Cape Lunacy Act (1 of 1897) the term *asylum* is defined to mean "an *asylum* for lunatics now existing or which may hereafter be declared by the Governor as an *asylum* or place for the reception or detention of lunatics." By the same Act (sec. 44) it is made a penal offence to receive or detain a lunatic or alleged lunatic in the Cape Colony in an *asylum*, or for payment take charge of, or board or lodge, or detain a lunatic or alleged lunatic, except under the provisions of the Act. The Transvaal has adopted the same definition for *asylum* as the Cape Colony; see Proclamation 36 of 1902, sec. 2; Ordinance 23 of 1904, sec. 2; and so too the Orange River Colony, see Ordinance 13 of 1906, sec. 2.

"At merchant's risk," see *Briscoe & Co.* v. *Powell & Co.* (22 T.L.R. 128).

Attempt to commit a crime. Mere acts of preparation, though done with criminal intent, do not amount to *attempt to commit crime*, and are not indictable under the common law (*Rex* v. *Sharpe*, [1903] T.S. 868). In *Regina* v. *Topken and Skelly* (1 A.C. 471) the prisoners had gone out with the intention of waylaying and robbing a post-cart, but as the cart did not pass that way they did nothing, and it was held they were not guilty of an attempt to commit the crime intended. DE VILLIERS, C.J., said: "If it were impossible for them, circumstanced as they were, to commit the crime of robbery and murder, it was equally impossible for them to be guilty of an attempt to commit either of those crimes." See also *Queen* v. *Kaplan* (10 S.C. 259); and *Misnum* v. *Rex* ([1906] T.S. 216). See Ordinance 26 of 1904 (T.), sec. 37.

Atterminatie (D.), a form of relief granted by the Dutch courts to a defendant whereby time was allowed to him within which to pay his creditors their debts on security being given for due payment on expiration of the time allowed. See Van der Linden's *Institutes*, 3, 7, 3. This security had usually to be provided within fourteen days. *Atterminatie* could not be granted against mortgage or secured creditors, or against the proceeds of the sale of houses, lands and other effects destined to form the capital funds the yearly revenue of which was appropriated for the maintenance of widows and orphans, or in cases where aliment would be reduced (Kersteman's *Woordenboek*, vol. 1, p. 32). *Atterminatie* is not now operative in South Africa; see Van Leeuwen's *Comm.* Kotzé's trans. vol. 2, p. 341, translator's note.

Attermination, Letters of, *see* ATTERMINATIE.

Attestatien (D.), derived from the Latin *adtestatum* (*adtestor*), are all such documents by which a person makes a solemn declaration. Attestations, which are made on oath, receive full credence in law. But attestations not made on oath have no such credence according to the maxim *Testis non juratus nullam meretur fidem* (Kersteman, *Woordenboek, sub voce*).

Attestation. (1) Of Wills. The signing by a person of his name as a witness to the due execution by the testator of a will or codicil in manner prescribed by law. It has been held in *Re Le Roux* (3 S.C. 56) that the signing by means of a mark was a sufficient subscription within the meaning of Ordinance 15 of 1845 (C.C.); and where a witness to a will, who was unable to write, held the pen at the top, whilst another person guided it and wrote the name of such witness, and it was proved to the satisfaction of the court that the transaction was *bonâ fide*, and that the witness held the pen with the object of thus attesting the will, it was held that his attestation was valid (*Van Niekerk* v. *Van Niekerk*, 15 S.C. 229). Wills to be valid in the Cape Colony must be executed as follows: (*a*) they must be signed at the foot or end by the testator or by some other person in his presence and by his direction; and (*b*) such signature must be acknowledged by the testator in the presence of two or more competent witnesses present at the same time; and (*c*) such witnesses must attest and subscribe the will in the presence of the person executing the same; and when the instrument is written on more leaves than one "the party executing the same and also the witnesses shall sign or shall have signed their names upon at least one side of every leaf upon which the instrument shall be or shall have been written" (Ordinance 15 of 1845 (C.C.), sec. 3). In *Re Trollip* (12 S.C. 243), where the testator and witnesses duly signed at the foot of a will written on more pages than one, but the only signature of the testatrix to the first leaf was made by means of her initials just above the initials of the witnesses, apparently made with the view of authenticating an erasure on the second page, it was held by the Supreme Court (C.C.) that the will should not be rejected, as not complying with the Ordinance just referred to, because of the signatures having been made by means of initials. *See* Sign. Similar provision is made for the attestation of wills in Natal by Law 2 of 1868, sec. 1; in the Transvaal by Ordinance 14 of 1903, sec. 1; in the Orange River Colony by Ordinance 11 of 1904, sec. 1; the law on the subject in Rhodesia is the same as that in the Cape Colony.

(2) Of Power of Attorney. Evidence of its due execution. As to the manner in which powers of attorney in the Cape Colony must be attested, see Act 10 of 1879.

(3) See Law 9 of 1859 (N.), for declaring the number of witnesses necessary to attest acts or deeds.

(4) *See* Attestatien.

Attorney (derived from O.Fr. *attorné;* p.p. of *attorner*, to assign or appoint) means one who has been appointed by another to act for him, and is the term specially applied in this country to practitioners of the Supreme Courts. It answers to the English term *solicitor*, but prior to 1875 solicitor in England denoted a practitioner in the Court of Chancery as distinguished from *attorney*, the name given to those who practised in the courts of common law (*see* SOLICITOR). As to admission of *attorneys* in Cape Colony, see Rules of Court 149–152, 199, 213, 293 and 362; Charter of Justice, secs. 19–24; Act 12 of 1858, secs. 3–7; Act 16 of 1873, sec. 21; Act 27 of 1883; Act 3 of 1892, secs. 2–7; Act 11 of 1903, secs. 3–6; in Natal, see Rules of Court of 14th July, 1904; in Transvaal, see Proclamation 14 of 1902, sec. 11; Ordinance 31 of 1904, secs. 7, 8 and 12; Government Notice 92 of 1906; Ordinance 1 of 1904; and Act 33 of 1908; in Orange River Colony, see Ordinance 4 of 1902, sec. 13, and Ordinance 13 of 1904.

Attributrix. Grotius (*De Jure Belli ac Pacis*, 1, 1, 8) divides justice into *justitia expletrix* and *attributrix*. Voet (*Comm.* 1, 1, 10) thus describes the distinction: "Under *expletrix* are included all things which one is not merely bound to give and fulfil from reasons of equity, but which when unwilling he can be compelled to give or fulfil by competent legal remedies. . . . On the other hand, the term *attributrix* is applied to all those things which one may be bound to do according to equity and natural reason, and doing which, he may be thought worthy of praise among good men, yet which, if he refuse to do them, thus laying aside shame and spurning the bonds of equity, no public authority can force him to fulfil." (See also Best on *Evidence*, sec. 36.)

Atturnatus extra-judicialis, one of the two classes of attorney recognised by the *Lex Romana* in the middle ages. He was a mere agent to assist in the transaction of business (Wessels' *History*, p. 195).

Atturnatus judicialis, one of the two classes of attorney recognised by the *Lex Romana* in the middle ages. He was "employed by a litigant to assist him in the conduct of his lawsuit" (Wessels' *History*, p. 195).

Auction, (1) an increasing; hence sales by auction.

(2) A public sale at which the bidding increases gradually and the highest bidder becomes the purchaser. "In sales by public auction each bidder is bound by his bid, and yet acquires no right if others bid higher" (Grotius' *Introd.* 3, 14, 30).

Auctioneer, a person duly licensed to sell goods or property by public auction. "*Auctioneer* means any person who sells any article or thing at any public sale where the highest bidder, whether the bidding be by the rise or by the fall, becomes the purchaser" (Act 38 of 1887 (C.C.), sec. 3). See Ordinance 23 of 1905 (T.), sec. 2; and *Dely & De Kock* v. *Civil Commissioner* ([1906] T.S. at p. 96). See also Ordinance 10 of 1903 (O.R.C.), sec. 2.

Audi alteram partem, hear the other side; a maxim of universal application in the administration of justice, according to which a man is entitled to have an opportunity of being heard before he is condemned in his person or property.

Auditor, an accountant appointed for the purpose of verifying and stating the true financial position of a company, firm or individual. In the case of companies he must see what exceptional duties, if any, are cast upon him by the articles of association (*Re Kingston Cotton Co.*, [1896] 2 Ch. 284).

The duties of an *auditor* were described by LINDLEY, L.J., in *Re London and General Bank* ([1895] 2 Ch. 673) as follows: "An *auditor* has nothing to do with the prudence or imprudence of making loans with or without security. It is nothing to him whether the business of a company is being conducted prudently or imprudently, profitably or unprofitably. It is nothing to him whether dividends are properly or improperly declared, provided he discharges his own duty to the shareholders. His business is to ascertain and state the true financial position of the company at the time of the audit, and his duty is confined to that. But then comes the question: How is he to ascertain that position? The answer is: By examining the books of the company. But he does not discharge his duty by doing this without inquiry and without taking any trouble to see that the books themselves show the company's true position. He must take reasonable care to ascertain that they do so. Unless he does this, his audit would be worse than idle farce. Assuming the books to be so kept as to show the true position of a company, the *auditor* has to frame a balance-sheet showing that position according to the books, and to certify that the balance-sheet presented is correct in that sense. But his first duty is to examine the books, not merely for the purpose of ascertaining what they do show, but also for the purpose of satisfying himself that they show the true financial position of the company. This is quite in accordance with the decision of STIRLING, J., in *Leeds Estate Building and Investment Co.* v. *Shepherd* (36 Ch. D. 787). An *auditor*, however, is not bound to do more than exercise reasonable care and skill in making inquiries and investigations. He is not an insurer; he does not guarantee that the books do correctly show the true position of the company's affairs; he does not even guarantee that his balance-sheet is accurate according to the books of the company. If he did, he would be responsible for an error on his part, even if he were himself deceived without any want of reasonable care on his part—say, by the fraudulent concealment of a book from him. His obligation is not so onerous as this. Such I take to be the duty of the *auditor:* he must be honest—*i.e.* he must not certify what he does not believe to be true, and he must take reasonable care and skill before he believes that what he certifies is true. What is reasonable care in any particular case must depend upon the circumstances of that case. Where there is nothing to excite suspicion, very little inquiry will be reasonably sufficient, and, in practice, I believe, business men select a few cases at haphazard, see that they are right, and assume that others like them are correct also. Where suspicion is aroused, more care is obviously necessary; but still an *auditor* is not bound to exercise more than reasonable care and skill even in a case of suspicion, and he is perfectly justified in acting on the opinion of an expert where special knowledge is required."

Aureus, the standard gold coin of Rome. It was the seventy-second part of a pound of gold (Troy), weighing 80 grains, equivalent to 120 grains avoirdupois, and was equal to about £1, 1s. 1d. (see Van Leeuwen's *Comm.* 4, 30, 4). It derives its importance with us from the rule of the Roman law, which has been adopted by the Roman-Dutch law, that donations exceeding the value of 500 *aurei* in order to be valid must be registered. For the purpose of this rule an *aureus* is regarded by us as equivalent to one pound sterling (*Thorpe's Executor* v. *Thorpe's Tutor*, 4 S.C. 488).

Authentica si qua mulier. The benefit conferred upon married women by Justinian in cases of suretyship for their husbands is known as the *beneficium authenticae "si qua mulier,"* and the constitution appertaining to the same is found in *Code*, 4, 29, 22: "If any woman becomes a party to an acknowledgment of debt, or signs it, and binds her property or her person, for and on behalf of her husband, we have determined that this transaction shall under no circumstances have validity, whether some act of this nature be performed once only or repeatedly, whether the debt be a private or a public one; indeed, it shall be accounted as never having been effected or signed, unless it is clearly established that the money has been expended for the woman's own benefit." See *Graaff-Reinet Board of Executors* v. *Maasdorp* ([1908] E.D.C. 431).

Authenticae. *Authenticum* is an original writing. Into the *Code* glossarists introduced what they called *Authenticae*—notes of the alterations made on the law by Justinian's *Novels* (Muirhead's *Roman Law,* p. 410). Thus appended to *C.* 4, 29, 22, we find an excerpt of *Novell.* 134, *cap.* 8.

Authenticum. *See* AUTHENTICAE.

Author, generally the original writer or composer of some literary work. In the Cape Copyright in Works of Art Act (46 of 1905) the term *author* is defined to mean "the inventor, designer, engraver, sculptor or maker of any work of art; provided that the *author* of a work of art made by the employé of any person or firm in virtue of his employment shall mean the person or firm under whose orders, or in the course of whose business, the work of art was made by such employé."

In the Natal Copyright Act (17 of 1897), sec. 3, "*author* means the author, inventor, designer, engraver or maker of any work, and in the case of a posthumous book means the proprietor of the manuscript." For definition in Play Rights Act, 1898, see Act 44 of 1898 (N.), sec. 2.

Authority. (1) Power; the right to command.

(2) A precedent. As to the binding force of text-books as *authorities*, see *Edmondson* v. *Edmondson* (23 N.L.R. at p. 373).

Autrefois acquit, formerly acquitted. *See* AUTREFOIS CONVICT.

Autrefois convict, formerly convicted. The general principle is *nemo debet bis vexari*, a man must not be put twice in peril for the same offence. Hence if he be indicted a second time he can plead as a complete defence his former conviction or accquittal (Cape Rule of Court 94), even though the conviction or acquittal took place in a foreign country. To determine in any particular case whether such a plea is available, it is necessary to ask:—

(1) Was the prisoner "in jeopardy" on the first indictment? A prisoner cannot have been in jeopardy if the indictment was legally invalid; for no conviction upon it would have been effectual. The prisoner may thus object to the jurisdiction of the court, or he may have the indictment quashed, but in such cases he would be amenable to a fresh indictment. Thus in *R.* v. *Myers* (2 S.C. 221) and *R.* v. *Twalutunga* (20 S.C. 425) the prisoners were convicted, but upon appeal the convictions were quashed upon a technicality, whereupon they were again indicted aud convicted, and the appeal court held that as the prisoners had not been in jeopardy under the first indictment, they were respectively properly tried under the second indictment.

(2) Was there a final verdict? If the jury cannot agree and they are discharged without a verdict, the prisoner may again be tried; but not if the indictment also has been withdrawn and the prisoner has been discharged (*Kerr* v. *Rex,* [1907] E.D.C. 324).

(3) Was the previous charge substantially the same as the second one? Dr. Kenny (*Outlines of Criminal Law*, p. 470) says: "They are sufficiently nearly identical, if evidence of the facts alleged in the second indictment would legally have sufficed to procure some conviction on the first indictment; whether it were a conviction for the offence actually charged in that first indictment, or even for some other, either of an equal or of a lower degree of heinousness. Hence the two indictments must refer to the same transaction. Yet the intent or the circumstances alleged in the one may be more aggravated than those alleged in the other. Thus an acquittal or conviction for a common assault bars a subsequent indictment for an assault with intent to murder, or even for an unlawful wounding; and an acquittal for manslaughter bars a subsequent indictment for murder, and *vice versâ*. On the other hand, an acquittal for an unlawful wounding does not bar a subsequent indictment for murder [cf. *R.* v. *Stuurman*, 1 Roscoe, 83]; and an acquittal on an indictment for murdering A by burning a house in which he was asleep, does not bar a subsequent indictment for arson. For in each of these two pairs of charges the pair are so dissimilar that it would not have been legally possible to obtain a conviction upon the first indictment by the evidence necessary to support the charge made in the second one."

Aval, a surety. A party who signs a bill otherwise than as drawer, acceptor or indorser becomes a surety or *aval*. The holder of the bill had by Roman-Dutch law his summary remedy against the guarantor *jure cambiali*, but the practice of giving provisional sentence against such indorsers has never been followed in the Cape Supreme Court (*Norton* v. *Satchwell*, 1 Menz. 77, and *Coetzee* v. *Tiran*, Foord, 42).

Avarye (D.), average. *See* AVERAGE.

Average. (1) IN SHIPPING LAW: Van der Keessel (*Thes.* 780) says: "Average, which is accurately treated of in the new law of Rotterdam, is there defined as 'the loss arising from any voluntary act done with the view of preserving the vessel and goods, or of averting greater and probable damage.' Such loss is to be made good by contribution from the vessel and goods, and is termed *gross average*." *See* GENERAL AVERAGE; PARTICULAR AVERAGE.

(2) IN FIRE INSURANCE LAW: Porter in his *Laws of Insurance* (5th ed. p. 277) says that conditions as to average "take two forms: (1) a condition declaring the property insured to be subject to the conditions of *average*; (2) a condition declaring that if any other subsisting insurance or insurances effected by the insured or any other person, covering any property by the policy in question insured, either exclusively or together with any other property in and subject to the same risk, should be subject to the conditions of *average*, the insurance on such property under the policy should be subject to the conditions of *average* in like manner." See also *McGrath* v. *South British Insurance Co.* (3 S.C. 81); *Kaffrarian Colonial Bank* v. *Grahamstown Fire Insurance Co.* (5 E.D.C. 61).

Averment, the allegation or statement of some thing as a positive fact.

Avulsio, avulsion, is a violent separation of a piece of ground which is carried by a river to the property of another and there annexed. Such ground continues the property of its rightful owner until it has become firmly attached to the estate to which it has been carried by means of roots of trees or plants growing thereon. See Holland's *Jurisprudence*, 10th ed. p. 208. *See* APPULSIO.

Award, the decision of arbitrators or an umpire in arbitration proceedings, made by virtue of a submission or other proper reference.

Azig (D.). "In Friesland the schepenen were called *azigen*. Grimm tells us that *azig* meant lawgiver" (Wessels' *History*, p. 160).

Azing or **Aafga** "was an ordinary judge in civil matters among the Frisians. He was well-born, but not noble, and had no persons of noble birth under his jurisdiction. He dispensed justice together with the neighbours or inhabitants of the vicinage (*gebuyren*)" (Meyer, *Woordenschat, sub voce,* referred to in an article by KOTZÉ, J.P., in 26 S.A.L.J. 59).

Azing en gebuyren (D.). "In regard to the ordinary tribunal of *azing en gebuyren* in the country, which exercised jurisdiction in lesser crimes and in civil matters, the *baljuw* of Rhineland had from very early times power to appoint two sworn persons, called *Azingen,* whose duty it was, the one on the upper and the other on the lower side of the Rhine, to appear on special court days in all the villages and courts of Rhineland in order to hold a court together with the neighbours and those brought by the parties, and to pronounce sentence upon the demand of the *schout* and *taalman* in a certain set form of words, which could not be departed from, and also to discover and ascertain what fines and offences had occurred and to report to the *baljuw* thereon. This mode of holding a court by means of *azing en gebuyren* in the country was in the year 1291 changed in Kennemerland into the practice of proceeding by means of schout and schepenen. But in some other parts of Rhineland this change took place at a much later date by means of an Ordinance of the States of Holland in the year 1577" (KOTZÉ, J.P., article on the *History of the Roman-Dutch Law,* in 26 S.A.L.J. 59).

Baargericht (D.), one of the forms of ordeal employed in early Dutch criminal procedure. "If a murder had been committed, and one or more persons were strongly suspected, they could be compelled to approach the corpse and touch it. If it began to bleed afresh at the touch of the suspected person he was declared guilty. This ordeal was used in the middle ages, and survived until the fifteenth century" (Wessels' *History*, p. 182).

Bail, the releasing of a prisoner from custody upon his entering into an undertaking or recognisance by himself alone, or by himself and one or more sureties according to the nature and circumstances of the case; the condition of the obligation being that the prisoner shall appear and answer to any indictment that may be presented against him, in any competent court, for the crime or offence wherewith he is charged, at any time within a specified period from the date thereof, and that he will accept service of any indictment and summons thereon at some certain place by him elected and expressed in the obligation. On the completion of such an obligation (which is only permitted and accepted in respect of bailable offences) the prisoner is released from custody and is said to be liberated on *bail* or admitted to *bail*. See Ordinance 40 of 1828 (C.C.), secs. 45 *et seq*. The rule of law "requires that there shall be a strict construction put on such recognisances as against the Crown" (*per* BARRY, J.P., in *Queen* v. *Long and Others,* 3 E.D.C. at p. 6).

See Ordinance 18 of 1845 (N.), sec. 54; Ordinance 1 of 1903 (T.), secs. 84, 97 *et seq.*; Ordinance 12 of 1902 (O.R.C.), secs. 52 *et seq.*; Ordinance 6 of 1905 (O.R.C.), secs. 6 *et seq.*

Bail bond, a written obligation or recognisance entered into by a prisoner either by himself or jointly with one or more sureties in the manner prescribed by law, and on the due execution of which he becomes entitled to be liberated on bail. *See* BAIL; RECOGNISANCE.

See Ordinance 18 of 1845 (N.), sec. 63; Ordinance 1 of 1903 (T.), sec. 105; Ordinance 12 of 1902 (O.R.C.), sec. 52.

Bailable offence, an offence in respect of which a prisoner is entitled to claim that he may be admitted to bail. See Ordinance 40 of 1828 (C.C.), secs. 46 to 52; Ordinance 18 of 1845 (N.), sec. 57.

Bailee, an English term, meaning the person to whom goods are delivered in trust upon a contract, express or implied, that the trust shall be faithfully executed on the part of the person to whom the goods are so delivered. *See* BAILMENT.

Bailluw (D.), an old form of spelling *baljuw*. *See* BALJUW.

Bailment, an English term denoting "a delivery of goods on a condition, express or implied, that they shall be restored by the bailee to the bailor, or according to his directions, as soon as the purpose for which they are bailed shall be answered" (Jones on *Bailments*, 4th ed. p. 1). "To constitute a *bailment* of goods the actual or constructive possession of a specific chattel must be transferred by its owner, or his agent duly authorised for that purpose, to another person, in order that that other person may perform some act in connection therewith for which such physical or constructive possession of the chattel is necessary, upon the understanding, either express or implied, that when the act is performed or the service rendered the recipient of the chattel shall redeliver it in specie to its owner or his nominee" (Paine on *Bailments*, p. 1). The nearest approach to *bailments* in Roman-Dutch law is that group of contracts which is regarded as being concluded by delivery of a thing *re*, and not by mere consent. On the question of difference between the English and Roman-Dutch law on the subject, consult Morice's *English and Roman-Dutch Law*, 2nd ed. p. 115.

Bailor, an English term, signifying the person who delivers goods to another person, called the bailee, in trust upon a contract, express or implied, that the trust shall be faithfully executed on the part of the bailee. *See* BAILMENT.

Baker. In the Orange River Colony *baker*, as defined by Ordinance 10 of 1903 (O.R.C.) means "every person who keeps a shop and exposes baked bread, cakes or pastry for sale, whether such person shall have baked such bread, cakes or pastry himself or not; provided that the holder of a general dealer's license who exposes for sale baked bread, cakes or pastry obtained from a licensed *baker* shall not be deemed to be a *baker* under this Ordinance."

Baliow (D.). *See* BALJUW.

Baljuw; Baliow; Ballif (*drossaart, ruwaart*) (D.), in mediæval Latin *bajulus*, a substituted or sub-count, whose duty it was to assemble the court in the first instance in criminal cases in regard to persons who were not of noble birth, and in appeal in civil matters, to prosecute and conduct the proceedings. This officer held in his hand a red staff or rod, or a drawn sword in order to indicate that he had summoned a criminal court, in the proceedings of which the well-born men took part. (See 26 S.A.L.J. 57, *note*).

Ballif (D). *See* BALJUW.

Ballot, a method of secret voting by means of a little ball, or ticket, or slip of paper with writing or printed matter thereon. If it be by ticket or slip of paper, such ticket or slip of paper is usually called a ballot-paper. The ballot by means of the little balls is usually conducted with white and black balls; hence the use of the expression "black ball" in club elections. Parliamentary, municipal and divisional council elections in South Africa are now conducted on the ballot system.

Ballot-box, a receptacle in which ballot papers or balls are placed at an election, where such election is conducted on the ballot system. *See* BALLOT; BALLOT-PAPER.

Ballot-paper, a ticket or slip of paper bearing the names of candidates at an election, and having spaces opposite each name in order that the elector or voter may put his mark against the name of that one of the candidates for whom he wishes to vote. When the ballot-paper has been so marked it is folded by the voter and placed by him in a receptacle prepared for the purpose, called a "ballot-box."

Ban (D.). (1) Formerly denoted jurisdiction.

(2) A public notification of any command or order. Hence *bannen*—to publish or proclaim, *e.g.* banns of marriage.

Banishment, enforced expulsion from a country; a form of punishment, now obsolete in South Africa.

Banker. In the Cape Bills of Exchange Act (19 of 1903) the word *banker* is defined to include a "body of persons, whether incorporated or not, who carry on the business of banking." See also Law 8 of 1887 (N.), sec. 1; Proclamation 11 of 1902 (T.), sec. 1; Ordinance 28 of 1902 (O.R.C.), sec. 1.

In the Transvaal Diamond Trade Ordinance (63 of 1903), sec. 43, *banker* means "any manager, cashier or other officer of a joint-stock bank, acting in his capacity as such." See also Ordinance 40 of 1904 (T.), sec. 9.

In the Orange River Colony Mining of Precious Metals Ordinance, (3 of 1904), sec. 124, *banker* includes "any manager, cashier or other officer of a joint-stock bank acting in his capacity as such."

Bank note. "A *bank note* may be defined as a promissory note issued by a banker payable to bearer on demand. It differs from an ordinary note in that it may be reissued after payment" (Chalmers on *Bills of Exchange*, 6th ed. p. 267). "Bank notes are payable to bearer and circulated freely from hand to hand; besides which they are in many cases legal tender. It may be years before they are presented for payment at the bank which issues them" (Sykes on *Banking and Currency*, 2nd ed. p. 58). The issue of *bank notes* is now generally regulated and restricted by statute. See Act 6 of 1891 (C.C.); Law 2 of 1893 (T.).

As to stolen *bank note*, see *Woodhead, Plant & Co.* v. *Gunn* (11 S.C. at p. 9).

Bankroetier (D.) (formerly *banqueroutier*), a bankrupt; an insolvent person.

Bankrupt, a term used in England to signify an insolvent or a state of insolvency. *See* INSOLVENT. It is sometimes used in South African statutes: see Law 8 of 1887 (N.), sec. 1.

Banks of loan, otherwise called "Lombard," were institutions in the fifteenth and sixteenth centuries, "where any one may pawn and pledge his property at a reasonable sum by the day or the week, as high as the value of the article pawned will fairly admit, for which the pawnbroker may enjoy a reasonable profit for his trouble and the use of his money. For this purpose certain persons are appointed by the Government, besides whom no one is admitted to such lending out on pawn; and in order that the profit may not be placed too high it is fixed at a certain sum" (Van Leeuwen's *Comm.* Kotzé's trans. vol. 2, p. 65). Formerly the supervision of these *banks of loan* was entrusted to the bishops, but in 1578 and 1584 this duty, by Resolution of the States of Holland, was vested in the magistrate of each town. In some places these banks were established by or on behalf of the town and managed by paid persons appointed for the purpose. See *Muller* v. *Chadwick & Co.* ([1906] T.S. at pp. 34 *et seq.*), where *banks of loan* are fully discussed.

Banns, the publication of an intended marriage during public divine service on a Sunday, in an audible manner by some person duly authorised by law to do so in order that persons knowing of any lawful objection to such intended marriage may have an opportunity of declaring their objections (see Marriage Order in Council of 7th

September, 1838, sec. 2, which, subject to certain amendments, is of force in Cape Colony, Natal and Rhodesia; for the Transvaal see Law 3 of 1871, as amended by Proclamation 34 of 1901, Ordinance 40 of 1903, Ordinance 39 of 1904 and Act 13 of 1909; and for the Orange River Colony see Law 26 of 1899).

Banns become void if the marriage is not celebrated within three months of their publication.

Ban-werk (D.). Compulsory service or labour performed by those living on adjoining lands, for the purpose of maintaining the public roads or highways and public waters. (See Van Leeuwen's *Comm.* Kotzé's trans. 2, 21, 7 and 9.)

Barrator, "a common *barrator* is one who habitually moves, excites or maintains suits or quarrels, either at law or otherwise" (Stephen's *Digest of the Criminal Law*, 5th ed. p. 112).

Base metals. *See* MINERAL.

Base minerals. In the Mineral Law Amendment Act (16 of 1907 (C.C.)), sec. 33, *base minerals* is defined as "asbestos, building stone, cinnabar, clay, coal, cobalt, copper, crocidolite, gypsum, iron, lead, manganese, magnesite, nickel, natural gas, oil, salt, slate, tin and such other minerals, not being gold, silver or platinum, as may from time to time be declared to be *base minerals* by Proclamation by the Governor." *See* MINERAL.

Bastard, a person born of parents not legally married. In South Africa the term *bastard* is usually applied to the offspring of a native woman by a European, or to certain coloured persons whose origin it is difficult to trace or describe. See *Queen* v. *Kirsten* (16 S.C. 510); *Rex* v. *Stern* (20 S.C. at p. 566).

Bazaar, a sale of fancy work, other articles, stock or produce in aid of some charitable object; the things so sold being, as a rule, supplied by the promoters of the *bazaar* or their friends gratuitously. To hold a *bazaar* it is not necessary that a license be taken out or auction duty paid. Where, however, the goods are put up to auction and sold to the bidder, the person acting as auctioneer must have a license. But see O.R.C. Law Book, ch. 107, sec. 10, according to which no auction duty or license is required in such cases.

Beacon, a natural or artificial object or erection, used as a landmark or distinguishing point for the purpose of defining or describing the division of land into portions; such as beacons defining the boundaries of farms, lots, erven, claims or water-rights. *Beacons* are also used for defining the boundaries of territory, or sections or areas of country. The size of *beacons* is frequently defined by statute.

Bearer. Under the Bills of Exchange Acts *bearer* means the person in possession of a bill or note which is payable to *bearer* (sec. 2, English Bills of Exchange Act, 1882). See also Act 19 of 1893 (C.C.), sec. 1; Law 8 of 1887 (N.), sec. 1; Proclamation 11 of 1902 (T.), sec. 1; Ordinance 28 of 1902 (O.R.C.), sec. 1.

Bedriegelijke insolventie (D.), fraudulent insolvency. *See* INSOLVENT (D.); FRAUDULENT INSOLVENCY.

Bedriegerijen (D.), cheating; deceit; fraudulent practices.

Bedrog (D.), fraud. Defined by Grotius (*Introduction*, Maasdorp's trans. p. 343) as "wicked deceit practised for the purpose of defrauding a person."

Beer is defined in the Cape Excise Beer Duty Act (11 of 1884), sec. 2, as follows: "Beer includes ale, porter, spruce beer and black beer, and any other description of *beer*, and shall be taken to mean any liquor made from infusion or decoction of malt, grain or saccharine matter which contains spirit, and to which any bitter flavour has been communicated by the addition of hops, herbs or other ingredients capable of being used as a bitter; and any fermented liquor which shall contain not less than" *two* [see Act 36 of 1904 (C.C.), sec. 2] "per centum of proof spirit, although the same shall not be included under the foregoing definition, or cannot be regarded as sweets or made wines, shall, for the purposes of the revenue, be deemed *beer*, and be subject to all regulations applicable to *beer*." See also Act 19 of 1908 (C.C.), sec. 11.

In Natal, in Act 37 of 1901, *beer* is defined to mean and include "ale, porter, spruce beer, lager beer, black beer, and every other spirituous liquor coming within the ordinary appellation of *beer*, and containing more than two per cent. of spirit."

In the Transvaal, in Act 9 of 1907, sec. 1, *beer* means and includes "ale, porter, spruce beer, lager beer, black beer, and every other spirituous liquor coming within the ordinary appellation of *beer* and exceeding three per cent. of proof spirit, but shall not include Kafir beer."

Bees. In the Cape Colony nests or hives of bees whether wild or domesticated are vested in the occupier of the land on which such nests or hives are located. See Act 9 of 1869 (C.C.), and Act 24 of 1886 (C.C.), sec. 178.

"Being thereunto required." This phrase appears in sec. 4 of Ordinance 6 of 1843 (C.C.), which was taken over from the former Insolvency Ordinance of the Cape (Ordinance 64 of 1829, sec. 4). In detailing the circumstances constituting insolvency the following occurs in the section referred to: "or having against him the sentence of any competent court *being thereunto required* shall not satisfy the same, or shall not point out to the officer charged with the execution thereof sufficient disposable property to satisfy the same," &c. In *Re*

Webster (3 Menz. 220) the Cape Supreme Court held that the words "*being thereunto required* shall not satisfy the same," as contained in sec. 4 of Ordinance 64 (C.C.)—now sec. 4 of Ordinance 6 of 1843 (C.C.)—constituted a distinct act of insolvency; and that the words *being thereunto required* had no connection whatever with the clause "or shall not point out," &c. The words *being thereunto required* also appear in sub-sec. (*h*) of sec. 4 of Law 47 of 1887 (N.); and in sub-sec. (*b*) of sec. 8 of Law 13 of 1895 (T.).

See REQUIRED.

Bekentenis (D.), confession; acknowledgment.

Belasting (D.), tax; taxation.

Beleening (D.), a mortgage; a loan on pledge.

Belofte, (D.). According to Van Leeuwen (*Comm.* Kotzé's trans. vol. 2, p. 4) *belofte* is a gratuitous promise, as where a person of his own accord, without having been asked to do so and without any debt, offers to do or give something to another, as opposed to *toezegging* (a promise upon request). A promise seriously and deliberately made gave rise to an action, according to the maxim *belofte maakt schuld.*

Benedicta est expositio quando res redimitur a destructione, an exposition (or a construction) is to be approved by which the matter is rescued from destruction. *See* UT RES MAGIS VALEAT QUAM PEREAT.

Beneficiary, one who is in possession of a benefice; a person who is in receipt of some gift, benefit or advantage. In English law *beneficiary* seems to be replacing the term *cestui que trust. See* TRUST.

Beneficium cedendarum actionum, the benefit of cession of actions. By raising this benefit one of several sureties, who is prepared to pay the whole debt, and does not or cannot avail himself of the benefit of division, may demand that the actions which the creditor has against the co-sureties and principal debtor shall be ceded to him by the creditor. The benefit may be claimed both before and after payment. Cession of action need not be tendered in the summons against a surety, it being sufficient that the creditor shall make such cession on being thereunto required (*Lippert & Co.* v. *Van Rensburg*, 1877, Buch. p. 42; *Horn* v. *Loedolff et Uxor*, 1 Menz. 405)

Beneficium de duobus vel pluribus reis debendi, the benefit of being sued together; the benefit of division. Where several principal debtors are bound jointly, but not severally, each is liable only for his *pro ratâ* share of the debt, and if sued for the whole amount may plead this benefit. The exception of the benefit, however, cannot be raised where it has been expressly renounced by the joint debtors. According to Grotius it also fails if one of the debtors is notoriously insolvent or is absent from the country (Grotius' *Introduction*, 3, 3, 11), but it has been held that in such cases the benefit does not cease (*Alcock* v. *Du Preez*, 1875, Buch. p. 132).

Beneficium divisionis, the benefit of division. It is available where several persons have intervened for payment of the same debt, without specifying their respective shares of liability. By means of this benefit, when pleaded, one of several sureties, who is called upon to pay the whole amount, claims that he shall not be condemned to pay more than his proportionate share of the debt. The other sureties must be solvent at the time of joinder of issue. The benefit may be renounced either expressly or tacitly.

Beneficium ordinis seu excussionis, the benefit of order or excussion. It is the right of defence given to a surety, when called upon for payment by the creditor, whereby he claims that the principal debtor shall first be excussed. The benefit may be renounced tacitly or specially. It must be pleaded before joinder of issue (*Mason & Co.* v. *Booth*, 20 S.C. 645; 13 C.T.R. 1154). Funds belonging to the principal debtor, but outside the jurisdiction of the court, cannot be excussed, nor can their non-excussion be pleaded in defence by sureties (*Rogerson, N.O.*, v. *Meyer and Berning*, 2 Menz. 38; *Wolfson* v. *Crowe*, [1904] T.S. 682). The insolvency of the principal debtor is a sufficient excussion (*Rogerson, N.O.*, v. *Meyer and Berning*, ibid.).

Benefit of clergy, exemption of clerical persons from arrest or punishment by the civil authority. Every one "for whatever offences he might be pursued, could take free refuge in the churches, monasteries, churchyards, and other ecclesiastical precincts, being places consecrated to God; nor could he be removed therefrom, nor suffer any molestation or restraint as regards his person" (Van Leeuwen's *Comm.* Kotzé's trans. vol. 1, p. 75). Van Leeuwen then proceeds to say that, as this privilege was much abused, an agreement was made between Rollotf van Diephout, Bishop of Utrecht, and Duke Philip of Burgundy, in his capacity of Count of Holland, on the 28th February, 1434, whereby the *benefit of clergy* was considerably restricted and modified and confined to ecclesiastical persons only.

Benefit of inventory, a privilege in Roman law, granted to an heir for the purpose of protecting himself from liability for the debts of the person to whose estate he was heir. "Any one entitled to the succession, either under a testament or by law, was accountable as heir, as soon as he declared his acceptance, or dealt with the property as heir. By the praetorian law the heir was allowed a certain time to deliberate whether he would undertake the representation of the deceased, and this was fixed by Justinian as a period not exceeding nine months if granted by the magistrates, and a year if granted by the emperor. A still more important privilege was conferred upon heirs by Justinian, when he introduced the principle of limited representation by the *benefit of inventory.* An heir who accepted with *benefit of inventory* protected himself from all liability for the debts of the ancestor beyond the value of the inheritance" (Mackenzie's *Roman Law,* 7th ed. p. 286). See also Justinian's *Institutes*, 2, 19, 6; Hunter's *Roman Law*, 4th ed. p. 754).

In *Fischer* v. *Liquidators of Union Bank* (8 S.C. at p. 50), after referring to the passage in Justinian's *Institutes* (2, 19, 6) on this subject, De Villiers, C.J., said: "The privilege here referred to is what the commentators have termed the *benefit of inventory.* Within thirty days after the heir became acquainted with the rights, an inventory of the property might be begun which was to finish within ninety days from the same. The inventory was to be made in the presence of a notary or else of three witnesses. If the heir chose to avail himself of this privilege he entirely separated the estate of the testator from his own, he could deduct anything that might be owing to him from it, and had to pay to it anything he might owe. He first paid the expenses of the funeral and of the inventory, and then the creditors in order in which they sent in their claims. If there was any surplus, he took it; if any deficiency, he was not liable. As has been justly remarked by Hunter (*Roman Law,* p. 755), the heir who took the benefit of inventory 'was now a mere executor, with the privilege of being residuary legatee and, if the testator did not forbid it, of retaining the Falcidian fourth.'"

The benefit of inventory was also introduced into Roman-Dutch law (*ibid.* at p. 51); *see* also Act of Deliberation. There is no "recorded case, at all events after the passing of the Ordinance [Ordinance 104 of 1833 (C.C.)], of any application to the court for the writ of *benefit of inventory*" (*per* De Villiers, C.J., *ibid.* at p. 52).

Bequest, something left by will; a legacy.

Beraad or **Berading** (D.), deliberation. The *regt van beraad* in Roman-Dutch law was the right of deliberation which was allowed to an heir before he accepted the inheritance. See Grotius' *Introduction,* 2, 21, 4; Benefit of Inventory.

Beschuldigde (D.), the accused person in a criminal prosecution. See Van der Linden's *Institutes*, 3, 2, 1, 1.

Beschuldiger (D.), the complainant in a criminal prosecution. See Van der Linden's *Institutes*, 3, 2, 1, 1.

Besluit (D.), pl. *besluiten,* a resolution. *See* Resolutien; Volksraad Besluit.

Betaaling (D.), payment or satisfaction of a debt.

Betichten (D.), to accuse, impeach, inform against. *See* Tichte.

Betrothal, a promise of marriage. "The Germans did not, like the Romans, allow a solemn betrothal to be lightly set aside at the desire of one of the parties (Hein. *Jus. Germ.* bk. 1, tit. 8, secs. 179, 184), and the refractory party could be compelled to complete his contract. This German custom prevailed in Holland, and became one of the important ancient customs of the country. In 1656 it obtained statutory recognition in the *Echtregelment* of that year, and the courts were empowered to compel the marriage to take place whatever might be the difference between the wealth or dignity of the parties. . . . In South Africa the action for specific performance of marriage has been abolished, and the only redress left to the injured party is to sue for damages for breach of promise to marry" (Wessels' *History*, p. 433).

The action for an order compelling the refractory party to complete the marriage was abolished in the Cape Colony by the Marriage Order in Council of the 7th September, 1838.

Better. "*Better* [referring to goods] means *better* as regards the purpose for which they are intended, and the question of *better* or worse in many cases depends simply upon one or two or three issues of fact. If an action will not lie because a man says that his goods are *better* than his neighbour's, it seems to me impossible to say that it will lie because he says that they are *better* in this or that or the other respect" (*per* Lord HERSCHELL, L.C., in *White v. Mellin*, [1895] A.C. at p. 165).

Beunhaazen (D.), persons who carried on the business of brokers in Holland without being duly admitted or licensed as such. See Van der Linden's *Institutes*, 4, 1, 9.

Bewaargeving (D.), equivalent to the Latin *depositum;* a contract whereby a person entrusts some movable property to the care of another, who undertakes the care thereof gratuitously, and binds himself to return such property when required to do so. See Grotius' *Introduction*, 3, 7, 2; Van der Linden's *Institutes*, 1, 15, 5; Kersteman's *Woordenboek*, vol. 2, p. 78.

Bewaarplaats (D.), a depository. Under the Transvaal Gold Law (15 of 1898) certain areas of land were given out by Government to claim-holders as storage sites, or for the purpose of depositing tailings or other refuse from the batteries, or for erecting settling tanks or pans, dams or reservoirs or for storing ores; the areas so given out were called *bewaarplaatsen;* the holder of a *bewaarplaats* acquired only a right to use the surface of the land. The Gold Law 15 of 1898 (T.) has been repealed by Act 35 of 1908 (T.).

Bewijs (D.), evidence. As to *bewijs* in Roman-Dutch law, see Van Leeuwen's *Comm.* 5, 20 *et seq.*; Van der Linden's *Institutes*, 1, 17 1.

Bezit (D.), possession; equivalent to the Latin *possessio*.

Bezitrecht (D.). (1) The right of possession, see Grotius' *Introduction* 2, 2, 1 *et seq.*

(2) A certificate of title granted by the Government of the Transvaal confirming and assuring the title, then already held by the registered owner, of a mijnpacht, claim, water-right or other description of mining right, upon a proclaimed public diggings, under sec. 110 of Law 15 of 1898 (T.) or sec. 54 of the Precious and Base Metals Act (35 of 1908 (T.)), which has repealed the former statute. Sec. 54 (1) of the latter Act provides that "any person in possession of ground held under mining title, or of a water-right, machinery site, or other right necessary or incidental to the development of a public digging, may at any time apply in writing to the Mining Commissioner for a certificate of *bezitrecht* in respect thereof." See sub-secs. 2–7 of the same section for form of application and conditions of grant. Sub-sec. 8 provides that "a certificate of *bezitrecht* shall include every right shown by the diagram transmitted with the application, whether such right was obtained under permission, contract or license under this Act or any prior law, and such certificate may be transferred, either wholly or in part, by the holder thereof; such certificate shall be conclusive evidence that the person to whom it was issued was, at the date of its issue, the lawful holder of the rights included therein, and shall further be indisputable and unassailable unless the same has been obtained by fraud on the part of the possessor thereof."

Bigamous marriage, a marriage entered into between two spouses, one of whom is at the time married to another person. A *bigamous marriage* is void (see *Hatch* v. *Hatch*, 9 S.C. 1; Schorer's *Notes*, note 8). *See* BIGAMY.

Bigamy. The crime of *bigamy* is committed when a person, being already lawfully married, marries any other person during the lifetime of his or her wife or husband. "Although the words of Van der Linden (*Inst.* 2, 7, 3), taken literally, would imply that under Roman-Dutch law *bigamy* was a crime whether or not the accused believed that the previous spouse was dead, the rule followed in South Africa is that laid down by the majority of the English judges in *R.* v. *Tolson* (23 Q.B.D. 168). The ruling in that case was that if the jury are satisfied of the prisoner's *bona fides,* and that he or she had reasonable grounds for believing in the death of his or her wife or husband, the prisoner ought to be acquitted. Probably also in South Africa a court would follow the English rule that if a seven years' absence is proved the onus is on the prosecution to show that the prisoner knew that his or her previous wife or husband was alive when he entered on the second marriage. In Roman-Dutch, as in English law, to constitute the crime of *bigamy* it is necessary that the first marriage should have been a valid one (*McIntyre* v. *Rex*, [1904] T.S. 804)" (Morice's *English and Roman-Dutch Law*, 2nd. ed. p. 365).

"By our law a person, whether husband or wife, is not punishable as for bigamy if he or she reasonably and *bonâ fide* believed that his or her spouse was dead at the time of the subsequent marriage. Whether the belief is reasonable and entertained in good faith is a question for the jury, but as a general rule it may be broadly stated that such belief is neither unreasonable nor *malâ fide* if the spouse has been absent for seven years or more and, notwithstanding due inquiries, has not been heard of or from during that period" (*per* De Villiers, C.J., in *Re Booysen*, Foord, at p. 190). See Act 24 of 1886 (C.C.), sec. 168; Law 46 of 1887 (N.), sec. 13.

Bill, under the Bills of Exchange Acts the term *bill* means a bill of exchange. *See* Bill of Exchange.

Bill of exchange is an unconditional order in writing, addressed by one person to another, signed by the person giving it, requiring the person to whom it is addressed to pay on demand, or at a fixed or determinable future time, a sum certain in money to, or to the order of, a specified person, or to bearer (sec. 3 of the English Bills of Exchange Act, 1882). This has been taken over in the Bills of Exchange Acts of the South African colonies; see Act 19 of 1893 (C.C.), sec. 2.; Law 8 of 1887 (N.), sec. 2; Proclamation 11 of 1902 (T.), sec. 1; Proclamation 12 of 1902 (T.). sec. 20 (1); Ordinance 40 of 1904 (T.), sec. 9; Ordinance 28 of 1902 (O.R.C.), sec. 2.

In Natal there are certain restrictions on contracts of natives founded on *bills of exchange*, promissory notes and the like (see Law 44 of 1887, sec. 8); also in respect of similar obligations executed by Indians (Act 48 of 1904).

Bill of lading. "In the case of goods sent from abroad by ship to a person resident in this country [England], or *vice versâ*, the transfer of the property therein is commonly authenticated, or (as the case may be) originally effected, by an instrument (not under seal) termed a *bill of lading*, which is in its form a receipt from the captain to the shipper (usually termed the consignor), undertaking on special conditions to deliver the goods (on payment of freight) to some person whose name is therein expressed, or indorsed thereon by the consignor. The delivery of this instrument (equally with the actual delivery of the goods) will suffice to pass and transfer to the party so named (usually termed the consignee), or to his indorsee for value, the property in such goods; and that so as even to put an end to the unpaid consignor's right to stop the goods *in transitu*" (Stephen's *Comm.* 14th ed. vol. 2, p. 50).

"The general rule for construing the conditions of a *bill of lading* is that a stipulation that the shipowners shall not be accountable for any specified cause of damage does not exempt them from responsibility for a loss by such cause when it arises from negligence" (*per* Buchanan. J., in *Clan Line of Steamers* v. *Alcock & Co.*, 13 S.C. at p. 112).

The law in the Cape Colony on this subject is similar to that in force in England; see Act 8 of 1879 (C.C.), sec. 2.

Birth. In the Cape Births and Deaths Registration Act (7 of 1894, sec. 2, the term *birth* is defined to mean and include "the *birth* of any viable child, whether such child shall be living or dead at the time of *birth*." For similar definitions see Ordinance 19 of 1906 (T.), sec. 2; Proclamation 15 of 1902 (O.R.C.), sec. 4.

Blackmailer. "The word *blackmailer* has been extended to include any one who, by threats of exposure or disclosure or adverse criticism, endeavours to extort money from another" (*per* INNES, C.J., in *Kernick* v. *Fitzpatrick*, [1907] T.S. at p. 391). To charge a person with being a *blackmailer* is highly defamatory (*ibid.*).

Blackmailing scoundrel. "If a man is a blackmailer, I do not know that to call him a *blackmailing scoundrel* makes any difference" (*per* INNES, C.J., in *Kernick* v. *Fitzpatrick*, [1907] T.S. at p. 391).

Blended whisky. "*Blended whisky* means whisky containing not less than 25 per cent. of malt whisky" (the Wine, Brandy, Whisky and Spirits Act, 42 of 1906 (C.C.), sec. 14). *See* MALT WHISKY; WHISKY.

Block of claims. In the Transvaal Precious Stones Ordinance (66 of 1903 (T.)), *block of claims* or *block* means "any number of contiguous claims"; so also in Ordinance 3 of 1904 (O.R.C.), sec. 5; and Ordinance 4 of 1904 (O.R.C.), sec. 5.

Bloedristen (D.), drawing of blood; a crime against the person. Decker in a note on Van Leeuwen's *Comm.* (4, 35, 1, Kotzé's trans.) says: "This word *bloedristen* will doubtless appear unintelligible to most readers. We must bear in mind that *quetsen* is even yet commonly used as synonymous with *wonden* (wounding), which is, properly speaking, the plural of the noun *een wonde* (a wound) or *vulnus*, derived from the Saxon verb *verwonden* (*inferre vulnus vel plagam*). So, on the other hand, the word *bloedreysen* or *bloedrysen* denotes, according to Kiliaan, *effundere sanguinem, infligere cruentum vulnus*, and therefore its meaning is the infliction of a *bloody* wound, hence called *bloedreese;* wherefore our author mentions it before wounding and the like, as being a more serious crime against the person of our neighbour."

Bloedverwantschap (D.), relationship by blood. Formerly spelt *bloedverwandschap*. As to degrees of relationship, see Grotius' *Introduction*, 2, 27.

Bode (D.), a messenger. *See* GERECHTS-BODE.

Bodemery or **Bodemry** (D.), bottomry.

Bodemery-brief (D.), a bottomry bond; a species of contract of assurance, or otherwise a loan upon the keel of a vessel. *See* BOTTOMRY BOND. See also Van Leeuwen's *Comm.* Kotzé's trans. vol. 2, p. 67.

Body. In the Cape Births and Deaths Registration Act (7 of 1894), sec. 2, the term *body* is defined to mean and include "any human dead body and the body of any still-born child." See also Ordinance 19 of 1906 (T.), sec. 2; Proclamation 15 of 1902 (O.R.C.), sec. 4.

Boedel (D.), an estate of a person or partnership.

Boedel erf (D.), a term used in the Boedel Erven Act (38 of 1905 (C.C,)), where it is defined as meaning "an erf granted or allotted as aforesaid, or any portion thereof, which at the present date remains registered in the name of the grantee or his successors in title, or is vested in the allottee or his heirs or assigns; and of which the persons now claiming to be owners shall not have received transfer."

The term *boedel erf* is not to be found in any Cape or other South African statute prior to Act 38 of 1905 (C.C), and, apparently, it was there only used as a convenient expression in connection with the circumstances specially dealt with in the Act. In 1836 the Governor at that time of the Cape Colony granted titles in freehold of defined portions of land to certain Hottentots in the Kat River settlement, in the division of Stockenstrom, Cape Colony, partly as a reward for their assistance in quelling a then recent rebellion, and partly for the purpose of keeping them together in one location. These Hottentots, about 100 in number, bequeathed or sold their holdings to their children, and in some cases those children succeeded their parents *ab intestato.* This system of succession continued until 1905, but no transfer was ever passed or registered in the Deeds Office to any one of the successors, whether by will, or by sale, or *ab intestato.* In each instance, however, the descendants of each original grantee held the plot of ground and occupied and cultivated it. In course of time many disputes arose among the occupiers, and the allotments became too small for the numerous children and grandchildren of the original grantees. The difficulties that had arisen were brought to the notice of the Government, when it was found that the then occupants had succeeded to the land of their ancestors, but had never taken transfer of the land, so as to secure a valid title, nor had they complied with the provisions of the Transfer Duty Acts by paying transfer duty. The properties could not be transferred under the Derelict Lands Act of 1881 (C.C.), because the land in question was not derelict. Those legally entitled thereto were in occupation, but without registered transfer. The correspondence between the magistrate of the division of Stockenstrom and the Government began in about the year 1900, and the magistrate then, for convenience and brevity, described the land in question as *boedel erven;* and in all subsequent correspondence, and in the subsequent parliamentary inquiry, the same term, *boedel erven*, was applied to these plots. To rectify the errors and omissions of the past, to provide for the settlement of the disputes that had arisen, and to enable the occupiers to secure valid title to their plots, the Boedel Erven Act (38 of 1905) (C.C.) was passed.

Boedelhouder (D.), estate-holder. A *boedelhouder* is the survivor of persons married in community of property, whom the first-dying has by last will appointed executor, guardian and administrator of the joint estate during the minority of the children. In this manner community of property continues between the survivor and the children until the majority of the children. "I have no doubt whatever that, where the will of the first-dying authorises such a continuation, the children are bound [by debts incurred by the survivor], more especially if, as in the present case, their tutors have consented to the continuation of the community after the death of the testator" (*per* DE VILLIERS, C.J., in *Cloete* v. *Cloete's Trustees*, 5 S.C. 68).

Boedel-recht or **Boedel-regt** (D.), the right to an estate, acquired by inheritance. See Van Leeuwen's *Comm.* Kotzé's trans. vol. I, p. 311.

Boedelscheiding (D.), a division of an estate.

Boete (D.), a penalty or fine.

Bona adventitia, adventitious property; property acquired by children from persons other than their parents. Such property belongs to the children in full ownership.

"Bona fide lunch or dinner," in defining these words in the Cape Liquor Act (25 of 1891), sec. 26, DE VILLIERS, C.J., said: "The test I would apply is this: was the food ordered and supplied merely as an excuse for the supply of the liquor, or was it ordered with the *bonâ fide* object of being taken as a fairly substantial meal with the liquor as a mere accessory. It is only by applying a test of that nature that effect can be given to the term *bonâ fide*, which we must assume the legislature to have inserted with a definite object. Whatever may be the etymology of the term 'lunch,' I take its ordinary modern meaning to be a light meal taken about midday, as distinguished from a heavy meal taken about midday, or towards evening, either of which would be better known as a 'dinner'" (*Queen* v. *Sutton*, 10 S.C. at p. 275).

Bona fide possessor, one who possesses in the belief that he is the legal owner or that no one has a better title.

Bona profectitia, profectitious property; property derived by children from their parents directly or indirectly. Such property belongs in full ownership to the parents. A parent may, however, in an open and *bonâ fide* manner make a valid gift to his or her child (*Elliott's Trustees* v. *Elliott*, 3 Menz. 86; *Thorpe's Executors* v. *Thorpe's Tutor*, 4 S.C. 488; *Russell* v. *Von Grossouw*, 1 Kotzé, 112; *Slabber's Trustee* v. *Neezer's Executor*, 12 S.C. 163).

Bona vacantia, unowned property, unappropriated by the Treasury. Such property is capable of acquisition by prescription.

Bond. *See* BAIL BOND; GENERAL MORTGAGE; MORTGAGE. For the purposes of the Cape Company Debenture Act (43 of 1895), the term *bond* is defined to mean "a mortgage bond or deed of hypothecation executed in conformity with the regulations and practice of the Deeds Registry of this [Cape] Colony."

In Natal the renunciation of the benefit of legal exceptions (*beneficia*) is rendered unnecessary by Law 40 of 1884.

Boni judicis est jurisdictionem ampliare, it is the duty of a good judge to extend his jurisdiction. Broom (*Legal Maxims*, ch. iii) points out that this maxim is erroneous, and that Lord MANSFIELD once suggested that the word *justitiam* should be substituted for *jurisdictionem*. "The true maxim is 'to amplify its remedies, and, without usurping jurisdiction, to apply its rules, to the advancement of substantial justice' (*per* Lord ABINGER, *Russell* v. *Smyth*, 9 M. & W. 818). The principle upon which our courts act is, to enforce the performance of contracts not injurious to society, and to administer justice to a party who can make his claim to redress appear, by enlarging the legal remedy, if necessary, in order to do justice" (Broom's *Legal Maxims*, 7th ed. p. 64). See *Stutterheim Municipality* v. *De Beer* (18 S.C. 288).

Bonorum possessio, possession of the goods. In the Roman law the equitable rules of the praetorian edict admitted to the succession to a deceased's estate many persons who would have been excluded by the strict and rigid rules of the *jus civile*. The praetor could not give the qualities of heirs to such persons, but he gave them *bonorum possessio* or the beneficial possession of the estate, and this possession in course of time ripened into ownership by *usucapio*. *Bonorum possessio* was of three kinds, viz.: (1) *secundum tabulas*, (2) *contra tabulas*, and (3) *ab intestato*. The first admitted the heirs named in a will notwithstanding the omission of the formalities prescribed by the early law, provided that the will was produced duly sealed with seven unbroken seals; the second recognised the claims of children who had been passed over in their father's testament; and the third enlarged the order of succession *ab intestato* fixed by the XII Tables.

Book. Under the Cape Copyright Act (2 of 1873), sec. 9, a *book* is construed to mean and include every volume, part or division of a volume, pamphlet, sheet of letter-press, sheet of music, and map, chart or plan separately published; for same definition see Natal Copyright Act (17 of 1897). By Act 4 of 1888 (C.C.), sec. 1, it is further provided that the term *book* "shall not include any publication which consists merely of a price list, sale catalogue, annual report, trade circular or trade advertisement, or any volume, pamphlet, sheet of letter-press, sheet of music, map, chart or plan intended for private circulation and not for sale, and of which not more than 50 copies shall be printed." For the purposes of the Cape Copyright Protection and Books Registration Act (18 of 1895), the term *book* is defined to mean and include "every volume, part or division of a volume, sheet of letter-press, sheet of music, and map, chart or plan separately published."

Booth, *see* POLLING BOOTH.

Borg (D.), surety; security; pledge; bail. *See* SURETY.

Borgtogt (D.), suretyship; a guarantee; a contract whereby a person binds himself for a debtor, for the benefit of the creditor, to pay him, the creditor, the whole or a part of that which the debtor owes him, and in this way becoming a party to the debtor's obligation (Van der Linden's *Institutes*, 1, 14, 10).

Borough, a town having a municipal organisation. See Law 19 of 1872 (N.), secs. 3 *et seq.*

Borrowing powers. A term applied to the power of a company, corporation or society to raise or borrow money. A trading company has usually an implied power to borrow money for the purposes of its business (*General Auction, &c., Co.* v. *Smith*, [1891] 3 Ch. 432); but such a power is not implied in the case of a non-trading company or a school board (*Regina* v. *Sir Charles Reed*, 5 Q.B.D. 483; 49 L.J. Q.B. 600; 42 L.T. 835). *Borrowing powers* are generally provided for in the articles of association of a company.

As to the *borrowing powers* of a building society, see *Langford* v. *Moore and Others* (17 S.C. at p. 19).

A deposit of money made with a building society is a borrowing (*ibid.* at p. 20).

Bottomry "is a contract whereby, in return for a loan of money to be expended on a ship or for the use and benefit of the owner in and about the ship, the master pledges the vessel as security. It is so called from the Dutch word *bodem*, meaning the keel of the vessel. Not merely the master, but the owners or part-owners, may effect a *bottomry bond* on a vessel. The bond remains in force on the vessel until the same is lost or destroyed" (Nathan's *Common Law*, sec. 950).

"In order to entitle the creditor to recover in full it is not sufficient that the keel of the vessel has been preserved; but it is necessary that the whole amount should be recoverable out of the vessel and its tackle and rigging; otherwise the master is discharged by delivering up the vessel to the creditor, who will thus have as much as can be realised from the vessel, according to the terms usually inserted in the contract—*zo verre deze bodem zo veel te land brengt*—so far as this bottom shall bring so much to shore" (Van der Keessel, *Thes.* 561). A higher rate of interest was allowed on money lent on bottomry than on money lent in the ordinary course of business.

As to the duties of a master before pledging goods on bottomry, see *Thomson, Watson & Co.* v. *Wieting and Others* (2 S.C. 197).

Bottomry bonds may be the subject of insurance, see Arnould's *Marine Insurance*, 7th ed. sec. 242.

Brand. In the Cape Brands Registration Act (12 of 1890) the term *brand* is defined to mean "the impression of any letter, sign or character branded upon any horse, cattle or ostrich;" and by Act 4 of 1897 (C.C.), sec. 3, it is extended to "include the impression of any letter, sign or character branded or tattooed on the body of any sheep or goat, or any pitch, paint or tar brand impressed on the wool of any sheep or goat." See sec. 3 of the Fertilisers, Farm Foods, Seeds and Pest Remedies Act (20 of 1907 (C.C.)).

For *brand* in Transvaal, see Ordinance 15 of 1904, sec. 1.

In Orange River Colony, see Ordinance 15 of 1903, sec. 1.

Brand directory. In the Cape Brands Registration Act (12 of 1890) the expression *brand directory* is defined to mean "the list of brands of horses, cattle or ostriches, compiled by the Registrar [of Brands] and published by the Government printers, whether in the shape of a book or of quarterly lists in the *Gazette*."

For Transvaal definition, see Ordinance 15 of 1904, sec. 1; for that in the Orange River Colony, see Ordinance 15 of 1903, sec. 1.

Branding instrument. In the Transvaal Great Stock Brands Ordinance (15 of 1904), sec. 1, *branding instrument* means "any other instrument [*see* BRANDING IRON] or tool by which any mark or symbol can be impressed, imprinted or cut on any portion of any horse or cattle."

Branding iron. In the Transvaal Great Stock Brands Ordinance (15 of 1904), sec. 1, *branding iron* means "the instrument prescribed for imprinting a brand or mark on great stock by this Ordinance or the regulations made under it."

Brandstigter (D.), (modern spelling, *brandstichter*), an incendiary; a person who maliciously and for the purpose of injuring others, sets fire to some building or other immovable property. Under old Dutch law *brandstigters* were on conviction burned alive.

Brandy. "*Brandy* means the distillate resulting from the distillation solely of (*a*) wine or must; (*b*) must and grape husks; (*c*) grape husks and water" (the Wine, Brandy, Whisky and Spirits Act (42 of 1906 (C.C.)), sec. 14). *See* DOP BRANDY; PURE GRAPE BRANDY; PURE WINE BRANDY.

Breach of promise of marriage. The injured party is entitled to an action for damages arising from the breach. "I cannot find that our law makes any distinction between the case of a man suing for damages for breach of promise of marriage and a woman suing for breach of promise of marriage. In either case damages are recoverable, if there has been a deliberate breach of the promise to marry and consequent damages sustained by the party" (*per* DE VILLIERS, C.J., in *Mocke* v. *Fourie*, 3 C.T.R. at p. 315).

Breach of trust. *See* TRUST.

Bread. In the Cape Ordinance amending the law relating to the baking trade (10 of 1846), wherein the sale of *bread* is regulated, it is provided in sec. 8 that "the term *bread* shall not extend to sweetened or spiced *bread* or cakes or any species of confectionery." See also the Cape Sale of Bread Act (29 of 1895).

Break. In the Transvaal Crimes Ordinance (26 of 1904), sec. 3, *break* means "the obtaining of entrance into or exit from any building by means of force, threat, fraud, stealth, or trick, or by the unfastening or opening of any door or window, or by the removal of any thing used to cover any opening into or within or from such building."

Brevi manu, by short hand; summarily. This expression is sometimes used in English and Scots law of an act done by a person of his own authority, without legal warrant, a practice somewhat equivalent to the *parate executie* of the Roman-Dutch law. In the earlier law both of England and Scotland it appears to have been permissible for a creditor to take at short hand property belonging to his debtor and to hold it as a pledge until the debtor paid the debt or found security for payment. Such a practice has for long been discouraged, and having been dealt with by statute, now survives in only one or two forms, *e.g.* in England in the law of distress. *See* PARATE EXECUTIE. In Roman law the expression *brevi manu* is used with reference to a kind of constructive delivery (*traditio*). In order that the *dominium* in the subject to be transferred should pass from one person to another delivery was essential. If, however, a thing before being sold to a person was held by him upon some other ground, such as hire, pledge, loan, or deposit, no fresh delivery was necessary when the sale took place, the property being considered to pass by the mere intention of the holder, now the purchaser, to retain the thing as his own (Voet's *Comm.* 41, 1, 34).

Brevi manu traditio. *See* BREVI MANU.

Breviarium Alaricum, the collection of laws made by Anianus, formerly called *Breviarium Aniani*, but after the tenth century usually called the *Breviarium Alaricum* (Wessels' *History*, p. 98). "This *Breviarium* contained not only a summary of the *Codex*

Theodosianus, but also extracts from the *Institutes* of Gaius and the *Sentences* of Paul" (*ibid.* p. 99).

Brewer. Under the Cape Excise Beer Duty Act (11 of 1884), sec. 2, a *brewer* is defined to mean a *brewer* of beer for sale; and in sec. 10 of the same Act it is provided that "every person who brews beer for sale, whether by wholesale or retail, or for any purpose of trade, shall be deemed to be a *brewer* within the meaning of this Act, whether the said person be licensed to deal in or retail beer or not." See Act 37 of 1901 (N.), sec. 1; Act 9 of 1907 (T.), sec. 1.

Bribery, the taking or giving, or procuring the taking or giving, of any money or valuable consideration; or office, place or employment; or gift, loan or promise of such, or of an advance of money; for the performance or non-performance of any public duty, or for false judgment or evidence, or for the performance of some unjust or illegal act. To bribe or attempt to bribe an official is a crime by Roman-Dutch law (*The State* v. *Aaron,* H. 146; 10 C.L.J. 238).

For definitions of *bribery* at elections of members of Parliament in Cape Colony, see secs. 1 and 2 of Act 21 of 1859; sec. 2 of Act 9 of 1883; and Act 26 of 1902.

As to *bribery* and corruption of witnesses, jurors, assessors or interpreters in Native Territories of Cape Colony, see Act 24 of 1886, sec. 113.

For statute law on *bribery* in Natal, see Law 13 of 1893, sec. 20.

In Transvaal, see Law 10 of 1894; Ordinance 38 of 1903, sec. 72; Act 20 of 1909, sec. 30.

Brief, originally an abridgment of the pleadings in a cause, together with concise instructions for counsel on the facts and law relating thereto. Generally, a copy of the pleadings, evidence of witnesses, and documents in a cause, together with special instructions by the solicitor to the counsel, for the use of the counsel engaged in the action, so that he may be fully instructed therein; or a copy of the petition, affidavits and instructions for the use of counsel in an application to the court.

Brieven van evocatie (D.), letters ordering the removal of a case from a lower to a higher court, granted in Holland upon the application of a litigant who could prove that either through impartiality or some other cause justice was being denied to him, or unreasonably delayed, in an action which he had pending in a lower court (Van der Linden's *Institutes,* 3, 3, 9; Van Leeuwen's *Comm.,* 5, 11, 4).

Brieven van inductie (D.), a legal remedy granted in Roman-Dutch law, whereby the debtor obtained time wherein to pay his debt on giving proper security. *See* BRIEVEN VAN RESPEYT. "The application for letters of induction is usually made to the court, as the common superior tribunal; and all the creditors are cited by the court, to answer before the judge of the debtor's domicile, concerning the grounds on which the delay is applied for, or suffer themselves to be induced to allow this indulgence. If the majority of the creditors consent to it, the judge by virtue of his office decrees the confirmation of the mandate" (Van der Keessel, *Thes.* 892).

Brieven van respeyt (D.), (modern spelling *respijt*), a legal remedy in Roman-Dutch law whereby the debtor was allowed time for the payment of his debt, also called *brieven van inductie*. In order to obtain letters of respite or induction it was required that the debtor should give good personal or other security to the satisfaction of his creditors for the payment of all his debts. The *cautio juratoria*, or security of his oath, was not sufficient (Van der Keessel, *Thes.* 890). See Wessels' *History*, p. 663.

Brieven van surete de corps (D.), a legal remedy granted in Roman-Dutch law, whereby the debtor obtained the benefit of safe conduct, or freedom of his person for a period of three, five, six or more months in order not to be troubled as to his person by his creditors within that time (Van Leeuwen's *Comm.* Kotzé's trans. vol. 2, p. 339). *Brieven van sureté de corps* "may be obtained from the States by debtors who are in concealment or residing in a foreign country, under apprehension of arrest, and who believe that they are able to effect an equitable arrangement with their creditors. It is not, however, granted except with the consent of the majority of the creditors; nor as against a sentence of the Supreme Court, or any other sentence which has passed into a *res judicata*" (Van der Keessel, *Thes.* 894).

British consular court "means any British court having jurisdiction under an Order in Council made in pursuance of the Foreign Jurisdiction Acts (1843 to 1878) or any of them" (Act 8 of 1888 (C.C.), sec. 1).

British medical register. These words appearing in sec. 3 of Proclamation 1 of 1902 (T.) were held not to include the medical register of any British possession, but that the word "British" was used with reference to the United Kingdom of Great Britain and Ireland, and in contrast with "colonial and foreign" (*Colonial Secretary* v. *Grice*, [1903] T.S. 361).

British possession is defined in the Interpretation Act, 1889 (Eng.), sec. 18, sub-sec. 2, as meaning "any part of her Majesty's dominions exclusive of the United Kingdom, and where parts of such dominions are under both a central and a local legislature, all parts under the central legislature shall, for the purposes of this definition, be deemed to be one *British possession*." See also Act 26 of 1906 (N.), sec. 30; Ordinance 1 of 1906 (T.), sec. 30 of schedule; Ordinance 30 of 1906 (T.), sec. 1; Act 7 of 1907 (T.), sec. 1; *Willis* v. *Rex* (27 N.L.R. at p. 374).

British subject. "Many modern jurists . . . maintain that the mere fact of annexation does not create the relation of sovereign and subject, but that there must be either an express or tacit submission for the purpose, and that remaining within the sphere of the new dominion and fulfilling the duties of subjects would amount to tacit submission" (*per* DE VILLIERS, C.J., in *Queen* v. *Jizwa*, 11 S.C. at p. 395).

Broker, an agent or middleman who, in consideration of a certain commission, is employed to negotiate and make purchases and sales on behalf of principals. He is obliged to buy or sell in the name of his principal. There are various kinds of *brokers,* such as share-brokers, stock-brokers, ship-brokers, and insurance-brokers. A *broker* of the present day is somewhat different to the *broker* of the seventeenth century. Decker in a *note* to Van Leeuwen's *Comm.* (Kotzé's trans. vol. 2, p. 222) says: "A *broker* is a sworn and qualified person, who inquires in all legitimate transactions concerning the will and intention of the contracting parties, and (if possible) brings them to an agreement and closes the bargain."

"*Broker*" means every person (other than an importer or an agent for a foreign firm) who shall in this [Cape] Colony carry on the trade or business of making bargains and contracts between other persons in matters of trade, commerce and navigation for a remuneration, commonly called a brokerage (Act 38 of 1877 (C.C.), sec. 3); see also *Queen* v. *Plockers* (5 H.C.G. at p. 371). As to the penalty for a *broker* in the Cape Colony using an unstamped note, see Act 38 of 1887, sec. 7.

As to Natal, see the Stock or Share Brokers' Admission Law of 1888 (Law 31 of 1888).

As to Transvaal, see Ordinance 23 of 1905, sec. 2, and Act 34 of 1909.

As to the Orange River Colony, see Ordinance 10 of 1903, sec. 2.

Brokerage, the remuneration or commission to which a broker becomes entitled for services rendered.

As to *brokerage* on sale of a lease, see *Steer & Co.* v. *Rowland* (14 S.C. 358).

Broker's note, a written or partly printed and partly written memorandum issued by a broker and signed by him, setting out the terms of a contract which he, as broker, has entered into on behalf of his principal or principals. In Proclamation 12 of 1902 (T.), sec. 26 (1), and for the purposes of that Proclamation, the expression *broker's note* means "a note sent by a broker or agent to his principal advising him of the sale or purchase of any marketable security." A *broker's note* when completed by the broker is handed to the principal, and affords him evidence of the bargain or contract.

Bruikleening (D.), the loan of the use of a thing. "Whenever the loan concerns such things as do not perish by use it is called *bruikleening,* being a contract whereby one person gratuitously hands over to another a certain thing to make use of it in a certain manner, and whereby he who receives it binds himself to return that thing after it has served the fixed purpose" (Van der Linden's *Institutes*, 1, 15, 4). Both movable and immovable property can be the subject of *bruikleening* (*ibid.*). See also Van Leeuwen's *Comm.* 4, 10, 1; Kersteman's *Woordenboek*, vol. 2, p. 108; Grotius' *Introduction*, 3, 9, 1.

Builder's lien, a tacit hypothec given to builders of new houses to secure the due payment to them of the balance of the contract price. Retention of possession of the building is necessary to secure the lien. In *Brown's Assignee* v. *Pote* (4 E.D.C. 50) it was held that a builder who retains possession of a house built by him has a lien on the house for the payment of his labour and of the value of the materials supplied; and that such lien is preferent to the claim of a mortgagee, who advanced his money upon the property after its value had been enhanced by the building. See Act 5 of 1861 (C.C.), sec. 8 (5); Proclamation 28 of 1902 (T.), sec. 130 (10). See also Maasdorp's *Institutes*, vol. 2, p. 251; Nathan's *Common Law*, sec. 1020; Voet's *Comm.* 20, 2, 28.

Building. "A *building* may not require masonry, but the word implies some degree of trouble, skill and elaboration in fixing or removing the structure" (*per* DE VILLIERS, C.J., in *Ex parte Greef*, 24 S.C. at p. 524). *See* CANVAS HOUSES; TENT.

Building society, a society mainly formed for the purpose of aiding those who desire to build. The shares are generally of a nominal amount, say £50 or £100, and are payable by means of small subscriptions weekly, fortnightly or monthly, according to the rules; fines of varying amounts are imposed if the subscriptions are not punctually paid. In addition to these subscriptions, which are placed to the credit of the member's liability on his shares, he usually receives credit for his proportion of such annual profits as may be divisible among the members. The funds accumulated from subscriptions are advanced on the security of mortgages of landed property; usually a member becomes entitled to a loan of £100 for each share of £100 value, so that if a member required a loan of £1000 he must hold ten shares of £100 each or twenty shares of £50 each; the shares are held by the society as additional security, and when the shares are in process of time fully paid the amount of the loan is also paid by a set-off against the shares. The rules of the society usually give limited borrowing powers to the directors. These societies frequently accept deposits of money from members at interest in the same manner as a savings bank. Generally speaking, *building societies* are not registered with limited liability. The question of the liability of the members of a *building society* for payment of the debts of the society arose in the case of *In re Cape of Good Hope Bank Permanent Building Society* (15 S.C. 323; 8 C.T.R. 360), where, after referring to the law regarding similar societies in England and Scotland, which are regulated by statute, DE VILLIERS, C.J., said: "The decisions proceed upon the ground that the contract itself is not of such a nature as to establish a partnership. It is a contract *sui generis*, which does not fall within any of the well-defined classes of contracts known to our law. Persons dealing with such societies know that they are English in their institution and constitution, and that the powers of the directors and the liabilities of the members are necessarily of a very limited nature. The directors are the agents of the members to carry out the rules of the society, and those rules furnish the only criterion by which the liability of the members *inter se* and towards outsiders can be ascertained. The status, then, of such a society in our law is that of an association of persons subscribing to a common fund for the assistance of one class of members by another class to the mutual advantage of both, and carrying on their business through the agency of a board of directors with certain limited powers, which powers persons dealing with the society must make themselves acquainted with. For the transaction of the necessary business of such an association some expenses must be incurred by the directors, and for the payment of such expenses all the members are personally liable. It is not, however, a necessary part of the business to borrow money. The rules provide for the contribution by the members themselves of funds to be lent to the advanced members. In fact, borrowing powers are conferred upon the directors, but those powers are limited, and cannot be exceeded so as to impose a personal liability upon the members to pay the excess." See definition of *building society* in Transvaal Companies Act (31 of 1909), sec. 202.

See also Natal Law for Regulating Building Societies (12 of 1858).

As to the nature of deposits made with a *building society*, see *Langford* v. *Moore and Others* (17 S.C. at p. 18).

As to deposits with a *building society* being a borrowing (*ibid.* at p. 20).

Burgerlijk recht (D.), municipal law, corresponding to the *Jus Civile* of the Romans. "Municipal law is that which derives its origin from the will of the supreme power of a state. It is either peculiar to one nation—for instance, the power of husbands over their wives, which is almost peculiar to Holland; or held in common with all or nearly all nations, but in such a manner that it may nevertheless be altered without the consent of other nations, as not affecting the mutual intercourse of nations—such are many laws with respect to trade and succession. Municipal law is either written or unwritten" (Grotius' *Introduction*, Maasdorp's trans. 1, 2, 13, 14, 15).

Burgermeester (D.) (modern spelling *Burgemeester*), the burgomaster or mayor of a town or place; he was entrusted with the government and direction of the town or place to which he was appointed.

Burgess, a person resident in a borough. See Law 19 of 1872 (N.), secs. 15 to 19.

Burg-graven or **Burgh-graven** (D.), or *Burg-graves*, were judges over certain villages called *vryheden* (manors), or custodians of certain canals and castles in Holland (Van Leeuwen's *Comm.* Kotzé's trans. vol. 1, p. 63). *See* GRAAF.

Burial. In the Cape Births and Deaths Registration Act (7 of 1894), sec 2, the term *burial* is defined to mean and include "not only any burial in earth, interment or other form of sepulture, but also the cremation of any body."

In the Transvaal (Ordinance 19 of 1906, sec. 2) *burial* means "burial in earth, interment or any other form of sepulture, or the cremation or any other mode of disposal of a body."

In the Orange River Colony, in Proclamation 15 of 1902, sec. 4, the definition of *burial* is similar to that in the Cape Act 7 of 1894.

Burial ground. In the Cape Public Health Amendment Act (23 of 1897), sec. 2, the term *burial ground* is defined to mean "any *burial ground*, whether public or private, or any place whatsoever wherein is buried or intended to be buried one or more human bodies." *See* BURIAL PLACE.

Burial place. In the Cape Births and Deaths Registration Act (7 of 1894), sec. 2, the expression *burial place* is defined to mean and include "any burial ground whether public or private, or any place whatsoever wherein is buried or intended to be buried one or more bodies." See also Ordinance 19 of 1906 (T.), sec. 2, where the definition is somewhat more extended and refers specifically to cremation. In the Orange River Colony the definition in Proclamation 15 of 1902, sec. 4, is similar to that in the Cape Act 7 of 1894.

Bushel, the old measure of a *bushel* was abolished in the Orange River Colony by Law 25 of 1898 (O.R.C.), sec. 15.

Bushel of malt. It is provided in the Cape Excise Beer Duty Act (11 of 1884) that "forty-two pounds weight of malt or corn of any description, or twenty-eight pounds weight of sugar, shall be deemed the equivalent of a *bushel of malt;* and the expression *bushel of malt* shall include either of its equivalents or any quantities of malt, corn and sugar, or any two of those materials, as by relation to such equivalents shall be equal to a *bushel of malt.*"

Business. "*Business* itself is a word of large and indefinite import. I have before me the last edition of Johnson's *Dictionary*, edited by Dr. Latham, and there the first meaning given of it is, 'employment, transaction of affairs'; the second, 'an affair'; the third, 'subject of business, affair, or object which engages the care.' Then there are some other meanings, and the sixth is, 'something to be transacted.' The seventh is, 'something required to be done.' Then, taking the last edition of the *Imperial Dictionary*, which is a very good dictionary, we find it a little more definite, but with a remark which is worth reading: '*Business*, employment; that which occupies the time and attention and labour of men for the purpose of profit or improvement.' That is to say, anything which occupies the time and attention and labour of a man for the purpose of profit is *business*. It is a word of extensive use and indefinite signification. Then, '*business* is a particular occupation, as agriculture, trade, mechanics, art, or profession, and when used in connection with particular employments it admits of the plural, that is, businesses.' Therefore the legislature could not well have used a larger word" (*per* JESSEL, M.R., in *Smith* v. *Anderson*, 15 Ch. D. at p. 258. It must be noted that on appeal the judgment of the Master of the Rolls, from which this extract is taken, was discharged, *ibid.* pp. 273 *et seq.*).

Business day. For purposes of the Bills of Exchange Laws business days are any days other than those defined as non-business days.

In Cape Colony (sec. 1, Act 19 of 1893) non-business days include (*a*) Sunday, New Year's Day, Good Friday, Easter Monday, Whit Monday, Ascension Day, Queen's Birthday [now called Victoria Day, see Act 15 of 1902], Christmas Day; (*b*) any day appointed by proclamation by the Governor as a solemn fast day or day of thanksgiving, or as a public holiday under the "Public Holiday Act, 1889," or any other law; see *Blanks* v. *Philip* ([1906] E.D.C. at p. 312).

In Natal (sec. 91, Law 8 of 1887, as amended by Act 18 of 1901) non-business days are: (*a*) Sunday, New Year's Day, Good Friday, Easter Monday, Whit Monday, the 24th May (known as Victoria Day), Michaelmas Day, (29th September), King's Birthday (the 9th November), Christmas Day; (*b*) any day appointed by proclamation of the Governor as a public holiday.

In Rhodesia (sec. 1, Government Regulations 23, 1895) non-business days include same as (*a*) of the Cape Act (as above), and (*b*) any day by law appointed as a solemn fast or day of thanksgiving or as a public holiday.

In the Transvaal (sec. 1, Proclamation 11 of 1902, as amended by Ordinance 37 of 1903) non-business days include (*a*) Sunday, New Year's Day, Good Friday, Easter Monday, Whit Monday, Victoria Day, first Monday in August, King's Birthday, Dingaan's Day, and Christmas Day; (*b*) any day appointed by the Governor under the authority of any law as a solemn fast or day of thanksgiving or as a public holiday.

For the Orange River Colony, see Ordinance 28 of 1902, sec. 1; Ordinance 31 of 1902; and Ordinance 37 of 1903.

Butcher. "If we look at the original derivation of the word *butcher*, it meant a man who killed what he sold. That is the case whether we take the derivation of the English word, which comes from the French, or whether we look at the derivation of the Dutch word *slachter*. The case of *Cleaver* v. *Bacon* (4 T.R. 27) was quoted to us, in which a dictum of Mr. Justice KEKEWICH supports the view that a man who sells what he does not kill is not a *butcher*. But there are earlier English cases to the contrary; and after considering those cases and also the Cape cases, I come to the conclusion that what may be called the original meaning of the word *butcher* is a meaning not consonant with the usage of modern times. At the present time in large cities the *butcher* who sells meat does not always kill it himself. Sometimes he has not the right to do so. The killing is done for him in certain places set apart, and the meat may be bought by the *butcher* after the killing has taken place. I do not think that modern circumstances allow one to restrict the word *butcher* to its original meaning and to its strict derivative significance. Take the case of a company which imports or buys livestock, and has, somewhere in this colony or in the neighbouring colonies, a depôt where that stock is slaughtered and is preserved by means of ice, and purchased by other people for sale. I think both those who buy such meat for the purpose of resale, and the company which sells it after having slaughtered it, come under the term *butchers*. Neither of them could escape the obligation of taking out a *butcher's* license" (*per* INNES, C.J., in *Imperial Cold Storage and Supply Co., Ltd.*, v. *Civil Commissioner*, [1904] T.S. at p. 694). In the Cape Colony, sec. 20 of Act 3 of 1864, after providing that persons exercising the trade or calling of a *butcher* must take out a *butcher's* license, goes on to say "that every person keeping a shop and exposing flesh meat for sale shall, whether he shall or shall not have himself slaughtered the same, be deemed to be a *butcher* for the purpose of requiring to have a *butcher's* license." As to whether a butcher should take out a general dealer's license, see *Papert* v. *Rex* ([1906] T.S. at p. 553).

See Act 15 of 1907 (C.C.), sec. 1.

As to the Orange River Colony, see Ordinance 10 of 1903, sec. 2.

Butter. In the Cape Sale of Food and Drugs and Seeds Act (5 of 1890) the term *butter* is defined to mean "the substances usually known as *butter*, made exclusively from milk or cream, or both, with or without salt or other preservative, and with or without the addition of colouring matter." A similar definition is found in the Natal Food and Drugs Act (45 of 1901). For further definition, see Ordinance 32 of 1906 (O.R.C.), sec. 1.

Butterine. In the Cape Sale of Food and Drugs and Seeds Act (5 of 1890) *butterine*, margarine or other similar articles are defined to mean "all substances, whether compounds or otherwise, prepared in imitation of butter, and whether mixed with butter or not."

Buuren (D.), the inhabitants living in the country (*ten platten lande*), who had the right of sitting in the court held by the Schout or Azing; neighbours.

Buurweg (D.), neighbour's road. *Buurwegen* are roads belonging to several neighbours in common, and may not be closed except by common consent (Grotius' *Introduction*, 2, 35, 10; Van Leeuwen's *Comm.* 2, 21, 9). *See* also VIA VICINALIS, which is the Latin name of this class of roads.

"Buyer to pay all expenses in connection with the completing of transfer." "In my opinion everything that is necessary to be done for the purpose of completing the diagram which formed part of the transfer is an expense in connection with the completing of the transfer. The preparation of the diagram itself is such an expense, and I am inclined to go further, and say that the cost of a survey made for the special purpose of enabling the surveyor to prepare such a diagram would be part of such expenses. But I cannot accept the view that the costs of a survey made before the sale for the purpose of a general subdivision form part of such expenses" (*per* DE VILLIERS, C.J., in *Van Wijk* v. *Smith & Co.*, 19 S.C. at p. 286).

By-law or **bye-law**, a standing rule or regulation made by a legislative body, a corporation, council, company or society for the management of its internal organisation and the conduct of its business. A *by-law* must be made in accordance with the constitution of the legislative or other body making it, and must, if the constitution so provides, be duly published. See Cape Interpretation of Statutes Act (5 of 1883), sec. 7.

"We have a distinction between crimes and quasi-crimes, but I think under our law this particular offence [a breach of a municipal *by-law*] would be a crime, and that breaches of *by-laws* would be called crimes under our law, and not quasi-crimes" (*per* BALE, C.J., in *Lawes & Co.* v. *Pietermaritzburg Corporation*, 27 N.L.R. at p. 305).

Bylbrief (D.), is a mortgage of a ship. A person who has a ship built, or buys one, and has not sufficient money to pay for it, may mortgage the vessel to his creditor in security of the loan. If the ship is lost the mortgagor still remains liable for the money, by virtue of the "general hypothecation" (Van der Linden's *Institutes*, p. 427). A *bylbrief* does not rank preferent to a bottomry bond later in date, the reason being that money advanced upon bottomry preserves the ship, which benefits the holder of the *bylbrief*. See Grotius' *Introduction*, 2, 48, 13; Van Leeuwen's *Comm.* 4, 13, 19.

By-road is defined in the Natal Road Boards Act (35 of 1901), sec. 17, as follows: "(*a*) A road or right-of-way, whether public or private, which has been established, or the right of which has been created, by prescription, or by deed, or in any other valid manner; (*b*) a way of necessity, including a reasonably necessary means of access to a public road or a railway station, stopping place or siding; and (*c*) foot or bridle path."

Cadit quaestio, the question falls to the ground; the dispute is at an end.

Caeteris paribus, other things being equal.

"**Call or other sum due.**" Where the articles of association of a company provide that after forfeiture of shares for non-payment of calls the company shall be entitled to recover the calls from the original holder, and also that no member shall have a vote so long as any calls or other sums are due and payable in respect of any share, the calls upon a forfeited share are "sums due in respect thereof," and the purchaser from the company of forfeited shares cannot vote so long as the calls have not been recovered from the former shareholder (*Rand Gold Mining Co.* v. *Wainwright*, 8 Manson, 61; 17 T.L.R. 29).

Cambiaal-recht (D.), the law of exchange.

Cambiale jus, the law of exchange. Van der Linden's definition of a contract of a bill of exchange is as follows: "By a contract of a bill of exchange is meant a transaction by which I give you, or bind myself to give you, a certain sum, at a certain place, for and in exchange of a sum of money which you bind yourself to pay to me at another place. In order to carry out this contract, and to bring it into operation, a *bill of exchange* is drawn, *i.e.* a letter, framed in a certain form defined by law, by which you request your correspondent at a certain place to pay me or my order, at that place, a certain sum of money or the value thereof, which you received from me here, either in cash or account" (Van der Linden's *Institutes*, Juta's trans. p. 470). The holder of a bill was entitled to proceed by the summary law of bills of exchange (by the cambial process or *paraat wissel-regt*), that is, by applying to the court for an order against the debtor, and an attachment of his goods. The law of bills of exchange is governed by statute law in the South African colonies. *See* BILL OF EXCHANGE.

Cambist, one who has knowledge of exchanges; one who deals in bills of exchange.

Camera. *See* IN CAMERA.

Camp followers, defined in the Natal Militia Act (36 of 1903) sec. 3, to mean "sutlers, servants, and all others who accompany the force, or any portion of the force when in camp or on military service." The same definition is found in Ordinance 33 of 1902 (T.), sec. 1, which is repealed by Ordinance 37 of 1904 (T.).

Cancellarii, a term sometimes applied to notaries in the middle ages. See Wessels' *History*, p. 198.

Cancellation, the act of cancelling, eliminating, striking out, or making void. As to cancellation of a bill of exchange and its effects, see Act 19 of 1893 (C.C.), sec. 61; Law 8 of 1887 (N.), sec. 62; Proclamation 11 of 1902 (T.), sec. 61; Ordinance 28 of 1902 (O.R.C.), sec. 61.

Candidate "shall mean any person elected to serve in Parliament, and any person who has received and accepted a requisition as in the 34th section of the [Cape] Constitution Ordinance mentioned, and any person who has been nominated as a *candidate* at an election, with his consent" (Act 9 of 1883 (C.C.), sec. 2). See also Act 26 of 1902 (C.C.), sec. 2.

Cannon. In the Transvaal Arms and Ammunition Act (10 of 1907), sec. 2, *cannon* is defined to mean and include "any firearm which is ordinarily moved by vehicular or animal transport, and is ordinarily fired from the ground or a fixed platform; but shall not include a *cannon bonâ fide* kept as a curio." The same definition is given in Act 23 of 1908 (O.R.C.), sec. 2.

Canton. The tribes of early Germans were "divided into hundreds (*centena*) and into thousands (*canton* or *gau*)." See Wessels' *History*, p. 19.

Canvas houses, such as frame tents, may be considered to be "houses or other buildings" (*Ex parte Greet*, 24 S.C. at p. 525).

Capax doli, capable of wrong-doing. As regards crimes children under seven years of age are absolutely free from criminal responsibility (*R.* v. *George*, 2 E.D.C. 392; *R.* v. *Lourie*, 9 S.C. 432). Between seven and fourteen they are presumed to be *doli incapax*, but the presumption may be set aside by evidence to the contrary, as where the circumstances or the nature of the crime are clearly such as to show that the offender was actuated by evil motives (*per* De Villiers, C.J., in *R.* v. *Lourie*). Where a child between seven and fourteen commits a crime in conjunction with his father it will be presumed that he was acting in obedience to his father's orders, and he will be held free from responsibility, unless the crime was so heinous as to absolve him from obedience (*R.* v. *Albert*, 12 S.C. 272). For the Roman-Dutch law on the subject see Van Leeuwen's *Comm.* Kotzé's trans. vol. 2, translator's note, pp. 252 *et seq.*

Where the case is not one of crime, but of delict or tort, it is not clear whether the same rules would in all cases apply. According to Voet a minor would be liable for damage caused under the *Lex Aquilia*, *i.e.* fraud or *culpa lata*, but not for *culpa levissima*. But if the rule as to freedom from responsibility, which holds good in the case of crime, should apply *a fortiori* to the case of tort or delict, a child between seven and fourteen years of age would not in all cases be liable even for *dolus* or *culpa lata*, while a child under seven would be free from responsibility for any degree of *culpa*.

In English law, where questions have arisen regarding a child's capacity to be guilty of contributory negligence so as to affect a claim for damages arising out of the injury to which the fault has contributed, the tendency has been to distinguish between what in an adult would be mere carelessness (*culpa levis* or *levissima*) and the commission of a wholly unlawful act, such as wilful and intentional trespass (*culpa lata*); it being held in the former case that contributory negligence will not avail as a defence, and in the latter case that it will disentitle the plaintiff to succeed. Thus in *Gardner* v. *Grace* (1 F. & F.), where a child, aged three and a half years, ran out into a road and was knocked down by the defendant's cart, the plea of contributory negligence was overruled. See also *Lay* v. *Midland Railway Co.* (54 L.T. N.S. 30), where the court laid down that what amounts to contributory negligence must have reference to the age of the child. Where, on the other hand, the child has been guilty of an act amounting to wilful misconduct (*culpa lata*) the plea of contributory negligence will afford a good defence. Thus in *Abbott* v. *Macfie* (33 L.J. Exch. 177), where the plaintiff, aged seven years, got upon the cover of a cellar left leaning against a wall by the defendant, and the cover fell and injured the child, it was held that the defendant was not liable. In *Mangan* v. *Alberton* (L.R. 1 Ex. 239; 35 L.J. Ex. 161; 14 L.T. 411) an oil-cake crushing machine was exposed for sale by the defendant in a public place, and left unguarded. The plaintiff, a child of four, at the suggestion of his brother, aged seven, put his fingers into the machine, while another turned the handle and crushed the plaintiff's fingers. It was held that the plaintiff was not entitled to succeed. The authority of this case, however, has been questioned, on the ground that a machine of this kind left unguarded and without the handle being secured is a dangerous instrument, to be treated in the same category as spring-guns (*Clark* v. *Chambers*, (1878) 3 Q.B.D. 327; 47 L.J. Q.B. 427; 38 L.T. N.S. 454). This view is supported by the Scotch case of *Campbell* v. *Ord* (Court of Session, 5th November, 1873, 1 Rettie, 149), where the facts were similar, the case being decided in favour of the plaintiff. See Clerk and Lindsell on *Torts*, 4th ed. pp. 507 *et seq.* For a South African case on contributory negligence of a child, see *Eagleson* v. *Argus Printing and Publishing Co.*, 1 Off. Rep. 264 *et seq.* (*per* KOTZÉ, C.J.).

Capital, the estate of a person or corporation; an accumulation of money or property or both, capable of being employed in a business or undertaking for the purpose of carrying on the same for profit. As to what is profit and what *capital*, see Palmer's *Company Precedents*, 8th ed. vol. 1, pp. 737 *et seq.*

"The word *capital* as used in the Acts 1867 and 1877 (E.) does not mean the capital assets of the company; it means share capital" (Rawlins and Macnaghten on *Companies*, p. 138). *See* SUBSCRIBED CAPITAL.

For definition of *capital* in the Profits Tax (Gold Mines) Proclamation, 1902, see Proclamation 34 of 1902 (T.), sec. 4. See also *Knights Deep, Ltd.*, v. *Colonial Treasurer* ([1905] T.S. 689).

Capital crime, a crime for which the penalty is death.

Capital offence. *See* CAPITAL CRIME.

Capital punishment, the penalty of death by hanging. Prior to 1869 prisoners sentenced to death were hanged in public, but in that year an Act was passed in the Cape Colony (3 of 1869) by which it became lawful for the Governor, if he were satisfied that fitting arrangements could be made for the execution within the gaol in which the prisoner was confined, to order by warrant under his hand that the sentence of death should be carried into effect within the walls of such gaol. This procedure has since become universal throughout British South Africa. As to *capital punishment* in Cape Native Territories, see Act 24 of 1886, sec. 7.

Capitis deminutio, loss of status, or change in one's previous civil rights in Roman law. This may happen in three ways: it may be the greatest, the less and the least. The greatest loss of status is the simultaneous loss of citizenship and freedom, as when a man becomes a slave. The less is loss of citizenship unaccompanied by loss of liberty, as when any one is forbidden the use of fire and water or is deported. The least form of loss of status occurs when citizenship and freedom are retained, but a man's domestic position is altered by arrogation and emancipation (*Inst.* lib. 1, tit. 16).

Capitularia "were the ordinances or statutes of the Carolingian monarchs. They were called *capitularia* either because they were divided into chapters or because they were made by the emperor in council: for *capitulum* means either the chapter of a book or a body of persons. . . . They constituted the body of laws passed by the Great Council under the presidency of the king" (Wessels' *History*, p. 42).

Caput. In Roman law *caput* signified all the rights that a man can possess, comprehended in the enjoyment of freedom, of citizenship, and the relation he bears to his family.

Carelessness. "It is new to me that *carelessness*, even if it be gross, is fraud, though I think it is laid down in the books that *culpa lata* is akin or near to fraud, *proxima dolo*" (*per* BALE, C.J., in *Natal Land and Colonisation Co., Ltd.*, v. *Rycroft*, 27 N.L.R. at p. 217).

Cargadoor (D.), a shipbroker, a shipfreighter.

Carriage, under the Roads Ordinance (9 of 1846 (C.C.)), sec. 45, is defined to comprehend "every description of vehicle whether upon two wheels or more, or whether drawn by one horse or more, except when there is something in the context to restrict the meaning of the said term."

Carrier, *see* COMMON CARRIER.

"Carrying on business." This phrase is found in the Cape Additional Taxation Act (36 of 1904), sec. 42, where it is defined as meaning "conducting any operation by means of which any income is derived." See *Colonial Government* v. *National Life Assurance Society* (16 S.C. 254); *Smith* v. *Anderson* (15 Ch. D. 247); *Re Capetown Club* (19 S.C. 424).

Case, a lawsuit; a term frequently applied to an action in a court of law. *See* "ONE UNBROKEN CASE."

Casting vote, the vote of a chairman or presiding officer of an assembly or council, when authorised by the regulations of such assembly or council, given by him for or against the resolution under consideration where the votes of the members at such assembly or council are equally divided. "If the number of votes at a general meeting is equal, the chairman has no *casting vote* by common right" (Palmer's *Company Precedents,* part 1, 8th ed. p. 594).

Casual conditions, an expression employed in connection with the institution of an heir. *Casual conditions* are such as depend upon the occurrence of some uncertain event; they can be fulfilled either during the lifetime of the testator or after it (Maasdorp's *Institutes*, vol. 1, p. 139).

Casual employment. In Act 38 of 1901 (N.), sec. 3, *casual employment* means "employment for the purpose of gain in streets or other places in vending any article, and employment of any other kind outside the child's home which, in the opinion of the magistrate, may be detrimental to a child's health" (the Act referred to is one making provision for the support and training of destitute children and juvenile offenders).

Casus fortuitus, fortuitous or unavoidable accident. This has been defined as an accident which no ordinary care or foresight could prevent. Such an accident gives rise to no right of action on the ground of either contract or tort. "This, however, must, of course, be understood with the qualification that even in respect of inevitable accident liability may, according to the civil law, arise where the person owing the duty is *in mora,* or has by express contract assumed liability, or has admitted negligence" (*per* SHIPPARD, J., in *Hume* v. *Cradock Divisional Council,* 1 E.D.C. 122). Nor from its essential nature will fortuitous accident in the case of contract include anything which was known when the contract was executed (*Jervis* v. *Tompkinson*, 26 L.J. Ex. 41). *See* VIS MAJOR.

Casus omissus, omitted case; a contingency not provided for by statute. The Cape Insolvency Ordinance (6 of 1843) lays down that when there is a competition for the office of trustee, the choice shall fall upon the candidate who receives the votes of the majority of creditors present and entitled to vote, and who represent not only the greater number among themselves, but also the greater value; but no creditor whose debt is below £30 shall be reckoned in number, the debt being computed in value only. In the case *Re Du Toit's Estate* (12 S.C. 162) the Master moved for the confirmation of the election of a trustee who had received two votes from creditors who proved for £28 and £7 respectively, while another creditor for £26 voted for another candidate. Strictly, therefore, according to the Ordinance there was no election. The magistrate, however, had declared elected as trustee the nominee who had the majority in value. DE VILLIERS, C.J., said: "As this is a *casus omissus* in the Ordinance, the most convenient course seems to be to uphold the magistrate's decision, and confirm the election of O as sole trustee of the estate." *Casus omissus et oblivioni datus dispositioni communis juris relinquitur* (a case omitted and consigned to oblivion is left to the disposal of the common law). "A *casus omissus* can in no case be supplied by a court of law, for that would be to make laws" (*per* BULLER, J., Broom's *Legal Maxims,* 7th ed. p. 32).

Casus-positie (D.). In the judicial practice of the Netherlands a *casus-positie* was a document annexed to the inventory or list of documents in a case which was to be argued orally; it contained a history of the case and of the pleadings; it also contained a statement of the questions at issue as they appeared from the pleadings. See Van der Linden's *Institutes*, 3, 1, 8, 3.

Cattle. Under the Roads Ordinance 9 of 1846 (C.C.), sec. 45, the "term *cattle* shall comprehend all animals used for draught."

"*Cattle* shall include bulls, cows, oxen, horses, mares, geldings, mules, asses, pigs, ostriches, sheep, goats, and generally all domesticated animals" (the Cape Forest Act, 28 of 1888, sec. 2). See also Law 22 of 1882 (N.), sec. 5; Law 21 of 1891 (N.), sec. 1; Act 1 of 1899 (N.), sec. 5; Act 42 of 1898 (N.), sec. 3; Ordinance 15 of 1904 (T.), sec. 1; Ordinance 31 of 1907 (O.R.C.), sec. 1.

Cattle killing, an expression employed in the Natal Cattle Stealing Act (1 of 1899), where it is provided "*cattle killing* and kindred words shall include killing of cattle, and any stabbing, wounding, maiming, poisoning, or the infliction of any physical injury on cattle."

Cattle road. Where a road called a *cattle road* was reserved in the grant of a farm, it was held that the narrowest road that could have been in contemplation of either party at the time of grant was at least 8 feet wide; that such a road would have been quite wide enough for vehicles to have passed over; and that it did include the right of going in vehicles over the road (*Breda's Executors and Another* v. *Mills,* 2 S.C. 189).

Cattle stealing, an expression used in Act 1 of 1899 (N.)—the Cattle Stealing Act, 1899—where it is provided that "*cattle stealing* and kindred words shall include the stealing, theft or robbery of cattle or any portion thereof, whether flesh, skin, horns, head, hoofs or carcass, or any other part, or ostrich feathers; as also receiving cattle, or any portion thereof as aforesaid, or ostrich feathers, knowing the same to have been stolen."

Caupo, innkeeper. An innkeeper is liable in every case of loss or damage, although happening without any default or neglect on his part, unless it happened by inevitable accident.

Causa, a term used in Roman law, in which it has a great variety of meanings, which will be found collected in Dr. Heumann's excellent *Handlexicon zu den Quellen des Römischen Rechts.*

Causa plays an important part in the Roman law of contracts, and here too it has more than one shade of meaning. Its chief meaning in the law of contract is that which gives a binding legal effect to a promise. Thus Ulpian defines *causa* as *ratio sufficiens a lege approbata, ob quam conventio actionem producit* (*Dig. de Pact.* 7, 4). An agreement which did not give rise to any action was called *nudum pactum*, and hence the maxim *ex nudo pacto non oritur actio. Causa* must, however, not be identified with the English "consideration." *See* CONSIDERATION.

Causa is also a term of the Roman-Dutch law, and its Dutch equivalent is *oorzaak*. In the Roman-Dutch law of contract *causa* or *oorzaak* denotes the ground, reason, motive or object for a promise, giving such promise a binding effect in law. It is, therefore, a term of much wider meaning than the English "consideration." The maxim *ex nudo pacto non oritur actio*, as understood in the English law, has no application in Roman-Dutch law, according to which any promise seriously and deliberately made and founded on a reasonable cause, *e.g.* the liberality which one of the parties desires to exercise towards the other (Grotius' *Introduction*, 3, 1, 53) will give rise to an action for its performance. Any cause is reasonable, which is not *contra legem aut bonos mores.* The present law of the Netherlands is still the same, in this respect, as the Dutch law in the time of Grotius (*Burgerl. Wetboek*, secs. 1356, 1371–73; *Transatlantic Trading Co. of Amsterdam* v. *De Roock, Weekblad van het Recht*, 17th November, 1905; 23 S.A.L.J. 102).

The ancient Germans attached the greatest importance to the faithful performance of a promise, and hence the above rule of Roman-Dutch law, as has been stated, which does not require a *quid pro quo* to give a promise a binding effect. A similar rule prevails in Germany. Thus Mackeldey (*Lehrbuch*, sec. 104, 6, and note) observes: "Those precepts of the Roman law are inapplicable which rest on principles that have never been acknowledged in Germany, *e.g.* the principle that a nude pact does not produce an action."

In South Africa there are some lawyers who hold that the *causa* of the Roman-Dutch law is the equivalent of the English consideration, but the opinion of a large number is decidedly opposed to this view. Judicial decisions are likewise conflicting on the point. So far as the Cape Colony is concerned the earlier cases in the Supreme Court adopted the rule of the Dutch law. Thus in *Louisa* v. *Van den Berg* (1 Menz. 472) it was held that a gratuitous promise, if accepted, gave a good right of action; and in *Jacobson* v. *Norton* (2 Menz. at p. 221) that a promise by the defendant to pay a debt due by K required no consideration to support it. In the more recent cases, however, of *Alexander* v. *Perry* (Buch. 1874, p. 61); *Malan and Van der Merwe* v. *Secretan, Boon & Co.* (Foord, 94); *Tradesmen's Benefit Society* v. *Du Preez* (5 S.C. 269); and *Mtembu* v. *Webster* (21 S.C. 323), DE VILLIERS, C.J., held that by Roman-Dutch law, and, therefore, by the law of the Cape Colony, a binding contract must be founded on some valuable consideration. But in the Transvaal, KOTZÉ, C.J., in *Van Beuge* v. *Coetzee* (1 Off. Rep. 314) and INNES, C.J., in *Rood* v. *Wallach* ([1904] T.S. at p 198), held the contrary view. In the latter of these two cases it was authoritatively laid down by the full court that by Roman-Dutch law consideration in the sense of the English law is not essential to give an agreement a binding legal effect. Chief Justice MAASDORP of the Orange River Colony (*Institutes of Cape Law*, vol. 3, pp. 35 *et seq.*) and Dr. M. Nathan (*Common Law of South Africa*, sec. 757) agree in the opinion expressed by KOTZÉ, C.J., and INNES, C.J. It seems that all the Roman-Dutch writers of authority agree that *ex nudo pacto non oritur actio* is not a rule of Roman-Dutch law. In Ceylon the Supreme Court has in the recent case of *Lipton* v. *Buchanan* likewise decided in accordance with this view (22 S.A.L.J. 169) and in the colony of British Guiana, where the Roman-Dutch law is also in force, a similar opinion seems to have been entertained by the Supreme Court of that colony (21 S.A.L.J. 347). See further on the subject Kotzé's *Note* to Van Leeuwen's *Comm.* 2, 4, 2; and Wessels' *History*, pp. 571 *et seq.*

Causa cadit, he falls from the case, *i.e.* loses his suit.

Causa causans, the inducing or immediate cause as distinguished from a cause which, although proximate, is not the inducing cause. See Pollock on *Torts*, 8th ed. p. 464, where he suggests the adoption of the term "decisive" instead of "proximate" cause to describe the act of negligence which fixes a defendant with liability or debars a plaintiff from recovering damages. *See* also PROXIMATE CAUSE.

Causa debiti (or **debendi**), the cause or ground of debt. A promissory note need not express its cause of debt, nor is it necessary for the plaintiff to prove it (*Watermeyer* v. *Denyssen*, 1 Menz. 26; *Low* v. *Oberholzer*, 1 Menz. 43). The *causa debiti* must be specifically set forth in the declaration when such is filed (*Jacobson* v. *Norton*, 2 Menz. 218).

Causation, the doctrine that one event is the unconditional result of some other event which preceded it. The term is not uncommon in American text-books, such as Labatt's *Master and Servant*, at secs. 802*a* *et seq.*, where, in treating of the liability of a master for injury to his servant, he discusses the proposition that the negligence proved was the legal cause of the injury received.

Cause. (1) An action in a court; a judicial proceeding. In the Natal Courts Act (49 of 1898), sec. 5, the term *cause* is defined as meaning "any action, suit, motion, application or other judicial proceeding."

(2) Reason; that which produces or contributes to an effect.

Cautio damni infecti, security against apprehended damage. In the Roman law a person whose property was threatened with damage owing to some act done by his neighbour on his own land, could claim from the latter the security *de damno infecto.* If the security were refused the praetor gave him a *missio in possessionem* of the neighbour's property (*Digest, De damno infecto,* lib. 4. sec. 1; Grotius' *Introduction*, 3, 3, 39; Schorer's *Note* 58). The procedure of the *cautio damni infecti* and of the *missio in possessionem* is obsolete in the Roman-Dutch law; it is now sufficient that the person who apprehends damage from his neighbour should serve him with a *protestatio*, which has the same effect as the *cautio* of the Roman law (Voet's *Comm.* 39, 2, 15; *Burnett and Taylor* v. *De Beers Consolidated Mines, Ltd.*, 8 H.C.G. at p. 19; *Central South African Railways* v. *Geldenhuis Main Reef G. M. Co., Ltd.*, [1907] T.H. at p. 291).

Cautio de sistendo. "Securities given by litigants under the Dutch system of procedure were of two kinds, viz., the *cautio de sistendo* and the *cautio judicatum solvi.* By the former he undertook to stand to, and abide by, the judgment of the court, by the latter he undertook to perform it" (*per* DE VILLIERS, C.J., in *Schunke* v. *Taylor and Symonds*, 8 S.C. 105, which case contains an exposition of the law on the subject of security for costs).

Caveat, "let him beware;" a notice to an official objecting for good reasons to the dealing by another person with his property. For example, a creditor may lodge a *caveat* against the surrender of his debtor's estate (*In re McLeod & Co.*, Buch. 1876, p. 1), or an objection to the transfer of certain property may be lodged with the Registrar of Deeds (*Van Wyk's Trustee* v. *Van Wyk and Others*, 13 S.C. 481). The term is borrowed from the English law, but the Cape statute law has made no provision for *caveats.* In Natal, however, Deeds Office Notice, 21st June, 1882, established the following practice: "It is hereby notified that any *caveat* or interdict against dealings with property which shall be lodged with this office must be followed up by the production of an order of the Supreme Court, confirming such prohibition, within forty-eight hours, as a general rule, of the delivery of such *caveat* or interdict, or within such other reasonable time as in the discretion of the Registrar of Deeds the circumstances of any special case may seem to warrant or require."

Caveat conductor, let the lessee beware. By English law, just as in the case of a purchaser of a business the rule is *caveat emptor*, so in the case of taking the lease of property the rule is *caveat* lessee, he must take the property as he finds it (*per* MELLISH, L.J., in *Erskine* v. *Adeane*, L.R. 8 Ch. App. 761), unless the lessor fraudulently concealed the defect from the lessee (*Gott* v. *Gandy*, 2 E. & B. 845). *Caveat conductor* is not the rule of South African law; but the lessor's knowledge of a material defect in the demised premises may affect his liability (*Watson* v. *Geard*, 3 E.D.C. 417).

Caveat emptor, let the purchaser beware. In English law the presumption, where there is no fraudulent concealment of defects on the part of the seller, is that the principle of *caveat emptor* applies. In other words, in English law warranty must be express, and will not be implied or inferred except in certain excepted cases. In Roman-Dutch law, on the other hand, the seller must expressly state that he does not warrant the things sold by him, otherwise warranty is presumed (*O'Brien* v. *Palmer*, 2 E.D.C. 344). There is, however, an exception to this rule of the Roman-Dutch law in the case where an article of a definite nature is ordered. In such a case the manufacturer warrants no more than that the article is as fit as any answering the description in the order (*Hall & Co.* v. *Kearns*, 10 S.C. 155).

Cedent, the person who has ceded, assigned or transferred some property, right or thing to another, the latter being called the cessionary.

Censor morum, censor of morals. "But a judge is not a *censor morum*" (*per* BUCHANAN, J.P., in *Preston & Dixon* v. *Biden's Trustee*, 1 A.C. 333).

Census. (1) The Roman land tax, imposed in respect of citizenship and of ownership of land. In Roman-Dutch law *census* means the right to receive a certain irredeemable annuity reserved by a person when he transfers the ownership in his property (see Van Leeuwen's *Comm.* 2, 12, 1).

(2) An enumeration of the inhabitants of a country or district, duly made under legislative authority, showing the number of persons in such country or district on a fixed day, their nationalities, sexes, ages, occupations, &c.

Census (D.), *see* CYNSEN; CYUS.

Certain, fixed; definite. See *Logan & Co.* v. *Colonial Government* (17 S.C. at p. 291).

Certe-partye or **Chertepartije** (D.) (modern spelling *Charterpartij*), a charter-party; a contract made between a merchant and a shipowner for the hire of a ship. *See* CHARTER-PARTY. See also Van der Linden's *Institutes*, 4, 4, 3.

Certificate of citizenship, a certificate granted by a resident magistrate to certain Fingoes, Kafirs and native foreigners in the Cape Colony, by virtue of Act 17 of 1864 (C.C.), certifying that the bearer, whose description is given in the certificate, is an inhabitant of the Cape Colony and a subject of his Majesty the King, and is not to be obstructed or impeded by any person upon the ground or supposition that he is a Kafir without a pass. As to the administration of the estate of a holder of such a certificate of citizenship, see Act 18 of 1864 (C.C.); also Act 22 of 1867 (C.C.), sec. 7.

Certification. The expression *certification* is employed in connection with the transfer of shares. Where a certificate of shares comprises other shares than those the transferor desires to transfer, the transferor usually lodges such certificate with the company, and then, at his request or at the request of his broker, the secretary certifies the transfers (before they are handed over to the transferees) by stamping in the margin the form of *certification* and signing the same (Palmer's *Company Precedents*, 8th ed. p. 575).

A *certification* by a secretary of a company on a transfer of shares, while it does not warrant the title of the transferor, does warrant that the certificates lodged are right on the face of them. If, therefore, a transfer which purports to deal with fully paid shares is "certificated," when in fact no certificate has been lodged, the company is estopped from afterwards saying that the shares in question are not fully paid up (*In re Concessions Trust,* 3 Manson, 274).

Cessante ratione legis cessat ipsa lex, when the reason of a law ceases, the law itself ceases. "If the sole and acknowledged reason of the law ceases entirely, the law must be considered as obsolete, because the intention of the legislator has ceased to exist; hence laws which apply only to war cease in time of peace, even without being repealed" (Grotius' *Introduction,* 1, 2, 23). "For instance, a member of parliament is privileged from arrest during the session in order that he may discharge his public duties and the trust reposed in him; but the reason of this privilege ceases at a certain time after the termination of the parliamentary session, because the public has then no longer an immediate interest in the personal freedom of the individuals composing the representative body" (Broom's *Legal Maxims,* 7th ed. p. 126).

The maxim does not, however, mean that when the circumstances which rendered necessary the passing of a law cease to exist the law itself will cease to exist in the sense that it cannot again become operative; for if the circumstances again arise the law, if still in force, will apply once more. Thus, although laws which apply to war cease in time of peace, they will revive when war breaks out again; and the privileges which a member of parliament loses at the end of a parliamentary session will again attach to him when parliament reassembles.

Cessie van actie (D.), cession of action. On this subject, see Anders' *Cession of Actions.*

Cessio bonorum, cession of goods or of an estate. It is a voluntary surrender of all one's property for the benefit of creditors in order to escape imprisonment, and not to be liable beyond this for the debts above one's means. Those who were guilty of fraud, or concealed their property with evil intent, or incurred debt through crime, were not accorded the privilege of ceding their estate. See Van Leeuwen's *Comm.* Kotzé's trans. vol. 2, p. 336.

By the insolvency laws prevailing throughout South Africa, *cessio bonorum* is specially abolished. It is, however, competent in an action by reason of fraudulent alienation by the insolvent to proceed not merely under the Insolvency Ordinance, but also under the provisions of the common law. "I can find nothing in the [Insolvent] Ordinance from which it would appear that it was intended to deprive creditors or trustees of any right they might have under the common law consistently with the provisions of the Ordinance" (*per* De Villiers, C.J., in *Smith's Trustees* v. *Smith,* Foord, 21).

Cessio fori, the giving-up of the market. *Cedere foro* in the Roman law is the equivalent of the expression to stop payment or become insolvent (see *Digest,* 16, 3, 7, 2).

Cessionary, the person to whom some property, right or thing, has been ceded, assigned or transferred.

Cestui que trust, a person who has the equitable and beneficial interest in property, the legal interest in which is vested in a trustee. "As a rule the trust property is not merely held for the benefit of the *cestui que trust;* but he is also entitled in equity to it. This, however, is not the case always. In what are known as 'illusory trusts,' or 'trusts of imperfect obligation' (such as trusts for the payment of the settlor's creditors and trusts for the benefit of animals) the *cestui que trust* has no claim in law or equity to the beneficial interest in the trust property (Stephen's *Comm.* 15th ed. vol. 3, p. 453). *See* Trust.

Cestui que use is he to whose use land is held.

Cestui que vie is he for whose life land is granted.

C.F.I. *See* C.I.F.

Champerty, "the unlawful maintenance of a suit, in consideration of some bargain to have part of the thing in dispute or some profit out of it" (*per* Tindal, C.J., in *Stanley* v. *Jones,* 7 Bing. at p. 377), quoted with approval by Kotzé, C.J., in *Hugo and Moller* v. *Transvaal Loan, Finance and Mortgage Co.* (1 Off. Rep. (Eng. ed.) at p. 339). See *Schweizer's Claimholders' Rights Syndicate, Ltd.,* v. *Rand Exploring Syndicate* (3 Off. Rep. (Eng. ed.) 140); Anders' *Cession of Actions,* p. 48.

An agreement to contribute towards the costs of a lawsuit in consideration of receiving a share in the result of the suit is not *per se* champertous; see *Patz* v. *Salzburg* ([1907] T.S. at p. 526).

Character, the moral qualities of a person; a verbal or written statement of the qualities, reputation or standing of a person. "No master is bound to give a *character* to any servant or apprentice, who is or has been in his service, or to assign any reason for refusing to give it" (Act 15 of 1856 (C.C.), ch. 6, sec. 1).

Charge-sheet. "When a criminal prosecution in a court of resident magistrate is instituted in respect of a statutory offence, the *charge-sheet*, which takes the place of the indictment in a superior court, should set out the particular section of the law which is alleged to have been broken, and should state shortly and distinctly the nature of the offence alleged to have been committed" (*per* INNES, C.J., in *Dada Gia* v. *Rex*, [1906] T.S. at p. 26). "I think, following, and perhaps somewhat extending, that [just quoted] rule we should hold that in a charge like the present the accused should be informed of the grounds upon which the Crown relies for its contention that they [the appellants] are liable to be removed, and upon which it is alleged that they are prohibited immigrants" (*per* INNES, C.J., in *Ismail and Others* v. *Rex*, [1908] T.S. at p. 1093).

Chattels, an English term, meaning things which in law are deemed personal property. "The words 'goods and chattels,' at the time when these terms were introduced into English law, were used to embrace all property not comprised under one or other of the terms, 'lands, tenements and hereditaments'; and they are used in that sense to the present day as equivalent to personalty" (Goodeve's *Personal Property*, 5th ed. p. 14).

Check, a means of comparison or verification for the purpose of proving correctness. *See* NOT CHECKED.

Cheese, in Ordinance 32 of 1906 (O.R.C.), sec. 1, means "the substance usually known as *cheese*, containing no fat derived otherwise than from milk."

Chemist. (1) A person versed in the science of chemistry.

(2) A person licensed to deal in drugs and medicines. In the Cape Medical and Pharmacy Act (34 of 1891) the terms *chemist* and druggist are defined to mean "every person duly licensed in this [Cape] Colony on the day before the taking effect of this Act as an apothecary or chemist and druggist, and also every person duly licensed under this Act as a chemist and druggist and holding an annual license as a chemist and druggist under tariff 15 of the Act 20 of 1884." The Natal Act (35 of 1896, sec. 3) is almost identical with that of the Cape; the reference to the Act is of course different. See

Ordinance 29 of 1904 (T.), sec. 3; Ordinance 1 of 1904 (O.R.C.), sec. 1.

As to when a *chemist* may be considered as practising as a medical practitioner, see *Boyd* v. *Rex* ([1906] E.D.C. 65).

Cheque. "By construing sec. 73 with sec. 3 [of the English Bills of Exchange Act, 1882], which defines a bill of exchange, we get the following definition of a *cheque*: 'A *cheque* is an unconditional order in writing addressed by one person to another, being a banker, requiring the person to whom it is addressed to pay on demand a sum certain in money to or to the order of a specified person or to bearer'" (Watson on *Cheques*, 3rd ed. p. 1). Sec. 73 of the English Bills of Exchange Act, 1882, reads as follows: "A *cheque* is a bill of exchange drawn on a banker payable on demand," and this definition is identical with that given in sec. 71 of the Cape Bills of Exchange Act, 1893, and the Cape Bank Act (6 of 1891), sec. 2; sec. 72 of the Natal Bills of Exchange Law, 1887; sec. 74 of the Rhodesian Bills of Exchange Regulations, 1895; sec. 71 of the Transvaal Bills of Exchange Proclamation, 1902; and sec. 71 of the Orange River Colony Bills of Exchange Ordinance, 1902.

"A *cheque* paid into a bank may be accepted in two ways—either for collection or as cash. If it is taken for collection it remains the property of the customer, and the bank in obtaining payment of it act merely as the customer's agents. If it is taken as cash the bank become holders of it for value. They place the amount of it to the customer's credit as cash, and they obtain the right to sue the drawer in their own name" (*per* BRISTOWE, J., in *Freeman* v. *Standard Bank of South Africa, Ltd.*, [1905] T.H. at p. 31). The payment must be made either (1) to the payee himself, or (2) to the person who presents the *cheque* with the indorsement of the payee upon it; a payment, therefore, to a person who presents the *cheque* (who is not the payee) without an indorsement by the payee is not a payment in the ordinary course of business; nor is a variance by the bank of the customer's order to pay within the ordinary course of business (*per* WESSELS, J., in *E. & J. Burke, Ltd.* v. *Standard Bank, Ltd.*, [1905] T.H. at p. 127).

Chertepartije (D.). *See* CERTE-PARTYE.

Chief, the head of a native tribe. In the Natal Code of Native Law (Law 19 of 1891, sch., sec. 9) the word *chief* is used to denote "any person who by virtue of the acknowledgment or appointment of the Supreme Chief is in charge of a tribe or section of a tribe of natives in this [Natal] colony, and entitled to have, use and possess the jurisdiction, powers and privileges conferred by this Code upon such persons. The term *chief* shall also include the persons appointed by the Supreme Chief to have charge over natives living upon or connected with mission stations." *See* NATIVE CHIEF; SUPREME CHIEF.

Child. *See* CHILDREN. See also Act 37 of 1904 (C.C.), sec. 1; Act 24 of 1906 (N.), sec. 3; Act 24 of 1909 (T.).

Child-bearing age. "No fixed rule of law can be laid down as to the age at which a woman must be conclusively presumed to be past child-bearing age. After a woman has reached the age of fifty the Court would not require the same degree of evidence as when she is under that age, but some further evidence would be required to support the presumption that she will not bear children" (*per* De Villiers, C.J., in *Re Meyer's Estate* (13 S.C. at p. 4). See also *Ex parte Francis* (13 C.T.R. 147), where the woman was seventy years of age, and the court held it was still possible she might remarry and have lawful issue; and *Ex parte Kok* (13 C.T.R. 213), where the woman was fifty-two years of age and the court was satisfied that there was no probability of further issue (see Best on *Evidence*, 10th ed. sec. 338, note (*t*)).

Children is a "flexible term, used sometimes to signify only sons and daughters and sometimes all descendants. . . The signification to be given to this term in any particular case is not a question of law, but of fact, namely, with what intention did the maker of the deed use the term?" (*Sequestrator* v. *Guardian of Slaves and Beck*, 1 Menz. at p. 333). See also *Pretorius* v. *Executors of Pretorius* (2 S.C. 293); *Re Bergh* (7 S.C. at p. 308); *Wright's Executors* v. *Wright* (18 C.T.R. 846); and Van Leeuwen's *Comm.* Kotzé's trans. 3, 6, 7, and 3, 8, 11 and 12. There is no presumption in the law of Cape Colony that the word "child" or "children" occurring in a statute refers to legitimate children only (*per* Kotzé, J.P., in *Davies* v. *Rex*, [1909] E.D.C. 149).

"Children and grandchildren." Where a testator had by his will appointed his *children and grandchildren* to be his sole and universal heirs, the Supreme Court of the Cape Colony held that, in the absence of any other indication to the contrary in the will, they were not all called together to the inheritance, but the children before the grandchildren, and on failure or predecease of one the other comes in his place by substitution (*Human* v. *Human's Executors*, 10 S.C. 172).

Child-stealing is a punishable offence. *See* Man-stealing; also *Queen* v. *Buchenroeder* (13 S.C. at p. 178).

Chirograph, a Roman law term meaning a note of hand; a written acknowledgment of debt.

Chirographarii, "creditors who have the security of 'private' writings under the hands of their debtors, as distinguished from those who are secured by 'public' instruments; but the term is also used to include all who have only a right to a personal action, and no hypothec, Matthaeus, *De Auct.*, lib. 1, cap, 20, sec. 1; Van Leeuwen's *Censura Forensis*, part 1, lib. 4, cap. 11, sec. 15; all of whom rank *pari passu* and without reference to priority of date; the only distinction being that preference is given to such of them as are 'privileged'" (Berwick's *Translation of Voet*, p. 320, *in notis*).

Chose-in-action, "any right, vested in a definite person or persons, to obtain from another, by legal proceedings, any money or money's worth, or any right in the nature of property, whether the aim of the proceedings be to get possession of a specific material object, or not" (Jenks' *Digest of English Civil Law*, bk. 1, sec. 41). *Chose-in-action* is an English legal term; it has not been adopted in South Africa.

Christian name, defined in the Cape Interpretation of Statutes Act (5 of 1883, sec. 3) as being "any name prefixed to the surname, whether received at Christian baptism or not." See also Proclamation 15 of 1902 (T.), sec. 2; Ordinance 3 of 1902 (O.R.C.), sec. 8.

Cider vinegar. In the Cape Wine, Brandy, Whisky and Spirits Act (19 of 1908), sec. 16, "'*Cider vinegar*' or 'Apple vinegar' means the product made by the alcoholic and subsequent acetous fermentation without distillation, of the juice of apples." *See* VINEGAR.

C.I.F., a commercial abbreviation of the words "cost, insurance and freight."

"The terms, at a price, 'to cover cost, freight, and insurance, payment by acceptance on receiving shipping documents,' are very usual and are perfectly well understood in practice. The invoice is made out debiting the consignee with the agreed price (or the actual cost and commission, with the premium of insurance and the freight, as the case may be), and giving him credit for the amount of the freight which he will have to pay the shipowner on actual delivery, and for the balance a draft is drawn on the consignee, which he is bound to accept, if the shipment be in conformity with his contract, on having handed to him the charter-party, bill of lading, and policy of insurance. Should the ship arrive with the goods on board he will have to pay the freight, which will make up the amount he has engaged to pay. Should the goods not be delivered, in consequence of the perils of the sea, he is not called on to pay the freight, and he will recover the amount of his interest in the goods under the policy. If the non-delivery is in consequence of some misconduct on the part of the master or mariners not covered by the policy, he will recover it from the shipowner. In substance, therefore, the consignee pays, though in a different manner, the same price as if the goods had been bought and shipped to him in the ordinary way" (Benjamin on *Sales*, 4th ed. p. 574). The transaction described in the foregoing quotation is commonly known by the abbreviations "*c.i.f.*" or "*c.f.i.*" See also *Hughes & Rogers* v. *White, Ryan & Co.* (17 S.C. 236).

Circuit courts, courts of record established in the Cape Colony in 1832 by the Charter of Justice, to be holden at least twice a year, and to be presided over by the Chief Justice or one of the puisne judges of the Supreme Court, for the purpose of visiting each of the circuit districts into which the colony has been apportioned. *Circuit courts* have both civil and criminal jurisdiction. This system of *circuit courts* has been extended to the other South African colonies. See Act 39 of 1896 (N.), secs. 11 *et seq.*; Ordinance 10 of 1903 (T.); Ordinance 4 of 1902 (O.R.C.), secs. 19 *et seq.*

Circuit district, a district within which a circuit court is held. Under sec. 37 of the Charter of Justice of 1832 (C.C.), the Governor of the Cape Colony was authorised to apportion the colony into districts in such manner as may appear to be best adapted for enabling the inhabitants to resort with ease and convenience to the circuit courts to be established in such districts. These districts are called *circuit districts,* and circuit courts are held therein at more or less regular intervals. A similar system has been adopted in the other South African colonies. See Act 39 of 1896 (N.), secs. 11 *et seq.*; Ordinance 10 of 1903 (T.); Ordinance 4 of 1902 (O.R.C.), secs. 19 *et seq.*

Circulation. In *Colonial Government* v. *Bank of Africa* (4 S.C. 477) it became necessary to construe the term *circulation* in reference to bank notes, as appearing in the Bank Note Duty Act (6 of 1864 (C.C.)), secs. 3 and 4. In doing so DE VILLIERS, C.J., said: "The company by allowing any of its offices to issue its own notes, confers on such office to that extent a certain individuality of its own. The notes are payable only at the office which issues them, and although the company may allow its other offices to pay those notes, it is not bound to do so. There is much force, therefore, in the argument that, in the absence of any interpretation clause defining the term *circulation,* and independently of the provisions of the 9th section of the Act, notes once issued are to be deemed to be in *circulation* and consequently liable to duty until they come back to the very office which first issued them. This argument acquires additional force in the case of notes which the issuing office has, for the purposes of Act 19 of 1865, represented as being in *circulation,* although in the possession of other offices of the same company. The argument is further strengthened, it certainly is not weakened, by the terms of the 9th section of Act 6 of 1864." See also *Colonial Government* v. *Standard Bank* (5 S.C. 43).

Citatie (D.), a summons. In Roman-Dutch law the *citatie* was the initial proceeding in a court of law whereby civil or criminal proceedings were instituted. A lawful citation had the effect of (*a*) bringing the defendant into court; (*b*) perpetuating jurisdiction; (*c*) interrupting prescription; and (*d*) transmitting the process to the heirs of the defendant. See Kersteman's *Woordenboek,* vol. 1, p. 62; Van Leeuwen's *Comm.* 5, 13.

Civil commissioners, officers appointed in the Cape Colony to perform the duties, or some of them, of the landdrosts upon the abolition of the office of landdrost in 1827. The duties were more particularly defined by Ordinance 77 of 1830 (C.C.). Civil commissioners at the present time are almost entirely confined to matters connected with the revenue and expenditure in their respective districts in the Cape Colony.

Civil fruits (*fructus civiles*), fruits that do not owe their origin to nature, but are merely the product of something; they include rents and interest.

Civil imprisonment, the confinement of a person in a public gaol or lock-up under a judgment of a competent court for not paying a judgment debt or any other sum of money he is ordered to pay; or for not doing any other act, thing or deed ordered by the court (Van Zyl's *Judicial Practice*, 2nd ed. p. 226). "At a comparatively early stage of its development the Dutch law gave the right to the creditor, if his debtor was unable to pay, to claim the custody of the debtor's person, in order that he might serve out his debt" (*per* KOTZÉ, J.P., in *Dold & Stone* v. *Wilson,* [1908] E.D.C. 480). Prior to 1813 there was no limited time for the duration of the imprisonment in the Cape Colony of any person or persons against whom an execution for debt, process of court, or precept or warrant of any court or competent authority was issued, but such persons were committed to prison until they could pay or satisfy such debt, &c. On the 5th February, 1813, a Proclamation was promulgated by Sir John Cradock, limiting the periods of *civil imprisonment.* See also Ordinance 6 of 1839, sec. 2; Act 20 of 1856, sec. 20; and Act 8 of 1879, sec. 6, of Cape Colony.

Civil jurisdiction, the jurisdiction granted to a court by law in civil matters—that is, matters relating to property and rights maintainable in law at the suit of the owner or claimant, as opposed to criminal jurisdiction, or to jurisdiction in ecclesiastical and naval or military matters.

Civil law, the municipal law of a state. It is also used to denote that portion of the municipal law of a country which deals in the civil rights and remedies as distinguished from the criminal law. It is sometimes employed as opposed to ecclesiastical law. When used without any qualification it is generally understood to mean the Roman law as contained in the *Corpus Juris Civilis.* "Among the primary systems the *civil law* holds the most prominent place. It is the great source from which most other systems of jurisprudence have been derived, and they still recognise the influence of its principles and doctrines. *Servatur ubique jus Romanum non ratione imperii sed rationis imperio.* The most important texts of the Roman law were collected and revised between 529 and 534 A.D., under the Emperor Justinian. This collection, known as the *Corpus Juris Civilis,* consists of (1) the *Institutes,* an educational text-book; (2) the *Digest,* or *Pandects,* a compilation of dicta, opinions, &c., from the writings of the most eminent Roman lawyers; (3) the *Code,* a chronological collection of Imperial statutes; and (4) the *Novels,* or new laws made subsequent to Justinian's codification" (Renton and Phillimore's *Colonial Laws and Courts,* p. 13; and Burge's *Comm.* new ed. vol. 1, p. 13).

Civil Service, that branch of the public service that is not military or naval. In the Cape Civil Service and Pensions Fund Act (32 of 1895), sec. 2, the term *Civil Service* is, for the purpose of that Act, defined to "include and consist of all persons continuously employed in the discharge of duties other than purely police or military in any department of the public service; not being ministers of the Crown, or judges of the Supreme Court, or their clerks, or private secretaries to the Governor, or aides-de-camp to the Governor, or officers of parliament; provided (*a*) that such persons are not remunerated solely by fees or allowances; (*b*) that their whole time is devoted to the public service, except in the cases of the Solicitor-General, the Crown Prosecutor at Kimberley, the Assistant Law Adviser to the Crown, and any other person to whom a retiring allowance may be granted under the provisions of the 47th section of this Act."

In the Natal Civil Service Act (21 of 1894), sec. 2, the term *Civil Service* is defined as "The body of persons, other than judges of the Supreme Court, who have been heretofore appointed and regarded as members of the permanent civil service of the colony, and all persons who may become members of such permanent civil service in terms of this Act." In the Transvaal the term used is *Public Service;* see the Pensions Ordinance (30 of 1906), sec. 1, which defines *public service* as "service in a department of the Government of this colony," and the Public Service and Pensions Act (18 of 1908), sec. 1, where the definition given is "the system of employment of persons of European descent by the Government of this colony in the discharge of public duties in a department or office of such Government."

Civiliter modo, in a reasonable manner; a phrase applied in Roman law to the exercise of servitude rights. The owner of the dominant tenement must exercise his right in the way least burdensome to the servient tenement, and with a due regard to the comfort and convenience of its owner (*Digest,* 8, 1, 9). Thus the holder of a *jus itineris* must keep the path, and cause no damage to the servient property.

Claim. (1) A right in a holding under some mining law. In Law 15 of 1898 (T.) *claim* is defined as "that portion of the field on which a person or persons or companies has or have lawfully obtained the right to dig or to prospect, or the right to dig or prospect on such piece of land." The Precious and Base Metals Act (35 of 1908 (T.)), which repealed the above Law, defines *claim* as "an area of ground which in accordance with this Act or a prior law has been lawfully pegged as a claim, and on which the right to prospect or dig for precious or base metals has been lawfully obtained."

The tenure under which *claims* held under license issued by virtue of the Transvaal Gold Law "is one *sui generis* specially created by statute, and the incidents of which must be gathered from the terms of the statute which established it" (*per* INNES, C.J., in *Neebe* v. *Registrar of Mining Rights*, [1902] T.S. 65). *See* PROSPECTING LICENSE.

In the Transvaal Precious Stones Ordinance (66 of 1903), sec. 2, *claim* means "the portion of ground assigned for mining purposes within any proclaimed alluvial diggings of a size fixed by this Ordinance, or the right to dig for precious stones in such portion of ground." See Ordinance 7 of 1905 (T.), sec. 1.

See Act 31 of 1898 (C.C)., sec. 3; Ordinance 63 of 1903 (T.), sec. 43.

See METAL CLAIM; MINERAL CLAIM.

In the Orange River Colony, in the Mining of Precious Metals Ordinance (3 of 1904,) sec. 5, *claim* signifies "an area of land situated on a public digging (not being a mijnpacht) assigned under the provisions of this Ordinance for mining purposes." And under the Mining of Precious Stones Ordinance (4 of 1904 (O.R.C.)) *claim* means "a portion of the land assigned for mining purposes within any proclaimed alluvial digging or any existing mine within the meaning of this Ordinance of a size fixed by this Ordinance, in respect of such existing mine or alluvial digging respectively. The land assigned for mining purposes as aforesaid with reference to existing mines shall be deemed to be the area respectively recognised as *claims* in the said mines at the time of the coming into operation of this Ordinance."

(2) An assertion of a right. "An editor supervising for the press the writings of judges and other lawyers has a special grievance in regard to the verb—not the noun-substantive—*claim*. In addition to being used as the equivalent of 'allege,' 'assert,' 'protest,' 'profess,' &c., . . . nothing is commoner than for *claim* also to do duty in place of 'contend,' 'argue,' 'urge.' In the same sentence we have often known it to mean, in the early part, allege, and in a later part, contend. In the forms of pleadings under the Judicature Act we have the proper use of the verb *claim*—and almost the only use to which it can be intelligibly put in legal writings. 'The plaintiff *claims* possession,' '*claims* a declaration,' '*claims* foreclosure,' '*claims* an injunction.' It seems possible that the substitution of '*claim*' for 'pray' or 'pray for,' authorised by the forms, has paved the way for the introduction into Canada, and we fear into England too, of the American use or misuse of the verb. English judgments are not quite free from such expressions as '*claims* that he was misled,' '*claims* to be entitled,' and the like, and Canadian judgments abound in them" (26 *Canadian Law Times*, 763). It is said that in America the verb *claim* "has been so disfigured by misuse and unsuitable tasks that the original significance, that of asserting a right, has been hopelessly weakened, if not entirely lost" (*ibid.*).

Claim in reconvention, a counter-claim made by a defendant against a plaintiff in a pending action.

"By looking at the text-books I think it will be found clearly laid down that the principle of reconventional claims was introduced into the Dutch law simply because it was for the interest of the State, *ut finis litium.* When an action was therefore brought against a defendant, if he had any kind of cross-action, of whatever nature, against the same party who brought the original suit, it was competent for him at once in pleading to make his *claims in reconvention*, so that the pleadings would go on *pari passu* to the day of trial, and prevent the plaintiff from getting judgment against the defendant when that defendant might have otherwise meritorious claims as a valid set-off. These reconventional claims, by being thus pleaded at once, prevented the necessity of defendant taking out fresh summonses, or beginning other proceedings which really might lead to very great injury" (*per* CLOETE, J., in *Brunette* v. *Stanford*, 3 Searle, at p. 225).

Claim inspector, an official appointed by Government to inspect and report upon claims, their beacons, &c., upon proclaimed diggings in certain South African colonies. As to *claim inspectors* in the Transvaal, see Law 15 of 1898, sec. 12 (since repealed).

Claimholder, the person who is entitled to a claim by license or other legal title on any proclaimed gold or other mineral-bearing field, or in a mine under the Precious Stones Acts. The tenure under which claims are held under the Transvaal Gold Law is one *sui generis* specially created by statute, and the incidents of which must be gathered from the terms of the statute which established it (*Neebe* v. *Registrar of Mining Rights*, [1902] T.S. at p. 83). As to the tenure in diamond mines in the Cape Colony, see *South African Loan and Mortgage Agency* v. *Cape of Good Hope Bank* (6 S.C. at p. 182).

In the Cape Precious Minerals Act (31 of 1898), sec. 3, the term *claimholder* is defined to include "partnership and joint-stock companies and any public body or body corporate to whom any portion of ground has been or may be assigned for mining purposes whether by way of absolute ownership, lease or otherwise." A similar definition is to be found in sec. 3 of the Cape Precious Stones Act (11 of 1899).

In the Transvaal Precious Stones Ordinance (66 of 1903), sec. 2, *claimholder* means "the registered holder of the right to dig for precious stones in a claim." And so also in Ordinance 4 of 1904 (O.R.C.), sec. 5.

Clandestine marriage, a secret marriage; a marriage contracted secretly without the consent of parents or in defiance of the will of parents or guardians.

"The Church recognised the validity of a marriage of minors where no parental consent had been obtained. . . . By the civil law the marriage was void, but the reason of that law did not apply to Holland, for the prohibition arose from the law regarding *patria potestas*, and this peculiar power of the Roman ancestor did not form part of the law of Holland. Public opinion was therefore the only influence which restrained *clandestine marriages.* In the sixteenth century, however, public opinion seems to have lost its restraining influence, and we find Charles V in 1540 attempting to check *clandestine marriages* by imposing severe penalties upon the parties. Notwithstanding that the parties could be punished, and that they forfeited the benefits arising from community, the number of *clandestine marriages* increased. In 1580, however, the States of Holland boldly broke away from the Canon law, and pronounced all marriages of minors void unless the consent of parents had been obtained, even though the marriage had been duly celebrated by an officer of the Church. The law was therefore brought into accord with that public opinion which had prevailed in the Netherlands from the earliest German period.

"Though the legal age has been reduced to twenty-one years, the requirement of the Political Ordinance that the parents must give their consent to the marriages of children under the age of majority has been retained (Order in Council, 7th September, 1838, sec. 10), and a marriage of minors without the consent of parents is as void with us as it was in Holland" (Wessels' *History*, pp. 442–43).

Clausula derogativa, the derogatory or derogative clause in a will. *See* CLAUSULE DEROGATOIR.

Clausule derogatoir (D.), a clause inserted in a testament or will whereby the testator expressly provided that whatever disposition he should afterwards make should not take effect except by special revocation and insertion of certain or particular words (Van Leeuwen's *Comm.* 3, 2, 17). Grotius says (*Introduction*, Maasdorp's trans. p. 117): "There is another cause which may render a will invalid *ab initio*, namely, if a previous testament contains a clause (*clausula derogativa*) to the effect that the testator does not wish any wills subsequently made by him to be valid; by which clause the testator does not indeed deprive himself of the right to alter his will (for that the law does not allow, even if a person imposes a penalty on himself in case he should subsequently make a will), but rather gives ground for suspecting that such subsequent will was extorted from him by compulsion or undue influence, and is consequently no indication of the testator's intention. If, therefore, a testator wishes to make a valid subsequent testament, he ought in such subsequent testament to refer to the clause contained in the previous one, and to revoke it. The lapse of ten years, however, after the making of the first will, the execution of the second will before the authorities, and such-like indications are also held as annulling such clause." See also Van der Keessel, *Thes.* 328. Kersteman (*Woordenboek*, vol. 1, p. 65) speaks of this clause with disapproval, and describes it as a corruption received into the Roman-Dutch practice.

Clausule reservatoir (D.), reservatory clause in a will. *See* RESERVATORY CLAUSE.

Clay. "It is clear that absolutely pure *clay* is a mineral, even in the narrow sense. It is called kaolin, but, scientifically speaking, it is hydrosilicate of alumina. When mixed with a proportion of basic metals it becomes a compound, and when hard and compressed it is called a rock. If the proportion of basic metals mixed with the pure kaolin is comparatively small then the substance is called fire-clay; and, not being easily fusible, it is used for purposes for which great heat-resisting properties are required. If, on the other hand, the proportion of basic metals is large, then the compound is comparatively easily fusible and is used as ordinary *clay* for making bricks for building purposes and such like" (*per* INNES, C.J., in *Blue Sky G. M. Co., Ltd.*, v. *Marshall*, [1905] T.S. at p. 26, *q.v.*). See *Donovan* v. *Turffontein Estate Co.* (2 Off. Rep. Webber's trans. 218); *Brick and Potteries Co.* v. *Registrar of Deeds* ([1903] T.S. 473); Ordinance 7 of 1905 (T.), sec. 1; MINERAL.

Clean certificate, an expression used in the Scab Acts. In the Cape Scab Act (20 of 1894), sec. 4, *clean certificate* is defined to mean "a certificate granted by a veterinary surgeon or inspector for and in respect of sheep, to the effect that such sheep are not infected." See Ordinance 14 of 1903 (O.R.C.), sec. 1.

Cleansed. In the Cape Cattle Cleansing Act (31 of 1908), sec. 2, "*cleansed* shall mean dipped, sprayed or otherwise cleaned in manner provided by regulations under this Act."

Clear days' notice, means a notice extending over a period of days, so that it does not include the day on which the notice is given or the day on which the thing or event, to which the notice refers, shall happen; thus seven clear days' notice convening a meeting means seven days' notice exclusive of the day on which the notice is given or that on which the meeting is held (see *Caldecott and Others* v. *Botha's Reef G. M. Co.*, 5 H.C.G. 249). In Natal "seven days' notice" has been held to mean seven *clear days' notice* (*Craig* v. *Tatham, Lyon and Thorrold*, 20 N.L.R. 29; and *Johnson* v. *Johnson*, 26 N.L.R. 142). See also Maxwell's *Interpretation of Statutes*, 4th ed. p. 519. *See* DAY.

Cloaca, sewer or drain. *See* SERVITUS CLOACAE.

Closed. In the Natal Shop Hours Act (36 of 1905), sec. 4, *closed* means "closed against the admission of any person for the purpose of buying or doing any shopping business, either for the whole day or for the remainder of the day, as the case may be." See also Act 32 of 1908 (T.).

Closed (or Close) will. "Written (otherwise called *close*) wills are those whereby the testator has expressed his intentions in writing; and having subscribed and sealed it, has handed the same, closed up, to a notary in the presence of two witnesses, together with a declaration that whatever is contained in the writing is his complete last will. The document is then superscribed by the notary, and an act thereof made, subscribed by the testator and the witnesses. It should, however, be specially observed with reference to this point, that a *close* *will* made by two spouses, whereby the one has conferred a benefit upon the other, must be written by a third person; for no one can write a will in his own favour" (Van Leeuwen's *Comm.* Kotzé's trans. vol. 1, p. 319). See also Van Zyl's *Notarial Practice*, p. 265; Maasdorp's *Institutes*, vol. 1, p. 121.

Club. "Clubs are associations of a peculiar nature. They are societies the members of which are perpetually changing. They are not partnerships; they are not associations for gain; and the feature which distinguishes them from other societies is that no member as such becomes liable to pay to the funds of the society or to any one else any money beyond the subscriptions required by the rules of the club to be paid so long as he remains a member. It is upon this fundamental condition, not usually expressed, but understood by every one, that clubs are formed; and this distinguishing feature has been often judicially recognised. It has been so recognised in actions by creditors and in winding-up proceedings" (*per* Lord LINDLEY, in *Wise* v. *Perpetual Trustee Co.*, 87 L.T. at p. 571). See *Re Panmure Club* (5 E.D.C. 170; 3 C.L.J. 213); *Reid and Stewart* v. *Rex* ([1904] T.S. 260).

As to what may not be a *bonâ fide club*, see *Goldman and Others* v. *Rex* ([1908] T.S. 895).

As to *club* being a descriptive word used in connection with a trade-mark, see *Wordon & Pegram* v. *Cantrell & Cochrane and Another* (18 S.C. 142).

As to whether a *club* is a shop in Natal, see *Ladysmith Corporation* v. *Cheeseman* (27 N.L.R. at p. 496).

Coasting trade is defined in the Cape Colony (sec. 2 of Act 26 of 1872) as being all trade by sea from any one part, port or place in the colony to any other part thereof, with certain exceptions mentioned in the Act, principally referring to ships arriving from or proceeding to ports beyond colonial limits. In Natal, *coasting trade* is defined as being "trade by sea from one port to any other port of the colony" (Act 13 of 1899, sec. 117).

Codicil, an instrument by which a testator makes some addition or alteration to his will by virtue of the reservatory clause. *See* Maasdorp's *Institutes*, vol. 1, p. 115; *Erasmus* v. *Erasmus' Guardians and Executors* ([1903] T.S. 843); *Joseph* v. *Joseph's Estate and Others* (17 C.T.R. 169).

Coercion, compulsion. "There is a rule of law that 'he is free from blame who is bound to obey' (*Dig.* 50, 17, 169). This rule, as pointed out by Matthaeus (*De Crim.* 1, 13), must be accepted with the limitation that the offence is not so heinous as obviously to absolve the person ordered to commit it from the duty of obedience. No assistance can be derived from the English law, which, in regard to crimes committed under compulsion, is most unsatisfactory. According to Stephen (*History of Criminal Law*, vol. 2, p. 106) 'As the law stands it produces this result: a husband and wife of mature age, and their daughter of fifteen, commit a theft. It is proved that the girl acted under actual threats used by her father. Nothing appears as to the wife's part in the matter, except that her husband was present when she committed the offence. The wife must be acquitted on account of the presumed *coercion* of her husband; the daughter must be convicted, notwithstanding the actual *coercion* of her father.' Even in England, however, there are, according to Sir M. Hale (P.C. 44), various crimes, such as those which are *mala in se*, from the punishment of which the wife is not privileged on the ground of *coercion*. As to our own law, I am not prepared to adopt the English rule that a wife who commits a theft in the presence of her husband must be presumed to have acted under his *coercion*. That rule was referred to, but not accepted by the majority of the court, in *Queen* v. *Barker* (2 S.C. 9). The Court has now to deal with the case of a child of eleven years assisting his father in committing a theft. It cannot be reasonably expected from a child under fourteen that he will disobey the illegal order of the father unless the offence he is ordered to commit is of an atrocious kind. If he has reached the age of fourteen he is presumed to have sufficient discernment between right and wrong, and sufficient strength of will to disobey unlawful orders. If he is under seven he is absolutely free from criminal responsibility. But between seven and fourteen, although he is presumed to be *doli incapax*, that presumption may, as was held in *Queen* v. *Lowrie* (9 S.C. 432), be rebutted by evidence to the contrary" (*per* De Villiers, C.J., in *Queen* v. *Albert*, 12 S.C. 272). See also *Queen* v. *Slinger and Klaas* (4 E.D.C. 279).

Whether a wife is acting under the *coercion* of her husband is a question of fact (*per* Smith, J., in *Queen* v. *Farley*, 2 S.C. at p. 229). See also *Queen* v. *Bruintjes* (4 E.D.C. 281).

Cogitationis poenam nemo patitur, no one suffers punishment for his thought. The mere intention to commit an offence or crime is not punishable. If, however, the intention has been manifested in some overt act, as in the case of an attempt to commit a crime, then the act, although unsuccessful, is punishable (Van Leeuwen's *Comm.* 4, 32, 2; Decker, *ibid. in notis*). According to Van Leeuwen (*Comm.* 4, 33, 1) an exception to this principle obtains in the case of high treason, intention alone being sufficient to constitute the crime. As regards English law, Act 36, Geo. III, cap. 7, in defining treason, strikes at mere intention to commit the crime; but it is nevertheless settled that such intention must be proved by some overt act, and it would appear that the same view must now be taken as regards this crime in Roman-Dutch law (*Rex* v. *Boers*, 21 N.L.R. 116).

Cognisable, that which is capable of being tried in, or adjudicated upon by, a court of law.

Cognoscement, (D.) (also spelt *cognossement* or *connossement*), bill of lading.

Cognossement (D.), *see* COGNOSCEMENT.

Cohabitatie (D.), cohabitation; the living together of spouses as man and wife.

Cohabitation, the state of a man and woman living together as husband and wife; generally implying sexual intercourse.

Coin. "*Coin* is metal used for the time being as money, and stamped and issued by authority of some state or sovereign power in order to be so used. Coin stamped and issued by authority of the Queen or any Government in the Queen's dominions is the Queen's coin" (Native Territories' Penal Code, Act 24 of 1886 (C.C.), sec. 228).

In the Cape Bank Act (6 of 1891) the term *coin* is defined to mean "gold, silver and bronze coin of British coinage current in the [Cape] Colony, and all gold coin coined by lawful authority in any of the colonies of the Crown, and such other coin as the Governor may by proclamation from time to time determine."

Coinage, pieces of metal stamped and issued by authority of some state or sovereign power in order that they may be used as money.

Coining, the crime of counterfeiting or knowingly performing any part of the process of counterfeiting coin. See Stephen's *Digest of the Criminal Law*, art. 409; see also the Native Territories' Penal Code (Act 24 of 1886 (C.C.)), secs. 228–30; Ordinance 26 of 1904 (T.), sec. 18.

Collateral relationship, a term denoting the relation of persons descended from the same stock or ancestor, but in a side or branch line; commonly known as "collaterals." Succession by representation among collaterals only extends to the fourth degree.

Collatie, (D), collation. *See* COLLATION.

Collation, "the duty incumbent on all descendants who wish to share in the succession to an ancestor or ascendant, either by will or *ab intestato*, of bringing into hotchpot or massing with the inheritance of the deceased any property acquired from or on account of such ancestor during his lifetime" (Maasdorp's *Institutes*, vol. 1, p. 152).

"A brief glance at the history of our law relating to *collation* will be useful to assist us in arriving at a decision upon the question now raised. By the ancient civil law emancipated children had no rights of succession *ab intestato* to their father or other ascendant, but the praetor in the exercise of his equitable jurisdiction gave them the *bonorum possessio*, just as if they had been in the ascendant's family at the time of his death. This right, however, was conditional upon their bringing into *collation* their own property, which was reckoned as part of the inheritance for the purpose of dividing it between them and their brothers and sisters living under their father's *potestas*. This was the origin of the doctrine of *collatio bonorum*, which was afterwards extended by statute and by judicial interpretation far beyond its original application. The Emperor Pius Antoninus extended it to the *dos* which a daughter had received from her father, and a similar extension was made by subsequent emperors to any substantial advancement made by a mother as well as by a father beyond the ordinary maintenance and education which a parent, according to his means, owed to his children. Justinian laid it down generally that whatever could be reckoned for the purpose of the legitimate portion should be brought into *collation* (*Cod.* 6, 20, 20), and he afterwards by his 18th *Novel* (c. 6) extended the principle still further by directing that it should apply to the testamentary succession as well as succession *ab intestato* of descendants. The right of the testator, however, to forbid its application was expressly reserved. It would serve no useful purpose to follow the applications and modifications of the doctrine which have been made in the law of the Netherlands. The 29th article of the Political Ordinance of 1580 substantially adopts the later Roman law on the subject, but contains no precise statement as to what benefits conferred on children or other descendants must be collated. Treatises have been written by Dutch lawyers upon the question whether or not a simple donation made to a child should form the subject of *collation*, and no agreement was ever arrived at by them. Vinnius (*De Coll.* c. 16, par. 15), after discussing the question at great length, comes to the conclusion that a simple and absolute gift made to a child by either parent need not be brought into *collation* except in two cases, namely, where the gift was made on condition that it should be brought into *collation*, and where the necessity of creating equality among the children gives occasion for applying the principle. The conclusion is a very lame one. If the gift was a conditional one it could not at the same time have been simple and absolute. The second exception must in many cases neutralise the rule, for if some only of the children obtained substantial gifts there must be an inequality requiring to be redressed, and if all the children received gifts, *collation* would not affect the ultimate result" (*Per* DE VILLIERS, C.J., in *Jooste* v. *Jooste's Executor*, 8 S.C. at p. 290). See *Meyer* v. *Estate Meyer*, 19 S.C. 227; *Re Correy's Estate* (27 N.L.R. 544).

Collusion. This term does not necessarily connote anything morally wrong, as literally it means nothing more than agreeing together, but it is generally applied in law to a secret agreement between two or more persons for the one to do or abstain from doing something in order that the other may by action obtain a remedy to which he would not otherwise be entitled. In divorce proceedings *collusion* is fatal if it is proved or even if the court has reason to believe in its existence.

Colonial forces is defined in the Cape Colonial Forces Act (32 of 1892) to include "the permanent forces as hereinafter [in the Act] defined, any volunteer corps, any colonial commissariat or transport force, attached to a field force, any corps of native levies, and any other corps raised and enrolled under the provisions of this Act."

Colonial legislature is defined in the Interpretation Act, 1889 (Eng.), sec. 18, sub-sec. 7, as follows: "The expression *colonial legislature* and the expression 'legislature' when used with reference to a British possession, shall respectively mean the authority, other than the Imperial Parliament or her Majesty the Queen in Council, competent to make laws for a British possession."

Colonus partiarius, a farmer whose land is leased to him at a rent which consists in a share of the produce; see *Oosthuizen* v. *Estate Oosthuizen* ([1903] T.S. 688).

Colony, a distant possession or dependency of a parent State. "Colonies are either gained by conquest or cession, or else they are acquired by right of occupancy only, that is, by finding them desert and uncultivated, and peopling them from the mother country. In conquered or ceded countries which have already laws of their own, those laws remain in force until changed by competent authority; the common law of England, as such, having no authority there. But it has been held that if an uninhabited country be discovered and planted by English subjects, all the English laws then in being, which are the birthright of every subject, are immediately there in force. But this must be understood with very many and very great restrictions. The colonists carry with them only so much of the English law as is applicable to the condition of an infant colony; such, for instance, as the general rules of inheritance and of protection from personal injuries" (Stephen's *Comm.* 15th ed. vol. 1, p. 62).

The expression *colony* is defined in the Interpretation Act, 1889 (Eng.), sec. 18, sub-sec. 3, as meaning "any part of her Majesty's dominions exclusive of the British Islands and of British India, and where parts of such dominions are under both a central and a local legislature, all parts under the central legislature shall, for the purposes of this definition, be deemed to be one *colony*." In *Re Koch* ([1902] T.S. 197) the Supreme Court of the Transvaal held that the definition contained in the Interpretation Act, 1889 (Eng.), just quoted, was not applicable to South African statutes.

Coloured person. Ordinance 39 of 1904 (T.), sec. 1, repealing the definition given in sec. 18 of Law 3 of 1897, regulating the marriage of coloured people, defines *coloured person* as "any person who is manifestly a *coloured person* and whose marriage on that account cannot be solemnised under the provisions of Law 3 of 1871." In the Precious and Base Metals Act 35 of 1908 (T.), sec. 3, *coloured person* means "any African or Asiatic native or any other person who is manifestly a *coloured person*."

In the Mining of Precious Metals Ordinance 3 of 1904 (O.R.C.), sec. 5, *coloured person* signifies "any African, Asiatic, or Polynesian aboriginal native, any coloured American person, Arab, Coolie or Chinaman, and all persons who in accordance with law or custom are called *coloured persons* or are treated as such, of whatever race or nationality they may be."

In the Poll Tax Consolidation Ordinance 2 of 1904 (O.R.C.), *coloured person* includes "Arabs, Chinese and other Asiatics, and also all other persons who are by law or custom in South Africa regarded as coloured." See also Ordinance 28 of 1907 (O.R.C.), sec. 1.

See *Salugee* v. *Rex* ([1903] T.S. 13); *Bosch* v. *Rex* ([1904] T.S. at p. 56).

Combined drain. The term *combined drain* is defined in the Capetown Municipal Act Amendment Act (25 of 1897 (C.C.)), sec. 1, to mean "any private drain used or intended to be used for the drainage of two or more houses or premises."

Commandeer. From the Dutch word *commandeeren*, to command. A term commonly applied to the requisition of property for the necessities of war in the late South African Republic and Orange Free State, where commandeering was carried out by virtue of the Krijgswet. In *Alexander* v. *Pfau* ([1902] T.S. 155) it was held that it was not in conflict with the principles of international law for a State to requisition the property of resident aliens, and *à fortiori* that of hostile resident aliens, in order to supply the necessities of war.

Commando (D), a collection of armed burghers called together or commandeered for military purposes under the statute law of the late South African Republic and Orange Free State. A *voet commando* was an infantry *commando* as above; a *paarde commando* was a commando of mounted infantry; and when a person had gone out with a commando he was said to be *op commando*.

Commit, to consign a person to prison, under warrant, for examination, further examination, trial or some other purpose.

Commitment, the act of consigning a person to prison under warrant. *See* COMMIT. For instance, one may speak of a "warrant for *commitment* for trial" or a "*commitment* for examination."

Committee. "A *committee* is a person or body to whom the discharge of certain duties is committed or delegated by another or others" (*per* INNES, C.J., in *Macintosh* v. *Pretoria School Board*, [1908] T.S. at p. 874).

See Act 3 of 1907 (T.), sec. 2; Act 6 of 1907 (T.), sec. 1; Act 12 of 1907 (T.), sec. 2.

Committee room, an expression used in statutes regulating parliamentary and other elections, and signifying the room officially used by the committee of a candidate for the purposes of an election. See Act 26 of 1902 (C.C.), secs. 2 and 11.

Commixtio, commixture; the term *commixtio* is used with reference to solids. *See* CONFUSIO.

Commodatum, a loan for use. *Commodatum* is a transaction whereby something is, without any gain, lent for a certain use, on condition that the same thing shall after the use be returned. The borrower must return the thing lent to him in the same state in which it was, and is liable for damage or injury caused to the property by his smallest neglect. He is, however, not liable for accidents. *See* also ACTIO COMMODATI.

Commodus usus, comfortable use. One of the duties of a lessor is to afford his lessee the use and comfortable enjoyment of the property let. Thus he is bound not to interfere with the lessee's use and enjoyment of the thing himself, and to guarantee the lessee against interference by way of legal process on the part of others (*Watson* v. *Geard*, 3 E.D.C. 422). Where during the currency of the lease the lessee has suffered eviction, without just cause, he can claim to be reinstated (*Diamond* v. *Gill*, 7 E.D.C. 194), or he may cancel the lease and claim damages (*Levy* v. *Rose*, 20 S.C. 194). So if the property has been leased for a certain definite object the lessor must afford the lessee the *commodus usus* of the property for such object. He will therefore be liable for any interference with the lessee's use of the property for that purpose, as where he himself has caused a nuisance or is responsible for it. But he will not be liable for any interference caused by third parties for which he is not responsible, *e.g.* where he has let the adjoining premises to a third party for a legitimate object, and they have been misused for the purpose of a nuisance, such as the keeping of a brothel (*Baum* v. *Rode*, [1904] T.S. 66). The lessor, again, is bound to keep the thing let in a proper state of repair. If he fails in this duty, the lessee will be entitled to an abatement of the rent to the extent to which he has been deprived of the means of enjoying the use and occupation of the thing or has himself incurred expenditure in placing it in a proper state of repair (*Bensley* v. *Clear*, Buch. 1878, p. 89). In certain circumstances the lessee will even be entitled to abandon the lease, in which event he will be liable for rent only for the time during which he has actually been in occupation of the premises. The lessee may also recover compensation for damage caused to him by reason of the disrepair of the thing let, if the lessor was aware of the disrepair, or from the nature of his trade or calling ought to have been aware of it (*Bensley* v. *Clear*; *ibid.*; *Armstrong* v. *Armstrong*, Buch. 1879, p. 23).

Common carrier. "A common carrier is one who makes carrying his business—who holds himself out to the world as prepared to transport the goods of any other person from place to place for hire.

It is not essential that he should hold himself out as ready to carry goods of all sorts. He may profess only to carry small parcels, and then he could not be required to carry large and bulky things. He may profess to carry one description of goods, as, for example, corn, in which case he would be a common carrier of corn, and could not be required to carry anything else. Again, he probably only professes to carry goods to certain places, or, perhaps, even only between two particular places. If this were the case, he would be entitled to refuse goods offered to him for carriage to places to which he did not profess to extend his operations. The essential part of the definition of a *common carrier* is that he holds himself out to the public as being ready to carry for any one whatsoever who wishes to engage his services and is prepared to pay his charges" (Disney's *Carriage by Railway*, p. 1).

"In England the well-established rule is that a *common carrier* is responsible for all losses, except those occasioned by the act of God or the king's enemies, but even then such responsibility does not extend to losses occasioned by some internal defect or some inherent tendency to damage in the goods carried. In this [Cape] Colony the liability of *common carriers* is not quite so wide as in England. It has never been expressly decided whether the praetor's edict relating to innkeepers, shipmasters and stablekeepers applies in this colony to carriers by land as well as by water. In the Netherlands the dearth of authority on this point may be accounted for by the fact that most of the carrying trade has always been done by water; but it is strange that in this colony, where there is no internal transport by water, the question has never been distinctly raised. The edict of the Roman praetor extended in terms to carriers by water only, but the reasons stated for the rules which it lays down are equally applicable to carriers by land. The praetor declared that if shipmasters, innkeepers and stablekeepers did not restore what they had received to keep safe, he would give judgment against them (*Dig.* 4, 9, 1). The reasons given by Ulpian for this edict are that it is for the most part necessary to place confidence in such persons and to commit the custody of things to them, and that unless this rule were thus established an opportunity would be afforded to them to combine with thieves against those who trusted them, whereas they now have an inducement to abstain from such frauds. The construction placed on this edict was that the bailees named were liable in every case of loss or damage occasioned by theft, injury or otherwise, although happening without any default on their part, unless it happened by superior force, or by what was called 'fatal damage,' as, for instance, by shipwreck or by the act of pirates. Among instances of superior force being used, Voet mentions the cases of an inn or a stable being broken into by burglars and the property of the guest or the horse of the bailor being stolen, but he adds that if the theft was facilitated by the negligence or default of the innkeeper or stablekeeper, he would be liable, and that the burthen of disproving negligence lies upon him (Voet, 4, 9, 2). Voet does not mention the case of carriers by land, but in the *Utrechtsche Consultatiën* (vol. 1, c. 21), such carriers appear to be placed on the same legal footing as carriers by water. Among French writers on the civil law, Domat (1, 16, 3 and 4) holds a similar view, which has been adopted in the *Code Civile* of France (art. 1782). In *Naylor* v. *Munnik* (3 Searle, 181), which was a case of a carrier by land, remarks were made by the then Chief Justice of this Court, and were concurred in by his three colleagues, which tend to show that in their opinion the principles of the edict were equally applicable to carriers by land. 'It appears to me,' said HODGES, C.J., 'that a carrier who undertakes to carry goods is bound to take faithful care of those goods, and is answerable for their loss even in the case of theft. It is for the interest of the public that this rule should be enforced, as otherwise a door would be opened for the perpetration of gross frauds when goods are handed over by their owners for the purposes of transit,'" (*per* DE VILLIERS, C.J., in *Tregidga & Co.* v. *Sivewright, N.O.*, 14 S.C., at p. 80). It should be added that in the same case MAASDORP, J., was of opinion that "the responsibilities of the defendants are not to be tested by the principles which have been founded on the rule of the civil law, but are similar to those of depositaries for hire. In that case they were bound to use ordinary diligence, and are liable for damage caused by their negligence," (*ibid.* at p. 86); but BUCHANAN, J., concurred with the Chief Justice (*ibid.* at p. 84).

See Carrier Law 11 of 1884 (N.); also Law 5 of 1891 (N.); and Law 21 of 1891 (N.).

Common employment. "Much objection has from time to time been taken to the expression *common employment*, and Mr. Joseph Brown, Q.C., has gone the length of saying that it is an expression incapable of definition (*Parlm. Com.* 1876, Q. 502). To give a precise definition, which will be applicable to every case that may occur, may be next to impossible; but that is no objection to the use of the terms in the absence of something better. . . . The difficulty suggested has arisen, not so much from the use of the expression *common employment*, as from its most unreasonable application and extension by different judges to wholly distinct departments of duty, and to persons in entirely different grades of service, under a common master or employer. . . . The mere fact of the servant injured and the servant injuring being fellow-servants—*i.e.* having the same master—is not enough to exempt the master from liability. It must be shown that the service which each servant performed was in some way connected, or that they were employed on what the law considers the same work or department of duty. This for practical purposes is well enough expressed by the words *common employment*" (*per* KOTZÉ, C.J., in *Lewis and Salisbury G. M. Co.*, 1 Off. Rep. Webber's trans. at p. 5).

Common fief, is a fief that is held without any noble titles or dignities attached, and without any incidents of nobility (Van Leeuwen's *Comm.* Kotzé's trans. vol. 1, p. 256).

Common form, *see* "USUAL COMMON FORM."

Common law. "Custom exists as law in every country, though it everywhere tends to lose its importance relatively to other kinds of law. It was known at Rome as the *jus moribus constitutum*. It is known in England as the *common law*, or 'the custom of the realm,' the existence of which is now usually proved by showing that it has been affirmed by the courts, or at least has been appealed to in the writings of great judicial sages" (Holland's *Jurisprudence*, 10th ed. p. 57). This definition is equally applicable to South Africa. In Ordinance 3 of 1902 (O.R.C.), sec. 1, it is specifically provided that "The Roman-Dutch law shall be the *common law* of the colony in so far as it has been introduced into, and is applicable to South Africa." See also Proclamation 14 of 1902 (T.), sec. 17.

Common wall, a wall between two properties, and in which the owners of both such properties have equal or common rights. (See Maasdorp's *Institutes*, vol. 2, pp. 177–80).

"The rights to a party wall partake of the nature of a servitude, but the wall itself is also regarded, in many important respects, as common property. The neighbouring proprietors are not co-owners, in the true sense of the term, of the wall, because the land on which the wall stands is not their common property, but they have the rights of co-owners to this extent, that each is entitled to the maintenance of the wall encroaching on his neighbour's property, as well as of the part standing on his own property. Such a wall is consequently termed in our law a *common wall*" (*per* DE VILLIERS, C.J., in *Wiener* v. *Van der Byl*, 21 S.C. at p. 26).

Commonage, town lands adjoining a town or village, and over which the inhabitants of such town or village have the right of grazing cattle, subject usually to municipal regulations or bye-laws.

Communal tenure, that form of title by which immovable or real property is held on behalf of a community, such community being so formed and organised as to protect and promote its general interests. As an example of such tenure, see sec. 26 of the Cape Glen Grey Act (25 of 1894).

Communis error facit jus, common error sometimes passes current as law. "It has been sometimes said," observed Lord ELLENBOROUGH (*Isherwood* v. *Oldknow*, 3 M. & S. 396) "that *communis error facit jus*; but I say that *communis opinio* is evidence of what the law is—not where it is an opinion merely speculative and theoretical, floating in the minds of persons; but where it has been made the groundwork and substratum of practice." This maxim must be applied with great caution, for it is apt to set up a misconception of the law in destruction of a law. "But where a decision of the courts, originally wrong, or an erroneous conception of the law, especially of real property has been made, for a length of time, the basis upon which rights have been regulated and arrangements as to property made, the maxim *communis error facit jus* may be applied. Indeed, this is strictly in accordance with the above cited view of Lord ELLENBOROUGH, and it will be found that, where the courts of justice have declined to correct misconceptions of long standing, the reluctance has been due to a wholesome fear of interference with rights based upon them" (Broom's *Legal Maxims*, p. 114; and cf. *Mtembu* v. *Webster*, 21 S.C. 345).

Community of goods, same as community of property. *See* COMMUNITY OF PROPERTY.

Community of property. (1) According to Roman-Dutch law the property of every description of the spouses becomes on marriage the common property of both, and this is known as *community of property*. This consequence can be avoided by the due execution of a contract, called an *antenuptial contract*, between the parties prior to the marriage providing for the exclusion of *community of property* and of profit and loss. *See* ANTENUPTIAL CONTRACT.

As to the law in Natal relating to parties married outside South Africa, see Law 22 of 1863, sec. 2.

(2) A real right belonging to two or more persons over the same thing (Grotius' *Introd.*, 2, 28, 2).

Commutative contract, a contract "in which the thing given or act done by one party is regarded as the exact equivalent of the money paid or act done by the other" (May on *Insurance* 4th ed. sec. 5).

Commutative justice, "treats of things *in commercio*. Things *in commercio* or *patrimonio* are those which are capable of individual possession and enjoyment, divided into *res corporales*, or such as are capable of corporeal possession (which might be *mobiles* or *immobiles*), and *res incorporales*, or such as are incapable of corporeal enjoyment. In *commutative justice* what is called the arithmetical proportion is observed, when there is only a comparison of thing with thing, and the equality of the things compared is regarded, not the equality of the persons between whom the transactions stand and the agreements are entered into (*i.e.*), whether nobles or plebeians, magistrates or private persons)" (Nathan's *Common Law*, sec. 5). See Grotius' *Introd.* 1, 1, 10; Van Leeuwen's *Comm.* Kotzé's trans. 1, 5, 3, *et in notis*.

Company, is defined in the Cape Companies Act (25 of 1892) to mean "every partnership whereof the capital is divided, or agreed to be divided, into shares, and so as to be transferable without express consent of all the partners; and also any partnership which at its formation or by subsequent admission shall consist, or have at any time consisted, of seven or more than seven members." As to the formation of a *company*, see sec. 23 of the same Act. *See* JOINT STOCK COMPANY; LIMITED COMPANY; see also the Cape Railways Extension Act (28 of 1895), sec. 1; Act 43 of 1895 (C.C.), sec. 1.

In the Transvaal, in Act 31 of 1909, *company* means "a limited or unlimited company which is incorporated and registered under chap. i of this Act, and shall include every company to which, by chap. vi, this Act is expressed to apply," *i.e* every existing *company* and every *company*, not being a foreign *company*, which was incorporated under Law 6 of 1874. In the Estate Duty Act 28 of 1909 (T.), sec. 2, *company* is defined as "any *company* incorporated or registered under the law for the time being of this colony relating to the incorporation or registration of companies, and shall include also a *company* which, though not so incorporated or registered, carries on business in this colony."

See O.R.C. Law Book, chap. C, sec. 1; Law 2 of 1892 (O.R.C.), sec. 1; Law 4 of 1892 (O.R.C.), sec. 1 (*a*).

Compensatie or **Schuld-vereffening** (D.), compensation; the payment and satisfaction of a debt or obligation; set-off. "Compensation is the setting off of one debt against another of equal amount and subsisting between the same parties" (Grotius' *Introd.* Maasdorp's trans. p. 333). See also Van Leeuwen's *Comm.* 4, 40; Van der Linden's *Institutes*, 1, 18, 4; Kersteman's *Woordenboek*, vol. 2, p. 118. *See* COMPENSATIO; SET-OFF.

Compensatio, set-off. It is the extinguishment of debts which two persons mutually owe each other by means of the claims which they mutually have against each other (Van der Linden's *Institutes*, Juta's trans. p. 168). In order that debts may be set off, it is necessary: (1) That they be of the same kind; (2) that they be due; (3) that they be liquidated; and (4) that they be due by the parties to the set-off in their personal capacities.

"By our law, set-off, whether admitted to be a set-off or not, extinguishes the debt *pro tanto* against which it is opposed. This extinguishment takes place *ipso jure*, and does not depend upon any admissions made by the parties" (*per* DE VILLIERS, C.J., in *Kruger* v. *Van Vuuren's Executrix*, 5 S.C. 166). See also *Symon* v. *Brecker* ([1904] T.S. at p. 747).

Compensation, (1) set-off. *See* COMPENSATIO.

(2) That which is given or received as an equivalent for services rendered or as amends or reparation for injuries done.

Competent evidence. "By *competent* (or admissible) *evidence* is meant that which the law requires, as the fit and appropriate proof in the particular case—such, for instance, as the production of a writing, where its contents are the subject of inquiry" (Taylor on *Evidence*, 10th ed. sec. 2).

Component part, a constituent portion or piece, such as a *component part* of machinery. See *Collector of Customs* v. *De Beers Consolidated Mines, Ltd.* (9 S.C. at p. 148).

Compounding a crime, an arrangement whereby, for a consideration, a person injured agrees to refrain from prosecuting, or if possible to discontinue a prosecution. "Where the punishment prescribed is merely a fine and no other punishment, the person injured is not criminally liable if, before a criminal suit has been instituted at all events, he compounds the offence, but . . . where the law provides any other punishment than a mere pecuniary penalty, no such private composition may be made" (*per* DE VILLIERS, C.J., in *Queen* v. *Thomas*, 1 A.C. at p. 207).

Compounds. This term is defined in the Cape Excise Spirits Act (18 of 1884), sec. 2, and in the Cape Additional Taxation Act (36 of 1904), sec. 2, as follows: "*Compounds* means spirits redistilled, or which have had any flavour communicated thereto, or ingredient or material mixed therewith."

Compromis (D), in Roman-Dutch law, was (1) an instrument usually passed before a notary and two witnesses, whereby the parties, in order to avoid the cost and trouble of a lawsuit, agreed to refer their differences to arbitration (see Kersteman's *Woordenboek*, vol. 1, p. 73).

(2) An agreement between litigants for the settlement of matters in dispute (see Grotius' *Introd.* 3, 4; Van Leeuwen's *Comm.* 5, 23).

Compromise, a mutual arrangement made between two or more persons for the settlement, by means of concessions, of the differences or disputes existing between them.

Compulsion. "An act which if done willingly would make a person a principal in the second degree and an aider and abettor in a crime, may be innocent if the crime is committed by a number of offenders, and if the act is done only because during the whole of the time in which it is being done, the person who does it is compelled to do it by threats on the part of the offenders instantly to kill him or to do him grievous bodily harm if he refuses; but threats of future injury, or the command of any one not the husband of the offender, do not excuse any offence" (Stephen's *Digest of the Criminal Law*, 5th ed. art. 32). See also the Native Territories' Penal Code (Act 24 of 1886 (C.C.), sec. 29). *See* COERCION.

Compulsory sequestration, an order of a competent court placing the estate of a debtor in insolvency for the benefit of his creditors upon the application of a creditor. A creditor having a claim against a debtor amounting to not less than a certain sum (usually £50) may, if such debtor has committed an act of insolvency, petition the court that the estate of such debtor be placed under sequestration for the benefit of his creditors, stating in such petition the amount of the debt, the cause thereof, and the alleged act of insolvency; the petition must be accompanied by an affidavit of the truth of the debt, and the security held by the creditor (if any) and the value thereof; security must also be lodged for the fees and charges for the due prosecution of the sequestration until the choice or appointment of trustees. Upon proof of the allegations to the satisfaction of the court, and provided the necessary affidavit and certificate of security have been filed, the court may order the estate of the debtor to be placed under sequestration in the hands of the Master of the Supreme Court. This is known as a provisional sequestration. The debtor is then summoned by the petitioning creditor to appear before the court on a certain day, to be appointed by the judge making the provisional order, to show cause why his estate should not by sentence of the court be adjudged to be sequestrated for the benefit of his creditors; on the return day the court may either adjourn the hearing, or grant the final order of sequestration or dismiss the petition. On the final order for sequestration being granted the insolvency is complete and the estate of the insolvent becomes vested in the Master of the Supreme Court, and is subsequently administered by trustees under supervision of the Master. See Ordinance 6 of 1843 (C.C.), secs. 4 *et seq*; Act 38 of 1884 (N.), sec. 3; Law 13 of 1895 (T.), secs. 7 *et seq.*; O.R.C. Law Book, chap. 104, sec. 5, and Ordinance 3 of 1906 (O.R.C.), sec. 9.

Computatio civilis et naturalis, civil and natural calculation. A policy of insurance dated 22nd January, 1857, was issued by the defendant company (*Cock* v. *Cape of Good Hope Marine Assurance Co.* 3 Searle, 114) to plaintiff upon the schooner *Onward* for a period of twelve calendar months from 14th January, 1857, to 14th January. 1858. It was held that the plaintiff could not recover on the policy, as the risk ceased at midnight on 13th January, 1858. WATERMEYER, J., said: "The Roman-Dutch law knows two modes of computation—the natural and the civil. In the natural, *de momento in momentum computatur* (computation is made from moment to moment), and in this fractions of a day are recognised. In the civil, *ultimus dies inceptus pro completo habetur* (the last day is held to be completed at its commencement) fractions of a day are not admitted, and the term expires at the first moment of the commencement of the last day. Voet (44, 3, 1) adduces some instances of the application of the 'natural computation,' in the prescription of actions not brought within the time limited by law, in favour of the maintenance of a subsisting right in danger of being lost; in the computation of majority where the benefit of restitution on the ground of minority is claimed; and in the time allowed for the fulfilment of a condition within a certain day. . . . Voet proceeds to instance the *computatio civilis*; and adduces the acquisition of property by *usucapio;* the attainment of the age of puberty, which gives the right of making a will. . . . It is clear, looking at the policy before us only, we must give the contract the civil interpretation. The year from 14th January to 14th January in law ceased at the first instant after midnight on 13th January, 1858, and therefore the plaintiff has no claim on the company under the policy."

Computation of time, *see* TIME; COMPUTATIO CIVILIS ET NATURALIS.

"**Concerned in,**" see remarks of LAURENCE, J.P., in *Cairncross and Another* v. *Fagan and Another* (24 S.C. at p. 126).

Concessionary, a person to whom some right in the nature of a concession has been granted. See the Cape Railways Extension Act (28 of 1895), sec. 1.

Conclusie (D.), a technical term in Roman-Dutch practice to denote a form of pleading which was filed of record. As soon as the case had been placed upon the roll the *conclusie van eisch* (conclusion of the claim) was filed, which set out the facts and claim with precision and in clear language. There were also other *conclusies, e.g. Conclusie van exceptie* (conclusion of exceptions), see Van der Linden's *Institutes*, 3, 1, 2, 16; *Conclusie tot absolutie van de instantie* (conclusion for absolution from the instance), *ibid.* 3, 1, 2, 15; *Conclusie van antwoord* (conclusion of plea), *ibid.* 3, 1, 2, 16.

Conclusive evidence. The provision of sec. 51 of the Companies Act, 1862 (E.), that the declaration of the chairman in the case of a special or extraordinary resolution, that the resolution has been carried "shall be deemed *conclusive evidence* of the fact, without proof of the number or proportion of the votes recorded in favour of or against the same," precludes the court from inquiring into the question whether the requisite proportion of votes was in fact given (*Arnot* v. *United African Land Co.*, 8 Manson, 179). The words quoted above as being portion of sec. 51 of the Companies Act, 1862 (E.), also appear in the Cape Companies Act (sec. 110 of Act 25, 1892); in the Transvaal Companies Act, 1909, sec. 67 (3); and in the Rhodesian Companies Ordinance (2 of 1895, sec. 62).

Conclusive proof "means evidence upon the production of which, or a fact upon the proof of which, the judge is bound by law to regard some fact as proved, and to exclude evidence intended to disprove it" (Stephen's *Digest of the Criminal Law*, 5th ed. p. 2).

Concurrent creditors, those creditors who rank concurrently or *pro ratâ* in the distribution of an estate after the preferent claims have been provided for or paid.

Concursus creditorum, gathering of creditors. "As to what should be the *locus concursus,* it was generally admitted that it should be the domicile of the insolvent. The assignment under the law of his domicile would operate as an assignment of his movable property wherever situate, subject, of course, to any rights which preferent creditors attaching any property before the date of the assignment may have acquired by the law of the country in which such property is situate" (*per* DE VILLIERS, C.J., in *Howse, Sons & Co's. Trustee* v. *Trustees of Howse, Sons & Co.*, 3 S.C. 20).

Concussie (D.), concussion; extortion. *See* CONCUSSIO.

Concussio, concussion; extortion. "Concussion or extortion" is the extorting of a contribution or something else in an improper way by officials and officers of Government from the common people, above that which they owe" (Van Leeuwen's *Comm.* Kotzé's trans. vol. 2, p. 262). This crime, however, includes not only extortion by officials, but also the obtaining of money or other things by private persons by means of threats (*State* v *Jacob and Jacob*, 6 Off. Rep., referred to in Van Hoytema and Raphaely's *Digest*, col. 147; *Brough* v. *Rex*, 26 N.L.R. 81). See also Voet's *Comm.* 47, 13, 1; and Kersteman's *Woordenboek*, vol. 2, p. 130; also EXTORTION.

Condictio causa data causa non secuta, an action which arises in respect of an innominate contract, where one person gives or does something with a view to receiving an equivalent in substance or deed, which the other party fails to give.

Condictio certi, the *lex Silia* of the Roman law introduced a new kind of action, termed *condictio*, for the enforcement of obligations binding a person to give the absolute ownership—*dare*—of a certain sum of money—*pecunia certa*. In course of time contracts *dare* or *facere* were enforced by a *condictio*, and this *condictio* was *certi* or *incerti* according as a definite or indefinite thing was demanded.

Condictio ex lege. If, says Paul (*Dig.* 13, 2) an obligation has been established by some new enactment, and it has not been provided in the same enactment by what form of action we are to sue, the action must be "on the law" (*ex lege*). The *condictio ex lege*, in other words, was the action allowed by Roman law when a *nova lex* provided a remedy, but was silent as to the mode of enforcing it. By *nova lex* some, among them Voet, understand a *lex* passed subsequent to the XII Tables, but Savigny takes it to mean one passed after the introduction of the formulary system.

Voet, without saying anything as to the application of the *condictio* in the law of Holland, states the following cases in which it was given in the Roman law, viz., to the donee in respect of a gift which one had agreed to make; to those to whom less was given by will than sufficed for their legitimate portion if they wished to claim suppletion; to the master whose slave was accused of adultery and at the instance of his accuser was put on trial, for the price of the slave if he should die or be rendered less valuable during the trial and be acquitted; to the fisc in proceeding by virtue of its privilege against the debtors of its debtor in order to compel them to pay their overdue debts before a fixed period; to States proceeding by a singular right (*i.e.* a right acquired otherwise than by succession) severally against each of those who possess *pro ratâ* property belonging to the debtors of the State; to more preferent mortgage creditors against less preferent creditors to whom an heir who has adiated with benefit of inventory, has paid the amount realised from the sale of goods belonging to the deceased's estate; to defendants who have sustained damage from the plaintiff making an excessive demand; and to one who wishes to recover what he has lost in gaming (Voet's *Comm.*, 13, 2, 2).

Condictio ex mutuo, a personal action on a loan; the action which lies against a person for the recovery of money which has been lent to him. The action is "personal, *stricti juris* and available to the lender and his heirs, provided the lender was the owner of the money or paid money belonging to another in his own name with the consent of the owner; in which latter case this action is not available to the owner of the money unless it has been ceded to him by the person who, not being the owner, paid (the money) in his own name; or unless provision was made in the document of debt that the debtor should restore the money lent to the holder of the writing, since in that case not only the owner of the money, but also any other holder of the writing without special cession will have a right of action against the debtor, unless it is proved that he holds the document in bad faith" (Voet's *Comm.* 12, 1, 15).

Condictio furtiva (sometimes written *condictio ex causa furtiva*), a personal action on the ground of theft; a personal action of Roman law which lay in favour of the owner against the thief or his heirs for the recovery of stolen property. In order that the action might lie, it was necessary that the person seeking to recover the property should have been owner both at the time when the theft was committed and the time when the action was brought. It was not available to a borrower (*commodatarius*), a depositary and other like persons who had not the ownership at either time. A pledgee from whom the thing pledged had been stolen was allowed to bring a *condictio incerti furtiva,* and according to Groenewegen the remedy was extended by custom to all who had an interest in the recovery of the property (Voet's *Comm.* 13, 1, 2 and 3). *See* ACTIO FURTI.

Condictio incerti, *see* CONDICTIO CERTI.

Condictio indebiti, a personal action for the recovery of money paid which is not owing. When a sum of money has been paid in settlement of a debt not in fact due, it may be recovered by the *condictio indebiti.* The payment must have been made in ignorance of fact, and not in ignorance of law. Money paid under a mistake of law cannot be recovered (*Rooth* v. *The State,* 2 Sth. Afr. Rep. 259; 5 C.L.J. 304; *Port Elizabeth Divisional Council* v. *Uitenhage Divisional Council,* Buch. 1868, p. 223).

"It is not every mistake of fact that will entitle a plaintiff to relief in the action known as *condictio indebiti.* The plaintiff's ignorance should not be, as stated by Voet, *supina aut affectata* (12, 6, 7), the meaning of which expression he explains in another passage (22, 6, 7), to be that the ignorance should not be of a fact concerning the plaintiff's own affairs or of a fact which, although concerning the affairs of others, is known to everybody except a few solitary individuals" (*per* DE VILLIERS, C.J., in *Divisional Council of Aliwal North* v. *De Wet,* 7 S.C. 234). "It must be *justus error,* that is to say, a mistake which is reasonable and justifiable" (*per* DE VILLIERS, C.J., in *Logan* v. *Beit,* 7 S.C. 216).

Condictio ob turpem vel injustam causam, a personal action for the recovery of whatever one has given for a dishonourable or unjust cause. This action lies where there is *mala fides* on the part of the recipient. When there is dishonourable conduct on both sides the maxim *in pari delicto potior est conditio possidentis* applies, while *mala fides* on the part of the giver alone disentitles him to relief.

Condictio sine causa, a personal action for recovery of whatever one has paid or given to another without lawful cause. For instance, when something is given in contemplation of marriage, and the marriage does not take place (Grotius' *Introd.* 3, 30, 15), or when rent has been paid in advance and the premises are subsequently destroyed by fire (*Wiley & Co.* v. *Mundinch & Co.,* 19 S.C. 450; and *Holtshausen* v. *Minnaar,* 23 S.A.L.J. 255).

Condictio triticaria, a personal action in the Roman law by which a claim was made for a corporeal thing, movable or immovable, or an incorporeal thing, belonging to any debtor, in whatever way it was due, whether *ex contractu* or *ex delicto* (Voet's *Comm.* 13, 3, 1).

Several conjectures have been made as to the origin of the term *triticaria,* of which an interesting one is cited by Voet (*ibid.*). According to Sandars (*Institutes of Justinian,* 10th ed. p. 427) the term derived its origin from *triticum* (wheat), one of the things to which the old *condictio certi* was extended by the *lex Calpurnia* of the Roman law, and when the principal obligation which was sought to be enforced was something else than the giving of a fixed sum of money, the *condictio,* whether *certi* or *incerti,* was called *triticaria.*

It was the nature of the principal obligation, it is to be observed, that decided whether the *condictio triticaria* was applicable to its enforcement or not, for although the thing principally due had to be something else than coined money, yet, as every *condemnatio* under the formulary system of the Roman law was in a pecuniary shape, the defendant was condemned in the money value of the wheat or other thing due. Besides that the thing principally due had to be something else than coined money, it was also necessary in order that the *condictio* might lie that the principal action which lay for the recovery of the thing itself should be personal like the *condictio;* for if the principal action were *in rem* the value would have to be claimed, not by the *condictio triticaria*, but by the action *in rem* itself. For this reason no one could regularly sue by this action for the recovery of his own property, save in those cases in which a condiction for one's property was permitted, as in the case of things which had been stolen or taken possession of by force, for the value of which the owners could properly sue by this action, just as if they had ceased to exist (Voet's *Comm., ibid.*).

Condiction, a Roman law term meaning "a personal action in which the contention is that some property should be conveyed to us or some service performed for us" (Justinian's *Institutes*, 4, 6, 15).

Conditie van triumphe (D.). So early as the year 1659 it was enacted in the Netherlands (apart from the common law on the subject) that advocates and attorneys were prohibited from undertaking the conduct of an action subject to the stipulation that they were not to be paid any reward for their services except in the event of their being successful in such action. This stipulation was called *conditie van triumphe*. *See* CHAMPERTY.

Conditio praepositionis servanda est, the condition of the appointment must be observed. A maxim of Roman law which applies to the English as well as the Roman-Dutch law of agency. Where the authority is express or special the agent is bound to act within it; and where it is of a more general nature still the agent cannot bind the principal beyond the manifest scope of the object to be accomplished by it (*Digest*, 17. 1, 46; see also Story on *Agency*, secs. 70 *et seq.*). Thus as regards special agents an authority to sell does not generally empower the agent to obtain payment of the price (*Tank & Co.* v. *Jacobs*, 1 S.C. 289); but the latter right may be implied from the circumstances (*Field & Co.* v. *Marks & Co.*, 12 E.D.C. 13). So an authority to purchase will not empower the agent to pay the price, in the absence of an express agreement or a trade custom to that effect (*Niebuhr and Another* v. *Joel*, 5 H.C.G. 335; see also *Noyce* v. *Gluyas*, 1 Off. Rep. 197; *Standard Bank* v. *Union Boating Co.*, 7 S.C. 267; *Harris* v. *Ruthven*, 2 Menz. 191; *Bowhay* v. *Ward*, [1903] T.S. 772). In the same way a general agent for a particular business is restricted in his dealings to that business, and cannot bind his principal by anything done beyond the scope of it. *See* VERBA GENERALIA RESTRINGUNTUR AD HABILITATEM REI VEL PERSONAM.

Conditio si sine liberis decesserit, the condition if he shall have died without children. *See* SI SINE LIBERIS DECESSERIT.

Condition. "A *condition* is a term in a contract or conveyance, to the effect that on the occurrence or non-occurrence of an uncertain event, act or forbearance, a right shall arise, or cease to exist" (Jenks' *Digest of English Civil Law*, vol. 1, sec. 109). As to when *conditions* prescribed by a statute are not considered as being indispensable, see Craies' *Statute Law*, p. 238.

Conditional acceptance. *See* QUALIFIED ACCEPTANCE.

Conditional delivery of a bill of exchange is where, as between immediate parties, and as regards a remote party other than a holder in due course, the delivery has been made subject to a condition or for a special purpose only, and not for the purpose of transferring the property in the bill. See Bills of Exchange Act, 1882 (Eng.), sec. 21 (2); Act 19 of 1903 (C.C.), sec. 19 (2); Law 8 of 1887 (N.), sec. 20 (2); Proclamation 11 of 1902 (T.), sec. 19 (2); Ordinance 28 of 1902 (O.R.C.), sec. 19 (2).

Conditional reprieve. *See* REPRIEVE.

Condominium, joint-ownership; ownership enjoyed in common with others.

Condonation. "The word *condonatio* is, so far as I am aware, foreign to Roman-Dutch nomenclature; but *condonation*, being a term apt and convenient to express a defence recognised by both systems, has been borrowed in South African practice from the English law. As interpreted by English courts, however, the word has acquired a legal meaning which differs somewhat from its literary and ordinary one. It means something more than mere pardon or forgiveness, which might conceivably be accorded by the injured spouse as a matter of Christian duty without any idea of restoring the *status quo ante*. It has been defined as 'a blotting out of the offence imputed, so as to restore the offending party to the position which he or she occupied before the offence was committed.' And there is high authority for the view that this blotting out can only be satisfactorily evidenced by subsequent cohabitation (see *per* Lord CHELMSFORD in *Keats* v. *Keats and Montezuma* (28 L.J. Mat. Cas. p. 61); Bishop on *Marriage, Divorce and Separation*, vol. 2, sec. 271; and *Bernstein* v. *Bernstein* ([1893] P.D. p. 313)). Turning to our law, we find that the expression used to denote substantially the same idea, which in English decisions is conveyed by the term *condonation*, is *reconciliatio*. That is the word used by Voet (24, 2, 5), Sande (*Decis. Fris.* 2, 6, 2), Van Leeuwen (*Cens. For.* 1, 1, 5, 7) and by other writers; and it is the test approved of by DE VILLIERS, C.J., in *Niemand* v. *Niemand*. To my mind we shall be correctly laying down the Roman-Dutch law if we hold that forgiveness by an injured spouse of the infidelity of his or her partner, if it is to operate as a bar to subsequent proceedings, founded on the offence, must contemplate the restoration of the offending spouse to his or her previous position, and must result in a reconciliation between the two. The injured spouse must have knowledge of the offence, must fully forgive it, and must be prepared to take back the guilty partner; the latter must be willing to accept forgiveness and to take advantage of the pardon, and a reconciliation must ensue. If sexual cohabitation is resumed after the injured spouse has full knowledge of the offence, then forgiveness and reconciliation will of course be implied. Indeed, there could be no better proof of full reconciliation than such resumption, and in the vast majority of cases where a real reconciliation has taken place it will be found to have been followed by cohabitation. But it is conceivable that there may be instances of forgiveness and reconciliation where, owing to absence, disease or some similar cause, the ordinary marital relationship between the parties has not been re-established. Such cases, however, must in the nature of things be extremely rare, and the evidence in support of them will always be most carefully scrutinised" (*per* INNES, C.J., in *Bell* v. *Bell*, [1909] T.S. at p. 508). "To establish *condonation* there must be evidence that the plaintiff agreed to take the defendant back as his wife *rectam et integram*; mere Christian forgiveness of the offence is not *condonation*" (*per* KOTZÉ, J., in *Weatherley* v. *Weatherley*, 1 K. 66). See *Wife* v. *Husband* (27 N.L.R. 349); *see* also CONSENSUS APERTUS.

Confession, the act of admitting or acknowledging a crime, debt, judgment or fault. 'Any *confession* of the commission of any crime or offence, which shall be proved by competent evidence to have been made by any person accused of such crime or offence, whether before or after his apprehension, whether on a judicial examination or after commitment, and whether reduced into writing or not, shall in every case be admissible evidence against such person; provided always that such *confession* shall be proved to have been freely and voluntarily made by such person in his sound and sober senses and without having been unduly influenced thereby" (Ordinance 72 of 1830 (C.C.), sec. 28). The same section goes on to provide, further, that when the *confession* is made in the course of a judicial examination before a magistrate the prisoner must have been previously cautioned; a further reservation is made in respect of certain *confessions* made on oath, and depositions made under the Insolvency Ordinance. A *confession* made by one person is not admissible as evidence against any other person (Ordinance 72 of 1830 (C.C.), sec. 31). See Ordinance 11 of 1902 (O.R.C.), sec. 24.

Confinium agrorum, quorum fines confusi sunt, regulation of land boundaries which are in dispute—a quasi-contractual obligation.

Confirmed, in the phrase "concessions *confirmed* by the late Chief Court," see *Sheldon* v. *Registrar of Deeds* ([1907] T.S. 97).

Confirmed diagram. In the Transvaal Precious and Base Metals Act (35 of 1908), sec. 3, *confirmed diagram* is defined as "a diagram confirmed by the Surveyor-General after notice of confirmation has been published in manner prescribed by regulation." A similar definition is given by the Transvaal Registration of Deeds and Titles Act (25 of 1909), sec. 2. *See* DIAGRAM.

Confiscatie van goederen (D.), confiscation of goods. Abolished by placaat in the Netherlands and at the Cape of Good Hope. See Kersteman's *Woordenboek*, vol. 1, p. 78. *See* also CONFISCATION.

Confiscation, the forfeiting of some property or thing by lawful authority. All laws and usages authorising the confiscation of the property of criminals (including those convicted of the *crimen perduellionis* or *læsæ majestatis*) were abolished in the Cape Colony by Placaat of the States-General of the United Netherlands, dated 10th August, 1778, published at the Castle of Good Hope on the 22nd April, 1779 (Van Leeuwen's *Comm.* Kotzé's trans. vol. 2, p. 564, note).

Confusie (D.), confusion. *See* CONFUSIO.

Confusio, confusion. Confusion or commixture takes place when materials belonging to different owners become mixed. If mixed inseparably—for instance, when silver belonging to two different persons is melted together—the united mass becomes common property, each party being entitled to a share proportionate to his original share in the material. If the materials are separable, as when one man's wheat is mixed with another man's barley, the ownership is not altered, unless the mixture takes place with the consent of the owners. *Confusio* is used with reference to the mixture of liquids, *commixtio* with reference to that of solids. The equivalent in Dutch is *confusie.* See Grotius' *Introd.* 2, 8, 8; Maasdorp's *Institutes,* vol. 2, p. 45; Kersteman's *Woordenboek,* vol. 2, p. 188; Nathan's *Common Law,* sec. 547.

Confusion. (1) The mixing together of materials belonging to two persons. *See* CONFUSIO.

(2) Or merger, is the union in one person of the characters of debtor and creditor (Holland's *Jurisprudence,* 10th ed. p. 308).

Connivance "is an act of the mind, and implies knowledge and acquiescence, and as a legal doctrine it has its origin and its limits in the principle *volenti non fit injuria*" (Gwynne Hall on *Divorce,* p. 256).

"*Connivance* exists where the plaintiff, by his acts and conduct, has either knowingly brought about, or conduced to the adultery of his wife; or where he has so neglected and exposed her to temptation, as under the circumstances of the case he ought to have foreseen would, if the opportunity offered, terminate in her fall. Here, then, if the wife commits adultery, he will be taken to have acquiesced in it, and, upon the principle *volenti non fit injuria,* he is the author of his own dishonour. So, where the plaintiff, having become aware of an improper intimacy between his wife and the co-respondent, remains passive and permits the intimacy to continue, taking no steps to protect his wife and to avert the coming danger, he will be held to have connived at her subsequent adultery" (*per* KOTZÉ, C.J., in *Weatherley* v. *Weatherley,* 1 K. 66).

"Here we have to deal with an expression taken over from the English law. When one married person is willing that the other should be unfaithful, then he cannot complain of any act of infidelity to which he mentally assented; he is said under such circumstances to have connived at the misconduct of the other. And *connivance* may be evidenced in various ways. A married person who actually procures, assists or gives express consent to the misconduct of his partner connives at such misconduct. And one who, knowing that misconduct is taking place, refrains from interfering because satisfied and willing for his own purposes that it should continue, is also guilty of *connivance*. But the principle may also apply in cases less gross than either of these. It has been held by the House of Lords (*Gipps* v. *Gipps and Hume*, 33 L.J. Mat. Cas. 161) that where a spouse wilfully abstains from any attempt to prevent misconduct, which he must know is likely to occur, then he also is held to have connived at such misconduct when it actually takes place. And that, of course, will be so where the only possible inference under the circumstances is that he was willing and satisfied for his own purposes that misconduct should ensue. But mere knowledge, mere negligence, or mere inaction is not sufficient; all these may be present, and yet the mind of the injured spouse not have been willing that a matrimonial offence should be committed. It is this willingness, this mental assent, with full knowledge of the circumstances, which lies at the root of the doctrine of *connivance*. The principle has been chiefly elaborated by the English courts; but it was recognised in Roman-Dutch law also. Thus Voet (24, 2, 5) remarks that a husband cannot condemn morals which he himself has corrupted, or the corruption of which he has countenanced. And in support of this view he refers to Brunneman. Now that remark really contains the kernel of the doctrine of *connivance* as enunciated by English decisions. For it is the acquiescence of the complaining spouse which is held to debar him from relief. *Volenti non fit injuria:* and a spouse who has been willing that misconduct should take place cannot be heard to complain of it" (*per* INNES, C.J., in *Bell* v. *Bell*, [1909] T.S. at p. 510). *See* CONSENSUS APERTUS.

Connossement (D.) [also spelt *cognoscement* or *cognossement*], bill of lading.

Consanguiniteit (D.), relationship by blood or descent from a common ancestor; consanguinity. *See* CONSANGUINITY.

Consanguinity, blood relationship. "*Consanguinity* consists in relationship by blood or by descent from a common ancestor, whether male or female" (Maasdorp's *Institutes*, vol. 1, p. 7).

Consensual obligation "is that which takes place by agreement between two persons, in good faith and with sincere intention, that the one shall thereby effectually bind the other, without any writing or delivery of the thing being necessary for the purpose. Of this kind are purchase, hire, partnership, mandate, and matrimony or marriage" (Van Leeuwen's *Comm.* Kotzé's trans. vol. 2, p. 129).

Consensus ad idem, the meeting of two minds in one and the same intention. "The first and most essential element of an agreement is the consent of the parties" (Pollock on *Contracts*, 6th ed. p. 3). "If it appears that each party mistook the meaning of the other, and they intended different things by the same expression, then the basis of agreement fails and the contract is avoided" (Leake's *Digest of the Law of Contracts*, p. 331). In the case of *Logan* v. *Beit* (7 S.C. 212), DE VILLIERS, C.J., said: "The result was that there was no *consensus ad idem;* the plaintiff understood one thing and the defendant another, and consequently there was no completed contract."

Consensus apertus, manifest consent. The right to a divorce on the ground of adultery is taken away by a reconciliation of the parties. According to Voet (*Comm.* 24, 2, 5) such a reconciliation may be evidenced by the manifest consent (*consensus apertus*) of the innocent spouse or by cohabitation after knowledge of the adultery. In the case of *Niemand* v. *Niemand* (15 S.C. 217; 8 C.T.R. 254), DE VILLIERS, C.J., said: "It is somewhat difficult to understand Voet's remark that such reconciliation may be evidenced by the 'manifest consent' of the innocent spouse. 'Consent,' in the proper sense of the term, can only be given before the act, whereas 'reconciliation' can only take place after the offence has been committed. Possibly Voet may have meant by the expression *consensus apertus* such a course of conduct after the commission of the offence as would justify the inference that the innocent spouse was a consenting party." See also *Wife* v. *Husband* (27 N.L.R. at pp. 353 *et seq.*) and CONNIVANCE.

Consent, to agree; to be in accord with. As to *consent* of lessor to subletting or cession of lease, see *Nieuwoudt* v. *Slavin and Jowell* (13 S.C. at p. 63). See *Smit* v. *Smit's Executrix* (14 S.C. at p. 147).

As to *consent* of a lessor to sublet where a lease prohibits subletting except with the consent of the lessor first had and obtained, see *Bonamour* v. *Dunne* (25 N.L.R. 138).

See CONSENSUS APERTUS.

Consideration, a term peculiar to the English common law, according to which every simple or parol contract, whether written or verbal, requires a *consideration* to support it. In other words, according to the law of England, differing in this respect from the law of Scotland and continental Europe, and from the Roman and Roman-Dutch law, a promise, however seriously and deliberately made, cannot be enforced unless it is founded on some *consideration* (*per* SKINNER, C.B., in *Rann* v *Hughes*, 7 Term Rep. 350, n.) A *consideration* is defined as "a detriment voluntarily incurred by the promisee, or a benefit conferred on the promisor, at the instance of the promisee, in exchange for the promise" (Jenks' *Doctrine of Consideration*, p. 26). "*Consideration* is that which is actually given and accepted in return for the promise. Ulterior motives, purposes or expectations may be present, but in a legal point of view they are indifferent. The party seeking to enforce a promise has to show the actual legal *consideration* for it, and he need not show anything beyond" (Pollock, *Contracts*, 6th ed. p. 165).

Jenks in his essay on the *Doctrine of Consideration* attempts to show that the requirement of a *quid pro quo*, which had become connected with the proof by suit in the action of debt, was carried over into the proof by suit in the action of assumpsit, and that in this way what had formerly been a mere rule of procedure became embodied as a rule or principle in the incipient law of contract. About the middle of the sixteenth century the practical amalgamation of these two actions tended to bring the doctrine of *consideration* to its present condition, especially by establishing the rule that detriment to the plaintiff was equally sufficient with benefit to the defendant. It is said by Mr. Justice HOLMES that the term *consideration* was first used in the reign of Queen Elizabeth, but, as Jenks has pointed out, the term occurs in the second dialogue to be found in the *Doctor and Student*, published *anno* 1530. On a reference to this dialogue it will be seen that there is a distinction drawn between "consideration of worldly profit" and "cause." This should serve as a warning to the English lawyer, unacquainted with the true principles of the Roman and Roman-Dutch law, not to confound the term *causa*, *cause* or *oorzaak* with the notion of *consideration*. The dialogue also negatives the theory that the idea of *consideration* found its way into the common law of England through the canon law. The doctrine of the doctor or canonist in the dialogue is plainly that of the Roman law, and considers the circumstances of the contract, and not the bargain itself, as the important point (Jenks, pp. 131 *et seq.*).

"The *consideration* must move from the plaintiff, but it must also move from him in contemplation of the promise, otherwise the objections to past *consideration* vanish. Mr. Justice PATTESON'S judgment in *Thomas* v. *Thomas* (2 Q.B. 859) is valuable as helping to explode the unscholarly and misleading doctrine, which confuses the *causa* of the Roman law and the *cause* of French law with the English *consideration*, which is, obviously, of an entirely different character (Jenks, p. 28; *see* CAUSA). The amount or adequacy of the *consideration* is immaterial, except in so far as it may be an element in a case of fraud. Thus a single penny or even a peppercorn will be a sufficient *consideration* in support of a legally binding promise."

Considerations are of various kinds: (1) *Executed* and *Executory*; an executed *consideration* is one already performed before the making of the promise, and unless this was at the request of the promissor it will not give rise to an action. An executory *consideration* is something to be done or rendered after the promise. (2) *Concurrent*, as where mutual promises are made; (3) *Continuing*, that is, executed in part only. The last three are sufficient to support a contract, which is not void for other reasons (Story on *Contracts*, p. 71). It is only a valuable *consideration* which will support an action brought to enforce a promise. Such a *consideration* is also sometimes spoken of as a *good consideration*, as opposed to *considerations* of nature or blood. It is so used in *Twyne's Case* (1 Sm. L.C. 9). Others, again, use the term *good consideration* as opposed to a *valuable consideration*. Thus, Blackstone says: "A good *consideration* is such as that of blood or of natural love and affection, and is founded on motives of generosity, prudence and natural affection. A valuable *consideration* is such as money, marriage or the like" (2 *Comm.* 297). *Considerations* of blood or natural affection and purely moral *considerations*, however seriously and deliberately made, and however binding they may be *in foro conscientiae*, do not, by the law of England, give a binding legal force to a promise.

For the history of the doctrine of *consideration* in English law, reference may be had to Holmes' *Common Law*; Pollock's *Contracts*, note E; Jenks' *Doctrine of Consideration*.

Consignatie (D.), consignation (*q.v.*).

Consignation, "the custody of money or something else, *i.e.* movable and of value, in the hands of the judge or public person authorised thereto, the expression being derived from *consignare*, to seal. *Consignation* takes place after refusal of a previously made oblation and offer of what we owe, and has this effect, that the debtor is thereby completely absolved, and consequently (there is) a stopping of the course of interest, a discharge of hypothecs, and release of sureties" (Van Leeuwen's *Comm.* Kotzé's trans. vol. 2, p. 81, Decker's *note*). *Consignatie* or consignation is classified by Grotius under the contract of *depositum*. See also Schorer's *Notes*, n. 331.

Consignee, the person to whom goods are transmitted by a person, called the consignor, for sale or delivery.

Consignor, the person who transmits goods to another, called the consignee, for sale or delivery.

Consilii non fraudulenti nulla obligatio est, there is no liability attaching to a person giving advice unless he acts fraudulently (*Digest*, 50, 17, 47). This legal maxim was relied upon by De Villiers, C.J., in the case of *Meyersohn* v. *Schmidt* (1 A.C. 375). In that case A, a sick man, came to B's hotel, and B telegraphed to C, who was understood to be a relative of A, asking what he should do with A. C replied: "Keep him there; do your best for him; his uncle is on the road." B thereupon attended A, who subsequently died at that hotel, and B sought to recover his disbursements on A's behalf from C. The court, however, held that C's telegram contained mere advice, and not a mandate, and that C was therefore not liable.

Consistory, an ecclesiastical court. In the Dutch Reformed Church it is the governing body of the local church.

Consolidated revenue account. In the Audit Act 14 of 1906 (C.C.), sec. 3 (*c*), the *consolidated revenue account* is defined to mean "an account of the cash income and the current expenditure forming part of the said Exchequer Account." *See* EXCHEQUER ACCOUNT.

Consortium omnis vitae, a partnership in the whole of life; from the definition of marriage given by Modestinus (*Digest*, 23, 2, 1), viz., *conjunctio maris et feminae, consortium omnis vitae, divini et humani juris communicatio* (the union of a man and woman as partners for their entire life and as sharers in divine and human rights).

Conspiracy. "When two or more persons agree to commit any crime they are guilty of the misdemeanour called conspiracy, whether the crime is committed or not" (Stephen's *Digest of the Criminal Law*, art. 48). "Those persons who abet in [the commission of] a crime to such an extent that but for their co-operation it could not have been committed, are called 'accomplices.' When the complicity is founded in a previous agreement and engagement to commit certain crimes in common, it is termed a 'complot' or '*conspiracy*'" (Van der Linden's *Institutes*, Juta's trans. 4th ed. p. 182; see also p. 183). A bare *conspiracy* to commit a crime is not an indictable offence, see *Queen* v. *Kaplan* (10 S.C. 259), where the point is fully discussed. See also *Queen* v. *February and Mei* (10 S.C. 382); *Queen* v. *Solomon and Others* (15 S.C. 107).

By the Transvaal Criminal Law Amendment Act (16 of 1908), sec. 7, however, it is provided that "Any person who (1) shall conspire with any other person to aid or procure the commission of any crime or offence; or (2) shall incite, instigate, command, counsel or procure any other person to commit any crime or offence; shall be guilty of an offence and liable on conviction to the punishment prescribed by law for an attempt to commit such crime or offence."

Constable, a policeman. *See* POLICE. The term *constable* is to be found in Ordinance 2 of 1840 (C.C.), sec. 6, where it is enacted that it shall be lawful for "the said Judge and Superintendent for the time being, subject to the approval of the Governor of this Colony for the time being, to nominate and appoint from time to time a sufficient number of fit and able men, who shall be sworn in by the said Judge and Superintendent to act as *constables* for preserving the peace, preventing the commission of crimes, and apprehending offenders when crimes have been committed." The word *constable* has since been generally used in South Africa.

Constablewick, an expression apparently first used in a South African Statute in Ordinance 2 of 1840 (C.C.), sec. 6; see also Ordinance 25 of 1847 (C.C.), sec. 4. The word *constablewick* is now rarely used; it signifies the place or assigned district within which a constable is authorised to act as such.

Constitution. "A *constitution* properly so called is a frame of political society, organised through and by law—that is to say, one in which law has established permanent institutions with recognised functions and definite rights" (Bryce's *History and Jurisprudence*, vol. 1, p. 159; see also Dicey's *Law of the Constitution*, 6th ed. pp. 22 *et seq.*).

Constitutional law. "*Constitutional law*, as the term is used in England, appears to include all rules which directly or indirectly affect the distribution or the exercise of the sovereign power in the State. Hence it includes (among other things) all rules which define the members of the sovereign power, all rules which regulate the relation of such members to each other, or which determine the mode in which the sovereign power, or the members thereof, exercise their authority. Its rules prescribe the order of succession to the throne, regulate the prerogatives of the chief magistrate, determine the form of the legislature and its mode of election. These rules also deal with ministers, with their responsibility, with their spheres of action, define the territory over which the sovereignty of the State extends, and settle who are to be deemed subjects or citizens" (Dicey's *Law of the Constitution*, 6th ed. p. 22).

Constitutum possessorium, possessory compact. The meaning of the doctrine of *constitutum possessorium* is "that a person who already has the lawful possession of a thing transfers the possession, or, in other words, effects delivery, merely by virtue of his own intention, expressed or implied, to hold the thing in future as agent for another" (*per* De Villiers, C.J., in *Mills & Sons* v. *Benjamin's Trustees*, Buch. 1876, p. 115). "The *constitutum possessorium* is thus a mode of acquisition by substitution through the declaration of the judicial possessor that for the future he will hold in the name of a third person that which he has hitherto held in his own name" (*per* Shippard, J., in *Stewart's Executor* v. *De Morgan*, 2 E.D.C. 220).

"That doctrine applies where a person who is already a legal possessor undertakes to become the possessor for some one else" (*per* De Villiers, C.J., in *Payn* v. *Yates*, 9 S.C. 497). "No principle is more clearly established than that a *constitutum* is not to be presumed unless its existence necessarily follows from the other circumstances of the case" (*per* De Villiers, C.J., in *Orson* v. *Reynolds*, 2 A.C. 105). "I have examined the cases and authorities quoted during the argument, and the conclusion to which they lead me is that by our law the doctrine of *constitutum possessorium* can have no place in a case of pledge where the pledged articles are to remain with the pledgor to be used by him for his own benefit. And for this simple reason—that such a doctrine would in practice destroy the very wholesome rule of the Roman-Dutch law, that for a pledge to be effectual against third parties there must be retention of possession by the pledgee" (*per* Innes, C.J., in *Lighter & Co.* v. *Edwards*, [1907] T.S. at p. 445).

Construction. (1) Of Contracts.—"No rule of law is more firmly established than this, that where the persons have entered into a formal written agreement, their intention must be deduced from the writing, and from that alone. If the language is clear and unambiguous, effect must be given to it, and in such a case a court of law has no right to speculate whether the real intention of the parties is expressed in the agreement, or to make for them a contract which they themselves have not made, but which it is believed they had intended to make. Occasionally, no doubt, we may feel very strongly that we are not giving effect to the real intention of the parties, but that after all is a small evil compared to the uncertainty and confusion that would be produced if we once allowed ourselves to depart from this well-recognised rule for the *construction* of written instruments" (*per* SOLOMON, J., in *Van der Merwe* v. *Jumpers Deep, Ltd.*, [1902] T.S. at p. 210).

(2) OF WILLS.—"What the Court has to do is to endeavour to arrive at the intention of the testators; and to arrive at that intention not by considering what we think it would have been a good thing if they did mean, or what they ought to have meant, but by ascertaining the plain meaning of the words used. If those words in a case like the present are capable of more than one *construction*, then of course the Court would lean towards the one most in favour of freedom of alienation. But if the testator's language admits of only one *construction*, then we must give effect to it, regardless of the consequences" (*per* INNES, C.J., in *Ex parte van Eeden and Others*, [1905] T.S. at p. 153).

(3) OF STATUTES.—Broadly speaking, the same rules that apply to the construction of wills must be applied to the construction of statutes. To this may be added the remarks of Lord Justice LINDLEY in *The Duke of Buccleuch* (15 P.D. 86): "You are not so to construe the Act of Parliament as to reduce it to rank absurdity. You are not to attribute to general language used by the legislature in this case, any more than in any other case, a meaning which would not carry out its object, but produce consequences which, to the ordinary intelligence, are absurd. You must give it such a meaning as will carry out its objects." *See* A VERBIS LEGIS NON EST RECEDENDUM; JUDICIS EST JUS DICERE NON DARE; QUOTIES IN VERBIS NULLA EST AMBIGUITAS, &c.; BENEDICTA EST EXPOSITIO QUANDO RES REDIMITUR A DESTRUCTIONE; UT RES MAGIS VALEAT QUAM PEREAT; IN POENALIBUS CAUSIS BENIGNIUS INTERPRETANDUM EST.

Consultatien (D.). (1) The *Hollandsche Consultatiën*, commonly known as *Consultatiën*, were opinions of eminent jurists given in the sixteenth and during the first half of the seventeenth century. They "have acquired by usage a foremost place in the legal literature of Holland. The opinions were given to private persons upon certain facts stated, and were quoted, if not before the higher courts, at least before the courts schout and schepenen" (Wessels' *History*, p. 242). They "have played a very important part in the development of the Roman-Dutch law" (*ibid.* p. 243).

(2) Consultations between a professional man and his client.

Consumer. The expression *consumer* is defined in the Cape Additional Taxation Act (36 of 1904) to mean and include "any person who is not by law entitled to sell or deal in spirits, and every other person who uses spirits in the preparation of drugs, medicines, perfumery and explosives, or in any art or manufacture."

In the Rand Water Board Further Powers Act (22 of 1909), sec. 3 (2), *consumer* means "any person to whom water may be supplied by the Board, other than local authorities or mines as defined in the Rand Water Board Statutes, 1903 to 1906."

Contempt of court, disobedience to the orders of a court of justice or conduct wilfully disregardful of its dignity or authority. *Contempt of court* is divided into acts of contempt committed within the court and those committed outside the court. Of the former kind are refusal of a person to obey an order addressed to him by the court, openly abusing or obstructing the court, refusing to be sworn or to answer questions as a witness. Among the latter kind are disobeying a subpœna; acts impeding or obstructing the course of justice, as *e.g.* detaining or corrupting witnesses, enticing them from attending court, preventing an officer of the court from performing his official duties, or attempting to do any of such things; commenting in the press upon matters *sub judice*, and generally saying or doing anything which tends to bring the court or its proceedings into contempt. Contempts within the court are then and there summarily dealt with, but where they are committed out of the court a distinct charge must be formulated against the accused.

See Van Zyl's *Judicial Practice*, 2nd ed. pp. 329 *et seq.*, and the cases there cited; also *In re Phelan*, 1 K. 5; *In re Dormer*, 4 S.A.R. p. 64; *Li Kui Yu* v. *Superintendent of Labourers*, [1906] T.S. 181; and *Fein and Cohen* v. *Colonial Government*, 23 S.C. 750; 16 C.T.R. 1101 (where the *Li Kui Yu* case is adversely criticised), for a full discussion of the doctrine of *contempt of court.*

Contempt of parliament. As to what constitutes *contempt of parliament* see Act 13 of 1883 (C.C.), sec. 7; Act 27 of 1895 (N.), sec. 6; Act 3 of 1907 (T.), sec. 16; Act 1 of 1908 (O.R.C.), sec. 16.

Content, a term used in statutes relating to Customs, signifying a written statement by the master of a vessel in which he sets out in detail the goods shipped in his vessel and some other particulars. It is used in the Natal law relating to Customs and Shipping (Act 13 of 1899, sec. 33), where it is provided that "before any such ship shall depart, the master or his authorised agent shall bring and deliver to the collector or other proper officer of Customs a *content* in writing, under his hand or that of the authorised agent, of the goods laden, and the names and addresses of the respective shippers of the goods, with the marks and numbers of the packages or parcels of the same, and shall make and subscribe a declaration to the truth of such *content*, as far as any such particulars can be known."

"**Contiguous to.**" In *Barrington and Others* v. *Colonial Government* (4 S.C. 408), a case involving the construction of a grant of land, DE VILLIERS, C.J. (at p. 417), said: "On the western and eastern sides were rivers forming the best possible natural boundaries. The grants of the farms describe the land granted as being *contiguous to* those rivers, and in the Dutch translation the words *strekkende aan* are used. In some of the grants, it is admitted, these words were occasionally used in the sense of 'adjoining to,' and it would be preposterous to suppose that either the grantor or the grantees attached a different meaning to the words where they are used to indicate the western and eastern boundaries. It is urged that the words may also mean 'in the direction of,' but why should this forced construction be placed upon them if their primary meaning is clear and intelligible. The primary meaning of the word *contiguous* is sufficiently obvious when we consider its derivation from *con* and *tango.* When Ovid said of Pyramus and Thisbe, *Contiguas tenuere domos,* he meant, not that they occupied houses in the vicinity of each other, but actually adjoining and touching each other, so that the lovers could converse with each other through the chinks of the walls. It is clear also that Milton, in speaking of extremes that are *contiguous,* meant that they meet and touch each other. But it is not only the poetical meaning of the word, but the common-sense meaning, which the grantees and all subsequent owners would reasonably have attached to it." See also *Reid* v. *Surveyor-General* (14 S.C. 34); ADJACENT and ADJOINING.

Contingency, the happening of some thing or event by chance that would not happen of necessity or in the ordinary course of events.

Contingent. (1) Depending upon a contingency. *See* CONTINGENCY.

(2) In a military sense *contingent* is defined in the Natal Militia Act (36 of 1903), sec. 3, to mean "two or more troops or companies combined together for administrative purposes, and also bodies of natives, Indians, or other coloured persons called out for service under this Act."

Contingent creditor, a term used in insolvency law signifying a person whose debt against the insolvent depends upon a contingency or an uncertain condition (see Ordinance 6 of 1843 (C.C.), sec. 31; Law 47 of 1887 (N.), sec. 37; Law 13 of 1895 (T.), sec. 63).

Continuing contract is a contract out of which rights and liabilities arise from time to time after the making of the contract (Jenks' *Digest of English Civil Law,* bk. 1, sec. 53).

Continuous crime, a crime or offence which proceeds without apparent interruption. "No matter how long a time an offence may take in its perpetration, it continues but one offence" (Wharton's *Criminal Law,* 10th ed. sec. 27). A conflict of jurisdiction sometimes arises when a *continuous crime* is commenced in one colony and continued in another. "If the theft was committed elsewhere, the offender could not be tried in this [Cape] Colony, unless he did some act here which amounts to a continuation of his original offence. It is not a mere legal sublety to hold that if he deals with the stolen property as his own in this colony he continues his original offence and exposes himself to prosecution in the courts of this country for theft. So far from such a rule being contrary to the comity of nations, it would rather tend to uphold that comity by preventing one country from becoming the refuge of thieves carrying stolen property from neighbouring territories" (*per* DE VILLIERS, C.J., in *Regina* v. *Lepal,* 9 S.C. at p. 265).

Continuous servitude, "a *continuous servitude* is one to the exercise or enjoyment of which no intervention of any act of man is necessary—*e.g. servitus stillicidii.* Such servitudes cannot be lost by non-user" (Van Leeuwen's *Comm.* Kotzé's trans., translator's *note* on p. 306).

Contra bonos mores, contrary to good morals; against morality. For the rules regarding contracts which are based upon an immoral consideration, *see* CONDICTIO OB TURPEM VEL INJUSTAM CAUSAM; and EX TURPI CAUSA NON ORITUR ACTIO.

Contract. "A *contract* is an agreement which creates, or is intended to create, a legal obligation between the parties to it" (Jenks' *Digest of English Civil Law,* 2, 1, 182). In Natal a writing is necessary in order to maintain actions in respect of certain contracts; see Law 12 of 1884 (N.).

"**Contract in writing,**" see *Richmond* v. *Crofton* (15 S.C. 183).

"**Contract in writing jointly executed,**" an expression used in the Natal Ordinance 1 of 1856 (see sec. 8), meaning "any contract duly signed and executed before any notary public, or in the presence of two witnesses, by the spouses or the intended spouses duly assisted, if need be, by their curators or guardians."

Contract made re "is where the agreement alone is not sufficient, but in addition the actual delivery of the thing must take place before it becomes fully effectual. Such are a loan for consumption (*mutuum*); a loan for use (*commodatum*); deposit (*depositum*); and pledge (*pignus*); giving that something may be given (*do ut des*); giving that something may be done (*do ut facias*); doing that something may be given (*facio ut des*); and doing that something may be done (*facio ut facias*)" (Van Leeuwen's *Comm.* Kotzé's trans. vol. 2, p. 51; see also translator's *note, ibid.*).

Contracting out. To *contract out* of a statute means to enter into an agreement whereby the right to a benefit conferred by the statute is relinquished. In the case of statutes which have been enacted from reasons of public policy such *contracting out* is not allowed in accordance with the maxim *Privatorum conventio juri publico non derogat;* and, moreover, is often expressly prohibited, notably in the Workmen's Compensation Acts.

Contractor, a person who engages to do or perform some work, act or service, or to supply some goods or things for a government, corporation or person in consideration of a certain payment. In the Cape Divisional Councils Act (40 of 1889), sec. 4, the term *contractor* is defined as meaning "every person who directly or indirectly has a pecuniary or valuable interest in any money or other valuable consideration paid or given, or to be paid or given by any council for services performed, for work or labour done, or for any goods or things of whatsoever nature or kind bought or hired by or supplied to such council;" in the Cape Railways Extension Act (28 of 1895), as meaning "any company or person who shall by any agreement undertake to the Governor to construct any line of railway authorised by this Act to be constructed by the Governor." See *Searle* v. *Parsons and Another* (12 S.C. 356).

Contractus aestimatorius. *See* AESTIMATORIUS CONTRACTUS.

Contractus innominati, innominate contracts; an expression of the Roman law denoting contracts having no name. *See* INNOMINATE.

Contrarie conclusie (D.), a form of pleading whereby the defendant simply denies the allegations in the plaintiff's declaration contained, without stating facts or reasons, and concludes to the contrary.

Contrectatio fraudulosa, fraudulent dealing. Theft was defined in Roman law (Justinian's *Institutes*, 4, 1, 1) as a fraudulent dealing with property, either in itself, or in its use, or in its possession; and the motive must be gain (*Dig.* 47, 2, 1, 3). *Contrectatio* implies that without an overt act there can be no *furtum* (theft), and *fraudulosa* implies unlawful intention. In *Rex* v. *Murphy and Another* ([1906] E.D.C. 62) the accused, when under the influence of drink, took horses, rode some distance upon them, turned them into an enclosed paddock, and continued their journey on foot. It was held that in the absence of proof of *animus furandi* the accused were not guilty of theft, KOTZÉ, J.P., remarking: "It is clear there was a taking, but it seems doubtful whether this taking was with a felonious or fraudulent intent. It is only *contrectatio fraudulosa* which constitutes theft in our law."

Contribution. *See* PLAN OF CONTRIBUTION.

Contribution account. *See* PLAN OF CONTRIBUTION.

Contributory. In the Cape Companies Act (25 of 1892), sec. 131, "the term *contributory* shall mean every person liable to contribute to the assets of a company in the event of the same being wound up under this Act; it shall also, in all proceedings for determining the persons who are to be deemed contributories and in all proceedings prior to the final determination of such persons, include any person alleged to be a *contributory*." This definition is taken verbatim (except for a slight transposition of words) from sec. 75 of the English Companies Act of 1862. See the Natal Winding-up Law (19 of 1866), sec. 44; Act 31 of 1909 (T.), sec. 108; Law 2 of 1892 (O.R.C.), sec. 18.

See *Cape of Good Hope Bank, in liqn.*, v. *Knight and Others* (8 S.C. 221).

Contrivance, the act of devising some arrangement or plan for some particular purpose; for example, a witness may have been kept away from a criminal trial "by means and *contrivance* of the prisoner."

Contumacie (D.), contumacy. A technical term in Dutch practice signifying the default made by a litigant in appearing, either in person or by his attorney, in court when lawfully required to do so. It also signifies contempt. *See* CONTUMACY.

Contumacy, wilful disobedience of a lawful order of a judicial or legislative body, and in some cases of its regulations or procedure. *See* CONTEMPT OF COURT; CONTEMPT OF PARLIAMENT; and EX CONTEMPTU VEL CONTUMACIA.

Conventio privatorum juri publico non derogat, an agreement between individuals does not derogate from public law (Van der Linden, *Supplement ad Voet,* 2, 1, 14). *See* PRIVATORUM CONVENTIO, &c.

Conventional mortgage, a mortgage arising out of the consent of the owner, and effected in an open and public manner; it may be a mortgage of either movable or immovable property. If the former, there must, as a rule, be actual delivery of the thing mortgaged; if the latter, it must be duly registered against the mortgaged property in the office of the Registrar of Deeds. *See* MORTGAGE.

A *conventional mortgage* is either general, of all the property of the mortgagor, otherwise known as a "general mortgage"; or of some special or particular property, in which case it is usually described as a "special mortgage." As to the question of delivery in the case of a pledge of movables by notarial deed, see a learned judgment by KOTZÉ, C.J., in *Francis* v. *Savage & Hill,* decided in the Supreme Court of the Transvaal in November, 1882, and quoted *in extenso* as a note to Van Leeuwen's *Comm.* Kotzé's trans. vol. 2, p. 107.

Conversion, the appropriation of the goods of another. "It is not for me to attempt to define what is meant by *conversion*, seeing that eminent English judges express doubt on the subject. But I desire to refer to a definition in *Hollins and Others* v. *Fowler and Others* (7 Eng. & Ir. App. 757), which is as follows: 'Any person who, however innocently, obtains possession of the goods of a person who has been fraudulently deprived of them and disposes of them, whether for his own benefit or that of any other person, is guilty of *conversion*'" (*per* BRISTOWE, J., in *Leal & Co.* v. *Williams*, [1906] T.S. at p. 558).

Conveyancer. Defined in sec. 2 of Act 11 of 1903 (C.C.) as being "a person duly authorised by any competent court to draw and prepare transfer deeds and deeds of hypothecation entitled to registration in a Deeds Office within this colony."

They were unknown to the law of Holland, and do not seem to have appeared in South Africa until 1844 (*per* INNES, C.J., in *Pienaar and Versfeld* v. *Incorporated Law Society*, [1902] T.S. at p. 18).

Act 12 of 1858, sec. 8 (C.C.), provides for admission of *conveyancers* in Cape Colony; see also Act 11 of 1903 (C.C.), sec. 3.

In the Transvaal their admission is regulated by sec. 15 (*b*) of Proclamation 14 of 1902; see also Rules of Court, and Ordinance 1 (Private) of 1905. In the Orange River Colony their admission is regulated by Ordinance 4 of 1902, sec. 17.

In Natal (by sec. 1 of Act 23 of 1904) a *conveyancer* is defined to mean "any person who prepares or executes on behalf of other persons deeds of transfer or other deeds proper for registration in the office of the Registrar of Deeds, or who for reward draws wills, marriage contracts or similar documents, or any instrument relating to property, movable or immovable." The definition of *conveyancer* is more extended in Natal than in the other colonies.

According to a ruling in the Transvaal a seller has the right to appoint his own *conveyancer* (*James* v. *Liquidators of the Amsterdam Township*, [1903] T.S. 653).

Convict. "*Convict* shall mean any convicted person under detention at a convict station" (Act 23 of 1888 (C.C.), sec. 2).

Convict prison, an expression used in the Transvaal Prisons and Reformatories Ordinance (6 of 1906), sec. 3; its definition is almost identical with that of *convict station* in the Cape Act. *See* CONVICT STATION.

Convict station is thus defined in the Convict Stations and Prisons Act (23 of 1888 (C.C.)): "*Convict station* shall mean any place which has already been appointed to be a station for the imprisonment, detention or confinement of persons convicted of any offence, or which shall hereafter by notice in the *Gazette* signed by or by direction of the Minister, be appointed to be such station or place, and shall include all branches or outstations, buildings or places to which convicts may be drafted or sent from any such station or place.

for the purposes of imprisonment, detention, confinement, labour or otherwise." A somewhat similar definition of *convict prison* is given in Ordinance 6 of 1906 (T.), sec. 3.

Conviction, the finding of any competent court that a prisoner, after being lawfully tried, is guilty of the offence with which he has been charged.

Convocation, an assembly of persons. The *convocation* of the University of the Cape of Good Hope consists of all graduates of the University and of the persons holding certificates in literature and science, granted by the Board of Public Examiners in the Cape Colony under Act 4 of 1858 (C.C.), sec. 9. Meetings of convocation may be called by the vice-chancellor at his own instance or upon requisition signed by ten or more members of convocation (see Act 16 of 1873 (C.C.), secs. 13 *et seq.*).

Convooibrief (D.) was, in the Netherlands, "a parcels ticket, by virtue of which merchandise was transported from one place to another. *Convooiloopers* were persons who gave such tickets" (Van der Linden's *Institutes*, Juta's trans. p. 393, translator's *note*).

Convooilooper (D.), a person who gave *convooibrieven. See* CONVOOIBRIEF. See also Van der Linden's *Institutes*, Juta's trans. p. 393, *in notis.*

Co-obligors, persons undertaking a joint obligation. "The general principle of our law relating to the liability of *co-obligors* and the rights of co-obligees is that, unless otherwise agreed upon, the liability is joint and the rights are held in common. If, therefore, two or more persons incur a joint obligation, the general rule, subject to certain well-known exceptions, as in the case of ordinary partnerships, is that each is liable only for his share, and not *in solidum*" (*per* DE VILLIERS, C.J., in *De Pass* v. *Colonial Government and Others*, 4 S.C. at p. 390).

Coolie, see *Superintendent of Police, Pietermaritzburg,* v. *Pillay* (26 N.L.R. 334).

Copy. In the Natal Copyright Act (17 of 1897), sec. 3, "*copy* in reference to a work of art means also repeat, colourably imitate, or otherwise multiply." See also Act 44 of 1898 (N.), sec. 2.

Copyright, the sole and exclusive liberty of printing or otherwise multiplying copies of any book, volume, part or division of a volume, pamphlet, sheet of letterpress, sheet of music, and map, chart or plan separately published (see the Cape Copyright Act (2 of 1873), sec. 9).

The term *copyright* is defined in the Cape Registration of Designs Act (28 of 1894) to mean "the exclusive right to apply a design to any article of manufacture or to any such substance as aforesaid in the class or classes in which the design is registered."

In the Cape Copyright in Works of Art Act (46 of 1905) it is defined as meaning "the sole and exclusive right of copying, reproducing, repeating or otherwise multiplying copies of any work of art and of the design thereof, of any size, in the same or any other material, or by the same or any other kind of art."

In the Natal Copyright Act (17 of 1897) "*copyright* means the sole and exclusive right of multiplying copies of any work, whether by printing, copying, engraving or otherwise." In the Natal Registration of Designs Act (19 of 1899), *copyright* is defined in the same way as in the Cape Registration of Designs Act (28 of 1894), see *supra*.

For Copyright Law in Transvaal, see Law 2 of 1887.

Coram judice loci rei sitae, in the presence of the judge of the place where the property is situated. This is another mode of expressing the same principle as that contained in the phrase *coram lege loci.* In the Netherlands there was not one particular court, such as the Court of Justice which existed in Cape Colony up to 1828, but several courts, before which land could be mortgaged and transferred. As the phrase indicates, the proper court in each case was the court of the place where the property was situated. From the Ordinance of 1529 it seems to have become the practice to mortgage land not before the court of the place where the property was situated, but before any court in the province. As purchasers of land were in many cases defrauded and the payment of the proper duties evaded by the practice, the Ordinance was passed to stop this custom, and provided that transfers and mortgages of immovable property which took place before any court other than that within the jurisdiction of which the land was situated should be null and void (see Wessels' *History*, p. 217).

Coram lege loci, before the court of the place. This phrase is used of the only valid mode of creating a real right in immovable property, whether by way of transfer or mortgage. The rule of our law as to the transfer of immovable property is not derived from the Roman law, which made little distinction between the mode of conveying movables and immovables, but has its origin in the customs of Holland. From an early period the rule was adopted in many parts of the Netherlands that the transfer of landed property should not be effective to transfer a *jus in re* to the purchaser unless the same was made before the court of the place in which the property was situated. This custom was by a Placaat of Charles V in the year 1529 declared of universal application throughout Holland and West Friesland, and was introduced into the Cape Colony on its first settlement (*Harris* v. *Buissinne's Trustee*, 2 Menz. 105).

Until 1828 all transfers and mortgages of immovable property and other acts affecting real rights in the Cape Colony were registered before the Court of Justice and in the presence of the Colonial Secretary. By Ordinance 39 (C.C.) of that year the Court of Justice was abolished, and it was provided that all such deeds were to be registered in future in the office of the Registrar of Deeds, by whom a register was to be kept for the purpose (see Maasdorp's *Institutes*, vol. 2, pp. 69 *et seq.*).

Co-respondent, a term used in proceedings for divorce; it denotes the alleged adulterer in actions for divorce on the ground of adultery.

Coroner, an official presiding over an inquest. *See* INQUEST.

Corporation. "A corporation, or *universitas personarum*, then, in our law is a legal fiction or incorporeal abstraction, consisting indeed of a collection or aggregation of real or natural persons, but having in itself no existence in nature, and existing merely in contemplation of law. Fictitious, however, though it be, it is endowed by legislative authority with the capacity and power of acting and of acquiring and having rights in the same way in most respects as a real human person" (Maasdorp's *Institutes*, vol. 1, p. 268).

Corporeal chattels, a division of chattels personal; they are "those which have an actual physical existence, which are capable of being touched, tasted or handled, such as money in specie, furniture, cattle, ships, and timber or minerals when severed from the land" (Goodeve's *Personal Property*, 4th ed. p. 1). It is an English law term, and is rarely used in South Africa.

Corporeal hereditaments, an English law term, signifying "land in the freeholder's possession" (Williams on *Real Property*, 20th ed. p. 31).

Corporeal thing, "a physical thing, *res corporalis* (*Sache* in the narrower, and proper, sense of the term), is sometimes defined as 'a locally limited portion of volitionless nature'; perhaps better as 'a permanent external cause of sensations.' The full meaning of any such definition is, of course, a question not of jurisprudence, but of metaphysics. The jurist need not go further than to lay down that a physical thing is something which is perceptible by the external organs of sense, and is capable of being so perceived again and again. By the latter characteristic it is distinguished from an 'event' which, as a cause of sensation, is transient" (Holland's *Jurisprudence*, 10th ed. p. 97). Nathan in his *Common Law* (sec. 530) defines *corporeal things* as "such as are tangible, or capable of actual physical possession." Grotius (*Introd.* 2, 1, 10) says: "*Corporeal things* are such as are visible to the outward sense, as this house, this book, &c., and are divided into movable and immovable." See *Ex parte Master of the Supreme Court* ([1906] T.S. at p. 566).

Corps is defined in the Natal Militia Act (36 of 1903), sec. 3, to mean and include "a naval corps, regiments and troops of mounted rifles, regiments and batteries of artillery, companies of engineers,

K 2

battalions and companies of infantry, transport, medical, veterinary and signalling *corps*, and any other *corps* which may be formed by direction of the Governor for military purposes. Troops or companies which are parts of a regiment shall not individually be deemed to be a *corps*." For further definition see Ordinance 37 of 1904 (T.), sec. 1; Ordinance 35 of 1905 (O.R.C.), sec. 1.

Corpus delicti, the body, substance or foundation of the offence. In all criminal prosecutions it is necessary first of all to prove that an offence has been committed before there can be any question as to the guilt or innocence of the accused. "In some offences the evidence establishing the existence of the crime also indicates the criminal, while in others the traces or effects of the crime are visible, leaving its author undetermined—the former being denominated by foreign jurists *delicta facti transeuntis*, and the latter *delicta facti permanentis*. Under the former—*i.e. delicta facti transeuntis*—are ranged those offences the essence of which consists in intention, such as various forms of treason, conspiracy, criminal language, &c., all which, being of an exclusively psychological nature, must necessarily be established by presumptive evidence, unless the guilty party chooses to make a plenary confession. In the other sort of cases—*delicta facti permanentis*, or, as they have been sometimes termed, *delicta cum effectu permanente*—the proof of the crime is separable from that of the criminal. Thus the finding a dead body, or a house in ashes, may indicate a crime, but does not necessarily afford a clue to the perpetrator. And here, again, a distinction must be drawn relative to the effect of presumptive evidence. The *corpus delicti* in cases such as we are now considering is made up of two things: first, certain facts forming its basis; and, secondly, the existence of criminal agency as the cause of them" (Best on *Evidence*, 10th ed. secs. 441, 442).

Corrupt practices include treating, undue influence, bribery and personation at parliamentary, divisional council or municipal elections. See Act 40 of 1889 (C.C.), sec. 70; Act 26 of 1902 (C.C.); Ordinance 38 of 1903 (T.), secs. 69 to 75.

Corruptie (D.), bribery; corruption. "With us all gifts and benefits which savour in the least degree of corruption and intrigue are entirely prohibited and disallowed; and very strict provision has been made by the placaten both against those who by promise of any gift or benefit to another seek to advance themselves, and those who accept such gifts" (Van Leeuwen's *Comm.* Kotzé's trans. vol. 2, p. 122). See *The State* v. *Benson Aaron* (10 C.L.J. 238; H. 125), where this subject is very fully dealt with.

Corruption, the vitiation or debasement of moral rectitude. *See* JUDICIAL CORRUPTION.

Corruption of public officers, the act of endeavouring by any means to force, persuade or induce any public officer to do or omit to do any act which the offender knows to be a violation of such officer's official duty (Stephen's *Digest of the Criminal Law*, 5th ed. art. 137). See Act 24 of 1886 (C.C.), sec. 104 (Native Territories' Penal Code).

"Cost laid down." As to whether the expression *cost laid down*, appearing in a contract for the supply of cold stored meat, includes London office and Capetown administration expenses, see *Imperial Cold Storage Co., Ltd.*, v. *Distributing Syndicate for Cold Storage* (24 S.C. 426), where it was held such expenses were so included.

Cost of production, the expenditure incurred in producing or bringing into being any wares or products.

For definition of *cost of production* in the Profit Tax (Gold Mines) Proclamation, 1902, see Proclamation 34 of 1902 (T.), sec. 3. See also *Knights Deep, Ltd.*, v. *Colonial Treasurer* ([1905] T.S. 689). *See* ACTUAL COST.

Costs of the day, such unnecessary or extra costs as have been or may be incurred, owing to a party to a suit applying for or causing the postponement or delay of the trial or hearing, which costs would not have been incurred but for such delay (Van Zyl's *Judicial Practice*, 2nd ed. p. 785; see also *Carlis* v. *Hay*, [1903] T.S. 317).

Costumen or **Costuymen** (D.), unwritten laws or usages; customs.

Co-tutor, a joint tutor; one of two or more persons who have been duly appointed to administer and manage any estate or property which may have devolved on, or come to belong to any minor, or to take care of the person of such minor, within a colony.

Council, an assembly of persons met together for the purpose of deliberation, consultation or advice; an authorised body of persons appointed for advisory or administrative purposes. In the Cape Divisional Council's Act (40 of 1889), sec. 4, *council* is defined as meaning "the divisional council of any division heretofore or hereafter by law locally constituted and defined, including divisions of all provinces or territories annexed to and forming portion of this [Cape] Colony."

Counterclaim, a claim set up by the defendant by way of cross-action; generally described in South Africa as a claim in reconvention; a claim put forward by the defendant as a set-off to the original claim of the plaintiff.

Counterfeit coin. In the Transvaal Crimes Ordinance (26 of 1904), sec. 3, *counterfeit coin* means "coin not current, but resembling or apparently intended to resemble or pass for current coin, and includes current coin prepared or altered so as to resemble or pass for coin of a higher denomination."

"Coupled with an interest." In discussing this phrase in *Fick* v. *Bierman* (2 S.C. at p. 35), SMITH, J., made the following remarks: "It is laid down by Story that a power of attorney, although irrevocable by the party giving it, and although founded upon a valuable consideration or given as a security, is nevertheless revoked by the death, and so by the bankruptcy, of the party unless it is *coupled with an interest* (Story on *Agency*, secs. 477, 482). What then is the meaning of *coupled with an interest?* This is well explained by Chief Justice MARSHALL in an American case, *Hunt* v. *Rousmaniere* (8 Wheaton, 174). He says: 'Is it an interest in the subject on which the power is to be exercised, or is it an interest in that which is produced by the exercise of the power? We hold it to be clear that the interest which can protect a power after the death of a person who creates it must be an interest in the thing itself. In other words, the power must be engrafted on an estate in the thing.' An ordinary instance of such an interest occurs when a factor has possession of the goods of his principal with a power to sell. He is entitled to sell and indemnify himself for any advance he may have made notwithstanding the insolvency of his principal, for he has a special property in the goods and can sell them in his own name. He has a lien upon the goods, and upon the purchase-price of goods lawfully sold. On the other hand, a mere broker having no special property has none of these rights, and his authority becomes extinct upon the insolvency of his principal. The power of the agent to transfer in his own name is said by Story to be the reason why (I would rather call it a test whether) a power *coupled with an interest* is irrevocable after the death or insolvency of the principal (Story on *Agency*, sec. 489)."

Courts of Request, inferior courts authorised to be established in the Cape Colony by sec. 48 of the Charter of Justice of 1832. The civil jurisdiction did not extend to any case in which the sum or matter in dispute exceeded the value of £40, nor did it extend to any case wherein the title to any lands or tenements, or any fee, duty or office may be in question or whereby rights in future may be bound; the criminal jurisdiction was limited to such cases as did not involve an accusation of any crime punishable by death, transportation or banishment from the colony. The *Courts of Request* were replaced by courts of resident magistrate (see Act 20 of 1856).

A *Court of Request*, which was otherwise known as a "Court of Conscience," was an English institution, wherein small debts could be recovered. *Courts of Request* in England are now superseded by the present County Courts, which were established by statute in 1846.

"Covered by the policy." "The interest of the assured is technically said to be *covered by the policy*, when the sum or aggregate of sums insured in the policy is sufficient to afford him full compensation for whatever loss that interest may sustain. If the value of his interest exceeds the sum insured, the excess of interest is said to be 'uncovered by the policy,' and the assured to be 'his own insurer to that extent'" (Arnold's *Marine Insurance*, 7th ed. sec. 2).

Covering, something that overspreads or conceals. In the Cape Merchandise Marks Act (12 of 1888), sec. 4 (2), the expression *covering* includes "any stopper, cask, bottle, vessel, box, cover, capsule, case, frame or wrapper."

Credibility, the state of being worthy of credit or belief. The expression is generally applied to witnesses; one speaks of the "*credibility* of a witness."

Credible witness, a witness who is competent to give evidence, and who is worthy of credit or belief.

Crediet-brief (D.), letter of credit; a letter in which a banker or merchant directs his correspondent in another place or places to pay the bearer of the letter of credit such moneys as he may from time to time require, not exceeding in all the amount stated in the letter.

Creditor, one who gives credit to another; a person to whom money is due and owing by a debtor; correlative to debtor. "*Creditor* and *debitor* denote respectively the person entitled to the benefit of an obligation and the person bound thereby. *Causa debendi*, therefore, is equivalent to *causa obligandi*" (Van Leeuwen's *Comm.* Kotzé's trans. vol. 2, p. 8, translator's *note*). *See Brink, N.O.*, v. *Norden* (3 Menz. 271).

As to the term *creditor* being taken in a wider sense so as to extend to persons to whom anything for whatever cause is due, see *MacMaster's Trustees* v. *Executor of Kruger* (4 Searle, at p. 210).

Creditores massae, creditors whose claims have reference to the costs of administration or of the liquidation and distribution of the estate of an insolvent or deceased debtor. These costs take precedence over all debts due by the debtor himself, and must be paid before there can be any question of a distribution of the estate among his creditors.

Crime "in a general sense is every punishable violation of the laws, done wilfully and with an evil intention, which is taken very narrowly and strictly, so that whatever is not connected with some open fraud or evil intention, cannot be punished as a *crime*. Such, however, that great negligence, although strictly not a fraud, and not to be considered as a *crime*, is yet punishable, although to a less extent at discretion" (Van Leeuwen's *Comm.* Kotzé's trans. vol. 2, p. 247); to which Decker in a *note* (*ibid.*) adds: "For this reason *crime* is thus defined by Moorman, 'Every act or neglect which is punishable by municipal law,' observing that just as it is a *crime of commission* to do something unlawful, so it is a *crime of omission* to allow anything to be done by another which we might have prevented."

Crimen expositionis infantis, the crime of exposing or abandoning a child to die from cold, hunger or neglect (*Rex* v. *Adams*, 20 S.C. 556).

Crimen falsi, the crime of falsity. *Falsum* is defined by Voet as "a designed perversion of the truth made with intent to deceive in fraud of another," and by Carpzovius and Matthaeus as a fraudulent misrepresentation of the truth made in prejudice of another. It includes such crimes as obtaining money under false pretences, forgery, perjury, coining of base money, use of false weights and measures, &c. In *Rex* v. *Brandford* (7 S.C. 169) it was laid down by DE VILLIERS, C.J., that in order to be the subject of a criminal prosecution the falsehood complained of must have caused actual prejudice to another. In that case the indictment alleged that the accused, having held a lottery under the disguise of an art union drawing, refused to deliver the prize to the person holding the winning number. It was held that "inasmuch as the lottery was illegal under the Placaat of 1787 the person holding the winning number had no legal claim to the prize, and that inasmuch as the refusal to deliver the prize, and not the false reason given for the refusal, constituted the prejudice stated in the indictment, the facts stated did not constitute the crime of fraud." It would, however, appear from the opinion of the same learned judge in *Queen* v. *Adelburg* (8 S.C. 234), and the cases of *Moolchund* v. *Rex* (23 N.L.R. 76); *Rex* v. *Jolosa* ([1903] T.S. 694), and *R.* v. *De Vos* (13 E.D.C. 145) that besides intent to deceive it is not necessary, to support a conviction for an offence falling under this generic term, that actual prejudice should be suffered by another, but only that the act was such as to be calculated to prejudice such other person. "It is not every fanciful, possible or remote risk of prejudice that will suffice, but the risk must be probable, direct or reasonably certain" (*The King* v. *Firling*, 18 E.D.C. 11).

Criminal intention. "It is a commonplace remark in the administration of the criminal law that there can be no crime, in the true sense of the term, without a *criminal intention*. This intention, which was sometimes expressed by the Roman jurists under the term *voluntas*, implies the existence of a power of exercising and controlling the will. This power every one is presumed to possess until the contrary is proved. Under the Roman law, as well as under the Dutch law, it was always admitted that no *criminal intention* could be held to exist where an offence was committed by an insane person, but the question whether insanity did or did not exist in any particular case was treated, as it ought to be treated, as a question of fact, and not of law. Under the law of England alsc insanity at the time of commission of an offence is a good defence to a criminal prosecution, but the test as to the existence of insanity has been treated as a question of law rather than of fact" (*per* DE VILLIERS, C.J., in *Queen* v. *Hay*, 16 S.C. at p. 297).

Criminal jurisdiction, the jurisdiction granted to a court by law in criminal matters; that is, in matters relating to crime, as opposed to civil jurisdiction or to jurisdiction in ecclesiastical or naval or military matters.

Criminal lunatic. In the Cape Lunacy Act (1 of 1897) the term *criminal lunatic* is defined to mean "any person convicted of any crime and certified to be insane under the provisions of this Act." *See* GOVERNOR'S PLEASURE LUNATIC. The Transvaal has adopted a similar definition of *criminal lunatic* to that of the Cape; see Proclamation 36 of 1902, sec. 2; and so too the Orange River Colony; see Ordinance 13 of 1906, sec. 2.

Crimineele zaken (D.), criminal cases.

Criminology, the science of crime.

Crown, kingly government; the sovereign power.

In the Transvaal Interpretation of Laws Proclamation (15 of 1902), sec. 13, it is provided that "in every Law references to the Sovereign reigning at the time of the passing of the Law or to the *Crown* shall, unless the contrary intention appears, be construed as references to the Sovereign for the time being."

As to actions against the Crown in the Transvaal, see Ordinance 51 of 1903.

As to land held by the Crown, see *Trading Board* v. *Germiston Town Council* ([1907] T.S. at p. 454).

As to holding an office of profit under the Crown, see *Hedley* v. *Celliers* (20 S.C. 271).

Crown forest, an expression used in the Cape Forest Act (28 of 1888), where it is defined as consisting of all demarcated forest and undemarcated forest (*q.v.*).

Crown land, land held by the Government of a South African British colony in its own right, and of which such Government has the power of disposal. The disposal of Crown lands is generally regulated by statute.

In the Transvaal, in Ordinance 40 of 1902, sec. 2, *Crown land* means and includes: (*a*) all unalienated *Crown land;* and (*b*) all land the property of the Government, however acquired. The same definition is found in sec. 2 of Ordinance 57 of 1903, which repeals the former statute. In the Precious and Base Metals Act (35 of 1908), sec. 3, *Crown land* means "(*a*) all land in respect of which the Crown is the holder of the mineral rights; and (*b*) all land which has or may become the property of the Transvaal Land Settlement Board in accordance with section fifty-two of the Transvaal Constitution Letters Patent, 1906, or the Land Settlement Act, 1907, unless the Crown is not the holder of the mineral rights in respect of such land or has alienated or contracted to alienate such rights." In the Precious Stones Ordinance (66 of 1903), sec. 2, *Crown land* means "all unalienated Crown land, and all land the property of the Government of this [Transvaal] colony in whatever way acquired; and any land alienated by the Crown with an express reservation to it of precious stones or minerals."

In the Orange River Colony, see Ordinance 3 of 1904, sec. 5, where the definition is very similar to that just quoted; Ordinance 4 of 1904, sec. 5, and Act 13 of 1908, sec. 1.

Crown Prosecutor, a person duly appointed by Government to prosecute in the name and on behalf of the king all crimes legally cognisable within a certain district or districts. See Act 39 of 1877 (C.C.), sec. 19; Act 43 of 1885 (C.C.), sec. 3; Act 35 of 1896 (C.C.), sec. 58; Ordinance 18 of 1845 (N.), sec. 2; Ordinance 18 of 1856 (N.), sec. 1 (where it is provided that the *Crown Prosecutor* of Natal should thereafter be designated and created the "Attorney-General of Natal"; by this Ordinance the office of "*Crown Prosecutor* of Natal" was abolished).

Cruelty, for definition of *cruelty* in regard to animals in the Orange River Colony, see O.R.C. Law Book, chap. 145, sec. 2.

Cuilibet licet juri pro se introducto renuntiare, any one may renounce a right made for his own benefit. *See* QUILIBET JURI PRO SE INTRODUCTO RENUNCIARE POTEST. At the present time this rule of law is not always applicable, for the legislature has at times enacted that certain rights for a person's own benefit may not be renounced, as, for instance, in the Workmen's Compensation Acts. *See* JUS PUBLICUM RENUNTIARI NON POTEST.

Cujus est commodum ejus debet esse periculum, his should be the risk who reaps the profit or advantage. In accordance with this maxim the risk attaching to a thing which has been sold, although not yet delivered, lies on the purchaser, for all fruits accruing from the thing after the time when the sale has been completed belong to him. *See* PERICULUM REI VENDITAE NONDUM TRADITAE EST EMPTORIS. This rule, however, does not apply in the contract of *commodatum*, or gratuitous loan for use, for although the borrower has the use and advantage of the thing, and is liable for the slightest degree of negligence, its deterioriation or accidental loss falls on the lender. Here the maxim is *res perit domino.*

Cujus est solum ejus est usque ad coelum, the owner of soil is owner up to the sky vertically above it, and may lawfully build without any limit as to height, but in length and breath not beyond his own land.

Cul de sac, a street or passage having no outlet at one end.

A *cul-de-sac* is as much a public highway or public street as any other street which is a thoroughfare (*Souch* v. *East London Railway Co.*, L.R. 16 Eq. 108; 42 L.J. Ch. 447).

Culpa, fault, negligence. There are three degrees or classes of *culpa*, namely, (1) *culpa lata*, gross fault or negligence, which consists in failing to show the slightest degree of diligence (*levissima diligentia*); this degree of negligence is treated as equivalent to *dolus;* (2) *culpa levis*, ordinary negligence, or the omission to take that care which a man of ordinary prudence would use in his own affairs (*diligentia*, sometimes termed *media diligentia*); and (3) *culpa levissima*, the slightest degree of negligence, which consists in the omission of extraordinary diligence (*exactissima diligentia*), *i.e.* the diligence which a most prudent man (*bonus paterfamilias*) observes in the conduct of his own affairs.

The degree of diligence for which persons are liable depends upon the kind of contract under which the obligation for diligence arises, whether it is for the benefit of only one of the parties, or for the benefit of both. Thus in the contract of deposit, which is for the benefit of the depositor, and confers no advantage on the depositary, being undertaken by him gratuitously, the latter will be liable only for *culpa lata*, which according to Grotius (*Introd.* 3, 7, 9) will be considered to be present when the depositary "does not take equal care of the deposit as he is accustomed to take of his own property." In the contract of *commodatum*, or gratuitous loan for use, as the contract is purely for the benefit of the borrower, he will be liable for *culpa levissima*. Again, where both parties benefit by the contract—as in letting and hiring, where one has the use of the thing lent and the other the hire paid for such use—each party is liable only for *culpa levis* or ordinary negligence.

Culpa caret qui scit sed prohibere non potest, no negligence is attributable to a person who is powerless to avoid the danger apparent to him (*Digest*, 50, 17, l. 17; *Philpott* v. *Whittal, Elston and Crosby & Co.*, [1907] E.D.C. at p. 207). In *Jones* v. *Boyce* (1 Stark, 493), where an accident happened to a stage-coach, upon which the plaintiff jumped down and broke his leg, Lord ELLENBOROUGH put it to the jury to consider whether the plaintiff's acts were such as a reasonable and prudent man would have adopted, and added: "If I place a man in such a situation that he must adopt a perilous alternative, I am responsible for the consequences." Cf. *Newman* v. *East London Town Council* (12 S.C. 61).

Culpa est immiscere se rei ad se non pertinenti, a person intermeddling with the affairs of others, which do not concern him, is guilty of negligence. As a rule a *negotiorum gestor* was not compelled to make good losses resulting from accident (*C.* 2, 19, 22) unless his interference was uncalled for. He was also liable for loss by accident when he made enterprises foreign to the habits of the principal.

Culpa lata dolo aequiparatur, gross fault or carelessness is equivalent to bad intention or wrong-doing.

Culpa praecederat casum, fault had preceded the accident. No one is liable upon contract for pure accident, but whenever fault or negligence has preceded the accident, the loss must be made good. (Grotius' *Introd.* 3, 8, 4; Schorer's *Note* 332). *See* CASUS FORTUITUS.

Culpa tenet suos auctores tantum, a man is only liable for his own fault. This is the rule of the German law. By that law the master is not, as a general rule, responsible for damage to third parties caused by his servant in the exercise of his employment, though, if he authorises or permits the damage to be caused, or has notice of the careless conduct of his servants, he would be liable. The Roman-Dutch law, however, recognises and adopts the principle that a master, or employer, is liable for the injuries caused by his servants, or workmen, within the scope of their employment (*Lewis* v. *Salisbury Gold Mining Co.*, 11 C.L.J. 137; 1 Off. Rep. 1).

Culpable homicide, the unlawful killing of a person without malice aforethought. On this subject see 19 S.A.L.J. at p. 132. In the Native Territories' Penal Code (Act 24 of 1886 (C.C.)), sec. 135, it is provided that "homicide is culpable when it consists in the killing of any person either by an unlawful act or by a culpable omission to perform or observe any legal duty, or by both combined; or by causing a person by threats or fear of violence, or by deception, to do an act which causes that person's death, or by wilfully frightening a child or sick person." See Ordinance 18 of 1845 (N.), sec. 28.

Culpable insolvency. In the Cape Colony an insolvent whose estate has been placed under sequestration is deemed to be guilty of the crime of culpable insolvency (sec. 71 of Ordinance 6 of 1843 (C.C.)) if (1) he shall fail to attend before his creditors at the first, second and third meetings or any adjournment of the second meeting, unless authorised not to attend by the Master or magistrate, as the case may be; or (2) shall, without good and lawful reason, fail to attend before his creditors at any meeting after having been personally served with a notice in writing, signed by the Master or the magistrate, as the case may be, requiring him to attend such meeting; or (3) shall not when thereto required by the Master or magistrate, as the case may be, at any meeting of his creditors account for or discover what has become of any money or valuable security or other property or effects which shall have been proved to have been in his possession so recently before the sequestration as to make it his duty so to do; or (4) shall not, when thereto required by the Master or magistrate, or when thereto required in writing by the trustee [printed as amended by sec. 10 of Act 38 of 1884 (C.C.)] give a true and sufficient explanation of the cause or causes of his insolvency; or (5) if he shall have given to any of his creditors an undue preference; or (6) shall have contracted any debt without any reasonable or probable expectation at the time of contracting the same of being able to pay the same: or (7) shall have incurred any debt by reason of any breach of trust; or (8) shall without having obtained his certificate and the allowance thereof, between the time of making the order for sequestration of his estate and the time of making the decree confirming the account and plan of distribution, have entered into any dealing or business, or taken upon him the buying and selling of any goods, wares or merchandise, whether for himself or any other person without the authority in writing of the trustee or Master, as the case may be; or (9) shall have granted, made or promised any gratuity, payment, security or other undue consideration in order to procure or obtain the concurrence or assent of any creditor either to any offer of composition or to the certificate as mentioned in the Ordinance; or (10) shall not have kept or caused to be kept such reasonable and proper books or accounts containing all such entries concerning and exhibiting the nature of his dealings and transactions as (regard being had to his particular trade or calling) might reasonably be expected or required [this is under sec. 9 of Act 38 of 1884 (C.C.)]. The punishment for *culpable insolvency* is imprisonment with or without hard labour for a period not exceeding six months.

The definition of *culpable insolvency* in the Transvaal is very similar to that of the Cape Colony; it differs from (6) above by making it applicable only to debts amounting to £50 or upwards; (7) and (8) are omitted. The punishment is the same as in Cape Colony (see sec. 147 of Law 13 of 1895).

As to Orange River Colony, see O.R.C. Law Book, chap. 104, sec. 71.

Cum nemo juri alieno renunciare possit, since no one may renounce or alienate the right of another. Privileges granted to corporations cannot be destroyed by the renunciation of individuals, nor by acts done by them contrary thereto.

"**Cum rights.**" "The phrase *cum rights* must *primâ facie* be taken to refer to rights accruing at or after the date of the sale, and not to bonus shares which had been distributed among the shareholders three weeks before the date of the sale" (*per* De Villiers, C.J., in *Logan* v. *Beit*, 7 S.C. at p. 215).

Cumulative, increasing in force, weight, number or effect by successive additions.

As to *cumulative sentences*, see Ordinance 1 of 1903 (T.), sec. 253.

Curatele or **curateele** (D.), guardianship; curatorship; trusteeship. *See* Curator; Guardianship.

Curatio funeris, the duty of burying a deceased person. It is a quasi-contractual obligation. A quasi-contractual obligation is an implied contract, that is, a contractual obligation which the law infers from the existence of a given set of circumstances, as binding upon the parties.

Curator, a person duly appointed to manage the affairs of another who, from some cause or other, is himself unable or unfit to manage his own affairs. "The XII Tables placed under the care of their agnates madmen (*furiosi*) and such spendthrifts (*prodigi*) as had been formally prohibited from dealing with their own estates" (Roby's *Private Roman Law*, p. 121). *Curators* may, in the Transvaal, also be appointed by persons bequeathing property, to administer and manage such property during the minority or insanity of the person to whom the property is bequeathed (sec. 73 of Proclamation 28 of 1902 (T.)). *See* CURATOR DATUR REI.

Curator ad litem, curator for the purpose of a suit, *i.e.* a curator appointed by the court to protect the interests of some party to a legal proceeding who is unable, or is alleged to be unable, to protect his own interests.

A minor who has no guardian must when suing or being sued have a *curator ad litem* appointed to conduct the suit upon his behalf. To have a person declared insane or incapable of managing his affairs a petition to the court for the appointment of a *curator ad litem* to the alleged lunatic is necessary. The duties of a *curator ad litem* are to watch and protect the minor or alleged lunatic's interests, and they end with the completion and final settlement of the case or inquiry. As regards the duties of a *curator ad litem* in lunacy proceedings, WATERMEYER, J., in the case of *Bathgate* (3 Searle, 187), said: "The duty of a *curator ad litem* (in lunacy proceedings) is this, to ascertain as far as he can, whether what is alleged respecting the individual to whom he is appointed curator is true or is not true, and to endeavour to prove in contradiction to what is alleged by the person stating it is a case of lunacy, that the alleged lunatic is sane and of sound mind. If he find he cannot do that, then his duty is to state that in court at all events."

Curator bonis, (1) persons appointed by the court to manage and control the property of those persons (not being minors) who, for reasons satisfactory to the court, are unable to manage and control their own property.

(2) Persons appointed by the Master of the Supreme Court: (*a*) in the estates of deceased persons, to take charge of such estates until letters of administration have been granted to executors testamentary or dative (*Melass's Estate*, 13 S.C. 97); (*b*) in insolvent estates, to take charge of such estates until the same have been finally sequestrated and a trustee appointed (*Wood* v. *Webb*, 4 E.D.C. 4; *Sprigg & Co.* v. *Fraser & Sons*, 15 C.T.R. 45); (*c*) pending letters of confirmation being granted to any one as tutor testamentary or dative or curator nominate or dative.

Curator datur rei, a curator is given to the property. In the Roman law curators were appointed to minors, lunatics and prodigals. They were said to be given to the property, as their exclusive duty was to see that the person under guardianship did not waste his goods. On the other hand, tutors or the guardians appointed to persons under puberty were said to be given to the person, for although they administered the property of the pupil they were appointed chiefly to supply what was wanting to complete the pupil's legal character. This distinction between the *tutela* of *impuberes* and the *cura* of minors does not exist in the Roman-Dutch law, according to which all persons under the age of majority are minors, whose guardians are appointed both to the care of the person and the administration of the property. *See* TUTOR DATUR PERSONAE.

Curators dative, persons appointed by the Master of the Supreme Court, after observance of the prescribed formalities, to take care of the estate, or property of absent persons.

Curators nominate, persons appointed by any one bequeathing or giving property to a minor, or to a person of unsound mind or weak intellect, for the purpose of administering or managing the property of such minor, or person of unsound mind or weak intellect, during the period of minority or other disability. *Curators nominate* may not enter upon the administration or management of any estate or property, except for the purpose of preservation or safe custody, until letters of confirmation have been granted to them by the Master of the Supreme Court.

Curia advisari vult, the court desires to consider; the phrase used when a court of law reserves its judgment; abbreviated in the reports to *cur. adv. vult.* and *C.A.V.*

Current coin. In the Transvaal Crimes Ordinance (26 of 1904), sec. 3, *current coin* means "any coin used in any place as money, and stamped by or under the authority of the Government of such place, whether within or without his Majesty's dominions in order that it may be so used; coins issued by the mint of the late South African Republic are *current coin.*"

"**Current value.**" The expression *current value* is found in the South African Customs Acts. In the Cape Customs Amendment and Tariff Act (6 of 1898), sec. 6, we find it provided: "The term *current value*, in the preceding section referred to, shall be taken to be the true *current value* in the open market for such goods at the place of purchase by the importer or his agent, including the cost of packing and packages; but not including agent's commission, if it does not exceed 5 per cent.: provided that in no case shall the true *current value* as above defined be less than the cost of the goods to the importer at the place of purchase." The Natal definition is precisely the same (see Act 13 of 1899, sec. 62).

Cursus curiae est lex curiae, the practice of the court is the law of the court. A well-established practice must be adhered to, for an inveterate practice in the law generally stands upon principles that are founded on justice and convenience. "Every court is the guardian of its own records and master of its own practice" (*per* TINDAL, C.J., in *Scales* v. *Cheese,* 12 M. & W. 687).

"Inasmuch as it is a mere matter of procedure, the maxim *cursus curiae lex curiae* must apply, and it is no argument to say that there was no actual contested case in which this procedure has been laid down; for a course of procedure may be adopted and hold good even though there has been no decision on the point" (*per* WESSELS, J., in *Wayland* v. *Transvaal Government*, [1904] T.S. at p. 758).

Curtilage, a piece of ground occupied by a dwelling-house and its outbuildings. It is an English law term: see 24 & 25 Vict. c. 96, secs. 55 and 56; and Stephen's *Digest of the Criminal Law*, art. 343. Probably its first appearance in South African statute law was in the Cape Public Health Amendment Act (23 of 1897), sec. 2.

Custody of children. "When the court grants a decree for the dissolution of a marriage or for a judicial separation, the *custody of the children* is in the discretion of the court, which must look to all the circumstances of the case and be chiefly guided by the consideration of what is best for the children. *Primâ facie* a guilty parent would not be a proper person to have the custody, but there might be circumstances that would make it desirable that the children, or some of them, should be brought up by him or her" (*per* SMITH, J., in *Simey* v. *Simey*, 1 S.C. at p. 176). See also *Ex parte Jansen* (18 S.C. at p. 156); *Painter* v. *Painter* (2 E.D.C. 147); *Mitchell* v. *Mitchell* ([1904] T.S. 128); *Hooper* v. *Hooper* ([1908] E.D.C. 474); *Coleby-Clarke* v. *Coleby-Clarke* ([1909] T.H. 60).

Custom. Law is divided into written and unwritten law, the latter consisting of customs which have been established by long usage. In order that a custom may acquire the force of law there are several requisites. In the first place, the acts must have been done freely and frequently and for a sufficient length of time. As to length of time, that question Schorer (*Note* 6) states is properly left to the discretion of the judge, but some authorities (he adds) require the same length of time as is necessary for prescription. Then the custom must be reasonable and just, and the acts which constitute it must be uniform (see Grotius' *Introd.* 1, 2, 21; Schorer *loc. cit.*; Van Leeuwen's *Comm.* 1, 3, 10 *et seq.*, and Decker, *ibid. in notis;* Van der Linden's *Institutes*, 1, 1, 7; *Zeiler* v. *Weeber*, 1 K. 18).

Customer. To create the relation of *customer* and banker there must be some sort of account between the parties—either a deposit or a current account. A person who is known to a banker as one accustomed to coming and getting cheques cashed at the bank without having an account is not a *customer* (*Great Western Railway Co.* v. *London and County Bank*, 15 L.T. 152; [1901] A.C. 414).

Cutting wood. *See* SERVITUDE OF CUTTING WOOD.

Cynsen (D.), census. *See* CENSUS. "The right to receive a certain irredeemable annuity, reserved by a person when he transfers the ownership in his property" (Grotius' *Introd.* Maasdorp's trans. p. 184).

Cynsgericht (D.), a court established in Holland about the fourteenth century for the purpose of dealing with disputes about taxes and contributions (Wessels' *History*, p. 152).

Cyus (D.), a burden or tribute imposed by a lord upon the villeins to whom land was given for cultivation. This was done by the lord at his own pleasure, without entering into any contract with his villeins. After villenage was abolished land continued subject to this burden or tribute (Meyer's *Woordenschat, sub voce* "*Cyus*"). Hence the expression *Cynsbaar-land, i.e.* land subject to such a burden or tax, continued in use after villenage ceased to exist in the Netherlands. *Cyus* is the same as *census*, which is defined by Van Leeuwen in his *Commentaries* (Kotzé's trans. 2, 12, 1) as the right by which a yearly rent is perpetually and hereditably imposed by the vendor over immovable property when sold, and is called by some perpetual and irredeemable rent; by others former or ancient ownership (*oudeygen*).

Daaden (D.), to do.

Daadigen (D.), to dispute, plead or argue; also to approve or ratify; to surrender on terms, to capitulate (*daadingen*).

Dadingsman (D.), an arbitrator.

Dagliedingen (D.), to sue or cite any one in law.

Dagvaarding (D.), a summons or citation. The initial proceeding in an action, whereby the defendant is required to appear in or before a court. See Kersteman's *Woordenboek*, vol. 2, p. 246.

Dairy, a place where milk is kept in quantity for the purpose of securing the cream, or for making butter or cheese. In the Cape Public Health Amendment Act (23 of 1897), sec. 2, the term *dairy* is defined to include "any farm, farm-house, cow-shed, milk-store, milk-shop, or other place from which milk or the product of milk is sold or supplied, or is kept for purposes of sale or profit." A similar definition is to be found in the Orange River Colony Public Health Ordinance (31 of 1907), sec. 1. See *Hulley* v. *Johannesburg Municipal Council* ([1909] T.S. at p. 119).

Dairyman, a person who keeps a dairy, or who deals in dairy produce. In the Cape Public Health Amendment Act (23 of 1897), sec. 2, the term *dairyman* is defined to include "any occupier of a dairy, dealer in milk, or person keeping any cow for the purpose of selling milk." The Orange River Colony Public Health Ordinance (31 of 1907), sec. 1, defines *dairyman* as including "any cow-keeper, purveyor of milk, occupier of a dairy, dealer in milk or milk products, and any person keeping a cow or cows who sells milk or milk products."

Dakschaer (D.), to sue or summon in law.

Dam, an "artificial storage or accumulation of water" (Act 43 of 1899 (N.), sec. 4).

Damnum absque (or sine) injuria, damage without legal injury—in other words, loss or damage caused by acts which do not give rise to any cause of action, because they do not constitute a breach of legal duty or an invasion of another's legal rights. Damage of this nature is that which is caused by an act done lawfully and without infringement of the rights of the injured person. *Injuria*, as used here, means that which arises from *dolus* or *culpa*, without which mere *damnum* will create no right of action. As instances of persons who cause *damnum sine injuria* may be mentioned he who erects upon his own land buildings which obstruct his neighbour's light or prospect where the latter has no servitude in favour of his property entitling him to either of these; he who places broken glass on a wall bounding his land, and the horse of another, in jumping over the wall in order to get into the enclosed land, is injured by the glass (*Pretorius* v. *Coetzee*, 1 S.A.R. 77); a person who destroys his neighbour's house as the only means of preventing a fire which has broken out from spreading to his own property; a trader who establishes a rival business and draws away the customers from a business previously established (cf. *Mission Trading Co.* v. *Hessel*, Buch. 1879, p. 74); claimholders in a diamond mine who have ceased to work their claims, and water having found its way by gravitation to their claims overflows and floods neighbouring claims (*Reed* v. *De Beers Consolidated Mines*, 6 H.C.G. 179). See also *Eastern and S. A. Telegraph Co.* v. *Capetown Tramways* (17 S.C. 95); *De Pass & Co.* v. *Rawson* (1 Roscoe, 108; and 5 Searle, 1).

Damnum emergens, loss arising; damage which has been actually done, as distinguished from *lucrum cessans*, or "loss of future benefits 'with respect to the thing itself or its value, of which the owner may be deprived by non-payment.'" When combined these constitute the *id quod interest*, or whole damage, including loss of profit, sustained by breach of contract (Berwick's *Translation of Voet*, p. 82, *in notis*).

Damnum fatale, inevitable loss; loss arising from inevitable accident. *See* CASUS FORTUITUS, the equivalent expression more commonly used in the Roman-Dutch law.

Damnum infectum, damage which has not been incurred, but which is anticipated, or which it is feared may be incurred. For instance, if a person built so high that his building threatened damage to his neighbour, the neighbour would be entitled to *cautio damni infecti*. See Grotius' *Introd.* 3, 3, 39; Schorer's *Notes*, n. 58; Kersteman's *Woordenboek*, vol. 2, p. 238. *See* also CAUTIO DAMNI INFECTI.

Damnum injuria datum, damage caused by an actionable wrong. Such damage may consist in injury to the person arising out of negligence or any other unintentional violence or injury to property, and is to be distinguished from damage caused by intentional wrongs involving the element of contumely or insult, such as assault, malicious prosecution, false arrest or defamation of character, which in Roman law fell under the class usually known as *injuriae*. See De Villiers' *Law of Injuries*, p. 22; Maasdorp's *Institutes*, vol. 4, p. 21; INJURIA.

Danger building, an expression used in the Transvaal Explosives Ordinance (4 of 1905), sec. 2, where it means "any building or part thereof used as an explosives factory or explosives magazine or in connection therewith, unless in respect of such building or part thereof a certificate has been granted under regulations framed under this Ordinance."

Datio in solutionem, giving in order to effect discharge, *i.e.* giving something else in place of that which is due. This is valid payment if accepted by the creditor.

Datio ob causam quae non sequitur. *See* CONDICTIO CAUSA DATA CAUSA NON SECUTA.

Datio ob turpem causam. *See* CONDICTIO OB TURPEM VEL INJUSTAM CAUSAM.

Datio sine causa. *See* CONDICTIO SINE CAUSA.

Day. A legal day consists of twenty-four hours, and begins and ends at midnight (Jenks' *Digest of English Civil Law*, bk. 1, sec. 148). *See* CLEAR DAYS' NOTICE. "When any particular number of days is prescribed for the doing of any act, or for any other purpose, the same shall be reckoned exclusively of the first and inclusively of the last day, unless the last day shall happen to fall on a Sunday, Christmas Day, New Year's Day, Good Friday, Easter Monday, Ascension Day, Whit Monday, Queen Victoria Day (24th May) or any other day appointed by Proclamation of the Governor as a solemn fast or day of thanksgiving, in which case the time shall be reckoned exclusively of the first and of every other such day also" (Act 5 of 1883 (C.C.), sec. 6, as amended by Act 15 of 1902 (C.C.), sec. 1); also Ordinance 3 of 1902 (O.R.C.), sec. 11.

Days of grace, certain days allowed to the parties to a bill after its due date (unless otherwise provided in the bill), for its payment, and before the expiration of which a right of action does not accrue. In England three *days of grace* are allowed (English Bills of Exchange Act, 1882, sec. 14).

"The number of *days of grace* allowed in different countries differs considerably. Originally, as the name implies, *days of grace* were a matter of favour, but they have [in England] long been a matter of right. Thus, presentment for payment on the second *day of grace* is invalid. The allowance of *days of grace* is regulated by the *lex loci solutionis,* irrespective of the country where the bill is drawn" (Chalmers' *Bills of Exchange,* 6th ed. p. 37).

As early as 1844 (in *Randall's Trustees* v. *Haupt,* 1 Menz. 79) it was held that there were no *days of grace* recognised in the law of the Cape Colony; but *days of grace* were allowed in the Transvaal until the year 1902. *Days of grace* were formally declared not to exist in the Cape Colony by sec. 12 of the Bills of Exchange Act, 1893; as also in Natal by sec. 13 of the Bills of Exchange Law, 1887; and in Rhodesia by sec. 12 of the Bills of Exchange Regulations, 1895. *Days of grace* were abolished in the Transvaal by sec. 12 of the Bills of Exchange Proclamation, 1902; and in the Orange River Colony by sec. 12 of the Bills of Exchange Ordinance, 1902.

Daytime "means the period between sunrise and sunset" (Ordinance 26 of 1904 (T.), sec. 3).

De bonis propriis, from his own property; out of his own pocket. A person suing or defending not in his own name, but in a representative capacity, *e.g.* as a trustee or executor, is not liable personally for the costs incurred by him unless he has been guilty of misconduct or has acted negligently or unreasonably. Thus, where a provisional trustee, without the creditors' authority, applied for an interdict and was unsuccessful, but the facts showed he had acted *bonâ fide* in order to protect the estate, and not without *primâ facie* grounds for the application, the court refused to mulct him in costs *de bonis propriis* (*Shapiro's Trustee* v. *Livingstone and Another,* [1907] T.S. 957). See also *Re Estate Potgieter* ([1908] T.S. 982); *Bell* v. *Bell's Trustee* ([1909] T.S. at pp. 61 *et seq.*). On the other hand, a trustee or executor who fails to file accounts of administration within the time prescribed by law is liable for the costs of an application at the instance of any interested person to compel him to do so, as it is the trustee's or executor's duty to apply immediately to the court for time to file his accounts (*Norden* v. *Brink,* 3 Menz. 270; see also *Kotze* v. *Kotze's Trustees,* 2 Menz. 414, and *Doornback* v. *Hofmeyr,* 17 C.T.R. 1134).

De duobus vel pluribus reis debendi. The *beneficium novae constitutionis de duobus vel pluribus reis debendi* (benefit created by a new constitution in regard to two or more debtors) was introduced by Justinian, by which, if several persons bind themselves as principal debtors, each is only liable for his proportionate share of the debt. If, however, he renounces this benefit, he becomes liable for the whole debt. *See* BENEFICIUM DE DUOBUS VEL PLURIBUS REIS DEBENDI.

De facto, according to fact; in point of fact, as opposed to *de jure,* in point of law.

De industria, purposely, intentionally; antithetical to *per incuriam*, by mistake or carelessness.

De jure, according to law; in point of law, as opposed to *de facto*, in point of fact.

De lunatico inquirendo, a judicial inquiry into a person's sanity, and his capacity of taking care of himself or of his property. Where the lunatic has no property it is unnecessary to have him judicially declared insane, but he may be placed and kept under restraint by order of a magistrate (Act 1 of 1897 (C.C.)).

De minimis non curat lex, the law does not concern itself about trifles. A thing is not capable of being stolen unless it possesses some value. Otherwise it would be a crime, as Lord Macaulay says, to dip one's pen in another man's inkstand, or to pick up a stone in his garden to throw at a bird.

De novo, afresh. When absolution from the instance has been granted a plaintiff, he may proceed *de novo* if equipped with further proof.

De plano, immediately; without formality.

De ventre inspiciendo, for inspection of the womb. This was the name given in Roman law to a procedure where a husband, after divorcing his wife, suspected she was pregnant by him. If she refused to admit the fact the husband could have her summoned before the praetor, and if she denied it in answer to the praetor, the latter could appoint three skilled midwives *de ventre inspiciendo*, whose decision, or the decision of two of whom in the event of a conflict of opinion, was accepted as the truth of the matter (Voet's *Comm.* 25, 4, 2). Where the woman was found not to be pregnant she had an *actio injuriarum* against the husband if he had acted *animo injuriandi* (Voet, *ibid.*). A *ventris inspectio* might also take place if a widow alleged she had been left pregnant by her husband. In this case the persons most nearly and immediately interested in the succession could have her examined by five respectable matrons and kept under restraint until the birth of the child (Voet, *ibid.* 25, 4, 3). Although no case appears to have arisen within the last century in which this procedure has been followed in the Roman-Dutch courts, it is quite in accordance with English practice, which gives to the presumptive heir a writ *de ventre inspiciendo* to establish the truth or otherwise of the widow's pregnancy.

So, where a woman, being sentenced to death, alleges, or the court has reason to believe, she is pregnant, a jury of twelve matrons is empanelled to decide whether she is quick with child, and if she is found to be so, the court suspends execution of the sentence until she is delivered or it is no longer possible that she should be so delivered (Archbold's *Criminal Pleading*, 23rd ed. p. 229).

Dealer. In the Cape Diamond Trade Act (14 of 1885), sec. 35, the words *dealer* and *deal* include "buyer, seller, broker and factor, and any sort of dealing in diamonds."

In the Transvaal Diamond Trade Ordinance (63 of 1903), sec. 43, *dealer* includes "buyer, seller, broker and factor." See *Bebro* v. *Rex* ([1904] T.S. 387).

Dealer in firearms is defined in sec. 23 of Ordinance 2 of 1853 (C.C.), as amended by Act 11 of 1875 (C.C.), as: "Every person being the keeper either individually or as one of some number of copartners in trade of any store, shop or other place where wares and merchandise are exposed for sale who shall have in his possession any guns, pistols or unconnected parts thereof, or percussion caps or lead, other than those used by him for the defence of his person or property or for sporting, shall be deemed and taken, until the contrary be proved, to be a *dealer in firearms* within the meaning of this section."

See Ordinance 13 of 1902 (T.), sec. 17 (2).

Dealer in gunpowder, "any person who sells gunpowder, explosives and explosive substances" (Act 38 of 1887 (C.C.), sec. 3).

Dealer in old metal, in Act 11 of 1907 (N.), sec. 1, is defined as "any person carrying on any business of dealing in, buying or selling old metal, scrap metal, broken metal, or partly manufactured metal goods, or defaced or old metal goods, whether such person deal in any such articles only or together with other goods, but not including founders or manufacturers who buy old metal for use only in their business as such."

Dealer in second-hand goods. The expression *dealer in second-hand goods* is defined in the Cape Second-hand Goods Act (10 of 1895), sec. 25, to mean "every person carrying on the trade, business or occupation of dealing in, buying or selling second-hand goods." *See* SECOND-HAND GOODS.

Death. As to presumption and proof of *death*, see *Re Kirby* (16 S.C. 245; 9 C.T.R. 217); *Re Kannemeyer* (16 S.C. 404; 9 C.T.R. 440); *Re Hoffmeister* (17 S.C. 539; 10 C.T.R. 753); *Re Fernandez* (3 C.T.R. 293); *Re Safodien* (3 C.T.R. 145); *Re Gledhill* (12 N.L.R. 43); *Re Selby* (13 N.L.R. 74); *McCubbin* v. *Knox* (14 N.L.R. 187); *Re Smit* ([1903] T.S. 12); *Re Chaddock* (15 C.T.R. 373 and 597).

As to alteration of the name of a deceased person in the Register of Deaths, see *Re Staehlin* ([1907] T.S. 68).

As to consent to *death* in Cape Native Territories, see Act 24 of 1886 (C.C.), sec. 76.

Death notice, a written statement, required in connection with the administration of the estates of deceased persons, containing certain prescribed particulars concerning a deceased person, such as (*a*) his name and birthplace, also the names of his parents; (*b*) his age; (*c*) his condition in life; (*d*) whether married or unmarried, widower or widow; (*e*) the day of decease; (*f*) at what house or where the person died; (*g*) names of his children, stating whether they are majors or minors; (*h*) whether the deceased has left any property, and of what kind; (*i*) the name of his surviving spouse, if any; (*j*) the name and approximate date of death of any predeceased spouse of the deceased; and (*k*) whether the deceased left a will or not. See secs. 9 and 10 of Ordinance 104 of 1833 (C.C.); sec. 4 of Act 27 of 1895 (C.C.); sch. 3 of Act 38 of 1899 (N.); secs. 5–7 of Proclamation 28 of 1902 (T.); sec. 3 of Ordinance 18 of 1905 (O.R.C); and sec. 4 of Government Notice 65 of 1896 (R.). The requirements of the *death notice* vary slightly in some of the colonies of South Africa. The *death notice* is filed in the office of the Master of the Supreme or High Court (as the case may be), and as it constitutes an important starting-point of the records of the estate of a deceased person, care should be taken to make it as complete as possible. It is the duty of the nearest relative or connection of the deceased, who shall at the time be at or near the place of death, to frame and file the *death notice*, or failing such nearest relative or connection, it becomes the duty of the person who at the time of or immediately after the death had chief charge of the house in, or of the place on, which the death occurred. Failure to perform this duty is punishable by fine or imprisonment, varying in the different colonies.

Death Register. (1) A register kept in the office of the Master of the Supreme Court of the Cape Colony (see sec. 11 of Ordinance 104 of 1833) in which he shall cause to be inserted every death notice transmitted to him in manner provided for in sec. 9 of Ordinance 104 of 1833 (C.C.) *See* DEATH NOTICE.

(2) An official register in which all deaths in the town or district are recorded. As to alteration of the name of a deceased person in the Register of Deaths, see *Re Staehlin* ([1907] T.S. 68).

Debenture. "Taking the test of conventional or commercial usage, a *debenture* may be roughly described as an instrument under the seal of a company providing for the payment of a principal sum at a specified date, and for the payment in the meantime of interest half-yearly, and being one of a series of like debentures charged or secured on the company's undertaking. In ninety-nine cases out of a hundred this description of a *debenture* will be found fairly accurate, but the description cannot be treated as an exhaustive definition, for the term *debenture* is of an extremely elastic character" (Palmer's *Company Precedents*, pt. 2, 9th ed. p. 3; see also the authorities there quoted).

In the Cape Colony, in Act 43 of 1895 (Company Debenture Act), sec. 1, *debenture* is defined to mean "a deed or document acknowledging indebtedness in a certain sum of money, and duly executed in accordance with law and with the provisions of the memorandum and articles of association or trust deed, if any, of the company granting the same."

Debiteur (D.), pl. *debiteuren*, a debtor. *See* DEBTOR.

Debitum in diem, a debt which is due, but is not yet payable. *See* DIES CEDIT.

Debt due. These words, as they appear in sec. 6 of Ordinance 12 of 1904 (T.), which provides for attachment under a garnishee order, must receive their ordinary meaning, so that the garnishee must be under an obligation to pay the judgment debtor, and therefore it is only debts actually due which can form the subject of attachment by garnishee order under the Ordinance (*per* INNES, C.J., in *White* v. *Municipal Council of Potchefstroom*, [1906] T.S. at p. 48).

"It seems to me that for a debt to be due there must be a liquidated money obligation presently claimable by the debtor, for which an action could presently be brought against the garnishee. If such an obligation exists, then, to my mind, a debt is due. And such an obligation need not necessarily arise from contract; it may, I think, be created by statute" (*per* INNES, C.J., in *Whatmore* v. *Murray*, [1908] T.S. at p. 970).

Debt registry, a register kept in the office of the Registrar of Deeds for the purpose of registration of all mortgages and hypothecations capable of registration. The first debt registry in South Africa was established by Proclamation of the 19th June, 1714, which, after reciting that owing to the absence of a proper system of registration "not only many difficult lawsuits are caused, but likewise the good inhabitants or the Company's servants who are inclined to put out their money at a proper interest are kept back, inasmuch as it can never be seen what may be due by any persons by *kustingbrieven* or obligations before Schepenen, Orphan Masters, and writings of mortgage on their immovable property, which, for the welfare of the good inhabitants, ought not to be," proceeds to provide for the production and registration of all existing *kustingbrieven*, obligations before Schepenen, Orphan Masters and other writings of mortgage within a certain time, and for the registration of all such deeds in future under penalty of forfeiture of such preference as would otherwise in that respect be awarded before other creditors. Further proclamations dated 22nd April, 1793, and 15th May, 1805, were issued on the same subject. These have been amended and improved upon from time to time, the result being the admirable system of debt registry which prevails in all the South African colonies. For the purpose of securing preference all mortgages and hypothecations must be registered in the office of the Registrar of Deeds.

Debtor, one who is indebted to another; a person by whom money is due and owing to a creditor. "*Creditor* and *debitor* denote respectively the person entitled to the benefit of an obligation and the person bound thereby. *Causa debendi*, therefore, is equivalent to *causa obligandi*" (Van Leeuwen's *Comm.* Kotzé's trans. vol. 2, p. 8, translator's *note*).

Decide. "To *decide* a matter means to take it into consideration and to settle it" (*per* INNES, C.J., in *Judes* v. *Registrar of Mining Rights, Krugersdorp*, [1907] T.S. at p. 1049).

Decision, a judgment or ruling upon some matter at issue.

As to the "*decision* of a Commissioner," see *Transvaal Chamber of Mines* v. *Tucker and Henderson* ([1904] T.S. at p. 521); *Stark* v. *Transvaal Chamber of Mines* ([1907] T.S. at p. 170).

Declaratory statutes "are where, the old custom of the kingdom being almost fallen into disuse or become disputable, the Parliament has thought proper, *in perpetuum rei testimonium*, and for avoiding all doubts and difficulties, to declare what the common law is and ever hath been" Stephen's *Comm.* 15th ed. vol. 1, p. 39; see also Craies' *Statute Law*, p. 59).

Declinatoire exceptie (D.), declinatory exception; an exception to the person of the judge by way of recusing him. See Van Leeuwen's *Comm.* Kotzé's trans. vol. 2, p. 456.

Decreet (D.), "the judicial order declaring the property executable. A cumbrous procedure was necessary after judgment before the *decreet* could be obtained" (*per* DE VILLIERS, C.J., in *Brink, N.O.*, v. *High Sheriff and Others*, 12 S.C. at p. 419). The term was used in the old Dutch courts, and is now obsolete in South Africa.

Decreta, the name given in the Roman law to judicial sentences pronounced by the Emperor in cases brought before him as supreme judge. The *decreta* formed one of three kinds of imperial constitutions, which came in time to be the only source of law. The other two kinds were: (1) *Epistolae,* answers by letter addressed to individuals or public bodies, *mandata,* orders given to particular officers, and *rescripta,* instructions or answers by letter given by the Emperor to magistrates who had submitted questions to him upon cases which had come before them; (2) *Edicta,* rules or laws published by the Emperor, and binding generally on all his subjects.

Dedication to the public, setting aside something, such as land, for the use of the public. See *London and South African Exploration Co.* v. *Kimberley Town Council* (1 H.C.G. 136); *Fleming* v. *Liesbeck Municipality* (3 S.C. 268); *Stuart* v. *Grant* (24 N.L.R. at p. 428). The dedication of a highway to the public does not deprive the owner of his *dominium* in the soil (*St. Mary, Newington, Vestry* v. *Jacobs*, L.R. 7 Q.B. 47, *per cur.*; 41 L.J. M.C. 72; 25 L.T. 800).

Deduction. *See* "WITHOUT ANY DEDUCTION OR ABATEMENT WHATEVER."

Deed. A *deed,* as it is known in English law, "is a writing (i) on paper, vellum or parchment, (ii) sealed and (iii) delivered, whereby an interest, right or property passes, or an obligation binding on some person is created, or which is in affirmance of some act whereby an interest, right or property has passed" (Norton on *Deeds*, p. 3). There are certain peculiarities connected with a *deed* in English law which are unknown in documents called *deeds* in South Africa. In South Africa the expression *deed* is applied to any formal document irrespective of its contents or the manner in which it is executed.

Deedingen, deedighen, (D.), to dispute, plead, defend.

Deedingslieden (D.), pleaders, disputants.

Deedingsman (D.), an arbitrator.

Deeds Office, the office set apart in each colony, under the control of a Registrar of Deeds, where the Land Register is kept and certain other deeds are registered. *See* DEBT REGISTRY; LAND REGISTER; REGISTRAR OF DEEDS.

Deel (D.), sentence, judgment (*oordeel*).

Deelen (D.), to pronounce judgment, to sentence.

Defaillant or **Defaut** (D.), default, as when a defendant who has been duly summoned to appear before a court does not appear in person or by his attorney.

Defamation was in Roman law a species of *injuria* by which the reputation of a person was affected as a member of society, so that he was not thereafter regarded by his fellow-citizens with the same esteem. This is also the case in the Roman-Dutch law. The essential requisite of *defamation* is an injury to the reputation of a person. A trading corporation does not stand in the same position as a person.

Defamatory libel, in England "consists in the writing and publishing of defamatory words of any living person, or words calculated or intended to provoke him to wrath or to expose him to public hatred, contempt or ridicule, or to damage his reputation, or in the exhibition of a picture or effigy, defamatory of him; and such a libel is an indictable misdemeanour if the publication or exhibition is calculated to cause a breach of the peace" (Archbold's *Criminal Practice*, 23rd ed. p. 1127).

As to *defamatory libel* in Cape Colony, see Act 46 of 1882, sec. 12.

Defaut (D.), [also spelt *default*], default, as when the defendant, duly summoned, does not appear before the court on the appointed day, and so makes default.

Defeating the course of justice is an indictable offence in the Cape Colony. See *Queen* v. *Foye Carlin* (2 App. Cas. 121): *Queen* v. *Kaplan* (10 S.C. 259).

Defective ownership "is where ownership does indeed belong to a person, but somebody else has the use, or something is wanting, so that he cannot do all he desires with the thing" (Van Leeuwen's *Comm.* Kotzé's trans. vol. 1, p. 155).

Defendant. "A defendant or summoned person is he who is cited and resists the plaintiff at law" (Van Leeuwen's *Comm.* Kotzé's trans. vol. 2, p. 367).

Deficiente probante remanet reus ut erat antequam conveniretur, when the proof fails the defendant remains as he was before he was sued. *See* ACTORI INCUMBIT ONUS PROBANDI.

Degree. (1) A certain distance between relations in the line of descent; a step in the line of direct descent from a common ancestor.

(2) In criminal law the term *degree* is used to denote the distinctions of culpability in criminals.

(3) A mark of distinction or honour conferred by universities on students and men of conspicuous learning or distinguished rank.

Degree honoris causa. *See* HONORARY DEGREE.

Del credere, an Italian equivalent for warranty, and applied to an agent who for an extra commission guarantees to his principal the solvency of the persons to whom he sells. "Like any other agent he is to sell according to the instructions of his principal, and to make such contracts as he is authorised to make for his principal" (*per* MELLISH, L.J., in *Ex parte White, Re Nevill*, L.R. 6 Ch. at p. 403). Although he warrants the solvency of the customer, he is not for that reason a party to the contract, and cannot sue in his own name (*Bramwell* v. *Spiller*, 21 L.T. 672). It is now settled that a *del credere* agent is not responsible to his principal in the first instance, but that his liability arises only when the customer is found unable to pay (*Hornby* v. *Lucy*, 6 M. &. S. 166; *Morris* v. *Cleasby*, 4 M. & S. 574, 575).

Delectus personae, choice of person. Those are considered as having *delectus personae* who have placed others in a relationship towards themselves which involves mutual trust and confidence. Thus a person who appoints another as his agent is regarded as having chosen him on account of his personal qualifications for the position. The latter, therefore, in the absence of a power of substitution, cannot appoint a sub-agent so as to divest himself of all liability to his principal, for, unless he has such authority to appoint another in his place, he will be liable for the acts of a sub-agent, except in matters in which it is customary to make such an appointment (*Gertenbach & Bellew* v. *Mosenthal and Others*, Buch. 1876,

p. 88). So in the contract of partnership, as each partner has a *delectus personae* with respect to the others, the heir of a deceased partner is not entitled, as such, to become a partner in place of the deceased (Grotius' *Introd.* 3, 21, 8; Van Leeuwen's *Comm.* 4, 22, 11); nor can any new member be introduced into the firm without the consent of all the partners.

Delegata potestas non potest delegari, a delegated power cannot be delegated. A person to whom powers have been delegated cannot as a general rule delegate these powers to another so as to release himself from liability, unless the power to delegate has been expressly conferred upon him. The reason of this is that in conferring the powers there has been a *delectus personae* or choice of a particular person on account of his character or ability, and this choice would be defeated if the delegate could substitute another person who might be unknown to the principal, or if known might be disapproved of by him. The following cases are enumerated by Story (*Agency,* sec. 14) as those in which the power to substitute may be implied, viz.: "Where it is indispensable by the laws, in order to accomplish the end; or it is the ordinary custom of trade; or it is understood by the parties to be the mode in which the particular business might or would be done. Thus if a person should order his goods to be sold by an agent at public auction, and the sale could only be made by a licensed auctioneer, the authority to substitute him in the agency, so far as the sale is concerned, would be implied. So where by the custom of trade a ship-broker or other agent is usually employed to procure a freight or charter-party for ships, seeking a freight, the master of such ship, who is authorised to let the ship on freight, will incidentally have the authority to employ a broker, or agent for the owner, for this purpose. And the same principle will apply to a factor, where he is, by the usage of trade, authorised to delegate to another the authority to substitute another person to dispose of the property."

Delegation is a transaction by which a creditor accepts one debtor in substitution for another (*Standard Bank* v. *Union Boating Co.*, 7 S.C. at p. 268).

Delict, a wrong; a tort; a violation of a person's rights.

Delinquanten or **Misdadigers** (D.), criminals; wrong-doers; persons who have committed crimes or delicts.

Delivery. (1) The placing another person in legal possession of a thing so that he may deal with it as his own; the ceding or giving to another the power over a thing in such a way that the physical control thereof is united to the legal right of disposing of it. *Delivery,* or something equivalent thereto, is essential to the transfer of ownership from one person to another, and without it any amount of intention will be of no avail. See *National Bank of South Africa, Ltd.*, v. *Beckett's Estate and Colonial Government* (26 N.L.R. at p. 258).

(2) Under the Bills of Exchange Acts *delivery* means transfer of possession, actual or constructive, from one person to another (sec. 2 of English Bills of Exchange Act, 1882; Act 19 of 1893 (C.C.), sec. 1; Law 8 of 1887 (N.), sec. 1; Proclamation 11 of 1902 (T.), sec. 1; Ordinance 28 of 1902 (O.R.C.), sec. 1.

Demarcated forest. "*Demarcated forest* shall include such area as has been surveyed or demarcated and declared by notice in the *Gazette* to be a *demarcated forest*, and shall include all pieces or portions of Crown land set aside as being forest, or the complement of a forest, or plantation, or intended for the site of a plantation, or for afforesting operations" (Cape Forest Act, 28 of 1888, sec. 2).

Dementia, a form of insanity; the condition of a person in whose mind ideas have been more or less formed, but have subsequently become entirely obliterated. See *Natal Land Colonisation Co.* v. *Molyneux* (24 N.L.R. at p. 286).

Demurrer, an English legal term. "After the plaintiff has delivered his statement of claim, it is the defendant's turn to consider in what manner it shall be encountered; and he is to address himself to this subject in the following manner. If the statement of claim appears on the face of it substantially insufficient, in point of law, to entitle the plaintiff to what he claims—in other words, if it does not show any cause of action—the defendant used to *demur*, that is, used to deliver a written formula, called a *demurrer* (from *demorari*), importing that he denied such sufficiency on some ground therein stated. But *demurrers* (*eo nomine*) have been abolished; and it is now provided that, in lieu of demurring, the defendant may raise in his defence the question of the sufficiency in law of the pleading. If, on the other hand, the statement of claim appears *ex facie* to show a good cause of action, then the defendant's course is to deliver his defence, the general object of which is to make answer, in point of fact, to the statement of claim" (Stephen's *Comm.* 14th ed. vol. 3, p. 575). In South African practice an "exception" takes the place of the old form of *demurrer*.

Denombrent (D.), a feudal term, denoting a command of the lord to render him on pain of forfeiture an account of all his feudal property with proper particulars.

Dentist. In the Cape Colony under the Medical and Pharmacy Act (34 of 1891), "*dentist* means every person duly licensed and *bonâ fide* engaged on or before the 1st June, 1891, in the practice of dentistry or dental surgery in this [Cape] Colony, either separately or in addition to his practice as a physician, surgeon, accoucheur, apothecary, or chemist and druggist, and also every person duly qualified by license and registration under this Act to practise as a *dentist* in this colony." The Natal definition (Act 30 of 1896, sec. 3) is almost identical with that of the Cape. See Ordinance 29 of 1904 (T.), sec. 3; Ordinance 1 of 1904 (O.R.C.), sec. 1.

Dependant, one who relies upon another for maintenance.

In the Cape Workman's Compensation Act *dependants* means "such members of the workman's family specified in the first schedule to this Act, as were wholly or in part dependent upon the workman at the time of the injury which caused his death." The persons so specified are: husband, wife, father, mother, grandfather, grandmother, stepfather, stepmother, son, daughter, grandson, granddaughter, stepson, stepdaughter, brother, sister.

In the Workmen's Compensation Act (T.), 36 of 1907, sec. 1, the word *dependants* is defined as meaning "such members of the workman's family specified in the schedule to this Act as are wholly or in part dependent upon the workman at the time of the injury which caused his death." The persons so specified, in the order of preference in which they are entitled to compensation, are as follows: (1) a husband or wife and any son or daughter (legitimate or illegitimate) or stepson or stepdaughter of the deceased workman; failing whom (2) a father, mother, stepfather, stepmother of the deceased workman; failing whom (3) a brother, sister, half-brother, half-sister of the deceased workman and any children of such persons; failing whom (4) a grandfather, grandmother, grandson, granddaughter of the deceased workman (whether the grandson or granddaughter be of legitimate or illegitimate birth); failing whom (5) any other relative of the deceased workman by consanguinity or affinity.

Deposit. (1) A contract whereby a person gives some movable property to be taken care of gratuitously, and to be reclaimed at his pleasure (Grotius' *Introd.* 3, 7, 2).

(2) A sum of money paid or entrusted by one person to another on account, or in part fulfilment, of some undertaking or agreement made, or about to be made, between them.

(3) The payment of a sum of money into a bank or corporation, or into the hands of some person, either with a stipulation that it is to bear interest or otherwise.

As to a *deposit* with a building society being in the nature of a *mutuum*, see *Langford* v. *Moore and Others* (17 S.C. at p. 18). Such a *deposit* is a borrowing (*ibid.* at p. 20).

Deposit accounts. In the Cape Audit Act (14 of 1906), sec. 3 (*j*), *deposit accounts* is defined to mean "the accounts relating to funds of which the Treasurer is, by statutory obligation or otherwise, a trustee and custodian, and such accounts as those of the Guardian's Fund, the Harbour Boards, the South African Widows' Fund as are not included in the Consolidated Revenue or General Loans Accounts."

Depositary. (1) The person to whom some movable property is given or entrusted to be taken care of gratuitously, and in such manner that it may be reclaimed by the depositor at pleasure. "The duty of the *depositary* is twofold. He must keep the thing delivered into his custody with reasonable care, and he must upon request restore it according to the original trust" (*per* De Villiers, C.J., in *Standard Bank* v. *Union Boating Co.*, 7 S.C. at p. 269).

"I am not prepared to say that under no circumstances can a *depositary* without the consent of the depositor sell goods deposited with him for safe keeping, but I am clearly of opinion that if he does so sell them, the burthen lies on him of proving that he acted in the interest and for the benefit of the depositor. It is a primary duty of a *depositary* to return the thing deposited when it is required of him, and if he is unable to do so he cannot escape liability without proving that his inability does not arise out of his own negligence. If it is lost or injured through his negligence, he is responsible to the extent of the loss or injury. It is no valid defence to the depositor's claim for the return of the goods that the *depositary* has sold them, unless it is clear that the sale was, under the circumstances, necessary and for the benefit of the depositor" (*per* DE VILLIERS, C.J., in *Medallie & Schiff* v. *Roux*, 20 S.C. at p. 440; see also *Kerr* v. *Banti*, 18 E.D.C. 277).

Parties may vary the liability which the common law imposes upon a *depositary;* see *Central South African Railways* v. *McLaren*, ([1903] T.S. at p. 733).

As to *depositary* for Private Bill Documents required to be deposited in accordance with the Standing Rules and Orders of either House of Parliament, see sec. 1 of Act 3 of 1906 (C.C.); sec. 1 of Act 6 of 1907 (T.); and sec. 1 of Act 41 of 1908 (O.R.C.).

(2) A bank, corporation or person who receives money as a deposit, either with a stipulation that it shall bear interest or otherwise.

Depositing site. In the Mining of Precious Stones Ordinance (4 of 1904 (O.R.C.)), sec. 5, *depositing site* means "a piece of land used for depositing and working of ground bearing precious stones, and for the accumulation of washed ground."

Deposition, either written evidence, or oral evidence reduced to writing, such evidence being given upon oath or affirmation before a magistrate, justice of the peace or other proper official. As to the admissibility in criminal cases of *depositions* taken at a preparatory examination of a witness since deceased, or who has been kept away from the trial by the means and contrivance of the prisoner, see sec. 41 of Ordinance 72 of 1830 (C.C.); or is too ill to travel, see sec. 5 of Act 17 of 1874 (C.C.). See also Law 16 of 1861 (N.), sec. 2 (whereby prisoners are entitled to inspect *depositions*) and Ordinance 1 of 1903 (T.), sec. 67.

Depositor. (1) The person who gives some movable property to another to take care of gratuitously, and to be reclaimed at the *depositor's* pleasure (Grotius' *Introd.* 3, 7, 2–8). As to *depositor* of Private Bill Documents required to be deposited in accordance with the Standing Rules and Orders of either House of Parliament, see sec. 1 of Act 3 of 1906 (C.C.); sec. 1 of Act 6 of 1907 (T.); and sec. 1 of Act 41 of 1908 (O.R.C.).

(2) A person who deposits or entrusts money with a bank, corporation or other person either with a stipulation that it shall bear interest or otherwise.

Derdeling (D.), a blood-relation in the third degree.

Derelict, anything forsaken and abandoned. The expression is usually applied to an abandoned vessel. Land that has been abandoned is spoken of as *derelict* land.

Descendants, the offspring of an ancestor in any degree; persons related to one another in the descending line from a common ancestor; opposed to "ascendants." See *Nieuwoudt* v. *Registrar of Deeds* (14 S.C. 244; 7 C.T.R. 238), where the term *descendant* was extended to the husband (married in community of property) of a *descendant* of the testator.

"**Deserting.**" "A seaman would not be guilty of *deserting*, who was driven by the cruelty of his officers to leave his ship" (Maxwell's *Interpretation of Statutes*, 4th ed. p. 145).

Design. The term *design* is defined in, and for the purpose of, the Cape Registration of Designs Act (28 of 1894), to mean "any design applicable to any article of manufacture or to any substance, artificial or natural, or partly artificial and partly natural, whether the design is applicable for the pattern or for the shape or configuration or for the ornamentation thereof, or for any two or more of such purposes, and by whatever means it is applicable, whether by printing, painting, embroidering, weaving, sewing, modelling, casting, embossing, engraving, pressing or stamping, staining, or any other means whatever, manual, mechanical or chemical, separate or combined, not being a design for sculpture."

Destitute child. The expression *destitute child* is defined in the Cape Destitute Children's Relief Act (24 of 1895) to mean "any child of European parentage who comes within any of the following descriptions, that is to say: (*a*) who is found habitually begging or being in any public place for the purpose of begging; (*b*) who is found wandering and not having any home or settled place of abode, or proper guardianship, or visible means of subsistence; (*c*) who is found in a state of destitution without any means of support, and who shall be without father, mother or lawful guardian, or whose father, mother or lawful guardian shall be unable to provide for its support and education; (*d*) who shall reside in any reputed brothel, or, being a female child, who shall reside with any known or reputed prostitute, whether such prostitute shall be the parent of the child or not; and (*e*) who shall associate or dwell with any person, not being the parent of the child, known or reputed to be a thief or drunkard, or with any such person convicted of vagrancy."

See also Act 10 of 1896 (N.); and for full definition, see Act 38 of 1901 (N.), sec. 3, also Ordinance 44 of 1903 (T.).

Destitution, a state of poverty; indigence; being without means of subsistence. "For the prevention of *destitution*, and to make provision for the relief of wives and families deserted and left destitute," which was extended to all native territories in Cape Colony by Proclamation 34 of 1897; see Act 7 of 1895 (C.C.). See also Act 10 of 1896 (N.); Ordinance 44 of 1903 (T.); and Ordinance 51 of 1903 (O.R.C.), for similar legislation.

Reciprocal regulations are in force in each colony for the recognition and enforcement of the orders made by the courts of any of the other colonies. The regulations in Cape Colony are to be found in Proclamations 27 of 1899, 377 of 1903, and 46 of 1904, which establish reciprocity with Natal, Transvaal and Orange River Colony respectively; in the Transvaal, in Proclamations 78 of 1903 (Natal), 82 of 1903 (Cape Colony) and 12 of 1904 (Orange River Colony); in Orange River Colony, in Proclamations 5 of 1904 (Cape Colony), 6 of 1904 (Transvaal) and 14 of 1904 (Natal).

Deurwaarder (D.), an usher. In the Netherlands a *deurwaarder* was the servant of a court of justice, and derived his name from the opening and keeping of the doors of the council chamber in which the president of the council and the court assembled (Kersteman's *Woordenboek*, vol. 2, p. 98). See Van Leeuwen's *Comm.* 5, 5.

Development. "As ordinarily used in mining matters *development* denotes that stage of work on mineralised ground which intervenes between prospecting and mining proper. First the ground is prospected in order to ascertain whether there are minerals in paying quantities. Then it is developed in order to test whether the minerals which have been found are such as to warrant the working of the property as a mining proposition. When that has been established the property is actually worked and the minerals are extracted. But the evidence given with regard to the nature of the tin deposits in Solomon's Temple satisfies me that in regard to that property we ought to give the word 'develop' a wider meaning than the one which it would ordinarily bear. And I think we shall be justified in taking 'to develop' as meaning 'to thoroughly prospect'" (*per* INNES, C.J., in *Douglas* v. *Baynes*, [1907] T.S. at p. 513).

In Ordinance 30 of 1907 (O.R.C.) *development* is defined to mean "such incline ways, shafts, drives, strippings and other work necessary for the opening up of a mine." See also Ordinance 3 of 1904 (O.R.C.), sec. 5, which defines *developed* as "opened up and prepared for the stoping of ore."

Diagram. In the Transvaal Precious and Base Metals Act (35 of 1908), sec. 3, *diagram* is defined as "a *diagram* prepared by a person lawfully admitted to practise as a land-surveyor and approved by the Surveyor-General without publication." The same definition is given by the Transvaal Registration of Deeds and Titles Act (25 of 1909), sec. 2. A diagram of a farm or piece of land is a picture or representation of the area of such land. It does not *per se* confer any title to the land (*Cumming* v. *Brown*, [1909] E.D.C. at p. 63). *See*

"BUYER TO PAY ALL EXPENSES IN CONNECTION WITH THE COMPLETING OF TRANSFER," also CONFIRMED DIAGRAM.

Diamondiferous, containing diamonds. See *London and South African Exploration Co.* v. *De Beers Consolidated Mines* (10 S.C. 231).

Dief (pl. *dieven*) (D.), a thief.

Diefstal (D.), theft. In Latin *furtum*. *See* THEFT.

Dienstbaarheid (D.), servitude; vassalage. *See* SERVITUDE.

Dienstbode (D.), a servant; a domestic.

Dienstman (D.), a slave, a bondman.

Dienstmanschap (D.), slavery, service, bondage.

Dies cedit, et dies venit. These words are defined by Ulpian (*Dig.* 50, 16, 1, 213) as follows: "*Cedere diem* means that the money has commenced to be due; *venire diem* means that the day has arrived upon which the money may be demanded." Voet (*Comm.* 36. 2, 1), distinguishing the case of contracts from that of legacies, explains the application of the maxim as follows: "In the case of contracts . . . where any one contracts unconditionally the obligation becomes at once due and exigible (*statim cedat ac veniat dies obligationis*); where he makes a contract for a future day (*i.e.* to take effect upon a future day), the obligation indeed becomes forthwith due (*dies cedit*), but cannot be exacted (*sed non veniat*), save upon the arrival of the day; where he contracts subject to a condition the obligation becomes neither due nor exigible (*neque cedat neque veniat dies*) while the condition is unfulfilled, but nevertheless an expectation (*spes*) of an obligation arises which is transmitted to heirs if the contracting party dies before the fulfilment of the condition. But in the case of legacies and *fideicommissa* the maxim is not applied wholly in the same way (as above); for if a legacy is left unconditionally it certainly vests (*dies cedit*) immediately from the death of the testator, . . . even before adiation of the inheritance, so that the legatee in surviving the testator transmits his legacy to heirs, but it becomes payable (*dies venit*) (only) when the inheritance is adiated, since before adiation there is no one who can be sued or of whom demand can be made. And it is of no consequence whether an heir who is burdened with an unconditional legacy is instituted unconditionally or subject to a condition, and owing to the legacy delays in adiating, as in either case the legatee is secure; nor, whether that which is bequeathed is due to the testator unconditionally or subject to a condition provided that which he has bequeathed is (in fact) due to him. On the other hand, if anything is bequeathed unconditionally, but is of such a nature that it perishes with the death of the legatee, the legacy vests (*dies cedit*) only from the adiation of the inheritance; since the effect of vesting (*cessionem*), namely, the transmission of the legacy to heirs, can have no place here; as is the case where freedom (of slaves) and personal servitudes are bequeathed by will. But a legacy of services vests only from the time when they are demanded. On the other hand, if the legatee dies during the testator's lifetime he transmits to his heirs no expectation at all of a legacy which has been unconditionally made."

Dies dominicus non est juridicus, Sunday is not a day for judicial or legal proceedings, "for that day ought to be consecrated to divine service." Parliament may in cases of necessity sit on Sunday, but the court cannot. Voet admits that in cases of necessity judicial acts can be done on a Sunday. In *R.* v. *Herman and Another* (1 A.C. 317) DE VILLIERS, C.J., said: "For my own part I am clearly of opinion that a sentence cannot, by our law, be set aside by reason of its having been passed on a Sunday; but even if it be essential to the validity of such a sentence that the necessity for its being passed on a Sunday should be proved, I am satisfied from the evidence that such necessity existed in the present case" (where the verdict of a jury in a criminal case was received at 2·30 A.M. on a Sunday).

Dies incertus pro conditione habetur, an uncertain day is regarded as a condition. Where an obligation is made payable on a day which it is quite uncertain will arrive or not, for example, on a person's marriage, it is regarded as a conditional obligation which will come into effect only when the condition is fulfilled.

Dies interpellat pro homine, the day makes demand on behalf of the man. The lapse or arrival of a certain day stands in the place of a proper demand, and places the debtor *in mora* (default). Interest runs from the day of default where this maxim applies, even if there is no promise to pay interest. In other cases interest runs only from the date of the letter of demand (*Snook* v. *Howard*, 8 E.D.C. 55).

Dieverij or **Diefstal** (D.), theft. *See* THEFT.

Digging, in the Transvaal Gold Law (15 of 1898, sec. 3) means "the intentional extraction of the precious metals mentioned in art. 2 [of the Law], including all work necessary for the purpose, irrespective of whether such extraction is effected by underground mining works, open cuttings, boring or otherwise." The above law is now repealed by the Precious and Base Metals Act, 35 of 1908 (T.), which in sec. 3 defines *dig* as "intentionally to win precious metals or base metals (as the case may be) from the earth," and as including "all excavating necessary for the purpose, whether by underground working, open cutting, boring or otherwise." *See* PUBLIC DIGGINGS. In the Precious Stones Ordinance, 66 of 1903 (T.), sec. 2, *digging* or "mining" means "the winning of precious stones, including all work necessary for the purpose, irrespective of whether such mining is effected by underground mining works, open cuttings or otherwise." A similar definition is found in Ordinance 4 of 1904 (O.R.C.), sec. 5, with the addition of the word "boring" after the word "cutting."

Dilatoire exceptie (D.), a dilatory exception in Dutch practice. (See Van Leeuwen's *Comm.* 5, 14.)

Diligentia, diligence; care. There are three degrees of diligence, viz., *levissima diligentia, diligentia,* and *exactissima diligentia.* They correspond respectively to the three degrees of negligence, *culpa lata, culpa levis,* and *culpa levissima.* Which of these three degrees of diligence a person is bound to show depends upon the nature of the contract under which the obligation for diligence arises. *See* CULPA.

Dipping tank. An expression used in the Scab Acts. In the Cape Scab Act (20 of 1894), sec. 4, *dipping tank* is defined to mean "a tank or dipping receptacle, portable or otherwise, constructed or provided to the satisfaction of the inspector."

Director, one who superintends or controls, such as the *director* of customs; a *director* of a company.

See the Transvaal Excise Act (9 of 1907), sec. 1.

Disabilities Removal Act, 1868. An Act passed in the Cape Colony in the year 1868 (11 of 1868) to annul all laws, if any, in the colony whereby any religious community or order or person was deprived of any rights or privileges in law, or whereby any penalties or disabilities were imposed upon such communities, orders or persons by reason only of their religious belief or profession. See also Act 6 of 1869 (C.C.), and Proclamation 80 of 1890 (C.C.).

Disannexation, the act of separating after having been annexed. The expression is to be found in Act 34 of 1883 (C.C.), which provided for the disannexation of Basutoland from the Cape Colony.

Discharge of insolvent. (1) The effect of a discharge of an insolvent person under sec. 106 of Ordinance 6 of 1843 (C.C.) is as follows: "(*a*) the insolvent, though freed from all debts proved, remains liable for his offer of composition; (*b*) the insolvent is reinvested with his estate, and is liable only for debts to the extent of his offer of composition" (Van Zyl's *Judicial Practice*, 2nd ed. p. 682).

(2) *See* REHABILITATION.

Discontinuous servitude "is one to the exercise or enjoyment of which some act on the part of man is necessary, *e.g. jus itineris, aquaeductus*," &c. (Van Leeuwen's *Comm.* Kotzé's trans. vol. 1, translator's *note* on p. 306).

Discoverer. (1) In mining laws the term *discoverer* signifies the person who first makes a discovery of minerals or precious stones upon a property, and thereby secures certain statutory rights.

In the Cape Precious Minerals Act (31 of 1898), sec. 3, the word *discoverer* is defined to mean "a duly licensed prospector who has discovered precious minerals, and has made the declaration referred to in this Act that he has found them in payable quantities;" in the Mineral Law Amendment Act, 16 of 1907 (C.C.), sec. 33, *discoverer* means "a duly licensed prospector who has discovered base minerals, and has made the declaration referred to in the 42nd section of this Act that he has found them in 'workable' quantities." In the Cape Precious Stones Act (11 of 1899), sec. 3, it is defined to mean "the prospector who has found precious stones while prospecting under a license issued under the provisions of this Act or any existing law dealing with Precious Stones and Minerals."

In the Transvaal Precious Stones Ordinance (66 of 1903), sec. 2, *discoverer* means "a duly licensed prospector who has discovered precious stones on Crown lands." The Precious and Base Metals Act (35 of 1908 (T.)), sec. 3, defines *discoverer* as "a person who holds a certificate under sec. 19," *i.e.* the certificate granted to a prospector who, having notified his discovery of precious metals to the Mining Commissioner of the district, and having received a notice from the Commissioner entitling him to peg, has complied with the terms of such notice.

For the Orange River Colony, see Ordinance 4 of 1904, sec. 5, also secs. 37 and 38.

See DISCOVERER'S RIGHTS.

Discoverer's claims, the claims to which a discoverer is entitled under the statutes relating to prospecting and mining for precious or base minerals or metals, or for precious stones. *See* DISCOVERER. As to *discoverer's claims* in Cape Colony, see Act 31 of 1898, secs. 3 *et seq.*; and Act 11 of 1899, secs. 3 *et seq.*

For those in the Transvaal, see Act 35 of 1908, sec. 19; Ordinance 66 of 1903, sec. 41.

For those in the Orange River Colony, see Ordinance 3 of 1904, secs. 37 and 38; Ordinance 4 of 1904, sec. 65.

Discoverer's rights, the statutory rights to which a discoverer is entitled on making a discovery and on compliance with the statutory requirements. *See* DISCOVERER. See also the Precious Minerals Act, 31 of 1898 (C.C.), secs. 12 *et seq.*, and 78 *et seq.*; the Precious and Base Metals Act, 35 of 1908 (T.), sec. 19; and the Precious Stones Ordinance, 66 of 1903 (T.), sec. 9.

In the Orange River Colony, see Ordinance 3 of 1904, secs. 37 and 38; Ordinance 4 of 1904, sec. 65.

Discretae, that form of alluvion which was known in Roman-Dutch law as *aanwas*. *See* AANWAS.

Discretion, personal judgment. "Where a *discretion* is conferred upon a public body to decide whether or not a certain thing shall be done, it appears to me that that is a condition inconsistent with the existence of an absolute duty to do that thing in all events" (*per* INNES, C.J., in *Thorpe* v. *Municipal Council of Pretoria*, [1905] T.S. at p. 789).

See *Nathan Bros.* v. *Pietermaritzburg Corporation* (23 N.L.R. at p. 128).

Dishonest, lacking honesty; having a disposition to deceive; having an element of fraud. See *Brown* v. *Rex* ([1908] T.S. at p. 212).

Disposable, that can be disposed of or sold, or used. The expression *disposable* is found in sec. 4 of Ordinance 6 of 1843 (C.C.), where the circumstances constituting insolvency are set forth. The paragraph of the section is as follows: "or having against him the sentence of any competent court being thereunto required shall not satisfy the same or shall not point out to the officer charged with the execution thereof sufficient *disposable* property to satisfy the same, if it shall appear from the return made by such officer or his affidavit that he has not found sufficient *disposable* property of such person to satisfy such sentence," &c. In *Van der Poel* v. *Langerman* (3 Menz. 307) the court held that where a creditor, who prays for the sequestration of an estate, holds a judgment on a first mortgage bond, the immovable property so mortgaged is not only *disposable* for the satisfaction of the judgment, but it can be disposed of by the plaintiff for that purpose by attachment and judicial sale as easily and in as short a time as under a sequestration of the defendant's estate. In the same connection the word *disposable* appears in sub-sec. (*h*) of sec. 4 of Law 47 of 1887 (N.), and in sub-sec. (*b*) of sec. 8 of Law 13 of 1895 (T.). See also *In re Webster* (3 Menz. 220).

"**Dispose of,**" to part with; to pass over the control of a thing to some one else. See *Queen* v. *Gontshe* (6 E.D.C. 280); *Reid and Stewart* v. *Rex* ([1904] T.S. at p. 267); *Platnauer* v. *Rex* ([1904] T.S. 979); *Rex* v. *Swartbooi* ([1906] E.D.C. 86).

Dissolution of partnership. "Partnerships become dissolved in one or other of the following ways: (1) By the death of one of the partners; (2) by the insolvency of the partnership or of one of its members; (3) by lapse or effluxion of time, if originally entered into for a limited period; (4) by completion of the partnership undertaking; (5) by mutual agreement; (6) by change in the membership of the firm; (7) by renunciation by one of the partners; (8) by decree of the court" (Maasdorp's *Institutes*, 3, 3, 28).

Dissolution of partnership is thus described in sec. 32 of the Partnership Act, 1890 (England): "Subject to any agreement between the partners, a partnership is dissolved (*a*) if entered into for a fixed term, by the expiration of that term; (*b*) if entered into for a single adventure or undertaking, by the termination of that adventure or undertaking; (*c*) if entered into for an undefined time, by any partner giving notice to the other or others of his intention to dissolve the partnership. In the last-mentioned case the partnership is dissolved as from the date mentioned in the notice as the date of dissolution, or if no date is so mentioned, as from the date of the communication of the notice." Under sec. 35 of the same Act the court may upon the application of a partner decree a dissolution of the partnership in certain other cases. At present there is no Partnership Act in any of the South African colonies.

Distance. *See* MEASUREMENT.

Distiller, one who extracts spirits by separating the volatile matters by means of heat from the substances in which they are contained, and then recondensing them into liquid form. A *distiller* is defined in the Cape Excise Spirits Act (18 of 1884), sec. 2, to mean and include "any person who conducts, works or carries on any distillery, or who distils or manufactures any spirits, by any process whatsoever, either by himself, or his agent or servant."

In the Additional Taxation Act, 36 of 1904 (C.C.), sec. 2, the following definition is given: "Any person not being an agricultural *distiller*, who conducts, works or carries on any distillery, or who distils or manufactures any spirits by any process whatsoever, either by himself or his agent or servant."

As to Natal, see Law 14 of 1868; Act 25 of 1905.

Distillery. "A *distillery*" is defined in the Cape Excise Spirits Act (18 of 1884), sec. 2, to mean and include "any place or premises where any process of distillation whatever of spirits is carried on, or where any process of rectification of spirits by redistillation or other process is carried on, or where any spirits are manufactured or produced from any substance whatever by any process whatever." A similar definition is given in the Additional Taxation Act, 36 of 1904 (C.C.), sec. 2.

As to Natal, see Law 14 of 1868 and several amending Laws and Acts.

Distinctive mark. An expression used in the Transvaal Great Stock Brands Ordinance (15 of 1904), sec. 1, where it means "a lawful mark (other than a registered brand) which a native is empowered by this Ordinance to mark upon the dewlap or head of any stock already bearing the brand of the location, native family or stad in which such native resides, to denote his ownership thereof."

Distress, an English term signifying the taking of the goods of another to satisfy some claim; usually a seizure of movables of a tenant by his landlord for payment of rent. This expression is found in the Crown Lands Ordinance of the Cape Colony, Ordinance 9 of 1844, secs. 4 and 5.

Distributive justice. In describing the two kinds of justice, commutative and distributive, Voet (*Elementa juris*, lib. 1, tit. 1) says: "That is called distributive which deals with the rewards and punishments to be awarded according to the merits [or demerits] of each individual. In this that proportion which is called geometrical is generally observed, or it has respect to persons; so that according to the difference in their condition, dignity, age, sex, &c., different rewards and punishments are adjudged for each kind of deed." See Van Leeuwen's *Comm.* Kotzé's trans. vol. 1, p. 38, *in notis;* Grotius' *Introd.* 1, 1, 10.

Distributor of stamps, a public official entrusted by Government, under statutory authority, with the custody of revenue stamps and their sale, issue and distribution.

District. In the Transvaal Interpretation of Laws Proclamation (15 of 1902), sec. 2, *district* means "the area subject to the jurisdiction of the court of any resident magistrate." See Ordinance 32 of 1902 (T.), sec. 3; Ordinance 40 of 1902 (T.), sec. 2; Ordinance 45 of 1902 (T.), sec. 1; Ordinance 43 of 1903 (T.), sec. 3.

District headman, a term employed in the Natal Code of Native Law (Law 19 of 1891, sch., sec. 10) to denote "any person nominated and appointed by a chief to preside over a district under such chief, and duly notified to the Administrator of Native Law as a *district headman*."

District road, in Ordinance 17 of 1905 (O.R.C.), sec. 1, means "a public trunk road or highway as aforesaid [*i.e.* as described in same Ordinance under 'main road'], and which has been proclaimed a *district road* in terms of this Ordinance."

Diverse akten (D.), (1) miscellaneous deeds; (2) the name applied to a certain register in the Deeds Office at Pretoria, prior to the Anglo-Boer war of 1899, in which miscellaneous notarial deeds were registered; the deeds so registered were not specially registered against the titles of the landed property to which they might refer; such registration could not be regarded as notice to the world in the same way as would be the case with registration in the land register. *See* LAND REGISTER.

Divestitive fact, a fact through which a right terminates. "A *divestitive fact* puts an end to a right altogether; so the right of a tenant terminates with the expiration of his lease, and the right of a creditor is at an end when his debt has been paid" (Holland's *Jurisprudence*, 10th ed. p. 152).

Divini juris, used in Roman law to denote things which were devoted to religious or quasi-religious purposes. Such things, together with *res communes,* belonged to that class of *res nullius* which could never become the subject of private property. *Res divini juris* were of three kinds, viz., *res sacrae, res religiosae* and *res sanctae.* The first kind consisted of things, such as churches, which had been consecrated to the service of God by a pontiff with the authority of the people, afterwards of the Senate, and finally of the Emperor. In the case of movables a sale was permitted for the purpose of supporting the poor in a time of famine and afterwards for the purpose of paying the debts of the church, but the inalienability of *res sacrae* was never relaxed in the case of immovables. The second kind, *res religiosae,* consisted of places devoted to the burial of the dead. *Res sanctae* were things which, without being sacred, were protected by heavy penalties against injury, such as the walls and gates of a city.

Things of this kind have long ceased to be *res nullius* (Van Leeuwen's *Comm.* 2, 1, 9). They may now be possessed in full ownership by individuals or communities who may, subject to any restrictions imposed by law, sell and encumber them like any other kind of property belonging to them (*Capetown and Districts Waterworks Co., Ltd.*, v. *Elder's Executors*, 8 S.C. 9).

Divisional area. This term is defined in the Cape School Board Act (35 of 1905), sec. 3, to mean "the area comprised within the limits of any duly constituted divisional council."

Divisional council, a council or assembly duly elected and constituted according to law in a division of a South African colony for the purpose of administering the affairs of such division, and more, especially the making, maintenance and supervision of the public roads and bridges therein. See Act 40 of 1889 (C.C.).

Dock. (1) The place in a court of justice where the prisoner is placed whilst undergoing preliminary examination or trial.

(2) A portion of a harbour, more or less enclosed, where a ship may float alongside a wharf or pier whilst being loaded or unloaded. In the Cape Harbour Boards Act (36 of 1896), sec. 82, it is provided that "the words *dock* or *docks* in this or any other Act relating to any harbour shall be taken to mean the docks, rivers, basins and other works or areas connected therewith, which the Governor has heretofore proclaimed or shall from time to time proclaim to be a dock or docks for the purposes of this Act."

Document. In the Native Territories' Penal Code (Act 24 of 1886 (C.C.)), sec. 219, a *document* is defined as being "any substance on which is expressed and described by means of letters, figures or marks, any matter which is intended to be or may be used in a court of justice, or otherwise, as evidence of such matter." See also Stephen's *Digest of the Law of Evidence*, under heading *Document*.

As to deposit of Private Bill *documents* required to be deposited in accordance with the Standing Rules and Orders of either House of Parliament, see Act 3 of 1906 (C.C.), sec. 1; Act 6 of 1907 (T.), sec. 1; Act 41 of 1908 (O.R.C.), sec. 1.

Doeme (D.), sentence, judgment.

Doemer (D.), a judge, one who pronounces judgment.

Dolus, fraud. The term *dolus* is only applied to fraud in civil cases, and especially in matters of contract.

The Roman lawyers held that gross neglect (*culpa lata*) was equivalent to *dolus*. A depositary is responsible only for gross neglect (*culpa lata*), but the term *dolus* in this connection must be understood in the mitigated sense of breach of good faith, or gross breach of duty, operating as a constructive fraud. *See* FRAUD.

Dolus bonus, as distinguished from *dolus malus*, is defined as *dolus* which is either wholly approved of by law, as where shrewdness (*solertia*) is employed against an enemy or robber, or is not so approved of, but is unpunished and permitted; of this latter nature being an advantage which one party takes of the other with regard to the price in a contract of purchase and sale (Voet's *Comm.* 4, 3, 1). In other words, although a vendor may not make a false statement upon which the purchaser is bound to rely, and by means of which he is induced to enter into the contract (*dolus dans locum contractui*), yet one party may praise or the other dispraise the goods with a view to obtaining a higher or paying a less price (see Van Leeuwen's *Comm.* Kotzé's trans. 4, 1, 5, translator's *note*).

Dolus cum dolo compensandus est, fraud is to be set off against fraud. An action for restitution ordinarily lies at the suit of a person who has been injured by the fraud of another, but if he himself has been guilty of fraud in connection with the transaction he will not be entitled to any action (Voet's *Comm.* 4, 3, 8).

Dolus dans causam (or locum) contractui, fraud giving rise to a contract. "Fraud is said to give rise to a contract where one is induced to contract who had no intention to do so for the reason that he would not have contracted if the fraud had been absent" (Voet's *Comm.* 4, 3, 3). In other words, it is such fraud that without it the contract would not have been made. The free consent of the parties being essential to a contract, its absence by reason of such fraud makes the contract *ipso jure* null and void. Thus, if a person is induced by fraud of this kind to enter into a contract of sale, and in pursuance thereof transfers or delivers the thing, the ownership will not pass to the other party, but will remain with the party defrauded, who may by a real action recover the thing not only from him who committed the fraud, but also from any possessor of the same, whether *bonâ fide* or *malâ fide* (Voet's *Comm.* (*ibid.*); *Vlotman* v. *Landsberg*, 7 S.C. 301; *Standard Bank* v. *Du Plooy and Another*, 16 S.C. 161).

Dolus incidens, fraud incidental, that is, which does not go to the essentials of the contract. "Fraud is considered to be merely incidental to a contract where any one voluntarily contracts, but is deceived in a term of the contract, as, for example, in the price or any other term" (Voet's *Comm.* 4, 3, 3). A contract affected by fraud of this nature is not *ipso jure* null, but the party defrauded will, upon proof of the fraud, be entitled to *restitutio in integrum* (Voet's *Comm.* 4, 3, 4).

Dolus latet in generalibus, fraud lurks in generalities.

Dolus malus, one of the Roman law divisions of fraud, and known in Roman-Dutch law as *arglist* (deceit). It is an artifice or deceit employed for the purpose of cheating or circumventing some person. See Kersteman's *Woordenboek*, vol. 2, p. 377; Nathan's *Common Law*, sec. 777.

Domicile "must not be confounded with mere residence. It is residence, but it is something more, its essential characteristics being residence combined or connected with an intention of permanently remaining at the place of residence (*animus remanendi*); in other words, a man's domicile is the place or country in which he lives and which he regards as his permanent home. This permanent home is either the domicile which he receives at birth, and which is spoken of as his *domicile of origin*, or one which is acquired by him afterwards by his own act, and which is known as his *domicile of choice*" (Maasdorp's *Institutes*, vol. 1, p. 4). Matrimonial *domicile* is the *domicile* of the husband at the time of his marriage, and such *domicile* on marriage also becomes the *domicile* of the wife. See *Ex parte Standring* ([1906] E.D.C. 169).

As to definition of *domicile* in Natal Immigration Acts, see Act 3 of 1906, sec. 1.

Domicilium citandi et executandi, domicile for the purpose of serving summons and levying execution. A domicile is often chosen by a defendant to facilitate service of process. Domicile in this connection is synonymous with address. Thus an accused who enters into a recognisance gives a certain address where the indictment may be served.

Dominant tenement, the land that benefits by a servitude, or that has the right of servitude over other land, called the servient tenement.

Dominium, ownership, "is the right by which each person's thing belongs to himself exclusively, whether he is in possession of it or not, for there may be a bare ownership without possession, and a mere possession without ownership. Ownership is therefore divided into full (*dominium plenum*) and defective (*dominium minus plenum*)" (Van Leeuwen's *Comm.* Kotzé's trans. vol. 1, p. 154). Decker, in a *note* to the first portion of this definition, says, "or rather the right by means of which a person has power over a corporeal thing, with the ability of immediately claiming the same wherever he may find it" (*ibid.*). According to Grotius (*Introd.* 2, 3, 1) *dominium* is "that attribute of a thing whereby a person, though not actually in possession of it, may acquire the same by legal process."

"Ownership or property is the right to use or deal with some given subject in a manner or to an extent which, though it is not unlimited, is indefinite" (Austin on *Jurisprudence*, Table II, 5th ed. p. 933).

Dominium directum, the name given to the right of the feudal superior in feudal law. "It is so called because at one time it was considered the direct and paramount right in the lands, the vassal's right being regarded as merely a burden upon it. This is a view not now entertained" (Trayner's *Latin Maxims and Phrases*, 4th ed. p. 169). In the Roman-Dutch law the name is applied to the right of the owner (*dominus directus*) in *emphyteusis* or quitrent tenure, as distinguished from that of the *emphyteuta*, which is termed the *dominium utile*. These terms, *dominium directum* and *dominium utile*, invented by feudal lawyers, were unknown to the Roman law (see Berwick's *Translation of Voet*, p. 53 and note, and p. 346 and note).

Dominium eminens (sometimes written *imperium eminens*), the power possessed by the sovereign as head of the State to compel particular individuals in case of public necessity or utility to part with their property subject to the right to compensation; "or in case of need to give it up without payment. But this cannot last longer than the necessity, for then compensation may justly be claimed" (Decker's *note* to Van Leeuwen's *Comm.* 2, 2, 1). This is the right exercised in statutes which authorise the expropriation of lands for public purposes, such as railways. See Decker (*ibid.*); Grotius' *Introd.* 2, 3, 2; Schorer, *Note* 65; *Jooste* v. *The Government* (4 Off. Rep. 147).

Dominium minus plenum, incomplete ownership. *See* DOMINIUM PLENUM.

Dominium plenum, full ownership. Ownership is of two kinds. The owner may be entitled to use the thing (*jus utendi*), to enjoy its fruits (*jus fruendi*), to consume it entirely where it is capable of consumption (*jus abutendi*), and to alienate or dispose of it as he pleases (*jus disponendi*). On the other hand, the ownership may be wanting in any of those rights owing to a real burden forming part of the property by way of servitude (real or personal) or *fidei-commissum* or mortgage. In the former case, where all the rights of ownership are present, the *dominium* is said to be *plenum*; in the latter case, *minus plenum* (Van Leeuwen's *Comm.* 2, 2, 1; Maasdorp's *Institutes*, vol. 2, p. 141).

Dominium rerum a naturali possessione coepit, ownership of things begins from (the time when one acquires) natural possession. This maxim is used in connection with the mode of acquiring ownership of property by *occupatio*. Things which are capable of being appropriated, but have never been acquired by any one, or things which, having once belonged to some one, have been abandoned by their owner, may be acquired by the first occupier, whose dominion begins from the moment when he takes possession with the intention of becoming owner.

Dominium utile, useful, indirect or equitable ownership; the term applied to the right of the *emphyteuta* in *emphyteusis* or quitrent tenure. *See* DOMINIUM DIRECTUM.

Dominus fluminum, owner of the streams. The Government remains *dominus fluminis*, and has the sole power from time to time to regulate the use of the water between all the parties through whose lands the stream naturally flows (*De Wet* v. *Cloete*, 1 Menz. 410).

Donatie (D.), donation. *See* DONATIO.

Donatio. Donation or gift is defined by Grotius in his *Introduction* (3, 2, 1) as a promise whereby a person, without being bound to another, out of liberality binds himself to give that other something belonging to himself without receiving anything from him in return or stipulating for anything for his own benefit.

Donations may be divided into two principal classes, viz., (*a*) donations *mortis causa* (donations made in contemplation of death); and (*b*) donations *inter vivos* (donations made otherwise than *mortis causa*).

Donations require acceptance, and if the donor revokes the promise, or dies, before such acceptance by the donee, the obligation does not take effect (See *Van Renen's Trustee* v. *Versfeld*, 9 S.C. 161: *Slubber's Trustee* v. *Neezer's Executor*, 12 S.C. at p. 167). Upon acceptance, however, before revocation the donation is complete and the donor is bound to make delivery.

Donations above the value of £500 must be registered (*Thorpe's Executors* v. *Thorpe's Tutor*, 4 S.C. 488).

In Roman-Dutch law when once a donation has been made it is irrevocable, except if the donor, who was childless at the time of the donation, begets children, or if the donee attempts the life of the donor, or strikes him, or attempts to ruin his estate, or maliciously slanders him. When the donation is so excessive that the children are thereby prejudiced in their legitimate portion, the whole gift is not annulled, but only the *pars inofficiosa*. Legitimate portions, however, have now been abolished throughout South Africa.

A minor cannot make a donation of his property.

A donation between husband and wife is of no force or effect unless or until the donor dies without having revoked the donation. If the donor becomes insolvent his or her creditors are fully entitled to the property forming the subject of the gift (*Union Bank* v. *Spence*, 4 S.C. 339).

A parent may donate to his child (*Elliott's Trustees* v. *Elliott and Another*, 3 Menz. 86: *Thorpe's Executors* v. *Thorpe's Tutor*, 4 S.C. 488; *De Kock* v. *Van de Waal's Executors*, 16 S.C. 463; *Slubber's Trustee* v. *Neezer's Executor*, 12 S.C. 163).

See DONATIO MORTIS CAUSA; DONATIO PROPTER NUPTIAS; DONATIO REMUNERATORIA.

Donatio mortis causa, a gift made in contemplation of death. There are three modes in which such a gift may be effected: (1) The donor gives something in mere general contemplation of death, but without any fear of an early death or imminent danger, and with the understanding that it is not to become the property of the donee until the donor's death; (2) when the gift is made in imminent peril of death, but with the understanding that the property shall only pass upon the donor's death; (3) under circumstances similar to those of the last case, but with the understanding that the ownership in the property shall pass immediately, though if the donor survives the peril the property shall be returned to him.

A gift *mortis causa* requires acceptance (*Clarke* v. *Executors of Castray and Beale*, 19 S.C. 498). A *donatio mortis causa* must be executed with the same formalities as a last will (Van der Keessel, *Thes.* 492, and *Clarke* v. *Executors of Castray and Beale*, 19 S.C. 498). It can only vest in the donee absolutely upon the donor's death. In *Oliphant* v. *Grootboom* (3 E.D.C. 11) the requisites to every *donatio mortis causa* were discussed: (1) It must be revocable; (2) it must be conditional on the death of the donor; (3) in the deed of donation some mention must be made of the death of the donor; (4) possession must be given to the donee. It is sufficiently clear, however, that the Roman-Dutch law does not insist upon possession being given. The authorities cited by counsel in support of this proposition were drawn from English reports.

By Act 5 of 1864 (C.C.) succession duty is payable on donations *mortis causa*.

Donatio non presumitur, donation is not presumed. "In case of doubt donation is not presumed as long as another construction is possible, and therefore he who alleges a donation, although it be by way of exception, must prove it, because no one is supposed readily to throw away his property, giving being really nothing but throwing away and squandering" (Voet's *Comm.* 39, 5, 5). The intention to make a donation must therefore be clear and manifest from the acts and language of the donor, and cannot be inferred from an indefinite expression of a desire to make a gift (*Brink's Trustees* v. *Mechau and Others*, 1 Roscoe, 209; *Van Renen's Trustee* v. *Versfeld*, 9 S.C. 161). It is not, however, necessary that the gift should be made in express terms, as the intention may be inferred from the conduct of the donor. Voet (*Comm.* 39, 5, 5) gives the following examples of implied donation, viz., if a person knowingly pays what is not due—donation being presumed and a claim for refund of the money being barred; if a person, having entered upon the land of another, gathers the fruits and lays out expenditure in cultivation; if a *malâ fide* possessor of another's land incurs useful expenditure upon it; if a *bonâ fide* possessor voluntarily restores the property to its owner without deducting the expenditure laid out upon it; if a man agrees with his son that the latter shall, for the purpose of assessment, report as his own property that which belongs to his father, or if the father himself reports the property in his son's name, unless he establishes by clear proofs that this was done without the intention of making a donation; and the various cases in which an action *negotiorum gestorum* is refused to the administrator, the expenditure incurred by him in such cases being presumed to have been made by way of gift. See also *Elliott's Trustee* v. *Elliott and Another*, 3 Menz. 91; *Pillans* v. *Porter's Executors*, 5 S.C. 420; Grotius, *Introd.* 3, 2, 12.

A donation, moreover, is strictly interpreted, and in such a way as to burden the donor least.

Donatio perficitur possessione accipientis, donation is completed by the possession of the donee. Although acceptance of a donation gives the donee a right of action against the donor for specific performance of the agreement to give (*Barratt* v. *Executors of O'Neil*, Kotzé, at p. 109), yet until the thing donated has been transferred or delivered to the donee the ownership or *jus in re* does not pass to him, but remains with the donor (*see* PACTUM DONATIONIS). Mere possession of the thing, however, is no presumption of a donation, and if the donor denies *animus donandi*, the onus of proof will be upon the person claiming to be donee.

Donatio propter nuptias, a gift made in contemplation of marriage; such gift must be returned to the donor in case the marriage does not take place. *See* DONATIO.

Donatio remuneratoria is a donation by way of reward. Such a donation is enforceable (*Melck* v. *David and Others*, 3 Menz. 468), requires no registration (*Slabber's Trustee* v. *Neezer's Executor*, 12 S.C. 168), and cannot be revoked on account of ingratitude (Grotius, 3, 2, 3; Voet's *Comm.* 39, 5, 15). *See* DONATIO.

Donee, one to whom a gift or donation is given or made.

Donor, one who gives something to another person gratuitously.

Donum matutinum or **Morgengave,** morning-gift. A gift wont to be given by the bridegroom to his bride on the day after the marriage as the reward of chastity. Van der Keessel (*Thes.* 258) says that, although from its nature the gift ought to accrue to the wife immediately, it is "according to our customs acquired only after the marriage has been dissolved and the creditors discharged."

Doodslag (D.), homicide. Van der Linden (*Institutes*, 2, 5, 5) says there are three kinds of homicide, (*a*) *opzettelijke doodslag*, wilful homicide; (*b*) *onvoorzigtige doodslag*, homicide by negligence; and (*c*) *toevalligen doodslag*, accidental homicide. *See* HOMICIDE.

Doodstraff (D.), capital punishment. The *doodstraffen* that were in use in Holland in Van der Linden's time (*Institutes*, 2, 2, 2) were (*a*) breaking on the wheel with or without decapitation; (*b*) the gallows; (*c*) the sword; and (*d*) strangling, with or without scorching. He tells us that at that period (beginning of nineteenth century) quartering, burning and drowning had fallen into disuse.

Dop brandy. "*Dop brandy* means the unrectified distillate resulting from the distillation solely of grape husks and water; the volatile constituents of which distillate (except water, as provided for in sec. 15 [of the Act]) are derived entirely from the above-named materials; provided that the alcoholic strength of such *dop brandy* be not lower than 25 degrees under proof" (the Wine, Brandy, Whisky and Spirits Act, 42 of 1906 (C.C.), sec. 14).

Dos, dowry.

Dos adventitia. This was the name given in the Roman law to a dowry contributed by any one else than a paternal ascendant of the wife, *e.g.* by the wife herself or by some third person for her. It could not be reclaimed by the donor or his heirs unless a special agreement to that effect had been made at the time when the dowry was constituted, in which case it was called *dos recepticia*. In the absence of such an agreement the dowry remained with the husband until Justinian enacted that in such a case it should go to the heirs of the wife. *See* DOS PROFECTITIA.

Dos profectitia, under Roman law, the dowry given by the father or other ascendant of the wife. Upon the wife's death the dowry could be reclaimed by the donor, but not by his heirs.

The division of dowries into *dotes adventitiae* and *dotes profectitiae* has no significance in the Roman-Dutch law, for in the absence of a special dotal agreement all property owned by the wife forms part of the statutory community of goods, and if anything in the nature of the *dos* of the Roman law is given by some third party, or by the wife herself, it will devolve at the dissolution of the marriage not according to the technicalities of the Roman law, but in terms of the dotal agreement under which it was given.

Douarie (D.). *See* DUARIE.

Double costs. Sec. 82 of Ordinance 6 of 1843 (C.C.)—the Insolvency Ordinance—provides that in certain events if a debtor does not pay the amount due by him to the trustee of the insolvent estate, the court may award the trustee *double costs.* In *Biccard's Trustee* v. *Visagie* (12 S.C. 413) it was held that *double costs* were allowed by way of penalty against such debtors, but only if they do not show cause to the satisfaction of the court for their neglect or refusal; and that due notice should be given to a debtor before the penalty is sought to be enforced.

Drain, a pipe or conduit for the purpose of conveying away surplus water or other fluids. See Act 32 of 1893 (C.C.), sec. 1; *see* also COMBINED DRAIN.

In the Cape Public Health Amendment Act (23 of 1897), the term *drain* is defined to mean "any *drain* of, and used for the drainage of one building only, or of premises within the same curtilage or enclosure, and made merely for the purpose of communicating therefrom with a sewer, cesspool or receptacle for drainage, into which the drainage of two or more such buildings or premises occupied by different persons is conveyed." For further statutory definitions see Act 25 of 1897 (C.C.), sec. 1.

Drankwet (D.), liquor law.

Drawer. Under the Bills of Exchange Acts, a *drawer* is a person who draws a bill (*see* BILL OF EXCHANGE). The drawer of a bill, by drawing it (*a*) engages that on due presentment it shall be accepted and paid according to its tenor, and that if it be dishonoured he will compensate the holder or any indorser who is compelled to pay it, provided that the requisite proceedings on dishonour be duly taken; and (*b*) is precluded from denying to a holder in due course the existence of the payee and his then capacity to indorse. See Act 19 of 1893 (C.C.), sec. 53; Law 8 of 1887 (N.), sec. 54; Proclamation 11 of 1902 (T.), sec. 53; Ordinance 28 of 1902 (O.R.C.), sec. 53.

Dredging claim, see sec. 17 of the Mineral Law Amendment Act, 16 of 1907 (C.C.).

Dredging lease, a lease to which a prospector becomes entitled under sec. 20 of the Mineral Law Amendment Act, 16 of 1907 (C.C.).

Dreef (D.), a drift-way, the right to drive cattle over the land of another.

Drench. A term used in the Natal Lung-sickness Prevention Act (30 of 1897), sec. 3, where it means "the internal administration of virus taken from the lung or chest of the animal infected with lung-sickness."

Droit, a French term, which expresses "not only 'a right,' but also 'law' in the abstract" (Holland's *Jurisprudence*, 10th ed. p. 80). This term is to be found in the Natal Escheat Law (11 of 1868), where "*droits* of the Crown" and "*droits* of the admiralty" are spoken of.

Dronkenschap (D.), drunkenness; intoxication. See Van der Linden's *Institutes*, 2, 1, 5.

Drop (D.), the right of letting one's rainwater drop on to the land of another.

Droppelspeet (D.), a spout or gutter used for leading off one's rainwater on to another's land.

Dropright, is a servitude whereby the owner of a house has a right to allow the rainwater from his roof to drop on to the land of another person (see Van Leeuwen's *Comm.* Kotzé's trans. vol. 1, p. 289, where this form of servitude is fully discussed).

Dropvang (D.), the right to catch up the rainwater of one's neighbour.

Drug. The term *drug* is defined in the Cape Sale of Food and Drugs and Seeds Act (5 of 1890) to include "medicine for internal or external use." See also Ordinance 32 of 1906 (O.R.C.), sec. 1.

Druggist, a person who deals in drugs. *See* CHEMIST.

Drunkenness. "Voluntary *drunkenness* is not regarded as a disease affecting the mind within the meaning of Article 28 [art. 28 refers to the exception of insanity]; but involuntary drunkenness and diseases caused by voluntary *drunkenness* fall, so far as they affect the mind, within that article" (Stephen's *Digest of the Criminal Law*, 5th ed. art. 30).

The Native Territories' Penal Code (Act 24 of 1886 (C.C.), sec. 27) provides that "nothing is an offence which is done by a person who, at the time of doing it, is by reason of intoxication incapable of knowing the nature of the act, or that he is doing either what is wrong or contrary to law: provided that the thing which intoxicated him was administered to him without his knowledge or against his will."

"Our law does not allow an accused to set up *drunkenness* as an excuse for a crime (Matthaeus, *de Criminibus*, p. 33). It draws a distinction between the man who becomes drunk on isolated occasions, led on by others, or by excessive indulgence at a feast or by ignorance of the strength of the liquor he has been drinking, and the man who deliberately becomes drunk. The former is called *ebrius*, the latter *ebriosus*. Both are liable for their acts if *drunkenness* was caused by voluntary drinking; but the punishment of the *ebrius* is less than that of the *ebriosus* (Matthaeus, *ibid.*). Moorman (*Misdaden*, p. 21) admits that this rule is subject to exceptions, and does not think that a person who through drinking has lost not only his reason, but his will power, should be classed with those whose *drunkenness* is not so complete. . . It is perfectly clear from a series of English decisions that *drunkenness* cannot as a rule be set up as an excuse for a crime, but it may sometimes absolve an accused from a particular crime which requires in addition to the ordinary *mens rea* some special intent. Thus if a person kills another without lawful cause he is certainly guilty of homicide. If, however, he was actuated by murderous malice he is not only guilty of homicide, but of murder as well. [Here the learned judge gave several illustrations, and continued.] This, I take it, is a fair statement of our general law upon the subject. In order, however, that *drunkenness* should have this effect, the circumstances of the particular case must show that the accused had taken drink, and that the effect of the drink upon him was such as to render him unconscious of the nature of the act he was doing. It is no sufficient excuse for the accused to say that he does not remember the act, or that he did not appreciate the moral import of his act. Whether the drink rendered an accused incapable of knowing what he was doing depends on many circumstances, such as the amount of drink taken, the effect of drink upon him, and no doubt in some cases the nature of the act committed. These facts must be submitted to the court by the accused, and from these facts the court, and not expert witnesses, must determine whether his *drunkenness* was such as to free him from the special intention which the Crown may be required to prove" (*per* WESSELS, J., in *Fowlie* v. *Rex*, [1906] T.S. at pp. 507 *et seq.*). "It is an extremely dangerous doctrine to excuse a drunken man for a criminal act, and if such excuse is to be allowed there must be clear proof not only of *drunkenness*, but of such *drunkenness* that the court must infer that there was lack of consciousness. An important element is the quantity of drink consumed by the prisoner" (*ibid.* at p. 510).

Dry wine. "*Dry wine* means wine produced by complete fermentation of the sugar contained in the juice or must of the fresh grapes from which it is made" (the Wine, Brandy, Whisky and Spirits Act, 42 of 1906 (C.C.), sec. 5).

Duarie or **Douarie** (D.) is a gift promised in an antenuptial contract by a man to the woman he is about to marry, as a provision against widowhood. It is validated by subsequent marriage, and is irrevocable. It does not constitute a preference upon the husband's estate. Van der Linden (*Institutes*, 1, 3, 4) describes it as a condition in an antenuptial contract to the effect that the survivor shall be benefited by way of gift or donation with a certain sum out of the estate of the deceased. Schorer (*Note* 130) discusses at some length the debatable point as to whether the legitimate portion was preferred to *douarie;* and he points out that *douarie* is entirely different from *dos*, with which some jurists confuse it. See also Van der Keessel, *Thes.* 259. Where mutual promises have been made in an antenuptial contract by each spouse to leave to the other by way of gift or donation a certain sum payable on the death of the first-dying, and one of them succeeds in obtaining a decree of judicial separation, the injured spouse, who elects to have his or her promise rescinded, can only obtain the order subject to a renunciation of the promise made in his or her favour (*Wessels* v. *Wessels*, 12 S.C. 468).

Dubii juris, of doubtful law; an unsettled point.

Dum se bene gesserit, so long as he conducts himself properly; during good behaviour. *See* "AD VITAM AUT CULPAM."

Dummodo constet de persona, provided it be clear who is the person meant. A legacy is valid although an error occurs in the name or description of the legatee, if from other circumstances it is sufficiently plain who is the person meant. But the legacy will be void "if the person is altogether mistaken, as where the testator has mentioned some one who is unknown altogether or in part" (Van Leeuwen's *Comm.* 3, 9, 5). So with regard to the thing bequeathed, the legacy will be valid notwithstanding that there is an error in the name or description of the thing, provided it is evident what was intended by the testator (Van Leeuwen, *ibid.*).

Duplicatio, or **Duplique** or **Duplicq.** Under the Dutch system of pleading the defendant was bound, after the plaintiff had filed his replication, to insist upon his defence by way of *duplique*, which corresponds to our "rejoinder" (*Meyer's Executors* v. *Gericke*, Foord, 17).

Duplicq (D). *See* Duplicatio.

Duplique. *See* Duplicatio.

Duress, actual compulsion or a threat of compulsion. "It is said that there must be some threatening of life or member, or of imprisonment, or some imprisonment or beating itself" (Pollock on *Contracts*, 7th ed. p. 596). As to *duress* in connection with salvage operations, see *Blackburn* v. *Mitchell* (14 S.C. 338).

Dwelling, a place of residence. The term *dwelling* is defined in the Cape Public Health Amendment Act (23 of 1897) to mean and include "any house, building or premises, *huur kamer* (hire room), hut, tent, caravan, vessel or boat, or other place, the whole or any part of which is used as a sleeping place, or habitually occupied by one or more persons."

In the Transvaal Crimes Ordinance (26 of 1904), sec. 3, *dwelling* means "a building or structure or any part thereof which is for the time being kept by the owner or occupier thereof for the residence therein of himself, his family or servants, or any of them, and whether or not such building or structure be from time to time uninhabited."

Dying declaration. "Upon an indictment for murder or manslaughter, the dying declarations of the deceased are receivable in evidence if it appears to the satisfaction of the judge that the deceased was conscious of his being in a dying state at the time he made them and was sensible of his awful situation, even though he did not actually *express* any apprehension of danger, and his death did not ensue until a considerable time after the declarations were made" (Archbold's *Criminal Practice*, 23rd ed. p. 321). See also Taylor on *Evidence*, secs. 714 *et seq.*; *Reg.* v. *Glosten* (16 Cox C.C. 471); and *Rex* v. *Elizabeth Perry* (25 T.L.R. 676).

"In order that a dying declaration may be admitted as evidence, the rule is that three things must have concurred: the person must have been in danger of impending death; he must have realised the extent of his danger so as to have given up all hope of life; and death must have ensued" (*per* Innes, C.J., in *Rex* v. *Abdul and Others*, [1905] T.S. at p. 122). See *Queen* v. *Le Roux* (14 S.C. 424).

Dykgericht (D.), a court established in Holland in about the fourteenth century. It was presided over by a *dykgraaf* or *dikereeve*, and "dealt with matters affecting the boundaries of farms and their protection from floods" (Wessels' *History*, p. 152).

Dykgraven (D.), pl. of *Dykgraf*, *dikereeves*, inspectors or judges of dikes (Van Leeuwen's *Comm.* Kotzé's trans. vol. 1, p. 62). *See* also Graaf.

Earnest money. "The practice of giving something to signify the conclusion of the contract, sometimes a sum of money, sometimes a ring or other object, to be repaid or redelivered on the completion of the contract, appears to be one of great antiquity and very general prevalence. It may not be unimportant to observe as evidence of this antiquity that our own word *earnest* has been supposed to flow from a Phœnician source through the ἀῤῥαβών of the Greeks, the *arra* or *arrha* of the Latins, and the *arrhes* of the French. It was familiar to the law of Rome, and without going into the distinctions of that law on the subject (see Vinnius on the *Institutes*, 3, 24; Pothier, *Contrat de Vente*, 6, 1, 3), it will be enough to observe that the general rule appears to have been that expressed in the *Institutes* (Vinnius, 3, 24, pr.): *Is qui recusat adimplere contractum siquidem est emptor, perdit quod dedit: si vero venditor; duplum restituere compellitur, licet super arrhis nihil expressum sit.* Furthermore, the *earnest* did not lose that character because the same thing might also avail as part payment. *Datur autem arrha vel simpliciter*, says Vinnius (3, 24, 8), *ut sit argumentum duntaxat et probatio emptionis contractae, veluti si annulus detur: vel ut simul postea cedat in partem pretii, data certa pecunia.* From the Roman law the principles relating to the *earnest* appear to have passed to the early jurisprudence of England. *Item cum arrarum nomine*, says Bracton (lib. ii, c. 27), *aliquid datum fuerit ante traditionem, si emptorem emptionis poenituerit et a contractu resilire voluerit perdat quod dedit: si autem venditorem, quod arrarum nomine receperit emptori restituat duplicatum.* Though the liability of the vendor to return to the purchaser twice the amount of the deposit has long since departed from our law, the passage in question seems an authority for the proposition that the *earnest* is lost by the party who fails to perform the contract. That *earnest* and part payment are two distinct things is apparent from the 17th section of the Statute of Frauds, which deals with them as separate acts, each of which is sufficient to give validity to a parol contract" (*per* FRY, L.J., in *Howe* v. *Smith*, 27 Ch. D. at pp. 101 *et seq.*). "In the Roman law the *arrhae* were either signs of a bargain having been struck, as, for instance, when the buyer deposited his ring with the seller (*Digest*, 19, 1, 11, 6), or consisted of an advance of portion of the purchase-money. They were also intended as a proof that the purchase had been made. Justinian gave these deposits a new character by making them the measures of a forfeit in case either party wished to recede from his bargain, it being open to either party to retract if he chose to incur this forfeit" (Sandars' *Institutes*, p. 363).

In Roman-Dutch law there was the same idea of *earnest* distinct from the purchase-price (see Grotius' *Introd.* 3, 14, 32; Van Leeuwen's *Roman-Dutch Law*, 4, 20, 2; Voet, 18, 3, 2). Grotius calls it *hand-gifte*, which suggests the *handsschlag*, or old custom of giving the hand as sign of the conclusion of a bargain (Holland's *Jurisprudence*, p. 205). The references of Grotius, Van Leeuwen and Voet to *earnest* or *arrha*, are in connection with sales under the *Lex Commissoria*, *i.e.* sales subject to the condition that the thing (movable or immovable) should be unbought, if the purchase-price was not paid. In case of non-payment the buyer forfeits the *earnest*; but according to Voet he does not forfeit any instalment of the purchase-price that may have been paid. When *earnest* is paid on immovables it is called in Dutch *rouwkoop*" (Morice's *English and Roman-Dutch Law*, 2nd ed. p. 130).

If *earnest money* is paid as such by a purchaser to a seller, without any further stipulation, the seller is entitled to retain it (*Brest and Ladon* v. *Heydenrych*, 13 S.C. at p. 21).

Ebriosus, a person who deliberately becomes drunk. *See* DRUNKENNESS.

Ebrius, a person who becomes drunk on an isolated occasion, led on by others, or by excessive indulgence at a feast or by ignorance of the strength of the liquor he has been drinking. *See* DRUNKENNESS.

Echte (D.), anciently meant law, but its modern meaning is marriage.

Echteren (D.), to slander.

Edelen (D.), the nobles in the Netherlands. In rank they came next to the overlord. "Their authority and prestige dated back to the early German period" (Wessels' *History*, p. 68).

Edicta, edicts, or general laws promulgated under the civil law by the emperor for the decision of cases which might arise. *See* DECRETA.

Eed (D.), an oath. *See* OATH. See also Van Leeuwen's *Comm.* 5, 22, 6; and Kersteman's *Woordenboek*, vol. 1, p. 115.

Eedelen (D.), nobles. Originally they were all the inhabitants of a country who possessed non-tributary lands as their own, and who filled or held some public office, and were accordingly obliged to take up arms in defence of their country. The term *eedelen* (nobles) was subsequently extended to all persons descended from them, although they neither possessed any land of their own nor filled any office. At a still later stage the term was further applied to those who were raised to the rank of nobility by the emperor, king or overlord (Meyer's *Woordenschat*).

Eeman (D.), a married man.

Eescheidt (D.), divorce.

Eestand (D.), the married state.

Eestui (D.), marriage penning.

Eewijf (D.), a married woman.

Eigendom (D.), property; equivalent to *dominium*.

Eisch (D.), formerly spelt *eysch*, a claim; the plaintiff's declaration. In Holland the declaration was called *conclusie van eisch;* in the Court of Holland it was made by means of a writ, and in the lower courts by a statement of the case followed by a conclusion or claim (see Van der Linden's *Institutes*, 3, 1, 2, 11; also Kersteman's *Woordenboek*, vol. 1, p. 133).

Eischer (D.), formerly spelt *eysscher*, a plaintiff in an action. *See* also AANLEGGER.

Ejus est interpretari cujus est condere, it belongs to him to interpret whose province it is to enact. This was a maxim used of the emperor in the later period of the Roman Empire. Where the words of a law were of doubtful meaning the judges were not allowed to construe or interpret them, but had to submit the point to the emperor for explanation. The maxim has no place in English or Scotch law or the Roman-Dutch law. When a statute has once been passed it admits of no explanation by the legislature, which is only concerned with the enactment of laws; the construction or interpretation of any ambiguities is the prerogative of the courts. "The province of the legislature is not to construe, but enact; and their opinion, not expressed in the form of law, as a declaratory provision would be, is not binding upon courts, whose duty it is to expound the statutes they have enacted" (*per* PARKE, B., in *Russell* v. *Ledsam*, 14 L.J. Exch. 358). Thus, where an interdict had been obtained under sec. 60 of the Gold Law (T.), to which the court in granting the interdict had attached a certain construction, and the legislature thereafter attached a different construction to the section by a resolution the effect of which was to deprive the person who had obtained the interdict of his rights under it, it was held that the resolution of the legislature was invalid, and that the proper course would have been for the legislature to modify the terms of the law to accord with its views, while accepting the court's decision (*Williams* v. *Geldenhuis Estate and G. M. Co., and Leyds, N.O.*, 11 C.L.J. 128; H. 237). *See* TESTING RIGHT.

Elder brethren, the Masters of Trinity House, a corporation in London, England, who have the control and management of lighthouses, buoys, &c., in England; and the licensing of pilots; they also have rights of supervision in Scotland and Ireland.

Election, the act of choosing or selecting. *See* GENERAL CAMPAIGN LITERATURE.

Election petition, a petition duly presented to a superior court having jurisdiction complaining of an undue return or undue election of a member to serve in either House of Parliament by reason of want of qualification, disqualification, corrupt practices, irregularity or otherwise (see Act 9 of 1883 (C.C.), sec. 3; Act 26 of 1902 (C.C.)). Also, in Cape Colony an *election petition* may complain that a member of the Legislative Council who has been elected has ceased to possess the qualification by law required (see Act 9 of 1883 (C.C.), sec. 3).

For *election petition* in Transvaal, see Ordinance 38 of 1903, sec. 102.

Elector, a person qualified, and registered within a certain area, to vote for a candidate at a public election; a person enjoying the franchise; a voter. *See* VOTER.

Ell, the old measure of an *ell* was abolished in the Orange Free State by Law 25 of 1898, sec. 15.

Ellendighen (D.), to banish. The word is derived from *ellendt* or *ellandt, i.e. el,* another, and *landt,* a country. Hence *ellendighen* signifies to send to another country, to banish (Meyer's *Woordenschat*).

Emancipation, one of the means by which children, whose parents are alive, become of age. *Emancipation* "takes place either judicially or tacitly, for instance, when a child is permitted to live and carry on business by himself. When children are released from the paternal power by one or other of these means [*i.e.* either marriage or *emancipation*], they acquire the right to administer their own property, and to appear for themselves in court" (Grotius' *Introd.* 1, 6, 4); see *Bosch* v. *Titley* ([1908] O.R.C. 27). As to *emancipation* among natives under the code of native law in Natal, see Law 19 of 1891, sec. 92; see also *Deyi* v. *Mbwzikazi and Another* (18 N.L.R. 227).

Embarrassed circumstances. "*Embarrassed circumstances* do not necessarily include and involve insolvency, and the consideration of the principles must be fixed upon the state of such circumstances immediately at the time of the payment" (*per* WILDE, C.J., in *Salom's Trustee* v. *Croll,* 1 Searle, at p. 15).

Empanel. *See* IMPANEL A JURY.

Emphyteusis, a form of tenure in Roman law, so called because of its being, as it were, a new or equitable ownership implanted or engrafted (ἐν φυτεύω) on the *dominium.* It was the alienable and heritable real right over the land of another on condition of cultivating and improving such land, subject to the payment of a fixed or yearly rent, variously called *canon, pensio, vectigal* or *reditus.* The owner of the land or grantor was called *dominus directus* or *emphyteuseos,* the person to whom the grant was made *emphyteuta,* and the subject of the grant *emphyteusis* or *ager emphyteuticarius.* At first only land formed the subject of an *emphyteusis,* but Justinian extended this form of tenure also to buildings (*Nov.* 7, 3, 1, 2). The *emphyteuta* possessed the right of the full and free enjoyment of the land or *praedium* and its fruits. He could dispose of the thing and alter it, provided he did not deteriorate it. He could transfer his right to another and dispose of it by will. He could mortgage the land and create servitudes over it. In these respects he differed from a usufructuary. On the other hand, the *emphyteuta* had to pay all the taxes imposed on the *praedium*, and had to cultivate, maintain and improve it. On a transfer of the right the *dominus directus* was entitled to be paid a fee or fine on alienation for his acceptance of the new *emphyteuta*. This fine consisted of a fiftieth part of the purchase money or of the value of the thing (*quinquagesima pars pretii vel aestimationis*, also called *laudemium*). In the absence of special agreement this fine had to be paid by the *new emphyteuta*. The *dominus* could, however, refuse his consent to the alienation.

Emphyteusis became extinguished in various ways: *e.g.* by effluxion of time, where the grantor had only a temporary ownership in the thing, or where the time, for which the thing was granted to the *emphyteuta*, had expired; by surrender of his right by the *emphyteuta;* by merger; by the death of the *emphyteuta* without heirs; by forfeiture, which might occur through waste on the part of the *emphyteuta* or through the non-payment of the rent for two years in the case of an ecclesiastical, and of three years in the case of a secular, *emphyteusis*. The owner or *dominus directus* could not, however, expel the *emphyteuta* on his own authority, but had to seek judicial intervention for the purpose.

Regard being had to the nature of *emphyteusis* and the rights of the *emphyteuta*, the ancient jurists were much puzzled as to the true classification of this contract. Some considered it as a contract of letting and hiring, others as a sale. The Emperor Zeno decided that it was to be regarded as a contract *sui generis,* and was to be regulated entirely by the pacts and agreements between the parties. In the absence of any agreement as to the risks which the thing might be subject to, Zeno decided that a total loss should fall on the *dominus* and a partial loss on the *emphyteuta*. This view was approved by Justinian (*Inst.* 3, 24, 3). The tenure of the *emphyteuta*, regard being had to its character and extent, was sometimes spoken of as *dominium bonitarium* or *dominium utile*. See further on the subject of *emphyteusis* Voet's *Comm.* 6, 3; Smith's *Dict. of Gr. and Roman Antiquities, sub voce;* Mackeldey's *Systema Juris* (*Lehrbuch*), secs. 295 *et seq.*

Emphyteusis also exists in Roman-Dutch law under the name of *erfpachtrecht* and its modern equivalent of *perpetual quitrent*. *Erfpachtrecht* is defined by Grotius (*Introd.* 2, 40, 2) as "the heritable usufruct of another's immovable property subject to an annual rent." The *emphyteuta* or *erfpachter*, unlike in the Roman law, could, in the absence of any agreement or special custom to the contrary, cede and transfer his right without the consent of the *dominus* or grantor, who would, however, have a *jus retractus* (*naasting*) within a year after becoming aware of the alienation (Grotius' *Introd.* 2, 40, 7).

The rights and duties of the *emphyteuta*, except where otherwise regulated by special agreement or local custom, are generally speaking the same as those of the *emphyteuta* in Roman law. There is, however, this important difference, that the Roman-Dutch law leaned more strongly against a forfeiture in case of non-payment of the rent for three years. Thus KOTZÉ, J., observed: "There can be no doubt that the equitable spirit of the canon law influenced Dutch jurisprudence, so far as the contract of *emphyteusis* or *erfpacht* is concerned, which is defined by Grotius as the hereditary usufruct of another's immovable property subject to the payment of a yearly rent or canon. It is, therefore, what we should call a perpetual quitrent tenure. By the law of Holland such a quitrent grant or *erfpacht* could be forfeited, if the rent was three years in arrear, but the *emphyteuta* or grantee, says Grotius, can readily escape forfeiture or purge his default by making payment shortly afterwards, or if he excuses himself on the ground of ignorance, or actually tenders the money; and the right of forfeiture is barred if the grantor or owner has by his conduct waived it, as where he accepts rent which has become due subsequently, or even rent which was due before, without any mention of his right to forfeiture. If, however, it can reasonably be inferred that the non-payment of rent proceeds *ex contemptu vel contumacia* of the *dominus directus*, no relief will be granted (Coren, *Obs.* 22). There are several decisions of the Dutch courts dealing with the matter, commencing as far back as four centuries ago. These decisions lay down that, where the grant contains an unequivocal condition that if the rent is not paid on the stipulated day it shall be forfeited, the court will decree a forfeiture, but not where no such forfeiture clause exists" (*Thomas' Estate* v. *Kerr*, 20 S.C. 354; 13 C.T.R. 538).

In British South Africa perpetual quitrent is a well-recognised form of tenure. The holder of land under this tenure has an hereditary alienable right in the land, and possesses all the powers and rights over it, which are enjoyed by the owner of land held in freehold (*eigendomsplaats*), except such rights as are respectively reserved by the Crown. By Roman-Dutch law the holder had only *jus utendi et fruendi*. He was not entitled to any minerals (Voet's *Comm.* 6, 3, 11), but by the Proclamation of 6th August, 1813, issued by Sir John Cradock, Governor of the Cape of Good Hope, the owner of land held in perpetual quitrent is entitled to all mines of iron, lead, copper, tin, coal, slate or ironstone. The Government, however, reserves to itself the right to all mines of precious stones, gold and silver, and the right of repairing all public roads and taking materials for the purpose from the land held in perpetual quitrent. (See Maasdorp's *Institutes*, vol. 2, pp. 142–43.)

Employee, in the Industrial Disputes Prevention Act, 20 of 1909 (T.), sec. 2, means "any white person engaged by an employer to perform, for hire or reward, manual, clerical or supervision work in any undertaking, trade or industry to which this Act applies." *See* SERVANT.

Employer. The term *employer* is defined in the Cape Workman's Compensation Act (40 of 1905) to mean "any person who hires or contracts with any workman in the [Cape] Colony or the territorial waters thereof, or between whom and any such workman there is an existing contract for the performance of any work to which the provisions of this Act apply, and shall include the legal personal representative of a deceased *employer* and the trustee of an estate of an *employer* when such estate has been sequestrated."

In the Transvaal Workmen's Compensation Act (36 of 1907) sec. 1, *employer* means "any person or any body of persons, corporate or unincorporate hiring or contracting before or after the date of the taking effect of this Act with any workman (as in this section defined) for the performance of any work (as in this section defined), and the term *employer* shall include his representative (as in this section defined)." See also Act 20 of 1909 (T.), sec. 2.

Employment, the state of being employed. As to *employment* in connection with Bribery and Corrupt Practices Acts, see *Burton* v. *Rhodes and Hill* (16 S.C. 3).

Emptio-venditio, the name given in the Roman law to the contract of sale, being a compound of the two elements of which the contract was composed, viz., purchase (*emptio*) and sale (*venditio*). The purchaser's rights were said to be *ex empto* and the seller's *ex vendito*.

En commandite. In the French Code of Commerce provision is made for partnerships in which, besides those members who are held out as such and who are jointly and severally responsible for the partnership debts, there are other members who merely provide capital to the concern, and whose liability, except probably in cases of insolvency, is limited to the amount of the capital so provided by them. Such partners are called *commandataires* or *commendataires*, and the partnership is styled a partnership *en commandite*. See Morice's *English and Roman-Dutch Law*, 2nd ed. p. 192.

Encroachment, the unlawful trespassing or intrusion upon the rights or property of another person.

Encumbrance, a burden or servitude affecting property. "*Encumbrance* means a real burden on the land, a portion of the *dominium* parted with by the owner" (*per* INNES, C.J., in *Hollins* v. *Registrar of Deeds*, [1904] T.S. at p. 607). But there may be an encumbrance on land and yet the owner may retain all the rights of ownership, as where a mortgage bond has been passed and registered against the title of the land.

Enemy. The term *enemy* is defined in the Cape Colonial Forces Act (32 of 1892) as follows: "The subject of any State at war with the [Cape] Colony and offering armed opposition to its forces; and also any armed mutineer, armed rebel or armed rioter, and any pirate."

Enter. In the Transvaal Crimes Ordinance (26 of 1904), sec. 3, *enter* means "the insertion of any part of the body of a person, or any part of an instrument used by such person within a building."

Entire contract is a term applied to building contracts. "An *entire contract* is a contract which cannot be divided up into parts, but must be treated and taken as a whole; the consideration is also indivisible, that is, the consideration cannot be divided up into parts; nor can one part of the work contracted for be treated as having been performed in respect of any specified part of the consideration. Whilst as to a contract which is not entire, the contrary obtains" (Macey's *Conditions of Contract*, p. 6). An *entire contract* for a building implies that the contractor must perform all works necessary to complete that building before he can claim payment.

Eo contra, on the contrary; on the other hand.

Eo converso, conversely.

Eo nomine, by that name.

Epistolae, letters. In the Roman law *epistolae* were letters, or answers to letters, addressed by the emperor to individuals or public bodies. *See* DECRETA.

Equipment is defined in the Natal Militia Act (36 of 1903), sec. 3, to signify "arms, accoutrements, and all articles, except clothing, worn or carried by a militiaman or his horse; and includes all ordnance, machine guns, harness, stores, tents and ammunition issued to militiamen individually or collectively." A similar definition, applicable to volunteers instead of militiamen, is found in Ordinance 33 of 1902 (T.), sec. 1.

Equipping, "in relation to a ship, shall include the furnishing of a ship with any tackle, apparel, furniture, provisions, arms, munitions or stores, or any other thing which is used in or about a ship for the purpose of fitting or adapting her for the sea or for naval service, and all words relating to *equipping* shall be construed accordingly" (the Foreign Enlistment Act of Natal, 26 of 1906, sec. 30). See also Ordinance 1 of 1906 (T.), sec. 30 of schedule.

Equitable mortgage. "There is no such thing in this [Cape] Colony as the *equitable mortgage* known in England created by the pledge of the title-deeds" (*per* BUCHANAN, J., in *De Bruyn* v. *Danvers & Co.'s Assignees*, 16 S.C. at p. 574). "The mere deposit of the documents or titles, together with a letter to the manager of the bank to the effect that these securities are handed to the bank against the debtor's overdraft, only shows that there was an intention to pass a mortgage, but it does not constitute or create any mortgage, especially as against the creditors of the insolvent" (*per* KOTZÉ, C.J., in *Collins* v. *Hugo and the Standard Bank*, H. at p. 182).

What is known in England as an *equitable mortgage* cannot have effect as against a subsequent special mortgage which has been duly registered; see *Van der Merwe's Estate* v. *Thorne* (24 S.C. at p. 71).

Equity. "*Equity* means to the Romans fairness, right feeling, the regard for substantial as opposed to formal and technical justice, the kind of conduct which would approve itself to a man of honour and conscience" (Bryce's *History and Jurisprudence*, vol. 2, p. 143). The same author (at p. 164) in speaking of the law of England says: "Our system of *Equity*, built up by the Chancellors, the earlier among them ecclesiastics, takes not only its name but its guiding and formative principles, and many of its positive rules, from the Roman *aequitas*, which was in substance identical with the law of nature and the *jus gentium*." Sir Henry Maine derives the term *equity* from the Latin *aequus*, in the sense of "levelling," and says it was precisely its levelling tendency which made the *jus gentium* most striking to a primitive Roman (*Ancient Law*, ch. 3). The system of *equity* as understood in England is unknown in Roman-Dutch law.

"The Court [Supreme Court of the Transvaal] has again and again had occasion to point out that it does not administer a system of *equity* as distinct from a system of law. Using the word *equity* in its broad sense, we are always desirous to administer *equity;* but we can only do so in accordance with the principles of Roman-Dutch law. If we cannot do so in accordance with those principles, we cannot do so at all" (*per* INNES, C.J., in *Kent* v. *Transvaalsche Bank*, [1907] T.S. at p. 774).

Erf (D.), (pl. *erven*), term applied to plots of land held in freehold into which many of the villages or townships in South Africa are divided. They are not of uniform size. See *Ex parte Myburgh* (23 S.C. at p. 670). See Act 44 of 1908 (C.C.), sec. 1.

Erfbesprek (D.), a last will or testament.

Erffennis (D.). *See* ERVENIS.

Erfgenamen (D.), heirs. There are two kinds of heirs (*a*) *erfgenamen ab intestato*, or heirs in intestacy; and (*b*) *erfgenamen ex testumento*, or testamentary heirs. "By the term *heirs* in the institution by will we do not understand the very nearest, but those who would be the nearest by succession *ab intestato*" (Van Leeuwen's *Comm.* Kotzé's trans. vol. 1, p. 363).

Erfgrondbrief (D.), the first title-deed or original grant of land held on a tenure that formerly existed in Cape Colony, called "loan freehold." The term was also applied to the first title-deed or grant of such land when under Sir John Cradock's Proclamation of 1813 the tenure was changed into "perpetual quitrent" (Maasdorp's *Institutes*, vol. 2, pp. 140–41; *De Villiers* v. *Cape Divisional Council*, Buch. 1875, p. 50).

Erflating (D.), a disposition or declaration of intention as to who is to be heir. See Van Leeuwen's *Comm.* Kotzé's trans. vol. 1, p. 343, where Chief Justice KOTZÉ points out that the Latin equivalent is *relictio hæreditatis*, and explains the distinction between *erflating* and *erfstelling*.

Erfpacht "is the term by which quitrent has always been known in this [Cape] Colony. It was used as the equivalent for quitrent in the Dutch version of the Proclamation (of Sir John Cradock of 1813) as officially published in the *Government Gazette* of the time. . . . It is also the term invariably used by the Dutch-speaking inhabitants of the colony to designate the quitrent tenure" (DE VILLIERS, C.J., in *De Villiers* v. *Cape Divisional Council*, Buch. 1875, p. 50). Quitrent is the English term for *emphyteusis*. *See* EMPHYTEUSIS.

Erfpachtrecht or **Erfpagregt** (D.), emphyteusis. *See* EMPHYTEUSIS; ERFPACHT. See also Van Leeuwen's *Comm.* Kotzé's trans. vol. 1, p. 220.

Erfstelling (D.), appointment of heir in a testament; the institution to the inheritance. In Latin *institutio heredis.* See Van Leeuwen's *Comm.* Kotzé's trans. vol. 1, p. 361.

Error. "'*Error*,' says Vinnius in his *Select Questions*, 'is twofold, being either of fact or law. An *error* of fact takes place either when some fact which really exists is unknown, or some fact is supposed to exist which really does not. On the other hand, when a person is truly acquainted with the existence or non-existence of the facts, but is ignorant of the legal consequences, he is under an *error* of law. If a person makes a payment knowing that he is not indebted, it is agreed on all hands that he has not any right of repetition; for a payment which is subject to repetition if made by mistake, amounts to a donation if made with full knowledge'" (*per* DE VILLIERS, C.J., in *White Bros.* v. *Treasurer-General*, 2 S.C. at p. 349). A payment made in error of law cannot be recovered (*Rooth* v. *The State*, 2 S.A.R. 259). *See* MISTAKE.

Error calculi, error of calculation. An exception of error in the calculation may be raised by a borrower when sued for the amount of the loan, unless it has been renounced by him.

Erumpens in suo, rising or bursting out on his own land. This phrase is used of water which rises on private land. In *Retief* v. *Louw* (Buch. 1874, p. 165) it was held that such water was the property of the land-owner, and that he might deal with it as freely as with any other part of his private property, might dispose of it or grant a servitude of *aquaeductus* over it. See also *Dreyer* v.

Ireland (Buch. 1874, p. 200); *Silberbauer* v. *Breda* (5 Searle, 231); and *Erasmus* v. *De Wet* (Buch. 1874, p. 204), in all of which cases the above principle was approved and followed. It is now, however, settled that the owner of land upon which water rises has the full ownership of the water and can use or dispose of it as he pleases only where the water has not for thirty years or more flowed beyond his land in a known and definite channel on to the lands of lower proprietors. If the water has so flowed beyond the limits of the land on which it rises, the stream is classed among public or perennial streams, to the accustomed use of which the lower proprietors are entitled (*Breda* v. *Silberbauer*, 6 Moore's P.C.C., N.S. 319; *Vermaak* v. *Palmer*, Buch. 1876, p. 25; *Struben* v. *Capetown Districts Waterworks Co.*, 9 S.C. 68; *Meyer* v. *Johannesburg Waterworks Co.*, H. 1; Maasdorp's *Institutes*. vol. 2, pp. 106 *et seq.*).

Ervenis or **Erffenis** (D.), inheritance; the right to the estate of a deceased person either in part or as a whole. "The right to an estate or *boedel* is acquired by *inheritance*, which is the administration of another's estate and heritage; and whereby we not merely acquire the actual possession of the property of the deceased existing at the time, but also his rights of action—that is, all the right of recourse and proceeding which the deceased had to and against another; and we also bind ourselves in the name of the deceased for everything owing by him and which another could claim from him" (Van Leeuwen's *Comm.* Kotzé's trans. vol. 4, p. 311). *See* HERES EST EADEM PERSONA CUM DEFUNCTO.

Escheat, the reversion of lands or moneys to the State; a reversion of lands to the lord of the fee or original grantor. See the Natal Escheat Laws (11 of 1868, and 6 of 1869): it may be noted that these Laws were passed whilst Natal was a Crown Colony. Law 6 of 1869 (N.) declares the law and practice in cases of *escheats*, and provides for the holding of an inquest in all cases of *escheat* to the Crown.

Escrow (from the Latin *scriptum* through the Norman-French *escrit*), an English law term signifying a deed or agreement delivered to a disinterested party in trust pending the fulfilment of some condition specified therein in favour of the other party to the deed or agreement. If the condition is performed it becomes a binding obligation, otherwise it fails. The term *escrow* is also applied to a payment to a disinterested party in trust pending the performance of some condition, such as the transfer of land. By analogy the term is sometimes applied to bills of exchange (Chalmers on *Bills of Exchange*, 5th ed. p. 56).

Espargne (D.), treasurer of the *espargne*, *i.e.* the receiver of everything forfeited to the count, or which accrued to the *fiscus*. *Espargne* or *epargnes* is a non-German or French word, denoting economy. In France the Royal Treasury of Francis I bore this name (Boey's *Woordentolk*).

Espousals (*trouwbeloften*) "are a mutual agreement and promise of a future marriage. Such a promise is confirmed and ratified like all other transactions which are completed by mutual consent" (Van Leeuwen's *Comm.* Kotzé's trans. vol. 2, p. 209).

"Establish themselves." "My decision in this case is based upon the meaning of the words *establish themselves.* To speak of a person establishing himself presupposes that he has independent freedom of action and choice, and that, of his own volition and for his own purposes, he comes into the Transvaal and settles there. The expression is not applicable to a child of tender years, nor to a boy of fifteen who comes in as a member of his father's family, is brought here by his father, and is supported by and lives with him" (*per* INNES, C.J., in *Rex* v. *Ebraham,* [1906] T.S. at p. 465; in this case the accused had been charged with contravening Law 3 of 1885 (T.) in that he settled in the Transvaal for the purpose of carrying on trade or otherwise without having registered himself in accordance with the provisions of the statute).

Estate, the property, whether movable or immovable, of a person, partnership or company.

In the Transvaal Insolvency Law (13 of 1895, sec. 180) *estate* comprises "all present and future property, whether movable or immovable, personal or real, and all rights of whatsoever description to such property, wherever they may be found to exist, belonging, to or due to the insolvent at the time of the granting of the order of sequestration, or which shall subsequently at any time before rehabilitation be acquired by or become due to such insolvent."

See *Master of the Supreme Court* v. *Maclean's Executrix* ([1904] T.S. 991).

Estoppel. "I do not wish to speak against the principle of *estoppels,* for I do not know how the business of life could go on unless the law recognised their existence; but an *estoppel* may be said to exist where a person is compelled to admit that to be true which is not true, and to act upon a theory which is contrary to the truth. I do not undertake to give an exhaustive definition, but that formula nearly approaches a correct definition of *estoppel*" (*per* BRAMWELL, L.J., in *Simm* v. *Anglo-American Telegraph Co.,* 5 Q.B.D. at p. 202). "The term *estoppel* is used in a very vague sense in the English law, and can generally be classed under some other head in our law" (*per* DE VILLIERS, C.J., in *Collector of Customs* v. *Cape Central Railways, Ltd.,* 6 S.C. at p. 405; see also his remarks on same subject in *Merriman* v. *Williams,* Foord, at p. 174). See *Re Reynolds Vehicle and Harness Factory, Ltd.* (23 S.C. at p. 712).

Et cetera, and other things. In a lease, where the subject let was described as "the farm K with buildings *et cetera* as it stands at present," it was held that the words *et cetera* must be restricted to things *ejusdem generis* as buildings, and did not include movables, such as machinery, furniture or cattle (*Van der Westhuizen* v. *Glastonbury*, [1908] T.S. 836).

Etula, a native word. *See* UKWETULA.

Euvelen (D.), to be hurtful, to cause damage or injury.

Event. "By an *event* is meant some motion or change, considered as having come about either in the course of nature, or through the agency of human will; in which latter case it is called 'an act' or 'an action'" (Best on *Evidence*, 10th ed. sec. 13). *See* "IN THE EVENT."

Evictie (D.), eviction. Decker in a *Note* to Van Leeuwen's *Comm.* (Kotzé's trans. vol. 2, p. 143) says: "Eviction consists in the total or partial loss of the thing sold, which the purchaser suffers in consequence of a right in a third party. . . . Further, eviction not only exists in case of sale, but the security arising therefrom also exists between co-heirs and in several other instances." See Kersteman's *Woordenboek*, vol. 2, p. 466.

Evidence "means (1) statements made by witnesses in court under a legal sanction, in relation to matters of fact under inquiry; such statements are called oral evidence: (2) documents produced for the inspection of the court or judge; such documents are called documentary evidence" (Stephen's *Digest of the Law of Evidence*, 5th. ed. p. 2).

For Cape Colony, see Ordinance 72 of 1830; Ordinance 14 of 1846; Act 4 of 1861; Act 13 of 1886.

For Natal, see Law 9 of 1859; Law 17 of 1859; Law 5 of 1870; Law 6 of 1884; Law 37 of 1888; Act 29 of 1899.

For Transvaal, see Proclamation 16 of 1902 and Ordinance 21 of 1904.

Ex abundanti cautela, from excessive caution.

Ex æquo et bono, in or according to equity and good conscience.

Ex cathedra, from the chair or seat of authority—referring to decisions of the Popes given from their *Cathedra*; with high authority.

Ex causa lucrativa, from a lucrative source. "Where it is clear that the testator knew it, and the legatee after the execution of the will acquires the property for valuable consideration (*titulo oneroso*), as by purchase, he may under the will claim its value from the heir, unless there were manifest indications of an intention on his part to renounce the legacy; but where he acquires the property without valuable consideration (*ex causa lucrativa*), as by gift, he is not entitled to claim either the thing itself or its value. If, therefore, property is bequeathed to a person under two distinct wills, he will do well first to obtain the value under one will, for he can then still claim the thing itself under the other; but having once acquired the thing itself without valuable consideration, he has no claim to its value" (Grotius' *Introd.* Maasdorp's trans. 2, 22, 41).

Ex concesso, from what has been conceded.

Ex contemptu vel contumacia, from contempt or contumacy. By the Roman law an *emphyteusis* or quitrent could be terminated by the *dominus* if the rent was for three years in arrear in the case of secular property and two years in the case of ecclesiastical property. In the same way a lease could be cancelled and the lessee ejected by the lessor where the rent had not been paid for two years. The Roman-Dutch law, following the Canon law, has modified this rule by allowing the court to inquire into the circumstances, and unless the quitrent holder or lessee in failing to pay his rent has acted in defiance (*ex contemptu vel contumacia*) of the rights of the *dominus* or lessor, the default may be purged and forfeiture avoided by tender of payment of the arrears (Voet's *Comm.* 6, 3, 36; Grotius' *Introd.* 2, 40, 19; *Thomas's Estate* v. *Kerr and Another*, 20 S.C. 354; 13 C.T.R. 538). *See* also CONTUMACY.

Ex curia, out of court.

Ex decreto judicis, by judicial decree. In *Lange and Others* v. *Liesching and Others* (Foord, 55) the question was discussed whether a sale by the trustee in an insolvent estate was, as regards preventing a *rei vindicatio,* a sale *ex decreto judicis,* such as referred to in Voet's *Comm.* 6, 1, 13; DE VILLIERS, C.J., said: "The only point upon which there may at first sight be some doubt is whether the sale was authorised, in the words of Voet, *ex decreto judicis.* Upon a closer examination of the subject this doubt also vanishes. A sale in insolvency is the necessary result of an order of the court placing the estate of the insolvent under sequestration in the hands of the Master of the Supreme Court." As the sale *ex decreto judicis* thus does not appear to be necessarily in consequence of the direct order of a court, it would seem that any sale in execution of a judgment is *ex decreto judicis.*

Ex delicto, from or arising out of a delict or crime.

Ex dividend, a Stock Exchange expression in connection with the sale of shares or stock, signifying that the shares or stock are sold exclusive of the accruing or declared dividend. Frequently abbreviated to "*ex div.*" or "*x. d.*"

Ex figura verborum, from the form of the words; by the form of words used.

Ex mera gratia, through mere favour.

Ex mero motu, of or from one's own free will or accord.

Ex necessitate legis, from the necessity of the law.

Ex necessitate rei, from the necessity of the case.

Ex nihilo nihil fit, out of nothing, nothing comes.

Ex nudo pacto non oritur actio, from a nude agreement no action arises; a rule of the civil, but not also of the Canon or the Roman-Dutch law. *See* CAUSA.

Ex officio, by virtue of office.

Ex officio judicis, by virtue of the office or power of the judge; said of things awarded by a judge, although not formally claimed. *See* NOBILE OFFICIUM.

Ex parte, on behalf of; from one side. An application to the court *ex parte* is made by the applicant only in the absence of the respondent.

Ex post facto, after the event; retrospective.

Ex quasi contractu, [arising] as if from a contract. See QUASI EX CONTRACTU.

Ex turpi causa non oritur actio, no action arises from a dishonourable cause or motive. Thus a woman cannot sue upon an unfulfilled promise made to her as a consideration for illicit intercourse. Where, however, the thing promised has been given or transferred to her, it cannot be reclaimed, following the maxim *In pari delicto melior est conditio possidentis* (*Aburrow* v. *Wallis*, 10 S.C. 214). The rule with respect to immoral contracts is as follows: if the immoral cause be on the side of the obligor the obligation is void, but any payment made under it cannot be recovered; if on the side of the obligee alone the obligation is also void and may be set aside at the instance of the obligor, and whatever has been paid under it by him may be recovered; if on both sides the above maxim will apply, *i.e.* he who is in possession will be in the better position.

Exactissima diligentia, the highest degree of diligence. Where such is obligatory, the person subject to the duty is liable for *levissima culpa*, the slightest degree of negligence. The person to whom a thing is lent for use (*commodatum*) is said to be liable for *exacta diligentia*, when the loan is entirely for his benefit (Voet's *Comm.* 13, 6, 4).

Exceptie (D.), exception. *Exceptions* formed a prominent feature in Dutch practice. See Van Leeuwen's *Comm.* 5, 14; and Kersteman's *Woordenboek*, vol. 1, p. 124.

Exceptio. This term in Roman law does not have precisely the same meaning as the term "exception" in modern practice. It was a plea allowed to a defendant, who, though liable according to the letter of the law, yet alleged facts that would make his condemnation inequitable. It was the means by which the magistrate gave effect to equitable defences not recognised by the *jus civile.* The *exceptio doli, exceptio metus, exceptio non numeratae pecuniae, exceptio pacti conventi* are examples of the Roman law *exceptio.*

Exceptio litis pendentis, exception of a suit depending. It affords *primâ facie* a good ground for a plea in abatement to any action, that another action between the same parties, for the same thing, and arising out of the same cause, is depending before another competent court. *See* LIS ALIBI PENDENS.

Exceptio non numeratae pecuniae, the exception that the money was not counted out or paid. This was an exception of the Roman law which could be pleaded by any one who was sued upon a written acknowledgment of debt. The exception was available only for a limited time—first one year, then five, and finally fixed by Justinian at two years—from the date of the writing. This rule has been adopted by the Roman-Dutch law with reference to written acknowledgments of a loan. "Not only is the exception *in rem,* being available to heirs and sureties, but also if opposed within two years reckoned from the date of the written obligation it is privileged to the effect of throwing the burden of proof upon the plaintiff, who says that payment followed, whereas generally a defendant in excepting becomes a plaintiff and is bound to prove his exception. But if he who holds the writing does not sue upon it within two years, so that the exception cannot be opposed to him by reason of his not suing, the writing itself within two years can be recovered by him who granted it and his heir in a *condictio sine causa,* or *causa data causa non secuta,* provided the holder of it is present. But if he is absent or in concealment, and cannot therefore be sued by those actions, the fact can be brought before a judge or otherwise be made the subject of a formal complaint; and by that course this privileged exception is rendered perpetual, so that the burden of proof that payment was indeed made will continue to be laid upon the plaintiff at whatever time he should afterwards sue" (Voet's *Comm.* 12, 1, 31).

The exception does not lie in the case of an acknowledgment given to a banker, or an acknowledgment of a previously existing debt, or if a pledge has been granted for a previously existing debt, not at the same time, but at a different time; for in those cases the person who has acknowledged the debt is bound to prove that the money was not paid to him, and has not a privileged, but a bare unprivileged, exception *non numeratae pecuniae.* If, on the other hand, he grants the acknowledgment and constitutes the pledge at the same time and by the same writing, the exception, as a privileged exception, will be available to him. Also if the debtor pays a part of the debt, or interest upon it, he cannot avail himself of the exception with regard to the remainder. The same principle applies if the parties enter into a compromise with regard to the money which was said not to have been paid.

The exception also does not lie in the case of an acknowledgment of a deposit, or in the case of receipts for public taxes (*publicarum functionum*); but as against receipts for private debts the exception is available for thirty days (Voet's *Comm.* 12, 1, 32). See EXCEPTIO NON SECUTAE SOLUTIONIS.

The exception, of course, ceases where it has been expressly renounced, the burden of proof in that case being transferred to the defendant (Schorer's *Note* to Grotius' *Introd.* 321).

After the lapse of two years it is still open to the debtor to plead the exception, but the burden of proof will then be transferred to him (Voet's *Comm.* 12, 1, 33; see also Van der Keessel, *Thes.* 523, 524).

Exceptio non qualificatae, the exception of non-qualification, that is, that a party has not the qualifications that he ascribes to himself in the case. If evidence is required on the point, the exception is now called a plea in bar. In *Aspeling, Executor of Low,* v. *Waldpot* (3 Menz. 350), after the plaintiff had closed his case, absolution from the instance was asked for, on the ground that the declaration alleged that the plaintiff was executor of Low, though he had not proved this; but the court held that the defendant, not having taking the exception of non-qualification before pleading and issue joined, must be taken to have admitted the plaintiff's title.

Exceptio non secutae solutionis, exception that payment did not follow. Somewhat like the *exceptio non numeratae pecuniae,* which may be opposed to a bond or written obligation, is the *exceptio non secutae solutionis,* which may be taken to a receipt by the creditor; but whereas the former exception, in its effect of throwing the burden of proof on the holder of the writing, is available at any time within two years, the plea of non-payment in the case of a receipt must be raised within thirty days after the date of the receipt, the onus of proof in that event being cast upon the debtor. After the thirty days, according to Schorer, the exception will not be available even though the creditor should be prepared to take the burden of proof upon himself (Schorer's *Note* to Grotius' *Introd.* 321; Voet's *Comm.* 12, 1, 32; 46, 3, 15).

Exceptio probat regulam, the exception proves the rule.

Exceptio procuratoris inhabilis. *See* INHABILITEIT VAN EEN PROCUREUR.

Exceptio rei judicatae vel litis finitae, the exception or plea that the point in dispute has already been decided by a competent court in a case between the same parties or their predecessors. *See* RES JUDICATA. In *Du Prez* v. *Rose* (3 Menz. 353) the court held that a plea of *rei judicatae et litis finitae,* although in the language of the civil law called the *exceptio rei judicatae et litis finitae*, was not an exception in the sense in which that word is used in the forms of procedure in the court, but a plea on the merits; and before giving judgment on the relevancy of this plea, allowed the defendant to call evidence.

Exchange. (1) "Is an agreement among merchants, whereby some one engages to pay to another, at a certain time and place, a sum of money received by him for a certain gain" (Van Leeuwen's *Comm.* Kotzé's trans. vol. 2, p. 224).

(2) Barter, a contract in which each party gives something in *exchange* for something given to him by the other.

Exchequer account. In the Cape Audit Act (14 of 1906), sec. 3 (*c*), *exchequer account* is defined to mean "the account in which all taxes, duties and all other revenues, the proceeds of all loans raised, the surplus funds available for investment of the Post Office Savings Bank, the Sinking Fund Commissioners, the Pension Fund Deposit Account, or the Guarantee Fund shall figure on the one side and the issues therefrom, authorised by the auditor, upon the other side."

'*Exchequer account* shall mean the account kept with the bank into which shall be paid all public revenues after deduction of any drawbacks, repayments or discounts, and into which shall further be paid all other public moneys" (Audit and Exchequer Act, 14 of 1907 (T.), and Audit and Exchequer Act, 17 of 1908 (O.R.C.)).

Excise, an internal or inland duty or tax, imposed and levied on the consumption of a commodity or upon the manufacture or the sale of it. In South Africa *excise* duties are chiefly confined to such commodities as spirits and beer.

Excise trader. The expression *excise trader* is defined in the Cape Excise Spirits Act (18 of 1884), sec. 2, as meaning "any person carrying on a business subject to any of the regulations of this Act, and includes any proprietor or occupier of an excise warehouse." The same definition is given in the Additional Taxation Act, 36 of 1904 (C.C.), sec. 2.

Executeur (D.), an executor. *See* EXECUTOR.

Execution. (1) The signing and attesting of contracts, wills, powers of attorney and other documents. The solemnities to be observed in connection therewith are governed by the law of the place of *execution*.

(2) The process by means of which a civil judgment of the court is enforced. After judgment a writ is issued and delivered to the sheriff or messenger of the court, as the case may be, who proceeds to attach and realise as directed in the writ. It is this attachment and realisation that is known by the term *execution*.

(3) The performance of capital punishment upon a prisoner by the executioner in accordance with the sentence of a court.

Executor. "If we look into the history of executorship we shall find that there always existed a difference between the testamentary *executor* and the *executor* dative. The former was in olden times a person appointed by the testator to see that the heir carried out his wishes, whilst the latter was a priest appointed by the bishop to safeguard in particular the interests of the Church, and in general those of the legatees. The testamentary *executor* was chosen by the deceased to represent him, whilst the *executor* dative was an appointee of the Church. In the old wills of the fifteenth and sixteenth centuries the testamentary *executor* is often called a *procurator in rem suam.* As *executors* in early days were mostly ecclesiastics, and as the Church was deeply interested in the disposition of the property, because it always got some gift *ad pias causas* or *pro salute animae*, it framed rules for the guidance of *executors*. These rules formed part of the Canon law. . . The rules of the Canon law were framed in order to regulate the acts of the *Ordinarius*, and they no doubt formed the basis of the later Roman-Dutch law; but in Holland, at any rate, the functions of a testamentary *executor* developed far beyond those of the Canon law. The *executor* of the Canon law could only pay the debts, hand over to the Church gifts made *pro salute animae*, and then place the balance in the hands of the heir for distribution. The testamentary *executor* under the Roman-Dutch law gradually acquired wider powers, and during the eighteenth century, amongst other duties, he had to liquidate the whole of the estate, to pay the debts, to pay out the legatees what was due to them, and then to hand over the balance to the heir" (*per* WESSELS, J., in *Ferguson and Huckell* v. *Langermann and Lorentz*, [1903] T.H. at p. 227). See also *Fischer* v. *Liquidators of Union Bank* (8 S.C. at p. 52).

"It is the duty of an *executor* to sell the assets when he requires funds, but not to pass bonds on the property unless thereto authorised by the will or by order of court" (*per* DE VILLIERS, C.J., in *Williams* v. *Williams*, 13 S.C. at p. 203).

Executor dative, a person elected to act as executor at a duly convened meeting of the next of kin and creditors of a deceased person who has died intestate, or having died testate the nominated executor testamentary is unwilling or unable to act; on such election being duly reported to him, the Master of the Supreme Court may grant letters of administration to such person appointing him the *executor dative* to administer the estate of the deceased person on the required security being given; the Master has certain discretionary powers in regard to such appointment; and in certain cases where the assets of the deceased do not exceed £100 or £200 (varying in the different South African colonies) the Master may summarily appoint an *executor dative* without his being elected at a meeting of next of kin and creditors. *See* EXECUTOR. An *executor dative* corresponds to the English "administrator" (*Hiddingh* v. *Denyssen and Others*, 3 S.C. 441).

Executor de son tort, executor of his own wrong. This is a term of English law denoting one who, not having been duly appointed executor or administrator, intermeddles with the estate of a deceased person or performs any act pertaining to an executor. The liability of such a person is with us regulated by statute—in the Cape Colony by sec. 29 of Ordinance 104 of 1833; in the Transvaal by sec. 43 of the Administration of Estates Proclamation (28 of 1902); and in the Orange River Colony by sec. 39 of the Administration of Estates Ordinance (18 of 1905). These statutes provide as follows: if before the granting of letters of administration to an executor, testamentary or dative, any person takes upon himself to administer, distribute, or in any way dispose of any estate or part thereof, except in so far as may be authorised by a competent court or by the Master, or may be absolutely necessary for the safe custody or preservation thereof, or for providing a suitable funeral for the deceased, or for the subsistence of the family or household or livestock left by the deceased, such person shall be personally liable to pay all debts due by the deceased at the time of his death or which have thereafter become due by the estate, and all legacies left by the deceased in so far as the assets of the estate may prove insufficient to pay the same, unless when sued for the payment of any such debt or legacy he can prove to the satisfaction of the court the true amount and value of the property which has been unduly administered, distributed, or disposed of by him, and that his administration, distribution or disposal was not fraudulent, in which case he will only be liable for such amount and value and for the amount of the costs incurred by him in the suit as well as for the plaintiff's taxed costs.

Executor testamentary, a person nominated and appointed as executor by the will of a deceased person. *See* EXECUTOR. *Executors testamentary* are recognised as such by letters of administration granted by the Master of the Supreme Court without being obliged to file security.

Exempli gratia, by way of example; usually abbreviated by use of the initial letters only, viz. "*e.g.*"

Exheredatie (D.), disinherison. In Roman-Dutch law *disinherison* took place by means of testamentary disposition, but it was necessary that such a testament should be executed before two of the *schepenen* (magistrates) of the place where the testator resided, and thus *disinherison* could never be effected by codicil or a closed testament; moreover, it was imperative that the lawful reasons for *disinherison* should be inserted in the will and should be thereafter proved.

Exheridation, a disinheriting. See *Van Schoor's Trustees* v. *Muller's Executors* (3 Searle, at p. 137).

Exhibition, a public display of productions whether in agriculture, mechanics, science, art, or the like. See the Cape Exhibition

Act (11 of 1898), which re-enacts, with slight amendment, the Cape Act 26 of 1892, regulating the holding of exhibitions in the Cape Colony.

Exigency, demand; urgency; necessity. In the Sheriff's Ordinance (37 of 1828) of the Cape Colony the sheriff is authorised, after arresting a defendant, to take security "that the said defendant shall appear according to the *exigency* of the said process," &c. The expression is used in several other places in the same Ordinance, as well as in other statutes dealing with sheriff's duties.

Existimatio circum colentium, the opinion of those living around or in the neighbourhood. This opinion is, according to Ulpian (*Dig.* 43, 12, 1), one of the tests for deciding whether a stream is a public or private stream (*Port Elizabeth Divisional Council* v. *Uitenhage Divisional Council,* Buch. 1868, p. 44).

Expenditure Act. In the Cape Audit Act (14 of 1906), sec. 3 (*e*), *Expenditure Act* is defined to mean "any Act, other than an Appropriation Act, under which any money is authorised to be expended for any purpose therein specified, whether the said money be authorised to be raised by loan or charged against the Consolidated Revenue Account.'

Expenses. *See* BUYER TO PAY ALL EXPENSES IN CONNECTION WITH THE COMPLETING OF TRANSFER.

Expert, a person skilled in some special department of knowledge, science or art. In the Cape Companies Act (25 of 1892), sec. 92, the term *expert* is defined to include "any person whose profession gives authority to a statement made by him." This definition is taken from the English Directors' Liability Act of 1890, sec. 3 (4). In the Transvaal Companies Act (31 of 1909), sec. 82, *expert* is defined to include "an engineer, valuer, accountant, and any other person whose profession gives authority to a statement made by him."

Expiration of tenancy. Where this expression appeared in a lease it was held that the tenancy terminated upon effluxion of time, upon default or upon forfeiture. See *Bennett and Tatham* v. *Koovarjee and Kasaw* (27 N.L.R. at p. 115).

Expletrix. *See* ATTRIBUTRIX.

Explosive. The term *explosive* in the Cape Explosives Act, (4 of 1887), has the following meaning: "(1) Means gunpowder, nitro-glycerine, dynamite, gun-cotton, blasting-powders, fulminate of mercury or of other metals, coloured fires, and every other substance, whether similar to those above mentioned or not, used or manufactured with a view to produce a practical effect by explosion or a pyrotechnic effect; and (2) includes fuses, rockets, detonators, cartridges, ammunition of all descriptions, and every adaptation or preparation of an explosive as above defined." *Explosive* is defined in Natal statute law in sec. 2 of Act 23 of 1899; in the Transvaal in Ordinance 4 of 1905, sec. 2; in the Orange River Colony in Ordinance 19 of 1907, sec. 1.

Explosive factory, in the Transvaal Explosives Ordinance (4 of 1905), sec. 2, means "any site licensed under this Ordinance for the manufacture of any explosives, together with every mound, building and work for whatsoever purpose used."

Exporter, a merchant or other person who ships goods or produce to a foreign country, or to some country beyond the boundaries of the country in which he resides or conducts his business. In the Natal Customs and Shipping Act (13 of 1899) sec. 4, *exporter* means the person who actually exports the goods, and also includes any person who acts on behalf of the *exporter*.

Express obligation "is properly described as the voluntary act of a person by which upon some reasonable ground, either by words or in writing, he promises another person something with the intention that the latter shall accept the same, and by such acceptance acquire against him a right to performance" (Van Leeuwen's *Comm.* Kotzé's trans. vol. 2, p. 3, Decker's *note*).

Expressio eorum quae tacite insunt nihil operatur, the expression of those things which are tacitly implied operates nothing. For example, as a bill of exchange or promissory note is presumed to be made for consideration, the addition of the words "for value received" has no operative effect. So, if as between master and servant a term of the engagement is that the latter may be summarily dismissed for fraud, such a stipulation has no special effect, for it is implied by law that a servant who is guilty of such conduct is not entitled to notice before dismissal. But if the master should desire to reserve to himself the right summarily to dismiss his servant for mere incompetence, that will require to be expressed in the agreement, as it is not a term that can be implied (*Allnatt & Rhode* v. *Piper*, 27 N.L.R. 90). Again, if a testator leaves his property "to his heirs," *i.e.* without indicating any particular persons who are to inherit, such a direction will have no operative effect, as it leaves the estate to devolve according to the rules of intestate succession, and therefore does no more than what the law itself provides.

Expressio unius est exclusio alterius, a legal maxim meaning that the expression of one thing implies the exclusion of the other. If, for example, a farm is let on condition that a rent be paid if there be a good harvest, the presumption would be that it was not the intention of the parties that any rent should be paid if there was not a good harvest. The maxim is a rule of interpretation applicable to statutes, contracts, wills and other documents. Its signification is similar to that of the maxim *expressum facit cessare tacitum* (see Broom's *Legal Maxims*, 7th ed. p. 491).

The maxim is discussed in the case *Uitenhage Municipality* v. *Colonial Government* (9 S.C. 375). See also *Abner Major* v. *John Makettra* (1 E.D.C. at p. 47): and *Re Estate Dugmore* (5 E.D.C. at p. 96).

Expressum facit cessare tacitum, the express ousts the tacit. In contracts there are frequently some conditions implied; for example, certain points may be left for regulation by the usage of trade. If, however, there is anything in the contract of the nature of an express agreement upon such points, the existence of such implied conditions is negatived. The maxim, which is a rule of interpretation, applies to statutes as well as contracts (*Thornton and Others* v. *Hugo, N.O., and the Mayor and Councillors of Graaff-Reinet,* 5 E.D.C. at p. 304). It is considered by Broom to be identical with *expressio unius est exclusio alterius* (Broom's *Legal Maxims,* 7th ed. p. 491); but there appears to be a distinct shade of meaning in the two maxims.

Expropriation, the dispossessing of an owner of certain of his property or rights for some public purpose and by lawful authority, usually subject to compensation (*Jooste* v. *Government of the S. A. Republic,* 4 Off. Rep. 147). *See* DOMINIUM EMINENS.

Extend. *See* RENEW AND EXTEND.

Extortion, the taking under colour of office or authority from any person, by means of illegitimate pressure, any money or valuable thing which is not due from him at the time it is taken. "The crime of extortion may be committed either by a public official or by a private individual under colour of authority, but illegitimate pressure in some shape is a necessary element to constitute the offence" (*per* INNES, C.J., in *Notaris* v. *Rex,* [1903] T.S. at p. 484). In Latin the crime is called *concussio* (*q.v.*), and in Dutch *afpersing*.

See Ordinance 26 of 1904 (T.), sec. 12; Act 8 of 1908 (O.R.C.).

Extra cursum curiae, outside the usual course of the court; applied to a judicial officer acting otherwise than in the discharge of his official functions. In *Lambrechts* v. *Van der Byl* (15 S.C. 402) DE VILLIERS, C.J., said: "The Court has more than once decided that the parties cannot by agreement extend the magistrate's jurisdiction over any subject-matter not included by statute within his jurisdiction, but that they may refer a dispute to him as arbitrator. A proceeding before him as arbitrator would be *extra cursum curiae,* and would not admit of appeal to a higher court."

Extra territorium jus dicenti impune non paretur, the sentence of one adjudicating beyond his territory is not obeyed with impunity. As a matter of absolute right no State can enact laws which will have any binding force outside the State territory. An exception to this rule exists in the case of what are called personal statutes or laws and mixed statutes or laws. The civilians divided laws into three classes, namely, personal, real and mixed statutes, meaning by the term statutes not legislative enactments, but the whole municipal law of a State. The difference between these three classes of laws, which are somewhat similarly defined by Voet (*Comm.* 1, 4, 2, 3, 4), Grotius (*Opinion* No. 1), and Van der Keessel (*Thes.* 26–29), may be stated as follows: (*a*) Personal statutes, whether they make mention of things or not, are those which are intended to define the condition or status of a person, such as the qualities of citizenship, legitimacy and illegitimacy, minority and majority, marriage and divorce, &c.; or which by reason of such status or condition declare any one as having capacity or incapacity for performing any personal act. (*b*) Real statutes are those in which, although mention is made of the person also, the intention is to treat concerning things. (*c*) Mixed statutes are those which prescribe the formalities and solemnities of acts or deeds.

Real laws do not operate beyond the territory of the enacting State. Personal laws, however, follow and govern the person subject to them even in other countries; they, however, give place to the real laws of another country or to contrary legislation of the place whither the person subject to the personal law may go, or where the property in question is situated. With reference to mixed laws, the rule is that acts done or deeds executed in accordance with the formalities and solemnities of the law of the place where they are so done or executed are valid everywhere, unless there is an express law to the contrary or they have been executed elsewhere in fraud of the law of the domicile (Van der Keessel, *Thes.* 39).

Extradition, the surrender of a fugitive criminal by one State to another in accordance with certain treaty or other lawful obligations. On this subject consult Clarke's *Law of Extradition*; also *The Attorney-General* v. *Anderson* (4 Off. Rep. 287). As to *extradition* in South Africa, see Bell and Nathan's *Legal Handbook*, 1905 ed. p. 566.

Extraordinary pension, an expression used in Ordinance 30 of 1906 (T.), sec. 1, where it means "a pension payable to an officer who has become unfitted for the public service by reason of an injury received in the discharge of duty involving special risk and as a result of such risk."

Extraordinary session. "*Extraordinary session* shall mean any session of Parliament other than an ordinary session" (Act 12 of 1907 (T.), sec. 2).

Fac simile, do or make the like; an exact copy of the original.

Facile princeps, easily first; eminent.

Faction fighting is defined in Natal in Act 11 of 1896, sec. 2, to mean "fighting with or without weapons, between natives, in which not less than eight persons are engaged, and includes any breach of the peace, riot, assault, injury or homicide, occurring in such fight." It is a crime cognisable in the courts of the magistrates (*ibid.* sec. 3). See also Act 9 of 1897 (N.). For further definition, where the minimum number of persons engaged is three, see Law 19 of 1891 (N.), sch., sec. 31.

Factor, an English term signifying a person who is employed to sell goods on behalf of his principal for a remuneration by way of commission; he has actual possession of the goods, and may buy and sell in his own name. See *Chiappini & Co.* v. *Jaffray's Trustees* (2 Menz. 192 (as paged)).

Factory, usually a building or combination of buildings, with machinery and appliances, appropriated for the manufacture of goods. See Act 11 of 1905 (C.C.), sec. 1.

Facts in issue, "means (1) all facts which, by the form of the pleadings in any action, are affirmed on one side and denied on the other; (2) in actions in which there are no pleadings, or in which the form of the pleadings is such that distinct issues are not joined between the parties, all facts from the establishment of which the existence, non-existence, nature, or extent of any right, liability, or disability asserted or denied in any such case would by law follow" (Stephen's *Digest of the Law of Evidence*, 5th ed. p. 2).

Falcidian portion, was introduced in Roman law by the *Lex Falcidia.* It conferred the right upon the heir to make such a proportionate deduction from all legacies with which he was charged, as to retain, over and above the debts of the deceased and the funeral expenses, a clear fourth of the estate or of that share of it to which he was instituted heir, the value of the estate being taken at what it was on the day of the death of the deceased, and debts due by the deceased to the heir being reckoned among the debts.

The *Falcidian portion* was abolished in Cape Colony by sec. 1 of Act 26 of 1873, which is also operative in Rhodesia; it was abolished in the Transvaal by sec. 126 of Proclamation 28 of 1902; in the Orange River Colony by chap. 92 of Law Book, sec. 2, and Ordinance 18 of 1905; and in Natal by Law 7 of 1885, sec. 2. *See* LEX FALCIDIA.

Falcidie or **Falcidique portie** (D.), Falcidian portion. *See* FALCIDIAN PORTION.

Falsa demonstratio non perimit legatum, a false description does not invalidate a legacy. Thus, if a testator bequeathed his house, describing it as situate in a certain place, whereas the only house owned by him was in another place, the legacy would nevertheless hold good. So the legacy of a piece of land would not be avoided by the fact that its extent was erroneously stated by the testator (Van Leeuwen's *Comm.* 3, 9, 5). The same applies with reference to the description of the legatee. For example, if a testator says, "I leave to my grandson John," and his only grandson is named James, the legacy to the grandson will be good, the name being regarded merely as descriptive. So if he bequeathed to his niece Mary, daughter of his sister Jane, and sister Jane has no children, but he has a niece named Mary, the legacy would also be valid, there being no doubt as to the person intended to be benefited by the testator. *See* AMBIGUITAS LATENS ET PATENS.

False pretences, as to theft by means of *false pretences, see* THEFT.

False trade description. "The expression *false trade description* means a trade description which is false in a material respect as regards the goods to which it is applied, and includes every alteration of a trade description, whether by way of addition, effacement or otherwise, where that alteration makes the description false in a material respect, and the fact that a trade description is a trade-mark or part of a trade-mark shall not prevent such trade description being a *false trade description* within the meaning of this Act" (Act 12 of 1888 (C.C.), sec. 2).

For Natal definition, see Law 22 of 1888, sec. 3. For that in the Transvaal, see Ordinance 47 of 1903, sec. 2 (1).

Falsiteit (D.), fraud. *See* CRIMEN FALSI; FRAUD.

Falsity. *See* CRIMEN FALSI; FRAUD.

Falsum, falsehood, falsity or fraud. *See* CRIMEN FALSI; FRAUD.

Fare, the price paid for conveyance of a person from one place to another by land or water; also sometimes the person so conveyed.

In the Transvaal Railway Ordinance (60 of 1903), sec. 3 [since repealed], *fare* included "any charge or other payment for the carriage of any passenger." For similar definition, see Ordinance 45 of 1903 (O.R.C.), sec. 3 [since repealed].

"*Fare* shall inclued all sums received or receivable, charged or chargeable for conveyance of passengers upon or along any railway (Act 13 of 1908 (T.), sec. 2; Act 29 of 1908 (O.R.C.), sec. 2).

Farm foods. "*Farm foods* shall mean all concentrated or artificially prepared feeding stuffs, whether mixtures or otherwise, intended for feeding domestic animals, sterilised bone meal, and all condimental stock foods claimed to possess nutritive as well as medicinal properties, but shall not include dog biscuits and dog food, hays and straws, the whole seeds nor the unmixed meals made directly from entire grains of wheat, rye, barley, oats, mealies, Kafir corn, buck-wheat, dried brewers' grains, wet brewers' grains, malt sprouts; nor shall it include wheat, rye and buckwheat brans or middlings not mixed with other substances, but sold separately as distinct articles of commerce, or pure grains ground together" (the Fertilisers, Farm Foods, Seeds and Pest Remedies Act, 20 of 1907 (C.C.), sec. 3).

Farm labourer, in the Transvaal Native Tax Act (9 of 1908), sec. 2, means "an adult who resides on a farm and is *boná fide*, but not necessarily continuously, employed by the proprietor thereof in domestic service or farming operations; provided that (*a*) if he resides on one farm and is employed on another farm of the same proprietor, he shall be deemed to have resided and to have been employed on one and the same farm; (*b*) he shall not be deemed to be *boná fide* employed unless ninety days' service, at least, on the farm occupied by the proprietor or on another and adjoining farm of the proprietor, has been rendered during the twelve months immediately preceding the date upon which demand is made for payment of the tax under this Act, and no rent is paid or valuable consideration of any kind, other than service, given by him to the proprietor in respect of residence on the farm." *See* FARM SERVANT.

Farm servant in Act 42 of 1908 (O.R.C.) (Rights of Coloured Persons in respect of Fixed Property Act), sec. 1, means "any person who is employed under contract of service with another person to engage either continuously or at such times as the employer may require his services in any bodily labour in farming or in piece work on a farm or in the care of livestock on any land owned or occupied by the employer; provided that such servant be resident on such land: and provided further that (*a*) if such contract be in writing it be for no longer a period than two years and have been signed by the parties thereto, and their signatures have been attested by two white witnesses; (*b*) if such contract be oral it be for no longer a period than one year and have been made in the presence of two white witnesses. The term *farm servant* shall be deemed to include the wife and daughters and minor sons of a *farm servant*."

Fees sometimes includes disbursements; see *Price* v. *Deputy-Sheriff, Witwatersrand* ([1903] T.H. at p. 468).

The charges made by a municipality for the use of its fire engines in extinguishing a fire may be *fees*; see *Lewis Bros.* v. *East London Municipality* (21 S.C. at p. 161).

Felon, an English law term signifying a person who has committed a felony or grave crime. The term is to be found in the Cape statute book in Act 1 of 1860 (C.C.).

Feme covert, a term of English law denoting a woman under the marital power of her husband. "Coverture is where a man and a woman are married together; now whatsoever is done concerning the wife in the time of the continuance of this marriage is said to be done 'during the coverture,' and the wife is called a woman covert" (*Termes* *de la Ley*). In English law where a wife commits a criminal offence in conjunction with, or in the presence of, her husband, she is presumed to have acted under his coercion; but no such rule exists in the Roman-Dutch law, it being settled that there must be sufficient evidence to show actual compulsion on the part of the husband (*Queen* v. *Barker*, 2 S.C. 9; *Queen* v. *Farley*, 2 S.C. 227; *Queen* v. *Albert*, 12 S.C. 272; *Bosch* v. *Rex*, [1904] T.S. at p. 58). *See* COERCION.

Fence, in the Transvaal Fencing Ordinance (7 of 1904), sec. 1, means "a substantial stock-proof fence, with gates at places where it crosses public or private roads, and suitable appliances where it crosses other obstacles. Any such fence shall be deemed to be a sufficient fence within the meaning of the Stock Theft Ordinance, 1904." This Ordinance was repealed by the Fencing Act (12 of 1908), in which the word *fence* is again defined. The definition in the Act is substantially the same as in the Ordinance.

Feoffer, the donor or grantor of a feud.

Ferae naturae, of a wild nature. This phrase is used of animals which are naturally wild, and which are classed as *res nullius* until captured, when they become the property of the captor (Justinian's *Institutes*, 2, 1, 12, 13). In *Graham* v. *Viljoen* (Buch. 1878, p. 126) DE VILLIERS, C.J., said that he inclined to the view of those writers who classed the dog with animals *ferae naturae*; his reason being that, though this state of the law might create occasional hardship, "it would obviate the still greater hardship which would result if an injured person can have no redress unless he proves that the owner knew, before the injury was done, of the dog's vicious propensity."

Fertiliser. "*Fertiliser* shall mean any substance containing, or purporting to contain, nitrogen, phosphoric oxide, potash or lime, manufactured, produced, or prepared in any manner, or imported into the colony and sold or intended for sale or distribution for the purpose of fertilising the soil or supplying nutriment to plants, but, shall not include farm-yard or stable manure, kraal manure and kraal manure ash, town refuse or crude night-soil; and all such *fertilisers* shall be considered to derive their entire value from the nitrogen, phosphoric oxide, potash or lime, as the case may be, which they contain" (the Fertilisers, Farm Foods, Seeds and Pest Remedies Act, 20 of 1907 (C.C.), sec. 3).

Feud "is a gift of certain immovable property, in an indivisible usufruct of inheritance, subject to the mutual condition of protection and homage between the lord and his vassal" (Van Leeuwen's *Comm.* Kotzé's trans. vol. 1, p. 250). Van Leeuwen explains that it is indivisible, for feudal property in Holland is not divisible, and can only descend and rest upon one head (*ibid.* p. 252). As to acquisition and loss of *feuds*, see Van Leeuwen's *Comm.* Kotzé's trans. vol. 1, pp. 257–64, and 270–73.

Feudatory, the holder of a feud. *See* FEUD.

Fiat, an order or authority authorising certain process. See Act 46 of 1882 (C.C.), sec. 8, where, in the Cape Colony, the *fiat* of the Attorney-General, Solicitor-General, or Crown Prosecutor, respectively, is required before a criminal prosecution for criminal libel can be commenced.

Fiat justitia, ruat coelum, let justice be done though the heavens should fall.

Fideicommissary heir, the heir who enjoys the benefit of a *fideicommissum;* he is frequently described as the "fideicommissary."

Fideicommissum, a grant of property to a person subject to a condition that he will hand over the same either wholly or in part, and that either immediately or after a certain time, and either simply or conditionally, to a third party (Grotius' *Introd.* 2, 20, 1; Voet's *Comm.* 36, 1, 6). A *fideicommissum* is usually created by last will, but it may also be constituted by deed *inter vivos*, such as an antenuptial contract. The Roman law form of *fideicommissum*, by which the heir was directed to hand over the property immediately to a third party, is obsolete, the usual form in the Roman-Dutch law being a grant or bequest of property to a person coupled with a direction that upon the happening of a certain event, usually the death of such person, the property will go to a third party. The person upon whom the trust is imposed of handing over the property is called the fiduciary; the person in whose favour it is created is called the fideicommissary.

Fideicommissum residui, a *fideicommissum* of the residue or remainder; a *fideicommissum* imposed by a testator, not upon the inheritance as a whole or upon any specific part of it, but upon what is left over at the death of the heir. Under Justinian's *Novel* (108, c. 1), which is incorporated in the Roman-Dutch law, a person who was instituted heir on condition that whatever was left over at his death should go to a third person was entitled to dispose of three-fourths of the estate during his lifetime, although he was bound to let whatever was left over go to the fideicommissary. An exception to this rule was admitted by the law of Holland, and has been recognised as of force in this country, viz., where two spouses married in community have by mutual will instituted each other reciprocally as heir with power of alienation, but on condition that whatever shall be left of the joint estate at the death of the survivor shall go to a third person or be divided equally between the heirs of the husband and the heirs of the wife. In that case the survivor is not bound to preserve even one-fourth for the fiduciary heir or heirs, but may spend the whole estate during his or her lifetime (*Brown* v. *Rickard*, 2 S.C. 314; *Klopper* v. *Smit*, 9 S.C. 167; Voet's *Comm.* 36, 1, 56; Schorer's *Note* 156).

Fideicommittens, he who by a testamentary or other disposition of his property creates a trust or *fideicommissum* in favour of some one.

Fidejussores, sureties. *See* SURETY.

Fiduciary heir, the heir who takes over property subject to a *fideicommissum*; he is often described as the "fiduciary."

Fief, synonymous with feud. *See* FEUD.

Field-cornetcy, the district or portion of a district over which a field-cornet has jurisdiction. See Act 48 of 1899 (C.C.), sec. 2; Act 26 of 1902 (C.C.), sec. 2; Act 20 of 1908 (O.R.C.), sec. 1.

Fieri facias (abbreviated *fi. fa.*), in English practice, a writ of execution.

Fieri feci, in English practice, the return of the Sheriff to the writ of *fieri facias.*

Filiation, the relation of a son or daughter to his or her parent; the act of adoption. Correlative of *paternity.*

Filius nullius, a son of no man; nobody's son.

Filum fluminis, the thread of a river; an imaginary line drawn down the centre of a river. *See* AD MEDIUM FILUM.

Final judgment, a judgment that finally disposes of the rights of the parties on a specific question. See *Colonial Government* v. *Dundee Coal Co.* (26 N.L.R. 346); *Inglis* v. *Durban Navigation Collieries* (27 N.L.R. 747); *Kimberley Waterworks Co.* v. *Kimberley Town Council* (19 S.C. 135).

Final order. "A final order is one settling the dispute between the parties (*per* INNES, C.J., in *Smith* v. *James,* [1907] T.S. at p. 448). See *Pretoria Racing Club* v. *Van Pietersen* ([1907] T.S. at p. 694).

Final order of sequestration, the judgment of a superior court placing the estate of an insolvent under sequestration for the benefit of his creditors. *See* COMPULSORY SEQUESTRATION.

Financial year, the year fixed by statute, articles of association, agreement or otherwise for the financial purposes of any government, corporation or person. See the Audit and Exchequer Act, 14 of 1907 (T.).

In the Cape Colony, by Act 14 of 1906, sec. 3 (*d*), it is defined to mean "the period from the first day of July in one year to the thirtieth day of June in the next following year, both days inclusive."

Fine (*boete*) "is a punishment consisting of money" (Van Leeuwen's *Comm.* Kotzé's trans. vol. 2, p. 563).

Firearms. Under the Cape Firearms and Ammunition Act (17 of 1892) "*firearms* means guns, pistols and all parts thereof, and any other description of *firearms* and all parts thereof wherein any explosive is capable of being used." See also Act 11 of 1862 (N.), sec. 58; Law 16 of 1862 (N.), sec. 9; Act 1 of 1906 (N.), sec. 3.

Fire-clay. "It is clear that absolutely pure clay is a mineral even in the narrow sense. It is called kaolin, but, scientifically speaking, it is hydrosilicate of alumina. When mixed with a proportion of basic metals it becomes a compound, and when hard and compressed it is called a rock. If the proportion of basic metals mixed with the pure kaolin is comparatively small, then the substance is called *fire-clay*; and, not being easily fusible, it is used for purposes for which great heat-resisting properties are required. If, on the other hand, the proportion of basic metals is large, then the compound is comparatively easily fusible, and is used as ordinary clay for making bricks for building purposes and such like. Applying those definitions, it seems to me that though *fire-clay* might not fall within the narrow meaning of the word 'mineral,' it would certainly be included in the wider definition of that term" (*per* INNES, C.J., in *New Blue Sky G. M. Co., Ltd.*, v. *Marshall*, [1905] T.S. at p. 367). In *Donovan* v. *Turffontein Estate Co.* (2 Off. Rep. 218) it was held that a clause in an agricultural lease, to the effect that the appearer of the third part will be entitled during the continuance of the lease to all minerals, precious stones or metals did not include the right to dig for clay in order to make and sell bricks or tiles. "The fact that in other countries clay is regarded as a metal, or rather as a mineral, is not *per se* sufficient. We must interpret the words in the contract according to the ordinary and common meaning in this country, even although the scientific meaning may be different" (*per* KOTZÉ, C.J., at p. 223). Similarly it was unanimously held by the House of Lords that sandstone is not a mineral within the meaning of sec. 70 of the Railway Clauses Consolidation (Scotland) Act, 1845 (*North British Railway Co.* v. *Budhill Coal and Sandstone Co.*, 26 T.L.R. 79).

Fire-insurance, that branch of insurance business which relates particularly to the risk of loss by fire. *See* INSURANCE.

Fire policy, a written contract of insurance, whereby for a consideration the person or corporation granting the policy indemnifies the person to whom it is granted against risk of loss by fire in respect of the property described in the policy, and subject to its conditions. The consideration so given or paid to the grantor of the policy is called a *premium*.

Firewood. "*Firewood* shall include parts of trees of all species made up into bundles, billets or loads; or cut up in the manner it is usual to cut wood for burning, and refuse wood generally" (the Cape Forest Act, 28 of 1888, sec. 2).

Firm, a partnership of two or more persons for the purpose of carrying on business; a commercial house; the name or style under which a partnership carries on its business. "Partners who have entered into partnership with one another are called collectively a *firm*, and the name under which their business is carried on is called the 'firm-name'" (Partnership Act, 1890, Eng., sec. 3).

In Natal in the Registration of Firms Act (35 of 1906) *firm* is defined to mean "any two or more persons lawfully associated for the purpose of carrying on any business, but shall not include a partnership registered under Law 1 of 1865, or a company registered or incorporated within the British Dominions under, by, or in pursuance of any Letters Patent, Royal Charter, or Act of Parliament other than this Act."

Firm contract, see *Cambrian Collieries, Ltd.*, v. *Smith & Ramsay* (23 N.L.R. at p. 343).

Firm-name, the name by which the business of a partnership is known and carried on. In Natal in the Registration of Firms Act (35 of 1906) provision is made for the registration of the *firm-name* of firms or persons carrying on business or having any place of business in Natal. In that Act *firm-name* is defined to mean "the name or style under which any business is carried on, whether in partnership or otherwise." *See* FIRM.

Firm offer, a definite offer or proposal made by one person to another for a certain period or pending a certain contingency, and subject to the acceptance of such other person within that period or pending that contingency (see *Ferguson* v. *Merensky*, [1903] T.S. 657). *See* OFFER.

First refusal. "An agreement by an owner of land to give to another person the *first refusal* of the land in certain events either means that he must on the happening of the events give the other person the opportunity of refusing a fair and reasonable offer, or that he must give the other person the opportunity of refusing the land at a price acceptable to the owner offered by some third person. The owner does not, on either view, comply with the condition if he offers the land to the first person at a price higher than he would accept from other would-be buyers in the event of the refusal of the first person to buy at that price" (Mew's *note* of *Manchester Ship Canal Co.* v. *Manchester Racecourse Co.*, [1901] 2 Ch. 37; 70 L.J. Ch. 468; 84 L.T. 436; 17 T.L.R. 410).

Firsts. Referring to the term *firsts* as used in the brick trade, GRAHAM, J., in *Scarrott* v. *Grahamstown Brick and Tile Co.* ([1907] E.D.C. at p. 285) said: "I am convinced on the evidence that the general meaning of *firsts* is hard bricks, and that quality and not colour is the test of a 'first' brick."

Fisc. Cloete, J., in *Chase, N.O.*, v. *Du Toit's Trustees* (3 Searle, 78), said: "I find that Boel, in his notes to Loenius' treatise on *Decisions of the Court of Holland*, is the first author who lays it down that by the word *fisc*, used in laws, is not to be understood the Crown or Government in its general sense, but only that branch of the Government which is expressly charged with the collection of the revenue."

Fiscus, the fisc or treasury. This was the name originally given by the Romans to the private purse of the emperor, as distinguished from the *aerarium*, which signified the moneys or goods belonging to the public or the State. Latterly the term was more commonly used in the sense of *aerarium*, to denote the public treasury. *See* Aerarium; Fisc.

Fish is defined in the Natal Coast Fisheries Act (31 of 1906, sec. 6) as follows: "Every description of fish and shell of fish and aquatic animal which is found in the waters to which this Act applies, together with the ova, spawn or eggs thereof."

Fixed deposit, the deposit of money in a bank or similar institution for a definite period; it is a loan to the banker, and is not a specific fund held by him in a fiduciary capacity.

Fixed establishment of the civil service, persons permanently appointed to positions in the civil service. See the Cape Civil Service and Pensions Funds Act (32 of 1895), sec. 3.

Fixed property, in Transvaal Proclamation 8 of 1902, sec. 2, is defined to include: (1) Land or the usufruct thereof or any other limited interest therein other than a lease; (2) mynpachts, claims and stands; (3) any right to minerals or precious stones on any land. In *Van der Hoven* v. *Cutting* ([1903] T.S. 299) it was decided that the words *limited interest therein* (in the above definition) refer only to interests *ejusdem generis* with usufruct, that is, to such interests as confer upon the possessors some real right. See also *Van Wyk and Others* v. *Dykerman* ([1904] T.S. at p. 915). See Ordinance 12 of 1906 (O.R.C.), sec. 2.

Stands let on ninety-nine years' lease under the Transvaal Gold Law are *fixed property*; see *per cur.* in *Collins, N.O.*, v. *Hugo and the Standard Bank* (H. 178); and *Ismail and Amod* v. *Lucas' Trustee* ([1905] T.H. at p. 81).

Flagrante delicto, in the act of committing a crime. Correctly written the expression is *in flagrante delicto*, and is applied to a person who is caught in the very act of committing a crime.

Floating capital, such portion of a company's or person's capital as is retained in hand for the purpose of meeting current expenditure.

Floating policy. "A *floating policy* is one in which there is no limitation of the risk to a particular ship, as where goods 'on ship or ships' are insured for the same voyage" (Arnould's *Marine Insurance*, 7th ed. sec. 9; see also secs. 185 and 186).

"The amount of goods covered by such a policy is ascertainable at the moment of loss only, and to protect the insurers, such a policy provides that the liability of the insurers shall be only rateable" (Porter's *Laws of Insurance*, 5th ed. p. 31).

Flock. In the Cape Scab Act (20 of 1894), sec. 4, the term *flock* is defined to mean "two or more sheep running together."

Flogging. In the Native Territories' Penal Code (Act 24 of 1886 (C.C.), sec. 10) it is provided that "*flogging* shall consist of the infliction on a male person, who shall have attained the age of sixteen years, of a number of strokes, not exceeding at any one time fifty, with an instrument specified by the court, and in default of such specification with such instrument as the Governor shall direct."

Flotation of a company, the act or process of forming and registering a company. "The term *flotation* is a technical one, and, as applied to companies, is of comparatively recent origin" (*per* De Villiers, C.J., in *Torva Exploring Syndicate* v. *Kelly*, 15 S.C. at p. 141. See also report of same case on appeal, [1900] A.C. 612; 69 L.J. P.C. 115; 83 L.T. 34; 16 T.L.R. 495, and 17 S.C. 301, where the term *flotation* is fully discussed).

Flotsam or **floatsam,** goods lost by shipwreck and which are found floating upon the water; such goods belong to the Crown if not claimed within a year and a day. See English Merchant Shipping Act, 1894, sec. 510.

Flumen, the name given in the Roman law to the servitude regarding rainwater collected in a spout from the roof of a house, and led on to a neighbour's land. When the rainwater was not so collected, but dripped from the eaves of the roof, the servitude was called *stillicidium*. *See* Servitus Fluminis.

Flumen privatum, a private river. Private rivers are rivers and streams which have not a perennial flow (Voet's *Comm.* 43, 12) and "streamlets which, although perennial, are so weak as to be incapable of being applied to the common use of the riparian proprietors" (*Van Heerden* v. *Wiese*, 1 Buch. A.C. 7; *De Wet* v. *Hiscock*, 1 E.D.C. at p. 257). Private streams belong to the owner of the land through which they flow, and in no way differ from other kinds of private property. See *Meyer* v. *Johannesburg Waterworks Co.* (H. at p. 10) *See* also Flumen publicum; Public Stream.

Flumen publicum, a public river. This term includes all streams which have a perennial flow, whether they are navigable or not (Voet's *Comm.* 39, 3, 1; 43, 12; 43, 13), and "all streams which, though not large enough to be considered as rivers, are yet perennial and capable of being applied to the common use of the riparian proprietors" (*Van Heerden* v. *Wiese*, 1 Buch. A.C. 7; *De Wet* v. *Hiscock*, 1 E.D.C. at p. 257). With regard to the term perennial, a stream is such that is always running, while a non-perennial stream is one the water of which runs only in rainy seasons. But the fact that a stream which is usually perennial ceases to flow during a very dry season will not make it non-perennial (Pothier on the *Pandects*, 43, 12, 1, sec. 2; *Vermaak* v. *Palmer*, 6 Buch. 28; *De Wet* v. *Hiscock*, 1 E.D.C. at p. 257). An interdict lies against any one who does anything upon a public river or stream or upon its banks whereby the navigation or mooring may be impaired (*ne quid in eo ripave ejus fiat quo deterior statio aut navigatio reddatur*) (Voet's *Comm.* 43, 12). So if anything is attempted by any one that may change the measure or character of the stream from what it was in the preceding summer (or dry season) any member of the public may apply for an interdict (*ne quid in flumine publico ripave ejus fiat, quo aliter aqua fluit atque priore aestate fluxit*) to prevent the alteration, or, if it has already been made, for an order of court to restore the stream to its original condition (Voet's *Comm.* 43, 13). See *Meyer* v. *Johannesburg Waterworks Co.* (H. 1). *See* also AD MEDIUM FILUM.

F.O.B., a commercial abbreviation of the words "Free on Board." When goods are sold *F.O.B.* the seller pays the expenses connected with such goods up to the time they are placed on board ship, after which all freight and further charges of delivery must be borne by the purchaser. It seems that when the goods have been so placed on board the ship they remain at the risk of the purchaser; see Benjamin on *Sales*, 4th ed. p. 289. As to the vendor's loss of lien under such a contract, see *ibid.* at p. 838.

Foenus nauticum, the high rate of interest claimed by persons who lend money on bottomry.

Folio, in legal documents is usually a page containing a specific number of words; in some instances it merely indicates a page of written or typed matter. The term *folio* also signifies the number of a page; or the largest size of book or volume.

Folteren (D.), to put to the torture.

Fons et origo, the source and origin.

Food. In the Cape Sale of Food and Drugs and Seeds Act (5 of 1890) the term *food* is defined to include "every article used for food or drink by man, other than drugs or water; see also Act 27 of 1906 (C.C.), sec. 1. The Natal Act (45 of 1901, sec. 3) adds the following to the foregoing definition: "and any article which ordinarily enters into or is used in the composition or preparation of human food; and also includes flavouring matters and condiments;" and so too in Ordinance 32 of 1906 (O.R.C.), sec. 1.

Forcible entry, the actual and violent entry upon lands or premises of another without lawful authority. A lease empowering the lessor, in the event of a breach of its conditions, to remove and expel the lessee from the premises without legal process and without liability for damages is illegal and void; and a lessee forcibly ejected under such an agreement for failing to perform a condition of the lease is entitled to be reinstated, for the lessor may not take the law into his own hands (*Blomson* v. *Boshoff*, [1905] T.S. 429).

Foreclosure, a term used in English law to signify the forfeiture by the mortgagor of his equity of redemption upon breach of a condition of the bond as to payment of capital or interest. It also signifies the act of foreclosing.

Foreign company is defined in the Transvaal Companies Act (31 of 1909), sec. 2, as "a company or other association of persons which has for its objects the acquisition of gain by the company or association, or by the individual members thereof, and is registered or incorporated in a foreign country under the laws of that country." For provisions as to foreign companies, see chap. V of Act.

Foreign Enlistment Acts, statutes having for their object the prevention of British subjects serving foreign countries in time of war. See statutes of the various colonies under this title. "A *Foreign Enlistment Act* makes it possible for the Ministry to check intervention in foreign contests or the supply of arms to foreign belligerents" (Dicey's *Law of the Constitution*, 6th ed. p. 356).

Foreign judgment, see *Smart* v. *Raymond & Smart*, 24 N.L.R at pp. 352 *et seq.*

Foreign Jurisdiction Acts, statutes in Great Britain regulating the exercise of the jurisdiction acquired by the Crown, whether by treaty or otherwise, in foreign countries.

Foreign liquidator. In the Transvaal Foreign Trustees and Liquidators Recognition Act (7 of 1907), sec. 1, *foreign liquidator* means and includes "a person duly appointed in any British possession for the purpose of liquidating any company." The same definition is given in Act 4 of 1908 (O.R.C.), sec. 1.

Foreign spirits. This expression is defined in the Cape Excise Spirits Act (18 of 1884), sec. 2, and in the Cape Additional Taxation

Act (36 of 1904), sec. 2, as follows: "*Foreign spirits* means all spirits and strong waters liable to a duty of Customs."

Foreign State, in the Natal and the Transvaal Foreign Enlistment statutes (Act 26 of 1906 (N.), sec. 30, and Ordinance 1 of 1906 (T.), sec. 30 of sch.) includes "any foreign prince, colony, province, or part of any province or people, or any person or persons exercising or assuming to exercise the powers of government in or over any foreign country, colony, province, or part of any province or people."

Foreign substance, see Wine, Brandy, Whisky and Spirits Act, 42 of 1906 (C.C.), sec. 7, as amended by Act 19 of 1908 (C.C.), secs. 6 and 7.

Foreign trustee. In the Transvaal Foreign Trustees and Liquidators Recognition Act (7 of 1907), sec. 1, *foreign trustee* means and includes "a person duly appointed in any British possession for the purpose of administering, liquidating and distributing any bankrupt or insolvent estate." The same definition is found in Act 4 of 1908 (O.R.C.), sec. 1.

Foreman, the presiding member of the jury, appointed by the jury to act as spokesman.

Forensic, pertaining to courts of justice or public debate; fitted for legal argument.

Forensic medicine, medical jurisprudence; the science which applies the principles and practice of medicine to the elucidation of doubtful questions in a court of justice.

Forensis strepitus, the clamour of the forum or law courts.

Foreshore, that portion of the beach or shore which is covered by the sea at an ordinary tide, and is left uncovered at low tide. See *Colonial Government* v. *Town Council of Capetown* (19 S.C. 87).

Forest offence. "*Forest offence* shall mean any contravention of any provision of this Act [Cape Forest Act, 1888], or of any regulation or rule made hereunder" (Act 28 of 1888 (C.C.), sec. 2).

Forest officer. "*Forest officer* shall mean any person duly appointed to be superintendent of woods and forests, conservator, assistant conservator, district forest officer, inspector, forest clerk, ranger, forester or forest guard" (Act 28 of 1888 (C.C.), sec. 2).

Forest produce. "*Forest produce* shall include the following things when found in or when brought from a forest: game, fish, minerals, stones, earth, trees, timber, firewood, wattles, kraal-wood, branch-wood, slabs, chips, sawdust, plants, grass, reeds, thatch, rushes, bedding, peat, creepers, fibres, leaves, moss, flowers, ferns, fruit, seeds, roots, bulbs, galls, spices, bark, gum, resin, sap, charcoal, honey, wax, shells, skins, horns, ivory, and generally everything growing or contained within the forest" (The Cape Forest Act, 28 of 1888, sec. 2).

Forfeiture in statutes "means *forfeiture* to the Crown, except when it is imposed for wrongful detention or dispossession; in which cases the *forfeiture* goes to the benefit of the party wronged" (Maxwell's *Interpretation of Statutes*, 4th ed. p. 526).

Forgery, the making of a false document with intent to defraud, coupled with an actual or potential prejudice to some person or persons. "Forgery under the Roman-Dutch law is merely a species of the crime of falsity, and the best definition of it I know is the one given by Matthaeus, viz.: 'A wilful perversion of the truth with intent to deceive and to the prejudice of another'" (*per* SOLOMON, J., in *Rex* v. *Jolosa*, [1903] T.S. at p. 699). In a prosecution for *forgery* (*crimen falsi*) it is not necessary to prove actual prejudice suffered by a third person, if only the act was of such a nature that in the ordinary course of things it was calculated to prejudice such person (*Rex* v. *Jolosa*, [1903] T.S. 694; *Crowe* v. *Rex*, [1904] T.S. at p. 583; see also *Rex* v. *Firling*, 18 E.D.C. 11; *Rex* v. *Lin Yunn Chen*, [1908] T.S. 634; and an article in 21 S.A.L.J. 194). See also sec. 7 of Act 3 of 1861 (C.C.); sec. 130 of Ordinance 1 of 1903 (T.); and sec. 15 of Law 17 of 1859 (N.); and FRAUD.

In the Cape Native Territories' Penal Code (Act 24 of 1886, sec. 221) *forgery* is thus defined: "*Forgery* is the making of a false document, knowing it to be false, with the intention that it shall in any way be used or acted upon as genuine whether within her Majesty's dominions or not. Making a false document includes altering a genuine document in any material part and adding to it any false date, attestation or other thing which is material, or making any material alteration in it either by erasure, obliteration, removal or otherwise. See also Act 16 of 1895, sec. 4.

Form, the manner or style in which a document is drawn, apart from its substance; a precedent constituting the basis of a document so far as its style is concerned.

Forma pauperis, in the form of a poor man. A person who is authorised by the court to sue or defend *in formâ pauperis* has, before such authority is granted, to satisfy the court that he is not possessed of means, apart from the subject of the action, above the value of a certain amount, the maximum being in the Transvaal, £25. The court then appoints an attorney and an advocate without remuneration to conduct his cause. If the pauper is successful in his action he will be entitled to the costs of suit.

Formulary, a precise statement or form of words made according to a prescribed form or rule; a precedent.

Fortes fortuna adjuvat, fortune favours the bold

Forthwith. "The word *forthwith* is not as peremptory as "immediately." This appears from the leading case of *The Queen* v. *The Justices of Worcester* (7 Dowl. 789). In that case it was held that where a statute requires that recognisances shall be entered into *forthwith* after notice of appeal, it means 'within a reasonable time'; and in giving judgment COLERIDGE, J., said, 'I agree that the word *forthwith* is not to receive a strict construction like the word "immediately," so that whatever follows must be done immediately after that which has been done before.' This decision has never been overruled" (*per* BARRY, J.P., in *Jamieson* v. *Rhind*, 4 E.D.C. at p. 318). See *Lok Jan* v. *Rex* ([1906] E.D.C. 28).

Fortior et potentior est dispositio legis quam hominis, the disposition of the law is stronger and more powerful than that of man. This maxim applies to those cases in which the individual is not allowed to vary the rules of law, any attempt on his part to do so being rendered void and ineffectual. For instance, by an antenuptial contract the community of property which marriage otherwise creates between spouses may be excluded, but if such a contract should not have been entered into no alteration can be afterwards made with respect to the community by an act *inter vivos*. So, a donation between husband and wife during marriage is null and void, and the donor cannot by any act make it effectual either as against himself or his or her creditors, even though the spouses may by antenuptial contract have reserved to themselves the right to make donations to each other (*Hall* v. *Hall's Trustee*, 3 S.C. 3).

Fortiter in re, with firmness in action.

Forum, a court; especially a court having jurisdiction to try a certain action. See Holland's *Jurisprudence*, 10th ed. pp. 398 and 412.

Forum domicilii, the forum or court of the domicile. A married woman takes upon marriage the domicile of her husband and—subject to certain cases in which she is considered to acquire a distinct domicile for herself—afterwards follows any new domicile which may be acquired by him (Voet's *Comm.* 5, 1, 95 and 101; 23, 2, 40). It has accordingly been held that the *forum domicilii* of the husband is also that of the wife, "whether she be at the time actually resident within the territory of the said *forum* or not, and this for the trial of all questions, not only arising between the wife and third parties, but between the wife and the husband, and respecting the rights and obligations and duties of both parties, which result from their relation as husband and wife" (*Reeves* v. *Reeves*, 1 Menz. at p. 249; see also *Bestandig* v. *Bestandig*, 1 Menz. 280; *Hawkes* v. *Hawkes*, 2 S.C. 109; *Ex parte Atkinson*, Off. Rep. 1895 (Webber's trans.), 212; *Ex parte Standing*, [1906] E.D.C. 169; and *Hudson* v. *Hudson*, [1907] E.D.C. 189).

Forum originis, the court of the country of a person's domicile by birth.

Forwarding agent, an agent who undertakes to receive goods for, and to despatch them to his principal or to his principal's order, in consideration of a certain commission or charge.

"Found." As to a charge against an accused person of contravening sec. 142 of Law 15 of 1908 (T.) by being *found* in possession of a quantity of unwrought gold, and not being able to prove that he became possessed of the same by lawful means, see *Rex* v. *Allen* ([1907] T.S. 59).

As to gaming appliances being *found* on a prisoner, see *Rex* v. *Moss* ([1908] T.S. at p. 802).

Frana (D.). *See* VROON.

Franchise, the right of voting at a public election, such as a parliamentary election. Also a privilege enjoyed by a subject of the sovereign by virtue of a royal grant or by virtue of prescription. *See* VOTER.

Frater consanguineus, a brother by the father's side.

Frater uterinus, a brother by the mother's side.

Fratricide, the act of killing a brother; or one who kills his brother.

Fraud, "the act of a person by which he premeditatedly causes damage to another with whom he is treating and who is ignorant thereof" (Van Leeuwen's *Comm.* Kotzé's trans. vol. 2, p. 13, translator's *note*).

"The word *fraud* as used in this [Cape] Colony is a very wide one, and embraces within its meaning the terms '*dolus malus,*' '*falsum*' and '*stellionatus,*' as used by the Roman-Dutch text-writers. The first of these terms is only used in civil cases, and especially in matters of contract; the two last terms are only applied to criminal offences. . . . A mere lie, which is foolishly acted upon by others to whom it is addressed, does not constitute a *fraud* in the legal sense of the term, unless the utterer intended or must, from the mode and circumstances in which he uttered it, be presumed to have intended that it should be acted upon" (*per* DE VILLIERS, C.J., in *Tait* v. *Wicht and Others,* 7 S.C. at pp. 165 and 164).

"Fair and honest competition, however active, is open to every one, but no one has the right to take an undue and improper advantage by means of falsehoods, the effect of which is to benefit himself at the expense of another" (*per* DE VILLIERS, C.J., in *Gous* v. *De Kock,* 5 S.C. at p. 409).

"If the defendant honestly believed his representation to be true, it cannot be relied upon as a fraudulent representation giving rise to an action for damages. Independently of contract, a false representation causing damage is not actionable unless it is fraudulent. If made recklessly without regard to its truth or falsehood, it would be fraudulent, but the defendant's honest belief in the truth of his statement is sufficient to negative *fraud* on his part" (*per* DE VILLIERS, C.J., in *Dickson & Co.* v. *Levy*, 11 S.C. at p. 36).

"There is no principle more clearly established in the administration of justice than that *fraud* must not only be alleged, but that it must be clearly and distinctly proved" (*per* DE VILLIERS, C.J., in *Standard Bank* v. *Du Plooy and Another*, 16 S.C. at p. 166; see also *Shauban* v. *Goveia*, 11 C.T.R. 289). *Fraud* is not to be presumed (Voet's *Comm.* 4, 3, 2 and 9, 2, 20).

"If the charges are true, the plaintiff would not be deprived of his right to relief by reason of thirty years having elapsed since the *fraud* was committed, provided, of course, his action is brought within a reasonable time after discovery of the fraud" (*per* DE VILLIERS, C.J., in *Bydien* v. *Samao's Estate*, 13 C.T.R. 667).

Wilful misrepresentation amounts in law to *fraud* (*per* BUCHANAN, Acting C.J., in *Schoeneman* v. *Cape Lime Co.*, 7 C.T.R. at p. 361).

An act fraudulently done with the intention of perverting the truth in *fraud* of another. See *Moolchund* v. *Rex* (23 N.L.R. 76).

As to *fraud* in commercial transactions, see also *Hain & Son* v. *Elandslaagte Colliery Co., Ltd., and Young* (24 N.L.R. at pp. 373 *et seq.*), and Van Leeuwen's *Comm.* Kotzé's trans. 4, 1, 6 and notes. *Fraud* renders a contract voidable at the election of the party sought to be defrauded (Voet's *Comm.* 4, 3, 7 and 18, 1, 5, *in fine*).

Fraudulent insolvency. In the Cape Colony an insolvent whose estate has been placed under sequestration is deemed to be guilty of the crime of *fraudulent insolvency* (sec. 70 of Ordinance 6 of 1843) if (1) he shall, either before or after the making of the order for sequestration, have alienated, transferred, given, ceded, delivered, mortgaged or pledged or shall have embezzled, concealed or removed any part of his estate or effects to the value of £10 or upwards; or (2) shall have concealed, removed, destroyed, falsified or mutilated any books of accounts, papers, writings, documents, bills or vouchers relating thereto with intent to defraud his creditors; or (3) shall have fraudulently contracted any debt; or (4) if he shall at the second meeting of his creditors or any adjournment thereof wilfully lodge any inventory containing any false statement of his estate or effects or any part thereof, or with respect to any debt due to or by him, or shall produce any books of accounts, papers, writings, documents, bills or vouchers which are false, or on which any erasure or alteration has been made or caused to be made by him, or with his knowledge, with the intent to defraud his creditors; or (5) if he shall at any time when examined before any court or commissioner, or by the Master or a resident magistrate, wilfully make any false answers to any lawful questions then put to him with intent to defraud his creditors; or (6) if he shall have connived at or concealed from the trustee his knowledge of the proof by any person of a false debt against his estate; or (7) if he shall (under sec. 63 of the same Ordinance) have been lawfully summoned to appear before a superior court or a commissioner, and shall depart from the colony, or abscond or conceal himself within the colony with the purpose and intent to evade appearing at any such examination to which he was summoned or to prevent a warrant under the Ordinance being executed upon him. On conviction for *fraudulent insolvency* the insolvent may be sentenced to transportation for life or for any shorter period not less than five years or imprisonment with or without hard labour for any period not exceeding five years (the penalty under sec. 63 is slightly different).

The definition of *fraudulent insolvency* in the Transvaal is almost identical with that of the Cape Colony (see sec. 146 of Law 13 of 1895). The punishment on conviction is imprisonment with or without hard labour for a period not exceeding seven years.

In the Orange River Colony the definition is also substantially the same as that in Cape Colony, omitting (7), and the punishment is imprisonment with or without hard labour for a period not exceeding five years.

Fraudulently. "The term *fraudulently* would imply the existence of the intention" [to defraud] (*per* DE VILLIERS, C.J., in *Tait* v. *Wicht and Others*, 7 S.C. at p. 166).

Fraus pia, a pious fraud; artifice employed for a good or laudable purpose.

Free occupation, discussed in *Crosbie* v. *Crosbie's Executors and Another* (21 S.C. at p. 606).

Free pass. *Free pass* shall mean an authority in writing given by the Administration (the Central South African Railways), or by an officer thereto appointed, for the person to whom it is given to travel as a passenger on a railway without the payment of any fare (Act 13 of 1908 (T.), sec. 2; Act 29 of 1908 (O.R.C.), sec. 2).

Free persons "were those who have lived of their own resources and have never engaged in any servile handiwork or trade" (Van Leeuwen's *Comm.* Kotzé's trans. vol. 1, p. 66).

Freehold. Where land is described as being held in *freehold*, it signifies that the owner holds it in his own right absolutely, according to registered title; opposed to leasehold title.

Freemen. (1) Men who, in the time of the Romans, were either free born or made free. "A freeborn man is one free from his birth, being the offspring of parents united in wedlock, whether both be free born or both made free, or one made free and the other free born. He is also free born if his mother be free, even though his father be a slave, and so also is he whose paternity is uncertain, being the offspring of promiscuous intercourse, but whose mother is free. . . . Those are freedmen, or made free, who have been manumitted from legal slavery" (Justinian's *Institutes*, Moyle's trans. 1, 4 and 5). "A slave on being set free assumed the name of his master, to whom he did not cease to belong. The relation of patron and freedman was in fact a continuance as regards the family in a modified form of the relation of master and slave. But his business relations with the world generally, including his patron, were now on a different footing: he could act and was responsible for himself. His children born after manumission were freeborn, and did not stand in any such quasi-servile relation to their father's patron" (Roby's *Roman Private Law*, vol. 1, p. 82).

(2) *Freemen* "(*poorters*) are those persons who, not having been born within a town, have purchased the rights of citizenship and of trading as citizens, which any one can obtain upon application and payment of a small sum, provided he takes the oath of allegiance Such persons, after having been for some years *freemen*, acquire the full right of citizenship, and, together with other citizens can be appointed to all the offices and dignities of the town" (Van Leeuwen's *Comm.* Kotzé's trans. vol. 1, p. 72).

Freight. (1) In shipping law "*freight* is the reward payable to the carrier for the safe carriage and delivery of goods; it is payable only on the safe carriage and delivery. . . . But a sum of money payable before the arrival of the ship at her port of discharge, and payable by the shippers of the goods at the port of shipment, does not acquire the legal character of *freight* because it is described under that name in a bill of lading, nor does it acquire the legal incidents of *freight*. It is in effect money to be paid for taking the goods on board and undertaking to carry, and not for carrying them" (*Kirchner* v. *Venus*, 12 Moore P.C. 361). "The term *freight* is ambiguous, and may by context be construed to mean a payment which is not strictly *freight*, but a sum of money to be paid at all events in consideration of the master receiving the goods on board and undertaking to carry them" (*Andrew* v. *Moorhouse*, 12 R.C. 369).

(2) As to *freight* payable for transport on a railway: "*Freight* shall include all sums received or receivable, charged or chargeable for the transport of goods upon or along any railway" (Act 13 of 1908 (T.), sec. 2; Act 29 of 1908 (O.R.C.), sec. 2).

Friendly action, an action brought in a court of law in a friendly manner, for the purpose of obtaining the court's ruling upon some doubtful point in dispute between the parties.

Friendly society, in the Transvaal Companies Act (31 of 1909), sec. 202 (from the operation of which Act such a society is excluded), is defined as "a society of persons formed solely or mainly for the purpose of raising by the voluntary subscriptions of its members, with or without the aid of donations, a fund—(*a*) for the relief or maintenance of members and their relatives during minority, old age, widowhood, sickness, or other infirmity, mental or bodily, or for the endowment at any age of members or their nominees; (*b*) providing medical attendance and procuring medicines and medical requirements for such members or relatives; (*c*) insuring a sum to be paid on the birth of a member's child or on the death of a member or for the funeral expenses of the husband, wife, child or relative of a member. See also secs. 2 and 3 of the Cape Friendly Societies Act (5 of 1892), and Natal Friendly Societies Law (20 of 1862), sec. 1.

Frone (D.). *See* VROON.

Fructus civiles, civil fruits; profits arising from things which yield no natural fruits, as rent of land and interest on money (Voet's *Comm.* 41, 1, 28).

Fructus industriales, industrial fruits; fruits which are produced by the aid of man's labour, such as corn and vintages.

Fructus naturales, natural fruits; fruits produced without the care or cultivation of man, such as apples, brushwood, grass, and the young of animals (Voet's *Comm.* 41, 1, 28).

Fructus pendentes, fruits hanging or ungathered, which are considered as part of the soil and immovable, as distinguished from *fructus percepti*, fruits which have been cut or gathered and which are regarded as movable (Voet's *Comm.* 41, 1, 28).

Fructus pendentes pro immobilibus habentur, ungathered fruits are regarded as immovables. Fruits and other things, such as sand, chalk or timber, which have been won or cut, do not pass to a purchaser of the land, but if still ungathered or adhering to the soil they will so pass as part of the land unless specially reserved by the vendor (Voet's *Comm.* 1, 8, 13). Upon the same principle, *fructus pendentes* on the death of a usufructuary will not pass to his heirs, but will belong to the *dominus*.

Fruits. "The term *fruits* denotes whatever the property possessed can annually produce, as all *fruits* of trees and *fruits* of the soil; also everything produced by and out of animals, as calves, foals, lambs, bees, chickens, young pigeons, geese, milk, butter, cheese and the like" (Van Leeuwen's *Comm.* Kotzé's trans. vol. 1, p. 183).

"The word *fruits*, as used in the authorities, has a very wide meaning indeed. The extensive nature of its meaning is referred to by Sir HENRY CONNOR, who says it includes grain, the *fruits* of the land, hire or the work of slaves. This particular question is also discussed by Mr. Chitty in his translation of Voet's title on *Vindication*, and he in turn refers to Burge, whose definition of the term *fruits* is exceedingly wide. It includes, according to him, 'all the profits which are to be derived from property, including those which are produced by cultivation (*fructus industriales*), those which spontaneously grow without any industry (*fructus naturales*), those which do not naturally grow from the property, but are accounted profits as being derived from the use or enjoyment of such property (*fructus civiles*), as interest, pecuniary rent or annuity'" (*per* BALE, C.J., in *Illing* v. *Lawford*, 23 N.L.R. at p. 391).

Fugam fecit, he has taken to flight.

Fugitive criminal is defined in the Natal Extradition Law (6 of 1892) to mean "any person accused or convicted of an extradition crime committed within the jurisdiction of the Orange Free State or the South African Republic who is in, or is suspected of being in, Natal."

Full age, the age of majority. *See* MAJORITY.

Full ownership "is where a person, in addition to the right of ownership, has also the full use" (Van Leeuwen's *Comm.* Kotzé's trans. vol. 1, p. 155).

Functus officio, having discharged his duty; said of a person holding an appointment when his duties have been fully performed or his appointment has come to an end.

Fundi publici, public lands. Among the Romans lands belonging to the State were so called, the revenues from them flowing to the State treasury.

Funeral expenses, the cost of burial. The funeral expenses of the first-dying of two spouses married in community of property "will have to be paid out of his or her half-share of the estate, and are not a debt due by the joint estate" (Maasdorp's *Institutes*, vol. 1, p. 93).

Fungibles, things that are weighed, measured or counted out. As to the risk of buyer or seller of fungibles, see Nathan's *Common Law*, secs. 879 *et seq.*

Furandi animus. *See* ANIMUS FURANDI.

Furtum, theft. In the Roman law theft is defined as "the fraudulent dealing with a thing or with its use or possession for the sake of gain" (*Institutes*, 4, 1, 1; *Digest*, 47, 2, 1, 3). In the Roman-Dutch law it is defined by Van Leeuwen (*Comm.* 4, 38, 1) as "a secret and fraudulent dealing with and retention of the property of another," and by Van der Linden (*Institutes*, 2, 5, 2) as the taking of any movable property without the knowledge and against the will of the owner with the object of obtaining some advantage for one's self or for others. The elements of the crime are thus (1) not mere intention, but an actual dealing with the thing with the object of deriving a gain or advantage; and (2) that the taking was without the consent of the owner or person in lawful possession and without a belief that he would consent. Only movable property can be the subject of theft (Voet's *Comm.* 47, 2, 3).

Furtum usus, theft of the use (*i.e.* the use of a thing). In the case of *R.* v. *Fortuin* (1 App. Cas. 290) it was unanimously decided that *furtum usus* is not a crime by the law of Cape Colony (see also *R.* v. *Dier*, 3 E.D.C. 436). KOTZÉ, C.J., who holds the contrary view (Van Leeuwen's *Comm.* 4, 38, 1, *in notis*), says with regard to the former decision: "On appeal DE VILLIERS, C.J., and SMITH, J., thought that as Voet and Groenewegen seem to leave the question in doubt, and the practice in the colony had been not to indict in such a case, the opinion of the court should be in favour of the prisoner. BARRY, J.P., while admitting that by Roman-Dutch law there could be the theft of the use, held that it is not an indictable offence in the colony. DWYER, J., and BUCHANAN, J.P., concurred. That there may be a theft of the use by Roman-Dutch law is clear. Grotius, 3, 37, 5; Huber. *Heed. Regts.* bk. 6, ch. 5, secs. 1 and 16; Voet, 47, 2, secs. 1, 5 and 8; *Cens. For.* 5, 29, 1; Math. *de Crim.* 47, 1, 8. This being so, the Roman-Dutch law, which is the common law of South Africa, must prevail in the Cape Colony, unless some legislative enactment, or a uniform series of judicial decisions exists to the contrary. There is no legislative enactment at the Cape of Good Hope on the subject, and the only judicial decision approaching the point under consideration is a ruling of BELL, J., in *Queen* v. *Meyer, Rish and Others*, A.D. 1862; the ruling in that case, however, is apparently based on the ground that *sine animo furandi furtum non committitur* (1 Roscoe, 31). It is true the learned CHIEF JUSTICE based his judgment in *Queen* v. *Fortuin* partly upon a written opinion of Porter, A.-G., that it was not the practice in the colony to indict in such cases. But the practice of the Attorney-General, however eminent in his profession, not to indict for *furtum usus* cannot alter the *substantive* law of the land. That *furtum usus*, on the authority of Voet and Groenewegen, is no longer a crime in the case of bailees and others *in a like position*, seems no sufficient ground for laying down the broad proposition that in no case can there be a theft of the use. Nor does it follow that because no indictment has in the Cape Colony been preferred for *furtum usus*, an accused cannot be convicted on an indictment for theft where the evidence shows a theft of the use merely was committed."

Fustages. "Their lordships inquired what was meant by *fustages*, and were told that it meant ullaged wine, which by a judicious blend might possibly be made consumable, and if so would be a valuable asset; but the word is to be found in Murray's *Dictionary*, and it is there defined as 'the vats and tubs and all the wooden utensils used in making wine'; and a quotation is given from a South African newspaper, the *Cape and Natal News* of 7th December, 1868, which shows clearly that there at least it is a known word bearing that signification. The quotation is 'a large vintage in prospect and no fustage in which to store it'" (*per* Sir ALFRED WILLS in *Hamburg* v. *Pickard*, decided by the Judicial Committee of the Privy Council, [1906] T.S. at p. 1016).

"**Future owner,**" discussed in *Krachmal's Trustees and Capetown Town Council* v. *Epstein* (17 S.C. 317).

Fylkisthing, an important and powerful council of the early Germans. See Wessels' *History*, pp. 19 and 20.

Gale (a contraction of the word *gavel, gabellum*), the payment of tribute, rent or interest. An old English law term, very rare in South Africa, but used in Natal in Law 13 of 1887 (to amend the law in respect to tacit hypothecs), where it is defined to mean "the interval between any two next consecutive days for payment of rent."

"The term *gale*, which is foreign to our law, and which was adopted by CONNOR, C.J., is defined to mean the interval between any two next consecutive days for payment of rent" (*per* BALE, C.J., in *Harwin's Estate* v. *Oates*, 27 N.L.R. at p. 242).

Galg (D.), gallows; gibbet.

Gallon, a liquid measure containing four quarts or eight pints.

In the Transvaal Excise Act (9 of 1907), sec. 1, *gallon* means "a liquid gallon imperial measure."

Game. "I am aware that the most general definition, and in fact the etymological meaning, of *game* includes any sport, fun, frolic or pastime. But, as my brother GRAHAM has remarked, if we accepted that meaning we should be going very far in curtailing the liberty of human beings" (*per* KOTZÉ, J.P., in *Oehley* v. *Rex*, [1908] E.D.C. at p. 43). It was therefore held that as a *game* is a contest of some kind, a person going round golf-links by himself on the Lord's Day was not playing the game of golf.

Gaming appliances, any appliances used for gaming; see *Bernstein* v. *Rex* ([1905] T.S. 418). See Ordinance 21 of 1902 (O.R.C.), sec. 13.

Gaol, *see* PRISON. See also Ordinance 6 of 1906 (T.), sec. 3.

Gaoler. "*Gaoler* shall mean the keeper of or officer for the the time being in chief control of any prison or lock-up" (Act 23 of 1888 (C.C.), sec. 2). See also Ordinance 6 of 1906 (T.), sec. 3; Ordinance 3 of 1903 (O.R.C.), sec. 1.

Garnishee, the person who, owing money to a judgment debtor, is called upon by order of court to pay over to an officer of the court (for the benefit of the judgment creditor) so much of the amount owing as will be sufficient to satisfy the debt of the judgment debtor and costs, or failing such payment to appear before the court on a day named in the order and show cause why he should not pay such debt. See Ordinance 12 of 1904 (T.), sec. 6. By the Magistrates' Courts Amendment Act, 30 of 1908 (T.), sec. 6, it is provided that nothing in the Ordinance of 1904 shall authorise a court of resident magistrate to make an order garnisheeing a judgment debtor's wages.

Garnishee order, the order of court granted against a garnishee. *See* GARNISHEE.

Gather, to collect together. In the Natal Coast Fisheries Act (31 of 1906), sec. 20, the word *gather* includes "destroying or disturbing." See Ordinance 1 of 1838 (C.C.), sec. 6, and *Oehley* v. *Rex* ([1908] E.D.C. 38).

Gau, *see* CANTON. A division of the tribes of the early Germans into thousands; a collection of *gauen* formed the tribe or nation (Wessels' *History*, p. 19).

Gedaagde (D.), the person summoned in an action; also called the defendant.

Geestelijken (D.), the clergy. As to their influence and power in the Netherlands, see Wessels' *History*, p. 69.

Gemaaghtaalde (D.), related, a relation or relative.

Gemeenschap van goederen (D.), community of property. "By the common law of Holland and West Friesland marriage effects community of property between the spouses, except in so far as the same has been excluded or limited by antenuptial contract; and excepting also that where a person marries a young man under twenty-five, or a young woman under twenty, without the consent of his or her parents or relatives or of the court, for in such a case, though the marriage remains valid, no community of property takes place" (Grotius' *Introd.* Maasdorp's trans. 2, 11, 8; see also Van der Keessel, *Thes.* 217–19; Maasdorp's *Institutes*, vol. 1, p. 34).

Genan (D.), of one and the same name.

Genealogy, the history of the descent of a person from his ancestor; a statement showing descent in the order of succession.

Genearch, the head of a family or tribe.

General acceptance. The acceptance of a bill of exchange may be either general or qualified. A *general acceptance* assents without qualification to the order of the drawer (Bills of Exchange Act, 1882 (Eng.), sec. 19; Act 19 of 1893 (C.C.), sec. 17; Law 8 of 1887 (N.), sec. 18; Proclamation 11 of 1902 (T.), sec. 17; Ordinance 28 of 1902 (O.R.C.), sec. 17).

See QUALIFIED ACCEPTANCE.

General agent "is an agent appointed to act as such: (*a*) in a course of dealing which comprises all the affairs of his principal, or all the affairs of his principal in a particular business or character; or (*b*) in the ordinary course of the agent's recognised trade or profession" (Jenks' *Digest of English Civil Law*, bk. 1, sec. 129). See *Muller Bros.* v. *Kemp and Others* (3 Searle, at p. 158).

General average. "The term *general average* is used indiscriminately, sometimes to denote the kind of loss which gives a claim to general average contribution, and sometimes to denote such contribution itself; in order to avoid confusion, it would have been better to use the term *general average loss* when speaking of the former, and *general average contribution* when speaking of the latter. A general average loss, and the consequent right to levy a general average contribution, can only arise out of a general average act. A general average act may consist either of the voluntary destruction of or parting with some tangible portion of the ship or cargo, or of the voluntary adoption of some extraordinary measure involving a subsequent loss or expenditure of money. In either case there is in reality a sacrifice: in the former case the sacrifice is itself the loss which is immediately apprehended, whilst in the latter case the sacrifice is in itself no present loss, but leads to loss or expenditure in the future. A loss of the former kind is generally called a *general average* sacrifice; a loss of the latter kind is generally called a *general average* loss or expenditure" (Arnould on *Marine Insurance*, 7th ed. sec. 906).

"**General campaign literature,**" an expression applied by INNES, C.J., in *De Visser* v. *Fitzpatrick* ([1907] T.S. at p. 375) to certain literature printed by a political association which was distributed to all its branches throughout the country, and amongst others to the branch in the town for which respondent was a candidate, and to the respondent's own offices.

General clause, a clause usually inserted in special mortgages, whereby the mortgagor declares to bind generally his person and property of every description as a further security for the debt. To be effective, like a special or general mortgage, it must be registered in the Deeds Office. A *general clause* has the same effect as a general mortgage, and becomes operative on the insolvency of the debtor. *See* "NECESSARY POWER."

General dealer. This term has received more than one statutory definition, as the following instances will show. "Any person who carries on the trade or business of selling, or offering or exposing for sale, barter or exchange any goods, wares or merchandise, not being the growth, produce or manufacture of South Africa" (Act 38 of 1887 (C.C.), sec. 3). See Act 28 of 1898 (C.C.), sec. 10, and Act 35 of 1906 (C.C.). See also *Rex* v. *Kukard*, 21 S.C. at p. 190; *Rex* v. *Warner*, 23 S.C. 483.

"Any person who carries on a trade or business in any shop, store or fixed place where goods are sold or offered or exposed for sale" (Ordinance 23 of 1905 (T.), sec. 2). As to whether a butcher should take out a *general dealer's* license, see *Papert* v. *Rex* ([1906] T.S. 553).

For the Orange River Colony, see Ordinance 10 of 1903, sec. 2; Ordinance 13 of 1905, sec. 5.

General issue, a plea which traverses the whole of the declaration or summons, as the case may be.

General mortgage, a bond executed before a notary public or the Registrar of Deeds and duly registered in the Deeds Office, whereby the debtor (called the mortgagor) mortgages in favour of the creditor (called the mortgagee) all his estate, and effects both movable and immovable as a security for a debt. What is known as the "general clause," usually inserted in special mortgages, operates as a *general mortgage*.

A *general mortgage* becomes operative upon the insolvency of the debtor. In *Francis* v. *Savage & Hill*, decided in the Supreme Court of the Transvaal in November, 1882, it was held, in a learned and elaborate judgment (quoted *in extenso* in a note to Van Leeuwen's *Comm.* Kotzé's trans. vol. 2, at p. 107), that a pledge of movables by notarial deed, duly registered, but unaccompanied by delivery, is valid not only against the debtor, but also gives the pledgee a right of preference against concurrent creditors in insolvency. But a registered notarial bond over movables, which have not been delivered to the pledgee, is of no force against an execution creditor (*Mangold Bros.* v. *Eskell*, 3 S.C. 48; *Meyer* v. *Botha and Hergenröder*, 2 Kotzé, 47; *Keet* v. *Dell*, *ibid.* 109; and *Natal Bank* v. *Martinus & Co.* 2 Off. Rep. 132).

General nursery an expression used in the Cape Nurseries Inspection and Quarantine Act (29 of 1905), where it is defined to mean "any nursery that is not a local nursery." *See* LOCAL NURSERY; NURSERY.

General power of attorney "is nothing more than a bundle or collection of special powers enumerated in one instrument. Yet if there are any general words which appear to govern the whole instrument, the court must so far regard the power as a whole, unless there is something to show that one or more clauses should be read apart from the rest" (*per* KOTZÉ, J.P., in *Grobbelaar* v. *Cockcroft*, [1906] E.D.C. at p. 113).

"**Generating the light.**" Where B W had agreed to supply electric light in B to the inhabitants, streets, public places and private property, and B M undertook to pay B W such sum as would yield a return of 10 per cent. over the "actual cost of *generating the light*, it was held that *generating the light* included generating the electric current as well as transmitting the current to the lamps, *i.e.* the whole process leading up to the production of the light in the street lamps (*Bulawayo Municipality* v. *Bulawayo Waterworks Co., Ltd.*, 16 C.T.R. 941; [1908] A.C. 241; 77 L.J. P.C. 70; 98 L.T. 600). *See* ACTUAL COST.

Generic, pertaining or belonging to a genus; of a distinctly characteristic kind; relating to a large class or group.

Genus, a kind; a sort; a class consisting of several species.

Gerechtsbode (D.), messenger of the court.

Gestation, pregnancy.

Getuige (D.), a witness.

Getuigenis (D.), evidence.

Gevangene (D.), a prisoner.

Gevangenis (D.), a prison. Formerly in Holland a *gevangenis* was a place set apart for the custody, and not for the punishment, of accused persons (see Kersteman's *Woordenboek*, vol. 1, p. 163).

Gheldeman (D.), a debtor.

Ghemaal (D.), a companion. *See* MAAL.

Ghenachte, Ghenachtdagh (D.), the day appointed or fixed for the holding of the court, or pronouncing judgment. So called because it was the custom of the ancient Germans and Franks to count time by the night and not by the day. It is said also to have been the practice of the ancient Britons (Meyer's *Woordenschat*).

Ghoedeins (D.), inheritance.

Ghoede-luiden (D.), literally, good or honest folk. They were citizens or inhabitants who were qualified and entitled to be present and vote in the determination of cases arising either in the towns or in the country (*ten platten lande*) (Meyer's *Woordenschat*).

Ghoeden (D.), to bestow or bequeath.

Ghoeding (D.), goods, property.

Ghoedmoeder (D.), a godmother.

Ghoedvader (D.), godfather.

Ghoggraaf (D.), a foot judge, one who judges without sitting on a judgment seat, in Latin *judex pedaneus.* Judges of this kind were chosen by the ancient Saxons to determine summarily as occasion arose upon an assault or violence committed. Consequently the term is derived by some from *goch, i.e.* quickly, and *graaf,* which formerly meant a judge.

Ghootrecht, Gootrecht (D.), the right to have a gutter or spout on or over another's land.

Ghouw or **Gouw**, (D.), a country, province or district.

Ghulde (D.), toll, duty, rent.

Gibbet, an upright post having an arm or cross-piece projecting at the top, from which persons were hanged; a gallows.

Gijzeling (D.), imprisonment for debt; civil imprisonment. See Van der Linden's *Institutes,* 3, 1, 9, 15 and 16.

Gild, an association or society formed for mutual protection or benefit.

"**Giving and supplying,**" in Cape Liquor Laws, see *Rex* v. *Francis* (18 S.C. at p. 59).

Glucose vinegar. In the Cape Wine, Brandy, Whisky and Spirits Act (19 of 1908), sec. 16, "*Glucose vinegar* means the product made by the alcoholic and subsequent acetous fermentation of solutions of starch, sugar, glucose, or glucose syrup." *See* VINEGAR.

"**God save the King.**" These words are usually to be found at the end of Proclamations, but they do not appear to have any special virtue as affecting the validity of a Proclamation (*Queen* v. *Wells,* 1 A.C. at p. 3).

Godspenning (D.), earnest money.

Goederen (D.), property, divided into movable and immovable property.

Goederen ter slete gelevert (D.), goods sold in small quantities, and of such a nature that they are consumed or become deteriorated by use (*per* WESSELS, J., in *Loteryman & Co.* v. *Cowie,* [1904] T.S. at p. 601). "The noun *sleet* is derived from *slyten,* which means 'to consume,' as well as 'to sell in small quantities.' *Koopmanschap ter slete gelevert* signifies goods sold not only by retail, but sold in small quantities for consumption or to be used up. *Sleet* is equivalent to consumption, and *ter slete gelevert* is nothing else than sold for consumption (see Sewell's *Lexicon;* and Oudeman's *Old*

Netherlands Dict. sub voce '*Sleet*')" *per* KOTZÉ, C.J., in *Little* v. *Rothman*, 2 Off. Rep. (1895) 201. See *Quick* v. *Luttey* ([1908] T.S. 708).

Gold. *See* NATIVE GOLD; UNWROUGHT GOLD.

Gold coins. "English *gold coins* are made of standard gold, which is an 'alloy' or mixture of eleven parts pure gold and one part of copper. Standard gold is therefore said to be 'eleven-twelfths' fine or twenty-two carats fine, a carat being a goldsmith's term for a twenty-fourth part of an ounce" (Sykes' *Banking and Currency*, p. 24).

Gold ore, in the Transvaal Gold Law (15 of 1908 (T.), sec. 3, since repealed) signifies "all auriferous ores, including concentrates, tailings and slimes."

Golf. The game of golf is played by two sides, each playing its own ball. Therefore a person going over golf-links by himself is not playing the game of *golf* within the meaning of Ordinance 1 of 1838 (C.C.), sec. 6 (*per* GRAHAM, J., in *Oehley* v. *Rex*, [1908] E.D.C. 38).

Good faith. The expression *good faith* is used in the Bills of Exchange Acts. "A thing is deemed to be done in *good faith*, within the meaning of this Act, where it is in fact done honestly, whether it is done negligently or not" (Act 19 of 1893 (C.C.), sec. 89; Law 8 of 1887 (N.), sec. 89; Proclamation 11 of 1902 (T.), sec. 89; Ordinance 28 of 1902 (O.R.C.), sec. 89).

Good for, a popular and brief form of an acknowledgment of debt. It is not a negotiable instrument.

Good Friday, a public holiday. *See* BUSINESS DAY.

Good order and condition. "The general statement in the bill of lading that the goods have been shipped 'in *good order and condition*,' amounts to an admission by the shipowner that, so far as he and his agents had the opportunity of judging, the goods were so shipped" (Carver's *Carriage of Goods by Sea*, 3rd ed. sec. 73; see following sections as to certain qualifications; see also *Porter & Co.* v. *Robinson*, 2 S.C. 16; and *Blaine & Co.* v. *Moller*, 2 S.C. 133).

Goods, merchandise. "*Goods* shall mean goods, luggage, or other movable property of any description, and shall include animals and birds whether live or dead" (Act 13 of 1908 (T.), sec. 2; Act 29 of 1908 (O.R.C.), sec. 2).

As to meaning of *goods* in Ordinance 23 of 1905 (T.), used in definitions of pedlar, hawker and general dealer, see *Papert* v. *Rex* ([1906] T.S. at p. 553).

Goodwill, all the advantages that are acquired by a business owing to its reputation, position or patronage, and which do not arise from the mere capital invested. *Goodwill* may be a partnership asset on the dissolution of a partnership; see *Sherry* v. *Stewart* ([1903] T.H. 13): see also *Wheeler* v. *Smith* ([1906] T.H. at p. 243).

Goograven (D.), pl. of *Goograaf*, officers who ruled over small districts. *See* GRAAF.

Gootrecht (D.). *See* GHOOTRECHT.

Goudwet (D.), Gold Law. See Law 15 of 1898 (T.), since repealed.

Gouw (D.), *See* GHOUW.

Government, the authority which directs and controls the affairs of a State; the executive power in which the administration of a State is vested.

As to *Government* in Cape Native Territories, see Act 24 of 1886 (C.C.), sec. 5 (*a*).

Government Gazette, the official publication of the Government. In South Africa *Government Gazettes* are published in each colony weekly, and in them are published Bills to be laid before Parliament, as also Acts of Parliament as soon as promulgated; Proclamations; Government Notices, and a variety of other matter of which public notice is required to be given through this medium.

Government securities. The expression *Government securities* is defined in the Cape Bank Act (6 of 1891) to mean "any bonds, scrip, certificates, stock or debentures of the Colony of the Cape of Good Hope."

Governor. In the Cape Interpretation of Statutes Act (5 of 1883, sec. 3) it is provided that the term "*Governor* shall mean the officer for the time being administering the government of the colony; provided that when any act, matter or thing is by any law directed or required to be done by the *Governor*, it shall mean the *Governor* with the advice of the Executive Council."

In the Transvaal Interpretation of Laws Proclamation (15 of 1902), sec. 2, *Governor* means "the officer for the time being administering the government of this [Transvaal] Colony;" see also Ordinance 1 of 1906 (T.), sec. 30 of schedule.

"*Governor* shall mean the officer for the time being administering the Government of this colony acting by and with the advice of the Executive Council thereof:" Act 13 of 1908 (T.), sec. 2; Act 29 of 1908 (O.R.C.), sec. 2; Act 4 of 1908 (T.), sec. 1; Act 14 of 1907 (T.), sec. 1: Act 15 of 1907 (T.), sec. 2.

Governor's pleasure lunatic. In the Cape Lunacy Act (1 of 1897), sec. 2, the expression *Governor's pleasure lunatic* is defined to mean "any person for whose detention during his pleasure the

Governor is authorised to grant an order." See also secs. 19 to 33 of the same Act. A similar definition of *Governor's pleasure lunatic* has been adopted in the Transvaal: see Proclamation 36 of 1902 (T.), sec. 2.

Graaf (D.), (1) originally signified a judge, a superior or leader; as if we said *grauuw*, a grey or old man, for probably at first none but grey-haired men of experience were appointed judges. Hence in this sense *graafschap* is also used to denote jurisdiction.

(2) He who, on behalf of the public, appoints the court, prosecutes and executes the judgment of the court. There were numerous officers of the kind. Thus *Burgh-graaf*, who ruled over a burgh; *Dykgraaf*, over a dike or dikes; *Goograaf*, over a small district; *Landtgraaf*, over a large district; *Markgraaf*, over the landmarks or boundaries; *Paltsgraaf*, over the palace; *Pluimgraaf*, over fowling, &c. All these various kinds of *graaf* were called in Latin *comites* or *judices*. See Van Leeuwen's *Comm.* Kotzé's trans. vol. 1. p. 62.

(3) In its modern sense the term denotes count. and *graafschap* denotes county (Meyer's *Woordenschat*).

Graafschap (D.). *See* GRAAF.

Graduate, a person upon whom a degree has, after examination, been conferred by a college, university or the like. In the Cape University Incorporation Act (16 of 1873, sec. 13) the term *graduate* is defined as meaning "any person upon whom the university shall have conferred any degree after examination, and also any *graduate* of another university whom the council shall, in the exercise of the power in that behalf hereinbefore bestowed, have admitted to any degree."

Grahven-gheding (D.), a dispute or trial held by the count in person, having in his hand a drawn sword.

Grant. In connection with land a *grant* is an original title issued by the Crown, with diagram attached, and duly registered in the Deeds Office. A *grant* contains all the conditions upon which the land is granted to the grantee. The *grant* of land is the fundamental title upon which all subsequent transfers of such land are based.

Grape brandy. *See* PURE GRAPE BRANDY.

Gratuitous promise (*belofte*) "is where a person of his own accord, without having been asked to do so and without any debt, offers to do or give something to another. If this promise be made in earnest and be accepted, it will bind the promisor to performance or fulfilment; according to the common saying, 'a promise incurs a debt' (*belofte maakt schuld*)" (Van Leeuwen's *Comm.* Kotzé's trans. vol. 2, p. 4. Chief Justice KOTZÉ adds a note to this definition as follows: "But every promise must have a definite and reasonable cause (*causa*) in order to create a right of action"). *See* CAUSA; see also *Scott* v. *Thieme* (14 C.T.R. 823; 21 S.A.L.J. 364).

Gravamen, that part of an accusation which is most serious against an accused person; the substantial cause of an action or complaint.

Gravity. In the Cape Excise Spirits Act (18 of 1884), sec. 2, *gravity* is defined as meaning "the *gravity* as ascertained by Bates's saccharometer." The same definition is given in the Additional Taxation Act, 36 of 1904 (C.C.), sec. 2.

Gray's Inn, one of the Inns of Court. *See* INNS OF COURT. Considerable inducement is offered to students by this Inn in the way of scholarships. It has a good library.

Great-grandchildren, a child in the third degree of descent.

As to whether the term "grandchildren" includes *great-grandchildren*, see *Re Cass' Will* (27 N.L.R. 262). In that case it was decided that it did not.

Great stock, "horses and cattle with their offspring" (Ordinance 15 of 1904 (T.), sec. 1.).

Griffier (D.), the registrar of a court. Formerly in Holland a *griffier* in a political sense was a principal secretary of a Minister of State, whose duty it was to take down in writing the resolutions and to sign the Ordinances of the States-General, as also to assist at the Assembly of the States (*lands vergaderingen*) and to take accurate notes of the proceedings and resolutions; in judicial practice the *griffier* was the secretary or registrar of a court of justice. See Kersteman's *Woordenboek*, vol. 1, p. 169.

Grondwet (D.), a written Constitution. In South Africa both the Orange Free State and the South African Republic (Transvaal) had written Constitutions. Of these, that of the Orange Free State is of earlier date. It was introduced and adopted on the 10th April, 1854, and was subsequently revised and amended in 1866, under the name of *Herziene Constitutie* (Revised Constitution). It consisted of 62 Articles, and was divided into different headings, dealing respectively with (1) the Volksraad or Legislature, (2) the President, (3) the Executive Council, (4) the Judiciary, (5) the Military System, and (6) Miscellaneous Provisions. By sec. 26 of this Constitution it was provided that it could only be altered after a three-fourths majority of the Volksraad had in two consecutive annual sessions voted in favour of the proposed alteration.

In the South African Republic (Transvaal) the Grondwet was introduced and adopted in February, 1858. Great disaffection and dissension had existed for some time previously in that country. In 1855 Mr. M. W. Pretorius, subsequently the first president of the Republic, and others induced the Volksraad to adopt a *Grondwet* or Constitution. This was done at Potchefstroom on the 9th November, 1855. The Volksraad, however, decided that the *Grondwet* should first of all be published and submitted to the people for their consideration and approval. Soon after this, differences unfortunately arose between Mr. Pretorius and Mr. Stephanus Schoeman, two of the four Commandants-General of the country. Schoeman was opposed to the *Grondwet* introduced by Pretorius, and seemed to think that it was the intention of Pretorius to have himself declared President under this Constitution. Early in 1858 the people assembled in an armed body at Rustenburg, but a collision was averted by means of a combined military council (*krygsraad*), which resolved that a Commission should be chosen to draw up and frame one general *Grondwet*. The Commission was elected by all the people present, and Pretorius and Schoeman were nominated joint chairmen. On the 13th February the committee was ready with a draft *Grondwet*, and on the 18th February, 1858, the Volksraad unanimously approved and accepted it as the *Grondwet* or Constitution of the South African Republic. This *Grondwet* consisted of 232 articles, and was divided into different headings similar to those of the *Grondwet* of the Orange Free State. Several of its provisions, however, dealt with minor matters of detail and administration, and should have been omitted from the Constitution altogether. Two supplements (*bylagen*) were added to this *Grondwet* in 1859, the one dealing with matters which were pending at the time of the adoption of the *Grondwet* in 1858 (*overgangsbepalingen*), and the other providing that the *Introduction of Grotius to the Jurisprudence of Holland*, the *Commentaries of S. van Leeuwen*, and the *Manual of Van der Linden* should be followed by the courts of justice where the local laws were silent. Besides being open to objection in other respects, this *Grondwet* did not, like that of the Orange Free State, contain any article or clause providing for its alteration; although some provision was made against hasty legislation by sec. 12, which enacted that any proposed law, except such as could brook no delay, must be published three months beforehand for the information of the people, to enable them to petition against it. This was, however, very inadequate, and in course of time this provision was very frequently departed from, so that what was originally intended as an exception often became a rule.

In 1877, while Sir Theophilus Shepstone was at Pretoria, on a mission from her Majesty's Government, the Transvaal was in a somewhat disturbed state and in an almost bankrupt condition. The people had for some time been very remiss in the payment of their taxes, the treasury was empty, and the authority of the Government was not respected. Sir Theophilus Shepstone had frankly informed President Burgers that, unless he could bring about a change for the better, the country would be annexed to her Majesty's Dominions. President Burgers, who was opposed by Mr. Kruger and his party, made heroic efforts to reform the unsatisfactory state of things. Among the various measures which he proposed should be adopted was the introduction of an amended *Grondwet*. In March, 1877, he introduced this measure, consisting of five chapters, into the Volksraad. That body was disposed only to adopt and approve two of these chapters, dealing respectively with the State-

President and Executive Council, and the judiciary. The chapter dealing with the judiciary was the first attempt to establish a Supreme Court and Circuit Court, such as existed in the other parts of South Africa. The Volksraad and people did not, however, support President Burgers in the measures which he proposed, in order to place the government on a more stable and satisfactory basis, and on the 12th April, 1877, the Republic was annexed to the British Dominions. On the retrocession in 1881, the Volksraad, by Law 3 of that year, re-enacted, with some modifications, the amendments to the *Grondwet* introduced by President Burgers in 1877. In 1889 a so-called new *Grondwet* consisting of 159 articles was introduced and adopted by the Volksraad, but it likewise did not provide for the manner in which alone the *Grondwet* could be altered. Again in 1896 the Government introduced and the Volksraad adopted the Law 2 of that year, which is described to be the *Grondwet* of the South African Republic, and consists of 183 articles. It is obvious that it is not a *Grondwet* or Constitution in the sense generally understood by that term, for, unlike the Constitution of 1858, it did not emanate from the people in any shape or form. In the case of *Brown* v. *Leyds, N.O.* (4 Off. Rep. 17), it was held by the High Court of the Republic (KOTZÉ, C.J., and AMESHOFF, J.) that the validity and binding force of Resolutions and Laws of the Volksraad could be tested by reference to the *Grondwet*, and that the Volksraad could not by Resolution or an ordinary Law alter the *Grondwet* or Constitution of 1858. *See* TESTING RIGHT.

Gross, the full and entire amount or weight, without deduction for charges, tare, waste or the like. Opposed to net.

Gross carelessness. In the Workman's Compensation Act, 40 of 1905 (C.C.), *gross carelessness* is defined to mean "any act done or duty omitted without safeguarding against the probable consequences, when such consequences are dangerous to human life or limb." Gross negligence or carelessness is ordinary negligence with a vituperative epithet (*per* ROLFE, B., in *Wilson* v. *Brett*, 11 M. & W. 113). See also *per* WILLES, J., in *Grill* v. *General Iron Screw Collier Co.* (L.R. 1 C.P. 600).

Grosse, sometimes spelt *gross*, a copy of a notarial instrument signed by the notary before whom the instrument is executed, but omitting the signature of the party executing the same and of the witnesses; the notary merely certifying above his signature that the original was passed in the presence of the subscribing witnesses (naming them), who, together with the appearer (party executing) and himself (the notary), had duly signed the original of the instrument then remaining in his protocol. See *Master of Supreme Court* v. *Berrangé* (11 S.C. 68).

The original Dutch word was *gros.* Its definition then was *het geen uit de kladde in het net gesteld is* (whatever has been reduced to writing from the original rough draft), in other words, "a neat copy of the original." This term was in use officially as early as the fifteenth century. It is to be found in several plakaten of Holland affecting notarial instructions, law and practice in 1540 and 1671. It is not a genuine Dutch classical word, but bastard Dutch. Frequently such a bastard Dutch word was used in technical legal expressions when no better words were available. It appears that this term had been in use among legal practitioners in the Netherlands long before it was used in the Dutch plakaten. The idea was that the first copy of the original draft of a notarial deed or instrument should be written neater and in larger characters, with the lines wider apart than those in the original *kladde* or *minut* in the notary's protocol. Hence followed the word *grosseren*, which means *in het net schrijven* (written neatly). *Grosse* or *grosseren* also means to extend according to the minute of the original instrument. The original first draft was called the *minut*, because it was written in small characters, with the lines and words close together—just the opposite way to that in which the *gros* was written.

The difference between a *gros* and a *copie authenticq* (authentic copy) is this: the first neat copy of the original was called the *gros*, and copies were called "duplicate," "triplicate" and "quadruplicate." Prior to the year 1540 notaries could issue any number of *grossen* of a *minut*, but in 1671 they were prohibited from issuing more than one *gros*; they could, however, issue as many copies of the *minut* as they desired; such copies were to be styled and certified as the "duplicate," "triplicate," &c., as the case might be.

Inasmuch as judicial instruments emanating from the courts in the Netherlands were, after having been formally recorded by the registrar (*griffier*) of the court, regarded as genuine, without requiring any further proof, so also were the different *grossen* issued by these registrars, and judicial credence was given to them. The registrar was not restricted in the number of *grossen*. And because the *gros* of the registrar was accepted as true, so also was the *gros* of the notary accepted by the courts as true. Hence in practice the courts of Holland have, from time immemorial—certainly prior to 1540—given provisional sentence on a *gros*, and so it is in practice in the courts of South Africa at the present time.

The Dutch word *gros* has been anglicised into *grosse* or *gross*; and the Dutch word *minut* has been anglicised into *minute*. See Van Zyl's *Notarial Practice*, pp. 17 *et seq.*; *Stanford* v. *Brunette* (3 Searle, at p. 111).

Guarantee, an undertaking given by a guarantor for the due performance and fulfilment, by a third party, of some specific contract or stipulation. "The tendency of the older authorities, Roman-Dutch and English, was to place a strict and adverse construction upon a document of suretyship. On the other hand, later cases—in England at any rate—rather tend in the opposite direction" (*per* Innes, C.J., in *Glenn Bros.* v. *Commercial General Agency*, [1905] T.S. at p. 741).

Guarantor. "A *guarantor* is practically the same person as the Roman law terms a surety for an indemnity—in other words, he guarantees that whatever part of the debt will not be paid by the principal or realised from the pledges will be made good by him (the guarantor)" (Nathan's *Common Law*, sec. 994, *in not.*).

Guardian, the person in lawful authority over another; one who has the right of exercising the powers and authority of guardianship. See *Van Rooyen* v. *Werner* (9 S.C. 425; 2 C.T.R. 295).

Guardian's Fund, a fund formed under sec. 30 of Ordinance 105 of 1833 (C.C.) under the control of the Master of the Supreme Court, in which are placed moneys coming into the hands of the Master in connection with persons or estates under guardianship. Moneys in this fund, not required for current expenditure, may be lent out on mortgage of immovable property within the colony after advising thereupon with certain officials as provided in the Ordinance (see sec. 33). See Proclamation 28 of 1902 (T.), secs. 100 *et seq.*; Ordinance 18 of 1905 (O.R.C.), secs. 92 *et seq.*; and Ordinance 8 of 1906 (O.R.C.), secs. 3 *et seq.*

Guardianship "is the lawful authority of one person over the person and property of another, introduced for purposes of special utility" (Grotius' *Introd.* 1, 4, 5). The person over whom the *guardianship* extends is called the ward. "The relation of guardian and ward is an artificial imitation of that of parent and child, and is entirely regulated by law" (Holland's *Jurisprudence*, 10th ed. p. 240). Van Leeuwen in his *Comm.* (Kotzé's trans. vol. 1, p. 124) says: "*Guardianship* is a legal custody of the person of another who, by reason of his tender years or incapacity, is unable to protect himself." See *Van Rooyen* v. *Werner* (9 S.C. 425; 2 C.T.R. 295).

As to *guardianship* of natives in Natal, see Law 19 of 1891, sec. 184 of schedule.

Guild. *See* GILD.

Guilty, indicating guilt or wrong-doing; having committed a crime or offence.

Haarstoot (D.), puberty.

Haarstootigh (D.), marriageable.

Habeas corpus. "In England the right to individual liberty is part of the Constitution, because it is secured by the decisions of the courts, extended or confirmed as they are by the *Habeas Corpus* Acts. . . . The *Habeas Corpus* Acts declare no principle and define no rights, but they are for practical purposes worth a hundred constitutional articles guaranteeing individual liberty" (Dicey's *Constitution*, 6th ed. pp. 193 and 195). For general explanation of the mode in which the law of England secures the right to persona freedom, see Dicey's *Constitution*, 6th ed. pp. 209 *et seq.*

Habitatio, a personal servitude conferring the right to live in a house belonging to another. It includes the right to let the house. It was for long doubted whether *habitatio* was a distinct servitude from *usus* until Justinian settled that it was (Justinian's *Institutes*, 2, 5, 5).

Hac voce, under this word or phrase; used as a means of reference and generally abbreviated "*h.v.*"

Hage-sette-rechters (D.), special judges appointed by a superior judge to settle a certain matter, in the same way as commissioners are appointed at the present day (Meyer's *Woordenschat*).

Haghemunt (D.), bad or base coin.

Hak (D.), a trader in inferior articles.

Half-blood, the relationship between persons born of the same father or the same mother, but not of the same father *and* mother.

Handelaar (D.), a dealer or trader; a merchant. A tailor who executes orders for garments, either supplying the material himself or making up cloth supplied by his customer, but who does not sell cloth or other articles, or make clothes except to order, is not a *handelaar* within the meaning of sec. 7 of Law 17 of 1899 (T.), and need not take out a license as such (*Bebro* v. *Rex*, [1904] T.S. 387).

Handtlichten (D.), to restore into possession.

Handtstelling (D.), arrest.

Handveste (D.), handwriting, signature. Its modern meaning is a privilege or charter.

Handvesten (D.). (1) Were in Holland special orders, confirmations or assurances under the count's own signature. They were written acknowledgments of anything that had been approved of by the ruler. They were thus not in their origin laws or orders, but an approval of what had been done in the name of law and then confirmed by the count's signature.

(2) Charters.

Handvulling (D.), more commonly known in Roman-Dutch jurisprudence as *provisie van namptissement.* It was a provisional payment made by a defendant of the amount awarded to the plaintiff by virtue of an interlocutory sentence of a court of justice, against proper security (*cautie de restituendo*) being given by the plaintiff for restitution of capital and interest in case the sentence should be reversed in the principal case. See Kersteman's *Woordenboek, sub voce "Namptissement,"* vol. 1, p. 300; 1 Menz. 6. *Handvulling* corresponds with the modern South African practice of "provisional sentence." See also Van Leeuwen's *Comm.* Kotzé's trans. vol. 2, p. 434.

Hangdief (D.). In about the thirteenth century the special hangman appointed to conduct the execution of condemned persons was called *hangdief* (Wessels' *History*, p. 165).

Hangman, a public executioner.

Harbour. In the Wrecks Removal Amendment Act, 46 of 1885 (C.C.) "the term *harbour* includes harbours and ports properly so called, whether natural or artificial, roadsteads, and anchorages of every description, estuaries, navigable rivers, piers, jetties and other works in or at which ships or vessels can obtain shelter, or ship or unship goods or passengers." See the Explosives Act, 4 of 1887 (C.C.), sec. 36.

Harbour boards, local boards of commissioners or persons invested with the necessary powers and authorities for the purpose of increasing, improving and regulating the safety and convenience of the several ports, harbours and roadsteads of the Cape Colony and Natal. Their creation was first authorised by Ordinance 21 of 1847 (C.C.), which was not applicable to Natal, and was confined to the ports of the Cape Colony. Since 1847 a number of Acts have been passed in Cape Colony dealing with the subject, until, in 1896, an Act was passed to assimilate and amend the law relating to the control and management of the harbours of Table Bay, Port Elizabeth and East London (these being the principal ports of the Cape Colony), and to amend in certain respects the law relating to ports and harbours of the Cape Colony (Act 36 of 1896). This Act exempted the harbours of Table Bay, Port Elizabeth and East London from the provisions of Ordinance 21 of 1847 and several subsequent Acts. The control and management of the harbour, together with the docks and breakwater of Table Bay, and the harbours of Port Elizabeth and East London, together with all works of construction and maintenance connected therewith, were by Act 36 of 1896 vested in *harbour boards* constituted under the provisions of that Act. Such boards consisted each of seven persons, of whom two were elected in manner provided in the Act, three were nominated by the Governor, and the other two were the nominees of the Incorporated Chamber of Commerce and the mayor of the towns of Capetown, Port Elizabeth and East London respectively. Each elected its own chairman, who held office for a year. By Act 38 of 1908 (sec. 1) the above *harbour boards* were abolished and their control and management transferred to the Government.

The principal statute in Natal dealing with this subject is Act 3 of 1894. See also Law 18 of 1883; Law 8 of 1884; and Act 3 of 1899.

By sec. 126 of the Act of Union all ports, harbours and railways belonging to the several colonies at the establishment of the Union are to vest from the date thereof in the Governor-General-in-Council.

Hard labour, a form of punishment usually added to the sentence of imprisonment.

Hawker, a person who carries about wares for sale in small quantities, generally on his person (*Solomon* v. *Rex*, [1905] T.S. 216). "Where a person goes round about a town or country [selling wares] he is hawking. The nearest definition of a *hawker* is given in schedule 15 of Act 3 of 1864 [C.C.], where it says '*hawker* or travelling trader'" (*per* SMITH, J., in *Queen* v. *Shortle*, 5 S.C. at p. 205; see also *Lezard* v. *The Queen*, 4 H.C.G. 1; *Queen* v. *Dickinson*, 4 C.L.J. 232; *Shortle* v. *Uniondale Magistrate*, 4 C.L.J. 286; and *Queen* v. *De Kock*, 3 H.C.G. 488). See Act 35 of 1906 (C.C.); Act 18 of 1897 (N.), sec. 2; Law 19 of 1872 (N.), sec. 71.

In the Transvaal, in the Revenue Licenses Ordinance (23 of 1905), sec. 2, *hawker* means "any person who travels with a wagon or other vehicle (other than a hand-barrow or hand-cart propelled by himself) or with a pack animal or carrier, and who carries goods for sale."

Hearing, the trial of an action or some other legal proceeding.

Hearsay evidence, second-hand evidence. For history of rule rejecting *hearsay evidence* see Best's *Law of Evidence*, 10th ed. sec. 115.

Heefdochter (D.), a stepdaughter.

Heefzoon (D.), a stepson.

Heemraden (D.), anciently *heimraden*, persons who form the court or tribunal with a president to determine minor civil cases (see Wessels' *History*, p. 152).

Heerenrecht (D.), transfer duty; a tax payable to Government on change of ownership of land. Probably in its old form of *heere regt* it denoted a tax or duty payable by the vassal to his lord. *Heerenrecht* has been known as a tax in South Africa since 1686. *See* TRANSFER DUTY.

Heerewegen (D.), roads common to all the people, highways free to be used by every one.

Heerghewade, Heergheweede, Hergheweide (D.), a feudal gift. The gift made by the new vassal to his lord, amounting to a year's income. Originally it signified the outfit presented to the lord by the new vassal.

Heiken (D.), father. *See* HYKEN.

Heimraden (D.), ancient form of *heemraden*. *See* HEEMRADEN.

Heir. "The expression *heir* in Roman-Dutch law is used with regard to both intestate and testamentary succession. In regard to intestate succession, the *heirs* are the persons who are entitled to succeed to the property of the deceased. In regard to testamentary succession, the *heirs* now mean the residuary legatees, the person or persons who receive what is left of the movable and immovable property after the debts and legacies have been paid" (Morice's *English and Roman-Dutch Law*, 2nd ed. p. 291).
See SOLE HEIR; UNIVERSAL HEIR.

Heiress, a female heir.

Heirloom is generally understood to mean some article or thing that passes from generation to generation in a family. Strictly speaking, in English law it means some personal chattel that accrues to the heir with the house itself by custom.

"Held by the Crown," discussed in *Trading Board* v. *Germiston Town Council* ([1907] T.S. at p. 454).

Herd is defined in the Natal Lung-sickness Prevention Act (30 of 1897), sec. 3, to include "a single animal, or any number of cattle running together."

Heredis institutio, the institution of the heir. In Dutch, *erfstelling*. See Van Leeuwen's *Comm.* Kotzé's trans. vol. 1, p. 343.

Hereditas, inheritance. It is defined in the Roman law as the succession to the whole estate which the deceased had (*Digest*, 50, 17, 62), and while including things of every kind, movable and immovable, corporeal and incorporeal, is itself incorporeal, being a *universitas* (or collection) of the rights and also of the obligations of the deceased (Voet's *Comm.* 28, 1, 1).

Hereditas directa, direct inheritance; an inheritance left absolutely and without condition, as distinguished from *hereditas fideicommissaria*, an inheritance burdened with a trust or *fideicommissum*. (See Berwick's *Translation of Voet*, p. 80 *in notis.*)

Hereditas fideicommissaria, a fideicommissary inheritance; an inheritance left subject to a *fideicommissum* or trust. *See* HEREDITAS DIRECTA.

Hereditas jacens, an inheritance or succession which has not yet been adiated or entered upon by the heir. "A *hereditas jacens* is in the property or possession of no one, and therefore theft cannot be made of a thing belonging to the inheritance unless another has some right over it, as where the deceased had given it in pledge or lent it upon commodate (to some one) or a usufruct over it belonged to another. Still in the meantime, until it is adiated, it represents the *persona* of the deceased as regards those things which have a legal aspect, but as regards those which require some act and which relate to the acquisition of property (it represents) rather the *persona* of the heir" (Voet's *Comm.* 22, 2, 1).

Heres est eadem persona cum defuncto, an heir is the same person with the deceased. In Roman law an heir by adiating the inheritance stepped into the shoes of the deceased, not only acquiring all his rights and property, but also becoming liable for all his debts and obligations, although these exceeded the assets of the estate. Various expedients were introduced by later Roman law for the protection of the heir. In accordance with the latest and most effectual remedy, viz., benefit of inventory (*q.v.*) the heir by making an inventory of the estate of the deceased limited his liability for the debts to the amount of the assets. The benefit of inventory is obsolete in South Africa. By statute law in the various colonies the administration of the estates of deceased persons has been transferred to executors, and the heir is merely a residuary legatee, succeeding to that portion of the estate which is left after the debts and legacies have been satisfied by the executors.

Heres personam defuncti sustinet, an heir sustains the person of the deceased. *See* HERES EST EADEM PERSONA CUM DEFUNCTO.

Hergheweide (D.). *See* HEERGHEWADE.

Hermeneutics, the art of interpretation.

Hertog (D.), a duke, "denoted a general of the army, chosen by the prince and stationed in a certain province" (Van Leeuwen's *Comm.* Kotzé's trans. vol. 1, p. 62).

Herwissel (D.), re-exchange, "that is, the costs which the holder had to incur by reason of his being embarrassed by the non-payment of the bill, in drawing for this amount upon the drawer or a third person, and thus to provide himself with the necessary funds" (Van der Linden's *Institutes,* Juta's trans. p. 481).

High seas, that part of the sea that lies more than three mil off the coast of any country.

Hijpotheek (D.), formerly spelt *hypotheecq*, a mortgage, whereby immovable property becomes bound as security for a debt or obligation without actual delivery. "In the Roman law, when the thing over which the right was given passed into the possession of the creditor, the right of the creditor was expressed by the word *pignus;* when the thing remained in the hands of the debtor, the right of the creditor was expressed by *hypothec*" (Sandars' note on Justinian's

Institutes, 2, 5, 6). Hypothec is used as equivalent to mortgage, which is either general or special, according as it embraces all property generally or only some specific property or thing belonging to the debtor. It is either created by contract between creditor and debtor, or is given by the law. In the former case the mortgage or hypothec is spoken of as express or conventional, and in the latter as tacit or legal. Tacit hypothecs are rather numerous in Roman-Dutch law, but their number has been reduced in South Africa by legislation (Van Zyl, *Judicial Practice*, 2nd ed. pp. 577 *et seq.* See also Grotius' *Introd.* 2, 48; Van Leeuwen's *Comm.* Kotzé's trans. 4, 12 and 13; Voet's *Comm.* 20, tits. 1 to 6 (Berwick's trans.); Kersteman's *Woordenboek, sub voce* "*Hypotheek*"; Maasdorp's *Institutes*, vol. 2, pp. 222 *et seq.* *See* MORTGAGE).

Hire, to undertake to pay a consideration for the use of a thing or for the services of a person, or the rent or wages paid or agreed to be paid for such use or services.

Hire goes before sale, an English translation of the old Dutch maxim *Huur gaat voor koop* (*q.v.*).

Hire purchase system, a contract whereby a person lets something to another (the hirer) on condition that the hirer shall pay the purchase-price of the thing by regular equal instalments in the way of rent, and that upon payment of the final instalment the thing shall become the property of the hirer. The contract generally contains a further condition that if the hirer fails to pay any instalment at maturity he shall forfeit his rights to the thing as well as all past payments. The *dominium* in the thing remains in the owner until the final instalment has been paid.

Hiring is "a contract whereby the use of a thing or the benefit of any service or act is promised for a certain price" (Van Leeuwen's *Comm.* Kotzé's trans. vol. 2, p. 167).

Hoc genus omne, all of this kind or description.

Hoc titulo, under this title; frequently used by commentators in referring to the *Digest*, and generally written "*h.t.*"

Hoflanden (D.), *i.e. agri fiscalini*, lands belonging to the State or the Count *qua* Count.

Hogshead, a liquid measure containing 52½ imperial gallons.

Holder, the payee or indorsee of a bill or note who is in possession of it, or the bearer thereof (sec. 2 of English Bills of Exchange Act, 1882; see also Act 19 of 1893 (C.C.), sec. 1; Law 8 of 1887 (N.), sec. 1; Proclamation 11 of 1902 (T.), sec. 1; Ordinance 28 of 1902 (O.R.C.), sec. 1.

"The term *holder* includes alike the payee, the indorsee and the bearer of a bill. It signifies the mercantile owner of the instrument, who may or may not be the legal owner of it" (Chalmers' *Bills of Exchange*, 6th ed. p. 5).

Holder for value. Where value has at any time been given for a bill, the holder is deemed to be a *holder for value* as regards the acceptor and all parties to the bill who became parties prior to such time; and where the holder of a bill has a lien on it, arising either from contract or by implication of law, he is deemed to be a *holder for value* to the extent of the sum for which he has a lien (sec. 27 of English Bills of Exchange Act, 1882). See also Act 19 of 1893 (C.C.), sec. 25; Law 8 of 1887 (N.), sec. 26; Proclamation 11 of 1902 (T.), sec. 25; Ordinance 28 of 1902 (O.R.C.), sec. 25; Regulation 23 of 1895 (R.), sec. 25.

Holder in due course is a holder who has taken a bill, complete and regular on the face of it, under the following conditions, namely: (*a*) that he became the holder of it before it was overdue, and without notice that it had been previously dishonoured, if such was the fact; (*b*) that he took the bill in good faith and for value, and that at the time the bill was negotiated to him he had no notice of any defect in the title of the person who negotiated it (sec. 29 of English Bills of Exchange Act, 1882). See Act 19 of 1893 (C.C.), sec. 27; Law 8 of 1887 (N.), sec. 28; Regulation 23 of 1895 (R.), sec. 27; Proclamation 11 of 1902 (T.), sec. 27; Ordinance 28 of 1902 (O.R.C.), sec. 27.

Holding. In the Transvaal Fencing Act (12 of 1908), *holding* is defined to mean: "(*a*) An area of land (not being an erf or stand) held by a white person under separate grant, deed of transfer, certificate of title, or lease; or (*b*) an area of land held under a lease or license by any person under the Settlers Ordinance, 1902, the Crown Land Disposal Ordinance, 1903, the Land Settlement Act, 1907, or any amendment of such laws; or (*c*) an area of land reserved under section *twelve* of the Crown Land Disposal Ordinance, 1903, for stock, forestry or agricultural purposes; or (*d*) any area of land used as a native location or mission station or held by a native under separate grant, deed of transfer, certificate of title or lease."

In Ordinance 15 of 1904 (T.), sec. 1, *holding* means "any farm or other place where great stock is kept."

Holiday. *See* Business Day.

Holograph, a deed or writing written entirely by the author with his own hand. A *holograph* will is written entirely by the testator.

Home Office, that branch of the Government in England in which the internal affairs of the State are administered.

Homicide "is the killing of a human being by a human being" (Stephen's *Digest of the Criminal Law,* 5th ed. p. 175). Van Leeuwen in his *Comm.* (Kotzé's trans. vol. 2, p. 268) says, "Crime against life is *homicide;* which is taken in a general sense to denote every act whereby one person improperly causes the death of another."

In the Native Territories Penal Code (Act 24 of 1886 (C.C.)), sec. 134, *homicide* is defined as "the killing of a human being by another directly or indirectly by any means whatever."

See Ordinance 18 of 1845 (N.), sec. 28.

Homing pigeon. "*Homing pigeon* shall mean and include all pigeons used as bearers of messages or as racing pigeons, and which have affixed or attached to either or each leg a rubber or metal ring" (Homing Pigeons' Protection Act, 22 of 1907 (C.C.), sec. 1).

Honeste vivere, to live honourably. This is one of the three precepts or maxims given by Justinian (*Institutes,* 1, 1, 3) as the basis of all rules of law. *Honeste* here has a wider significance than the mere legal, embracing the whole field of moral obligation, for *non omne quod licet honestum est* (not everything which is lawful is morally right).

Honorarium, a fee or gratuity given for professional services rendered.

Honorary degree. In discussing this term as it appears in sec. 5 of Act 6 of 1896 (C.C.), De Villiers, C.J., said: "Reading the section as a whole I can come to no other conclusion than that an *honorary degree* was intended to mean a degree conferred without examination on persons who have obtained an equivalent degree from another university, and that a degree *honoris causa* was intended to mean a degree conferred without examination on persons who are deemed worthy of such distinction, although they may not have obtained an equivalent degree from any other university" (*Ex parte McIlwaine,* 15 S.C. at p. 269).

Hooger beroep (D.), appeal to a superior court. Also termed *appel,* and formerly spelt *Hoger beroep.*

Hoon (D.), insult, affront. Anciently the word meant favour or grace.

Hoor (D.). *See* Oir.

Hoorigen (D.), one of the classes of people into which the early Germans were divided. They were also called *lites, liti,* or half free (Wessels' *History,* p. 21).

Horse, in the Transvaal Great Stock Brands Ordinance (15 of 1904), sec. 1, means "any *horse,* mare, gelding, colt, filly, ass or mule."

Hospital. As to whether a *hospital* is rateable under the Cape General Municipal Act (45 of 1882), see *Claremont Sanatorium* v. *Claremont Municipality* (14 S.C. 236).

Hostile witness, a witness who, when giving his evidence, exhibits a hostile mind towards the party calling him.

Hotel, a building arranged for the accommodation and convenience of travellers and strangers. In Act 11 of 1905 (C.C.), sec. 1, *hotel* means "*hotels* duly licensed by the licensing court; temperance *hotels*, whether requiring a license or not; and boarding-houses.". See also Act 25 of 1905 (C.C.), sec. 1.

Houder (D.), the holder of a promissory note or bill of exchange.

Houdvester en Meesterknapen (D.), a special court of Wood-Reeve and Companions instituted in Holland prior to 1376, which decided matters relating to hunting and waste lands (Van Leeuwen's *Comm.* Kotzé's trans. vol. 1, p. 19).

House. In the Cape Births and Deaths Registration Act (7 of 1894), sec. 2, the term *house* is defined to mean and include "the whole or any part of any tenement, any hut, tent, convict-station, prison, lock-up, hospital, asylum, public or charitable institution, cart, carriage, wagon, truck, van, and any other place of residence, vehicle or premises in or upon which any person may be born or die."

In the Natal Code of Native Law (Law 19 of 1891, sec. 16) the word *house* denotes "the family and property, rights and status which commence with, attach to, and arise out of, the marriage of each woman. It also includes the dwellings used and occupied by the natives, commonly called huts."

For the Transvaal, see Ordinance 19 of 1906, sec. 2 (the Births, Marriages and Deaths Ordinance, 1906).

In the Orange River Colony the definition in the Registration of Births and Deaths Proclamation (15 of 1902) is the same as that in the Cape Act 7 of 1894.

House of Commons, the lower House of the English Parliament, consisting of elected members. "Parliament means, in the mouth of a lawyer (though the word has often a different sense in ordinary conversation), the King, the House of Lords, and the *House of Commons;* these three bodies acting together may be aptly described as the 'King in Parliament' and constitute Parliament" (Dicey's *Law of the Constitution,* 6th ed. p. 37).

"Being a representative body, the *House of Commons* contains persons who are presumably above the average in knowledge of the world and its affairs as well as in intellectual capacity. Among these there are to be found many men (though a smaller proportion than is found in the American Congress or in some colonial legislatures) who possess a technical acquaintance with the laws of the country, and ought to be specially well fitted to amend them, while at the same time any such tendency as professional men might have to indulge in mere technicalities is likely to be corrected by the presence of a majority of laymen. They deliberate in full publicity, and thereby can obtain from all quarters suggestions that may direct or help them. They are responsible to those who have sent them up, and who can closely watch their conduct. Ample opportunities are provided for the discussion of every measure, and for curing any defect which may lurk in any Bill brought forward either by the Ministers of the Crown, liable through their position to a fire of hostile criticism, or by a private member. Every Bill has to pass through seven stages in the *House of Commons* [now reduced to six], and six in the House of Lords, and at each of these stages it may be debated at indefinite length [now, however, subject to the power of imposing the closure of debate]" (Bryce's *History and Jurisprudence*, vol. 2, p. 324).

House of Lords, the upper House of the English Parliament, consisting of lords spiritual and temporal. *See* HOUSE OF COMMONS. "The House of Lords. . . . contains, among the fifty or sixty persons (out of nearly six hundred members) who habitually attend its sittings, not a few possessing intellectual power and practical experience, with (usually) some seven or eight distinguished lawyers, the flower of the legal profession" (Bryce's *History and Jurisprudence*, vol. 2, p. 324).

House property. (1) A term commonly applied to urban lands upon which houses are built.

(2) An expression used in the Natal Code of Native Law (Law 19 of 1891, sec. 18 of sch.) denoting "all property vested in and pertaining specially to the several houses in a kraal. *House property* may be acquired by donations or apportionments, and by the *lobolo* of the girls of the house."

Household furniture (*huisraad*) "includes everything which properly belongs to the service of the house and daily use, as chairs, tables, benches, chests," &c. (Van Leeuwen's *Comm.* Kotzé's trans. vol. 1, p. 439).

Houtvester (D.). *See* WALDVESTER.

Huisraad (D.), household furniture; household goods. Formerly spelt *huysraad*.

Hulk, the body of a ship: but generally the body of an old or disabled ship which is unfit for further service. "I think a distinction may be drawn between a *hulk* and a condemned vessel. To be a *hulk* it is not necessary a vessel should be without spars and rigging; it is enough if she lies in the harbour and is used as a storehouse there, or for some other purpose for which she was not in the ordinary use of trade or commerce intended. The legislature never meant to allow the harbour to be used for storage purposes without payment. That the vessel now in question is occasionally taken out of harbour in tow does not in my opinion prevent her being a *hulk*" (*per* JUTA, Acting J., in *Watson* v. *Rex,* [1908] E.D.C. at p. 148).

Hunt. In Ordinance 6 of 1905 (T.), sec. 2, *hunt* means "shooting at, pursuing, taking, killing, or wilfully disturbing."

Hush-money, a bribe given for the purpose of securing silence and so avoiding prosecution.

Hustings, an electioneering expression, signifying the platforms from which candidates deliver their electioneering speeches.

Huur (D.), the contract of hire. *Huur* also denotes the rent payable in respect of such a contract. The Dutch jurisprudents speak of the "contract van *huur* en verhuuring," *i.e.* the contract of hiring and letting (see Van der Linden's *Institutes,* 1, 15, 11). Grotius says, "Letting and hiring is an agreement whereby one party binds himself to let another have his labour or that of some other person or animal, or the use of some other thing, and the other binds himself to the payment of rent" (*Introd.* Maasdorp's trans. p. 260). See Kersteman's *Woordenboek,* vol. 1, p. 181.

Huur gaat voor koop (D.), a Dutch legal maxim meaning "Hire goes before sale." "The contract of hire does not become void by the sale of the property leased, as the rule *hire goes before sale* prevails in our law" (Van der Linden's *Institutes,* Juta's trans. p. 145). This maxim means "that if a vendor sold his property, the purchaser was obliged to recognise leases not *in longum tempus,* and according to good authority short leases were those for periods under ten years" (*per* INNES, C.J., in *Rolfes, Nebel & Co.* v. *Zweigenhaft,* [1903] T.S. at p. 195). See also *Canavan and Rivas* v. *New Transvaal Gold Farms, Ltd.* ([1904] T.S. at pp. 141, 153).

"I fully concur in the view contended for by Mr. Schreiner, that the rule 'Hire goes before sale' applies only to leases actually in existence, and not to a mere right of renewal. I agree also that even in regard to leases actually in existence at the time when the land under lease is purchased, the rule giving a real right to the lessee, as against the purchaser, does not extend to terms exceeding ten years without notarial registration of the lease upon the title-deeds of the property" (*per* DE VILLIERS, C.J., in *Hite's Executor* v. *Jones,* 19 S.C. at p. 244).

Huurcontract (D.), a lease.

Huwelijk (D.), marriage. *See* MARRIAGE.

Huwelijksche voorwaarden (D.), antenuptial contract. *See* ANTENUPTIAL CONTRACT.

Hyken, heiken (D.), father. Hence *pithyken*, a grandfather.

Hypotheca, hypothec or mortgage. *See* JUS PIGNORIS.

Hypothecation. *See* HIJPOTHEEK; MORTGAGE; TACIT HYPOTHEC.

Ibidem, also written *ibid.* and *ib.*, in the same place, or in the same matter or case.

Id certum est quod certum reddi potest, that is certain which can be made certain. For example, it is a requisite of a valid contract of sale that the price should be certain. If, however, the price is not fixed at the time by the parties, but is left to be ascertained by reference to some standard, as, for example, the current market price, or to the decision of a third party, the contract is good, for *id quod certum est quod certum reddi potest* (Voet's *Comm.* 18, 1, 23).

Id est, that is; usually abbreviated and written "*i.e.*"

Id genus omne, all of that kind or description.

Id quod interest, lit. that which is of interest; an expression used in the Roman law for damages, denoting not only actual loss suffered, but also the profit which has not been made, by reason of the breach of a contract. *See* DAMNUM EMERGENS.

Identity, sameness of an individual, thing or event; the state of being the same person in all respects as some other particular person. *Identification*, the act of identifying. This subject is fully discussed in Best on *Evidence,* 10th ed. sec. 517; see also Phipson on *Evidence.*

Ides, a division of time among the Romans; the eighth day after the nones. The *Ides* were on the thirteenth day of the months of January, February, April, June, August, September, November and December, and on the fifteenth day of the months of March, May, July and October.

Idiot, a person who is deficient in, or has no intellectual faculties. See *Natal Land and Colonisation Co.* v. *Molyneux* (24 N.L.R. at p. 286).

Idiotcy (or **Idiocy**), the state of being an idiot; the mental condition of a person in whom no ideas have ever been formed. See *Natal Land and Colonisation Co.* v. *Molyneux* (24 N.L.R. at p. 286).

Ignorance of law. The Native Territories' Penal Code (Act 24 of 1886 (C.C.)), sec. 30, provides that "the fact that an offender is ignorant of the law is not an excuse for any offence committed by him; but nothing is an offence which is done by any person who is justified by law, or who by reason of a mistake of fact and not by reason of a mistake of law, believes himself to be justified by law in doing it." See also Stephen's *Digest of the Criminal Law,* 5th ed. art. 34.

Ignorantia facti excusat, ignorantia juris non excusat, ignorance of a fact excuses, ignorance of the law does not excuse. As every one is presumed to know the law, no one can plead ignorance in excuse of a breach of it. With regard to the repayment of money paid by mistake, some writers, such as Voet (*Comm.* 12, 6, 7, and 22, 6, 5), and Schorer (*Note* 457) hold that the *condictio indebiti* lies where the mistake is one of fact but not of law; while others, such as Grotius (*Introd.* 3, 30, 6), Van Leeuwen (*Cens. For.* 1, 4, 14, 3) and Van der Keessel (*Thes.* 796) maintain that money paid under a mistake of law can be recovered. In South Africa it has been held that the *condictio indebiti* will not lie on the ground of a mistake of law. (See the judgment of KOTZÉ, C.J., in *Rooth* v. *The State,* 2 S.A.R. 263, where the authorities upon the point are fully reviewed.)

Ignorantia legis neminem excusat, ignorance of the law excuses no one. *See* IGNORANTIA FACTI EXCUSAT, &c.

Ikohlo, a native term used in the Natal Code of Native Law (Law 19 of 1891, sec. 21 of sch.), denoting "the chief house of the right-hand side of the kraal, as viewed from the *indhlunkulu,* looking towards the gate."

Illegal, unlawful. In the Native Territories' Penal Code (Act 24 of 1886) (C.C.), sec. 5 (*g*), it is provided that "the word *illegal* is applicable to anything which is an offence, or which is prohibited by law, or which furnishes grounds for a civil action; and a person is said to be 'legally bound to do' whatever it is *illegal* in him to omit."

"**Illegal game,**" as to *illegal games* under the Gaming Law of 1892 (T.), see *Rex* v. *Moss* ([1908] T.S. at pp. 800, 802 and 803).

Illegitimate children, persons who are not born in lawful wedlock, and who have not been legitimated by the subsequent marriage of their parents. See Maasdorp's *Institutes,* vol. 1, p. 8.

The status of an *illegitimate child* is derived from and depends upon the status of its mother. See *Govu* v. *Stuart* (24 N.L.R. at p. 441).

Illicit, unlawful; clandestine; such as the illicit sale of gold, diamonds or liquor, being the sale of gold, diamonds or liquor without license or contrary to law.

Imaum, the chief priest of a Mohammedan church. As to appointment or election and powers of the *imaum,* see *Ian and*

Others v. *Ismael and Others* (5 Searle, 102); *Du Toit and Others* v. *Domingo* (14 S.C. 126); and *Salie* v. *Connelly and Others* ([1908] E.D.C. 97).

Imbecility, the state of being an imbecile. The state of a person whose condition is such that ideas have been partially formed in his mind and then arrested. See *Natal Land and Colonisation Co.* v. *Molyneux* (24 N.L.R. at p. 286). The term is also applied to bodily weakness or incapacity.

Imboedel (D.), includes all that is found in a house without any exception, not only as regards furniture, but also silver work, clothing and materials, thus differing from *huisraad.*

Immediately. "When a statute requires that something shall be done 'forthwith,' or '*immediately,*' or even 'instantly' it would probably be understood as allowing a reasonable time for doing it" (Maxwell's *Interpretation of Statutes,* 4th ed. p. 520). *See* FORTHWITH.

Immemorial, extending back for a lengthy and unknown period; beyond the memory of man.

Immissie (D.). The *mandament van immissie* or writ of *immissie* was a form of proceeding in Dutch practice, and was applicable where a person was ousted by a co-heir, who had equal rights, out of the possession of the estate (Van der Linden's *Institutes,* 1, 13, 3).

Immissio in possessionem damni infecti causa, putting in possession on account of (*i.e.* as security for) apprehended damage. *See* MISSIO IN POSSESSIONEM.

Immissio in possessionem legatorum vel fideicommissorum servandorum causa, putting in possession for the purpose of securing legacies or *fideicommissa.* *See* MISSIO IN POSSESSIONEM.

Immoral contract, a contract that is inconsistent with or contrary to law; a contract that is against public policy and contrary to good morals. Such contracts cannot be enforced.

Immovable property, land and whatever is permanently attached to the land. "Things in their nature movable are sometimes considered immovable, when they are regarded as a part of, or an accession to immovable things" (Schorer's *Notes to Grotius,* note 54). Correlative to movable property. May be said to be equivalent, roughly speaking, to the "real property" of English law. See Act 7 of 1907 (T.), sec. 1.

In *Olivier and Others* v. *Haarhof & Co.* ([1906] T.S. at p. 500) INNES, C.J., in discussing whether a wood and iron building of considerable size, having five rooms and resting on wooden posts projecting some six or nine inches from the ground, was movable or immovable, said: "The conclusion to which I come is that it is impossible to lay down one general rule: each case must depend on its own circumstances. The points chiefly to be considered are the nature and object of the structure, the way in which it is fixed, and the intention of the person who erected it. And of these the last point is in some respects the most important." See also *Victoria Falls Power Co.* v. *Colonial Treasurer* ([1909] T.S. 140); *Deputy-Sheriff of Pretoria* v. *Heymann* ([1909] T.S. 280); *Van Wyk and Others* v. *Dykerman* ([1904] T.S. at p. 915).

As to the lease of a stand *in longum tempus* specially registered under sec. 107 of the Gold Law of 1898 (T.), see *Ex parte Master of the Supreme Court* ([1906] T.S. at pp. 564 *et seq.*), where the common law meaning of the term *immovable property* is fully discussed.

Impanel a jury, to call certain jurymen who have been duly summoned to attend a court of justice, and to swear them in for the purpose of hearing the parties, their counsel, and the summing up of the judge, and thereafter to deliver their verdict on the issues submitted for their decision. Sometimes spelt "empanel." *See* JURY.

Impeach, to accuse; to prosecute a person before the House of Lords, or to charge a public official before a competent tribunal with some offence or misconduct; to discredit. *See* IMPEACHMENT.

Impeachment, the prosecution by the Commons before the Lords of a commoner for high misdemeanours, such as treason, or of a peer for any crime; also the ancient method of enforcing parliamentary authority. "Though it may well be conceded—and the fact is one of great importance—that the habit of obedience to the constitution was originally generated and confirmed by *impeachments*, yet there are insuperable difficulties to entertaining the belief that the dread of the Tower and the block exerts any appreciable influence over the conduct of modern statesmen. No *impeachment* for violations of the constitution (since for the present purpose we may leave out of account such proceedings as those taken against Lord Macclesfield, Warren Hastings and Lord Melville) has occurred for more than a century and a half. The process, which is supposed to ensure the retirement from office of a modern Prime Minister, when placed in a hopeless minority, is, and has long been, obsolete. The arm by which attacks on freedom were once repelled has grown rusty by disuse; it is laid aside among the antiquities of the constitution, nor will it ever, we may anticipate, be drawn again from its scabbard. For, in truth, *impeachment*, as a means for enforcing the observance of constitutional morality, always laboured under one grave defect. The possibility of its use suggested, if it did not stimulate, one most important violation of political usage; a minister who dreaded *impeachment* would, since Parliament was the only court before which he could be impeached, naturally advise the Crown not to convene Parliament" (Dicey's *Law of the Constitution*, 6th ed. p. 387).

Imperial, pertaining to an empire, an emperor, a sovereign, or a supreme authority.

Imperial officer. The Supreme Court of the Cape Colony has no jurisdiction without an order of her Majesty that right should be done, in an action brought against an officer of the Imperial Government in his official capacity (*Fraser* v. *Sievewright*, 3 S.C. 55; see also *Palmer* v. *Hutchinson*, 6 App. Cas. 619).

Imperialism, the state of being imperial; the spirit of empire.

Imperitia culpae adnumeratur, want of skill is regarded as negligence (*Digest*, 50, 17, 132). *See* SPONDET PERITIAM ARTIS, &c.

Imperium eminens. *See* DOMINIUM EMINENS.

Imperium in imperio, a supreme power within a supreme power, hence a government within a government.

Impetrant (D.), a technical term used in practice before the courts of justice in Holland, synonymous with *aanlegger* or *eischer*, plaintiff. It was, however, not so frequently employed before the judges in the towns as the word *eischer*.

Impignoration, the act of pawning or pledging.

Implication, the inference that may be drawn from something that has been said or observed.

Import, (1) to bring goods into a country from abroad; (2) significance; meaning.

Importer is defined in the Cape Stamp Duties and Licenses Act (38 of 1887), sec. 3, as follows: "*Importer* means every person who imports any goods other than the produce of South Africa for the purpose of trade or barter: provided that such importation shall be of the value of at least £1200 during the year ending 31st day of December." See *Queen* v. *Poppe* (9 S.C. 506); *Queen* v. *Ohlsson* (10 S.C. 22). For definition in Natal, see Act 13 of 1899, sec. 4; Act 45 of 1901, sec. 3.

Impossible agreement. "An agreement is void if the performance of it is either impossible in itself or impossible by law" (Pollock on *Contracts*, 7th ed. p. 399).

Impotence, the incapacity of a husband or wife to procreate children; complete absence of sexual power. *Impotence* prior to the celebration of a marriage is a ground for a decree of nullity of such marriage; it is otherwise if *impotence* supervenes after marriage (see Maasdorp's *Institutes*, vol. 1, p. 80).

Impressment is the act of seizing for public purposes. The term *impressment* is not in common use in South Africa, but it is to be found in the Natal Militia Amendment Act (30 of 1905), sec. 2. It is equivalent to the more usual expression "commandeer."

Imprimatur, lit. let it be marked or printed; a license to publish.

Imprint, the name and address of the printer or publisher, or both, of any printed book, periodical, newspaper or printed sheet. In books the *imprint* of the publisher is usually placed at the foot of the title-page, and that of the printer at the back of the title-page or at the end of the book; in newspapers and other printed matter the *imprint* is usually placed at the end.

Imprisonment. The Native Territories' Penal Code (Act 24 of 1886) (C.C.), sec. 9, provides that "the punishment of *imprisonment* consists in the detention of the offender in prison, and in his subjection to the discipline appointed for prisoners, during the period expressed in the sentence. *Imprisonment* shall be with or without hard labour, or with or without spare diet. If it is with hard labour, the sentence shall so direct. No prisoner shall be sentenced to, or suffer solitary confinement for any part of the term of his *imprisonment*, except the same may be unavoidable, or necessary for the purpose of carrying out any sentence of spare diet. No female shall be sentenced to hard labour on any road, street or public place. No offender sentenced to *imprisonment* with hard labour for any period exceeding three months shall be sentenced to spare diet, except for offences against the discipline of the gaol or other place at which he may be lawfully confined or employed."

"*Imprisonment* shall mean *imprisonment* with or without hard labour as the court which passes sentence for an offence may determine, except where *imprisonment* with hard labour is expressly provided by this Act as a punishment for an offence" (Act 13 of 1908 (T.), sec. 2; Act 29 of 1908 (O.R.C.), sec. 2).

Improvements. The question of compensation for improvements was fully discussed in *Bellingham and Another* v. *Bloommetje* (Buch. 1874, at p. 38), where De Villiers, C.J., said: "All the Roman-Dutch authorities are agreed that, where a *bonâ fide* occupier has built upon land belonging to another, he is entitled to compensation for the useful expenses incurred by him, that is to say, for the expenses to the extent to which the value of the land has been enhanced by the building, and that he cannot be compelled to relinquish possession of such building until such compensation has been tendered or paid to him. As to a *malâ fide* possessor, there is no doubt that under the ancient Roman law a person who built on land which he knew, or had reason to know, did not belong to him, lost all property in the materials, and was considered to have voluntarily alienated them." Proceeding then to discuss the Roman-Dutch authorities on the subject, the Chief Justice added: "It would therefore be impossible to reconcile the conflicting authorities on the point under consideration, but considering the high respect which this Court has always paid to the opinion of

Groenewegen, Voet and Van Leeuwen, it is not too much to say that the weight of authority is in favour of the right of even a *malâ fide* possessor to compensation for useful expenses." The point was again fully discussed in a learned judgment of DE VILLIERS, C.J., in *De Beers Consolidated Mines* v. *London and South African Exploration Co.* (10 S.C. at p. 366).

As to the rights of parties where the owner of land refuses to compensate the *bonâ fide* possessor, see *Barnard* v. *Colonial Government* (5 S.C. 122). See *Parkin* v. *Lippert* (12 S.C. 179); *Lippert* v. *Parkin* (13 S.C. 189).

For statutory definition of *improvements* in Natal, see Act 44 of 1904, sec. 3.

In aequali jure melior est conditio possidentis, where the right is equal the possessor is in the better position. *See* IN PARI CAUSA MELIOR EST CONDITIO POSSIDENTIS.

In ambiguo, in doubt; in a doubtful case.

In articulo mortis, at the point of death. A declaration made by a person *in articulo mortis* as to the cause and circumstances of his death is admissible as evidence on the trial of a person who is charged with his murder or manslaughter (Ordinance 72 of 1830 (C.C.), sec. 43; Proclamation 16 of 1902 (T.), sec. 43; Taylor on *Evidence*, secs. 714 *et seq.*). To ensure the admissibility of the declaration it is necessary that the declarant should have been in actual danger of death, that he should have been fully conscious of his danger, and that death should have actually ensued (*State* v. *Dyer*, 4 S.A.R. 291; *R.* v. *Le Roux*, 14 S.C. 424; *Rex* v. *Abdul and Others*, [1905] T.S. 119: *Rex* v. *Rolston*, [1907] T.S. 681).

In camera, in chambers; privately; with closed doors. All proceedings in connection with the hearing of an action must be carried on in open court (Charter of Justice (C.C.), sec. 32; Proclamation 14 of 1902 (T.), sec. 18; Ordinance 4 of 1902 (O.R.C.), sec. 22). It would appear that the terms of these statutes will not permit of an application being granted to have the evidence of a case heard *in camera* on the ground that it is of such a nature that publicity should be avoided (*W* v. *W*, 7 S.C. 104).

In curia, in the court.

In diem. The creditor or debtor in an obligation which is due, but not yet exigible, is called a creditor or debtor *in diem*. *See* DIES CEDIT.

In dubio, in doubt; in a doubtful case.

In emptis et venditis potius id quod actum quam id quod dictum sequendum est, in purchase and sale that which has been done rather than that which has been said is to be followed. For example, if there is no clear evidence of an agreement to give credit to a purchaser, and only accessories of the things sold have been delivered to him, while the things themselves remain in the possession of the seller, the property cannot be held to have been delivered on credit so as to transfer the ownership to the purchaser. In such a case that which has been done rather than that which has been said is to be followed (*Friis* v. *British United Diamond Mining Co.*, 7 S.C. 17). According also to this maxim the real transaction of the parties will be looked to, and not what they called it. Thus, where A wished to purchase a portion of a piece of land, and B would only sell the entire land, and in order to avoid payment of transfer duty on the whole of the land A guaranteed to B the sale of the entire land in whole or in lots to one or more purchasers for the sum of £9000, retaining the sole control of such sale or sales, and for that purpose received from B an irrevocable power of attorney "granting him the fullest power over the said property so as to enable him to deal with it as he thinks fit"; and A further guaranteed the payment of interest on the said sum of £9000, or so much thereof as should remain due, and undertook that if the land should remain unsold in whole or in part after a certain date he would be bound to take it over for £9000 or to pay the balance still unpaid, it was held by the Privy Council, reversing the decision of the Supreme Court of Cape Colony, that as the transaction was to give B every right which a seller could claim and A every right which a purchaser could demand, the word "guarantee" could not disguise its real nature as a sale, and that A was liable to pay transfer duty (*Treasurer-General* v. *Lippert*, 2 S.C. 172).

In esse, in being; in actual existence, as opposed to *in posse*, that which may, but at present does not, exist.

In extenso, at full length.

In extremis, at the point of death. *See* IN ARTICULO MORTIS.

In forma pauperis, *see* FORMA PAUPERIS.

In foro conscientiae, in the court of conscience.

In foro seculari, in a secular or civil court.

In gremio, in the body of. Any clause, term or condition contained in a deed or writing is said to be *in gremio* of the deed or writing.

In hoc statu, in this position; as matters now stand.

In infinitum, without limit; for ever.

In initio litis, at the beginning or outset of the suit. *See* IN LIMINE LITIS.

In limine (or in initio) litis, at the outset of the suit. All exceptions and special pleas of which a defendant intends to avail himself should be raised by him *in limine* before pleading over on the merits of the action.

In lineas, in or according to lines; a form of intestate succession in which the estate of the deceased person is divided into two equal portions, one going to the relations on the side of the father and the other to those on the side of the mother of the deceased. This takes place upon failure of descendants, parents, brothers and sisters and their descendants.

In loco parentis, in the place of a parent. Those who have been entrusted by the parents with the custody and control of children under age are said to stand *in loco parentis* to the children. Where a person carries a child out of the possession of such custodians without their consent for the purpose of marriage or from motives of lust, he will be guilty of the crime of abduction just as if he had carried the child out of the possession of the parents themselves (*Queen* v. *Wilderman*, 6 S.C. 295).

In nomine, in the name (of).

In obscuris minimum est sequendum, in matters of doubt the least doubtful view is to be followed; a maxim of Roman law (*Digest*, 50, 17, 9). Thus in an action for the value of a thing or for damages, the court, where the evidence is conflicting, will adopt as a rule the lowest measure of damages, in accordance with the above maxim (*Emslie* v. *African Merchants, Ltd.*, [1908] E.D.C. at p. 95). *See* ACTORI INCUMBIT ONUS PROBANDI.

In omnia paratus, prepared for all things.

In pace, in peace.

In pari casu, in an equal or similar position.

In pari causa melior est conditio possidentis, in an equal case (*i.e.* where both parties have an equal title) the possessor is in the better position. As possession of a subject is a good title against all not having a better title, he who is in possession is not bound to give up possession to another who has only an equal title. Thus a *bonâ fide* purchaser who has lost possession cannot recover from another who after such loss of possession purchased *bonâ fide* (Voet's *Comm.* 6, 2, 6). This maxim is variously rendered, *In aequali jure melior est conditio possidentis* (where the right is equal the possessor is in the better position) and *In pari causa possessor potior haberi debet* (in an equal case the possessor ought to be considered the stronger).

In pari delicto potior est conditio possidentis vel defendentis, in equal delict the position of the possessor or defendant is the stronger. Where money or property has been given or promised by one person to another for an immoral or illegal purpose the law will not assist a claim for its recovery at the instance either of him who has handed it over for the improper purpose or of him who, having performed the illegal or immoral act, demands the promised reward (Van Leeuwen's *Comm.* 4, 14, 4; Voet's *Comm.* 12, 5, 2). Thus no action lies for the recovery of money which has been lost or won in gambling, for the possessor is in the stronger position whether he be the loser who has not yet parted with his money or the winner who has received payment of his gains (*Sonnenberg* v. *Flower*, Buch. 1875, p. 4; *Lucas* v. *Reston*, 1 Kotzé, p. 45). In the same way, as prize-fighting is illegal, if two persons agree to meet each other and each hands over his portion of the stake to a third party, the loser cannot, upon the stake being paid over to the winner, maintain an action for the recovery of his money (*Clarke* v. *Bruning*, [1905] T.S. 295).

In perpetuum, for ever.

In persona, in person.

In pleno, in full.

In poenalibus causis benignius interpretandum est, in penal matters a more liberal interpretation is to be adopted. "No doubt it is a rule both of English law and of our own that a penal enactment is more strictly construed than a remedial one. The observation of Paulus, *In poenalibus causis benignius interpretandum est* (*Dig.* 50, 17, *lex* 155) is a just and sound one, for it imports that where the language is obscure or ambiguous the court should give the benefit of the doubt in favour of the defendant or of the accused. That is clear from what Gaius observes in *lex* 56 of the same title of the *Pandects*, and is a well-recognised principle of universal recognition. But the strict interpretation, in a sense more favourable to the defendant or the accused, is only permissible where the circumstances will justify its application. It must not be stretched or extended beyond that. It cannot be applied in order to vary the plain and clear language of the legislature in framing the Act, and induce us to give an interpretation at variance with the obvious intention" (*per* KOTZÉ, J.P., in *Moss* v. *Sissons and McKenzie*, [1907] E.D.C. at p. 167).

In posse. *See* IN ESSE.

In potestate parentis, under the power or authority of a parent.

In praesenti, at the present time.

In propria causa, in one's own suit.

In propria persona, in one's own person.

In quantum lucratus est, to the extent to which he has profited or benefited. Minors who enter into contracts without the assistance of their guardians are liable on such contracts only to the extent to which they have benefited thereby. So under the Roman-Dutch law an heir who adiated with benefit of inventory was liable for the debts of the deceased only in so far as he had profited by the succession, just as now an executor to whom letters of administration have been granted is liable for the debts of the estate of the deceased only to the extent of its assets.

In re, in the matter of.

In rem suam, in one's own affair; regarding one's own interest. A *procurator in rem suam* is an agent who has been appointed with regard to a matter which it is his interest or advantage to carry out. According to Voet (*Comm.* 17, 1, 17), where a person is appointed a *procurator in rem suam* and action is ceded to him, his mandate is irrevocable, that is, it neither falls by death nor can be recalled by the mandant. In *Marcus' Executor* v. *Mackie, Dunn & Co.* (11 E.D.C. 33) it was laid down that the principle that an authority coupled with an interest is irrevocable applies only to cases where the authority is given for the purpose of being a security. (See also *Koch* v. *Mair, N.O.*, 11 S.C. 83; *Fick* v. *Bierman*, 2 S.C. 35; *Natal Bank, Ltd.*, v. *Natorp and Registrar of Deeds*, [1908] T.S. 1016).

In rerum natura, in the nature of things.

In rixa, in a quarrel or brawl. As the essence of slander is the *animus injuriandi*, or intent to injure, defamatory words spoken *in rixa* and under the impulse of anger (*ab irae impetu*) are not actionable. It is, however, for the defendant to show by evidence of provocation that the words were uttered by him while in a state of anger (*per* De Villiers, C.J., in *Wilhelm* v. *Beamish*, 11 S.C. 15; *Foxcroft* v. *Meiring*, [1907] E.D.C. 113).

In solidum, for the whole. Where several debtors have bound themselves *in solidum* they may be sued separately for the whole debt, but in the absence of any special agreement to that effect each is liable only for his *pro ratâ* share (*Alcock* v. *Du Preez*, Buch. 1875, p. 132). The same applies to the liability of joint contractors for the non-fulfilment of an indivisible obligation, *i.e.* if they have not agreed to be liable *in solidum* they are only liable each for his own portion of the secondary obligation of damages into which the primary obligation is converted, for although the latter obligation is indivisible the damages are divisible (*Henwood & Co.* v. *Westlake & Coles*, 5 S.C. 341).

In solutum, in payment or satisfaction.

In statu quo ante, in the condition in which it was before.

In subsidium, in aid of. A debtor under an accessory obligation, who cannot be sued unless the principal debtor has been excussed or is manifestly unable to pay, *e.g.* a surety who has not renounced the benefit of order or excussion, is said to be liable *in subsidium* of the principal debtor.

In tali conflictu magis est ut jus nostrum quam jus alienum servemus, in case of such conflict (of laws) it is preferable to observe our own rather than a foreign law. As one State recognises the law of another State only from comity and considerations of mutual interest, it is not bound to grant such recognition where the foreign law is contrary to its own law or policy or would prejudice the interests of its own subjects (*Paterson's Marriage Settlement Trustees* v. *Paterson's Trustees in insolvency,* Buch. 1869, at p. 111).

In terrorem, by way of warning or intimidation.

In testimonium, in testimony.

"**In the event.**" "The use of the phrase *in the event* seems to imply that the thing may or may not take place; perhaps one might even go so far as to say that it implies that in the normal course it would not take place" (*per* LAURENCE, J.P., in *Eastern and S. A. Telegraph Co.* v. *Capetown Tramways Co.*, 17 S.C. at p. 117).

"**In the presence**" "of two witnesses, has been construed as meaning the actual visual presence" (Maxwell's *Interpretation of Statutes*, 4th ed. p. 10).

In totidem verbis, in so many words.

In toto, altogether; entirely.

In transitu, in transit; in course of conveyance. The right of stoppage *in transitu*, a doctrine of English law which has been adopted by Cape Colony (General Law Amendment Act, 8 of 1879, sec. 1), is the right of an unpaid seller who has delivered goods to a carrier for conveyance to the purchaser to recover possession of the goods so long as they have not yet reached the purchaser's hands. The right can be exercised only where the buyer has become insolvent, but is competent whether the sale was for cash or on credit (*Truter* v. *Joubert's Trustee*, 16 S.C. 375).

In utero, in the womb; not yet born. Although a child in the womb is generally regarded as only a part of the mother (*portio mulieris*), yet in all matters where its own interest is concerned it is treated by law as already born, *i.e.* as a *persona*, upon the maxim *Nasciturus pro jam nato habetur quoties de commodo ejus agitur* (A child about to be born is considered already born in all matters which are to its advantage.) Thus, in the Roman law a father in making his will had to appoint a tutor or tutors not only for his children already born, but also for a child that might be born. Further, he had to disinherit or institute as heirs in his testament *nascituri*, otherwise the testament would be rendered invalid upon the subsequent birth of a child. So, if a man died leaving a widow who was pregnant, the agnates of the deceased were excluded from the succession so long as there was any possibilty of a child being born to the widow. In the Roman-Dutch law the institution of heir might be set aside if to the testator a posthumous child was born of whom no mention was made in the testament (Grotius' *Introd.* 2, 18, 10; Van Leeuwen's *Comm.* 1, 3, 46). Since, however, the abolition of the legitimate portion throughout the South African colonies a testament is no longer avoided by the passing over of children, whether born or unborn.

In the same way, if a person should die before the birth of a child who may be entitled to succeed him, the estate will have to be administered for the benefit of the unborn child until the time when it is born or until it is clear that no such child will be born (Voet's *Comm.* 28, 5, 12).

In utroque jure, in both laws, *i.e.* the civil and the canon law.

Inaedificatio, building; a form of acquiring ownership by *accessio*, or the acceding of one thing to another. *See* AEDIFICIUM SOLO CEDIT.

Inaedificatio solo cedit, building accedes to the soil. *See* AEDIFICIUM SOLO CEDIT.

Inalienable, incapable of being sold, ceded or transferred.

Inalienable things "are those which belong to a person in such a manner that they cannot in any way be acquired by another: and this whether they are altogether *extra commercium*, as the air, the sea; or only in a particular sense, as those things the alienation and disposal of which have been prohibited by the laws, or by the will of the previous owner, such as fideicommissary and mortgaged property" (Van Leeuwen's *Comm.* Kotzé's trans. vol. 1, p. 153).

Inboorlingen (D.), aboriginal natives.

Inbreng (D.), collation.

Incapax doli, incapable of wrong-doing. *See* CAPAX DOLI.

Incendium, arson or incendiarism; the crime of setting fire to property with the intention to injure others. While *incendium* applies to immovable property generally, it is doubtful whether it includes movables, but a person setting fire to these may certainly be indicted for malicious injury to property (*R.* v. *Enslin,* 2 App. Cas. 69). It is essential to the crime that there should be an intention to injure another. Accordingly if a person sets fire to his own house or to that of his wife where he is married in community of property, without intending that the fire should cause injury to another, he will not be guilty of *incendium* (*R.* v. *Van Vliet,* 9 S.C. 273). But setting fire to one's own property will be criminal if it has been done with the object of defrauding an insurance company.

Incest "is the sexual union of two persons who cannot intermarry, because they are too nearly related by blood or affinity, whether this union takes place in the form of marriage or without it" (Van Leeuwen's *Comm.* Kotzé's trans. vol. 2, p. 308; see also *Rex* v. *Delport,* 18 S.C. at p. 360, where this subject was fully discussed, and Van Leeuwen's definition was approved; see also *Queen* v. *Piet Arends,* 8 S.C. 176). According to the Native Territories' Penal Code (Act 24 of 1886 (C.C.), sec. 123) "*incest* is the carnal connection of persons related by consanguinity within the third degree."

Incestuous marriage, a marriage between two persons who are related together within the degrees within which marriage is by law prohibited. Under Roman law marriages forbidden by public morals (*moribus, jure gentium*) were deemed incestuous (Roby's *Private Roman Law,* vol. 1, p. 129).

Inchoate, incipient; incomplete. As to completing *inchoate* bills of exchange, see Bills of Exchange Act, 1882 (Eng.), secs. 12 and 20; Act 19 of 1893 (C.C.), secs. 10 and 18; Proclamation 11 of 1902 (T.), secs. 10 and 18; Law 8 of 1887 (N.), secs. 11 and 19; Ordinance 28 of 1902 (O.R.C.), secs. 10 and 18.

Inchoate instrument, an agreement, bill, or other document that is not completely formed.

Incola, an inhabitant; the term applied to a litigant who resides within the country, as opposed to a *peregrinus,* one who resides elsewhere. All except *incolae* must give security before they can sue, unless they have immovable property of sufficient value within the jurisdiction (*Witham* v. *Venables,* 1 Menz. 291; *Lumsden* v. *Kaffrarian Bank,* 3 S.C. 366). "It is very difficult precisely to define what was intended by the word *incola,* but the authorities cited showed that a person who is a foreigner and who is in the colony for a temporary purpose, and does not intend permanently to reside within the jurisdiction of the Court, must, before he can sue in court, give security" (*per* BUCHANAN, J., in *Gordon* v. *Berliner,* 13 S.C. 300). *See* PEREGRINUS.

Income, the payments, rents and profits to which a person or corporation becomes entitled or receives for services rendered, investment of capital, rents of land or the like, either at stated periods or annually.

In the Cape Additional Taxation Act (36 of 1904), sec. 42, the term *income* is defined to mean "any gains or profits derived or received by any company or person in any year or by any means from any source within this [Cape] Colony, and includes profits, gains, rents, interest, salaries, wages, allowances, pensions, stipends, charges, annuities, and all profits derived from mining or quarrying." See Ordinance 18 of 1907 (O.R.C.), sec. 1.

Income tax, a tax levied in England and some colonies by statute upon the incomes of persons and corporations exceeding a certain amount. In the Cape Additional Taxation Act (36 of 1904), sec. 42, *income tax* is defined to mean "the tax or duty imposed or charged in respect of income as assessed under this Act, or any Act amending the same."

Inconvertible currency. *See* INCONVERTIBLE PAPER.

Inconvertible paper. "Speaking briefly, any system of inconvertible notes is bad, and should only be resorted to in the direst national extremity. . . . An issue of *inconvertible paper,* that is, paper money the payment of which in gold or silver cannot be legally enforced, may retain its value and perform all the functions of money so long as its amount is restricted, but experience shows that the power of issuing an inconvertible currency can rarely be used in moderation for any length of time, and that the temptation to abuse the power of issue is so great as to be almost irresistible" (Sykes on *Banking and Currency,* 2nd ed. p. 59; see also *ibid.* pp. 65 *et seq.*).

Incorporated accountant. It has been held in England (*Society of Accountants and Auditors* v. *Goodway and Another,* [1907] 1 Ch. 489; 23 T.L.R. 286) that the designation *incorporated accountant* was a fancy and not a descriptive term, and had come to denote membership of the Society of Accountants and Auditors, and that therefore the unauthorised use of it inflicted an injury on that society, which entitled it to an injunction. *See* ACCOUNTANT.

Incorporated Law Society, a society of attorneys incorporated by statute for the purpose of exercising general control over the admission and conduct of attorneys, notaries and conveyancers. There are incorporated law societies in the Cape Colony, Natal, Transvaal, and Orange River Colony.

Incorporeal, being of an intangible nature; not having a material body, such as legal rights.

Incorporeal chattels, the term applied in English law to things which have only an ideal existence, such as debts, shares in companies, patents and copyrights, otherwise called choses in action; as opposed to corporeal chattels, which are styled choses in possession (Goodeve's *Personal Property,* 4th ed. p. 1). These terms are rarely used in South Africa.

Incorporeal hereditaments, an English law term, signifying "mere rights to or over land, which is in another's possession. For example, a right to enjoy land in fee upon the determination of the interest of another, who is in possession thereof for his life or for a term of years, is a mere right regarded in law as an incorporeal thing" (Williams on *Real Property*, 20th ed. p. 31).

Incorporeal things "are such as are not tangible, in other words, which are incapable of physical possession; and they consist in rights 'of which exercise is the proof'" (Nathan's *Common Law*, sec. 530). Grotius (*Introd.* 2. 1, 14) says: "*Incorporeal things* are such as are not visible to the sense, as a right of way over land, for though the land is corporeal, the right of way is not." Holland, in his *Jurisprudence* (10th ed. p. 99), writes: "Intellectual or artificial things, '*blos gedachte dinge*,' '*res incorporales*,' '*quae tangi non possunt*,' '*quae in jure consistunt*'; as a usufruct, a *hereditas*, a *dos*, a *peculium*, an obligation; where the *ipsum jus* is incorporeal, though it often relates to corporeal objects. This class might of course include all Rights, though as a matter of fact the Roman lawyers abstain from treating under it of *dominium*. German writers express the idea by the term *rechtsgesammtheit*. It will be observed that some 'things' of this class are aggregates of duties as well as of rights; *e.g.* a *hereditas*, which imposes on the heir liabilities as well as profit; and that modern civilisation has added to the class those groups of rights known as 'copyright,' 'patent right,' and the like, and collectively described as 'intellectual property.'" See *Ex parte Master of the Supreme Court* ([1906] T.S. at p. 566).

Incumbrance. *See* ENCUMBRANCE.

"**Incur liability,**" see *Federal Supply and Cold Storage Co.* v. *Schultze & Fly* (27 N.L.R. at p. 89).

Indebiti solutio, the payment of that which is not due. Money paid under a mistake of fact and not of law may be recovered. *See* CONDICTIO INDEBITI.

Indecent assault. *See* RAPE.

Indefeasible, that cannot be set aside or made void.

Indemnity, an undertaking securing a person from loss; security given as compensation for, or guarantee against, damage, injury or expense that may be incurred by a person who is acting, or has acted, for another; an exemption from liability.

Indent, a commercial expression signifying a written order for goods sent by a merchant to another merchant or manufacturer.

Indenture, an English legal term signifying a deed made between two or more parties. In South Africa *indentured* means that a person has been bound to another to serve him as apprentice or servant.

Indhlunkulu, a native term signifying the great house. A term used in the Natal Code of Native Law (Law 19 of 1891, sec. 19 of sch.) to denote the chief house in a native kraal.

Indictment, a formal charge or complaint preferred against an accused person by or on behalf of the Crown, and upon which the accused is brought to trial before a jury. Two elements are essential to an *indictment:* (*a*) it should contain allegations which, if proved, would constitute the crime with which the accused is charged; and (*b*) it should set out the particulars of the offence in such detail as to enable the accused to know the case he has to meet (*Rex* v. *Schapiro and Saltman*, [1904] T.S. 355).

By the Criminal Law Amendment Act (4 of 1861) of the Cape Colony it is provided that in the construction of that Act the word *indictment* shall be understood to include any charge or complaint in any court of resident magistrate or in any other court, and also any plea, replication or other pleading. See *Van Zyl and Another* v. *Graaf* (24 S.C. at p. 75).

As to *indictment* in Natal, see Law 16 of 1861, secs. 8 *et seq.*; in the Transvaal, Ordinance 1 of 1903, secs. 114 *et seq.*; in the Orange River Colony, Ordinance 12 of 1902 (O.R.C.), sec. 76.

"**Indirectly.**" This term was discussed in *Van Niekerk* v. *Blake* (10 S.C. 43) in connection with a contract in which the words "shall not directly or *indirectly* sell," &c., appeared.

Indorsee. "The term *indorsee* is used to denote not only the person to whom a bill is specially indorsed, but also the bearer of a bill indorsed in blank, *i.e.* any person who makes title to a bill through an indorsement" (Chalmers' *Bills of Exchange*, 6th ed. p. 6).

Indorsement, a signature or other writing on the back of a document. In the Bills of Exchange Acts *indorsement* means an *indorsement* completed by delivery (sec. 2 of English Bills of Exchange Act, 1882; see also Act 19 of 1893 (C.C.), sec. 1; Law 8 of 1887 (N.), sec. 1; Proclamation 11 of 1902, sec. 1; Ordinance 28 of 1902 (O.R.C.), sec. 1). *See* RESTRICTIVE INDORSEMENT.

Indorser primarily denotes the holder of a bill who indorses it, but the term is also used to denote any person who backs a bill with his signature, and thereby incurs the liability of an *indorser* (Chalmers' *Bills of Exchange*, 6th ed. p. 6). Where a person signs a bill otherwise than as drawer or acceptor, he thereby incurs the liabilities of an *indorser* to a holder in due course (sec. 56 of English Bills of Exchange Act, 1882; sec. 54 of Cape Bills of Exchange Act, 1893; sec. 55 of Natal Bills of Exchange Law, 1887; sec. 54 of Rhodesian Bills of Exchange Regulations, 1895; sec. 54 of Transvaal Bills of Exchange Proclamation, 1902; sec. 54 of O.R.C. Bills of Exchange Ordinance, 1902). It is also provided in the Bills of Exchange Acts that the *indorser* of a bill by indorsing it (*a*) engages that on due presentment it shall be accepted and paid according to its tenour, and that if it be dishonoured he will compensate the holder or a subsequent *indorser*, who is compelled to pay it, provided that the requisite proceedings on dishonour be duly taken; (*b*) is precluded from denying to a holder in due course the genuineness and regularity in all respects of the drawer's signature and all previous indorsements; and (*c*) is precluded from denying to his immediate or a subsequent indorsee that the bill was at the time of his indorsement a valid and subsisting bill, and that he had then a good title thereto. See Act 19 of 1893 (C.C.), sec. 53 (2); Natal Bills of Exchange Law, 1887, sec. 54; Rhodesian Bills of Exchange Regulations, 1895, sec. 53; Transvaal Bills of Exchange Proclamation, 1902, sec. 53; Orange River Colony Bills of Exchange Ordinance, 1902, sec. 53.

Induciae, days of grace allowed for the performance of a legal act, *e.g.* the number of days allowed to a defendant to appear in answer to a plaintiff's summons.

Inductie (D.), a technical term in the judicial practice of Holland, signifying a remedy permitted to a defendant whereby he was entitled to apply to the High Court for an order directing that his creditors should be summoned before the court to show cause why payment of his debt should not be delayed upon his giving proper security. See Van der Linden's *Institutes*, 3, 1, 7, 4; BRIEVEN VAN INDUCTIE.

Industrial dispute, in the Industrial Disputes Prevention Act, 20 of 1909 (T.), sec. 2, means, "Any dispute or difference between an employer and any of his employees in relation to (*a*) matters affecting work done or to be done by such employees; or (*b*) rights, privileges, or duties of employers or employees, not involving such a violation thereof as would constitute a criminal offence; or (*c*) the wages, allowances or other remuneration of employees, or the price paid or to be paid to them in respect of their employment; or (*d*) the hours of employment, the qualification or status of employees, and the terms, conditions and manner of their employment; or (*e*) the employment of any persons or class of persons, or the dismissal of, or refusal to employ, any particular persons or class of persons; or (*f*) claims on the part of an employer or any employee that preference should be given, or not be given, to one class of persons over another class of persons (whether as members of a trade-union or not, as British subjects or aliens, or as white or coloured persons), and the circumstances under which such preference, if allowed, should, or should not, be given; or (*g*) materials supplied and alleged to be bad, unfit, or unsuitable, or damage alleged to have been caused to work; or (*h*) any custom or usage recognised, whether generally or in a particular district, or on particular industrial premises; or (*i*) the interpretation of any agreement between an employer and employee, or a portion thereof."

Industrial fruits (*fructus industriales*), fruit or crops that are produced by the aid or labour of man.

Inebriate. In the Cape Inebriates Act (32 of 1896), sec. 2, the term inebriate is defined to mean "a person who, though not by law subject to be declared a lunatic, is notwithstanding by reason of habitual intemperate drinking of intoxicating liquor, or habitual intemperate use of anæsthetics or narcotics, at times dangerous to himself or others, or incapable of managing himself or his affairs."

Infamous, having a notoriously bad reputation; detestable.

Infanticide, child murder; the killing of an infant, whether newly born or still *in utero*. See Nathan's *Common Law*, sec. 2627.

Infants. "The word *infants* is not in ordinary parlance confined to children of very tender age. If one looks at its derivation etymologically it would apply to children so long as they are not able to articulate distinctly—not able to speak—and nobody would hesitate to refer to children, I should say, at least under two years of age as *infants*, just as much as they would to children under six months of age" (*per* Lord HERSCHELL, L.C., in *White* v. *Mellin*, [1895] A.C. 157). In the Transvaal Infant Life Protection Act (24 of 1909), sec. 1, *infant* means a child under the age of seven years.

Infected, tainted with disease or the germs of disease. For a definition of the term *infected* as (*a*) applied to a flock of sheep, and (*b*) as applied to sheep, see the Cape Scab Act (20 of 1894), sec. 4. See also Ordinance 14 of 1903 (O.R.C.), sec. 1.

Infectious disease, in the Orange River Colony Public Health Ordinance (31 of 1907), sec. 25, comprises "any of the following diseases, namely — plague, cholera, leprosy, tuberculosis, small-pox, amaas, varicella (or chicken-pox), diphtheria, erysipelas, puerperal septicaemia, scarlatina (or scarlet fever), dysentery, and the fevers known by and of the following names—typhoid (or enteric), puerperal, undulant (or Malta) fever, and such other diseases as the Governor by notice in the *Gazette* or the local authority by resolution may from time to time declare to be infectious diseases within the meaning of this part of this Ordinance within any district or part of the colony."

Inferior courts, courts the jurisdiction of which is limited by statute and is below that of the superior courts. *Inferior courts* are subject to superior courts, and, generally speaking, are presided over by resident magistrates. *See* SUPERIOR COURTS.

Informer, a person who gives information as to the commission of a crime; generally a person who gives such information in the expectation, or on the promise, of some remuneration or reward.

Infringement. "The *infringement* of a patent is the doing of that which the patent prohibits from being done" (Terrell on *Patents*, 4th ed. p. 274).

Ingqutu. *See* UNQOLISO.

Inhabiliteit van een procureur (D.), unskilfulness of an attorney. It was a species of *dilatoire exceptie* that could be proposed in Dutch practice before as well as after *litis contestatio*. Its equivalent in Latin was the *exceptio procuratoris inhabilis*.

Inhabitant, one who dwells or resides in a place. "The question is whether Mr. Dipstaple is an *inhabitant* householder. It is a mere question of fact whether he is or not. In all these cases it is a question of degree. There is no precise line to be drawn. A person may inhabit a place without sleeping there, and he may sleep there without inhabiting it. The fact that a person sleeps in a place is generally a very important ingredient in deciding whether he inhabits it, but it is not conclusive" (*Dipstaple's Case*, L.R. 4 Q.B. 114). Where the applicant had only an office in a certain ward, and there was no evidence that he lived in his office, the court held that he was not an *inhabitant* of that ward (*Rogers* v. *Hancock*, 1 Off. Rep. 67; see also Maxwell's *Interpretation of Statutes*, 4th ed. p. 93).

Inheemsch, Inheimsch (D.), inland, native. *Uitheemsch*, foreign.

Inherent, inseparable; existing as an element of something.

Inherent vice, "some fault or defect latent in the thing itself, which by its development tends to the injury or destruction of the thing carried" (Disney's *Carriage by Railway*, p. 7).

Inherit, to succeed to an ancestor by virtue of descent; to have the right of succession either as to a part or the whole of the estate of a deceased person.

Inheritance. "An *inheritance* is the net balance of the estate of a deceased person which is left after the debts and legacies have been paid, and which has to be handed over by the executor to the heir" (Maasdorp's *Institutes*, vol. 1, p. 104). It is thus defined in Nathan's *Common Law* (p. 729): "An *inheritance* is that collection of possessions, real and personal, movable and immovable, which belonged to a deceased person, and which has not yet been taken into possession, by way of ownership, by any living person." Inheritance is either by last will or *ab intestato*.

"**Inheritances and legacies**" is an expression used in chapter 68 of the Orange River Colony Law Book, where it is understood to mean "all such portions which devolve on persons according to law, either by will or intestacy, from the estates of their deceased relatives in the ascending, descending and collateral lines, as well as all testamentary inheritances or legacies of money or other property to persons who are not related by blood to the testator."

Inhibitie (D.), inhibition; a clause inserted in a petition for the prosecution of an appeal, addressed to a superior court in Holland,

and having for its object the prevention of any steps being taken in the action pending the appeal. See Van der Linden's *Institutes*, 3, 1, 6, 5; Van Leeuwen's *Comm.* 5, 25, 2.

Initial, placed at the beginning; the first letter of a name. *See* SIGN.

Injunction. An English law term. "An *injunction* was under the old procedure a writ issuing by order and under seal of the Court of Chancery. A writ of *injunction* may be described as a judicial process whereby a party was required to do a particular thing or to refrain from doing a particular thing according to the exigency of the writ. . Under the present procedure no writ of *injunction* is to issue. An *injunction* is by judgment or order, and such judgment or order has the effect which a writ of *injunction* previously had" (Kerr on *Injunctions*, 4th ed. p. 1). *See* INTERDICT.

Injuria, injury; *injurie* (D.). "The word *injuria* is derived from the word *jus* (right), and implies a negation of that which is denoted by the latter word. In its original and more general sense, therefore, it signified any infraction of right or wrongful or illicit act. As a term of law it is, however, as a rule, used in either of the two following senses: firstly, in the expression *damnum injuriâ datum*, damage done to or in respect of property, means or prospective gains (patrimonial loss), the term *injuria* relates to an unintentional, or not necessarily intentional wrong, and is considered to be used as signifying an act due to negligence or fault (*culpa*); and, secondly, in its most usual sense when standing by itself, it expresses an unlawful, vexatious and intentional act of one person whereby another is assailed in respect of his absolute rights of personality" (De Villiers' *Law of Injuries*, p. 21).

Injuria non excusat injuriam, one wrong does not justify or excuse another wrong. *See* IN RIXA; RETORSIO INJURIARUM.

Injuria sine damno, injury without damage. Where an action is brought for an *injuria*, not committed under circumstances amounting to *contumelia*, or insult, the action being solely for damages, and not to establish any right which has been violated by the *injuria*, the plaintiff must prove that he has actually sustained some damage; in the absence of such proof he will not be entitled to nominal damages (*Edwards* v. *Hyde*, [1903] T.S. 381; *Steenkamp* v. *Juriaanse*, [1907] T.S. 980).

Injury, the violation of a right or legal duty to the prejudice of another person. In the Native Territories' Penal Code (Act 24 of 1886 (C.C.), sec. 5 (*g*)) it is provided that "the word *injury* denotes any harm whatever illegally caused to any person in mind, reputation or property."

See *Hart* v. *Cohen* (16 S.C. 363); INJURIA.

Inmates, persons dwelling in or occupying a dwelling or place. In the Natal Code of Native Law (Law 19 of 1891, sec. 15 of sch.) *inmates* is, when used in connection with a kraal, defined to denote "the persons usually residing therein, and subject to the kraal head."

Inner Temple, one of the Inns of Court. *See* INNS OF COURT. In common with the other three Inns it is the resort of students not only from the Universities of Oxford, Cambridge and others, but also from all portions of the British Empire, for the purpose of studying law and being called to the Bar. It is said to have now the largest membership of all the Inns. The library attached to this Inn is excellent, and so are all the arrangements connected with it.

Innkeeper, one who keeps an inn or hotel. In the original Roman sense the word "inn" "was limited to houses of refreshment only, but in modern usage these houses are employed for the purpose of providing lodging as well as board" (Nathan's *Common Law,* sec. 1058). As to liability of innkeepers, see Nathan's *Common Law,* secs. 1059 *et seq.*

Innominate, having no name. "When an agreement did not take the shape of any of the ten forms of contract recognised in the civil law, it was, strictly speaking, not a contract at all; but if one party to it had executed it, the praetor would force the other party to execute it also. These contracts, as having no special name, have been termed *contractus innominati,* and as the contract sprang into existence by a thing having been done or given, by the fact, that is, of the contract being already executed by one party to it, these *contractus innominati* may be looked on as belonging more immediately to the head of contracts made *re*" (Sandars' *Institutes of Justinian,* 12th ed. p. 322).

Inns of Court. There are in England four *Inns of Court,* viz., Lincoln's Inn, Inner Temple, Middle Temple, and Gray's Inn. Formerly there were several others attached to the principal Inns, such as Clifford's Inn, Clement's Inn, Sergeants' Inn (from which the judges were selected), Old Sergeants' Inn, New Inn and Staple Inn. The *Inns of Court* are of ancient origin; they are voluntary, self-governed societies possessing the exclusive privilege by prescription of admitting persons to practise at the Bar. Each Inn is governed by a bench of masters, who are called Benchers. They have control over the morals and conduct of the members, and they may disbar any member on sufficient cause shown. Applications are made to the Benchers by students who desire to be called to the Bar. The Benchers may refuse to call a member to the Bar. They may likewise disbar a member, in which case an appeal lies to the judges. See H. Bellot, *The Inner and Middle Temple: History and Antiquities of the Inns of Court and of the Nine Inns of Chancery,* Lond. 1780; W. Herbert, *Antiquities of the Inns of Court and Chancery,* Lond. 1804; S. Ireland, *Inns of Court;* and Spilsbury, *Lincoln's Inn and* *its Library*; C. E. A. Bedwell, *The Middle Temple*, Lond. 1909). *See* LINCOLN'S INN; INNER TEMPLE; MIDDLE TEMPLE; GRAY'S INN.

Innuendo (fr. Latin *innuo*, to nod), a term used in actions of defamation to signify a defamatory inference to be drawn from words which are not *primâ facie* actionable. The words may be incapable of the defamatory construction put upon them by the plaintiff, and if so an exception to the summons or declaration as bad in law will be upheld (*Rudd* v. *De Vos*, 9 S.C. 491). In that case DE VILLIERS, C.J., said: "There could be no defamation unless the words alleged to have been used by the defendant were defamatory. To decide whether words are defamatory or not, their plain meaning is of course the first consideration, but the context in which, the circumstances under which, and the tone in which they were spoken are not to be lost sight of. For instance, to say that a certain individual is an 'honest attorney' is at first sight perfectly harmless, but the words may be spoken under such circumstances and in such a tone as clearly to convey to the hearer the imputation of dishonesty in his profession to the attorney. But the language must be such as to be capable of the construction. The mere fact that the hearers understood it in a defamatory sense does not make it defamatory unless they were reasonably justified in so understanding it." See also *Grossman* v. *Lewis* (10 C.T.R. 337). If the words are capable of the meaning with which it is alleged they were used it is a question of fact whether they did convey such meaning to the persons to whom they were communicated (*De Villiers* v. *Viljoen*, Transvaal High Court, 1899, not reported; *Finlason* v. *The State*, Transvaal High Court, 13th June, 1898).

Inoculation. In the Natal Lung-sickness Prevention Act (30 of 1897), sec. 3, the term *inoculation* is defined to mean "the subcutaneous introduction into the system of cattle of the specific virus of lung-sickness."

Inquest. (1) An official inquiry in cases where persons die suddenly or are found dead, or are supposed or suspected to have come by their death by violence, or otherwise than in a natural way; an *inquest* is presided over by a coroner. The first statute in the Cape Colony making provision for such *inquests* was Act 22 of 1875; see also Act 7 of 1894 (C.C.), secs. 16, 26 and 27. See Act 10 of 1897 (N.); Transvaal Act 8 of 1909; and Orange River Colony Proclamation 14 of 1901.

(2) An official inquiry where any house, building or property is destroyed or injured under suspicious circumstances; see Act 33 of 1883 (C.C.); Law 5 of 1884 (N.).

Insanity. "Where the defence of *insanity* is interposed in a criminal trial the capacity to distinguish between right and wrong is not the sole test of responsibility in all cases; in the absence of legislation to the contrary, courts of law are bound to recognise the existence of a form of mental disease which prevents the sufferer from controlling his conduct and choosing between right and wrong, although he may have the mental capacity to distinguish between right and wrong; the defence of *insanity* is established if it be proved that the accused had, by reason of such mental disease, lost the power of will to control his conduct in reference to the particular act charged as an offence; the capacity of the accused to control his own conduct must be presumed until the contrary is proved" (*per* DE VILLIERS, C.J., in *Queen* v. *Hay*, 16 S.C. 290). See *Natal Land and Colonisation Co.* v. *Molyneux* (24 N.L.R. at p. 286).

Inschult (D.), a claim which the creditor or obligee has against the obligor or promisor.

Insolvency, the state or condition of being insolvent. *See* COMPULSORY SEQUESTRATION; INSOLVENT; VOLUNTARY SEQUESTRATION.

Insolvent (equivalent to the English term "bankrupt"), inability to meet or pay one's liabilities; a person who is unable to pay his liabilities, and who in consequence has surrendered his estate for the benefit of his creditors, or whose estate has been compulsorily sequestrated by a creditor or creditors.

An *insolvent* person has a reversionary interest in his insolvent estate (*Mears* v. *Rissik and Others*, [1905] T.S. at p. 305; *Coetzee* v. *Wentzell*, 4 E.D.C. 2).

As to the application of the term *insolvent* to a person whose estate has not been placed under sequestration, see *Acutt* v. *Bennett* (27 N.L.R. at p. 723).

The Dutch term is also *insolvent*. *Insolventie wet* is the insolvency law; *insolvente boedel* is an insolvent estate; *bedriegelijke insolventie* is fraudulent insolvency; *strafbare insolventie* is culpable insolvency.

Insonyami, a native term used in the Natal Code of native law (Law 19 of 1891, sec. 27 of sch.) to denote "that portion of a slaughtered animal which is the perquisite of a superior person or house from an inferior person or house."

"**Instalment system,**" as to whether these words have acquired in trade the technical meaning of hire-purchase system, see *Burroughs & Watts, Ltd.*, v. *Campbell* (22 S.C. at p. 231).

Instanter, immediately; at once.

Instelling (D.), the appointment in a valid written or nuncupative will made by a person, since deceased, as to who should succeed him as heir. See Van Leeuwen's *Comm.* Kotzé's trans. vol. 1, p. 362.

Institor, the name given in Roman law to the person who was put in charge of a shop, business or undertaking. The contracts of an *institor* bound his principal (*praeponens*), the action which was given against the latter being called the *actio institoria*. The *institor* was the equivalent of the modern factor or agent.

Institute. (1) A society or organisation, especially one established for literary or scientific purposes.

(2) To appoint in a will, as in the case of a father instituting his children as heirs. See Maasdorp's *Institutes*, vol. 1, p. 137.

Instruct, to impart information or directions to a person, as in the case of a solicitor instructing counsel; to authorise and direct counsel to appear in court on behalf of a client.

Instructions, directions; information.

"**Instrument of pledge,**" a term used in the Natal Share Pledge Act (33 of 1899), where it is defined as meaning "a document stating the fact of the pledge signed by the pledgor in the presence of a witness, and dated at the time of the signature."

Insured or **assured,** the party interested in some property or thing the subject of an insurance, or whose life is the subject of the insurance.

Insurer, the party who indemnifies the assured against loss (see Arnould's *Marine Insurance*, 7th ed. sec. 2).

Intendit (D.), a term employed in Dutch practice. An *intendit* was a document containing a statement of the plaintiff's case, describing the defendant's defaults, and the reasons for the plaintiff's conclusion or prayer. See Van der Linden's *Institutes*, 3, 1, 2, 13. As a rule an *intendit* was not allowed to be served except in cases where the defendant was in default in respect of four citations. The term *intendit* is in use in South African practice in proceedings by edictal citation, and is equivalent to the modern declaration.

Intent, the intention of a person; purpose or design; the purpose of an action or of the omission to perform a duty.

"**Intent to defraud.**" "The words 'with *intent to defraud*' seem to me to import more than a mere intent to deceive. They can only mean an intent to deceive to the detriment or loss of another. They are so defined by Stephen in his *History of the Criminal Law*, where he says, 'With *intent to defraud* means with intent to deceive in such a manner as to expose any person to loss or the risk of loss' (vol. 3, p. 187; vol. 2, p. 121, ed. of 1883). It is true the section (sec. 7 of Act 3 of 1861 [C.C.]) provides that an indictment may be sustained without alleging or proving that the prisoner intended to defraud any particular person. Now in certain cases a prisoner may be guilty of forgery without having a fraudulent intention against any one in particular, and yet his intention is clearly to defraud, as where a person forges bank-notes for circulation; but in most cases an *intent to defraud* is generally directed against one or more particular persons" (*per* KOTZÉ, J.P., in *Rex* v. *Firling*, 18 E.D.C. 11).

Intention. An important element in the construction of all written instruments and of all contracts is the *intention* of the parties. "The one universal principle is that effect is to be given to the *intention* of the parties collected from their expression of it as a whole. It must be collected from the whole; that is, particular terms are to be construed in that sense which is most consistent with the general *intention*. It must also be collected from what is expressed, not from a mere conjecture of some *intention* which the parties may have had in their minds, and would have expressed if they had been better advised" (Pollock on *Contracts*, 7th ed. p. 255). "The main object always is to ascertain what the parties intended; but we can only adopt what we think was their *intention* so far as the words of the contract permit us to do so" (*per* INNES, C.J., in *Van der Merwe* v. *Jumpers Deep, Ltd.*, [1902] T.S. at p. 207. See also remarks of SOLOMON, J., *ibid.* at p. 210). See Anson's *Law of Contract*, 11th ed. pp. 2 and 232.

In criminal procedure, "where a special *intention* has to be proved, and where a person is so deprived of will and reason that he cannot be said to have had any *intention*, that special *intention* cannot be said to have existed" (*per* WESSELS, J., in *Fowlie* v. *Rex*, [1906] T.S. at p. 508).

As to *intention* of a legislature, see Craies' *Statute Law*, pp. 66 and 67; *Salomon* v. *Salomon* ([1897] App. Cas. at p. 38).

Inter alia, among other things.

Inter arma silent leges, in the midst of arms the laws are silent; meaning thereby that in war time martial law takes the place of civil law.

Inter nos, between ourselves.

Inter se, between themselves.

Inter vivos, between living persons. An ordinary act or deed of transfer by which property is conveyed from one person to another is called an act or deed *inter vivos*, as distinguished from a will or other like deed transferring property to another in the event of the grantor's death, which is called an act or deed *mortis causa*.

Interdict, a mode of procedure for the purpose of enforcing one's proprietary or possessory rights. "An *interdict* may be applied for with the object of either acquiring or retaining or recovering possession. In some respects the Roman and Roman-Dutch mode of procedure by *interdict* corresponds to the English remedy of injunction, but in the majority of cases *interdicts* discharge a function to which injunctions can lay no claim—not merely affording relief, partial or total, against the wrongful or tortious acts of another, but conserving and protecting to the fullest extent one's rights of property." See Nathan's *Common Law*, secs. 641 *et seq.*

"According to our established practice a clear *primâ facie* case must be made out before such an *interdict* can be granted" (*per* DE VILLIERS, C.J., in *Anderson & Murison* v. *Colonial Government*, 8 S.C. at p. 295).

Interest. (1) "That which is stipulated for the benefit of property or money lent is commonly called *interest* or money-profit (because it generally consists of money): for here, besides the return of the same thing of the like kind and quality, we also stipulate for what we lose through being deprived of the thing or money. This is also improperly called by some usury (*usura*)" (Van Leeuwen's *Comm.* Kotzé's trans. vol. 2, p. 56). See *Dyason* v. *Ruthven* (3 Searle, 282).

Interest is either *simple*, being at the rate of so much per cent. per annum, or *compound*, which is a charge of interest upon interest.

In the Cape Usury Act (23 of 1908), sec. 2, the word *interest* includes "any charges for discount, commission, expenses, inquiries, fines, foregift, bonus, renewals and any other charges not being taxable conveyancing charges or revenue charges. It shall also include any valuable consideration for a loan of money, whether such consideration be in cash, in goods, in kind or in any other form whatsoever."

In Natal (Law 6 of 1858) money may be lent at any rate of *interest*, but where no special rate has been agreed upon no higher rate of interest may be charged than 6 per cent. per annum. This fairly expresses the common law in South Africa generally on this subject.

Interest is unknown in native law in Natal, and natives without exception claiming interest as having accrued upon any debt or claim are obliged to prove a distinct contract to pay the same (Law 19 of 1891, sec. 221 of sch.).

In the Orange River Colony the rate of *interest* does not seem to be limited; see O.R.C. Law Book, chapter 98, sec. 1.

(2) *Interest* in land, discussed in *Bennett & Green and Bank of Africa, Ltd.* (22 N.L.R. at p. 407).

Interest in land, a phrase employed in the Johannesburg Rating Proclamation, 38 of 1902 (T.), sec. 2, to denote certain rights over or *interests in land* within the municipal limits as in the section specified, which are subject to the terms of the Proclamation, and thus rateable property. Also found in the Local Authorities Rating Ordinance, 43 of 1903 (T.), sec. 3, where it is used in connection with the definition of "rateable property." See also *In re Bennett & Green and Bank of Africa, Ltd.* (22 N.L.R. at p. 407).

Interest policy. "An *interest policy* is one in which it appears by its terms that the insured is interested in the thing insured, or, in other words, runs a risk. He has something at stake, and, in case of loss, something to be indemnified for. Policies are usually in this form, and import, unless otherwise expressed, that the assured is interested in the subject-matter" (May on *Insurance*, 4th ed. sec. 33; see also Arnould's *Marine Insurance*, 7th ed. sec. 9).

Interest reipublicae ut sit finis litium, it is to the interest of the State that there should be an end of lawsuits (see Best on *Evidence*, 10th ed. sec. 41). To this maxim may be referred the doctrine of *res judicata* and the prescription of rights of action. So affidavits relative to statements made by jurors as to the verdict found by them are not admissible to furnish grounds for an application for a new trial, as well on the principle of the maxim as according to the law of evidence (*Sidman* v. *McLoughlin*, Buch. 1879, p. 156). Upon the same ground a successful litigant who has taxed a bill of costs against the unsuccessful party, and obtained payment of the taxed amount from him, cannot afterwards bring the taxation in review and claim to be entitled to sums which were disallowed on taxation (*Michaelis* v. *Weston & Co.* 4 E.D.C. 306).

Interim, meanwhile; in the meantime.

Interim dividend, a dividend paid on account, and in anticipation of the ordinary or annual dividend, and prior to the ordinary general meeting of shareholders of a company.

Interlocutoire sententie. *See* INTERLOCUTORY ORDER.

Interlocutory order (in Dutch *interlocutoire sententie*), a term applied to a proceeding or an order made during the course or pendency of a suit; an order which is not final and from which there is no appeal. In Roman-Dutch law, however, a decision or order, although interlocutory, may be definitive and consequently appealable, *e.g.* where it is not reparable. Merula in his *Manier van Procederen*, bk. 4, tit. 91, ch. 1, distinguishes between simple *interlocutory orders* and *interlocutory orders* affecting the principal case and possessing the force of a definitive sentence. "The general rule of the Roman-Dutch law is that it is open to any one to appeal from sentences and judgments or other decrees by which he conceives himself aggrieved. There are, however, exceptions to this rule; for instance, in the case of *interlocutory orders* and judgments, which are definitely reparable and can be redressed by final judgment (Van Leeuwen's *Comm.* 5, 25, 13). Interlocutory judgments do not, however, always denote the opposite of final or definitive judgments, for it may happen that the former may indeed have the effect of definitive judgments. Voet (*Comm.* 42, 1, 4) gives us much the same definition which we find in Van Leeuwen, and proceeds to mention instances in which interlocutory judgments are indeed appealable. Gail (1, *Obs.* 130, nn. 5 and 6) lays down the same principle. He says that an interlocutory sentence has the force of a definitive sentence when thereby, *inter alia*, the office of the judge ceases and determines, or when the sentence directs something to be given or done. An application, therefore, for an interdict pending action, whereby the opposite party or defendant shall be restrained from alienating or mortgaging certain immovable property, the subject of the suit, is not of a purely interlocutory character. If the judge refuses the application irremediable injury or loss may indeed be caused to the applicant and plaintiff, for the opposite party would be able, pending the action, to alienate or encumber the property, and in this way frustrate the whole object of the suit" (*per* KOTZÉ, C.J., in *Donoghue and Others* v. *Executor of Van der Merwe* (4 Off. Rep. 1); see also *Middelvlei Syndicate* v. *Tucker* (*ibid.* 10).

"The Roman-Dutch lawyers gave to the term *interlocutoire sententie* a very wide, but, regard being had to the derivation of the words, a very correct and logical meaning. They applied it to any order made at any stage between the inception and the conclusion of the litigation upon any incidental matter which did not finally determine the original dispute. According to Gail (*Obs.* 129), whose words are approved by Merula, *Dicitur autem interlocutoria sententia illa, quae inter principium et finem causae super aliquo incidenti vel emergenti profertur.* And Voet (*ad Pandectas*, 42, 1, 4) defines an *interlocutory order* as follows: *Interlocutoria est pronunciatio aliqua de plano super incidenti aliquo in principio vel mediis litis facta, causam principalem non plene determinans.* All orders comprised within these general limits are in theory merely ancillary to the settlement of the main dispute. But it is obvious that in practice the differences in degree between them must be so great as to approximate to a difference in kind. Some would have little or no bearing upon the merits of the action, others might involve consequences practically decisive of the ultimate issue. This was fully recognised by the practitioners of Holland, and we find that all the authorities divide decisions of this kind into two classes—*interlocutory orders* proper and *interlocutory orders* which have the effect of definitive or final decrees. Various tests are suggested to determine whether any particular order falls within the one category or the other. Some of them are of little practical use, and many of the numerous illustrations to be found in the books require for their correct appreciation a more accurate acquaintance with the intricacies of Dutch procedure in the sixteenth and seventeenth centuries than, it is to be feared, all present-day judges possess. But the more important of them are intelligible and useful. When an order incidentally given during the progress of the litigation has a direct effect upon the final issue, when its execution causes prejudice which cannot be repaired at a later stage, when it disposes of a definite portion of that suit, then in essence it is final, though in form it may be interlocutory. . . . Neither our statute law nor our Rules of Court draw any distinction between the two classes of *interlocutory orders.* They treat all judgments, decrees or orders as being either *interlocutory* or final. And it will be convenient in future to follow the same lines, and to hold that the *interlocutory orders* of our rules correspond with the simple *interlocutory orders* of the books; while what Dutch lawyers would have styled *interlocutory orders* having the force of definite decrees are to be classed with all other definite decisions as final judgments. In that way we shall be giving full effect to our own terminology, while at the same time preserving the principles and spirit of the Roman-Dutch procedure" (*per* INNES, C.J., in *Bell* v. *Bell*, [1908] T.S. at p. 890). See also *Pretoria Racing Club* v. *Van Pietersen* ([1907] T.S. at p. 694).

Intermarriage, the marriage of persons nearly related by blood.

Intermittent stream. "*Intermittent stream* means a stream which is not a perennial stream, and into which the natural surface drainage waters flow from the lands of more than one riparian property. Provided that a stream shall not be deemed to be an *intermittent stream* above the highest point of its course at which the natural surface drainage waters from the lands of more than one riparian property unite, or for such lower portions of its course as satisfy the conditions of a perennial stream" (Irrigation Act, 32 of 1906 (C.C.), sec. 3).

Interpleader, a form of action, generally allowed in the magistrate's court, to test the right to certain movable property (or its proceeds) attached in execution and claimed by a third party (see sec. 53 of Act 20 of 1856 (C.C.)).

The interpleader action in the magistrate's court has been derived from the English law (*per* DE VILLIERS, C.J., in *Beattie* v. *Fennell*, 5 S.C. at p. 38).

Interpolate, to insert additional words in a written document.

Interpret, to translate; to explain.

Interpreter. (1) One who interprets or translates from one language to another. Most South African courts have an interpreter attached to the court. A person appointed as interpreter of the Supreme Court of the Cape Colony becomes an officer of that court, and as such holds his office during the pleasure of the Crown (*Fauré* v. *Colonial Secretary*, Foord, 82).

(2) An *interpreter*, "otherwise called a procurator [in the Netherlands in the seventeenth century], so named because he keeps a record of the pleadings, acts in the prosecution of the cause in all its stages, sees that no delay takes place therein, and in everything assists the advocate, who, when the case is completed by his advice and the assistance of the attorney, further pleads and defends the cause at law, either orally or in writing" (Van Leeuwen's *Comm.* Kotzé's trans. vol. 2, p. 378).

Interregnum, the period intervening between the end of the reign of one sovereign and the commencement of that of another.

Interrogatories are questions in writing administered, under an order or authority of a competent court, to a defendant by a plaintiff, or *vice versâ*, on matters relevant to a pending action. The practice of taking evidence by interrogatories is not universal in South Africa. It is authorised in the Cape Colony; see Rule 335 (*b*), and sec. 52 of Act 20 of 1856 (C.C.); Rule of Court 60 (T.).

Interventie (D.), intervention. The joinder, by leave of the court, of a person interested in an action, but who was not originally either plaintiff or defendant; such a person, on being granted leave to intervene, becomes either co-plaintiff or co-defendant as may be directed by the court. *Interventie* was a term used in old Dutch practice, and corresponds with the modern word "intervention." See Kersteman's *Woordenboek*, vol. 1, p. 216.

Intestate estate, the estate of a person who has died without leaving a valid will. "The expression *intestate estate* means the estate of a deceased person who died without a will; or without having appointed an executor; or in respect of whose will or estate an executor is at any time required, and no provision is made in such will for the appointment of an executor" (Act 38 of 1899 (N.), sec. 2).

Intestate succession, the succession to the estate of a deceased person who died without leaving a will, or who died leaving a will which, after death, was declared void. This form of succession is also known as succession *ab intestato*. (For a full account of the origin and development of this branch of law see Wessels' *History*, p. 540.)

Intimidation, the use of violence or threats for the purpose of compelling a person to do or abstain from doing something that he has a right to do or abstain from doing. Archbold's *Criminal Practice*, 23rd ed. p. 1161; Stephen's *Comm*. 15th ed. pp. 201 and 214.

Intonjane dance, a native dance common among the South African native tribes, except the Zulus with whom it has ceased to be a custom. It is a function to celebrate the attainment of the age of puberty by female natives, and consists of a dance more or less continuous extending over a period of three or four months—the length depending much upon the custom of the tribe. At the commencement of the ceremony the girl in question joins in the dance; the Fingo maiden, however, does not join in the dance when she enters the "school" (as it is called), but only on being discharged therefrom. On entering the school the girl is confined in a hut in the kraal, and scrupulously guarded against visitors by an old and trusted woman; but among the Xosa and Fingo tribes she is looked after by young women, and the owner of the hut is held responsible for her. At the termination of her period of seclusion she is brought forth and joins in the dance; but on this occasion she is no longer regarded as a girl: she has become a woman, and has arrived at a marriageable state. This dance corresponds with the *abakweta* dance of the young men. In the Cape Colony the *intonjane* dance is prohibited in certain districts proclaimed and to be proclaimed by the Governor under Act 16 of 1891; this Act is extended to the district of Elliot by Proclamation 396 of 1896.

Intoxicating liquor "means any spirits, wines, liqueurs, ale, beer, porter, cider, perry, or other fermented, distilled, spirituous, or malt liquor of an intoxicating nature, methylated spirits, and every drink with which any such liquor shall have been mixed" (Act 38 of 1896 (N.), sec. 4; see also Act 36 of 1899 (N.), sec. 2).

For definition in Transvaal, see Ordinance 32 of 1902, sec. 3.

Intoxication. *See* DRUNKENNESS.

Intra vires, within the power or authority.

Intruder, one who thrusts himself in, or unwarrantably enters, some place where he has no right or permission to be. In Law 5 of 1888 (T.), sec. 1, an *intruder* is "any person who shall have effected such entrance [*i.e.* in or upon any dwelling or enclosed place, &c.] by means of breaking or climbing in, or by means of skeleton or false keys or other implements not intended for the opening of the dwelling-place, or erf, the stand or werf, or by means of a forged order or disguise, or who without the previous knowledge of the person entitled to the property, intruded upon, or in any way other than as the result of mistake shall have entered upon and be found therein or thereon during the time intended for the night's rest."

Intuitu mortis, in the prospect of death.

Inure, to take effect; to serve to the use or benefit of.

Invalid, of no binding force; void.

Invalid pension, in Ordinance 30 of 1906 (T.), sec. 1, means "a pension payable to an officer on retirement under the prescribed age applicable to such officer owing to mental or bodily infirmity."

Invecta et illata, things brought and carried in; used with reference to things brought on to leased premises. Over these the landlord has a lien or hypothec in security of rent due, not only where the things belong to the lessee, but also where they belong to others and have been brought on to the premises with the consent of the owner and with the object of their remaining, not for a merely temporary purpose, but for the period of the lease or indefinitely (Voet's *Comm.* 20, 2, 5). In the latter case the goods will be regarded as subject to the landlord's lien from the fact of their having been brought on to the premises under such circumstances as would lead the landlord to believe that they belonged to the lessee. Thus it has been held that the lien has effect over the separate property of a wife married by antenuptial contract, who has brought such separate property into a house rented by the husband, and in which she resided without notifying the landlord that the property belonged to her (*Crowley* v. *Domony*, Buch. 1869, p. 205; see also *Ulrich* v. *Ulrich's Trustee*, 2 S.C. 319, and *Russell* v. *Savory*, [1906] E.D.C. 100). Where, however, the circumstances are not such as to lead the landlord to believe that the goods belong to the lessee, they will not be subject to his lien. Thus the lien will not attach to a hired piano brought on to the leased premises with the owner's name engraved upon it (*Lazarus* v. *Dose*, 3 S.C. 42); nor to a hired piano of which the owner has given notice of his ownership to the landlord (*Mackay Bros.* v. *Cohen*, 1 Off. Rep. 342).

Inventaris (D.), an inventory.

Inventio, discovery; a form of acquiring title by occupation, consisting in the discovery and seizure of *res nullius, i.e.* things movable or immovable which have never been in the possession of any one, or which have been abandoned by their owners with the intention of no longer owning them. (See Voet's *Comm.* 4, 1, 9 and 10.)

Invention. By sec. 46 of the English Patents Act, 1883, an *invention* is defined as follows: "*Invention* means any manner of new manufacture, the subject of letters patent and grant of privilege within sec. 6 of the Statute of Monopolies (that is, the Act of the twenty-first year of the reign of King James the First, Chapter 3, intituled 'An Act concerning monopolies and dispensations with penal laws and the forfeiture thereof'), and includes an alleged *invention.*" This definition has been taken over by the Cape Colony (Act 17, 1860, sec. 1), and by Natal (Law 4, 1870, sec. 1).

In the Transvaal "the expression *invention* means any new and useful art, process, machine, manufacture or composition of matter, or any new and useful improvement thereof capable of being used or applied in trade or industry and not known or used by others in this colony (save as provided by secs. 23 and 53 respectively of this Proclamation) and not patented or described in any printed publication in this colony or any foreign country before the application for a patent in respect of the same and not in public use or on sale in this colony or any foreign country for more than two years prior to such application, unless the same is proved to have been abandoned" (Proclamation 22 of 1902, sec. 5); in reference to the exceptions referred to above it may be added that sec. 23 of the Proclamation provides that a grant of a foreign patent is no bar if the application is made within twelve months of the grant of such foreign patent, and sec. 53 provides that the exhibition at an industrial exhibition (subject to certain conditions) shall not prejudice the inventor in his rights.

In Rhodesia sec. 3 of Ordinance 7 of 1904 provides: "*Invention*, save as provided by secs. 24 and 54 respectively of this Ordinance, [shall mean] any new and useful art, process, machine, manufacture or composition of matter, or any new or useful improvement thereof capable of being used or applied in trade or industry and not known or used by others; and not (1) either patented in Rhodesia or any foreign country before the application for a patent in respect to the same; or (2) in public use or on sale in Rhodesia or any foreign country for more than two years prior to such application, unless the same is proved to have been abandoned"; the exceptions in secs. 24 and 54 of the Ordinance are similar to those in secs. 23 and 53 of the Transvaal Proclamation referred to above.

Inventory, a detailed list of assets belonging to a person, or to the estate of a deceased person, or to the estate of a person under guardianship. *See* BENEFIT OF INVENTORY.

Investitive fact, a fact by means of which a right comes into existence. "An *investitive fact* finds its nearest equivalents in classical Latin in the terms *justa causa, justum initium,* and *titulus.* In some, but not in all, cases, it is possible to detect two stages in the acquisition of a right, a more remote and a nearer, and it has been proposed to distinguish them by describing the *causa remota* as *titulus,* the *causa proxima* as *modus adquirendi. Cavendum est ante omnia,* says Heineccius, *ne confundamus titulum et modum adquirendi, quippe qui toto coelo differunt;* and he goes on to assert that *dominium* can never be gained without the combination of a *titulus,* giving a *jus in personam,* and a *modus adquirendi,* which superadds the *jus in rem.* These two stages are undoubtedly traceable in such a transaction as a Roman contract of sale followed by delivery, but they are by no means universally present in the acquisition even of real rights, and it is now admitted that the importance of the distinction has been much overrated" (Holland's *Jurisprudence,* 10th ed. p. 151).

I.O.U., a popular and brief form of an acknowledgment of debt or undertaking to pay. Generally speaking an I.O.U. is not a negotiable instrument (see Chalmers' *Bills of Exchange,* 5th ed. p. 264); but an I.O.U. may be a promissory note (see *Vos* v. *Marsh,* 16 S.C. 224).

Ipse dixit, he himself said it; a dogmatic assertion; a saying without proof.

Ipsissima verba, the identical words; the precise language.

Ipso facto, by the fact itself; by the mere fact.

Ipso jure, by the law itself.

Iqadi, a native term used in the Natal Code of Native Law (Law 19 of 1891, sec. 20 of sch.) denoting "the chief house of the left-hand side of the kraal, as viewed from the *indhlunkulu,* looking towards the gate."

Irreducible, that cannot be reduced.

Irrelevant, not relevant. The converse of relevant. *See* RELEVANT.

Irrevocable, not capable of being revoked or annulled.

Irrevocable power of attorney, a power of attorney given for a consideration, and which the grantor undertakes shall not be cancelled or revoked by him. "In order to make the power *irrevocable* there must be consideration for the undertaking, or if there was no such consideration it must be shown that the agent has done such acts under the power that its revocation would be to his prejudice" (*per* DE VILLIERS, C.J., in *Koch* v. *Mair, N.O.*, 11 S.C. at p. 83).

Irrigation district, an expression employed in Act 8 of 1877 (C.C.) for the promotion of irrigation; it there signifies an area proclaimed by the Governor as an irrigation district upon the petition of three or more owners of land situate within the area for which in their opinion it is expedient that there should be a combined system of irrigation, or that recourse should be had to artificial means of storing or supplying water.

Isanusi, a native term signifying a witch-doctor, witch-finder or sorcerer, who is supposed to possess supernatural powers derived from lions, leopards, elephants, boa-constrictors, alligators, and the like, thereby enabling him to provide and supply charms that will protect the natives with whom he is concerned from evil influences, and to "smell out" or ascertain those who exert such evil influences. As to penalty in Cape Colony for being by habit or repute an *isanusi*, see Act 2 of 1895 (C.C.), sec. 2.

Isityimiyana, a native term used in the Natal Code of Native Law (Law 19 of 1891, sec. 30 of sch.) to denote "an intoxicating liquor made of treacle or sugar mixed with water." *See* Act 38 of 1896 (N.), sec. 78; Act 27 of 1905 (N.).

Issue. (1) In the Bills of Exchange Acts means the first delivery of a bill or note, complete in form, to a person who takes it as a holder (sec. 2 of English Bills of Exchange Act, 1882; Act 19 of 1893 (C.C.), sec. 1; Law 8 of 1887 (N.), sec. 1; Proclamation 11 of 1902 (T.), sec. 1; Ordinance 28 of 1902 (O.R.C.), sec. 1).

(2) In the Transvaal Law concerning banks (Law 2 of 1893, sec. 13) the word *issue* "includes, *inter alia*, the payment or the depositing as security of any bank-note by the bank responsible for the payment of the amount thereof, or by any other bank, or by any agent of a branch office or official of such bank, irrespective of such note ever having been issued before or not at the same or at any other place."

(3) The children of a marriage.

(4) The result of the pleadings in an action, disclosing the precise points on which the decision of the court is required.

"It shall be lawful." *See* "SHALL BE LAWFUL."

Ita est, it is so.

Ita lex scripta est, thus the law is written.

Iter, a rural servitude. *See* SERVITUS ITINERIS.

Izinyanga zemeti, a native expression signifying herbalists, being native medicine men and women allowed to practise for gain under the Natal Code of Native Law (Law 19 of 1891, sec. 192 of sch.); see also Act 21 of 1899 (N.), sec. 33. As to bad results due to blunders or negligence of herbalists, see Law 19 of 1891 (N.), sec. 193 of sch.

Izinyanga zo kwe lapa, a native expression meaning those skilled in healing; native medicine men and women who, under the Natal Code of Native Law (Law 19 of 1891, sec. 192 of sch.) are allowed to practise for gain. See also Act 21 of 1899 (N.), sec. 33. These people are licensed by the Administrator of Native Law, and all "blunders or negligence of medicine men, women or herbalists entailing bad results, lay the party causing such bad results open to an action for civil damages, independent of any criminal charge which may lie against them." See also Law 19 of 1891 (N.), sec. 193 of sch. *et seq.*

Jetsam, goods thrown overboard during a storm or time of danger to lighten the ship.

Jettison, the throwing of goods overboard during a storm or time of danger to lighten the ship.

Joint and several, an expression commonly used in connection with suretyship. A person binding himself jointly and severally with others is liable to a joint action against himself and all others bound with him, as well as to a separate action against him personally.

Joint stock company. *See* COMPANY. See also definition of *joint stock company* in the Cape Stamps and Licenses Amendment Act (43 of 1898), schedule ii.

In the Natal Joint Stock Companies' Limited Liability Law (10 of 1864), sec. 1, the term *joint stock company* is defined to mean "every partnership whereof the capital is divided, or agreed to be divided, into shares, and so as to be transferable without the express consent of all the partners; and also every partnership which at its formation or by subsequent admission shall consist of more than ten members; provided that nothing in this law contained shall apply to any *joint stock company* formed for the purpose of banking."

See Act 31 of 1909 (T.), sec. 1; O.R.C. Law Book, chapter C, sec. 1; Law 2 of 1892 (O.R.C.), sec. 1; Law 4 of 1892 (O.R.C.), sec. 1 (*a*).

Juala, Kafir beer. See Ordinance 8 of 1903 (O.R.C.), sec. 43; *John M'Tati* v. *Rex* ([1908] O.R.C. 24).

Judex damnatur cum nocens absolvitur, the judge is condemned when the guilty person escapes punishment.

Judex suspectus, judge suspected. Where a judge himself or his near kinsman has an interest in the cause, or he has been guilty of malice or corruption, the party to the suit who is adversely affected thereby may object to his trying the case by raising the *exceptio judicis suspecti*. Such an act of objection is known as recusation. For the grounds upon which a judge may be so recused, see Voet's *Comm.* 5, 1, 44 *et seq.* and Nathan's *Common Law*, sec. 1993.

Judge, a person learned in the law appointed by the Government to administer justice in a court of law. He is "the recognised and permanent organ through which the mind of the people expresses itself in shaping that part of the law which the State power does not formally enact. He is their official mouthpiece, whose primary duty is to know and to apply the law, but who, in applying it, expands it and works it out authoritatively, as the jurists do less authoritatively. He represents the legal intelligence of the nation, somewhat as upon one theory of papal functions the bishop of the old imperial See represents the religious intelligence and spiritual discernment of the Christian community on earth; and therefore, like the Pope, he represents the principle of that development which it is his function to guide" (Bryce's *History and Jurisprudence*, vol. 2, p. 272).

"Our *judges* are independent, in the sense of holding their office by a permanent tenure, and of being raised above the direct influence of the Crown or the Ministry; but the judicial department does not pretend to stand on a level with Parliament; its functions might be modified at any time by an Act of Parliament; and such a statute would be no violation of the law" (Dicey's *Constitution*, 6th ed. p. 152). *See* TESTING RIGHT.

Judgment, the sentence or decision of a judge sitting in his court.

A court has no power to amend its own judgment; see *Caledonia Landing S. and S. Co., Ltd., and Another* v. *East London Harbour Board* (24 S.C. 434).

Judicature, judicial authority; a court of justice.

Judicial, pertaining to a judge or a court of justice.

Judicial commission. (1) A commission appointed under sec. 10 of the Articles of Peace, dated 31st May, 1902, for the purpose of inquiring into and assessing claims for compensation for losses suffered through the Anglo-Boer war of 1899.

(2) In the early days of the Cape Colony the transfer of land took place before Judicial Commissioners. The present office of Registrar of Deeds is said to be the direct representative of these Judicial Commissioners. See Wessels' *History*, p. 500.

Judicial Committee of the Privy Council, a final court of appeal in England from the decisions of various courts of judicature in the East Indies, and in the plantations, colonies and other dominions of his Majesty abroad. It was established by 3 & 4 Will. IV, c. 41, in the year 1833. This Act has been since frequently amended. The members of the Committee now include the President for the time being of the Privy Council; the holder of the office of Lord Keeper or First Commissioner of the Great Seal of Great Britain; all members of the Privy Council who have been President thereof or who have held any of the above offices; and two other persons appointed under sign manual; two judges of India or of his Majesty's dominions beyond the seas (being Privy Councillors) appointed for that purpose by his Majesty; four Lords of Appeal in Ordinary; past and present Lords Justices of Appeal who are members of the Privy Council; every person holding or who has held in England the office of Lord Justice of Appeal, if a member of the Privy Council; and certain chief justices or judges of the superior courts in certain of the colonies, not exceeding five in number. The quorum of the Judicial Committee is three.

Judicial corruption, the act of corruptly accepting or obtaining, or agreeing to accept or attempting to obtain, by any person holding any judicial office, for himself or any other person, any money or valuable consideration, office, place, or employment whatever, on account of anything already done or omitted, or to be afterwards done or omitted by him in his judicial capacity; or corruptly giving to any person holding any judicial office, or to any other person, any money or valuable consideration, office, place or employment whatever on account of any such act or omission. See Act 24 of 1886 (C.C.), sec. 103 (Native Territories' Penal Code); also Stephen's *Digest of the Criminal Law*, 5th ed. art. 136.

Judicial mortgage, a hypothecation in favour of the creditor arising from attachment of the goods of the debtor by the Sheriff or a messenger of a magistrate's court. A *judicial mortgage* is only effective while the goods are under attachment; encroachment may be made thereon by subsequent attachment within certain periods by other creditors; and it lapses entirely on the insolvency of the debtor or withdrawal of attachment. *See* PIGNUS PRAETORIUM.

Judicial proceeding. "An examination ordered by a judge to be taken before the registrar of the court ceases to be a *judicial proceeding* as defined by Crim. Code, sec. 171 (2) of Criminal Code (Canada) if the registrar after administering the oath leaves the room and the examination is proceeded with in his absence. A false statement under oath made by a witness at such an examination, but in the absence of the registrar as aforesaid, is not perjury as defined by sec. 170 of the Criminal Code (Canada); *Queen* v. *Lloyd*, (1887) 56 L.J.M.C. 119, followed" (*Rex* v. *Rulofson*, 44 Canada Law Journal, 712).

Judicial separation, a judicial decree of a competent court suspending the marriage between husband and wife, and separating them from bed, board and cohabitation. Where the spouses are married in community of property the decree may also include an order dividing their joint estate.

Judicis est jus dicere, non dare, it is the duty of the judge to declare, not to give or make law. The function of the judge is limited to interpreting and giving effect to what has already been made law by the legislative authority; he cannot add to or alter the actual words of the law (*Hess* v. *The State*, 2 Off. Rep. at p. 118).

Jurat, a memorandum at the foot of an affidavit or solemn declaration, above the signature of the justice of the peace, stating when and where the affidavit or declaration was sworn or declared to.

Jure divino, by divine right.

Jure naturae aequum est neminem cum alterius detrimento et injuria fieri locupletiorem, by the law of nature it is just that no one should be enriched with the detriment and injury of another. *See* NEMO DEBET LOCUPLETARI CUM ALTERIUS DETRIMENTO.

Juris executio non habet injuriam, the carrying out of the law inflicts no wrong (*Digest*, 47, 10, 13, sec. 1). Upon this principle a person who sues another is not liable in an action of damages because his suit should be proved to be groundless or to have been taken against the wrong person. In such a case the Roman law maxim (*Dig.* 50, 17, 55) also applies, *Nullus videtur dolo facere qui suo jure utitur* (No one is considered to act wrongfully who exercises his legal right). If, however, in suing out execution upon his judgment the creditor should issue his writ against the goods of some other person than his judgment debtor—an action will lie for the recovery of damages. So if it can be shown that the process of the court has been used as a means of extortion or oppression, the fact that the wrong-doer has acted with legal formality will not protect him from liability for damages.

The maxim also applies to exempt officials from liability for anything done by them while properly carrying out their official duties, as where a gaoler with proper authority puts a person into prison (Voet's *Comm.* 47, 10, 2).

Jurisconsult. "The *jurisconsults* at Rome were distinct from the pleaders of causes. They were for the most part specialists, who confined themselves to the study of one particular branch of the law" (Nathan's *Common Law*, sec. 11).

Jurisdictie (D.), jurisdiction.

Jurisprudence "is the science of living according to justice" (Grotius' *Introd.* 1, 1, 1).

"The term *jurisprudence* is wrongly applied to actual systems of law or to current views of law, or to suggestions for its amendment, but it is the name of a science. This science is a formal, or analytical, rather than a material one. It is the science of actual or positive law. It is wrongly divided into 'general' and 'particular' or into 'philosophical' and 'historical.' It may therefore be defined provisionally as 'the formal science of positive law.' The full import of this definition will not be apparent till after the completion of an analysis of the all-important term 'Law'" (Holland's *Jurisprudence*, 10th ed. p. 13).

Jurist, one versed in the law, especially the civil law; a writer on law. As to the Roman *jurists,* see Bryce's *History and Jurisprudence*, vol. 2, p. 155.

Juror, a duly qualified person liable to serve on a jury. In the Cape Colony every man residing within the colony between the ages of twenty-one years and sixty years who is the owner or occupier of any immovable property of the value of not less than £300 according to the valuation of the divisional council or municipality, or is in receipt of salary or wages amounting to not less than £150 per annum, and who is not disqualified or exempted by the Act, is qualified and liable to serve as a *juror* on any jury empanelled for any trial or inquiry within the jury district in which such person resides. See Act 22 of 1891 (C.C.), consolidating and amending the law relating to juries; also Act 2 of 1894 (C.C.), providing for the payment of persons summoned to serve as *jurors* in criminal cases.

In the Transvaal as to *jurors* see Ordinance 10 of 1902; in the Orange River Colony, see Ordinance 17 of 1902.

Jury, a body of qualified persons (called jurors), empanelled for any trial or inquiry. The jurors are sworn to deliver a true verdict upon the facts submitted to them during the course of the trial or inquiry. Trial by *jury* is of early Anglo-Saxon origin, and was introduced into Cape Colony by sec. 34 of the Charter of Justice of 1832, which directed that in any criminal case depending before the Supreme

Court, "the trial of any person or persons accused shall be before any one or more of the judges of the said court and a *jury* of nine men, who shall concur in every verdict to be given on the trial of any such accused party or parties; and every such verdict shall be delivered in open court by the mouth of the foreman of every such *jury*, and shall be thereupon recorded and read over to such *jury* before they are discharged from attendance on the said court." Trial by *jury* has since been adopted by the other South African colonies.

The law relating to *juries* in criminal cases in Cape Colony was consolidated by Act 22 of 1891; payment to persons summoned to serve as jurors in criminal cases is provided for in Act 2 of 1894; and the trial by jury in civil cases is regulated by Act 2 of 1894.

As to trial by *jury* in civil cases in Natal, see Act 39 of 1896, sec. 41; and as to trial in criminal cases see Law 10 of 1871; see also Law 24 of 1874; Law 8 of 1878; Law 14 of 1883; Law 4 of 1892; Act 15 of 1895; and Act 5 of 1899.

For trial by jury in the Transvaal, see Ordinance 10 of 1902; Ordinance 1 of 1903, secs. 187 *et seq.*

For the Orange River Colony, see Ordinance 17 of 1902.

Jus. This word signifies either the law which defines a man's right or the right as defined by the law. In the Roman law the word is also used with a variety of other meanings. In the first place *jus* signifies the customary or unwritten law, dealt with in the writings of the jurists, as opposed to *leges* or imperial statutes. It also sometimes denotes secular law as opposed to *fas*, or law with a religious sanction, and sometimes it is used in the sense of strict law as opposed to equity (*aequitas*). Again, it is used to signify the presence of a magistrate, corresponding in this sense to the use of our word "court," as in the phrases *in jure cessio*, surrender into court; *in jus vocatio*, a summons into the presence of a magistrate. So the proceedings in an action were divided into those *in jure*, before the magistrate, as opposed to those *in judicio*, before the *judex*.

Jus accrescendi, right of accrual. In the Roman law if one of several instituted heirs died in the testator's lifetime, or failed for any reason to become heir, his share went to his co-heirs by the *jus accrescendi*. This arose from the rule of Roman law that no one could die partly testate and partly intestate. As that rule, however, does not hold good in the Roman-Dutch law, the question whether a surviving heir takes a deceased co-heir's share is one depending upon what was the intention of the testator. (Voet's *Comm.* 29, 2, 40; Schorer's *Notes*, 152, 163 and 182; Van Leeuwen's *Comm.* 3, 4, 4.)

In the case of co-legatees the intention of the testator is presumed from the way in which they are conjoined in the will. They may be named together in one of three different ways, viz., (1) *re*, where the testator leaves a certain thing to A and in another part of the will to B; (2) *re et verbis, i.e.* the conjunction being both with regard to the subject of the legacy and by the words used, as where the testator says, "I leave my farm to A and B;" (3) *verbis tantum*, the conjunction being by words only, as where the same thing is bequeathed to A and B in equal shares. In the first two cases there is a *jus accrescendi*, but in the third there is none. (See Nathan's *Common Law*, sec. 1876.)

Jus accrescendi inter mercatores, pro beneficio commercii, locum non habet, for the benefit of commerce there is no right of accrual among merchants. In English law where property is held by the form of co-ownership called joint-tenancy the presumption at common law, although not in courts of equity, is that the survivor is entitled to the whole of the property upon the death of his joint-tenants. In accordance with the above maxim the presumption is excluded by mercantile law, the share of each partner upon his death going to his heirs, and not to the other members of the partnership. This right of accrual among joint-owners is not known in the Roman-Dutch law, according to which if one joint-owner dies, his share goes to his heirs by will or intestacy.

Jus ad rem, the right to a thing; a personal right, as distinguished from a *jus in rem*, or real right. *See* JUS IN REM.

Jus civile, the civil or Roman law. In the sense in which the term is used in the Roman law *jus civile* means the ancient, technical and formal law of Rome prior to the *jus honorarium*. In another sense civil law is the law which any State makes for its own Government, but when this term occurs in the text-writers reference is generally made to the Roman law. *See* CIVIL LAW.

Jus disponendi, the right of disposal; one of the rights of full ownership. *See* DOMINIUM PLENUM.

Jus eundi, the right of going. *See* SERVITUS ITINERIS.

Jus feciale, the law of negotiation and diplomacy; the branch of Roman law which corresponded to modern international law.

Jus gentium, the law of nations. The *jus gentium* was a branch of Roman law which arose from the increasing contact between the Romans and peregrine peoples. In the early Roman republic foreigners were denied any share in the institutions of the *jus civile*, which applied to and bound only Roman citizens. They could not, for example, be parties to a *mancipatio*, the mode used alike to transfer property and to effect a contract. As the Roman dominions extended and the commercial relations of Rome spread on every side, it became more and more necessary to devise some method of regulating and enforcing the rights and duties of foreigners. The Roman lawyers refused to apply to the new cases the principles of the *jus civile*, and, on the other hand, they declined to recognise the law of the particular State to which the foreign litigants belonged. The expedient adopted by them was that of selecting the rules of law common to Rome and the different States from which the foreigners came. Thus, in the case of the transfer of property it was seen that delivery (*traditio*) was the common ingredient of the forms used in the different States as well as of *mancipatio*, the form of conveyance peculiar to Rome, and *traditio* was adopted as the *jus gentium* mode of conveyance. The new law was administered throughout the Roman dominions by the peregrine praetors, who gradually rose to sixteen in number. In course of time, by means of the edict of the urban praetor and later through the *responsa* of the jurists, the rules of the *jus gentium* were grafted on to the old *jus civile*. *Traditio* in this way came to take the place of *mancipatio*, in the law of contract *stipulatio* and the consensual contracts displaced *nexum* and *sponsio*, and even *agnatio*, relationship based on the *patriapotestas*, made way for *cognatio* or relationship by blood. *Jus gentium* does not mean international law. It was the law common to all the nations whom the Romans had the means of observing, and therefore in modern law it is to be likened more to comparative jurisprudence. See Maine's *Ancient Law*, chap. 3.

Jus honorarium, the law introduced by the Roman praetors through their edicts "for the purpose of assisting and supplementing the *jus civile*" or old law of Rome (*Digest*, 1, 1, 7).

Jus in personam, a right against a person; a personal as distinguished from a real right, or *jus in rem*. *See* JUS IN REM.

Jus in rem (or *in re*), a right in a thing; a real right, as distinguished from a *jus ad rem* or *in personam*, a personal right. He who has a *jus in re* has a right to the thing against all other men, and may enforce it against any one who interferes with his possession or control of the thing. A *jus ad rem*, on the other hand, is a mere right to oblige a particular person to give or do or not do something, as, for example, to give transfer of immovable property to a purchaser. After transfer the purchaser will have a *jus in rem* in the property, but until then his right is only a *jus ad rem* or right against the seller to fulfil his obligation to pass transfer (*Harris* v. *Buissine's Trustee*, 2 Menz. 104; *Van Aardt* v. *Hartley's Trustees*, 2 Menz. 134).

Jus itineris, a right of going. *See* SERVITUS ITINERIS.

Jus mariti, the right of the husband. This right includes the guardianship of the wife and the management and administration of her property. As regards the latter, the husband may alienate or encumber both movables and immovables without his wife's consent, even although community of property and of profit and loss have been excluded by antenuptial contract, unless the *jus mariti* has also expressly been excluded (Grotius' *Introd.* 1, 5, 22 and 24; Van Leeuwen's *Comm.* 1, 6, 7; Voet's *Comm.* 23, 2, 52). A provision that the wife's property is to be secure to her will not, in the absence of an express exclusion of the *jus mariti*, deprive the husband of his right to alienate his wife's property.

Jus naturale, the law of nature; the principles which the highest reason commands to all men. Some writers adopt a threefold division of law, viz., civil law (*jus civile*), the law of nations (*jus gentium*) and the law of nature. As, however, the *jus gentium* and the *jus naturale* are but the complement of one another, the law common to all nations being the indication of what right reason commands to all men, a twofold division of law is adopted by other jurists. *See* LAW OF NATURE.

Jus papirianum, a collection of the *leges regiae* or laws made during the regal period at Rome, so styled from the name of the supposed compiler, *Sextus Papirius*, who lived during the reign of Tarquinius Superbus, towards the close of the sixth century B.C.

Jus pascendi pecoris, the right of pasturing cattle; a rural servitude entitling the owner of the dominant tenement to pasture or graze his cattle upon the servient tenement. The right of pasturing is limited to the stock of the dominant farm, and will not entitle the owner to graze stock belonging to strangers or stock belonging to himself, but used by him in connection with another farm (Voet's *Comm.* 8, 3, 10; *Heidelberg Municipality* v. *Uys*, 15 S.C. 156). The owner of the servient tenement cannot plough the pasture land or do any other thing which would interfere with the exercise of the right of the dominant owner; but if the pasture is sufficient he may graze his own stock upon it (Voet, *ibid.*; *Heidelberg Municipality* v. *Uys*, *ibid.*). The right may be acquired not only by express grant, but also by prescription (*Municipality of Swellendam* v. *Surveyor-General*, 3 Menz. 578). See *Nolan* v. *Barnard* ([1908] T.S. 142).

Jus pignoris, the right of pledge; a real right given to a creditor over a thing belonging to another as security for the payment of his debt. The term includes *pignus* or pledge, properly so called, where the possession of the thing is given to the creditor, and *hypotheca* or mortgage, where the thing remains in the possession of the debtor.

Jus possessionis, the right of possession. *See* POSSESSION.

Jus postliminii, the right of postliminy or reverter. Postliminy was a fiction of Roman law by which persons and in some cases things, captured by an enemy were, upon being again brought under the power of their own State, regarded as if they had never left it, and restored to their original legal status. The doctrine of postliminy is frequently applied in modern international law in the case of property taken by an enemy and afterwards recaptured. (See Taylor's *International Public Law*, sec. 559; Phillimore's *International Law*, 3rd ed. vol. 3, p. 615; also *Mshwakezele* v. *Gudusa*, 18 S.C. 167).

Jus publicum privatorum pactis mutari non potest, a public law cannot be altered by agreements or pacts between private individuals. *See* PRIVATORUM CONVENTIO JURI PUBLICO NON DEROGAT.

Jus redimendi, the right of redeeming. By an agreement added to a contract of sale the seller may reserve to himself the right to redeem or purchase back the thing sold. *See* PACTUM DE RETRO-VENDENDO.

Jus representationis, the right of representation; the right of a person to step into the place of a predeceased parent and to succeed to the share of an inheritance to which the parent would have been entitled if he had survived. Succession by representation, or *per stirpes,* takes place amongst descendants *ad infinitum,* but as regards collaterals it does not extend beyond the grandchildren of brothers and sisters or the children of uncles and aunts, *i.e.* the fourth degree, upon failure of which the inheritance is divided *per capita* amongst those collaterals in the fifth or more remote degree who are most nearly related to the deceased.

Jus retentionis, right of retention or lien; the right to retain a thing until the owner has paid what is due to the holder in respect of it. Thus a seller has a right to retain the thing sold until he has been paid the purchase-price. The right especially applies where goods have been entrusted to persons for the purpose of having work done or expense incurred in connection with them, *e.g.* workmen and artificers can retain goods until they have been paid the price of the work or labour employed by them in connection therewith. Carriers have the same right over the goods carried by them for the payment of their charges, and innkeepers over goods brought by a guest to the inn until the board and lodging has been paid. So also an agent can retain the property of his principal until he has been reimbursed the expense incurred by him in connection with it, while an attorney or conveyancer has a lien upon documents for the cost of services rendered or expenses incurred by him in respect of them. As regards immovable property, one who builds or repairs a house, as well as one who builds or repairs a ship, has a right of retention until he has been paid for his labour and material (*see* BUILDER'S LIEN; also *United Building Society* v. *Smookler's Trustees and Golombick's Trustee,* [1906] T.S. 623). A *bonâ fide* possessor of land has also a right of retention until he has been compensated for improvements made by him upon the land (*De Beers Consolidated Mines* v. *London and South African Exploration Co.,* 10 S.C. 359). See also Kersteman's *Woordenboek, sub voce* "*Retentie.*"

Jus retractus, the right of retraction. This right is of two kinds, conventional and legal. Conventional *retractus* is an agreement annexed to a contract of sale that if the purchaser again sells the thing he shall sell it not to another, but to the original vendor. Where such an agreement is made the purchaser before selling again must intimate to his vendor the price offered, so that the latter may decide whether he will repurchase the thing at the same price. This right of retraction must be exercised within two months, after which the purchaser will be free to sell to the third party who has offered to buy. The right applies only to the case of a sale, and not where the first purchaser transfers the thing by some other title than that of sale, such as exchange, donation, testamentary disposition, intestate succession (Voet's *Comm.* 18, 3, 10). If the property sold under such an agreement is land the vendor will be entitled to have the agreement inserted in the transfer (*Smuts' Executrix* v. *Meyer*, 3 Searle, 75). The legal right of retraction, also called *naasting*, was the right belonging to the blood relations of the seller of immovable property to step into the place of the purchaser if the property should be again sold (Grotius' *Introd.* 2, 16; Voet's *Comm.* 18, 3, 11–30). The right of *naasting* was also sometimes claimed in case of a lease of land. Legal *retractus* or *naasting* does not appear to have formed part of the general law of Holland, and has been held to be of no force in South Africa (*Seaville* v. *Colley*, 9 S.C. 39).

Justice "is the moral virtue of doing what is just" (Grotius' *Introd.* 1, 1, 2).

Justice of the peace. The office of *justice of the peace* was originally created in the Cape Colony by Sir Richard Bourke's Ordinance (32 of 1827), in which it is recited that whereas it was "expedient for the preservation of the public peace, the security of individuals and the due execution of the laws, that magistrates be appointed in the several districts of this [Cape] Colony, with power to apprehend, commit to prison or hold to bail all vagrants, rioters, robbers or other notorious offenders found within their several jurisdictions, in order that such offenders may be brought to trial, and with power to do all other such matters and things as the said magistrates may by law be appointed to do." The Ordinance then proceeded to enact that it should be lawful for the Governor from time to time as occasion might require to appoint *justices of the peace* under the Great Seal of the Colony of the Cape of Good Hope, for Capetown and district and the several country districts respectively, who should take and subscribe the oath of allegiance and prescribed oath of office. Such *justices of the peace* were authorised and required to preserve the public peace, and for that purpose to call to their aid and assistance all field-cornets, constables, and peace officers, military officers, and others, his Majesty's subjects, to quell all riots, brawls or other disturbances; and to lodge all rioters, brawlers, vagrants and disturbers of the peace in any prison within their respective jurisdictions to be dealt with according to law; they were also authorised and required to inquire of all crimes and offences committed, or alleged to be committed, within their respective jurisdictions, and for that purpose to summon and examine witnesses, and to apprehend criminals and deal with them according to law; they were also authorised and required, upon information or complaint in writing upon oath made to them, or any of them, to cause to come before them all those who had used any threats towards any person or persons, whether regarding their bodies or the firing of their houses, and to require adequate security for the peace and their good behaviour, failing which to keep them in prison. This Ordinance is still of force, but as a matter of fact the ordinary *justice of the peace* no longer exercises magisterial functions, although some judicial power has since been vested in special *justices of the peace* (*q.v.*). The principal duty of a *justice of the peace* at the present day is to administer oaths (see an article on "*Justices of the Peace* in the Cape Colony" in 22 S.A.L.J. 179).

As to special statute law in Natal on this subject, see Ordinance 6 of 1846).

Justitia attributrix. *See* ATTRIBUTRIX.

Justitia nihil expetit praemii, justice seeks no reward.

Justus error, reasonable error. In order that a person may successfully plead an error of fact as a ground of obtaining relief from the effects of a contract entered into by him, he must show that his error was reasonable or justifiable. Thus, if land is purchased by a person under the *boná fide* belief that a house built on the land is included in the sale, and the circumstances are not such as to justify an opposite contention, the seller cannot plead *justus error* and endeavour to show that he did not intend to sell the house (*Heatlie* v. *Colonial Government*, 5 S.C. 356). So a person, who at a public sale has purchased certain land marked and numbered on a general plan exhibited at the sale, cannot afterwards refuse to accept transfer on the ground that he believed he was purchasing certain other lots. This is not a *justus error*, as it was the duty of the purchaser to inquire what lots he was buying (*Merrington* v. *Davidson and Others*, 22 S.C. 148). In *Logan* v. *Beit* (7 S.C. 197) the principle was laid down that if the terms of a contract are unambiguous a misapprehension of one of the parties as to its meaning will not found a claim for relief unless it is proved that the other party knew or had reason to know at the time when the contract was made that it was so misapprehended.

Justus titulus, a just title. In addition to the *prescriptio longissimi temporis*, or prescription of thirty years, the Roman law recognised another form of prescription, viz., usucapion, the period of which was three years as regards movables, and as regards immovables ten years against persons present and twenty years against persons absent. For the purpose of usucapion, differing in this respect from the *prescriptio longissimi temporis*, both *bona fides* and *justus titulus* on the part of the possessor were necessary; that is, he must have commenced his possession in the belief that he had a right to possess (*bona fides*), and have acquired it by some mode recognised by law (*justus titulus*). In the Roman-Dutch law the only prescription recognised for acquiring ownership of property is the prescription of a third of a century, which is generally taken as applying to both movable and immovable property (Voet's *Comm.* 44, 3, 8; Van der Linden's *Institutes,* 1, 18, 8; Schorer, *in notis,* 80), although Van Leeuwen (*Comm.* 2, 8, 5) and Van der Keessel (*Thes.* 206) hold with Groenewegen that thirty years is sufficient for movable property. For this prescription, as in Roman law, neither *bona fides* nor *justus titulus* is required.

Kamp (D.), portion of a farm enclosed for the purpose of depasturing stock therein so as to enable them to run and live there, if necessary day and night (*Bronkhorst* v. *Aberfeldy Diamond Developing Co., Ltd.*, [1904] T.S. 477). For a comparison between a *kamp* and a *kraal*, *see* KRAAL.

Kanonieke recht (D.), Canon law.

Kaolin, a hydrosilicate of alumina; a fine variety of clay resulting from the decomposition of feldspar. *See* FIRE-CLAY.

Keeper of the Great Seal, a high State official in England. He was the Keeper of the Great Seal of Great Britain. Since 5 Eliz. c. 18, the Lord Chancellor is the Keeper.

Keeper of the Privy Seal, now known as the Lord Privy Seal, is the officer in England through whose hands all charters, pardons, &c., pass before they come to the Great Seal. This office is held by a Cabinet Minister. The *Keeper of the Privy Seal* is a Privy Councillor.

Keeper of the Touch, the Master of the assay in the British Mint.

Keuren (D.), local enactments in the Netherlands. In Friesland they were called *Kesten.* *Keuren* were issued by the counts, and were purely local laws and statutes for local purposes, issued for the general welfare of the people under the government of a count (18 S.A.L.J. 279). See Wessels' *History,* p. 210.

Keurwond (D.), was in Kennemerland a statutory wound of the length of a nail of one of the two first-fingers (Van Leeuwen's *Comm.* Kotzé's trans. vol. 2, p. 285). A penetrating wound in the fleshy part of the body was equal to nine *keurwonden,* and if the wound went right through from side to side it was equal to eighteen *keurwonden* (*ibid.* p. 286).

Key plan, a small diagram or plan showing how several other plans on a larger scale are pieced together. As to alleged misrepresentations by means of a *key plan*, see *Jenkins* v. *Durban Bay Lands Co., Ltd.* (26 N.L.R. 455).

"Kill or catch," in the Natal Game Act (8 of 1906), sec. 2, includes "intentionally disturbing, chasing, capturing, shooting or shooting at, injuring or destroying in whatever manner or by whatever means; and also includes any attempt to do any of such things; and also includes aiding or being knowingly a party to any of such acts."

Kin, relationship.

Kinderbewys (D.), a deed of hypothecation or mortgage passed by a surviving spouse, married in community of property, for the purpose of securing to the minor children of the marriage the portions due to them from the estate of the deceased spouse. Before entering upon a second or other marriage a surviving spouse is obliged, in South Africa, to pay the portions due to the minor children from the estate of the deceased parent to the Master of the Supreme Court or to secure such portions by a deed of *kinderbewys*.

Kindermoord (D.), infanticide.

Kindskinderen (D.), grandchildren.

King, the supreme ruler of a State. Dicey, in his *Law of the Constitution* (6th ed. p. 11), throws some doubt upon this definition, and points out "that the true position of the Crown, as also the true powers of the Government, are concealed under the fictitious ascription to the sovereign of political omnipotence."

K.B., an abbreviation of *King's Bench*. *See* KING'S BENCH.

King's Bench, one of the divisions of the High Court of Justice in England. It is the court of common law, having cognisance of both civil and criminal causes, and is presided over by the Lord Chief Justice.

K.C., an abbreviation of *King's Counsel*. *See* KING'S COUNSEL.

King's Counsel. The position of Queen's Counsel, which seems to have been the earliest appointment, was first created in the time of Queen Elizabeth. Lord Bacon was the first who bore that title. The next appointment of *King's Counsel* was made in the reign of Charles II, when Sir Francis North (Lord Guildford) was created *King's Counsel*. From that date the title seems to have grown, and to have gradually assumed its present significance (Dillon, *The Laws and Jurisprudence of England and America*, p. 69). *King's Counsel* occupy the first place among the members of the bar. Next came the sergeants-at-law, but that degree has been abolished. The barristers-at-law hold the lowest rank at the bar. The patent to a K.C. describes him as "one of our counsel learned in the law." A K.C. "leads" in the case, receives double the fees of an ordinary barrister, and does not admit pupils in his chambers. When the order of sergeant-at-law still existed, a member of that order, who had obtained a patent of precedence, stood on the same footing as a King's or Queen's Counsel, and their relative precedence depended on the date of their respective appointment. A *King's Counsel* appears in a silk gown, whereas the ordinary barrister is robed in a black stuff gown. Hence the expression "to take silk" is equivalent to being raised to the dignity of a *King's Counsel.* A K.C. cannot act against the Crown except with leave of the Crown.

King's Proctor, a public functionary representing the Crown in the Courts of Probate and Divorce in England to prevent collusion in actions for divorce.

King's warehouse, equivalent to *Queen's warehouse.* *See* QUEEN'S WAREHOUSE.

Klick steenen (D.). In Nijmegen, about the thirteenth century, the hangman's "assistants were called *klick steenen;* these were entitled to the underclothing of the person executed" (Wessels' *History*, p. 165).

Knevelarij (D.), extortion, that is to say, "when a person with a view to benefiting himself by abusing his office or authority, or by pretence of an order from the Government, frequently by threats, compels and forces another to submit to that which he desires" (Van der Linden's *Institutes*, Juta's trans. p. 208). The crime of extortion can be committed by any private person, and is not confined to officials (see *The State* v. *Jacob and Jacob*, 6 Off. Rep., referred to in Van Hoytema and Raphaely's *Digest*, col. 147). See also Van Leeuwen's *Comm.* 4, 33, 8; CONCUSSIO; EXTORTION.

Kohlo. *See* IKOHLO.

Koop (D.), purchase; bargain.

Kooper (D.), a purchaser; a buyer.

Koophandel (D.), commerce, trade.

Kraal (D.). (1) An enclosure used solely for confining stock. In deciding whether an enclosure is a *kraal* or a *kamp* the use to which it was put should be taken as the test; a *kraal* is an enclosure used solely for the purpose of confining stock, chiefly at night; whereas a *kamp* is used for enclosing stock depasturing in it so as to enable them to run and live there if necessary day and night (*Bronkhorst* v. *Aberfeldy Diamond Developing Co., Ltd.*, [1904] T.S. 477).

(2) In the Cape Native Territories' Penal Code (Act 24 of 1886), sec. 5 (*k*), "the word *kraal* denotes any hut, house or enclosure occupied by any single family or member of a family, or any aboriginal tribe, or any collection of huts, houses or enclosures occupied by several families of any aboriginal tribes, with a recognised head known as *umninimzi.*"

In Act 1 of 1899 (N.), sec. 5, it includes "the hut, house, residence, or place of abode of whatever description of any native." *Kraals* in Natal are exempt from the operation of the Mines and Collieries Act (43 of 1899, sec. 92 (*c*)). In the Natal Code of Native Law (Law 19 of 1891), sec. 14 of schedule, *kraal* is defined as "the domestic establishment and ordinary place of residence of natives. It is subject to and under the control of a 'kraal head,' and may consist of one or more houses. For the purposes of this Code individual dwellings occupied by natives on mission stations or private lands or elsewhere are to be deemed *kraals*." *See* KRAAL HEAD; KRAAL PROPERTY.

For the Orange River Colony, see Ordinance 14 of 1903 (O.R.C.), sec. 1.

Kraal head, an expression used in the Natal Code of Native Law to denote "the head of a family and the possessor or occupier of the kraal or kraals containing such family, either in his own right or by the right of guardianship. The term *kraal head* shall also include the heads of families living on mission stations or private lands, whether living in kraals or in separate dwellings" (Law 19 of 1891, sec. 13 of sch.).

Kraal property. These words in the Natal Code of Native Law (Law 19 of 1891), sec. 17 of schedule, "denote all the property in a kraal or kraals being the absolute property of the kraal head. They do not denote property specially apportioned or gifted to any of the houses of the kraal or kraals, nor to the property of an inmate of a kraal not related to or belonging to the family of the kraal head."

Krijgswet (D.), the equivalent for martial law; the law pertaining to war and the military. The late South African Republic and Orange Free State had each a *krijgswet* providing for the military establishment of the State and the conduct of military operations.

Kustingbrief (D.), a special mortgage bond over immovable property securing to the seller the balance of the purchase-price of such property. See Grotius' *Introd.* 2, 48, 40; Van Leeuwen's *Comm.* Kotzé's trans. vol. 2, p. 84.

Kustingpenningen (D.), the balance of the purchase-price of immovable property, together with interest thereon. See Van Leeuwen's *Comm.* Kotzé's trans. vol. 1, p. 114, *in notis*. *See* KUSTINGBRIEF.

Kwijtschelding (D.), release. A *kwijtschelding van schuld* is a release of a debt.

Laat (D), a farmer, a husbandman. It also denotes an inferior judge who decides petty cases. *Laatbank*, the court held by such officer.

Labour agent, a person engaged in recruiting native labour. The term *labour agent* is defined in, and for the purposes of, the Cape Native Labour Agent Act (6 of 1899) to mean and include "any person who shall himself or by means of runners or messengers in his own name or otherwise, for the purpose of work or labour beyond the borders of the [Cape] Colony procure or attempt to procure, ply, seek for, or engage natives, or shall supply or contract or undertake to supply natives to be employed or engaged in work or labour of any kind beyond the borders of the colony." See also sec. 5 of the same Act.

In the Transvaal *labour agent* is defined in sec. 2 of sch. A of Proclamation 38 of 1901 to be "any person who shall himself or through agents or messengers, in his own name or otherwise, procure or attempt to procure, seek for, engage, conduct, take charge of, supply or undertake to supply natives to be employed in work or labour of any kind within the Transvaal; provided that the term *labour agent* shall not include any person who procures or engages or conducts natives for his own *bonâ fide* domestic or personal business exclusively; provided that the total number of natives so employed by him does not exceed twenty at any one time." Sec. 1 of the schedule to the Proclamation referred to makes it unlawful for any person to act as a *labour agent* within the Transvaal unless he is in lawful possession of a license issued by the Commissioner of Native Affairs or by any officer appointed by him thereto. In *Gerandeau* v. *Rex* ([1903] T.S. 458) it was held that sec. 1 did not apply to a person who, without any pecuniary or other interest in the transaction, engages a native servant for another. See Ordinance 6 of 1906 (O.R.C.), sec. 2. *See* TOUT.

Labour tout. *See* LABOUR AGENT; TOUT.

Laches, remissness; neglect in the assertion of a right.

Lacuna, a hiatus; a blank caused by an omission or obliteration.

Laesio enormis, enormous lesion. In Roman-Dutch law contracts, such as sale, lease, partnership, &c., may be set aside on the ground of *laesio enormis*, which is regarded as having taken place when one of the contracting parties has been damnified to the extent of more than one-half of the subject-matter of the contract, as where a purchaser pays more than twice the market value of the thing sold or the vendor has received less than half of that value. The party who has been damnified may at his option hold by the contract, and claim damages or sue for cancellation of the contract. In determining whether *laesio enormis* has taken place, the value to be considered is the value of the subject-matter of the contract at the time when the contract was made, not the value at the time when the action is raised. *Laesio enormis* does not apply to sales made by order of court, sales of a testator's property at a price fixed upon by his will, or sales of a chance (*spes*), such as the sale of a crop which is still to be produced. This remedy of the common law has been abolished in Cape Colony by Act 8 of 1879, sec. 8, and in the Orange River Colony by Ordinance 5 of 1902, sec. 6.

Lagan. *See* LIGAN.

Lager beer. Defined in the Cape Additional Taxation Act, (36 of 1904), sec. 2, to mean "beer the mash of which is made or partially made by the process of decoction, and the worts of which are fermented at a low temperature by means of 'low' or 'bottom' yeast."

Laity, the people as distinguished from the Church.

Land. In the Transvaal Municipalities Powers of Expropriation Ordinance (64 of 1903), sec. 2, *land* means and includes: "(*a*) land with or without buildings thereon; (*b*) land or the usufruct thereof; (*c*) all land held under any tenure or under lease or stand or claim license: and (*d*) any servitude over land." *See* PRIVATE LAND. For further definition see Ordinance 44 of 1904 (T.), sec. 1; Ordinance 11 of 1905 (O.R.C.), sec. 1.

Land-graven; Landtgraven (D.), or *landgraves,* were the judges of a certain province in Holland (Van Leeuwen's *Comm.* Kotzé's trans. vol. 1, p. 63). *See* GRAAF

Land Register, a special register kept in the office of the Registrar of Deeds for the registration of the title to land as well as servitudes and other encumbrances relating thereto. "In the Roman law we find nothing about registration in the transfer of land. In western Europe, however, a custom sprang up in many places which required the seller and purchaser to appear before some official and to state in the presence of witnesses that a sale of the land had taken place. The transaction was then noted in a book kept specially for the purpose. This custom prevailed throughout the greater part of the Netherlands, and was in the time of Grotius regarded as an inveterate custom. In many parts of the Netherlands, in addition to the registration, the sale had to be publicly proclaimed on three Saturdays or on three church days (*Rechts. Obs.* pt. 3, obs. 32). There can therefore be but little doubt that the registration *coram judice loci rei sitae* was for the purpose of publicity, partly that land should not be sold twice over to different purchasers, and partly so that persons who had any claim upon the land might assert these claims before the purchaser took possession. In Holland the registration took place before the schepenen of the district where the land was situated. The system of registration was afterwards, by various Placaats, extended to hypothecations, servitudes and other burdens. When the Dutch settled in the Cape Colony they brought over from Holland this system of registration, and the titles to land granted by the Governors were registered before the Commissioners of the Court of Justice. No sales of this land and no servitudes imposed thereon were recognised, unless these were registered against the title before the Commissioners. Later on in the Cape Colony the office of Registrar of Deeds was created, and he continued the functions of the Commissioners as regards the registration of sales and burdens on land. The Registrar of Deeds therefore took the place of the Commissioners, as these had taken the place of the schepenen. The only register kept by them which affected land was the register of titles or *Land Register*, as it is frequently called" (*per* WESSELS, J., in *Houtpoort Mining and Estate Syndicate, Ltd.*, v. *Jacobs*, [1904] T.S. at p. 108).

The Cape system of land registration was subsequently introduced into the other South African colonies, each of which has a separate Deeds Office and *Land Register*. In practice the system works admirably, and it enables the transfer or conveyance of land to be effected with precision, expeditiously, and at little cost. Reference to the *Land Register* is facilitated by means of a very complete index.

The effect of a transfer of land duly registered is to divest the transferor of all right to the property transferred and to vest the same in the transferee, and this is the case whether the purchase-price has been paid or not.

Landed property "means land, including houses, buildings, &c., upon the soil" (*per* INNES, C.J., in *Van Wyk, Burger and Nefdt* v. *Dykerman*, [1904] T.S. at p. 915).

Landerij (D.), portion of a farm broken up and used for agricultural purposes, whether irrigated and enclosed or not, and such land does not cease to be *landerij* merely because it has lain fallow for a year or two, in the absence of proof that the use of it for agricultural purposes has been definitely abandoned (*Bronkhorst* v. *Aberfeldy Diamond Developing Co., Ltd.*, [1904] T.S. 477).

Landlord, the owner of immovable property; the proprietor of an hotel or boarding-house.

Landlord's lien, the hypothec possessed by landlords over goods brought on to the premises let, for the use of the lessee, with the consent of the owner of the goods, and with the intention that they should remain there indefinitely. The landlord's lien only lasts, as a general rule, while the goods are on the leased premises, and the court will not interfere after the goods have been once removed, if a third person has acquired rights in the goods *bonâ fide* (*Alexander* v. *Burger*, [1905] T.S. 80).

Landmeter (D.), a land surveyor. In South Africa land surveyors or *landmeters* are authorised by Government to practise as such after passing the prescribed examinations.

Landrecht (D.). "It is clear that besides the keuren and handvesten there existed a kind of common law or *landrecht* composed of what was called the *oude costumen*. What these old customs were our authorities do not state, but from numerous charters and extracts Van der Spiegel concludes 'that it is certain that these old customs were nothing but the old laws and customs which had grown up with our forefathers; they were the *mores Germanorum*, the laws of the Franks and the neighbouring nations, and the then known *Lex Romana'* (Van der Spiegel, p. 95)" (Wessels' *History*, p. 108).

Landsdieverij (D.), theft of public moneys. This crime is committed by those who steal public money entrusted to their care.

Landwinning (D.), a license of non-molestation, whereby a person who had killed another in necessary self-defence, or if the killing was attended by such slight negligence as not to merit punishment, was allowed to remain undisturbed in the country (Van Leeuwen's *Comm.* 4, 43, 3); a *sureté de corps.*

Lapse, to pass away; to become void. Sec. 85 of the Gold Law of 1898 (T.) (now repealed) provided that in certain circumstances if claim licenses were not duly renewed the claims should "*lapse* to Government"; it was held by SOLOMON, J., in *Van Ryn Gold Mines Estate, Ltd.*, v. *Frames* ([1904] T.S. at p. 986) that in case claims so *lapse* "the original or former claimholder ceases to be the holder of the claims, and those claims *lapse* to the Government; they pass from the claimholder and they vest in the Government; the *dominium* in the claims ceases to be in the original claimholder, and the *dominium* is, by those words of the legislature, transferred to the Government."

Lastbrief (D.), a warrant.

Lastering (D.), slander.

Lastgeving (D.). *See* MANDAAT.

Latent, concealed; not apparent.

Latent ambiguity. "The admission or rejection of parol evidence is commonly said to depend in all cases on the canon, which rejects it in the case of a patent ambiguity, or 'that which appears to be ambiguous upon the deed or instrument,' and admits it in the case of a *latent ambiguity*, or 'that which seems certain and without ambiguity for anything that appeareth upon the deed or instrument, but there is some collateral matter, outside of the deed, that breedeth the ambiguity.' In the latter case ambiguity being raised by parol evidence, may, it is said, be fairly removed by the same means. But upon examination the maxim proves not to be an universal guide; for, on the one hand, there are many recognised authorities for the admission of parol evidence to explain ambiguities appearing on the face of the will, while, on the other hand, the evidence of a *latent ambiguity* will certainly not, as appears sometimes to have been supposed, warrant the admission in all cases indiscriminately of parol evidence to show what the testator meant to have written as distinguished from what is the meaning of the words he has used" (Jarman on *Wills*, 5th ed. p. 400). Also see full discussion of the subject in *Re Herold; Ex parte Rademeyer* (1 S.C. at p. 164).

Lateral, pertaining to, or proceeding from the side.

Lateral support. *See* SUPPORT.

Laundry foreman. *See* SERVANT.

Law agent, a person of full age, and of good fame and character, enrolled in a court of resident magistrate to practise therein on payment of a small fee.

In Cape Colony a *law agent* may not be admitted in a district where not less than two attorneys are in practice. None can be admitted in Natal since the passing of Act 22 of 1896.

In the Transvaal only *law agents* who were entitled to practise in the courts of landdrost of the late South African Republic, or who have passed the examinations which under the laws of the Republic would have entitled them to admission, could be admitted; no provision has been made for further enrolment or admission.

In the Orange River Colony Ordinance 7 of 1902 authorises the enrolment of persons of full age and of good fame and character to practise in the courts of resident magistrate in districts where less than three attorneys are carrying on practice as such independently of one another; in that colony they are called "admitted agents."

In Rhodesia the same power to admit applies as in Cape Colony.

Law agents are not authorised to practise in the superior courts. They must not be confounded with the Scotch *law agent,* who ranks as a solicitor. Before the Anglo-Boer war the South African Republic stood alone in requiring *law agents* to pass an examination in law. Now in the Transvaal, by Act 33 of 1908, *law agents* may at any time within four years from the passing of the Act be admitted as attorneys upon their passing any of the examinations in law prescribed by the Act for the purpose. In the Orange River Colony provision was made by Ordinance 13 of 1904, sec. 7, for admission of *law agents* as attorneys under similar conditions at any time within three years from the taking effect of the Ordinance.

Law Lords, peers in Great Britain who hold or have held high judicial office.

Law of Nations "is that which is universally adopted by all nations for upholding the great society of mankind" (Grotius' *Introd.* 1, 2, 11). The *Law of Nations* is what obtains, and is uniformly observed, among all nations, or at least among such as are more civilised" (Nathan's *Common Law,* sec. 8). "The body of rules regulating those rights in which both of the personal factors are States, is loosely called the '*Law of Nations,*' but more appropriately '*jus inter Gentes*' or 'International Law.' It differs from ordinary law in being unsupported by the authority of a State. It differs from ordinary morality in being a rule for States and not for individuals" (Holland's *Jurisprudence,* 10th ed. p. 380).

Law of Nature. "The natural law of man is the dictate of reason pointing out what things are in their very nature honourable or dishonourable, with an obligation to observe the same imposed by God"

(Grotius' *Introd.* 1, 2, 5). The *Law of Nature* is defined by Van der Linden as "including all the duties, both perfect and imperfect, which natural reason teaches us must be observed in order to advance our own happiness and that of our fellow-men" (Van der Linden's *Institutes*, 1, 1, 3). "That portion of morality which supplies the more important and universal rules for the governance of the outward acts of mankind is called the *Law of Nature*. . . . While there has been much difference of opinion as to the contents of the *Law of Nature*, the existence of such a law has been very generally admitted" (Holland's *Jurisprudence*, 10th ed. pp. 30, 31).

"We owe to the theory of Natural Law far more than is usually imagined. We owe to it our modern International Law, and a great deal of the law reform of the seventeenth and eighteenth centuries. A correct appreciation, therefore, of the philosophy of law as accepted by Grotius and adopted by nearly all the great writers on the Roman-Dutch law is not unnecessary, and not the waste of time which so many believe it to be. It was only after the Roman-Dutch law had been supplanted by the Code Napoléon that these hypotheses were seriously attacked, and that the system of jurisprudence based on Natural Law fell into discredit. In order, therefore, to understand the scientific development of the Roman-Dutch law the student should never lose sight of the fact that Natural Law or the *Law of Nature* was the corner-stone of the whole fabric" (Wessels' *History*, p. 293).

Law Reports, reports of the proceedings and judgments of the superior courts of law. Bryce in his *History and Jurisprudence* (vol. 2, p. 266) points out that the Reports fill a place in English legal studies corresponding in a general way to that which the treatises of the great Roman jurists filled in the Roman Empire.

Law Society. *See* INCORPORATED LAW SOCIETY.

Lawful, conformable to law; legitimate.

Lawsuit, a civil action or proceeding in a court of law between two parties.

Lawyer, a person learned in the law, who has been duly admitted to practise in the superior courts.

Lay days, the agreed number of days allowed to the charterer of a vessel for shipping or discharging cargo.

Leading cases, cases decided in the superior courts containing great principles of law, or containing some point of law of real practical importance.

"Leaf." In *Re Ebden's Will* (4 S.C. 495) the question arose as to the validity of the execution of a will which was written page-wise on the three first pages of an ordinary sheet of folded note-paper, and duly signed by the testator, and attested by the witnesses at the foot or end thereof, on the third page; at the bottom of the first and second pages the witnesses signed their names, but not the testator; and the body of the will was in the testator's handwriting, including his name at the commencement. The point for decision was whether this was a sufficient compliance with the provisions of Ordinance 15 of 1845 (C.C.), which requires that where wills are written on more *leaves* than one, the testator and witnesses shall sign their names upon at least one side of every *leaf*. DE VILLIERS C.J. (at p. 498), said: "The only requirement is that the testator and witnesses shall sign their names upon at least one side of every *leaf*. It is obvious that this requirement was introduced for the purpose of authenticating those portions of the instrument which are disconnected from the signatures at the end. There is force in the argument of the applicant's counsel that this object could have been attained by a direction that one side at least of every sheet should be signed, and he follows up this argument by contending that by the word *leaf* the legislature really meant 'sheet.' But the meaning of the word *leaf* is too clearly established to admit of this construction. Where a sheet of paper is folded and written upon page-wise, no one would speak of the whole sheet as a *leaf*, but the parts into which the sheet is divided by the folding, each consisting of two pages, would be called *leaves*. . . . A *leaf* is a *leaf*, whether it forms part of a will or of a book." See also *Re Walter's Estate* (9 S.C. 311).

Leak, a breach or hole which lets in water; also the passing of water or other fluid through a crack or aperture. As to whether an escape of electricity from rails, uninsulated, on its way to the earth, constitutes a *leak*, see *Eastern and S. A. Telegraph Co.* v. *Capetown Tramways Co.* (17 S.C. at p. 107). As to difference between *leak* and *leakage*, see *ibid.* In the same case LAURENCE, J.P. (at p. 117), points out that "a *leak*, so to speak, is a thing, while leakage is a process."

Lease. *See* LETTING AND HIRING.

"Leave and bequeath." "We understand that the terms *leaving* and *bequeathing* (*laten en maken*), which would be deemed to amount to a simple bequest where they refer to a single thing, denote a complete institution to the inheritance (*erfstelling*) if they relate to the entire administration of the estate and no one else is appointed heir, or if used between children and parents who must be left a certain portion of the inheritance" (Van Leeuwen's *Comm.* Kotzé's trans. vol. 1, p. 363). It must, however, be borne in mind that the right to claim legitimate portion has been abolished throughout British South Africa (*see* LEGITIMATE PORTION).

Lectores, a term sometimes applied to notaries in the middle ages. See Wessels' *History*, p. 198.

Leen (D.). (1) A feud or fief.

(2) A loan. Grotius in his *Introduction* (Maasdorp's trans. p. 229) says: "In Dutch the word *leenen* is applied not only to the case where the same identical article is to be returned, but also where not the same article, but an equal quantity is to be returned; but, as the characteristics of these two contracts are widely different, it is necessary to qualify this ambiguous term by some adjective." *See* BRUIKLEEN; VERBRUIKLEEN.

Leenbankhouder (D.), a pawnbroker. This term is thus used in Law 13 of 1894 (T.).

Leenheer (D.), feudal lord.

Leenrecht (D.), the Dutch equivalent of *jus feudi*, defined by Grotius (*Introd.* 2, 41, 1) as "an hereditary indivisible usufruct over the immovable property of another, coupled with the mutual obligation of protection on the one side and the duty of homage and service on the other."

Legaat (D.) [pl. *legaten*], a legacy; "a voluntary gift which the deceased directs his heir to satisfy; and may be left by and to every one who may make or take by last will" (Van Leeuwen's *Comm.* Kotzé's trans. vol. 1, p. 389).

Legacy. Justinian (*Institutes*, 2, 20, 1) defines *legacy* as a kind of gift left by a person deceased. Grotius (*Introd.* 2, 14, 13, 14) says: "A *legacy* or bequest is a declaration of intention whereby something is left to a person by last will, but not as heir. That is, not in his capacity as heir, whether instituted jointly with others or not." "*Donatio quaedam a defuncto relicta* is a deduction from an inheritance for the benefit of some one. It is the creation of a claim upon the universal successor, and a distinction is drawn between the vesting of a *legacy*, *dies cedit*, and its becoming payable, *dies venit*. It may be revoked by the testator, or it may lapse. It will be void if inconsistent with any rule of law as to the amount of *legacies*, or as to the proportion which they may bear to the property which is to remain with the heir, or as to the persons who may receive them. A *legacy* must be distinguished from a *donatio mortis causa*, which, though it takes effect on the death of the donor, does not do so by way of deduction from the inheritance" (Holland's *Jurisprudence*, 10th ed. p. 158).

Legal, pertaining to the law; lawful; having the force of law.

Legal duty, a duty imposed upon a public body or an individual by the legislature. See *Jordaan* v. *Worcester Municipality* (10 S.C. 159); *Haarhoff's Trustee* v. *Frieslich* (11 S.C. 339).

Legal mortgage (also known as "tacit mortgage" or "tacit hypothecation"), such mortgage as arises by operation of law.

Legal proceedings. In the Cape Bankers' Books Evidence Act (21 of 1877) *legal proceedings* means and includes all proceedings in courts of justice, both criminal and civil, and all proceedings by way of arbitration, examination of witnesses, assessment of damages, compensation or otherwise, in which there is power to administer an oath. The same definition is given in Ordinance 11 of 1902 (O.R.C.), sec. 1. See *Page* v. *Burtwell* (99 L.T. 542).

Legal tender. *See* TENDER.

Legalise, to make lawful.

Legatee, one who becomes entitled to a legacy. "It is no doubt quite true that besides the personal action which a legatee has under the will against the heir or executor, he also possesses certain real rights by virtue of which he may either bring an action *in rem* to recover the subject of the legacy itself, or may institute an hypothecary action in respect of property belonging to the estate of his testator" (*per* DE VILLIERS, C.J., in *Booysen and Another* v. *Colonial Orphan Chamber*, Foord, 48).

Legatum rei alienae, legacy of a thing belonging to another. If a testator bequeaths property believing that it is his, while in fact it belongs to another, the legacy is void. If, however, he knew that the property did not belong to him the legacy will be valid. In the latter case if the subject of the legacy belongs to the heir himself he will be bound to deliver it to the legatee. If it belongs to a third party, the heir must endeavour to purchase it for the legatee, and if this is impossible he must pay the legatee the value of the property (Grotius' *Introd.* 2, 22, 38 and 39; Van Leeuwen's *Comm.* 3, 9, 9; see also Schorer, note 161).

Leges Barbarorum, one of the sources of law in the Netherlands at the time of the Carolingian monarchy. See Wessels' *History*, p. 41.

Leges et constitutiones futuris certum est dare formam negotiis, non ad facta praeterita revocari, it is a rule that laws and ordinances make provision for future matters and do not apply to past acts; that is, laws are prospective, and not retrospective in their effect. This maxim expresses the general principle of law that no statute can be applied to cases occurring previous to its operation unless it is clear from its terms that the statute is intended to have a retroactive effect. In *Colonial Government* v. *Standard Bank* (9 S.C. 25) this maxim was referred to. That was an action for the recovery of bank-note duty alleged to be due under Act 6 of 1864 (C.C.). This Act had provided that every bank should pay a yearly duty of 1½ per cent. upon the average issue of bank-notes of each year ending the 31st December, such average issues to be ascertained by adding together the amounts set forth in the several monthly returns of such bank for such year and by dividing the result by twelve. Upon the 23rd October, 1891, Act 6 of that year came into operation, and, in imposing a new bank-note duty, repealed the Act of 1864. It was claimed that duty was due under the 1864 Act upon the issue of bank-notes for the nine months ending the 30th September, 1891. The bank contended that the effect of the repeal of the Act was to extinguish its liability for such duty. It was, however, held that although demand could not be made nor an action brought until after the 31st of December of any year, the liability for the duty had been incurred under the law, and that although repealed the law remained in force for the purpose of sustaining any action to enforce such liability. See also *Guinsberg* v. *Scholtz* ([1903] T.S. 748). The rule that new laws cannot have a retroactive effect does not apply to laws which are declaratory (Van Leeuwen's *Comm.* 1, 3, 1; Decker *ibid. in notis*). Remedial statutes are often given retroactive effect.

Leges regiae, regal laws; laws made during the regal period at Rome. *See* JUS PAPIRIANUM.

Legislature, the assembly or assemblies of persons in a State vested with the authority to make, amend or repeal laws in that State. Professor Dicey draws a distinction between sovereign and non-sovereign *legislatures.* He says: "We perceive without difficulty that the Parliaments of even those colonies, such as the Dominion of Canada, or the Australian Commonwealth, which are most nearly independent States, are not in reality sovereign *legislatures.* This is easily seen, because the sovereign Parliament of the United Kingdom, which legislates for the whole British Empire, is visible in the background, and because the colonies, however large their practical freedom of action, do not act as independent powers in relation to foreign States; the Parliament of a dependency cannot itself be a sovereign body" (Dicey's *Constitution*, 6th ed. p. 117).

When used in reference to a British possession the term *legislature* is defined in the Interpretation Act, 1889 (Eng.), sec. 18, sub-sec. 7, to mean the authority, other than the Imperial Parliament or her Majesty the Queen in Council, competent to make laws for a British possession.

Legislation, the laws introduced into or enacted by a legislature. The term is also applied in a secondary sense to rules of law laid down by judicial authority. Professor Dicey points out that a large proportion of English law is in reality made by the judges; this, he says, is not inconsistent with the supremacy of Parliament, as the English judges do not claim or exercise the power to repeal a statute, whilst Acts of Parliament may and do override the law of the judges; "judicial *legislation* is, in short, subordinate legislation, carried on with the assent and subject to the supervision of Parliament" (Dicey's *Constitution*, 6th ed. p. 58). See Bryce's *History and Jurisprudence*, vol. 2, pp. 269 *et seq.*

Legist, one skilled in the laws.

Legitima persona standi in judicio, the legal character entitling a person to appear in a lawsuit. This character is possessed by all except those who have been deprived of it by law or those who have not yet attained it. Thus as a general rule a married woman, who has by herself no *persona standi* in a lawsuit, must sue or defend with the assistance of her husband. In the same way a minor, unless he has been emancipated from parental control, as where he is allowed to carry on a trade or business in his own name, cannot appear in law without the assistance of his guardians.

Legitimate, in accordance with law; born of parents legally married.

Legitimate portion "is a legal share [under Roman-Dutch law] of what is due to one *ab intestato,* which (the law directs) must of necessity be left to those who may not, on account of near relationship, be disinherited except for sound reasons" (Van Leeuwen's *Comm.* Kotzé's trans. vol. 1; Decker's *note* on p. 354). See *Van Schoor's Trustee* v. *Muller's Executors* (3 Searle, at p. 136).

If the children were four or less in number the *legitimate portion* was one-third, but if they were five or more it was one-half of what they would have inherited *ab intestato;* in the case of parents, brothers or sisters it was always one-third. There were, however, certain cases in which the near relation might be disinherited.

The right to claim *legitimate portion* has been abolished throughout British South Africa. Sec. 2 of Act 23 of 1874 (C.C.) enacts that no *legitimate portion* shall be claimable of right by any one out of the estate of any person who may die in the Cape Colony after the taking effect of that Act. The Cape Act is operative in Rhodesia. A similar statutory provision has been made in the Transvaal by sec. 128 of Proclamation 28 of 1902; in Natal by sec. 3 of Law 22 of 1863 (see also Law 7 of 1885); and in the Orange River Colony by chap. 92 of the Law Book, sec. 3.

Legitimated children, children who were originally illegitimate, but who have been made legitimate by the subsequent marriage of their parents. *Legitimated children* "are in exactly the same position as if they had originally been legitimate by birth; and therefore they succeed to both father and mother and to their relations equally with those who are legitimate by birth" (Maasdorp's *Institutes,* vol. 1, p. 109).

Legitimatio per subsequens matrimonium, legitimation by subsequent marriage. Children born out of wedlock are considered in all respects legitimate if their parents should afterwards marry one another. This principle, although not recognised by English law, has been adopted in all countries which follow the Roman system.

Legitimation, the act of rendering legitimate.

Legitime. *See* LEGITIMATE PORTION; PORTIO LEGITIMA.

Legitime portie (D.), the legitimate portion. *See* LEGITIMATE PORTION; PORTIO LEGITIMA.

Leonina societas, a leonine partnership; a partnership in which one receives all the profits (therefore the lion's share) and another bears all or a share of the loss. It is lawful to stipulate that one partner shall have a larger share in the profits and a less share in the losses, or for a share in the profits without a share in the loss, but an arrangement of the above nature, whereby one receives no share in the profits at all, was void in the civil law (*Dig.* 17, 2, 29, 2), and is equally forbidden in the Roman-Dutch law (Voet's *Comm.* 17, 2, 8; Grotius' *Introd.* 3, 21, 5).

Lessee, the person to whom a lease is given or granted. For a more extended definition of the term see *Barrett* v. *New Oceana Transvaal Coal Co., Ltd.* ([1903] T.S. at p. 438), where in certain circumstances it was held to signify the holder of a lease for the time being. "A *lessee* is a person in whom no *dominium* is vested" (*per* WESSELS, J., in *Ward and Salmons* v. *Phillips*, [1902] T.H. at p. 140).

Lessor, the person who lets a property to another on lease.

Letter of allotment, a formal written notification to an applicant for shares that the shares (or a portion thereof) for which he applied have been allotted to him.

Letter of appointment. In the Non-Cape Trustees and Liquidators Recognition Act, 7 of 1907 (C.C.), sec. 1, *letter of appointment* includes "every document issued and delivered, or a copy of such document duly certified by any lawful and competent judicial authority in any British colony in South Africa, other than in the Cape Colony, under which document any person shall be appointed to perform in such part of South Africa, in regard to any bankrupt or insolvent estates, or to any company that is being wound up there, duties similar to those which are performed in this [Cape] Colony by trustees of insolvent estates or by liquidators under a winding-up as the case might be." See also Act 7 of 1907 (T.), sec. 1, and Act 4 of 1908 (O.R.C.), sec. 1.

Letter of credit, a letter addressed by a banker or merchant in one place to a banker or merchant in another place or places, requesting the latter for account of the former to pay to a person named in the letter any sums of money, not exceeding a specified amount.

Letter of renunciation, a letter signed by an allottee of shares in a company, renouncing his right to such shares in favour of some other person accepting the same. *Letters of renunciation* "must be signed by the members to whom the shares are allotted, and in cases of joint accounts all the persons named in such accounts must sign the renunciation" (Palmer's *Company Precedents*, pt. 1, 8th ed. p. 906).

Letters of administration, a certificate granted by the Master of the Supreme or High Court (as the case may be) of the various South African colonies, except Natal, authorising some person, nominated in a will or elected at a meeting of next of kin and creditors, or assumed, and after due compliance with certain other requirements of law, to act as executor testamentary or executor dative (as the case may be) in the estate of a deceased person and as such to administer the estate (see secs. 19, 20, 24, &c., of Ordinance 104 of 1833 (C.C.); Government Notice 379 of 1893 (C.C.); Act 19 of 1894 (N.); secs. 25–39 of Proclamation 28 of 1902 (T.); and sec. 22 of Ordinance 18 of 1905 (O.R.C.)). The Cape laws also apply to Rhodesia.

In the Cape Foreign Letters of Administration Act (8 of 1888), Proclamation 28 of 1902 (T.), sec. 39, and Ordinance 18 of 1905 (O.R.C.), sec. 36, the expression *letters of administration* is defined to "include every document issued and delivered, or a copy of every such document duly certified by any lawful and competent judicial or other public authority in any State, under and by which document any person or body corporate shall be authorised and empowered to act as the personal representative of any deceased person or as executor or administrator, either testamentary or dative, either of the whole estate of any deceased person which shall be legally situate in such State, or of so much of such estate so situate as consists of immovable, movable, real or personal property, as the case may be."

"*Letters of administration* should not be granted by the Master to any person who is absent from the [Cape] Colony at the time when he applies for them" (*per* De Villiers, C.J., in *Re Schoeman's Estate*, 10 S.C. at p. 5).

In Natal, *letters of administration*, instead of being granted by the Master, are granted by the Registrar of Deeds (see Act 19 of 1894, secs. 3 and 4, also 10 as to foreign *letters of administration*. In the same Act (sec. 2) *letters of administration* are defined to include "every document issued and delivered, or a copy of every such document, duly certified, under and by which document any person or body corporate shall be authorised and empowered to act as the personal representative of any deceased person, or as executor or administrator testamentary either of the whole estate of any deceased person which shall be legally situate in the State in which such *letters* have been granted, or of so much of such estate so situate as consists of immovable, movable, real or personal property, as the case may be." Foreign *letters of administration* are defined in the same section. In Natal *letters of administration* are also granted to tutors and guardians testamentary or dative (*ibid.* secs. 5 and 6).

Letters of confirmation, a certificate granted by the Master of the Supreme Court certifying to the due appointment and authority to act of some person as tutor testamentary or dative, or curator nominate or dative. See Ordinance 105 of 1833 (C.C.), secs. 3 and 4; Proclamation 28 of 1902 (T.), secs. 74, 76, 78 and 83. In Natal letters of administration are granted by the Registrar of Deeds to tutors and guardians testamentary and dative, in place of *letters of confirmation* as above (see Act 19 of 1894, secs. 5 and 6).

Letters of exemption, an expression used in Law 28 of 1865 (N.). Under this statute male natives and unmarried female natives resident in Natal may, by petition to the Lieutenant-Governor, pray for a *letter of exemption* declaring the petitioner exempt from the operation of the Native Law (28 of 1865); and if the necessary formalities have been observed and the necessary requirements fulfilled, the Lieutenant-Governor, with the advice and consent of the Executive Council, may grant such *letter of exemption.*

Letters patent. Edmunds in his work on *Patents* (2nd ed. p. 1) says: "The sovereign, as the fountain of honour, office and privilege, the arbiter of trade, and the chief guardian of the common weal, has from time immemorial exercised the prerogative of making grants to subjects. Such grants are in general made by *letters patent* (*litterae patentes*), that is, according to Blackstone, 'open letters; so called because they are not sealed up, but exposed to open view with the Great Seal pendent at the bottom; and are usually addressed by the sovereign to all the subjects of the realm.' *Letters patent* commence with the formula, 'Victoria, by the grace of God of the United Kingdom of Great Britain and Ireland Queen, Defender of the Faith: To all to whom these presents shall come, greeting,' and then, after such recitals as may be necessary, proceed to grant the privilege which is conferred, 'of Our *especial grace*, certain knowledge, and *mere motion*.' Among grants which are made by *letters patent* we may cite as examples titles of honour, such as peerages and baronetcies; appointments to offices such as those of many of the ministers of the Crown and of the judges of the superior courts; special privileges, such as charters of incorporation to bodies of persons; and, vastly more numerous for many years past than all other grants by *letters patent* taken together, *letters patent* to the true and first inventors thereof for the monopoly of 'making, using, exercising and vending' new inventions. It is this last form of royal grant which it is the object of this work to discuss." See also Terrell on *Patents*, 4th ed. p. 1.

Letting and hiring is defined by Grotius (*Introd.* Maasdorp's trans. 3, 19, 1) as "an agreement whereby one party binds himself to let another have his labour or that of some other person or animal, or the use of some other thing, and the other binds himself to the payment of rent" (see also Voet's *Comm.* 19, 2, 1; Van Leeuwen's *Comm.* 4, 21, 1; and Van der Linden's *Institutes*, Juta's trans. p. 141).

As regards the lease of lands and houses, the Roman-Dutch law, differing in this respect from the Roman law, gives the lessee not only a personal claim against the lessor, but a real right to the subject of the lease enforceable against trespassers and even purchasers.

Level-crossing, a point at which a road crosses the track of a railway line on the level or on the surface of the ground. "A *level-crossing* must always have a certain element of danger, and any person, before crossing the railway, should exercise due and proper care in order to see that a train is not approaching; and neglect on the part of the railway officials in not giving warning of its approach is in my opinion no excuse whatever for neglect on the part of any one travelling along the road" (*per* SOLOMON, J., in *Worthington and Others* v. *Central South African Railways,* [1905] T.H. at p. 151). See also *French* v. *Hill's Plymouth Co. and Others*, 24 T.L.R. 644).

Levering (D.), delivery. *See* DELIVERY.

Levy, the seizure and taking into possession by the Sheriff or a messenger of the court, by virtue of a writ duly issued.

Lex Anastasiana, a law of the later Roman Empire (*Code*, 4, 35, 22), which enacted that he who purchased a right of action from another could not exact from the debtor more than the price he had paid for the claim. This rule was adopted by the law of Holland to the effect that when a debtor was sued upon a ceded right of action he could within a year of the time when he became aware of the cession require the plaintiff to declare on oath what sum he had paid for it and discharge himself by paying the same amount. It has been decided that this law is not of force in South Africa (*Seaville* v. *Colley*, 9 S.C. 39; *Deschamps* v. *Van Onselin*, 6 E.D.C. 22; *MacHattie* v. *Filmer*, 1 Off. Rep. 55).

Lex Aquilia. In the Roman law an action was granted by the *Lex Aquilia*, passed about the year 286 B.C. for loss wrongfully (whether wilfully or only negligently) caused to another (*damnum injuria datum*) for injury to his property. The first head of the law provided for any one killing another's slave or four-footed beast, being one of those reckoned among cattle, *i.e.* horses, mules, asses, sheep, oxen, goats, pigs, but not wild animals or dogs; and the measure of damage was fixed at the greatest value which the thing possessed at any time within a year previously (*Institutes*, 4. 3, pr.). The third head (the second head being unimportant) provided for the wounding of any slave or four-footed beast of those reckoned among cattle and for the killing or wounding of any other animal or damaging any other thing belonging to another. Here the measure of damage was the greatest value which the thing possessed within the preceding thirty days (*Institutes*, 4, 3, 13 and 14).

The *actio legis Aquiliae* did not apply to injuries to the person. Under the later Roman law, however, the praetor granted an equitable action under the *Lex Aquilia* for personal injuries not involving the element of contumely or insult. Where that element was present the remedy was the *actio injuriarum.*

Lex Cincia, a law passed at Rome in the year 204 B.C. It prohibited gifts to advocates and all gifts exceeding a certain amount. Gifts above the amount fixed were not null, but they were revocable during the lifetime of the donor.

Lex commissoria. "The *lex commissoria,* prohibited in the case of pledge, but allowed here (*i.e.* in the contract of sale), is simply a pact annexed to a purchase at the time when it is contracted, to the effect that unless the price be paid by a certain time the thing shall be considered unbought. It is probably called *commissoria* because a person who violates such a provision (*lex*) or pact strikes at the sale in its entirety, so that thereafter, by force of this pact, the whole sale is committed to the discretion of the vendor either to confirm or to annul it as he may think fit" (Voet's *Comm.* 18, 3, 1). A *lex commissoria* may be so expressed as to make the sale conditional, as where it is agreed that the thing shall be considered as sold if the price is paid within six months, in which case the sale is in the meantime suspended. As a general rule, however, the effect of a *lex commissoria* is to make the sale immediately binding, so that the risk and by delivery the ownership passes to the purchaser, subject to the right of the seller to demand back the thing sold should the price be not paid by the appointed time (Voet's *Comm. ibid.*). Upon the expiry of the time the seller must declare whether he will avail himself of the pact or not, and if he has once elected to waive his right he cannot afterwards alter his decision. He will be regarded as having waived his right if after the appointed time he accepts from the purchaser the price or interest thereon (Voet's *Comm.* 18, 3, 2). An agreement that the seller shall be entitled in the event of non-payment of the price by the time fixed to put up the property for sale at the risk of the purchaser is not a *lex commissoria.* In such a case the sale remains in force notwithstanding the lapse of the appointed time without payment of the price, and the seller is simply in the position of a *procurator in rem suam,* empowered to put the property up for resale, which may be prevented at any time by the purchaser tendering the price together with interest to date of tender (*Port Elizabeth Town Council* v. *Rigg,* 20 S.C. 257). *See* PACTUM COMMISSORIUM.

Lex domicilii, the law of the domicile. The *lex domicilii* determines all questions with regard to personal capacity and status, while the *lex rei sitae,* or the law of the place where the thing is situated, regulates all rights to immovable property.

Lex Falcidia. Under the Roman law it was essential to the validity of a testament that an heir should be validly instituted, and, secondly, that he should accept or adiate the inheritance. If the instituted heir adiated he had to carry out the terms of the testament, and was in addition liable for the entire obligations of the deceased as sustaining his *persona*. Where, therefore, the testator had disposed of the whole or the greater part of his estate by way of legacies the heir had no inducement to take up the succession, for while conferring no benefit on himself it rendered him liable for the whole of the deceased's debts. The effect of the heir's refusal to adiate was that the testament fell and the deceased was regarded as having died without a will, his estate being distributed according to the law of intestacy. To remedy this state of things several measures were passed, the last of which was the *lex Falcidia*. By this statute a testator was bound to leave at least one-fourth of his estate to his heir, and if he left him nothing or less than a fourth, then the heir was entitled to reduce the legacies *pro ratâ* so as to retain a fourth for himself. This fourth was called the *portio* or *quarta Falcidia*. It could not be deducted if such deduction was expressly forbidden by the will; and, even without such prohibition, legacies in favour of hospitals or almshouses were exempted therefrom, as also was property so bequeathed that it could not be alienated. The heir also who was negligent in fulfilling the will of the deceased, or who had omitted making an inventory, lost this right (Grotius' *Introd.* 2, 23, 20). Schorer in his *Notes to Grotius* (note 166) says that the *lex Falcidia* also failed where the heir had, either knowingly or through an error of law, paid the legatees the whole of the legacies; where he had concealed the testament or codicils from the legatees; and where, knowing that the property bequeathed was still in existence, he had falsely stated that it had perished by accident. The *lex Falcidia* formed part of the Roman-Dutch law, but as the failure of the instituted heir no longer invalidates a testament, and the administration of the estates of deceased persons has, further, been transferred to executors, the reason for the enactment has ceased, and the Falcidian portion has now been abolished throughout South Africa (Act 26 of 1873 (C.C.), sec. 1; Law 7 of 1885 (N.), sec. 2; Proclamation 28 of 1902 (T.), sec. 126; chap. 92 of Law Book (O.R.C.), sec. 2).

Lex fori, the law of the *forum*, *i.e.* the country in which action is brought. Although a contract may require to be construed according to the law of the place where it was entered into (*lex loci contractûs*), the *lex fori* will regulate the mode of procedure for its enforcement. Thus, for example, all questions of evidence and of the limitation of actions, which affects not the right itself, but the remedy, are governed by the *lex fori*. *See* LEX LOCI CONTRACTUS.

Lex hac edictali, an enactment of the Roman law, adopted by the Roman-Dutch law, which imposed a restriction on second marriages by prohibiting a widow or widower, having children by the first marriage, from giving or leaving to the second spouse, either by act *inter vivos* or *mortis causa*, more than was given or left to that one of the children of the first marriage to whom least was given or left by him or her. This law has now been abolished in South Africa.

Lex loci contractus, the law of the place of contract, *i.e.* of the place where the contract was made. "The validity of a contract will, as a general rule, depend upon the law of the place where it is concluded. Such contract will not necessarily be enforced in every country in which action is brought upon it, for where the *lex loci contractûs* comes in direct conflict with the law of the latter place (*lex fori*), the comity of nations, which requires the observance of the *lex loci contractûs*, will have to give way to the positive law of the place of action (*lex fori*). This will, amongst other things, be the case where the contract sought to be enforced violates the principles or policy of the law of the *forum, e.g.* where it is usurious or unconscionable in character; or where the interest of third parties, beings citizens of the *lex fori*, such as creditors of the parties to the contract, are concerned" (Maasdorp's *Institutes*, vol. 3, p. 13). "The rights of the parties under a contract must as a general rule be regulated according to the law of the country where it is contracted. This, however, is not an absolute and universally applicable rule, but applies only in those cases, the circumstances of which are such as to give rise to a legal presumption that the parties intended that their contract should be regulated by that law, and ceases to apply whenever the circumstances are such as to afford stronger grounds for presuming that they intended it to be regulated by some other law, as, for example, the law of the place where the contract has to be carried out (*lex loci solutionis*)" (Maasdorp, *ibid.* p. 78). As regards the formalities required for the execution of contracts, these are governed by the *lex loci contractûs.*

Lex loci solutionis, the law of the place of payment, *i.e.* the law of the place where an obligation is to be fulfilled.

Lex rei sitae, the law of the place where a thing is situated. All rights, including questions of succession, to immovable property are regulated by the *lex rei sitae.* Thus a child legitimated by the subsequent marriage of his parents, although regarded by the law of his domicile for all purposes as if born after their marriage, will not be entitled to succeed *ab intestato* to immovable property in England, the law of which country admits to intestate succession only those born in lawful wedlock. Upon the same principle immovable property can only be conveyed in accordance with the forms prescribed by the *lex rei sitae.*

Lex Rhodia de jactu, the Rhodian law concerning property thrown overboard. "If goods have been thrown overboard for the purpose of lightening the ship, the loss should be made good by the contribution of all, because it has been done for the common benefit" (*Dig.* 14, 2, 1, 1). This equitable rule, under the name of gross or general average, has been adopted by the Roman-Dutch law, and with several modifications is common to the law of all commercial countries in Europe. More fully stated, the rule is that where a ship is in imminent danger, and in order to ensure the safety of the ship and cargo goods are thrown overboard, or the vessel is run ashore, or its masts, cables, &c., are cut away, the loss occasioned has to be borne by the owners of the ship and cargo *pro ratâ* (Van Leeuwen's *Comm.* 4, 31, 1; Van der Keessel, *Thes.* 781–95; Grotius' *Introd.* 3, 29, 9–17). *See* GENERAL AVERAGE.

Lex Ripuaria, the laws of the River Franks, probably compiled in the sixth century. See Wessels' *History*, p. 39.

Lex Romana, the Roman law. As to its introduction into Holland, see Wessels' *History*, p. 95.

Lex Salica, the laws of the Salii or Sea Franks, dating back to the sixth century. See Wessels' *History*, p. 37.

Liabilities, the debts and obligations due by a person to his creditors, whether ascertained or contingent.

Liability. *See* "INCUR LIABILITIES."

Licensable, suitable to be, or capable of being, licensed.

License or **licence.** (1) An authority or permission to do, or to forbear from doing, some act which, without such authority or permission, it would be illegal to do or omit to do. "If people went outside their *license*, they were trespassers. A *license* must be limited, and it was a thing which was liable to be revoked" (*per* DARLING, J., in *French* v. *Hills Plymouth Co. and Others*, 24 T.L.R. 644).

(2) In the Cape Excise Spirits Act (18 of 1884), sec. 2, *license* is defined to mean "a *license* in the form prescribed granted by any distributor of stamps or by any officer duly authorised"; and the same definition is to be found in the Additional Taxation Act, 36 of 1904 (C.C.), sec. 2.

As to Transvaal, see Ordinance 32 of 1902, secs. 3 and 7; Ordinance 45 of 1902, sec. 1; Act 33 of 1909, sec. 2 (4).

As to Orange River Colony, see Ordinance 8 of 1903, sec. 3.

Licensee, the person in whose favour a license is granted. *See* MERE LICENSEE.

Licentie (D.), a license.

Lien, the right to retain possession of certain property belonging to another person as security for some claim in respect of that property, until such claim has been paid. *See* LANDLORD'S LIEN. See also *United Building Society* v. *Smookler's Trustees and Another* ([1906] T.S. 623). *See* JUS RETENTIONIS.

Life insurance. "The contract commonly called *life assurance*, when properly considered, is a mere contract to pay a certain sum of money on the death of a person, in consideration of the due payment of a certain annuity for his life; the amount of the annuity being calculated in the first instance according to the probable duration of the life, and when once fixed it is constant and invariable. The stipulated amount of annuity is to be uniformly paid on one side, and the sum to be paid in the event of death is always (except where bonuses have been given by prosperous offices) the same on the other. This species of insurance in no way resembles a contract of indemnity" (*per* PARKE, B., in *Dalby* v. *India and London Life Assurance Co.*, 24 L.J.C.P. at p. 6). With reference to the statement that *life insurance* in no way resembles a contract of indemnity, May, in his work on *Insurance* (4th ed. sec. 7), says: "A distinction has sometimes been taken between marine and other insurances and *life insurance*, on the ground that while the former have for their object to indemnify for loss, the latter is an absolute engagement to pay a fixed sum on the happening of a certain event, without reference to any damage in fact suffered by the insured in consequence. But this distinction is superficial, and rests rather upon the mode of applying the principles and of determining the amount of indemnity, than upon any difference in the principles themselves."

By Act 8 of 1879 (C.C.) the law of the Cape Colony having reference to questions of *life assurance* is assimilated to that of England, except where repugnant to or in conflict with Cape statute law.

Life policy, a policy of insurance granted in respect of a person's life. *See* LIFE INSURANCE.

In Proclamation 12 of 1902 (T.), sec. 29 (1), the expression *policy of life insurance* means "a policy upon any life or lives, or upon any event or contingency relating to or depending upon any life or lives, except a policy of insurance against accident."

Ligan, anything sunk in the sea, but tied to a buoy with a view to its ultimate recovery.

Ligeantia trahit protectionem, allegiance brings about protection; a maxim of constitutional law indicating the reciprocal obligations of subject and state, viz., allegiance on the one hand and protection on the other.

Lijf-eygen (D.), the same as servants, domestics, *liti*, *lassi*. They were all such persons as had to cultivate the land and to render out of it annually a certain tax or return to the lord or owner, and to perform certain court or religious services.

Lijfstraffen (D.), corporal punishments. The corporal punishments in use in Holland in Van der Linden's time (early part of nineteenth century) were (1) flogging, with or without the halter round the neck, and with or without branding; (2) confinement in a house of correction (*tuchthuis*); (3) hard labour; (4) waving the sword over the head; (5) exposure in the pillory, with or without rods; (6) praying on bare knees for the forgiveness of God and the court; and (7) imprisonment for some days with spare diet (bread and water).

Lijftochtenaar (D.), a usufructuary.

Like. The word *like* appearing in the expression "like jurisdiction" in sec. 4 of the Fugitive Offenders Act, 1881 (Eng.), is "not equivalent to 'the same,' but means 'similar' or 'not less than,' the object apparently being to secure that the important powers conferred by this part of the Act shall only be exercised by certain superior judicial or magisterial officers" (*per* BALE, C.J., in *Willis* v. *Rex*, 27 N.L.R. at p. 225).

Lime. In the Cape Fertilisers, Farm Foods, Seeds and Pest Remedies Act (20 of 1907), sec. 3, *lime* is defined to mean "anhydrous oxide of calcium."

In Ordinance 7 of 1905 (T.), sec. 1, it includes "limestone, marble, chalk, dolomite and gypsum."

Limited company. In the Cape Colony under the Companies Act (25 of 1892), sec. 2, a *limited company* is defined to mean "a company, the liability of the members of which is by their registered memorandum of association limited to the amount, if any, unpaid on the shares respectively held by them or by the operation of any Act of Parliament." The Transvaal Companies Act (31 of 1909), sec. 2, gives a similar definition.

Limited partnership is a partnership (other than a joint stock company or partnership established for the purpose of banking) for the transaction of any mercantile, mechanical or manufacturing business in the Cape Colony duly registered in accordance with the provisions of Act 24 of 1861 (C.C.), known as the Special Partnerships' Limited Liability Act, 1861, as amended by Act 12 of 1906 (C.C.).

Lincoln's Inn, one of the Inns of Court. *See* INNS OF COURT. This Inn is chiefly the Inn of Chancery barristers. It is said to have the best of all the Inn libraries. In the middle of the nineteenth century it had by far the largest membership of all the Inns.

Lineal ascent, direct ascent from descendant to ancestor in a direct and unbroken line, as from grandson to grandfather.

Lineal descent, direct descent from ascendant to descendant in a direct and unbroken line, as from grandfather to grandson.

"**Liquidated.**" "An estate is *liquidated* when it is reduced into possession, cleared of debts and other immediate outgoings, and so left free for enjoyment by the heirs" (judgment of Judicial Committee of the Privy Council in *Hiddingh's Heirs* v. *De Villiers, Denyssen and Others*, 5 S.C. at p. 308; see also *In re Best*, 9 S.C. 488).

Liquidated damages, an agreed amount of damages stipulated in a contract to be paid by the contractor to the employer in case of breach, especially breach in regard to time limit for completion of the contract. See *Capetown Town Council* v. *Linder* (6 S.C. 410); *Davey-Paxman & Co.* v. *Langlaagte Star G. M. Co.* (16 C.L.J. 57); *Peach & Co.* v. *Committee of Jewish Synagogue* (12 C.L.J. 69); and *Clyde Engineering and Shipbuilding Co.* v. *Castaneda and Others* (91 L.T. 666). *Liquidated damages* are fully discussed in an article in 23 S.A.L.J. 145, where the writer sums up the result of the decisions as follows: "(1) The question whether the stipulation was for a penalty or for *liquidated damages* is one of intention, to be gathered from the agreement between the parties and from the circumstances; (2) if the payment or payments are made proportionate to the extent to which the defaulting party may fail to perform his obligation, the presumption is that the stipulation is for *liquidated damages* and not a penalty; (3) the burden of proving that the sum agreed on as *liquidated damages* is excessive lies on the party in default who has to pay such sum; (4) where the amount stipulated is not exorbitant with reference to the circumstances of the case, it will be regarded as *liquidated damages*, and not as a penalty; (5) where the stipulation is clearly a penalty, it will not be enforced."

Liquidated demand. "It may perhaps be said that a liquidated debt is one whose exact amount can be finally determined by the creditor without either the consent of the debtor or the assistance of a court of law" (Buckle's *Transvaal Magistrates' Court Practice*, p. 36). Where in an action a certain piece of land was claimed, it was held that the claim was in the nature of a *liquidated demand* (*Grundling* v. *Grundling*, 3 S.C. 45). See also *Kruger* v. *Van Vuuren's Executrix* (5 S.C. 162), where the question was fully discussed; and *Havinga and Others* v. *Swart* ([1906] E.D.C. 54).

Liquidation, the realisation, distribution and winding up of the affairs of a person, partnership or corporation.

Liquidator, the person duly appointed to carry out a liquidation.

Liquor. In the Transvaal, in Ordinance 32 of 1902, sec. 3, *liquor* means "any spirit, wine, ale, beer, porter, cider, perry, hop beer, Kafir beer, and any liquor containing more than two per cent. of alcohol and any other *liquor* which the Lieutenant-Governor may from time to time declare by Proclamation in the *Gazette* to be included in this definition."

In the Cape Native Reserve Location Act (40 of 1902), sec. 1, "intoxicating *liquor*" or "*liquor*" is defined as meaning "any spirits, wine, beer (including Kafir beer, as defined and interpreted in the first proviso of the seventh section of the Liquor Law Amendment Act 1898), or other fermented, distilled, spirituous or malt *liquors* of an intoxicating nature, or any other intoxicating brew or mixture." In the Cape Railway Refreshment Catering Act (44 of 1902), sec. 1, *liquor* means "any such intoxicating *liquor* as is commonly sold in licensed premises."

In the Natal Liquor Act (38 of 1896), sec. 4, "intoxicating *liquor*" or "*liquor*" is defined as "any spirits, wines, liqueurs, ale, beer, porter, cider, perry or other fermented, distilled, spirituous or malt *liquor* of an intoxicating nature, methylated spirits, and every drink with which any such *liquor* shall have been mixed."

Lis alibi pendens, a suit elsewhere depending; a plea in abatement, the requisites of which, according to Voet (*Comm.* 44, 2, 7), are the same as those of a plea of *res judicata*, viz., that the actions are between the same persons, for the same thing, and arise out of the same cause. "He (Voet) does not, however, touch upon the question whether, in the case of foreign litigation, a greater discretion should be allowed to the court in regard to suits still pending in foreign courts than in regard to suits finally concluded in such foreign courts. For myself, I am not prepared to say that the plea of *lis pendens* in a foreign State would be a good defence in every case in which the plea of *res judicata* in such foreign State would have been a good answer. But I do hold that the fact that a suit has been commenced by a plaintiff and is still pending in the court of a foreign State having jurisdiction over the defendant affords, *primâ facie*, a good ground for a plea in abatement to an action instituted in this Court by the same plaintiff against the same defendant for the same thing, and arising out of the same cause, in the absence of proof that justice would not be done without the double remedy" (*per* DE VILLIERS, C.J., in *Wolff, N.O.*, v. *Solomon*, 15 S.C. 297). It would appear that as between England and Scotland the courts of each country mutually reject this plea of *lis alibi pendens* in the other country, but that in Scotland at least the courts, where an action is brought by any one having a depending suit in England against the same defendant, frequently in their discretion stay proceedings until the previously depending action in England has been concluded (see Trayner's *Latin Maxims and Phrases*, *h.v.*).

Lis finita, suit concluded. This signifies not only that the action has been brought to an end, but also that the matter at issue between the parties has been finally determined, so that if a fresh action should be raised with regard to the same subject-matter it will be effectually met by an *exceptio litis finitae vel rei judicatae.* An action in which absolution from the instance has been granted is not regarded as concluded in this sense, the plaintiff in such a case being entitled to take fresh proceedings.

Lis pendens, suit depending. *See* EXCEPTIO LITIS PENDENTIS and LIS ALIBI PENDENS.

Literature. *See* GENERAL CAMPAIGN LITERATURE.

Lites. *See* HOORIGEN.

Lithographic artist. *See* SERVANT.

Litis contestatie (D.), equivalent to the Latin *litis contestatio.* *See* LITIS CONTESTATIO.

Litis contestatio. In the Roman system of civil process it was always considered necessary that the time when a contested right was to be considered as really made the subject of litigation should be clearly marked and ascertained. In the early Roman times under the system of *legis actiones* the parties to the suit appeared first before a judicial officer, the magistrate, who was, as a rule, the praetor. The object of these proceedings *in jure* was to ascertain whether the plaintiff's claim was legally admissible. These proceedings culminated in and terminated with *litis contestatio,* the "knitting of the issue." The litigants appealed to witnesses to testify that the litigation had duly begun, and tacitly bound themselves to abide by the judgment. Thereupon a private individual (*judex*) was appointed by the *magistratus* to ascertain the facts of the case and to pronounce judgment.

Under the system of *formulae, litis contestatio* took place when the praetor appointed the judge, whereupon the proceedings *in jure* immediately gave place to the proceedings *in judicio.*

Finally, under the system of *extraordinaria judicia, litis contestatio* took place after the statement of the plaintiff and the counter-statement of the defendant (*C.* 3, 1, 14, 1). The service of the summons was thus not the legal commencement of the suit or *litis contestatio. Lis enim tunc contestata videtur quum judex per enarrationem negotii causam audire coeperit* (*C.* 3, 9, 1).

In Holland the mode of procedure was somewhat cumbrous, and it was far from easy to mark the exact moment when *litis contestatio* took place.

In the case of *Meyer's Executors* v. *Gericke* (Foord, 17), DE VILLIERS, C.J., examined various modes of proceedings under the old Dutch law, and came to the conclusion that in defended cases the rule was that the *litis contestatio* was not complete until after *duplicatio* had been pleaded. The *duplicatio* or *duplique* corresponds to the "rejoinder" of our law, but in Holland issue was not actually joined until the defendant had filed his *duplicatio,* while with us pleadings may extend beyond the rejoinder. "The pleadings are deemed to be closed as soon as either party has joined issue upon any pleading of the opposite party without adding any further or other pleading thereto. In the Supreme Court, therefore, the *litis contestatio* in an ordinary defended suit may be considered to take place as soon as the pleadings are closed." "Broadly stated, the answer [to the question: at what stage of the action does the *litis contestatio* take place?] must be that it takes effect as soon as the case is ripe for hearing, or, if the defendant is in default, as soon as he is debarred from defending the action" (*per* DE VILLIERS, C.J., *ibid.*).

With regard to criminal cases, *litis contestatio* takes place when the plea of "not guilty" is recorded. From that moment the accused has the right to demand that he shall be acquitted or found guilty, and, the suit having been brought to a termination, he cannot afterwards be arraigned upon the same charge (*Queen* v. *Robertson*, 4 E.D.C. at p. 196; *Kerr* v. *Rex*, [1907] E.D.C. 324; 25 S.C. 91). As to when a criminal suit is terminated so as to bar subsequent proceedings upon the same charge, see *Kerr* v. *Rex* (*ibid.*). See also *The King* v. *Jack Zulu* (9 H.C.G. 164); *Ormond* v. *Rex* (27 N.L.R. 401); and article in 26 S.A.L.J. p. 345.

L.J., in England signifies a Lord Justice of Appeal.

Lloyd's underwriters. "In the time of William III and of Queen Anne, Lloyd's Coffee-house, at the corner of Abchurch Lane in Lombard Street [London], became the celebrated resort of seafaring men, and those that did business with them. There, and subsequently in Pope's Head Alley, and ultimately on the west side of the old Royal Exchange, at this coffee-house congregated the underwriters of London. For some time they had no organisation; but in the latter part of the eighteenth century they formed themselves into an association or club with a committee of management, which became famous under the name of Lloyd's. In connection with this association they have developed a ramified system of agency radiating everywhere to the ports of the world, which is now become of imposing magnitude, essential to the business of marine insurance whether in the hands of individuals or of companies, and to the general interests of British commerce" (Arnould's *Marine Insurance*, 7th ed. sec. 77).

Loan for use "is a transaction whereby something is without any gain lent for a certain use, on condition that the same thing shall after the use be returned" (Van Leeuwen's *Comm.* Kotzé's trans. vol. 2, p. 77). Property lent on a *loan for use* must be returned in the same state as it was in when lent, the borrower being responsible for all damage. *See* COMMODATUM.

Loan place, a common form of tenure in the early days of the settlement of the Dutch in the Cape Colony, under which small garden plots were granted "on loan," subject to reassumption by the Government; the title being a loan lease. On the 6th August, 1813, Sir John Cradock issued an important Proclamation in which it was recited that agriculture constituted the chief source of prosperity in the Cape Colony; that encouragement of the industry depended upon the certainty of tenures, so that improvements of the soil and increase of fertility should indisputably belong to the holder; that although the establishment of loan leases might have been suitable to the early state of the colony when the wants of Government were not foreseen, "it now appears from experience that loan tenure is injurious to that certainty, so essential to the happiness and the interest of the inhabitants, and equally injurious to the public interest, by preventing the holders from appropriating as much of their means to the improvement and extension of agriculture as they would do, in case they had no right of reassumption to apprehend, and might dispose of the ground as they please, by subdividing the same among their children, letting, selling or otherwise alienating it in lots, cultivating it in the prospect of remote benefit, by the planting of timber, &c.;" the Proclamation then proceeded "to grant to the holders of all lands on loan, who may regularly apply for the same, their places on perpetual quitrent" with the rights, privileges and conditions fully set out in the Proclamation. Among the conditions may be mentioned that no *loan place* should exceed 3000 morgen; the holder should "hold the land hereditary" with power to alienate; the Government reserved the rights "on mines of precious stones, gold or silver" as also the right to make roads and raise material for the purpose; that a small yearly rent should be paid to the Government not exceeding 250 rix dollars; that no alienation should be legal without survey of the property, together with proper transfer and registration; and that the title-deed (*erfgrondbrief*) would be granted after survey. The following are among the concluding paragraphs of this Proclamation: "Thus at length is this great measure matured and brought forward. It is the one that has long engaged the attention and anxious wish of each preceding Government, but which could not well admit of conclusion, except in times like the present—of unexampled tranquility, uniform progress in civilisation and good order, and the unbounded prospect of universal prosperity. I feel the greatest gratification in giving effect to these beneficent and paternal designs of his Majesty's Government; and persuade myself that the gratitude of the inhabitants of this colony will be equal to the value of the inestimable gift thus extended to them on the part of the Crown, which, by graciously offering to their acceptance a perfect title to lands, that enables them to provide for their children and descendants, and dispose of them as they please, grants them, in fact, possession of an estate, and the high character and station of 'a real landholder.'"

Loan service. In the Cape Audit Act (14 of 1906), sec. 3 (*f*), *loan service* is defined to mean the "purpose specified in any Loan Act."

Lobolo, a native term defined in the Natal Code of Native Law (19 of 1891), sec. 23 of sch., to denote "a delivery of cattle or other property by or on behalf of an intended husband, to the parent or guardian of an intended wife." This may be accepted as a correct definition of *lobolo* throughout South Africa, the consideration for the delivery of the cattle or other property being that the girl is given by the parent or guardian to the man as his wife. Under the same Natal

Code (sec. 177 of sch.) it is provided that "all the *lobolo* must be delivered on or before the day of marriage. If any cattle are delivered before that day they shall be considered and treated as *sisa* cattle, and any increase or decrease in such cattle previous to the day of marriage shall be the profit or the loss of the person delivering the *lobolo*. Should any of the *lobolo* cattle die within fourteen days after the marriage, the cattle so dying shall, if duly reported, be replaced by the person on whose behalf the delivery was made." The *lobolo* claimable in respect of the marriage of any girl or woman being the daughter of an ordinary native (without rank) is ten head of ordinary cattle or their equivalent (*ibid.* sec. 178 of sch.).

Local acceptance. *See* QUALIFIED ACCEPTANCE.

Local authority, an expression frequently used in statutes where it is variously defined. See Act 11 of 1882 (C.C.), sec. 1; Act 27 of 1882 (C.C.), sec. 2; Act 29 of 1885 (C.C.), sec. 2; Act 4 of 1887 (C.C.), sec. 29; Act 25 of 1894 (C.C.), sec. 54; Act 19 of 1895 (C.C.), sec. 2; Act 30 of 1895 (C.C.), sec. 1; Act 42 of 1895 (C.C.), sec. 1; Act 23 of 1897 (C.C.), sec. 2; Act 32 of 1902 (C.C.), sec. 2; Act 34 of 1905 (C.C.), sec. 1; Act 26 of 1906 (C.C.), sec. 1; Ordinance 32 of 1902 (T.), sec. 3; Ordinance 43 of 1903 (T.), sec. 3; Ordinance 14 of 1904 (T.), sec. 2; Ordinance 44 of 1904 (T.), sec. 1; Ordinance 21 of 1902 (O.R.C.), sec. 3; Ordinance 9 of 1904 (O.R.C.), sec. 1; Ordinance 5 of 1906 (O.R.C.), sec. 1; Act 27 of 1908 (T.), sec. 2; Act 25 of 1909 (T.), sec. 2.

Local creditor. In the Transvaal Foreign Trustees and Liquidators Recognition Act (7 of 1907), *local creditor* means and includes "(1) a creditor resident or carrying on business in this colony; (2) a creditor who is such by virtue of any right or claim against the estate first accruing to a creditor resident or carrying on business in this colony; (3) a creditor who is such by virtue of any debt or obligation registered in the office of the Registrar of Deeds or Registrar of Mining Rights or other registration officer."

Local newspaper is defined in the Cape Public Bodies Private Bills Act (35 of 1885) to mean "any newspaper circulating in the neighbourhood wherein all or most of the persons reside who are liable to pay rates to such public body."

Local nursery. The term *local nursery* is defined in the Cape Nurseries Inspection and Quarantine Act (29 of 1905) to mean "any nursery, the nursery stock of which by the provisions of this Act may not be despatched by railroad or other public carrier, or distributed by any means beyond the boundary of the fiscal division in which such nursery is situated." *See* GENERAL NURSERY; NURSERY.

Local option, a term used in connection with the grant of liquor licenses; its object is "to leave to a large extent the question of the granting of a new license to the voters resident in the district and to give them an opportunity of expressing their wishes in the matter" (*per* De Villiers, C.J., in *Strydom* v. *Uniondale Licensing Court and Others,* 20 S.C. at p. 390).

Locatio, letting or leasing.

Locatio conductio, letting and hiring; the name given to the contract by which one person agrees to let the use of a thing or the use of his services to another, who agrees to hire the same.

Locatio custodiae, letting of custody; that form of the *locatio operis* by which one person agrees to receive goods on deposit from another for a consideration.

Locatio operarum, letting of services; the form of the contract of *locatio* whereby one person lets his services to another, called the hirer.

Locatio operis faciendi, that form of the contract of letting and hiring by which one person entrusts the performance of a particular piece of work, such as the erection of a house, to another, who contracts to do it.

Locatio operis mercium vehendarum, letting of the work of carrying goods; the contract for the carriage of goods.

Locatio rei, the letting of a thing; the form of the contract of *locatio* whereby one person (*locator*) lets a thing and another person (*conductor*) hires it.

Location, an area of land set apart for the exclusive use of natives; see *Smith* v. *Germiston Municipality* ([1908] T.S. at p. 248); *Scrutton* v. *Ehrlich & Co. and Others* ([1908] T.S. at p. 307); *De Vos and Others* v. *Rex* ([1909] T.S. 214); *Essop and Others* v. *Rex* ([1909] T.S. 480).

Lockout, in the Industrial Disputes Prevention Act, 20 of 1909 (T.), sec. 2, is defined as "the closing by an employer of his employment premises, or a suspension by him of work, or the refusal by an employer to continue to employ any number of his employees when such closing, suspension, or refusal is for the purpose of compelling his own employees, or of aiding another employer, to accept specific terms of employment."

Lock-up is defined in the Cape Convict Stations and Prisons Act (23 of 1888) as follows: "*Lock-up* shall mean any building, cell or place in which any person lawfully arrested or detained in custody is placed with a view to his being brought to trial or removed to a prison, or any building, cell or place provided for the detention in custody of prisoners at or in the neighbourhood of any place where there is no ordinary prison and where any court is holden." See also Law 19 of 1872 (N.), sec. 94; Ordinance 6 of 1906 (T.), sec. 3; Ordinance 3 of 1903 (O.R.C.), sec. 1.

Loco citato, in the place quoted; generally abbreviated *loc. cit.*

Locus classicus, a classical passage; the reference of acknowledged authority upon any point.

Locus concursus creditorum, the place of competition of creditors: a phrase used in connection with the distribution of an insolvent's property. As the object of this distribution is to secure perfect equality among those who have equal rights and no preferent claims, it has been held that this can only be conveniently and effectually attained in one place, which is called the *locus concursus creditorum*; and if any other place is selected by the creditor for the recovery of his debt, he may be met by the plea *ne continentia causae dividatur*. As to what should be the *locus concursus*, this is generally admitted to be the domicile of the insolvent. An assignment under the law of his domicile will operate as an assignment of his movable property wherever situate, subject, however, to any rights which preferent creditors attaching any property before the date of the assignment may have acquired by the law of the country in which the property is situate (*Howse, Sons & Co.'s Trustee* v. *Howse, Sons & Co.'s Trustee—Jocelyne* v. *Shearer & Hine*, 3 S.C. 14).

Locus poenitentiae, place for repentance or withdrawal. While an agreement is inchoate or incomplete either party has the right to withdraw from it. Thus, a mere offer which has not yet been accepted constitutes no binding contract, and may be receded from at any time before acceptance. So, where the parties to a sale have agreed that the contract shall be in writing, the sale is not complete until the writing has been signed by the parties, and in the meantime either party may change his mind and exercise the right to withdraw. In the same way, although a person who has paid money which he has lost in gambling cannot recover it, yet if he has given the money to a stakeholder to abide the event which is to decide the bet or wager there is a *locus poenitentiae*, and the owner of the money may demand it back at any time before that event (*Sonnenberg* v. *Flower*, Buch. 1875, p. 4; *Sloman* v. *Berkovitz*, 12 N.L.R. 216). This doctrine of *locus poenitentiae* applies also in criminal law to acts which are yet incomplete and have produced no result. Thus, where a person was convicted of having contravened Act 20 of 1861 (C.C.), sec. 10, by sending a false telegram, and it was proved that after handing the telegram to the postal clerk the accused had requested its return, as he did not wish it despatched, but the clerk could not return the telegram, but was obliged by postal regulations to despatch it, the conviction was quashed on the ground that the accused was not aware of such regulations and had a *locus poenitentiae*, which he had exercised (*Regina* v. *Russouw*, 1 C.T.R. 113).

Locus regit actum, the place governs the act. An act done or a contract made is to be governed as to validity and construction by the law of the place where the act is done or the contract is entered into. An exception to this rule holds in the case of immovable property, which can only be conveyed in accordance with the forms prescribed by the law of the place where the property is situated, *i.e.* the *lex rei sitae.*

Locus standi, lit. place of standing. He who has a right to sue in an action is said to have a *locus standi* in such action, and *vice versâ*. *See* LEGITIMA PERSONA STANDI IN JUDICIO.

Locusts, defined in Act 40 of 1904 (N.), sec. 3, to mean "insects called respectively *acridium purpuriferum* and *pachytylus migratorius*, while in the stage known as hoppers or *voetgangers;*" and in Ordinance 27 of 1907 (O.R.C.), sec. 1, "the insects called respectively *pachytylus migratorius* or brown locust and *acridium purpuriferum* or red locust."

Lottery, the distribution of prizes by lot or chance; a scheme for raising money by the sale of tickets or other things which will entitle the successful drawer of the lot to a prize.

Lotteries were forbidden in England by the Gaming Act, 1802, 42 Geo. 3, c. 119, sec. 2; see Stone's *Justices' Manual* under heading "Lottery."

In Cape Colony *lottery* "means every *lottery* in the common and received acceptation of that term, and more particularly every scheme, arrangement, system, plan or device by which any prize or prizes is or are, or is or are intended to be, gained, won, drawn for, thrown or competed for, by lot, dice or any other mode of chance, either with or without reference to the happening of any uncertain event other than the issue or result of the application or employment of such lot, dice or mode of chance" (Act 9 of 1889, sec. 3); and "any person who in any way personally or by representative takes any part in the establishment, management or conduct of a *lottery* or who has any beneficial interest therein, or sells or disposes of or purchases any *lottery* ticket, or allows any premises under his control to be used for the purposes of a *lottery*," is liable on conviction for a first offence to a fine not exceeding £200 or imprisonment not exceeding six months, and for any subsequent offence to a fine not exceeding £500 or imprisonment not exceeding twelve months, or to both fine and imprisonment (Act 9 of 1889, sec. 4).

In the Transvaal *lotteries* founded on subscription are illegal; sec. 6 of Law 7 of 1890 reads as follows: "*Lottery* shall mean any *lottery* in the general and accepted meaning of that word, which is founded on subscription, and more especially any scheme, institution, system, plan or design by means of which a prize or prizes shall or may be won, or drawn, or awarded according to what may be determined by lot, or by a throwing of dice, or by any other method of selection by chance, irrespective whether the happening of any accidental occurrence, other than the result of the application or use of such dice or other methods of selection by chance, be an element in determining such award or selection or not." See *Rex* v. *Clapp* ([1902] T.S. 106); *Ming Soo and Others* v. *Rex* ([1906] T.S. 2).

In Natal "all *lotteries* commonly termed selling lotteries, *lotteries* for goods, all games of chance, such as 'rouge et noir' and 'roulette,' and all betting stands or betting booths" are declared common nuisances and against the law, and as such are punishable (Law 25 of 1878).

For definition of *lottery* in the Orange River Colony, see chap. 143 of Law Book, sec. 2.

"**Low-life fellow,**" these words were held to be not defamatory in the sense of being derogatory to plaintiff's character; see *Mann* v. *Booker* (19 S.C. 419).

Low wines. This expression is defined in the Cape Excise Spirits Act (18 of 1884), sec. 2; and in the Cape Additional Taxation Act (36 of 1904), sec. 2, as follows: "*Low wines* means spirits of the first extraction conveyed into a *low wines* receiver."

In Natal, in Act 33 of 1901, sec. 3, *low wines* means "spirits of the first extraction by a single still, and conveyed into a *low wines* receiver."

Lucrum cessans, profit ceasing. *See* DAMNUM EMERGENS.

Luggage. *See* PASSENGERS' LUGGAGE.

Lumen, light. *See* SERVITUS LUMINUM and SERVITUS LUMINIS.

Lunatic. This term is, in the Cape Lunacy Act (1 of 1897) defined to include "any idiot or person of unsound mind incapable of managing himself or his affairs." See also Law 1 of 1868 (N.); Proclamation 36 of 1902 (T.), sec. 2; and Ordinance 13 of 1906 (O.R.C.), sec. 2.

"**Lunch.**" "Whatever may be the etymology of the term *lunch*, I take its ordinary modern meaning to be a light meal taken about midday, as distinguished from a heavy meal taken about midday or towards evening, either of which would be better known as a 'dinner'" (*per* DE VILLIERS, C.J., in *Queen* v. *Sutton*, 10 S.C. at p. 275). *See* "BONÂ FIDE LUNCH OR DINNER."

Lung-sickness, defined in the Natal Lung-sickness Prevention Amendent Act (15 of 1907), sec. 2, to mean "the disease known as contagious pleuro-pneumonia in animals of the ox tribe."

Lymph is defined in the Cape Public Health Act (4 of 1883), sec. 51, to mean "*lymph* taken from a heifer or from a fully formed vaccine vesicle, on the day week after vaccination, and before any areola has been formed; the subject from which such vaccine *lymph* is taken being a healthy infant or child who has not previously been vaccinated, or a healthy young heifer." See Ordinance 29 of 1903 (O.R.C.), sec. 2.

Maaghsibbe, Maaghtaale (D.), relationship.

Maaking (D.), a testamentary disposition or bequest.

Maal (D.). This word has various meanings. (1) The same as *ghemaal*, that is, companion, and hence also a spouse; (2) time or turn; (3) with the ancient Saxons it denoted limit, boundary, end; also law, right, judgment; (4) an assemblage of persons in order to deliberate over public matters, in mediæval Latin *mallus* or *mallum*.

Maatschappij (D.), a company; society; or partnership. In the late South African Republics the term *maatschappij* was most frequently applied to what are known as joint-stock companies. For definition of *maatschappij* in Law 5 of 1874 (T.—since repealed), *see* COMPANY.

Machine stand, a term used in statutes relating to mining operations. It signifies an area of land set apart as a site for the erection of machinery or deposit of tailings, &c., in connection with a mine. See Act 31 of 1898 (C.C.), sec. 51; Act 43 of 1899 (N.), sec. 81.

Machinery. In *De Beers Consolidated Mines* v. *Collector of Customs* (7 S.C. at p. 147), DE VILLIERS, C.J., adopted the definition of the word *machinery* in the *Imperial Dictionary*, viz., 'A complicated apparatus or combination of mechanical powers designed to increase, regulate or apply motion and force, as the machinery of a watch or other chronometer;" and held that certain water piping imported by the plaintiffs could in no sense be considered as a complicated apparatus, unless it were attached to something else which could rightly be called *machinery*. See also *Rudd* v. *Colonial Government* (11 S.C. at p. 134); *Wesselton Syndicate* v. *Colonial Government* (10 S.C. 221).

In the Transvaal Mines, Works, Machinery and Certificates Act (32 of 1909), sec. 2, the term *machinery* means and includes "stationary and portable boilers, steam apparatus, steam and other engines, including locomotives and all appliances or combinations of appliances which can be used for developing, receiving, transmitting or converting either mechanical or natural power."

"**Made to appear,**" discussed in *Johnstone* v. *Byrne & Lamport* (1 Searle, at p. 159).

Magisterial area. This term is defined in the Cape School Board Act (35 of 1905), sec. 3, to mean "any area under the jurisdiction of a magistrate or assistant magistrate, and not forming by itself a fiscal division."

Magistrate, a person appointed by the Governor under the seal of the colony to act as such within a certain place or district, with such jurisdiction both civil and criminal as is provided by law. *Magistrates* in South Africa are usually known as *resident magistrates.* Not only do they preside over the court or courts of their respective districts, but in addition a number of public duties are entrusted to them as the local representatives of the Government. In the Transvaal and Orange River colonies the duties of *magistrates* were, prior to the war, performed by landdrosts. See *Willis* v. *Rex* (27 N.L.R. at p. 377); ROAD MAGISTRATE.

Main road, in Orange River Colony Ordinance 17 of 1905, sec. 1, means "a public trunk road or highway over or along which the general road traffic of the colony passes, and which has been proclaimed a *main road* in terms of this Ordinance."

Maintenance. (1) "*Maintenance* denotes a collection, as food, clothes, lodging, washing and attendance in sickness and health" (Van Leeuwen's *Comm.* Kotzé's trans. vol. 1, p. 396). Parents are obliged to maintain their children until they are capable of maintaining themselves; so too the children, when able to do so, are bound to maintain their parents. See Maasdorp's *Institutes,* vol. 1, p. 232. In like manner a brother is obliged to support a brother or sister in case he or she has become reduced to poverty (Van Leeuwen's *Comm.* 1, 13, 7; Voet's *Comm.* 25, 3, 8).

(2) "*Maintenance* is the act of assisting the plaintiff in any legal proceeding in which the person giving the assistance has no valuable interest, or in which he acts from any improper motive" (Stephen's *Digest of Criminal Law,* art. 156; see also Anders' *Cession of Actions,* p. 48, and *Hugo and Moller, N.O.,* v. *Transvaal Loan, Finance and Mortgage Co.,* 1 Off. Rep. 336).

Maintenue (D.), legal process in Dutch practice whereby a person sought the aid of the court to protect, maintain and confirm him in his right of actual possession. See Van Leeuwen's *Comm.* 5, 12, 4; Van der Linden's *Institutes,* 3, 1, 5, 2. The writ of *maintenue* was called the *mandament van maintenue.*

Major, person of full age; one who is *sui juris.* Under Roman-Dutch law a person became a major at the age of twenty-five years, but in South Africa the age of majority is fixed at twenty-one years.

A person may also become a major by marriage, and formerly also by being granted *venia aetatis*, but this procedure seems now to be obsolete. *See* MAJORITY.

Majority. (1) A person becomes a major or attains full age, or *majority*, as it is termed, at the commencement of the day immediately preceding his twenty-first birthday (Jenk's *Digest of English Civil Law*, bk. 1, sec. 2). But *see* MINORITY. He might also formerly attain majority by being granted *venia aetatis*, but this procedure seems now to have become obsolete (see *In re Cachet*, 15 S.C. 5; 8 C.T.R. 9: and *Ex parte Moolman*, [1903] T.S. 159). Maasdorp in his *Institutes* (vol. 1, p. 3) puts it thus: "A person becomes of age when he attains the age of twenty-one years, and, until he does so, is subject to certain disabilities or incapacities in the eyes of the law, as also are persons of unsound mind and persons labouring under any other infirmity which necessitates their being placed under curatorship."

According to the law of Holland the age of *majority* was twenty-five years. In 1829 an Ordinance (62 of 1829) was promulgated in the Cape Colony which fixed the age of *majority* at twenty-one years, and this rule has since been adopted in all the other South African states and colonies. A minor also attains *majority* on marriage.

Makelaar (D.), a broker. In connection with the term *makelaar* Decker's *note* to Van Leeuwen's *Comm.* (Kotzé's trans. vol. 2, p. 222) is of interest. He says: "I will here observe that a broker is a sworn and qualified person, who inquires in all legitimate transactions concerning the will and intention of the contracting parties, and (if possible) brings them to an agreement, and closes the bargain. Budaeus says, not inelegantly, *Est quasi conglutinator hominum inter se stipulantium et spondentium.* And if we derive the word broker, *maaklaar* (*vulgo makelaar*, but improperly so), from the verb *klaarmaken* (*i.e.* to make ready or arrange), we will, I think, at once approve the definition. Further, it is a general rule of law that a broker is not liable in a transaction in which he has acted. But this admits of some exceptions, as, for instance, where he has intervened in an unlawful matter, stipulated for usury, &c., or is under suspicion of fraud. With reference to the remark of Cepol. and others, *Proxenetae abundant mendaciis et in ambiguo praesumuntur mendaces, i.e.* 'Brokers are full of falsehood, and in case of doubt are presumed to be liars,' we are altogether of a different opinion. . . . Brokerage being indeed an important matter in a commercial town, the magistrates of the town of Amsterdam have as usual made several very wholesome provisions and regulations with respect thereto, among which, that no broker shall himself trade, or advance money in trade, or have any share therein (which not infrequently is the case, to the prejudice of traders and merchants), nor may he participate in any brokerage, provision or profits, with any one else under any pretext whatever, either directly or indirectly; of which he must at all times clear himself upon solemn oath before the honourable members of the Court." *See* BROKER.

Maker of a promissory note is the principal debtor on the instrument (Chalmers' *Bills of Exchange*, 6th ed. p. 274). The *maker* of a promissory note by making it, (*a*) engages that he will pay it according to its tenour; and (*b*) is precluded from denying to a holder in due course the existence of the payee and his then capacity to indorse (sec. 88 of English Bills of Exchange Act, 1882; sec. 87 of Cape Bills of Exchange Act, 1893; sec. 87 of Natal Bills of Exchange Law, 1887; sec. 87 of Rhodesian Bills of Exchange Regulations, 1895; sec. 87 of Transvaal Bills of Exchange Proclamation, 11 of 1902; sec. 87 of O.R.C. Bills of Exchange Ordinance, 28 of 1902).

Mala fide possessor, one who possesses a thing knowing that another is the owner and that he himself has no title thereto. *See* POSSESSIO BONÂ FIDE ET POSSESSIO MALÂ FIDE.

Mala in se, things bad or wrong in themselves. This term is applied to acts which are wrong by their own nature, being contrary to the laws of morality. Some of such acts are regarded simply as moral offences, while others, such as murder and theft, violate in addition the law of the land and are criminally punishable.

Mala quia prohibita, things bad or wrong because prohibited. As distinguished from *mala in se, mala quia prohibita* are acts which are wrong not in themselves, but by virtue of their having been prohibited by law, such, *e.g.* as the carrying on of a trade without a license.

Malay. As to Malay marriages, see *Mashia Ebrahim* v. *Mahomed Essop* ([1905] T.S. 59).

Malfeasance, the commission of a wrongful act; the doing of an act that is unlawful.

Malice, "a conscious violation of the law to the prejudice of another" (*per* Lord CAMPBELL in *Ferguson* v. *Earl of Kinnoul*, 9 Cl. & F. 321). See *Fyne* v. *African Realty Trust, Ltd.* ([1906] E.D.C. at pp. 257 and 258).

Malicious desertion, the wilful desertion by one of two spouses of the other spouse without good and sufficient cause. *Malicious desertion* has since the seventeenth century been a ground for divorce in Roman-Dutch law. The form of action is to sue for restitution of conjugal rights; at the trial evidence is led, and if the plaintiff proves his case an order for restitution of conjugal rights by the defendant within a specified time is made; failing such restitution, and on proof of such failure, a decree of divorce is granted. See *Mostert* v. *Mostert* (2 Searle, at p. 132).

In Natal special provision is made by statute in regard to the period of desertion; Law 13 of 1883, sec. 1, reads as follows: "No divorce shall be obtainable on the grounds of *malicious desertion* unless such desertion shall at the commencement of any suit, the object of which is to obtain such a divorce, have continued uninterruptedly for eighteen months next before such commencement;" the summons must allege that the desertion commenced more than eighteen months before the date of summons (*Roberts* v. *Roberts*, 7 N.L.R. 128). As to matrimonial relief by means of edictal process in Natal, see Law 18 of 1891.

Malicious injury. "In order to substantiate a charge of *malicious injury* to property, it is essential for the Crown to prove a malicious intention. From the nature of the act malice can be inferred" (*per* WESSELS, J., in *Fowlie* v. *Rex*, [1906] T.S. at p. 507).

Malitia supplet aetatem, badness or evil disposition supplies age. Children between seven and fourteen years of age are presumed to be incapable of wrong-doing so as to be free from criminal responsibility. Such presumption, however, will be set aside if it is proved that the child knew he was doing something forbidden or if the nature of the crime is such as to show that the child, notwithstanding his age, was actuated by evil motives. In other words, his evil motives will supply his want of years (*Queen* v. *Lourie*, 9 S.C. 432).

Malitieuze desertie (D.), malicious desertion of husband by wife, or *vice versâ*, otherwise known in Dutch practice (especially modern) as *moedwillige verlating*. *See* MALICIOUS DESERTION.

Mallum was the term adopted by Latin writers on the ancient laws and customs of the Germans to signify the place where the court was held. See Wessels' *History*, p. 145, where the origin and use of this term are fully discussed; also at p. 150.

Malt vinegar. In the Cape Wine, Spirits, Beer and Vinegar Act (19 of 1908), sec. 16, "*malt vinegar* means the product made by the alcoholic and subsequent acetous fermentation without distillation, of an infusion solely of cereal grain, whose starch has been converted into fermentable sugar by the direct agency of malt." *See* VINEGAR.

Malt whisky. "*Malt whisky* means whisky derived solely from malt" (the Wine, Brandy, Whisky and Spirits Act, 42 of 1906 (C.C.), sec. 14). The words "by pot-still distillation" were added to the foregoing definition by Act 19 of 1908 (C.C.), sec. 9 *See* WHISKY.

Management. As to the obligations included in the *management* of a property in India, see *Amar Chunder Kundu* v. *Soshi Bushan Roy and Others* (20 T.L.R. 128).

See "MANAGEMENT OF THE VESSEL."

"Management of the vessel." Sec. 3 of the Harter Act (U.S.A.) was incorporated in certain bills of lading under which certain butter was shipped from New York to London; thereby it was provided that if the owner of any vessel transporting merchandise should exercise due diligence to make the vessel seaworthy and properly manned and equipped, the owner would not be held responsible for damage or loss "resulting from faults or errors in navigation or in the management of the said vessel;" in consequence of the negligence of the persons in charge of the refrigerating apparatus on the vessel the butter was damaged; it was held that *management of the vessel* meant the management of the ship *quâ* ship; that is not *quâ* navigation, but *quâ* ship. See *Rowson* v. *Atlantic Transport Co.* ([1903] 2 K.B. 666; 72 L.J. K.B. 811; 89 L.T. 204; 19 T.L.R. 668). See also *The Rodney* ([1900] P. 112; 69 L.J.P. 29; 82 L.T. 27; 16 T.L.R. 183).

Manager, a person charged with the direction or control of some business or undertaking. In the Natal Mines and Collieries Act (43 of 1899, sec. 4) the term *manager* is defined to mean "the person appointed by the mine owner or his agent as responsible under this Act for the control, management and working of the mine."

Mandaat (D.), also called *lastgeving;* equivalent to mandate. *Mandaat* may be either in writing or verbally, see Van Leeuwen's *Comm.* 4, 26, 5; Kersteman's *Woordenboek,* vol. 1, p. 268. *See* also MANDATE.

Mandament (D.), a writ granted by the Court in Holland upon the petition of the plaintiff. The *mandament* was drawn up in the name of the president and members of the Court, it recited the contents of the petition and authorised the usher (*deurwaarder*) to summon the defendant as prayed in the petition. See Van der Linden's *Institutes,* 3, 1, 2, 8.

Mandament poenaal (D.), an important privilege granted to litigants in Dutch practice, equivalent to an interdict, whereby the Supreme Court of Holland "under a heavy penalty forbids or commands something, in cases where another suffers damage, which he cannot prevent by any ordinary remedy, or where something has been done against which he cannot well be restored, or which may lead to considerable damage, or where the case admits of no delay" (Van Leeuwen's *Comm.* Kotzé's trans. vol. 2, p. 429). See also Kersteman's *Woordenboek,* vol. 1, p. 273; *Commissioner of Mines* v. *Solomon and Others* ([1907] T.S. at p. 54).

Mandamus, an order granted by a competent court directing some person, official or corporation to do some specific thing. In Law 19 of 1872 (N.), sec. 130, it is spoken of as "writ of *mandamus,*" which corresponds with the same term as used in England.

Mandata, orders. Under the Roman law *mandata,* with *epistolae* and *rescripta,* formed one of the three kinds of imperial constitutions or ordinances; by *mandata* orders were given by the emperor to particular officers. The other two kinds of imperial constitutions were *decreta* and *edicta.*

Mandataris (D.), the person who has accepted a mandate; an agent or mandatory who has undertaken to act for another in some business or transaction.

Mandate, a consensual contract under Roman-Dutch law, "whereby one person entrusts to another something lawful to be done for himself or a third person, and the other person accepts such trust gratis" (Grotius' *Introd.* 3, 12, 2; see also Van der Linden's *Institutes*, Juta's trans. p. 147). There is, however, authority for the statement that the mandatory may receive a gratuity or honorarium for his services (see Voet, 17, 1, 2; Schorer's *Notes to Grotius*, n. 340; and Van der Keessel, *Thes.* 570). Voet (*Comm.* 17, 1, 1) says: "It is called *mandate* from a giving of the hand, because, as Isidorus says, in olden times one used to give another his hand in conducting business, and the hand was a sign of good faith; and it [*mandate*] takes its origin from friendship, and differs from *commendatio* in this respect, that he who has given a *mandate* is bound, whereas he who has [merely] advised [lit. commended] is not." Van Leeuwen (*Comm.* Kotzé's trans. vol. 2, p. 219) defines *mandate* as follows: "*Mandate*, or authority, is a transaction whereby any one accepts a commission to execute something for another without stipulating for any remuneration; as, for instance, a commission to buy or sell something for another, or to transact some business or other for him, which begets a grateful acknowledgment at discretion, but not any debt."

Mandator, the principal in a contract of mandate. *See* MANDATE. The *mandator* "is bound to indemnify the mandatory for all reasonable expenses incurred and damages suffered on account of the mandate, even though the mandatory may have been prevented by some obstacle or other from completing the mandate" (Grotius' *Introd.* 3, 12, 9).

Mandatory, the agent who is entrusted with a mandate. *See* MANDATE. Under the contract of mandate "the *mandatory* is bound to fulfil the mandate, and that according to the directions of the mandator, without deviating from them in any way, unless indeed he does something clearly equivalent to what he has been directed to do" (Grotius' *Introd.* 3, 12, 8). "A sudden and unexpected emergency wholly excuses a *mandatory* who either has not thoroughly fulfilled the mandate or has exceeded his limits" (Van der Keessel, *Thes.* 571).

Manslaughter "is unlawful homicide without malice aforethought" (Stephen's *Digest of the Criminal Law*, 5th ed. p. 182).

Man-stealing is the wrongful and unlawful carrying away or concealing a human being with a view to depriving him of his liberty; in Dutch law it was regarded as a grave offence, and punishable with the severest penalties (see judgment of DE VILLIERS, C.J., in *Queen* v. *Buchenroeder*, 13 S.C. at p. 177). "Upon the facts stated the charge should have been that of *man-stealing*, which is the nearest equivalent of *plagium*, the term 'man' being used in the generic sense of 'a human being, and the term 'stealing' in a somewhat wider sense than 'theft'" (*per* DE VILLIERS, C.J., *ibid.* at p. 178). *Man-stealing* is a punishable offence (*ibid.*). *See* PLAGIUM.

Manu fortiori, by superior force. *See* VIS MAJOR.

Manufacture. In *Dugall* v. *Riches* (23 N.L.R. at p. 97), and *Buxton* v. *Barfield* (23 N.L.R. at p. 198), BALE, C.J., adopted with approval the definition of *manufacture* given in the *Century Dictionary*, as follows: "A manufacture is the operation of making goods or wares of any kind; the production of articles for use from raw or prepared materials by giving to these materials new forms, qualities, properties, or combinations, whether by hand-labour or by machinery." See *R.* v. *Wheeler* (2 B. & Ald. 349); Ordinance 4 of 1905 (T.), sec. 2.

Manuscript, something that has been written by the hand.

Margarine, a pearl-like substance extracted from lard; also taken from the concrete part of olive oil; a term applied to an artificial imitation of butter. In the Cape Sale of Food and Drugs and Seeds Act (5 of 1890) the expression *margarine*, butterine, or other similar articles is defined to mean "all substances, whether compounds or otherwise, prepared in imitation of butter, and whether mixed with butter or not." The Natal Food and Drugs Act (45 of 1901) contains a similar definition; and so does Ordinance 32 of 1906 (O.R.C.), sec. 1.

Margarine cheese, in Ordinance 32 of 1906 (O.R.C.), sec. 1, means "any substance, whether compound or otherwise, which is prepared in imitation of cheese, and which contains fat not derived from milk."

Marine, relating to the sea.

Marine insurance or **assurance.** "A policy of *marine insurance* is a contract of indemnity against all losses accruing to the subject-matter of the policy from certain perils during the adventure. This subject-matter need not be strictly a property in either the ship, goods or freight, for, as has been long said, if a man is so situated with respect to them that he will receive benefit from their arriving safely at the end of the adventure, or sustain loss in consequence of their not arriving safely, he has an insurable interest. If the assured, before the termination of the adventure, has parted with all interest in the subject-matter of the insurance, he can suffer no damage from any subsequent loss, and consequently, from the nature of the contract being one of indemnity, he cannot recover in respect of any loss subsequent to his transfer of the property, and, for exactly the same reason, an attempted transfer of the beneficial interest in the policy, before loss, to a person having no beneficial interest in the subject-matter is inoperative; for the *cestui que trust* of the contract, having nothing in respect of which to be indemnified, could recover no indemnity. But after the loss has happened, and the adventure is over, this reason ceases at once. The assured may sell the damaged subject of insurance, thereby, as it were, ascertaining how much his loss is, and yet recover for the loss he has sustained" (*per* BLACKBURN, J., in *Lloyd* v. *Spence*, 41 L.J. Q.B. 94).

Decker in a *note* to Van Leeuwen's *Comm.* (Kotzé's trans. vol. 2, p. 70) says: "Assurance or insuring is a contract, whereby one of the contracting parties takes upon himself, for a certain fixed time, the uncertain risk to which the other party is or will be exposed, and for which the latter is bound to pay him the stipulated sum or praemium;" and Van Leeuwen (*ibid.*) says: "Assurance or securing is a transaction by which a person, for a certain money gain, paid at the time of completing the agreement, takes upon himself the risk of the sea or water, wind, enemies, pirates and other dangers, on the ship and its belongings; or also on certain goods or merchandise, until it arrives safely at its destination."

It is thus defined in Arnould's *Marine Insurance* (7th ed. sec. 1): "*Marine insurance* is a contract whereby one party, for an agreed consideration, undertakes to indemnify the other against all loss arising from certain perils or sea-risks to which his ship, merchandise, or other interest in a maritime adventure, may be exposed during a certain voyage, or a certain period of time."

In the Cape Colony by Act 8 of 1879, sec. 2, the law relating to questions of marine insurance is assimilated to that of England, except where the latter is repugnant to, or in conflict with Cape statute law.

Marital power, the authority or power of a husband over his wife at common law. On marriage a wife becomes a minor under the guardianship of her husband. By virtue of the marital power a husband controls the wife's estate; appears for her in court; and may alienate or encumber her property, unless otherwise stipulated by antenuptial contract. *Maritale macht* is the Dutch equivalent.

Marital rights, the rights of or pertaining to a husband.

Maritale macht (D.). *See* MARITAL POWER.

Maritime law, the law relating to shipping and the sea, and to persons or things connected therewith. In the Cape Colony by Act 8 of 1879, sec. 1, it is provided that "in all questions relating to maritime and shipping law in respect of which the Supreme Court has concurrent jurisdiction with the Vice-Admiralty Court, the law of this colony shall hereafter be the same as the law of England, so far as the law of England shall not be repugnant to or inconsistent with any Ordinance, Act of Parliament, or other statute having the force of law in this colony."

Market overt, in Dutch, *vrije markt,* free market, endowed by charter with certain local privileges. Whether any such markets exist in South Africa other than pound sales is a disputed point among the lawyers. See Maasdorp's *Institutes,* vol. 2, p. 62; Van Leeuwen's *Comm.* Kotzé's trans. vol. 2, p. 134, translator's note; and Wessels' *History*, p. 506. This controversy arises in connection with the statement of law that the purchaser of stolen property in *market overt* is entitled to retain possession of it against the true owner until the latter pays to him the purchase-price (see Grotius' *Introd.* 2, 3, 6; Van Leeuwen's *Comm.* 2, 7, 3). The leading cases on this subject, *pro* and *con*, are: *Van der Merwe* v. *Webb* (3 E.D.C. 97); *Retief* v. *Hamerslach* (1 C.L.J. 346); *Woodhead, Plant & Co.* v. *Gunn* (11 S.C. 4); see also *Muller* v. *Chadwick & Co.* ([1906] T.S. 35). The subject is impartially discussed as a controverted point of law at 5 C.L.J. 70.

Market overt is a term also known in English law, and it is thus described in Stephen's *Comm.* 15th ed. vol. 2, at p. 134: "*Market overt*, in the country, is a market held on the special days provided as market days, for particular towns, by charter or prescription; but in the City of London every day, except Sunday, is a market day. The market place or spot of ground set apart by custom for the sale of particular goods is also, in the country, the only *market overt*, but in the City of London every shop in which goods are exposed publicly for sale is a *market overt*, though only for such things as the owner ordinarily trades in there." See also Benjamin on *Sales*, 4th ed. p. 8, where a similar description is given.

Marketable security, an expression used in the Natal Licenses and Stamps Act (43 of 1898), where it is defined to include "any stock, debenture, security, share, or the like, of such a description as to be capable of being sold in any share market or exchange in South Africa." *Marketable securities* are subject to a special stamp duty in Natal. A fire insurance policy is not a *marketable security* within the meaning of the Act just referred to (*In re License and Stamp Act*, 1898, 21 N.L.R. 6).

The term *marketable security* is also found in Proclamation 12 of 1902 (T.), sec. 1; the definition there given is similar to that of the Natal statute.

Markgraven (D.) (pl. of *markgraaf*) were the judges of certain marshes, or boundary poles of countries in Holland (Van Leeuwen's *Comm.* Kotzé's trans. vol. 1, p. 63). *See* GRAAF.

Marriage "is a contract between a man and a woman to live together for life as man and wife to the exclusion of all other men and women. But though it is a contract, it is a contract of a very special kind, inasmuch as though it may, like all other consensual contracts, be constituted by the consent of the parties, testified and confirmed by certain solemnities required by law, it differs from other consensual contracts in that it cannot be again dissolved by such consent" (Maasdorp's *Institutes,* vol. 1, p. 10).

"The contract of *marriage*, then, is something more than a mere contract, for it is a contract which not only creates a legal relationship, but also creates a civil status entailing obligations and rights which are ascertainable, not according to the *lex loci contractus*, but according to the municipal law to which the parties become subject, and which is dependent upon the law of the 'matrimonial home.' The status itself (as contra-distinguished from the contract) is *juris gentium*, and its relations extend so far beyond the parties themselves that, unlike other contracts, the contract on which the status is founded cannot be made by the parties themselves to confer whatsoever rights and obligations they please; but it is the municipal law which takes upon itself to define and declare what are the rights, duties and obligations which shall be incident to the status of *marriage*, whether that status has been originally constituted under its own law or under that of any other country. The consequences, therefore, resulting from *marriage* involve different considerations from the fact of *marriage*, and do not form any part of the *jus gentium*" (Gwynne Hall on *Divorce*, p. 717).

As to Malay marriages, see *Mashia Ebrahim* v. *Mahomed Essop* ([1905] T.S. 59).

As to native marriages in Natal, see Law 19 of 1891, secs. 146 *et seq.* of sch.

Marriage record book, a book kept by magistrates of the Cape Colony, in which copies of the register of all marriages solemnised before them are entered (see sec. 12 of Act 16 of 1860 (C.C.)).

Marriage settlement, a contract for settling some money, property or thing upon one or both spouses or their children, before, and in consideration of the marriage. In South Africa such a settlement is usually embodied in an antenuptial contract. *Marriage settlements* "may provide either (1) for the immediate settlement of property, movable or immovable, by one of the intended spouses upon or for the benefit of the other, or upon or for the benefit of the children of the marriage or their descendants; or (2) for the payment out of the estate of the spouse making the settlement, at his or her death or at any other time, of any sum of money or annuity, or for making any other provision for the benefit of the other spouse or of the children of the marriage or their descendants" (Maasdorp's *Institutes*, vol. 1, p. 67).

Martial law. "*Martial law*, in the sense in which the expression is here used, means the power, right or duty of the Crown and its servants, or, in other words, of the Government, to maintain public order, or, in technical language, the King's peace, at whatever cost of blood or property may be in strictness necessary for that purpose. Hence *martial law* comes into existence in times of invasion or insurrection, when, where, and in so far as the King's peace cannot be maintained by ordinary means, and owes its existence to urgent and paramount necessity. This power to maintain the peace by the exertion of any amount of force strictly necessary for the purpose is sometimes described as the prerogative of the Crown, but it may more correctly be considered, not only as a power necessarily possessed by the Crown, but also as the power, right, or duty possessed by, or incumbent upon, every loyal citizen of preserving or restoring the King's peace in the case, whether of invasion or of rebellion or generally of armed opposition to the law, by the use of any amount of force whatever necessary to preserve or restore the peace" (Dicey's *Law of the Constitution*, 6th ed. p. 503). "The proclamation of *martial law* does not, unless under some statutory provision, add to the power or right inherent in the Government to use force for the repression of disorder, or for resistance of invasion. It does not confer upon the Government any power which the Government would not have possessed without it. The object and the effect of the proclamation can only be to give notice, to the inhabitants of the place with regard to which *martial law* is proclaimed, of the course which the Government is obliged to adopt for the purpose of defending the country, or of restoring tranquility" (*ibid.* p. 510).

Mason. *See* SERVANT.

Master. (1) One who by contract or in some other legal manner has the right to, and control over, the services of another person. "A master has a right, as against the world, to the services of his servant, and can sue not only any one by whose act the servant is rendered less capable of, or is hindered from, performing his duties, but also any one who entices him away from the performance of them; and this principle has been declared to apply not only to domestic service, but also to any kind of employment" (Holland's *Jurisprudence*, 10th ed. p. 175). See Master and Servants Statutes of the various colonies, and especially Ordinance 7 of 1904 (O.R.C.), sec. 2.

(2) The *Master* of the Supreme Court is an official who is charged with the supervision of the estates of deceased persons, insolvent estates, the Guardians' Fund, and other matters in most of the South African colonies; he appoints executors, tutors, curators and trustees, and cares for the interests of minors. His duties in many respects are similar to those of the Probate Branch of the High Court of Justice in England.

Master companions, the judges in the Netherlands in the sixteenth century who, with the *woodreeve*, constituted a special court for the trial of matters concerning the chase and wildernesses. They were three in number, and were selected by the county of Holland from among the principal of the nobility. See Van Leeuwen's *Comm.* Kotzé's trans. vol. 2, p. 595.

Mater non habet nothos, a mother has no bastards. Although illegitimate children are regarded as having no father, and are unable to inherit any property from him or his relations unless it has been left to them by will, yet they are entitled to succeed *ab intestato* to their mother and her relations, for a mother makes no bastards. On the same principle the mother of illegitimate children, and not the father, is their natural guardian (*Van Rooyen* v. *Werner*, 9 S.C. at p. 431).

Matrimonial domicile, the domicile of the husband at the time of his marriage; such domicile is also the domicile of the wife, for a married woman is deemed by law to assume the domicile of her husband by the fact of marriage without inquiry as to her intention.

In South Africa "the law of the *domicile of marriage* regulates the rights of spouses with regard to all property, whether possessed at the time of marriage or after-acquired, even though it may have been acquired in a country to which they had removed after marriage" (*per* INNES, C.J., in *Schapiro* v. *Schapiro*, [1904] T.S. at p. 677). "The expression *matrimonial domicile* is to some extent an unfortunate one" (*per* KOTZÉ, J.P., in *Ex parte Standring*, [1906] E.D.C. at p. 176).

"By the *matrimonial domicile* is to be understood that of the husband at the date of the marriage, with a possible exception in favour of any other which may have been acquired immediately after the marriage, in pursuance of an agreement to that effect made before it" (Westlake's *Private International Law*, 4th ed. p. 71).

"**May,**" as to whether this term is permissive or obligatory when used in statutes, see Maxwell's *Interpretation of Statutes*, 4th ed. pp. 360 *et seq.*; Craies' *Statute Law*, pp. 251 *et seq.*

Measurement. In the Transvaal Interpretation of Laws Proclamation (15 of 1902), sec. 14, it is provided that "in the *measurement* of any distance for the purpose of any law that distance shall, unless the contrary intention appears, be measured in a straight line on a horizontal plane."

Medical practitioner. The expression *medical practitioner* is defined in the Cape Medical and Pharmacy Act (34 of 1891) to mean "every person duly admitted and lawfully entitled to practise in this [Cape] Colony as a physician, surgeon or accoucheur, on the day before the taking effect of this Act, and also every person duly qualified by license and registration under this Act to practise as a physician and surgeon within this [Cape] Colony." See Act 1 of 1897 (C.C.), sec. 2, and Ordinance 29 of 1904 (T.), sec. 3. See also Proclamation 36 of 1902 (T.), sec. 2; Ordinance 23 of 1904 (T.), sec. 2; Proclamation 15 of 1902 (O.R.C.), sec. 4; Ordinance 29 of 1903 (O.R.C.), sec. 2; Ordinance 1 of 1904 (O.R.C.), sec. 1; Ordinance 13 of 1906 (O.R.C.), sec. 2; Act 35 of 1896 (N.), sec. 3.

Medicinal purposes, purposes connected with the healing or alleviation of bodily disorders. See *Regina* v. *Bell* (8 E.D.C. 3); *Queen* v. *Armstrong* (13 S.C. 408).

Meerderjarig (D.), a person who has attained the age of majority; a major. In Holland and West Friesland the legal age of majority was twenty-five years; in Gelderland twenty-one years; and in some other places it was twenty years. *See* MAJOR; MAJORITY; MINDERJARIG.

Meineed (D.), perjury. *See* PERJURY.

Melioratien (D.), also called *verbeteringen*, improvements to buildings or immovable property.

Meliorations, improvements.

Member. The term *member* as applied to joint-stock companies is defined in the Cape Companies Act (25 of 1892), sec. 74, as follows: "The subscribers of the memorandum of association of any company under this Act shall be deemed to have agreed to become *members* of the company whose memorandum they have subscribed, and upon the registration of the company shall be entered as *members* on the register of *members* hereinafter mentioned; and every other person who has agreed to become a *member* of a company under this Act, and whose name is entered on the register of *members*, shall be deemed to be a *member* of the company." This definition was taken verbatim from the English Companies Act of 1862, sec. 23. *See* Transvaal Companies Act (31 of 1909), sec. 24.

Memorandum of association, the fundamental and (except in certain particulars) the unalterable law of statutory corporations; such corporations are incorporated only for the objects and purposes expressed in that memorandum (*per* Lord SELBORNE in *Ashbury & Co.* v. *Riche*, L.R. 7 H.L. 693). See Act 31 of 1909 (T.), sec. 2.

Mens rea, criminal intention. *See* ACTUS NON FACIT REUM NISI MENS SIT REA.

Mensa et thoro, from board and bed. *See* A MENSA, THORO ET COMMUNIONE BONORUM.

Mercantile law, the law merchant; the law relating to commercial matters. See the General Law Amendment Act (8 of 1879) of the Cape Colony.

"**Mere licensee.**" "The distinction between a *mere licensee* and other licensees was pointed out in *Holmes'* case (24 L.T. 69). A *mere licensee* is there stated to be one who has permission to go on the ground of another for his own purposes without any relation to the occupier, and who goes taking all risks attendant on his being there; whilst a licensee is one who is invited upon the land by the owner or occupier for some purpose in which he and the owner or occupier have a common interest" (*per* SMITH, J., in *Skinner* v. *Johannesburg Turf Club*, [1907] T.H. at p. 191).

Merger, the union in the same person of the characters of creditor and debtor in respect of the same debt. See Van der Linden's *Institutes* (Juta's trans.), p. 169.

Servitudes are extinguished by *merger*. See *Salmon* v. *Lamb's Executor and Naidoo* ([1906] E.D.C. at p. 360).

Mero motu. *See* EX MERO MOTU.

Merx, merchandise; used, in connection with the contract of sale, of a thing which is capable of being bought and sold (see Voet's *Comm.* 18, 1, 13). In letting and hiring (*locatio conductio*) *merces* is the hire-money, *i.e.* rent in the case of lands and houses, and wages, &c., in the case of personal services.

Messuage, an English legal term signifying a dwelling or manor house with adjacent buildings, together with garden and land required for the proper use and enjoyment thereof.

Met den voet te stooten (D.), literally, to push with the foot. An expression used in connection with sales, whereby, "in order to escape making compensation for any defect, the property is often sold as good and bad as it is; . . . in which case we are only obliged to deliver the property as good and bad as it is" (Van Leeuwen's *Comm.* vol. 2, p. 146). Such sales are commonly described as being made *voetstoots*, and amount to sales of property without any warranty.

Metal claim, one of the three classes into which claims are divided under the Natal Mines and Collieries Act (43 of 1899, sec. 8); it is of a size not exceeding 300 yards by 300 yards (18·595 acres), and is granted for the purpose of prospecting or mining for gold and other minerals, including coal, but excepting precious stones and alluvial minerals. The other two classes of claim under the Natal Mines and Collieries Act are "alluvial claims" and "mineral claims." As to issue of licenses for *metal claims* under the Act see sec. 28 thereof.

Methylate. The term *methylate* is defined in the Cape Additional Taxation Act (36 of 1904), sec. 2, to mean "to mix spirits with any substance or combination of substances in such manner and under regulations to be framed by the Treasurer as to render the mixture unfit for human consumption as a beverage."

In the Natal Act to amend the Excise Act (25 of 1905, sec. 2) *methylate* means "to mix spirits of wine under approved regulations with some substance in such manner and quantity as to denaturate or render the spirits unfit for drinking."

Methylated spirits, in the Transvaal Ordinance 32 of 1902, sec. 3, means "spirits mixed with some substance in such manner and quantity as to the satisfaction of the Director of Customs to render the mixture unfit for use as a beverage." See also Ordinance 8 of 1903 (O.R.C.), sec. 3.

Middle Temple, one of the Inns of Court. *See* INNS OF COURT. His Majesty the King is one of its Masters of the Bench. It has the reputation of being the most catholic and democratic of the Inns of Court. It is conducted on liberal lines, and is specially a common law Inn.

"**Might,**" discussed in *Ismail and Others* v. *Rex* ([1908] T.S. at p. 1091).

Mijnpacht (D.), a mining area granted in the Transvaal under lease by the Government to the owner of a farm or piece of land upon which precious metals have been found, for a specified period, with the right of renewal, subject to a certain rental and to the provisions of the Gold Law. A *mijnpacht* on private property under Law 15 of 1898 (T.), sec. 25, is equal to 10 per cent. of the area of the land. The above Law has been repealed by Act 35 of 1908 (T.), under which a *mijnpacht* is to be equal to not more than one-fifth or 20 per cent. of the area of the land (see secs. 20 *et seq.* of the Act for provisions as to selection of the *mijnpacht,* issue and renewal of *mijnpacht* brief and conditions of tenure).

Mijnpacht-brief (D.), the deed of lease under which a *mijnpacht* is granted. *See* MIJNPACHT.

Military service. The expression *military service* is defined in the Cape Colonial Forces Act (32 of 1892), sec. 2, as follows: "(*a*) The permanent forces will be considered to be on *military service* during the whole period of their commission or enrolment; (*b*) volunteers shall be considered to be in *military service* (i) when being trained or exercised with any portion of her Majesty's regular forces or of the permanent forces; (ii) when assembled in a camp of training or instruction; (iii) when called out to aid the civil power in the protection of life and property by proclamation of the Governor, under the powers conferred upon him by the 85th section of this Act."

In the Natal Foreign Enlistment Act (26 of 1906, sec. 30) *military service* includes "military telegraphy, and any other employment whatever in or in connection with any military operation." In the Militia Act, 36 of 1903 (N.), sec. 3, the definition of *military service* or active service provides that "militia-men shall be considered to be on military or active service when called out by the Governor under this Act, or when assembled in, or during the time of any camp of training or instruction, or when going to or returning from any such camp, or while engaged in any military exercise or drill, or when called out for any escort, duty or guard of honour, or while in uniform on duty, at any time or place."

For Transvaal, see Ordinance 37 of 1904, sec. 1; Ordinance 1 of 1906, sec. 30 of sch.

For Orange River Colony, see Ordinance 35 of 1905, sec. 1.

Minderjarig (D.), a person who has not attained the age of majority; a minor. *See* MEERDERJARIG; MINORITY; MINORS.

Mine, one or more excavations in the earth, either from the surface downwards or by means of an adit or adits into the sides of hills or mountains, for the purpose of prospecting for or winning minerals or precious stones.

In the Natal Mines and Collieries Act (43 of 1899, sec. 4) "*mine*" is defined to mean "all workings of minerals, including quarrying and other methods of excavation on the surface, and from the surface downwards, and underground, together with all erections and appliances, matters or things of what nature soever connected therewith or belonging thereto, above and below ground for the purpose of prospecting for or winning minerals."

In the Transvaal, in the Mines, Works, Machinery and Certificates Act (32 of 1909), sec. 2, *mine* means and includes "all excavations for the purpose of searching for or winning minerals, as well as working of mineral deposits, whether abandoned or actually being worked on the surface, from the surface downwards and underground, together with all buildings, erections and appliances belonging or appertaining thereto above and below ground for the purpose of prospecting for or winning metals, minerals or precious stones by boring, excavating or dredging."

In the Orange River Colony Mining of Precious Stones Ordinance (4 of 1904), sec. 5, *mine* means "any area of ground bearing precious stones, which is continuous in its formation and is contained within a pipe or similar geological formation, together with any directly connected overflow or extension of the same." See also Ordinance 28 of 1907, sec. 1.

For statutory definitions in Cape Colony, see Act 18 of 1894, sec. 2; Act 11 of 1899, sec. 3; Act 27 of 1907, sec. 3.

Mine owner, the owner of a mine, whether an individual or a corporation. In the Natal Mines and Collieries Act (43 of 1899, sec. 4) the expression *mine owner* is defined to mean "any person or body of persons, being the immediate holder or lessee of any mine or part thereof, and not being a person or body of persons who merely receive a royalty or rent from a mine, or who is merely the owner of a mine subject to any contract for the working thereof. Where a mine is owned by a company or syndicate not registered in this [Natal] colony and having its board of directors beyond the [Natal] colony, the duly appointed agent of such company or syndicate in the colony will be considered to be the *mine owner*."

Mineholder, a term used in the Orange River Colony Mining of Precious Stones Ordinance (4 of 1904), sec. 5, where it means "the person entitled under the provisions of this Ordinance to work a mine." *See* MINE OWNER.

Mineral. In the Cape Colony *minerals* is defined in the Precious Minerals Act (31 of 1898) as gold, silver or platinum.

"As to the scientific definition of the word *mineral*, after hearing a great deal of evidence from experts it appears to me that the word may be used in at least two senses. First, in a very wide sense it may be taken to mean any portion of the earth's crust, not being animal or vegetable. But in its more specific sense it means an inorganic substance having a definite chemical composition and possessing characteristics not easy to define. Speaking generally, it has a crystallisation of its own and a certain degree of hardness and specific gravity" (*per* INNES, C.J., in *New Blue Sky G. M. Co., Ltd.*, v. *Marshall*, [1905] T.S. 367). See also *Midland Railway Co.* v. *Haunchwood Brick and Tile Co.*, 20 Ch. Div. 552; 46 T.L.R. 301; *Great Western Railway Co.* v. *Carpalla United China Clay Co.*, 24 T.L.R. 804 and 25 T.L.R. 91.

In the Transvaal the Precious and Base Metals Act (35 of 1908), defines "precious metals" as:—

"(*a*) gold and silver, and their ores and gold or silver found in combination with a base metal, where such gold or silver cannot be worked apart from such base metal, and the value of the gold or silver exceeds the cost of producing both such precious and base metal;

(*b*) any other metal (not being a base metal) declared by proclamation of the Governor in the *Gazette* to be a precious metal for the purposes of this Act and the regulations,"

and the term "base metals" is defined as "quicksilver, iron, lead, copper, tin, zinc, cobalt, nickel, arsenic, manganese, antimony, bismuth, as well as the ores of such metals, and sulphur, coal, graphite, or any other mineral substance, for the exploitation of which no special provision is made by law." The Precious Stones Ordinance (66 of 1903) defines "precious stones" as including diamonds and any other gems or stones proclaimed such by the Lieutenant-Governor. In the Mines, Works, Machinery and Certificates Act (32 of 1909), sec. 2, *mineral* means and includes "all substances (including mineral oils) which can be obtained from the earth by mining, digging, dredging, hydraulicing, or quarrying operations for purposes of profit." *See* CLAY; FIRE CLAY.

In the Natal Mines and Collieries Act (43 of 1899) the word *minerals* is defined as being "all substances which can be extracted from the earth by mining operations for the purpose of profit; provided that the term *mineral* shall not apply to any stone or clay for use for building, road-making or kindred purposes, except such as are mentioned in this Act, nor to any *minerals* which, not being so mentioned, may be excepted from the operation of this Act by Government Notice by order of the Governor in Council."

In the Orange River Colony the Precious Metals Ordinance (3 of 1904) applies to gold and silver "and to such other precious metals as the Lieutenant-Governor shall from time to time by proclamation declare to be included within its provisions;" the Precious Stones Ordinance (4 of 1904), sec. 4, applies to "diamonds and to such other precious stones as the Lieutenant-Governor shall from time to time proclaim as included within its provisions;" the Base Metals Ordinance (8 of 1904) applies to tin, copper, iron, zinc, lead, cinnabar, coal, petroleum, oil shale, sulphur and chloride of sodium (salt) "and such other metals or *minerals* other than gold, silver or precious stones as the Lieutenant-Governor shall from time to time by proclamation declare to be subject thereto." *See* BASE MINERALS.

Mineral claim, one of the three classes into which claims are divided under the Natal Mines and Collieries Act (43 of 1899, sec. 8); it is of a size not exceeding 700 yards by 700 yards (101·239 acres), and is granted for the purpose of prospecting or mining for coal, limestone, stratified ironstone, slate, soapstone, and such other minerals as may from time to time be included by Government Notice by order of the Governor in Council. The other two classes of claims under the Natal Mines and Collieries Act are "alluvial claims" and "metal claims." As to issue of licenses for mineral claims under the Act, see sec. 28 thereof.

Mining, in the Transvaal Gold Law (15 of 1898, sec. 3—now repealed) means "the intentional extraction of the precious metals mentioned in art. 2 [of the Law], including all work necessary for the purpose, irrespective of whether such extraction is effected by underground mining works, open cuttings, boring or otherwise." See also Ordinance 4 of 1904 (O.R.C.), sec. 5.

Mining district. In the Transvaal Precious and Base Metals Act (35 of 1908), sec. 3, *mining district* means one of the districts into which the colony is divided in accordance with the Act, *i.e.* any of the districts of Johannesburg, Boksburg, Krugersdorp, Pretoria, Heidelberg, Klerksdorp, Pietersburg, Barberton, Pilgrim's Rest and Ottoshoop; and when used in reference to land, means the *mining district* in which such land is situate. This definition is adopted by the Transvaal Registration of Deeds and Titles Act (25 of 1909), sec. 2.

Mining ground. In Ordinance 44 of 1904 (T.), sec. 22 (*a*), *mining ground* means "ground held under any mining title." *See* MINING TITLE.

Mining property. In the Orange River Colony, in the Mining of Precious Metals Ordinance (3 of 1904), sec. 5, *mining property* means and comprises "any claim, block of claims or mijnpacht, or any mijnpacht together with any claim or claims contiguous thereto on a public digging occupied by any person as the registered holder thereof under the provisions of this Ordinance."

"**Mining purposes.**" In construing the expression *mining purposes* within the meaning of Act 1 of 1889 (C.C.), in *Collector of Customs* v. *De Beers Consolidated Mines, Ltd.* (9 S.C. at p. 149) DE VILLIERS, C.J., said: "The words *mining purposes* include all purposes necessary to win diamonds from the mine [the defendant company being a diamond mining company], and include all works necessary for this, both on the surface and underground; and if it is necessary in order to win the diamonds that the blue ground should be constantly watered, then the pipes used for watering the blue, if attached to and forming component parts of any machinery used for that purpose, are used for *mining purposes.* The same remark applies to the piping used for feeding the boiler of the engine: it is attached thereto, and forms part of a complicated apparatus, and as the engine is used only for *mining purposes* the piping must be treated as such also."

In the Natal Mines and Collieries Act (43 of 1899), sec. 4, the expression *mining purposes* is defined as follows: "The purpose of searching for, mining and removing minerals, including the erection of machinery and the construction of works connected with such purposes, and the doing of all lawful acts incident or conducive thereto."

Mining right, a term employed in the mining laws of the Transvaal to denote certain rights relating to, or connected with, the prospecting or mining for minerals or precious stones, and as such recognised by the Government as being in the nature of a real right. See Proclamation 35 of 1902 (T.), sec. 1, repealed by Act 29 of 1908 (T.), which substitutes the term "mining title" (*q.v.*). The latter Act has now in turn been repealed by Act 25 of 1909 (T.).

Mining title, in the Transvaal Registration of Deeds and Titles Act (25 of 1909), sec. 2, means:—

"(*a*) All such rights as are included in the definition of *mining title* in the Precious and Base Metals Act, 1908, or any amendment thereof." [*Mining title* in the latter Act is defined as "(1) a mynpacht-brief issued under this Act or Law No. 15 of 1898, or a prior law; (2) a prospecting or digger's license issued under this Act, under Law No. 15 of 1898, or a prior law; (3) a mynpacht-brief issued under Article 31 of Law No. 15 of 1898; (4) any right to mine granted by the Governor under section forty-six or forty-seven of this Act; (5) a license for a base metal claim issued under Part III of this Act, or under Law No. 14 of 1897 or a prior law, and shall include a lease granted under the Base Metal Law Amendment Ordinance, 1903; (6) any other right to mine existing at the commencement of this Act and lawfully granted."]

"(*b*) Discoverers' certificates and alluvial claim licenses held under the Precious Stones Ordinance, 1903, or any amendment thereof, and discoverers' certificates held under the Precious and Base Metals Act, 1908, or any amendment thereof;

(*c*) Any such interest in a mine as is mentioned in Chapter V of the Precious Stones Ordinance, 1903, and is held by the owner as therein described."

Minnelijke aanmaning (D.), a friendly demand made by the creditor upon the debtor before instituting his action. See Van der Linden's *Institutes*, 3, 1, 2, 1.

Minority, the period of a person's existence prior to the attainment of majority. *See* MAJORITY; MINORS.

Minors are persons who have not attained full age or the age of majority (*see* MAJORITY). "The last day of minority is regarded as completed at the moment of its inception, when it is to the *minor's* advantage that this should be so; but when the *minor* seeks *restitutio in integrum*, the period of minority is reckoned to extend to the close of the last day of minority, *de momento in momentum* (to the very minute) (Nathan's *Common Law*, sec. 168). Grotius (*Introd.* 1, 4, 3) says that minors are such from one or other of three causes, to wit, by marriage, by birth, or from incapacity to take care of themselves. A contract made by a minor without the authority of his guardian is voidable, unless it can be proved that it was for the minor's benefit (Morice's *English and Roman-Dutch Law*, 1st ed. p. 22). In Natal an exception has been made to this rule in favour of minor native servants, who are entitled to sue for any claim against their masters without the intervention of a guardian (Act 40 of 1894, sec. 58).

Minute, from the Dutch word *minut*. It was originally the first draft of a notarial deed or instrument, and was so called because it was written in small characters and the lines and words were close together. The word *minute* now signifies the original of a notarial deed or instrument which remains in the notary's protocol. *See* GROSSE.

Miscellaneous register. *See* DIVERSE AKTEN.

Misdaadén (D.) [sing. *misdaad*], crimes. Van der Linden says (*Institutes*, 2, 1, 1): "By crimes [*misdaaden*] are understood the voluntary and injurious acts which are not only contrary to law, but to which also punishments are affixed by law."

Miserabile depositum, the name given in Roman law to a deposit which the depositor had been forced to make by sudden and unforeseen misfortune, such as fire, shipwreck or tumult. If the depositary denied having received the thing, he was condemned in double its value (*Institutes*, 4, 6, 17). The double penalty fell into disuse in the Roman-Dutch law, the depositary in such a case being liable only for compensation (Schorer, *Note* 325).

Misfeasance, a trespass; the improper and injurious exercise of lawful authority; the improper performance of a lawful act.

Misprision of treason. "Every one who knows that any other person has committed high treason, and does not within a reasonable time give information thereof to a judge of assize or a justice of the peace, is guilty of *misprision of treason*" (Stephen's *Digest of the Criminal Law*, 5th ed. p. 121). The expression *misprision of treason* is used, probably for the first time in a South African statute, in sec. 49 of Ordinance 72 of 1830 (C.C.). *See* TREASON.

Missio in possessionem, putting in possession; a process of Roman law granted by the praetor to one of the parties to an action for the purpose of protecting property to which the latter claimed to be entitled. One of the forms of the *missio in possessionem* was that given to legatees or fideicommissaries (*legatorum vel fideicommissorum servandorum causa*) when the heir did not give proper security, the effect being to put them in possession of the whole estate of the deceased until security was given. The *missio in possessionem rei servandae causa* was that given to a creditor where the debtor had been ordered to give security for the delivery of property to which the creditor would be entitled at a future date and had failed to give such security. Another kind was the *immissio damni infecti causa*, given to a person against a neighbour whose property was in a dangerous condition, and who had failed to give security against apprehended damage (*cautio damni infecti*). The procedure by way of the *missio in possessionem* is now obsolete in our law (*Central South African Railways* v. *Geldenhuis Main Reef G. M. Co., Ltd.*, [1907] T.H. 270).

Mistake, to act or to be under a misapprehension or misconception; to commit an error. *See* ERROR. See also *Van der Byl and Others* v. *Van der Byl & Co.* (16 S.C. 338).

Mixed statutes or laws. Civilians divided laws into three classes, namely, personal, real and mixed statutes, meaning by statutes not legislative enactments, but the whole municipal law of a State. *Mixed statutes or laws* are those which prescribe the formalities and solemnities of acts or deeds. The rule with reference to them is that acts done or deeds executed in accordance with the formalities and solemnities of the law of the place where they are so done or executed are valid everywhere, unless there is an express law to the contrary or they have been executed elsewhere in fraud of the law of the domicile (Van der Keessel, *Thes.* 39). *See* EXTRA TERRITORIUM JUS DICENTI IMPUNE NON PARETUR; LOCUS REGIT ACTUM.

Mobilia non habent sequelam, movables cannot be followed up. This was a rule of Teutonic law, according to which if the owner of a movable lent it to another, and the latter sold it openly to a third person, the owner lost his right of vindicating the property, the title of the innocent purchaser being regarded as better than that of the owner. A contrary principle obtained in the Roman law, which allowed the *dominus* to follow up and recover his property by a real action from any person in whose hands it might be. Here the maxims were *nemo potest in alium transferre plus quam ipse haberet* and *id quod nostrum est sine facto nostro ad alium transferri non potest.* The law of Holland followed the Roman law subject to certain exceptions (see Ant. Matth. *Paroem.* No. 7), one of which, viz., where goods have been sold in market overt, has given rise to considerable diversity of opinion in South Africa. In the Transvaal it has been held in *Retief* v. *Hamerslach* (1 C.L.J. 346) that goods which have been sold in market overt cannot be recovered by the true owner unless he tenders the price paid for them. The courts of Cape

Colony, on the other hand, hold that the doctrine of market overt does not form part of the law of the colony, and that even in this case the rightful owner may vindicate his property (*Van der Merwe* v. *Webb*, 3 E.D.C. 97; *Woodhead, Plant & Co.* v. *Gunn*, 11 S.C. 4).

The maxim, however, applies so as to exclude the preference afforded by a general mortgage, conventional or legal, or a special mortgage of movables without delivery, where the property is subsequently alienated by the pledgor, or pledged by him to a third party who has obtained delivery, or where it has been taken in execution by a judgment creditor of the pledgor (see Maasdorp's *Institutes* (2nd ed.), vol. 2, p. 306). A contrary rule prevails in Natal, where it has been held that a pledge without possession by a registered bond over movables is good against a *bonâ fide* purchaser (*Turner* v. *Colville*, 4 N.L.R. 6) or an execution creditor (*Trew & Snow* v. *Crabb*, 26 N.L.R. 150, where the subject is fully discussed from the Natal Supreme Court view).

Mobilia non habent situm, movables have no locality. *See* MOBILIA SEQUUNTUR PERSONAM.

Mobilia sequuntur personam, movables follow the person. Movable property is said to have no locality, by which is meant not that it has no visible locality, but that it is subject to the law which governs the person of the owner, *i.e.* the *lex domicilii* or law of the place of his domicile. Thus the disposition of such property and its transmission by succession is governed by that law. For example, a transfer or conveyance of movables executed according to the law of the domicile of the owner would be valid even though it was not in accordance with the requisites of the law of the place where it was situated (Story, *Conflict of Laws*, secs. 377 and 380). The *lex domicilii* in the case of the *inter vivos* transfer of movables does not, however, operate to the exclusion of the *lex rei sitae*, for it is settled that if movables are disposed of according to the law of the country where they are the disposition is valid everywhere, as where the property in a movable is transferred in virtue of a judgment of the courts of the country in which it is situated. (See *Cammell* v. *Sewell*, 3 H. & N. 138; 27 L.J. Exch. 447; 29 L.J. Exch. 350; *Castrique* v. *Imrie*, L.R. 4 H.L. 414, and at p. 429; *Hooper* v. *Gumm*, L.R. 2 Ch. App. 282; *City Bank* v. *Barrow*, 5 A.C. 664.) So, too, the succession to the movable estate of a person is determined by the law of his domicile at the time of his death. Thus where a person domiciled in this country dies intestate, leaving movable property situated in England, the succession to such property is regulated by Roman-Dutch and not by English law; while the succession in such a case to immovable property situated in England would be governed by English law as being the *lex rei sitae*.

Modus, mode or manner. Where a legacy is bequeathed for some object or purpose, *e.g.* "to build a house for John," it is said to be left subject to a *modus*.

Moedwillige verlating (D.), malicious desertion of husband by wife or *vice versâ*. Also known as *malitieuze desertie*. *See* MALICIOUS DESERTION.

Molliter manus imponere, to lay one's hands gently on (another). As a general rule no one is entitled to take the law into his own hands, but where he can by a gentle degree of force prevent an infringement of his rights of person or property, he may employ such force without being legally answerable for the act. Thus a person may push aside another who wilfully obstructs him while walking along a public path, and in an action for assault may state that he laid hands on the other gently. So, if a proprietor in erecting a fence takes in part of his neighbour's land, the latter may throw down the fence and remove the trespass (*Incorporated Diamond Mining Co.* v. *Gordon Mining Co.*, 1 A.C. 135).

Momboir (D.), a guardian; a manager and protector of parentless children (Van Leeuwen's *Comm.* Kotzé's trans. vol. 1, p. 125).

Mond-borg (D.), a guardian; a manager and protector of parentless children (Van Leeuwen's *Comm.* Kotzé's trans. vol. 1, p. 125).

Money, current coin. In statutes regulating parliamentary or other elections the term is usually employed in a wider sense. See Act 26 of 1902 (C.C.), sec. 2; Ordinance 1 of 1903 (T.), sec. 3.

Monopoly, an exclusive privilege granted by the sovereign power to an individual or corporation. Van Leeuwen in his *Comm.* (Kotzé's trans. vol. 2, p. 163) describes *monopoly* as the buying up of articles and the causing of dearth in all transactions, commerce, handicraft and trade; and adds it was expressly forbidden in the Netherlands by several placaats and ordinances. *Monopolies* were also forbidden in England (with certain exceptions, such as patents) by the Statute of Monopolies, 21 Jac. 1, c. 3.

Month. In the Cape Interpretation of Statutes Act (5 of 1883), sec. 3, a *month* is defined as a calendar *month*. See Act 34 of 1886, sec. 5 (*h*), where a similar definition is given.

As to Natal, see *Paruk* v. *Hayne & Co.* (27 N.L.R. at p. 382), where *month* was held to mean a calendar *month;* also schedule to Law 3 of 1887.

As to Transvaal, see Proclamation 15 of 1902, sec. 2.

As to Orange River Colony, see Ordinance 28 of 1902, sec. 1.

In England in the construction of a document the meaning of *month* is lunar month, except where a contrary custom of a trade or place be proved, or a contrary intention appears either from the document to be construed or from surrounding contemporaneous circumstances; see *Bruner* v. *Moore* ([1904] 1 Ch. 305; 89 L.T. 738; 20 T.L.R. 125; 73 L.J. Ch. 377).

Moord (D.), murder. "The meaning of murder [*moord*] implies: (*a*) that some one was killed or mortally wounded; (*b*) that this was done with a premeditated and wilful intention; (*c*) that the object of the person committing the act was to derive some gain or advantage from it" (Van der Linden's *Institutes*, Juta's trans. p. 216). In Holland at the beginning of the nineteenth century "breaking on the wheel" was the usual capital punishment for the crime of *moord*. *See* MURDER.

Moordbrand (D.). "*Moordbrand* was arson committed with the view of burning to death those inside a house. The houses were constructed of wood and roofed in with reeds or straw. If the doors were closed the inmates, together with all the property in the house, could easily be destroyed. Hence the seriousness of this offence" (article by Mr. Justice Kotzé on *History of Roman-Dutch Law* in 26 S.A.L.J. 58, *in not.*).

Morgen-gave (D.), the gift which either of the spouses presented to the other on the morning after the marriage night. "The *morgen-gave*, or morning gift, wont to be given on the morning after the marriage as the reward of chastity, although it ought from its nature to accrue to the wife immediately, is according to our customs acquired only after the marriage has been dissolved and the creditors discharged" (Van der Keessel, *Thes.* 258).

Morghen spraak (D.). To hold a *morghen spraak* meant to assemble and deliberate upon matters concerning the country, town or village. This was a practice of the citizens of the towns of Holland. The term owes its origin to the fact that according to the customs of the ancient Germans public matters were disposed of in the morning or early part of the day when people were sober.

Mortgage is that privilege over the property of another which tends to the security of a debt or personal claim (Grotius' *Introd.* 2, 48, 1). "The word *mortgage* is a generic term comprising *hypothec* or mortgage proper on the one hand, and *pledge* on the other, the latter being constituted by actual delivery of possession and the former without. The word also covers what is more usually expressed by the term *lien*, that is, the right of retaining property, of which one is in actual possession, until a debt is paid" (Maasdorp's *Institutes*, vol. 2, p. 222). *Mortgages* are divided into three classes: conventional, tacit or legal, and judicial.

"A *mortgage* of immovable property in Roman-Dutch law is a document declaring the property to be security for the debt, made out by a conveyancer and registered in the Deeds Office against the title of the mortgaged property. The mortgagor remains the owner of the property. If the debt is not paid at the stipulated time, an action is brought for an order of court condemning the mortgagor to pay the sum due with interest and costs of the action, and declaring the property executable" (Morice's *English and Roman-Dutch Law*,

2nd ed. p. 57). Berwick, in a note to his *Translation of Voet* (new ed. p. 269), says the word *mortgage* is not known to the civil law, but is an invention of the middle ages.

In Natal there are certain restrictions on contracts of natives founded on *mortgage* bonds, promissory notes and other liquid documents of debt (see Law 44 of 1887, sec. 8); also in respect of similar obligations executed by Indians (see Act 48 of 1904).

Mortgagee, the person in whose favour a mortgage is passed. As to rights of mortgagees in Natal in reference to judicial sales, see Law 17 of 1866; and as to rights of mortgagees in insolvency, see Law 47 of 1887, sec. 122.

Mortgagor, the person who passes or grants a mortgage in favour of another person, called the mortgagee.

Mortis causa capio, acquisition *mortis causa*; a term which includes all kinds of acquisition in respect of a person's death (Voet's *Comm.* 39, 6, 9 and 10).

Movable property, otherwise called movable things. "Movable things are such as are capable of being moved about from one place to another, however heavy they may be, and whether they be individual things or what are called *fungibles,* that is, things which are dealt with by number, weight or measure. A ship, for instance, is movable property" (Maasdorp's *Institutes*, vol. 2, p. 5). Correlative to immovable property. May be said to be equivalent, roughly speaking, to the "personal property" of English law.

The question whether a structure is movable or immovable is one which depends upon the circumstances of each case. In *Olivier and Others* v. *Haarhof & Co.* ([1906] T.S. 497) Innes, C.J., said: "The points chiefly to be considered are the nature of the structure, the way in which it is fixed, and the intention of the person who erected it. And of these the last point is in some respects the most important." See also *Victoria Falls Power Co.* v. *Colonial Treasurer* ([1909] T.S. 140), and *Deputy-Sheriff of Pretoria* v. *Heymann* ([1909] T.S. 280).

In the Native Territories Penal Code (Act 24 of 1886 (C.C.), sec. 5) the expression *movable property* is defined to "include corporeal property of every description, except land and things attached to the earth or permanently fastened to anything attached to the earth."

In the Transvaal Foreign Trustees and Liquidators Recognition Act (7 of 1907), *movable property* means "every kind of property, and every right, interest or asset which is not immovable property."

Muid, the old measure of a *muid* was abolished in the Orange River Colony by Law 25 of 1898, sec. 15; it was equivalent to four bushels.

Mumba, a native term. *See* Ungoliso.

Municipal area. This term is defined in the Cape School Board Act (35 of 1905), sec. 3, to mean "the area comprised within the limits of any duly constituted municipality, or under the control of a village management board."

Municipal law is that law which derives its origin from the will of the supreme power of a State. Grotius' *Introd.* 1, 2, 13; Wessels' *History*, p. 286; Stephen's *Comm.* vol. 1, p. 12.

Munitions of war. This expression is defined in Law 16 of 1862 (N.), sec. 12, to mean and include "gunpowder, gun caps, flints, cartridges, saltpetre, sulphur, lead, zinc and pewter."

Murder "is unlawful homicide with malice aforethought" (Stephen's *Digest of the Criminal Law*, 5th ed. p. 182). *See* MOORD.

Mutatis mutandis, things being changed which are to be changed.

Mutual life insurance company. This expression is defined in the Cape Additional Taxation Act (36 of 1904), sec. 42, to mean "a company carrying on the business of granting policies of assurance, or endowment or annuities on human life, and which is not a company that pays or credits dividends or profits to shareholders in such company."

Mutual will, a will made by husband and wife in the one document. The *mutual will* of a husband and wife, notwithstanding its form, is to be read as the separate will of each. The dispositions of each spouse are to be treated as applicable to his or her half of the joint property. Each is at liberty to revoke his or her part of the will during the co-testator's lifetime, with or without communication with the co-testator, as also after the co-testator's death; but where a spouse who first dies has bequeathed any benefit in favour of the survivor, and has afterwards limited the disposal of the property in general after the death of such survivor, then such survivor, if he or she accepts such benefits, may not afterwards dispose of his or her share in any manner at variance with the will of the deceased spouse (*South African Association* v. *Mostert*, Buch. 1873, p. 31).

Naamlooze societeit, an anonymous partnership, that is, where two or more persons agree to participate in a certain business and it is stipulated that the same shall be carried on by one of them in his own name (Van der Linden's *Institutes*, 4, 1, 12). *See* ANONYMOUS PARTNERSHIP.

Naasten (D.), to retract, *naasting*, retraction (*retractus*). *See* JUS RETRACTUS; NAASTING.

Naasting (D.), the right of retraction, equivalent to the *jus retractus*. "*Naasting* (*jus retractus*) is the right of a person over immovable property, as also against the purchaser and seller thereof, to step into the place of the purchaser whenever the property is sold" (Grotius' *Introd.* Maasdorp's trans. p. 254. See also Van Leeuwen's *Comm.* 4, 19; Van der Keessel, *Thes.* 645). The right of *naasting* does not apply to transactions of barter, see Grotius' *Introd.* 3, 31, 6. *See* JUS RETRACTUS.

Nagelvriendt (D.). *See* NAGHELMAAGHE.

Naghelmaaghe, nagelvriendt (D.), a blood relation in the seventh degree.

Nahuur (D.), the right of retraction set up by the prior lessee against a new lessee. See Van Leeuwen's *Comm.* Kotzé's trans. vol. 2, pp. 168 and 176, translator's notes.

Named policy "is one in which the adventure is limited to a ship specifically named therein, as where goods by the ship *Emma* are insured from Hamburg to London" (Arnould's *Marine Insurance*, 7th ed. sec. 9).

Namptissement (D.), a technical term for "provisional sentence." Sometimes called *handvulling*. It "is a provisional payment by means of an interlocutory judgment, and by which the defendant, if he does not deny the debt, is condemned provisionally to pay the sum subject to security *de restituendo*. In course of time this technical term was gradually dropped by practitioners in Holland in favour of the words *provisie* or *provisioneel*, or *provisie van namptissement*, and hence the use of the term 'provisional sentence' in our practice" (Van Zyl's *Judicial Practice*, 2nd ed. p. 65, *q.v.*). See 1 Menz. 6; and PROVISIONAL SENTENCE.

"*Namptissement* is also founded upon this, that a person who cannot deny his signature or other debt may not have any extension of time, and whatever he has to urge against it (in defence) must immediately appear, or if he sets up a defence, which requires further investigation, he must pay provisionally (*namptiseeren en handvulling doen*)" (Van Leeuwen's *Comm.* Kotzé's trans. vol. 2, p. 125).

Native case, an expression used in Natal in the Courts Act (49 of 1898), where, with certain exceptions, it means "a civil case in which all the parties are natives, or a criminal case in which the accused person, or, if more than one, all the accused persons are natives."

Native chief, a person holding the position of chief in a native tribe. But see Act 49 of 1898 (N.), sec. 5, where the term is used in a more extended sense and includes district headmen. *See* CHIEF.

Native foreigner. Under the Cape Native Pass Law (Act 22 of 1867) a *native foreigner* is defined as follows: "For the purposes of this Act the term *native foreigner* shall be taken to mean any member of any tribe, other than a Fingo, of which the principal chief shall live beyond the borders of the colony."

Native gold is defined in the Natal Mines and Collieries Act (43 of 1899), sec. 4, as follows: "*Native gold* includes gold or precious metal in whatever form, although smelted, which is not manufactured or made up into any article suitable for trading purposes. It also includes raw gold or other precious metal and amalgam." *See* UNWROUGHT GOLD.

Native High Court, a court established in Natal by Act 49 of 1898 for the trial of certain native cases. For its constitution, jurisdiction, &c., see the Act just referred to.

Native law, that law which is specially applicable to natives. As to *Native law* in Natal, see Law 28 of 1865; Law 26 of 1875; and Law 19 of 1891, which legalises the Code of *Native law* in Natal.

Native Territories Penal Code. A penal code passed in the Cape Colony by Act 24 of 1886. It took effect on the 1st January, 1887, throughout the whole of the territories known as the Transkei (including Gcalekaland), Griqualand East, Tembuland (including Emigrant Tembuland and Bomvanaland), and the port and territory of St. John's River, all which are styled in the Code the "Transkeian Territories." By Proclamation 112 of 1886 this Code was extended to all Native Territories; by Proclamation 340 of 1894 it was extended to East and West Pondoland; and by Proclamation 180 of 1905 to Walfish Bay. The Code has been amended by the Transkeian Territories Penal Code Amendment Act (41 of 1898); and by the Better Administration of Justice Act (35 of 1904).

Native township.—In the Cape Establishment of Native Townships Act (44 of 1908), sec. 1, "*native township* shall mean any area being private property which has been divided, or which it may hereafter be proposed to divide, into more than fifteen erven or more than such greater number of erven as the divisional council may fix by resolution duly approved by the Governor, and thereafter notified to the Registrar of Deeds, and by notice published in the *Gazette* and in a local paper circulating in the division in which such private property is situate, the said erven being owned or occupied by natives or under offer of sale or lease to natives."

Natives. The term *natives* is defined in the East London Municipality Amendment Act (12 of 1895 (C.C.)), to mean "any person or persons belonging to any of the native races of Africa, such as Kafirs, Fingoes, Basutos, Zulus, Hottentots, Bushmen and the like." See also Act 28 of 1898 (C.C.), sec. 5; Act 6 of 1899 (C.C.), sec. 23, where the definition is extended to "any Kafir, Zulu, Fingo, Basuto, Damara,

Hottentot, Bechuana, Bushman, Koranna or other aboriginal native of South or Central Africa;" Act 31 of 1899 (C.C.), sec. 26; Act 40 of 1902 (C.C.), sec. 1; Act 44 of 1908 (C.C.) sec. 1.

For definitions in Natal, see Law 28 of 1865, sec. 37; Act 49 of 1898, sec. 5; Act 1 of 1899, sec. 5; Act 38 of 1896, sec. 4; Law 19 of 1891, sec. 12; and especially Law 14 of 1888, and Law 10 of 1891, which define the meaning of the word *native*. Also see Act 1 of 1906, sec. 3; *Superintendent of Police, Pietermaritzburg*, v. *Alfred* (27 N.L.R. 368).

For Transvaal, see Transvaal Proclamation 37 of 1901, sec. 4; Proclamation 28 of 1902, sec. 72; in Ordinance 43 of 1902, *native* includes "every person belonging to any of the aboriginal races or tribes of Africa south of the equator, and every person one of whose parents belongs to any such race or tribe as aforesaid." In Ordinance 58 of 1903 *native* means "any person both of whose parents belong to any aboriginal race or tribe of Africa," and Act 9 of 1908 (Native Tax Act) gives the same definition. See also Urban Areas Native Pass Act (18 of 1909), sec. 2.

See *Queen* v. *Parrott*, 16 S.C. 452.

Natural fruits, fruits produced without the aid of man; *fructus naturales*.

Natural guardian. "The father is . . . the natural guardian of his children, looks after their interests during their minority, and can bring actions on their behalf. If the father dies the mother always retains the control over her children to which she is entitled by natural law" (Wessels' *History*, p. 422; see also Maasdorp's *Institutes*, vol. 1, p. 230; Grotius' *Introd.* 1, 7, 8).

Natural law. *See* LAW OF NATURE.

Natural wine. "*Natural wine* or *pure natural wine* means the product solely of the alcoholic fermentation of the juice or must of fresh grapes without the addition of any foreign substance as hereinafter [in the Act] defined, before, during or after the making of the same" (the Wine, Brandy, Whisky and Spirits Act, 42 of 1906 (C.C.), sec. 5).

Naturalisation, one of the modes in which British nationality may be acquired; the procedure by which, under certain circumstances, an alien is converted into a British naturalised subject. See Act 2 of 1883 (C.C.) and amending statutes; Act 18 of 1905 (N.); Ordinance 46 of 1902 (T.); Ordinance 10 of 1904 (T.); Ordinance 1 of 1903 (O.R.C.) and Ordinance 7 of 1905 (O.R.C.).

Naturellen (D.), natives.

Naval service, in the Natal Foreign Enlistment Act (26 of 1906), sec. 30, is defined to include "as respects a person . . . service as a marine, employment as a pilot in piloting or directing the course of a ship of war or other ship when such ship of war or other ship is being used in any military or naval operation, and any employment whatever on board a ship of war, transport, store ship, privateer, or ship under letters of marque; and as respects a ship include any user of a ship as a transport, store ship, privateer, or ship under letters of marque." See also Ordinance 1 of 1906 (T.), sec. 30 of sch.

Navvy. *See* SERVANT.

Ne continentia causae dividatur, that the contents of the cause should not be divided; an exception which may be opposed to the creditor of an insolvent who seeks to recover his debt in any other place than the *locus concursus creditorum*. *See* LOCUS CONCURSUS CREDITORUM.

Ne exeat familia, that it shall not go out of the family; a prohibition which is sometimes attached to a testamentary bequest of property. Such a prohibition does not extend beyond the fourth generation, unless there is clear proof of the testator's intention that it should be so extended. Grotius (*Introd.* 2, 20, 11) states that a prohibition of alienation out of the family, even if made perpetual by the testator, cannot extend beyond the fourth generation, but this is not supported by the weight of authority (Schorer, *Note* 144; Groenewegen, note 22 on above passage of Grotius; Voet's *Comm.* 36, 1, 33; Van Leeuwen's *Comm.* 3, 8, 7). It would, however, appear from the case of *Ryklief's Heirs* v. *Rykliefs Executors* (13 S.C. 64) that a very strong expression of the testator's intention will be required to rebut the presumption that the prohibition is not to be extended beyond the fourth generation.

Ne luminibus officiatur, that lights shall not be obstructed. *See* SERVITUS LUMINIS NON OFFICIENDI.

Ne quid in flumine publico ripave ejus fiat, quo aliter aqua fluat, atque uti priore aestate fluxit, that nothing be done upon a public river or stream or upon its banks whereby the water may flow otherwise than it did in the preceding summer. An interdict in these terms may be obtained by any member of the public against any one who attempts to interfere with the accustomed flow of the water of a public stream. *See* FLUMEN PUBLICUM.

Ne quid in flumine publico ripave ejus fiat, quo pejus navigetur, that nothing be done on a public stream or its banks whereby it may be worse to navigate; the interdict which is given against those who interfere in any way with the navigation of a public stream.

Nec vi, nec clam, nec precario, neither by force, nor by stealth, nor by request. The Roman law of possession of immovable property was secured by the interdict called, from the first words, *uti possidetis*, but the party applying for the interdict was entitled to it only where he had not obtained possession by force or by stealth, or by request, from the person against whom the interdict was sought. So, although neither *bona fides* nor *justus titulus* is required for the acquisition of immovable property by the *prescriptio longissimi temporis*, it is necessary in the Roman-Dutch as in the Roman law that the person should have possessed the property *nec vi, nec clam, nec precario.*

Necessariae impensae, expenses that are necessary for the preservation of the property. See *United Building Society* v. *Smookler's Trustees* ([1906] T.S. at p. 627).

Necessaries, reasonable household expenses for food and clothing, in respect of which a wife may bind herself and her husband (*Grassmann* v. *Hoffman*, 3 S.C. 282). See *Mason* v. *Bernstein* (14 S.C. 504).

"**Necessary power.**" An authority to the trustees of a company to sign the *necessary power* to mortgage its property is such a power as is necessary to have the mortgage bond passed, and includes the "general clause" (*Ex parte Grand Hotel and Theatre Co., Ltd., in liqu.*, [1908] O.R.C. at p. 22).

Necessity. *See* "Road of Necessity."

Negative servitude "prevents the owner of the soil from doing something thereon or making some use thereof, which, but for the existence of the servitude, he would have been entitled to do; *e.g. Servitus non altius tollendi; ne luminibus officiatur*, &c." (Van Leeuwen's *Comm.* Kotzé's trans. vol. 1, Decker's *note* on p. 306).

Negligence. "From a general view of the subject it may be concluded that legal *negligence* consists for the most part in the breach, or omission, of a legal duty, which may be either unintentional, as is usually the case, or intentional, as is sometimes the case. This duty may be either one imposed by the rules of civil society, in which case the violation of it is a tort, or one voluntarily assumed by contract, in which the failure is a breach of contract. Whence it appears that *negligence*, in its legal aspect, is of two distinct sorts, the one springing out of relations resting in contract, and the other not. In the one case there is an action sounding in tort, and in the other there is an action for breach of contract. It is clear that the same definitions and the same rules of law cannot equally apply to each, and that in consequence it is always necessary to consider *negligence* in this dual aspect. While accurate and scientific knowledge, clear thinking and precise expression as to the principles of law governing this subject are possible, to define the term *negligence* in its legal sense—in its application to all human interests as they may become subjects of litigation, or to reduce the law of *negligence* to rules of mathematical completeness and precision, as one writes magic squares—is hopelessly out of the question" (Beach on *Contributory Negligence*, 3rd ed. sec. 6). See *Jameson's Minors* v. *Central South African Railways* ([1908] T.S. at p. 586).

Negotiation. "A bill is negotiated when it is transferred from one person to another in such a manner as to constitute the transferee the holder of the bill; a bill payable to bearer is negotiated by delivery; a bill payable to order is negotiated by the indorsement of the holder completed by delivery" (sec. 31 of English Bills of Exchange Act of 1882; Act 19 of 1893 (C.C.), sec. 29; Law 8 of 1887 (N.), sec. 30; Proclamation 11 of 1902 (T.), sec. 29; Ordinance 28 of 1902 (O.R.C.), sec. 29; Regulation 23 of 1895 (R.), sec. 29).

Negotiorum gestio, lit. management of affairs; unauthorised management; the name given in Roman law to the quasi-contract which arises where a person undertakes the management of the affairs of another in his absence without having received any mandate, express or implied, from him (Voet's *Comm.* 3, 5, 1; Grotius' *Introd.* 3, 27, 1). The person who takes upon himself such management, called *negotiorum gestor*, is entitled to be reimbursed for the expenses incurred by him. On the other hand, he is bound to exercise the highest degree of diligence in the course of his actings (Voet's *Comm.* 3, 5, 4; Grotius' *Introd.* 3, 27, 3). In some cases, however, he is liable only for *culpa lata*, as where he intervenes in affairs which have already been neglected (Voet, *ibid.*; Schorer, *Note* 439).

Neighbour, one who lives in close proximity to another. The expression *neighbour* was discussed in *Nel and Others* v. *Potgieter and Others* (1 A.C. 22), where the following condition was embodied in a deed of grant: "That he [the grantee] shall have only four days at a time during the seasons the use of the water [meaning a stream called the Congo River] in succession with his *neighbours,* who now or hereafter may be dependant on the stream for the use of their respective lands;" De Villiers, C.J., held that the servitude must be construed strictly, and that the word *neighbour* in that case must be confined to the proprietor of the next adjoining farm.

Nemine contradicente, no one objecting; without opposition.

Nemo alteri stipulari potest, no one can stipulate for another. It was a rule of Roman law that a person could not make a binding promise that an act should be done by a third person, unless a penalty was added for non-performance, or unless from the question and answer of the *stipulatio* it was clear that the promisor undertook to do the act himself in the event of non-performance by the third party. This principle was rejected alike by the Canon and the Roman-Dutch law, according to which if a person promises the performance of an act on the part of another he is understood to oblige himself to see that the act is performed or to pay damages for non-performance (Grotius' *Introd.* 3, 3, 3; Voet, 45, 1, 5).

Nemo dat quod non habet, no one gives that which he has not. *See* NEMO PLUS JURIS AD ALIUM TRANSFERRE POTEST QUAM IPSE HABET.

Nemo debet bis vexari, the maxim in which is expressed the principle of law that no one ought to be put twice to trouble for the same offence. *See* AUTREFOIS CONVICT; RES JUDICATA.

Nemo debet esse judex in propria causa, no one should be a judge in his own cause. No rule in connection with the administration of justice is more settled than that contained in the above maxim, which applies equally to the case where the judge has an interest in the cause as to where he is a direct party to it. Thus, where a servant was under the Master and Servants Law (C.C.) convicted before his master, sitting as a special justice of the peace, of having used abusive and insulting language to his master, it was held that the conviction must be quashed (*Queen* v. *Plaatjes*, 12 S.C. 351; see also *Paarl Board of Executors* v. *Paarl Civil Commissioner*, Buch. 1870, p. 1; *Binda* v. *Simpkins*, 5 E.D.C. 239; *Pretorius* v. *Richmond Divisional Council*, Buch. 1875, p. 78; *Dyke* v. *De Villiers*, 1 S.C. 375; *Queen* v. *Phillip and Jack*, 6 E.D.C. 194; *Vos* v. *Colonial Government*, 15 N.L.R. 228; Ordinance 40 of 1828 (C.C.), sec. 5 (ii); Proclamation 14 of 1902 (T.), sec. 19 (2); Ordinance 4 of 1902 (O.R.C.), sec. 26 (2).

Nemo debet locupletari cum alterius detrimento, no one should gain profit to the detriment of another; a maxim of Roman law which is applied to cases where the person seeking the profit has suffered no loss, and the person from whom the profit is sought has incurred no legal obligation. Thus where a *bonâ fide* possessor makes improvements on land belonging to another, the owner, although entitled to the improvements as an accessory of the land, is bound to compensate such *bonâ fide* possessor for the improvements to the extent to which the land has been enhanced in value (*De Beers Consolidated Mines* v. *London and South African Exploration Co.*, 10 S.C. 359; 3 C.T.R. 438). In the same way, while a lessee is deprived after the expiration of his term of the ownership of materials affixed by him, he is allowed to recover from the lessor the cost of those materials if they have been affixed with the landlord's consent (*ibid.*). So, where a person loses his property by *specificatio, confusio, commixtio*, or any other like mode of accession, he must be compensated by the person who acquires the same. Again, although a minor is not bound by contracts made by him during minority, he is always liable where he has benefited by such contracts to the extent of the benefit. It is upon the same principle that a *negotiorum gestor* is entitled to recover the amount expended by him on behalf of the absent person whose affairs he has managed.

Nemo errans rem suam amittit, no one loses his property by mistake. Mistake as to the ownership of a thing, where it is such as to be inconsistent with the intention to alienate, prevents transfer of the property by delivery. Thus if an agent or the guardian of a minor transfers to another his own property as if it belonged respectively to his principal or the minor the ownership is not lost and the alienation is null, because no one loses his property by mistake

(*Digest*, 41, 1, 35; Voet's *Comm.* 41, 1, 35; see also *Digest*, 18, 1, 15, 2). Voet (*ibid.*), following Marcellus, lays down a contrary rule where a person in good faith purchases from another a thing which belongs to his agent, and takes possession of it, and thereafter this agent upon his mandate sells the thing to another in ignorance of the fact that it is his own property. In such a case the agent is bound to make transfer to the purchaser, and if he has already done so he has no right to vindicate the property.

Nemo in dubio praesumitur donare velle aut suum jactare, no one, in a case of doubt, is presumed to intend to give or to make away with his own property. *See* DONATIO NON PRAESUMITUR.

Nemo mori potest pro parte testatus pro parte intestatus, no one can die partly testate and partly intestate. This rule of the civil law (*Dig.* 50, 17, 7) does not apply in the Roman-Dutch law, according to which an heir may be instituted either wholly or in part, the remaining part in the latter case being distributed according to the rules of intestate succession (Voet's *Comm.* 28, 5, 26; Grotius' *Introd.* 2, 18, 19; Van der Keessel, *Thes.* 309).

Nemo moriturus praesumitur mentiri, no one is presumed guilty of falsehood when he is about to die. *See* IN ARTICULO MORTIS.

Nemo plus juris ad alium transferre potest quam ipse habet, no one can transfer to another a greater right than he has himself. Thus if a person grants a servitude over a piece of land which only belongs to him for his life, the servitude will lapse at his death. So where a person comes into possession of stolen property, the real owner may recover it from him whether he acquired the property *bonâ fide* or *malâ fide*, and whether from the thief directly or from some one who acquired from the latter. To this rule as to the right of the owner to follow up and recover his property when stolen there are some exceptions, one of which, namely, that with regard to property sold in market overt, has been the subject of conflicting decisions in South Africa (see *Retief* v. *Hamerslach*, 2 Kotzé, 177; *Van der Merwe* v. *Webb*, 3 E.D.C. 97; and *Woodhead, Plant & Co.* v. *Gunn*, 11 S.C. 11). There are also other exceptions to the rule expressed in the maxim. For example, a holder in due course may enforce payment of a bill of exchange notwithstanding defects of title of prior parties and of personal defences available to prior parties among themselves. Thus where a bill has been drawn and accepted for a gambling debt, the drawer would have no right of action against the acceptor, but if he indorsed the bill for value to one who was ignorant of the ground of debt, such indorsee would be entitled to sue upon the bill.

Nemo potest exuere patriam, no one can disclaim his native country. This was a maxim of British constitutional law until 1870.

By the Naturalisation Act, however, of that year a British subject may become naturalised in a foreign State, and will thereupon cease to be a British subject.

Nemo praecise ad factum cogi potest, no one can be compelled specifically to do a thing. This maxim, which was once considered to express a principle of our law (*Schmidt* v. *Francke*, 1 Menz. 334), is no longer held to be applicable. It is now settled that a person who has come under an obligation either to do or to give a thing may be ordered to make specific performance, and, failing performance, as decreed, may be compelled thereto by means of civil imprisonment. Thus if a seller refuses to deliver the thing sold the purchaser need not be content with a claim for damages for the loss caused by non-delivery, but may compel the purchaser to deliver the property if it is still in his power to do so (*Cohen* v. *Shires, McHattie and King*, Kotzé's Rep. 1880–84, p. 48; *Thompson* v. *Pullinger*, 1. Off. Rep. Webber's trans. 298; *Westhuizen* v. *Velenski*, 8 C.T.R. 273; *Silverton Estates Co.* v. *Bellevue Syndicate*, [1904] T.S. 467; Grotius' *Introd.* 3, 15, 6; Van der Keessel, *Thes.* 512; Van Leeuwen's *Comm.* 4, 2, 13; 4, 18, 1). Where it has become impossible for the promisor to fulfil his obligation, as where a seller has resold to a third party, who was ignorant of the prior sale, specific performance will not be decreed; the only remedy in such cases being a claim for damages.

Nemo sibi causam possessionis mutare potest, no one can change for himself the ground of his possession. In other words, a possessor cannot change the ground upon which he has hitherto held possession by a mere declaration of intention. Thus a person who has unlawful possession of a thing cannot become its lawful possessor by assuming that he holds the thing upon some lawful ground or title. A new ground of possession may, however, be acquired by the intervention of some external act or fact, either actual or constructive. Thus an unlawful possessor who purchases the ownership begins from the time of the purchase to possess lawfully as owner. In the same way a depositary who converts the thing deposited with him to his own use, ceases to hold the thing as depositary, and commences to possess it as stolen property (Voet's *Comm.* 41, 2, 13; *Orson* v. *Reynolds*, 3 H.C.G. 231; *Stewart's Executors* v. *De Morgan*, 2 E.D.C. 218; *O'Callaghan's Assignees* v. *Cavanagh*, 2 S.C. 122).

Net profits, that portion of the profits of a business or undertaking which represents the clear gain for a certain period or at a certain date, after deduction of all working costs, losses and depreciation.

In the Cape Precious Stones Amendment Act (27 of 1907), sec. 20, "the term *net profits* shall be taken to mean that profit left after paying all amounts not being capital outlay actually expended during the year in winning and disposing of precious stones, together with salaries, wages, director's fees, auditor's fees, taxes, insurance, printing, stationery, advertising, maintenance of plant and buildings, agencies, legal expenses, survey expenses, arbitration expenses and office expenses."

See Ordinance 4 of 1904 (O.R.C.), sec. 48.

New license, in Ordinance 32 of 1902 (T.), sec. 3, means "a license applied for in respect of premises not licensed for the sale of intoxicating liquor at the date of the application therefor." See also Ordinance 8 of 1903 (O.R.C.), sec. 3.

New street, *see* STREET. See also *Davis* v. *Board of Works for Greenwich Dist.* ([1905] 2 Q.B. 219); *Capetown Town Council* v. *Shenker* (19 S.C. at p. 105); *Woodhead, Plant & Co.* v. *Capetown Town Council* (23 S.C. at p. 354).

Newspaper. For the purposes of the Cape Post Office Act (4 of 1882), a *newspaper* is defined as follows: "Any publication consisting wholly or in great part of political or other news, or of articles relating thereto, or to other current topics, with or without advertisements, and with or without engravings, prints or lithographs illustrative of articles in such newspaper, subject to these conditions: that it be published in numbers or parts at intervals of not more than seven days; that it be printed on a sheet or sheets unstitched; that it have the full title and date of publication printed at the top of the first page, and the whole or part of the title and the date of publication printed at the top of every subsequent page." Newspapers in the Cape Colony must be registered under Act 29 of 1884. As to newspapers in Natal, see Law 9 of 1858.

Next-of-kin, blood relations. "*Next-of-kin* or blood relations, or heirs by blood, when mentioned in a will, are understood as intended to be instituted to the same inheritance to which they would be entitled under the common law of the locality, unless there are clear indications of a different intention" (Grotius' *Introd.* Maasdorp's trans. p. 99). "The term *next-of-kin* means the same thing as "successors *ab intestato*" (Maasdorp's *Institutes*, vol. 1, p. 194).

Night, "the period between sunset and sunrise" (Ordinance 26 of 1904 (T.), sec. 3).

"**No longer needed,**" in reference to the closing of roads by a road board, see *Symons* v. *Estcourt Local Road Board* (25 N.L.R. 38).

Nobile judicium. *See* NOBILE OFFICIUM.

Nobile officium, the discretionary power vested in a judge to award what has not been expressly claimed in an action (Voet's *Comm.* 2, 13, 13). Thus if in a possessory and petitory action, *i.e.* an action in which not only preliminary possession of a thing is claimed, but also the full ownership of it is finally sought, no mention is made of the latter or petitory claim, the court may nevertheless give judgment for both claims, or for the possessory one alone if sufficient evidence has not been adduced to support the petitory claim, or it may give a petitory judgment where the issue between the parties is petitory, but the plaintiff has framed his claim for only a possessory judgment. In the same way a judge may award costs to a successful litigant even though these have not been claimed in the action (Voet's *Comm. ibid.*; see also Van Leeuwen's *Comm.* 4, 4, 2; *Weatherley* v. *Weatherley*, Kotzé's Rep. p. 66). A similar function, under the same name, is regarded as inherent in the Supreme Court of Scotland, but there it seems to have a much wider application than the above, being resorted to in order to "modify or abate the rigour of the law, and, to a certain extent, to give aid where no remedy could be had in a court confined to strict law" (Bell's *Dictionary*, *h.v.*; see also Erskine's *Institutes of the Law of Scotland*, 1, 3, 22).

Nolle prosequi, to be unwilling to prosecute. In each of the South African colonies the right of prosecuting all crimes and offences committed throughout the colony is vested in the Attorney-General. In Cape Colony the Solicitor-General has the same right as regards crimes and offences committed in the Eastern Districts, and the Crown Prosecutor as regards those committed in Griqualand West and Bechuanaland. A refusal on the part of such Crown law officers to prosecute does not operate as *res judicata* so as to prevent a future prosecution for the offence charged. Thus in Cape Colony the Attorney-General can prosecute after the Solicitor-General or the Crown Prosecutor has decided not to do so (*Queen* v. *Pushtu and Hlekiso*, 6 E.D.C. 116). Nor is the Attorney-General barred from taking up the case upon further evidence even if he has himself declined in the first instance to prosecute (*ibid.*). Moreover, should the Attorney-General decline to prosecute there may be a private prosecution at the instance of any person who can show a substantial interest in the issue of the trial arising out of some injury which he individually has sustained by the commission of the alleged crime. As regards actions for malicious prosecution, which cannot be brought until the prosecution is at an end, it has been held that the refusal of the Attorney-General to prosecute gives a sufficient termination to the criminal proceedings to allow of the civil action being tried (*Lemue* v. *Zwaartbooi*, 13 S.C. 403).

The phrase *nolle prosequi* is in current use in Natal (*Ormond* v. *Rex*, 27 N.L.R. 401), but not in the other South African colonies.

Nominal, existing in name only; trivial.

Nominal rent (*tyns regt*) "very much resembles the old emphyteusis, and is a return or rent, often of only a farthing, or the fourth of a stiver, annually, and if it be not paid on the precise day, the property charged with it will be lost and become forfeited" (Van Leeuwen's *Comm.* Kotzé's trans. vol. 1, p. 237, *q.v.* as to origin of *tyns* and the customs observed in Holland in connection therewith). Nominal rents were, in the singular, called *tyns*, and in the plural *tynsen*.

Nomine officii, in name of office; used with reference to a person who sues or is sued in an official character, and generally abbreviated to "*N.O.*"

Non omne quod licet honestum est, not everything which is permitted is honourable or moral. This maxim refers to the distinction which exists between the field of law and that of morality. Many things are permitted or not prohibited by law, which are yet considered unjust or immoral. For example, a man is morally bound to pay even a debt with regard to which the prescriptive period has expired, yet if he should refuse to do so and should avail himself of the plea of prescription the law will give no assistance to his creditor. Again, by the Transfer Duty Proclamation, 8 of 1902 (T.), sec. 30, no contract of sale of fixed property is of any force or effect unless it be in writing and signed by the parties or their agents duly authorised in writing; if, therefore, a person enters into a verbal agreement to sell a farm in the Transvaal, he may afterwards refuse to sign a written deed of sale in respect of the purchase of the property, and the law will not compel him to do so, although his conduct is neither just nor honourable (*Davis* v. *Prinsloo's Executors,* 16 C.L.J. 213; *Auret* v. *Kernick*, 21 S.A.L.J. 64). In the same way, although there is a natural obligation upon a parent to make suitable provision for his children after his death, yet since the abolition of the legitimate portion (Act 23 of 1874 (C.C.), sec. 2; Proclamation 28 of 1902 (T.), sec. 28) he may legally disregard this duty and pass over his children in favour of strangers.

Non quod dictum, sed quod actum est inspicitur, not what has been said, but what has been done, is regarded. This maxim is frequently applied in the construction of contracts, wills and other deeds, where the language used is ambiguous or terms are erroneously employed and it is necessary to determine the true intention of the parties, *i.e.* what they did rather than what they said. The maxim also applies to those cases where the parties for some reason pretend to enter into a certain kind of contract, such as a sale, while the real contract made by them is of another description, such as a pledge (*Fitzpatrick* v. *Dawes,* [1907] E.D.C. at p. 322; see also PLUS VALET QUOD AGITUR QUAM QUOD SIMULATE CONCIPITUR).

Non-business day. *See* BUSINESS DAY.

Non-Cape. In the Non-Cape Trustees and Liquidators Recognition Act, 7 of 1907 (C.C.), sec. 1, *non-Cape* means and includes "every British colony in South Africa other than this [Cape] Colony."

Non-Cape liquidator. "*Non-Cape liquidator* shall include every person duly appointed in any British colony in South Africa, other than in the Cape Colony, for the purpose of winding up any company in such part" (the Non-Cape Trustees and Liquidators Recognition Act, 7 of 1907 (C.C.), sec. 1).

Non-Cape trustee. In the Non-Cape Trustees and Liquidators Recognition Act, 7 of 1907 (C.C.), sec. 1, *non-Cape trustee* includes "every person duly appointed in any British colony in South Africa other than in the Cape Colony for the purpose of administering, liquidating and distributing any bankrupt or insolvent estate in such part."

Nonfeasance, the omission to perform some act which should have been performed. See *O'Shea* v. *Port Elizabeth Town Council* (12 S.C. at p. 158).

Non-joinder, failure to join a necessary and interested party as a plaintiff or defendant in an action.

Noodtweg (D.), a way of necessity.

Noodweer (D.), self-defence. As to killing in self-defence, see Van Leeuwen's *Comm.* Kotzé's trans. vol. 2, p. 277, translator's note.

Noon, the hour of twelve in the daytime. The word *noon,* used to denote the beginning and termination of the risk under an insurance policy, was held, in *Rochester German Insurance Co.* v. *Peaslee-Gauldert Co.* ((Ky.), 1 L. R.A. (N.S.) 364), to be properly interpreted to be standard, and not sun, time, where the use of the former system of reckoning time had been the prevailing custom in the community for a long period.

"**Not checked.**" The words "not checked" added by the checker of common carriers on signing a consignment note, render the document, in the absence of *aliunde* evidence, not binding as a receipt for delivery of the specific number of goods therein stated (*Woolfe, Woolfe & Co.* v. *Central South African Railways,* [1903] T.H. 76).

"**Not guilty**" "is the proper plea, wherever the prisoner means either to deny or to justify the charge in the indictment" (Stephen's *Comm.* 15th ed. vol. 4, p. 339).

"**Not less than.**" When in computing time "*not less than* so many days are to intervene, both the terminal days are excluded from the computation" (Maxwell's *Interpretation of Statutes,* 4th ed. p. 520).

Not negotiable. These words are frequently written across a cheque; the "effect is that the cheque remains transferable, but is deprived of the full character of negotiability. However honestly and for value a transferee may take it, he cannot acquire any better title to the cheque or its proceeds, or any better right against any prior party to it, than his transferor had" (Paget on *Banking,* 2nd ed. p. 70).

"Every one who takes a cheque marked *not negotiable* takes it at his own risk, and his title to the money got by its means is as defective as his title to the cheque itself" (*per* LINDLEY, L.J., in *Great Western Railway Co.* v. *London and County Bank,* [1901] A.C. at p. 418; 85 L.T. 155; 17 T.L.R. 702).

Notae hieroglyphicae, the memoranda taken down by a Roman notary in abbreviated characters of which he alone knew the meaning (Wessels' *History,* p. 197).

Notarial act, any deed or document formally executed before or by a notary public in his capacity as such.

Notarial attestation, a formal act executed by a notary public in testimony of some fact.

Notarial bond, a mortgage bond duly executed in the presence of a notary public. *See* GENERAL MORTGAGE.

Notarial will, a will executed by the testator in the presence of a notary public and two witnesses. The testator or the witnesses to the will should be known to the notary, and it is necessary that the testator should declare to the notary that he understands the contents of the instrument, and that it contains his last will and testament, before it is executed. This declaration is usually recorded at the end of the will. When completed the original will is lodged in the notary's protocol. After death of the testator the Master of the Supreme Court may demand that the original will shall be filed in his office. It has been held in the Supreme Court of the Cape Colony (in *Re Proctor's Estate,* 5 S.C. 159; 4 C.L.J. 232) that the witnesses need not actually sign, but they must be present. In that case DE VILLIERS, C.J., said: "Notarial wills are valid even although they are not signed by any witnesses at all. . . . If the witnesses do not subscribe, the will must, it would seem, be read to the testator in their presence. In the present case the notary knows that the will was read over, and in the absence of any proof to the contrary we must presume the truth of this solemn averment on the face of the will." It is, however, safer in every case to get the witnesses to sign the will.

Notaris (D), a notary. *See* NOTARY PUBLIC.

Notarius, a notary. See Wessels' *History,* p. 197.

Notary public. The word *notary* is derived from the Latin *notarius,* which is again derived from *notae,* the signs or abbreviations made by notaries of the matters for which their testimony was required, and from which notes the notarial act was afterwards drawn. A notary is a person duly appointed by the court as a notary public and sworn in as such. Notaries with us must also be attorneys. For the duties of notaries public see Van Zyl's *Notarial Practice,* pp. 70 *et seq.*

Note. (1) *See* To Note.

(2) In the Bills of Exchange Acts the term *note* means promissory note; see Act 19 of 1893 (C.C.), sec. 1; Law 8 of 1887 (N.), sec. 1; Proclamation 11 of 1902 (T.), sec. 1; Ordinance 28 of 1902 (O.R.C.), sec. 1.

Notice, a notification either verbal or in writing.

In the Cape Scab Act (20 of 1894), sec. 4, "*notice* means a verbal notice or a *notice* in writing delivered in manner following, that is to say, by delivering the same personally or by leaving the same at, or posting the same addressed to the office or address of any inspector, or at or to the usual or last-known place of abode in the colony of the owner or other person, or by affixing such *notice* at the dwelling-house, homestead or other conspicuous place on the farm of such owner or person."

In the Cape Additional Taxation Act (36 of 1904), sec. 42, *notice* is defined as meaning "a *notice* in writing given or causing the same to be personally served on any person, or by leaving the same at his usual or last-known place of abode or business in the [Cape] Colony, or by sending the same by post addressed to his usual or last-known place of abode or business; and, in the case of a company, means a *notice* given by being served upon or sent by post or delivered to the public offices of such company at the address for service, given under this Act, or, if there should be no address for service, then by serving, leaving or sending the same as aforesaid at or to any office or place where the company carries on business in this [Cape] Colony." *See* Public Notice.

In Natal law, see Law 30 of 1887, sec. 7; also *Johnson* v. *Johnson* (26 N.L.R. 142), where it was held that when a certain number of days' *notice* must be given, such *notice* must be clear days' *notice*, whether the word "clear" is used or not.

See Clear Days' Notice.

Nova constitutio futuris formam imponere debet non praeteritis, a new law ought to make provision for the future, not for the past. *See* Leges et constitutiones futuris certum est dare formam negotiis, non ad facta praeterita revocari.

Novatie (D.), novation. It arises "where an obligation is discharged by another obligation being made in its stead, whereby the first obligation is destroyed" (Van Leeuwen's *Comm.* Kotzé's trans. vol. 2, p. 335. See also Grotius' *Introd.* 3, 43). *See* Novation.

Novation, the discharge of an obligation in such a manner that another obligation is substituted in its stead (Grotius' *Introd.* 3, 43, 1). The question is one of intention to be gathered from all the circumstances (*Derkson* v. *Wrensch*, 3 S.C. 163). See *Ewers* v. *R.M. of Oudtshoorn*. (Foord, at p. 35).

"Now in force." Where the words "in the absence of any greater or special penalty provided by the law *now in force*" occurred in an Act of Parliament, it was held that the words *now in force* must be taken to mean in force immediately before the Act received the assent of the Crown or Governor (*Queen* v. *Vorster*, 1 S.C. 390).

Noxae deditio, surrender of the guilty thing. In Roman law if a son under power or a slave caused damage to another without the knowledge of his father or master, the latter could elect whether he would pay the damage or free himself from that liability by surrendering the wrong-doer. The action that lay was called the *actio noxalis*, the principle of which was extended to the case of damage done by irrational animals without fault on the part of their owners (*pauperies, q.v.*). In South Africa it has been held that *noxae deditio* is obsolete, and that no action lies for damage done by animals without negligence on the part of their owners (*Parker* v. *Reed*, 21 S.C. 496).

Noxalis actio, noxal action. *See* NOXAE DEDITIO.

Noxious weed, in the Transvaal Noxious Weeds Act (12 of 1909), sec. 1, means "*Xanthium Spinosum*, or any other plant which the Governor may declare by proclamation in the *Gazette* to be a *noxious weed*, either throughout the whole colony or in one or more districts or portions of districts thereof."

Nuda proprietas, bare ownership. Where one person is indeed the owner of a thing, but another has the usufruct, the right of the former is called a *nuda proprietas*.

Nudum pactum, a bare agreement; a promise made without consideration. *See* CAUSA.

Nuisance. "A *nuisance* may be defined as 'the wrong done to a man by unlawfully disturbing him in the enjoyment of his property, or, in some cases, in the exercise of a common right'; but it will be found, on examination, that all *nuisances* primarily affect the enjoyment of land. A *nuisance* is either *public* or *private*" (Stephen's *Comm.* 15th ed. vol. 3, p. 405). *See* PRIVATE NUISANCE; PUBLIC NUISANCE.

Nulla bona, no goods; the name given to the return of the sheriff or messenger to a writ where the judgment debtor has failed, upon being required to do so, to point out sufficient disposable assets to satisfy the judgment. Upon such a return being made the judgment creditor may obtain a decree of civil imprisonment against the debtor, or he may have the debtor's estate compulsorily sequestrated as insolvent.

In the Transvaal Ordinance 12 of 1904, sec. 7, a penalty is provided in the case of a person making a false return of *nulla bona*. The section reads as follows: "If any person being required by the messenger of the Court to point out property to satisfy any writ shall (*a*) falsely declare to the messenger that he possesses no property or not sufficient property to satisfy such writ; or (*b*) although owning such property shall fail or refuse to point out the same, he shall on conviction be liable to a fine not exceeding fifty pounds and in default of payment to imprisonment with or without hard labour for any period not exceeding six months."

Nullum tempus occurrit regi, no time runs against the King. Prescription runs against the Crown as to rights which can be alienated by the Crown, but not as to inalienable rights (Voet's *Comm.* 44, 3, 12; 44, 3, 11). It will thus run against land which can be alienated (*Municipality of Frenchhoek* v. *Hugo*, 2 S.C. 248; 3 S.C. 346; *Blake* v. *Goldman and Others*, [1903] T.S. 764). And this applies even although the legislature has fixed certain conditions upon which such alienation will take place (*Blanckenberg* v. *Colonial Government*, 11 S.C. 90).

Nullus idoneus testis in re sua intelligitur, no one is considered a suitable witness in a matter in which he himself is interested. In accordance with this maxim the heir under the Roman law could not be one of the witnesses to a will. The Roman-Dutch law also excluded legatees, the will being regarded as void *ab initio* if any such interested person so attested it. In the Cape Colony Act 22 of 1876 provides that if a person attests a will to whom or to whose wife or husband a benefit or appointment is given, such person forfeits the benefit or appointment, but the will remains valid. A similar provision is made in the Transvaal by Ordinance 14 of 1903, secs. 3 and 4; and in the Orange River Colony by Ordinance 11 of 1904, secs. 3 and 4. See also Law 2 of 1868 (N.), sec. 7.

The application of the maxim in Roman law to the parties to a lawsuit is not followed by us, although the fact that a person has an interest in an action may have some bearing on his credibility as a witness.

Nunc pro tunc, now for then. A proceeding which is not taken at the proper time, but afterwards, is sometimes held to have been taken at the proper time, *i.e.* now for then, *nunc pro tunc.*

Nuncupative will. "A nuncupative testament was made by the testator declaring his will consecutively by word of mouth, even though it were reduced to writing for the purpose of being better remembered" (Grotius' *Introd.* Maasdorp's trans. p. 90). See also Maasdorp's *Institutes*, vol. 1, p. 115, where he points out that "at the present day all wills, with the exception perhaps of a privileged military testament, have to be in writing."

Nunquam indebitatus, never indebted.

Nursery, in the Cape Nurseries Inspection and Quarantine Act (29 of 1905), means "any land or premises whereon is grown or cultivated any nursery stock." *See* GENERAL NURSERY; LOCAL NURSERY.

In the Natal Plants Diseases Act (45 of 1904), sec. 3, *nursery* means "any land or premises whereon are grown any plants intended for sale or distribution for the purpose of being grown elsewhere."

Nursery stock. The expression *nursery stock* is defined in the Cape Nurseries Inspection and Quarantine Act (29 of 1905) to mean "trees or plants of any kind, not being vegetables, grown or cultivated for purposes of trade and with the intention of their being sold or distributed for the purpose of their being grown elsewhere than on the premises where they stand."

Oath. Van der Linden in his *Institutes* (Juta's trans. 3rd ed. p. 162), in dealing with the subject of Evidence, says: "The *oath* is also a kind of proof. Parties often make use of it to perfect a proof which cannot be deemed conclusive, or to defend themselves against a presumption raised against them. Such a tender of *oath* does not, however, become evidence until the judge by his judgment has allowed one of the two parties to take it, and when such party has taken this *oath*, the statements thus sworn to are deemed to be proved as between the parties." The practice on this point has been considerably modified since the days of Van der Linden. Generally speaking, all evidence is given in the courts on *oath*. "*Oaths* are binding which are administered in such form and with such ceremonies as the person sworn declares to be binding" (Stephen's *Digest of the Law of Evidence*, 5th ed. p. 141).

In the Native Territories' Penal Code (Act 24 of 1886 (C.C.), sec. 5 (*i*)) it is provided in the interpretation clause that "'*oath*' and all expressions relating to 'the taking of *oaths*' include all such affirmations and declarations as may by law be substituted for an *oath*, and the making of such affirmations and declarations." See an article on *Oaths* in 1 C.L.J. 325: and the Cape Oaths and Declarations Act (18 of 1891).

As to *oaths* in Natal, see Law 13 of 1862; Law 14 of 1869; Law 5 of 1870, sec. 6; and Act 14 of 1904, sec. 9.

For the Transvaal, see the Interpretation of Laws Proclamation, 15 of 1902, sec. 2.

Ob turpem causam, on account of a dishonourable or immoral cause or consideration. *See* Ex turpi causa non oritur actio; and Condictio ob turpem vel injustam causam.

Obiter dictum, said incidentally; an opinion which a judge expresses in the course of his judgment, but which is not essential to the decision of the matter at issue. Such opinions have not the authority of decisions, but they sometimes receive great weight from the reputation of the judge who has pronounced them.

Obligatie (D.), an obligation; a special form of contract or acknowledgment of debt, which binds only one party to the contract, namely, the debtor. *Obligatien* in favour of lawful creditors were usually passed in Holland in three ways: (*a*) judicially, that is, before the secretary and two schepenen; (*b*) notarially, that is, before a notary and two witnesses; and (*c*) under the hand and confirmed by the signature of the debtor (Kersteman's *Woordenboek*, vol. 1, p. 315).

Obligation "is a legal bond with which we are bound by a necessity of performing some act according to the laws of our State" (Justinian's *Institutes*, 3, 13). "An *obligation*, as its etymology denotes, is a tie, whereby one person is bound to perform some act for the benefit of another. In some cases the two parties agree thus to be bound together, in other cases they are bound without their consent. In every case it is the law which ties the knot, and its untying, *solutio*, is competent only to the same authority" (Holland's *Jurisprudence*, 10th ed. p. 236). Grotius (*Introd.* 3, 1, 24) says that an *obligation* "is an act of one man, from which a personal claim results in favour of another."

See Van Leeuwen's *Comm.* Kotzé's trans. vol. 2, p. 2, where, in a note, Mr. Justice Kotzé fully discusses the term *obligation* and its several meanings.

Obligation quasi ex contractu "embraces every transaction, whereby one person binds another without any contract, in such a way just as if a contract had been made. Such an obligation arises through the undertaking and execution of the affairs of another, whether the person transacts the business for an absent friend out of friendship and without any mandate, or whether the execution of another's affairs proceeds in consequence of a certain accepted mandate or service, as in the case of guardians, attorneys, agents and the like" (Van Leeuwen's *Comm.* Kotzé's trans. vol. 2, p. 229). *See* Quasi ex contractu.

Obligation quasi ex delicto "arises either through the act of those whom we have in our power or service, or through damage caused to another by our property. For this we are obliged to make compensation, as if we had caused the damage ourselves; but are not liable to punishment, which is not extended beyond the person of the wrong-doer" (Van Leeuwen's *Comm.* Kotzé's trans. vol. 2, p. 322). *See* Quasi ex delicto.

Obreptijf or **Subreptijf** (D.), a term used in Dutch practice signifying that the plaintiff has, by request or otherwise, obtained something from the judge by untruthfulness or craftiness.

Obsolete, gone out of use; antiquated.

Obstringitur ne in suum factum veniat, he is prevented from going back upon his own deed. Thus, if a person consents to an article belonging to him being sold to another, he cannot afterwards claim the thing or its value from the purchaser. In such a case he is regarded either as having given a mandate or as having held out that the seller had a right to sell, and is therefore estopped from denying to the contrary (*Smit* v. *Smit's Executrix*, 14 S.C. 142).

Obstruct. "To make false signals, and thereby to bring a train to a stand on a railway, was held to be within the enactment which made it an offence to *obstruct* a railway" (Maxwell's *Interpretation of Statutes*, 4th ed. p. 416).

Obtain, to acquire possession of a thing; to procure. See *John M'Tati* v. *Rex* ([1908] O.R.C. at p. 25).

"Obtain and purchase." See *De Beers Consolidated Mines* v. *Kimberley Waterworks Co.* (12 S.C. 52), where these words, appearing in an agreement between plaintiffs and defendants, were construed.

Occupation. (1) The legal apprehension or taking of corporeal things, which are common (*res communes*) by the *jus gentium*, with the intention to acquire the ownership thereof; and by this such things as belong to no one in particular (*res nullius*) go to the first occupier, by natural reason" (Nathan's *Common Law*, sec. 537). In Roman law it is known as *occupatio*. *See* RES NULLIUS.

(2) Being in possession; the state of being occupied; see *Capetown Town Council* v. *Kaiser* (17 S.C. 282 *et seq.*).

Octrooy (D.) [modern spelling *octrooi*], a patent; a privilege granted by the supreme power of a state.

Offence, such a transgression of the law as will subject the accused to summary trial and punishment. A contravention of municipal regulations is not a crime, but it is an *offence* (*Hunt* v. *Hoare*, 1 S.C. 379). "The word *offence* appears to be used in two senses: firstly, in a more general sense (for instance, in the preamble of Act 3 of 1861 [C.C.]) as inclusive of crimes and of transgressions of a less degree than crimes; and, secondly, in a more restricted sense, as distinguished from crimes and as expressive of such minor transgressions. In this latter sense it is more particularly used in the Police Offences Act [C.C.]." (See "Notes on Controverted Points of Law," 26 S.A.L.J. p. 227).

In the Native Territories' Penal Code (Act 24 of 1886 (C.C.), sec. 5) the word *offence* denotes "anything made punishable by this Code." As to parties to the commission of *offences* under the same Code, see secs. 77–84; as to various *offences*, see subsequent sections of the Code.

In the Transvaal Criminal Procedure Code (Ordinance 1 of 1903, sec. 3) *offence* is "an act or omission punishable by law."

"Offences summarily triable." *See* SUMMARY TRIAL.

Offer, a proposal presented by one person to another for acceptance. "An *offer* does not bind the offeror until acceptance, and may lapse or be revoked at any time before acceptance" (Jenks' *Digest of English Civil Law*, 2, 1, 192). *See* FIRM OFFER.

Office of profit. "An office may be an *office of profit* without any salary being attached to it, provided, of course, that the holder is entitled, by virtue of such office, to some fees or other emoluments" (*per* DE VILLIERS, C.J., in *Hedley* v. *Celliers*, 20 S.C. at p. 280).

As to *office of profit* under the Crown, see *ibid.* at p. 271.

Officer, one who performs an office or service, generally applied to a public functionary. As to an officer in municipal employment, see *Winterbach* v. *Worcester Municipality and Lindenberg* (16 S.C. 247).

Officer of Parliament. In the Transvaal Powers and Privileges of Parliament Act (3 of 1907), sec. 2, *officer of Parliament* means "the clerk or clerk-assistant of the Legislative Council, the clerk or clerk-assistant of the Legislative Assembly, the gentleman usher of the black rod, the sergeant-at-arms, and such other officers or persons as may be appointed from time to time to the staff of either House."

"Officer of the Court." As to the signification of this term, see *Price* v. *Deputy-Sheriff, Witwatersrand* ([1903] T.H. at p. 467).

Official liquidator, a person appointed by the court for the purpose of conducting the proceedings in winding up a company, and assisting the court therein. See the Companies Act, 25 of 1892 (C.C.), sec. 146, and the Companies Act, 31 of 1909 (T.), secs. 125 *et seq.*

Official referee, a person appointed by the court to act as referee under the statutes relating to arbitrations. *See* SPECIAL REFEREE. See Act 29 of 1898 (C.C.), sec. 2; Act 24 of 1898 (N.), sec. 3; Ordinance 24 of 1904 (T.), sec. 2.

Official witness, an expression used in the Natal Code of Native Law (19 of 1891), sec. 11, to denote a person duly appointed and confirmed as such to attend at the celebration of native marriages.

Officium judicis, the function or power of a judge. *See* NOBILE OFFICIUM.

Oir, oor, hoor (D.), an heir, a descendant.

Oirkouden (D.), to bear testimony, give evidence.

Old metal, in Act 11 of 1907 (N.), sec. 1, is defined as including "scrap metal, broken metal, partly manufactured metal goods, metal fittings or parts of old machinery or other things, second-hand sheets, pieces or lengths of iron, wire or any other metal, and generally all second-hand, old or broken goods, consisting wholly or chiefly of metal."

Omission. For meaning of the term *omission* in Native Territories' Penal Code, Act 24 of 1886 (C.C.), see sec. 5 (*d*) of that Act.

As to *omission* in particulars of certain conditions of sale, see *In re Leyland and Taylor's Contract* ([1900] 2 Ch. 625; 69 L.J. Ch. 764; 83 L.T. 380; 16 T.L.R. 566).

Omkooping (D.), bribery. As to *omkooping* of officials, see Law 10 of 1894 (T.). Attempting to bribe is a crime; see *The State* v. *Benson Aaron* (10 C.L.J. 238); *Friedmann and Sonn* v. *The State* (4 Off. Rep. 244). See Van der Linden's *Institutes*, 2, 4, 9; Nathan's *Common Law*, secs. 2503 *et seq.*

Omne quod inaedificatur solo cedit solo, everything which is built upon the ground accedes to the ground. *See* AEDIFICIUM SOLO CEDIT.

Omnis ratihabitio retrotrahitur et mandato priori aequiparatur, every ratification has a retrospective effect and is equivalent to a prior mandate. Thus if an agent makes a contract with another, the subject-matter of which is beyond the scope of his authority, the contract will not be binding on his principal. If, however, the principal should afterwards ratify the contract, the ratification will have the effect of making the contract as binding on the principal as if the agent had been authorised to enter into it at its date. But in order to establish a valid ratification it is essential to prove not only that the principal intended so to ratify the particular act, but that he expressed his intention with full knowledge of all the circumstances or with the object of confirming the agent's acts in all events (*Page, N.O.*, v. *Ross*, 2 A.C. 52; *Braude* v. *Verdoes' Executors*, 12 S.C. 159; *Reid and Others* v. *Warner*, [1907] T.S. 961).

"On his behalf." "The popular meaning of those words is that everything done for a man's benefit or in his interest or to his advantage is a thing done *on his behalf.* On the other hand, the more legal view is that they mean something done by a man's representative or agent" (*per* INNES, C.J., in *De Visser* v. *Fitzpatrick*, [1907] T.S. at p. 363).

Onder correctie (D.), under correction. An expression used by advocates in the Netherlands in the old Dutch courts to relieve themselves from personal responsibility (Wessels' *History*, p. 193).

Onderhoud (D.), maintenance. *See* ALIMENTATIE. See also Kersteman's *Woordenboek*, vol. 3, p. 970.

Onderstelling (D.), substitution; the nomination of some other person as heir in case the instituted heir should fail to enter upon the inheritance. See Van Leeuwen's *Comm.* Kotzé's trans. vol. 1, p. 372; Maasdorp's *Institutes*, vol. 1, p. 142.

"One unbroken case," a term used in connection with a wholesale dealer's license. See *Rex* v. *Reece* (21 S.C. at p. 199).

Oneris ferendi, of bearing a weight or burden. *See* SERVITUS ONERIS FERENDI.

Onmondig (D.), under full age; a minor. *See* MINDERJARIG.

Onus probandi, the burden of proof. *See* ACTORI INCUMBIT ONUS PROBANDI.

Oor (D.). *See* OIR.

Oorkenner (D.), of the king, a public notary, *tabellio regis*.

Oorzaak (D.), the origin of a debt; the *causa debiti* of an obligation. See Van Leeuwen's *Comm.* Kotzé's trans. vol. 1, p. 123. *See* also CONSIDERATION.

Opdragt (D.), transfer of immovable property. Also termed *Overdragt* or *Transport*.

Open policy. "An *open policy* is one in which the sum so to be paid [as an indemnity in case of loss] is not fixed, but is left open to be proved by the claimant in case of loss, or to be determined by the parties, and the determination is called 'the adjustment of the loss.' The difference between a valued and *open policy*, in point of *form*, is this, that the blank which is intended to be filled up by the sum at which the parties agree to fix the value of the property insured, and the amount of damages to be recovered in case of loss, as between themselves, is filled up in the former, while it is not filled in the latter, or, at least, is not stated as an agreed valuation or sum to be recovered in case of loss. The difference between them in point of *effect* is, that under an *open policy*, in case of loss, the insured must prove the true value of the property insured, while under a valued policy he need never do so, the sum agreed being taken as conclusive both at law and in equity, unless in cases of fraud, or of such excessive overvalua tion as to raise a presumption of fraud" (May on *Insurance*, 4th ed. sec. 30). In *Harman* v. *Kingston* (3 Camp. at p. 152) Lord ELLENBOROUGH said: "Where there is an insurance on goods, as may be thereafter declared and valued, this gives the assured a power, by duly declaring or valuing before the loss, to make it a valued policy; but that if the assured do not so declare and value, it is then an *open policy*, and the interest is matter of evidence at the trial." See also Arnould's *Marine Insurance*, 7th ed. secs. 9 and 336 *et seq.*

Open space, see *Lewis and Lensen* v. *Rex* ([1907] T.S. at p. 1021).

Operae servorum et animalium, the services of slaves and animals. *See* SERVITUS OPERARUM SERVORUM ET ANIMALIUM.

Opheffing van sequestratie (D.), a Dutch term for the discharge from sequestration as used in the original of the Transvaal Insolvency Law (13 of 1895), secs. 132 *et seq.* See also *Simon* v. *Jackson* ([1904] T.S. 116). Also termed *Ontheven* or *Ontheffen van sequestratie.*

Opstal (D.), a *building.* A word used in the early days in South Africa to denote the homestead, that is, the buildings and garden ground, on loan places. The most common tenure in the early days of the settlement of the Dutch in the Cape of Good Hope was that "under which small garden plots were granted 'on loan.' No rent was charged for these temporary concessions, and the grants were gradually enlarged to allow of the grazing of stock. As the population and requirements of the Government of the colony increased these gratuitous loans were converted into concessions of the use of land for a certain period at a fixed rent, the Crown retaining in law the right of resuming the land at any time, though in practice that right was never exercised, except in the case of a breach of the conditions of the grant or of the land being required for public purposes. The homestead, that is, buildings and garden ground, of the 'loan place' was called the *opstal,* and the sale or bequest of such *opstal* was impliedly allowed by the Government, seeing that a transfer duty was placed upon such alienation. This, however, did not give the purchaser or legatee of the *opstal* a superior right to that of the original grantee. The whole system, in fact, rested upon a confidence in the indulgence of the Government which, as a general rule, was not misplaced" (1 C.L.J. 317).

Option, the right granted to a person to choose whether he will do, purchase or accept a certain thing or not—generally within a specified time. So soon as the *option* is accepted—or "exercised" as is frequently said—the contract is complete. See *Bal* v. *Van Staden* ([1902] T.S. at p. 131).

"I cannot agree in the view that an *option* is capable of formal transfer and registration in the Deeds Office. It is a personal contract, giving the purchaser of the *option* the right to purchase the farm for a certain price, and until the farm is purchased there is no real right which is capable of registration" (*per* DE VILLIERS, C.J., in *Kotzé* v. *Civil Commissioner of Namaqualand,* 17 S.C. at p. 39).

See OPTION TO PURCHASE.

Option to purchase is "in effect an offer to sell which may be accepted at any time within the period fixed by the contract, and on such acceptance being notified a contract is formed" (*per* SMITH, J., in *Bal* v. *Van Staden,* [1902] T.S. at p. 148).

See OPTION.

Or. "To read *or* as 'and' is a violent expedient which ought not to be adopted except in the last resort, for the simple reason that *or* does not mean 'and,' and when the legislature uses *or* it must, *primâ facie* at all events, be taken to mean *or* and not 'and'" (*per* BRISTOWE, J., in *Colonial Treasurer* v. *Great Eastern Collieries, Ltd.*, [1904] T.S. at p. 719; see also *Colonial Treasurer* v. *African Agricultural and Finance Corporation*, [1905] T.S. at p. 79; *James, James & Co.* v. *Vanderwagen*, 27 N.L.R. at pp. 287 and 289). It occasionally becomes necessary to read *or* for "and"; see Maxwell's *Interpretation of Statutes*, 4th ed. pp. 357 *et seq.*

See *Raphael* v. *Rex* ([1907] T.S. at p. 71); *Sanch* v. *Groves* ([1907] T.S. at p. 246).

"Or otherwise," for construction of this expression, see *Baerselman* v. *Bailey and Others* ([1895] 2 Q.B.D. 301); *Eastern and South African Telegraph Co.* v. *Capetown Tramways Co.* (17 S.C. 95).

Oral contract, a contract made by word of mouth, as opposed to a written contract.

Oral evidence. *See* EVIDENCE.

Orchard, in the Natal Plants Diseases Act (45 of 1904), sec. 3, *orchard* means "any land or premises where are grown and cultivated any fruit-bearing plants or trees, and extends to and includes a garden or vinery."

"Ordinarily resident," an expression used in Law 4 of 1890 (N.), sec. 2 (a law to provide for certain expenses incurred under the Foreign Jurisdiction Acts), where it is provided that "a person shall be deemed to be *ordinarily resident* in this [Natal] Colony who has resided here continuously for a period of not less than five years."

"Ordinary course of business," an expression employed in the Insolvency Laws of South Africa; see sec. 86 of Ordinance 6 of 1843 (C.C.). See *Hiddingh, Manuel's Trustee,* v. *Eaton* (3 Menz. 295); *De Wet's Trustees* v. *Krynauw & Co.* (Buch. 1879, p. 179); *Du Plooy's Trustee* v. *Plewman* (7 S.C. 334); *Jordaan's Trustee* v. *Fletcher & Co.* (11 S.C. 47); *Horwitch's Trustee* v. *Twentyman & Co.* (12 S.C. 321); *Van Heerden's Trustees* v. *Wagenaar* ([1906] E.D.C. at p. 149); *Green's Estate* v. *S. A. Mutual Insurance Society* (21 S.C. 47).

Ordinary session. "*Ordinary session* shall mean the session of Parliament at which the estimates of expenditure for the ordinary administrative services of a financial year are considered" (Act 12 of 1907 (T.), sec. 2).

Orphan Chamber, a Government department in the Netherlands, presided over by an Orphan Master, and having the supervising control over guardians and the management and administration (unless excluded by testament; see Van Leeuwen's *Comm.* Kotzé's trans. vol. 1, p. 127) of the persons or property of orphans. The Orphan Chamber was introduced into the Settlement of the Cape of Good Hope under the old Dutch Government, and it continued to exercise authority until abolished in 1832 by sec. 35 of the Charter of Justice. In the following year, by Ordinances 104 and 105 of 1833, the duties of the late Orphan Master were transferred to the Master of the Supreme Court. The Orphan Chamber was abolished in the Transvaal by Proclamation 28 of 1902, sec. 1.

Oude costumen (D.), ancient customs, a kind of common law that existed in the Netherlands. See Wessels' *History,* p. 108.

Oudeygen (D.). *See* CYUS.

"**Outsider,**" in *Thompson* v. *Brown* (14 S.C. 488) this expression was, in the circumstances, held to be not defamatory.

Outspan place, or public outspan; an area of land set apart for grazing cattle when being moved from one place to another—especially oxen engaged in transport—on or in the neighbourhood of a public road, for the convenience of the travelling public. In the early days of the South African colonies, when goods were conveyed from the seaports inland almost entirely by ox-wagon, it was necessary that there should be, at convenient intervals along public roads, places where the oxen could be unyoked from the wagons and sent to graze and rest; such places were properly set apart for the purpose either by grant or servitude, and were called *outspans.* Most of them still exist. In the Cape Colony all public *outspans* in each division are placed under the management and control of the divisional council for the division; see Act 40 of 1889, sec. 207, and Act 13 of 1906.

For statute law in Natal regarding *outspans*, see Law 9 of 1870; Law 14 of 1872; and Act 15 of 1896.

In the Orange River Colony, see Ordinance 17 of 1905, secs. 24 *et seq.*

Overdaging (D.), was a summons in Dutch practice whereby a person was summoned before a judge of another jurisdiction than that within which he resided. *Overdaging* commonly occurred where there was process between two inhabitants residing in the same province of Holland, but under different jurisdictions (Kersteman's *Woordenboek*, vol. 1, p. 338).

Overdragt (D.), transfer; a transfer of the ownership in some movable or immovable property according to law. The Latin equivalent is *traditio.* See Grotius' *Introd.* 2, 5, 11 and 13. *See* TRANSFER.

Overlap, that portion of one piece of ground which on survey is found to encroach upon an adjoining piece. In the early days of the South African territories, when boundaries of farms were often defined in a crude and elementary manner, *overlaps* were frequent, but now they seldom occur. The expression is to be found in the Cape Land Beacons Act (7 of 1865), sec. 47.

Overspel (D.), adultery.

Overt, open; unconcealed. *See* MARKET OVERT.

Overwonne bastaarden (D.), children who have been procreated in adultery or incest. They cannot inherit from their parents *ab intestato*, and by last will they may receive no more than is necessary for their bare maintenance (Van Leeuwen's *Comm.* Kotzé's trans. vol. 1, pp. 48, 337 and 425 *in not.*).

Owner, the person who is entitled in law to exercise the right of ownership, and in whom the *dominium* is vested.

In the Cape Crown Lands Ordinance (9 of 1844), sec. 13, *owner* is defined as "the person in whom, whether in his individual or in some fiduciary capacity, the complete *dominium* or legal right in any place or property held by any quitrent grant, or lease or other title from and under the Colonial Government, shall for the time being be vested."

As to *owner* under the Cape Roads Ordinance, see sec. 38 of Ordinance 9 of 1846; see also the Cape Vagrancy Law Amendment Act (27 of 1889), sec. 1.

As to *owner* under the Pound Laws (C.C.), see *Conradie* v. *Gray* (21 S.C. at p. 456).

In the Cape Scab Act (20 of 1894), "'*owner* as applied to sheep' means every person claiming jointly or in severalty any right, title or interest in any sheep in his possession, and shall include every person having charge, control or management of sheep, as well as the *owner* of land in respect of sheep belonging to his servants and running on such land;" and in the same Act "'*owner* as applied to land' means every person, partnership, association, council, board or corporation in whom land, whether held jointly, severally or as commonage is vested, or who have the charge, control or management of any land; or the lessee or the occupier of any land."

In the Cape Railway Regulations Amendment Act (36 of 1895) *owner* is defined to mean "the person or persons, local authority or company actually responsible for the direction or control of any railway undertaking."

In the Capetown Municipal Act Amendment Act (25 of 1897), sec. 1, *owner* is defined to mean and include "(*a*) the person or persons in whom from time to time shall be vested the legal title to any immovable property; (*b*) in any case where a property has been leased for a period of fifty years or upwards, the lessee of such property; (*c*) in cases where the person in whom the legal title is vested is insolvent or dead, the person in whom the administration of such property is vested as trustee, executor, administrator or otherwise; (*d*) in cases where the *owner*, as above described, is absent from the [Cape] Colony, the agent or person receiving the rent of the property in question." See *Capetown Town Council* v. *Royal Hotel* (1906), *Ltd.* (23 S.C. at p. 701). For further definitions in Cape statutes see Precious Minerals Act (31 of 1898), sec. 62; Irrigation Act (32 of 1906), sec. 3; and Act 44 of 1908.

In Natal statute law, see Law 16 of 1872, sec. 3; Law 26 of 1891, sec. 1; Act 43 of 1899, sec. 4. In Act 44 of 1904, sec. 3, *owner* is defined to mean "the registered holder of land held under freehold or quitrent tenure, or the purchaser of Crown lands to which title has not yet been given;" see also Act 8 of 1906, sec. 2; Act 40 of 1904, sec. 2.

In the Transvaal Criminal Procedure Code (1 of 1903), sec. 3, "Person, *owner* and other like terms, when used with reference to property or acts, include corporations of all kinds, and any other associations of persons capable of owning or holding property or doing acts; they also, when relating to property, include his Majesty." See also Ordinance 43 of 1903, sec. 3; Ordinance 46 of 1903, sec. 2, and in this connection *Hovent* v. *Rex* ([1905] T.S. at p. 25); Ordinance 58 of 1903, sec. 2. As to meaning of *owner* under the Precious Stones Ordinance, see Ordinance 66 of 1903, secs. 25 and 37; see also Ordinance 44 of 1904, sec. 22 (*b*); Ordinance 6 of 1905, sec. 2; Ordinance 31 of 1905, sec. 1; Act 27 of 1907; Act 33 of 1907, sec. 2; Act 12 of 1908, sec. 2.

In the Orange River Colony, see Ordinance 14 of 1903, sec. 1, as amended by Ordinance 12 of 1905, sec. 1; Ordinance 25 of 1903, sec. 6. In the Mining of Precious Stones Ordinance (4 of 1904), sec. 5, *owner* means "the registered *owner* of any land on which any mine or alluvial digging is situated;" see also sec. 57. See also Ordinance 11 of 1905, sec. 1, and Ordinance 31 of 1907, sec. 1.

Owner was discussed in *London and South African Exploration Co.* v. *Bultfontein Mining Board and Another* (7 S.C. at p. 49).

The word *owner* "can never be held to refer to lessees of pieces of ground, however long the leases may run" (*per* WESSELS, J., in *Ward & Salmons* v. *Phillips*, [1902] T.H. at p. 140).

"An *owner* may always vindicate his property wherever it is found" (*per* DE VILLIERS, C.J., in *Salvage Association of London* v. *S. A. Salvage Syndicate Ltd.*, 23 S.C. at p. 171).

Owner's agent. This expression is used in the Natal Mines and Collieries Act (43 of 1899, sec. 4), where it is defined to mean "the representative of the mine owner, but who is not necessarily the responsible person under this Act for the control, management and direction of the mine."

Owner's claims, a term applied to those claims to which an owner of land is entitled on the proclamation of such land as a public diggings. The number of *owner's claims* is regulated according to the area of the land proclaimed. They are entitled to certain privileges. See Act 35 of 1908 (T.), secs. 20 *et seq.*; Act 16 of 1907 (C.C.), sec. 6. *See* MYNPACHT.

As to alluvial diggings for precious stones, see Ordinance 66 of

1903 (T.), sec 42; Ordinance 3 of 1904 (O.R.C), sec. 44; Ordinance 4 of 1904 (O.R.C.), sec. 66.

Owner's risk, an expression employed by carriers in their contracts, consignment notes, or the like with the object of relieving them from liability. The effect of a contract with a railway administration for the carriage of goods at *owner's risk* was very fully discussed in *Central South African Railways* v. *Adlington & Co.* ([1906] T.S. 964), where WESSELS, J., in delivering judgment said, *inter alia*, at p. 973: "Where parties agree that a carrier shall carry at *owner's risk* for a lower rate than the usual charge, it is undoubtedly within the contemplation of both parties that there is to be a limitation to the carrier's risk. As the carrier is by law excused from the consequences of *casus fortuitus*, the carrying at *owner's risk* must mean something more than exemption from damage arising from inevitable accident. There has been a judicial expression of opinion that *owner's risk* does not include freedom from liability arising from gross negligence or from malfeasance. From what liability then does it exonerate the carrier? The fact that the word 'owner' is used in defining the risk seems to us to show that the parties must be held to have contemplated that the carrier is not to be held liable if he shows such diligence as an ordinary owner is expected to show when transporting and handling his own goods. He is not exempted if he displays gross negligence or malfeasance, or if he employs such servants as are likely to be guilty of gross negligence or wilful misconduct, for the court cannot assume that an ordinary owner conveying his own goods would be guilty of gross negligence or would employ servants grossly incompetent. If the carrier, however, employs suitable servants, and by some error of judgment on their part, but through no malfeasance or gross negligence, an accident occurs by which the goods are damaged, then the carrier will not be liable if he takes the goods at *owner's risk* and at a lower rate. An error of judgment on the part of a servant is a condition to which the owner who carries his own goods may reasonably be considered to be exposed."

Ownership. "Full *ownership* is that whereby a person may, for his own benefit, do with a thing whatever he pleases so long as it is not forbidden by law. Qualified ownership is where something is wanting to this general power of doing everything" (Grotius' *Introd.* 2, 3, 10, 11). Maasdorp in his *Institutes* (vol. 2, p. 32) defines *ownership* as "the exclusive right of disposing of a corporeal thing combined with the legal means of alienating the same and coupled with the right to claim the possession and enjoyment thereof." The right of *ownership* is "unlimited only in comparison with other rights over objects. In accordance with the maxim *sic utere tuo ut alienum non laedas*, it must always be enjoyed in such a way as not to interfere with the rights of others, and is therefore defined in the French Code as *le droit de jouir et disposer des choses de la manière la plus absolue, pourvu qu'on n'en fasse pas un usage prohibé par les lois ou par les règle-*

ments. It may also, as we shall see hereafter, continue to subsist although stripped of almost every attribute which makes it valuable, in which condition it is described in Roman law as *nuda proprietas.* A really satisfactory definition of a right thus wide, yet necessarily limited in several respects and conceivably limited in many more, has perhaps never been suggested. It is difficult to do more than to describe it, with Austin, as a right 'over a determinate thing, indefinite in point of user, unrestricted in point of disposition, and unlimited in point of duration'" (Holland's *Jurisprudence*, 10th ed. p. 199).

Oyer. *See* PROFERT AND OYER.

Pacta adjecta, stipulations annexed to *bonae fidei* contracts at the time of their conclusion, *i.e.* to the bilateral contracts of purchase and sale, letting and hiring, partnership and mandate, *depositum, commodatum* and *pignus*, and the quasi-contracts of *negotiorum gestio*, the administration of common property and guardianships. They are, in other words, accessory agreements which modify the principal contract, of which they are regarded as a part. As instances of *pacta adjecta* in the case of the contract of sale, Voet (*Comm.* 18, 1, 26) enumerates the following: that the seller shall be allowed to hire the thing purchased for a certain sum; that the purchaser shall not build on the land sold; that the thing shall be considered unbought if within a certain time the purchaser is dissatisfied with it, or, *vice versâ*, that it shall hold good if within a certain time the purchaser is satisfied with it; that the seller shall give the thing for sale on trial to be returned within a certain time if not approved of, and that in the event of the purchase falling through something shall be paid for the use of the thing. To the class of *pacta adjecta* belong the *pactum commissorium* and the *in diem addictio.*

Pacts. "An agreement, *pactum*, not coming under the ten heads of contract, nor binding as an innominate contract by having been executed on one side, was, as a general rule [in the time of the Romans], a *nudum pactum;* that is, it could not be enforced by an action. But such an agreement might be used as the basis of an exception. *Nuda pactio obligationem non parit, sed parit exceptionem* (*D.* 2, 14, 7, 4). There were, however, some *pacts* to which an action was attached, either by express enactment, *pacta legitima*, such as, after the time of Justinian, the agreement to give, or by the praetors (*pacta praetoria*), such as the *pactum constitutae pecuniae*, an agreement by which a person agreed to pay what he already owed. *Pacta* might also be added (*adjecta*) as subsidiary to a main obligation" (Sandars' *Justinian*, 12th ed. p. 323). These *pacta* are commonly spoken of as *pacts.*

Pactum antichreseos. *See* ANTICHRESIS.

Pactum commissorium, an agreement of forfeiture, one of the *pacta adjecta* or agreements which may be annexed at the time of their conclusion to *bonae fidei* contracts, *i.e.* the bilateral contracts of purchase and sale, letting and hiring, partnership and mandate, *depositum, commodatum* and *pignus*, &c. Where such an agreement is annexed to a contract of purchase and sale, for example, the effect is that if the price be not paid by a certain date, the thing shall be considered unbought. *See* LEX COMMISSORIA. In the case of letting and hiring a *pactum commissorium* may be added to provide that if the tenant should sublet, the lease will determine and the thing let revert to the owner (Voet's *Comm.* 19, 2, 5). Where it is added to a contract of pledge or mortgage, the effect of the agreement is that if the debt be not paid on the due date the property pledged or mortgaged shall belong to the creditor for the amount of the debt, or, in other words, it shall be *committed* to the pleasure of the creditor to hold the property as his own. According to Grotius (*Introd.* 2, 48, 41) such an agreement in the case of pledge is invalid, but Voet (*Comm.* 20, 5, 6) and Matthaeus (*De Auctionibus*, l. 1, c. 3, 11) contend that the agreement will be valid if the debt due be equal to a reasonable price for the property (see Schorer, *Note* 256), and Decker in his *Notes* to Van Leeuwen's *Comm.* (4, 12, 4) supports this latter view.

Pactum de non petendo, an agreement not to sue. Such an agreement may be absolute or conditional, and may affect the whole or only a portion of the debt. In the Roman law an agreement not to sue had not the effect of a formal release, as a pact was not a mode of dissolving an obligation. The debtor thus remained bound, but if sued upon his obligation he was allowed by the praetor to plead the defence of bargain agreed. A nude promise of this kind is also recognised in our law as a good defence to an action, however much the authorities may differ upon the question whether an action can be maintained on a promise made without consideration (*Roos* v. *Roos's Executors*, 1 Menz. 89; *Jones and Another* v. *Goldschmidt*, 1 S.C. 109).

Pactum de retrovendendo, an agreement for selling back. This was the name given in the Roman law to an agreement which was sometimes added to a contract of sale. By it the seller reserves to himself the right within or after a certain time or at any time to purchase back the thing sold. For the enforcement of his right the seller has only a personal action *ex vendito*, unless it has been agreed that on the price being repaid within a certain time the thing is to be considered as unpurchased or the seller is to have the thing back, in which case the seller may recover the thing by a real action, provided in the case of immovables such an agreement is inserted in the transfer (Voet's *Comm.* 18, 3, 7).

Pactum donationis, an agreement to give in donation. Such an agreement does not confer upon the donee a *jus in re* in respect of the subject agreed to be given, and if, therefore, the donor, who retains the *dominium* until delivery, makes a gift of it to another perfected by delivery, the latter will acquire a complete title to the thing, notwithstanding the previous agreement. The pact, however, gives the first donee a *jus ad rem*, which will entitle him to sue the donor for delivery of the thing or for damages for non-performance of the agreement if the donor has by his own act rendered himself unable to fulfil it (*Barrett* v. *O'Neil's Executor*, Kotzé, 1877–81, p. 109).

Palsgraven; Paltsgraven (D.), pl. of *Palsgraaf*, Counts Palatine, were judges who acted as lieutenants of the king in a conquered town or province in Holland (Van Leeuwen's *Comm.* Kotzé's trans. vol. 1, p. 63); officers appointed over a palace. *See* GRAAF.

Pand (D.), pledge, pawn. *See* PLEDGE.

Pand ter minne (D.), a pledge of movables by simple delivery to the creditor. See Van Leeuwen's *Comm.* Kotzé's trans. vol. 2, pp. 83 and 106.

Panden (D.), to execute process against or levy distress upon the property of another.

Pandgenot (D.), the use of the thing pledged; equivalent to the *pactum antichreseos*. See Decker's *Note* on Van Leeuwen's *Comm.* Kotzé's trans. vol. 2, pp. 85, 86.

Pandgever (D.), a borrower on pledge; one who pawns. See Van Leeuwen's *Comm.* 4, 8.

Pandgeving or **Pandschap** (D.), the act of pawning.

Paper. In the Cape Stamp Act (3 of 1864), sec. 34, *paper* is "taken to comprehend parchment and vellum as well as *paper*."

Parate executie (D.), summary execution. It is sometimes stipulated in a contract of pledge that the pledgee shall be entitled to sell the property pledged on his own authority, without an order of court, in the event of the pledgor failing to pay the debt on the due date. According to Grotius (*Introd.* 2, 48, 41), Van Leeuwen (*Comm.* 5, 8, 3), Voet (*Comm.* 20, 5, 6), Groenewegen (*De Legibus Abrogatis*, 2, 8, 1), and others such a stipulation for immediate execution without a previous order of court is void, and this view has been adopted by the late Transvaal High Court in the case of *Gundelfinger* v. *De Villiers* (not reported). "In his notes to his translation of Van Leeuwen's *Commentaries*, Chief Justice KOTZÉ says, 'It is possible that in South Africa the courts of law may sanction a private sale by the creditor of a chattel, *e.g.* a watch or a horse given in pledge, where such has been agreed upon; but they will not favour such a practice, and will certainly not extend it to immovable property or movable property of considerable value.' This dictum as to movable property of considerable value is in conformity with the law as stated by Paul Voet (*Mobilium et Immobilium Natura*, ch. 6, sec. 5), where he says that *res pretiosa* is on the same footing as immovable property" (De Bruyn's *Opinions of Grotius*, p. 521).

Pardon "is a complete forgiveness of the crime committed for special reasons" (Van Leeuwen's *Comm.* Kotzé's trans. vol. 2, p. 350). See Law 9 of 1876 (N.); Ordinance 1 of 1903 (T.), secs. 275 *et seq.* *See* also CONDONATION.

Parent, the father or mother of a child. "The analogy of the patron guardian led to another kind of so-called statutory guardianship, namely, that of a *parent* over a son or daughter, or a grandson or granddaughter by a son, or any other descendant through males, whom he emancipates below the age of puberty: in which case he will be statutory guardian" (Justinian's *Institutes*, Moyle's trans. 1, 18).

In the Cape Public Health Act (4 of 1883, sec. 51) it is provided that "the word *parent* shall include the father and mother of a legitimate child, and the mother of an illegitimate child." For similar definition see Act 24 of 1906 (N.), sec. 3; Law 12 of 1895 (T.), sec. 29; Ordinance 29 of 1903 (O.R.C.), sec. 2.

In the Transvaal Education Act (25 of 1907), sec. 2, *parent* means "the father of a child, and if there be no father, the mother of such child, and if the father and the mother of a child be dead or absent from such child's usual place of residence, the person having actual custody or control of such child." The same definition is to be found in the Orange River Colony School Act (35 of 1908), sec. 2.

See PATERNAL POWER.

Parliament. "*Parliament* means, in the mouth of a lawyer (though the word has often a different sense in ordinary conversation), the King, the House of Lords and the House of Commons; these three bodies acting together may be aptly described as the 'King in Parliament' and constitute *Parliament*. The principle of parliamentary sovereignty means neither more nor less than this, namely, that *Parliament* thus defined has, under the English constitution, the right to make or unmake any law whatever; and, further, that no person or body is recognised by the law of England as having a right to override or set aside the legislation of *Parliament*" (Dicey's *Law of the Constitution*, 6th ed. p. 37). *See* also Bryce's *History and Jurisprudence*, vol. 1, p. 152). In the same way there are *Parliaments* of the British colonies enjoying responsible government.

Parliamentary agent, a person, usually an attorney, authorised to act as such in promoting or opposing Bills and the like, before Parliament.

Parochial, pertaining to a parish.

Parole, a statement made by word of mouth.

Parricide, one who kills a near blood relation (see Van Leeuwen's *Comm.* Kotzé's trans. vol. 2, p. 270).

Partial acceptance. *See* QUALIFIED ACCEPTANCE.

Partial assurance. "*Partial assurance* is a loose and indefinite expression. It may mean insurance of part of a building as distinguished from the rest of it, or it may mean insurance of part of the value of the building, distinguished or not distinguished, as it may be, from the rest of the value" (*Lange & Co.* v. *South African Fire and Life Assurance Co.*, 5 Searle, at p. 365).

Particeps criminis, a partaker or sharer in crime; an accessory. Those who are present as aiders and abettors at the commission of a crime are in Roman-Dutch law equally punishable with the actual perpetrators as principals (*R.* v. *Abrams*, 1 S.C. 393). Besides actually assisting in the commission of the crime, a person may become liable as an accessory in various ways. Thus he may counsel, command or incite the actual perpetrator to commit the crime, and in such a case he is punishable as a principal (*R.* v. *Abrams, ibid.*). So a person may become a partaker in a crime after its commission by harbouring or assisting the criminal or by sharing with him the profits of the crime. According to Van der Linden the non-prevention of a crime may render a person criminally punishable, especially where he had an opportunity or was under any obligation to prevent the crime. As regards the concealment of a crime, the same author states that the concealment of a crime about to be committed renders one liable as a criminal, but if the crime has already been committed concealment is not criminal "unless the welfare and security of the State depended upon its discovery, or if some special law or official position imposed this obligation" (Van der Linden, *Inst.* 2, 1, 8).

Particular average. "A *particular average* loss is a loss arising from damage accidentally and proximately caused, by the perils insured against, to some particular interest, as the ship alone or the cargo alone" (Arnould's *Marine Insurance*, 7th ed. sec. 1008). "*Particular average* is also used, however, to denote a partial, as distinguished from a 'total loss,' and not merely in contrast to general average" (*ibid. in notis*).

Partition, action for, an action for the division of land as held by several owners in undivided ownership.

Partition of immovable property, the division by survey, and registration in the Land Register (as kept in the office of the Registrar of Deeds) of land held by several owners in undivided ownership, so that each owner shall become the registered proprietor of his defined share.

"Under the ordinary law one of two or more co-proprietors is entitled to claim a partition of the land, but that rule is subject to exceptions, one of those exceptions being that where it was impracticable or inequitable to allow such a partition, the court would in such a case make such an order as the justice or the equity of the case might require. The court under such circumstances would be quite justified in awarding the whole of the farm to one of the co-proprietors, and ordering him to pay a fair compensation to the co-proprietor" (*per* DE VILLIERS, C.J., in *Dickson* v. *Stagg*, 3 S.C. at p. 116).

Partnership. "*Partnreship* is a consensual contract between two or more persons to place their money, food, labour and skill, or some or all of them, in lawful commerce or business, and to divide the profit and bear the loss in certain proportions" (*per* DE VILLIERS, C.J., in *Poppe, Russouw & Co.* v. *Kitching and Others*, 6 S.C. 307; quoted with approval in *Uys* v. *Le Roux*, [1906] T.S. 429). "A partnership is where two people agree to conduct a business jointly, and the partners have each of them power to bind the other in respect of the business" (*per* MASON, A.C.J., in *Brown & Co.* v. *Letchford*, 22 N.L.R. at p. 212). See also *Davidson's Estate* v. *Auret* (22 S.C. at p. 15).

A partnership is not recognised as a *persona* apart from the partners; see *Ehrig & Weyer* v. *Transatlantic Fire Insurance Co.* ([1905] T.H. at p. 121).

Partnership en commandite is a partnership "whereby the parties on entering into the partnership agree that one partner alone shall contribute money to the partnership, while the other shall give his services and have the sole management of the business, while the partner contributing money shall not be liable as to losses for more than the amount of money contributed by him" (Nathan's *Common Law*, sec. 927). See *Butcher & Sons* v. *Baranov Bros.* (26 N.L.R. at pp. 592 *et seq.*).

Partus sequitur ventrem, the offspring follows the mother. By natural accession the ownership of the young of animals follows the ownership of the animals. Under the Roman law the children of a female slave, on the same principle, belonged to the owner of the slave (*In re Beck's Insolvent Estate*, 1 Menz. 332).

Party wall. *See* COMMON WALL.

Passage by water, an old form of Dutch servitude. It "is the right of passing over the waters belonging to another, and is generally limited to a width of 12 ft., and at such a depth that a laden Rhenish ship can float through; whereas otherwise common boundary ditches need not be more than 7 ft. wide and of a reasonable depth, so that the cattle cannot stray on to the adjoining lands" (Van Leeuwen's *Comm.* Kotzé's trans. vol. 1, p. 298).

Passengers' luggage. "We hold the true rule to be that whatever the passenger takes with him for his personal use or convenience, according to the habits or wants of the particular class to which he belongs, either with reference to the immediate necessities, or the ultimate purpose of the journey, must be considered as personal luggage. This would include not only all articles of apparel, whether for use or ornament, but also the gun-case or the fishing apparatus of the sportsman, the easel of the artist on a sketching tour, or the books of the student, and other articles of an analogous character, the use of which is personal to the traveller, and the taking of which has arisen from the fact of his journey. On the other hand, the term 'ordinary luggage' being thus confined to that which is personal to the passenger, and carried for his use or convenience, it follows that what is carried for the purposes of business, such as merchandise or the like, or for larger or ulterior purposes, such as articles of furniture or household goods, would not come within the description of ordinary luggage, unless accepted as such by the carrier" (*per* COCKBURN, C.J., in *Macrow* v. *Great Western Railway Co.*, L.R. 6 Q.B. 612). This definition has, however, to some extent been qualified by the judgment of CHANNELL, J., in *Britten* v. *Great Northern Railway Co.* ([1899] 1 Q.B. 243), where he said: "I think there are certain requirements which must exist in order that the thing may be ordinary luggage: first of all, that it must be for the passenger's personal use; and next, that it must be for use in connection with the journey, which, I understand, means that it must be something that is habitually taken by the person when he is travelling, for use not merely during the actual journey, but for use during the time he is away from home. He is not to take his furniture, and such like articles of permanent use, under the category of luggage. So far that excludes things which are not taken for those purposes, but it does not seem to me at all necessary to say that it includes everything which is taken for personal use. It seems to me that, overriding it all, in the word 'luggage' there is involved the idea of a package or something of that sort, and it seems to me that an article which is taken, as it were, loose, as a bicycle is taken, is subject to rather different considerations."

"*Luggage* shall mean such articles of necessity or personal use and convenience as, being enveloped in some kind of package, are usually carried by passengers for their personal use, but shall not include merchandise or other valuables, which, though carried in the trunks of passengers, are not designed for any such use, but are for sale or other like purposes" (Act 13 of 1908 (T.), sec. 2; Act 29 of 1908 (O.R.C.), sec. 2).

Patent means letters patent for an invention. *See* INVENTION; LETTERS PATENT.

Patent ambiguity. *See* LATENT AMBIGUITY.

Patentee, the person for the time being entitled to the benefit of a patent.

Pater est quem nuptiae demonstrant, he is the father to whom the marriage points. All children born of a lawfully married woman are presumed to be the children of her husband. This presumption may be rebutted by evidence that the husband is impotent or that he was absent from the home or had no access to his wife for a time inconsistent with the period of gestation. According to Voet (*Comm.* 1, 6, 4) this period is fixed from the beginning of the seventh to the beginning of the eleventh month, but he adds that as the health and mode of living of the mother are important factors in determining the period of pregnancy, no rigid rule can be adopted, and that each case should be left to the decision of the judge. See also Grotius' *Introd.* 1, 12, 3; Schorer, *in notis* 49 and 50; and Van Leeuwen's *Comm.* 1, 7, 2. The presumption that children born of a lawful marriage are the children of the husband is not rebutted by the wife's declaring that they are not his children (*Abraham* v. *Adams,* Buch. 1878, p. 86; *Johnson* v. *Story,* N.L.R. 1869, p. 116; *Ex parte Venter,* 13 C.T.R. 620); or by the fact that the mother has been found guilty of adultery, or by the fact that at the time of their birth he was over eighty years of age, or by all these facts combined in the absence of any evidence of incompetence on his part or of non-cohabitation with his wife (*Ex parte Venter, ibid.*).

Paternal power. "Under the early Roman law the power of a father over the person and property of his minor children was absolute. The father, in fact, was considered to be the owner of his child, and could deal with his person and property as he thought fit. Gradually the powers of the father in respect of his children's persons were abridged until they were practically as limited as they are in this country at the present day, but his powers over his children's property, although also considerably abridged, remained, as justly remarked by Maine (*Ancient Law,* p. 143), 'far ampler and severer than any analogous institution of the modern world.' The father still retained the absolute right to acquisitions derived from his own property, but as to acquisitions of the child derived in any other way, the father retained only an usufruct during his own life. It would serve no useful purpose to cite the different authorities of the Dutch law, showing the gradual further relaxation of the father's rights and the gradual recognition of the mother's claims in the different provinces of the Netherlands, except in Vriesland, or to refer to the different colonial statutes, regulations, and instructions which were framed during the Dutch occupation of this colony. The instructions of Governor De Mist of the year 1804 served as a guide to the old Orphan Chamber until it was abolished by the Charter of Justice, when a new code of regulations was introduced for the guidance of the Master of the Supreme Court by Ordinances Nos. 103, 104 and 105. In considering what the powers of parents are in this country [Cape Colony] at the present day, it should be remembered that they exercise those powers subject to the supervision of this Court as the upper guardian of all minors. So long as the authority of parents is not abused and in the absence of any order of court declaring them to be prodigals, of unsound mind, or otherwise unfit to have the custody of the person or property of their children, their powers, so far as they fall within the scope of the present inquiry, may be briefly summed up as follows: Firstly, as to the father, he is the natural guardian of his legitimate children until they attain majority. During his lifetime he alone may appoint tutors to take his place after his death, during his children's minority (Ordinance 105, sec. 1). He alone is entitled to their custody, has control over their education, and can consent to their marriage. On the other hand, he is bound to maintain them until they can maintain themselves. He no longer enjoys a life interest in any part of their property; but where they have means of their own, derived either from their own earnings or otherwise, he can recoup himself for his expenses of maintenance out of such means. He has the right to administer their property, but he may lose this right by allowing them to live apart from him, and openly to exercise some trade or calling. Until they have thus been virtually emancipated, or until they become majors, either by marriage or by attaining the age of twenty-one years, he has the management of their property, except such property as has been left to them by others, and placed under a different administration. . . . Coming next to the mother, her rights of control over the person and property of her legitimate children do not arise until after the death of the father. If he has appointed tutors, these tutors, after being duly confirmed, obtain the guardianship over the person and property of the minors. It is only on failure by the father to appoint such tutors that the surviving mother acquires her full rights. She then has all the powers which the husband enjoyed until his death, and she may then by will appoint tutors for her children to act after her death (Ordinance 105 (C.C.), sec. 1)" (*per* DE VILLIERS, C.J., in *Van Rooyen* v. *Werner*, 9 S.C. at p. 428).

Patriapotestas, the name given in the Roman law to the power which a *paterfamilias* or head of a family had over all the members of his family. The persons included in such family and subject to the *patriapotestas* were his sons and daughters, his wife, who ranked in law as a daughter, and all the children and other descendants of sons in his power. When a daughter married she passed into the family of her husband. Upon the death of the *paterfamilias* each of his sons became *sui juris* and the *paterfamilias* of all his descendants; his daughters also became *sui juris* if unmarried, but upon marriage each fell under the power of her husband, or, if he was not *sui juris*, under that of the ascendant who stood in the position of *paterfamilias* to him.

In the early Roman law the power of the *paterfamilias* over the persons of those in his power was absolute and unfettered; thus, he could sell or put a child to death. In course of time, however, this power was extremely limited, until the father had the mere right to inflict moderate chastisement.

As regards the property of children under power, the *paterfamilias* had the full ownership of everything acquired by the children from whatever source. The first change was made in the case of property acquired by a son in military service (*peculium castrense*), of which the son was allowed the complete *dominium*. The favour granted to the *peculium castrense* was afterwards by Constantine extended to the property acquired by a *filiusfamilias* as an officer of the imperial Court, which was called a *quasi-castrense peculium.* The same emperor also introduced the *peculium adventitium,* which in the time of Justinian included all that came to a son from any other source than from his father. Of this *peculium* the father had only the usufruct during his lifetime, the ownership being held by the son. It was now only property that a son had acquired from or through his father, called *peculium profectitium,* that belonged in full ownership to the father. *See* PATERNAL POWER.

Patrimony, the estate or inheritance which becomes, or should become, due, or to which a person is entitled, on the death of his father or other ancestor.

Pauper, a person in a wholly destitute condition.

Pauper suit, a proceeding brought or defended *in formâ pauperis.* "It is a privilege granted by the court to sue or defend, *gratis,* given to those who have a good right of action in law, but no means to assert it" (Van Zyl's *Judicial Practice,* 2nd ed. p. 337; *Spring* v. *Coetzee's Executor and Others,* [1905] T.S. 347). *See* PROBABILIS CAUSA.

Pauperies, the name given in Roman law to damage caused by an animal. An action, called the *actio de pauperie,* lay against the owner of the animal even although he had been guilty of no negligence, the mere fact of his ownership being sufficient to fix him with liability. When sued, however, the defendant could free himself from paying damages by giving up the animal to the plaintiff (*noxae deditio*). The *actio de pauperie* applied only to animals which are tame by nature. In the case of animals which are naturally wild the owner could not escape liability by surrendering the animal, but had to make full compensation for the damage caused. It has been held that the *actio de pauperie* and the right of *noxae deditio* are obsolete in South Africa, and that the owner of an animal without negligence on his part is not liable for damage done by it (*Parker* v. *Reed,* 21 S.C. 496).

Pawn, a pledge; something deposited with a lender as security for money advanced, the ownership of the *pawn* remains in the borrower or debtor although the creditor has possession.

Pawnbroker, "any person who carries on the trade or business of taking movable property in pawn or pledge" (Act 38 of 1887 (C.C.), sec. 3; and Act 36 of 1889 (C.C.), sec. 2). For Natal statute law on the subject, see Act 22 of 1895, secs. 5 and 6; for that in the Transvaal, see Ordinance 13 of 1894; Ordinance 23 of 1905, sec. 2. See *Muller* v. *Chadwick & Co.,* [1906] T.S. at pp. 34 *et seq.,* where *pawnbrokers* are historically discussed as from the earliest times by MASON, J.

Pawner, in the Cape Pawnbroker's Act (36 of 1819) *pawner* is defined as meaning "a person delivering an article for pawn to a pawnbroker."

Payee, a person to whom money is payable; the person to whom a bill of exchange or other similar liquid document is made payable.

Payment "is the delivery of the thing which a person owes, made either by the debtor himself or by some one else on his behalf, provided he be competent to do so, to the creditor, who is competent to receive the same" (Grotius' *Introd.* 3, 39, 7). See the Cape Illegal Practices Act, 26 of 1902 (C.C.), sec. 2.

Payment is thus defined by Voet: "*Payment* (*solutio*) sometimes includes any extinction and satisfaction of an obligation, *e.g.* when we say that a man *solvit* if he has performed what he has promised to do. This is the sense in the definition 'an obligation is a tie of law by which we are placed under the necessity to pay something.' But in its specific meaning, wherein it differs from acceptilation, novation and the numerous other methods of extinguishing an obligation, *payment* is the natural rendering of that which is due" (Voet's *Comm.* Swift & Payne's trans. 46, 3, 1).

"The *payment* and satisfaction of a common debt must be precisely of that to which the obligation binds, whether it consists in doing or giving something. Except only that the debtor may in the *payment* bring in by way of compensation and set-off whatever the creditor owes him of the same quality and value" (Van Leeuwen's *Comm.* Kotzé's trans. vol. 2, p. 328).

"By our law a *payment* made by a third person to a creditor on behalf of a debtor, even if the debtor is ignorant of the *payment* or objects to it, constitutes a valid discharge of the debt" (*per* De Villiers, C.J., 19 S.C. 70; see also Voet's *Comm.* 46, 3, 1).

"Where a man is forced by menaces to his person to make *payments* which he is not legally bound to make, it cannot be said that there is a total absence of consent—but, inasmuch as his consent is forced and not free, the *payment* is treated as involuntary, and therefore subject to restitution. There is a similar absence of free consent where goods are illegally detained, and a sum of money is paid simply for the purpose of obtaining possession of those goods again. There is, however, this difference between the case of menaces to the person and that of duress of goods, that in the former the menaces—if sufficient to affect the mind of a person of ordinary firmness—might *per se* be enough to prove the absence of free consent, although no objection may have been made to the *payment* at the time it was made, whereas in the latter case—all reasons for fear of bodily danger being absent—it is impossible to know whether the *payment* is voluntarily or involuntarily made unless some unequivocal objection to the *payment* is raised at the time it is made" (*per* De Villiers, C.J., in *White Bros.* v. *Treasurer-General,* 2 S.C. at p. 353; see also *De Beers Mining Co.* v. *Colonial Government,* 6 S.C. 155; *Vergotine* v. *Ceres Municipality,* 21 S.C. 28).

Payment in due course means payment made at or after the maturity of the bill to the holder thereof in good faith, and without notice that his title to the bill is defective (sec. 59 of English Bills of Exchange Act, 1882); see also Act 19 of 1893 (C.C.), secs. 1 and 57; Law 8 of 1887 (N.), sec. 58; Proclamation 11 of 1902 (T.), secs. 1 and 57; Ordinance 28 of 1902 (O.R.C.), secs. 1 and 57; Bills of Exchange Regulations (R.), 1895, secs. 1 and 57.

Payment into court without admitting liability. "The practice of paying money into court is derived from the English, and not from the Roman-Dutch practice. It is said to have been first introduced in the reign of Charles II, to avoid the hazard and difficulty of pleading a tender. If the action was founded on contract, it operated as an acknowledgment of the contract. Since 1833 various statutes have been passed dealing with payment into court, and at present the English practice is regulated by the Rules of Court framed under the Judicature Act. The present English practice, as laid down in a recent case (*Coote* v. *Ford*, [1899] 2 Ch. 93), allows a defendant to plead a denial of liability in addition to payment into court; and such payment into court with denial of liability cannot be twisted into an admission of liability. Our [Transvaal] Rules (38*a*) merely state that a defendant may pay money into court by way of satisfaction and amends, and may plead such payment. Nothing is said about pleading other pleas inconsistent with such payment into court. No doubt as a general rule a payment into court will be considered as equivalent to an admission of the cause of action in respect of which the money has been paid. Where, therefore, a defendant pays money into court and denies liability, a plaintiff may possibly raise the point that he is embarrassed by the procedure; but unless he does so the court must pay due regard to the intention of the defendant as shown by his pleadings, and to judge whether he wished to admit or to deny the existence of the contract. Now in this case no exception has been taken to the amended plea, and the whole case manifestly proceeded on the assumption that the contract was denied. It is therefore too late now for the appellant to contend that the Court is to take no notice of the denial of liability as contained in the amended plea, and to decide that the payment into court should be accepted as an unequivocal admission of the contract, and that the words 'without admitting liability' should be regarded *pro non scriptis*. On this point, therefore, the appeal also fails" (*per* WESSELS, J., in *Shepherd* v. *Commissioner of Railways*, [1905] T.S. at p. 195). See also *Grabie* v. *Pretoria Municipal Council* ([1908] T.S. 862).

Peace, Justice of the. *See* JUSTICE OF THE PEACE.

Peace officer, in the Transvaal Criminal Procedure Code (1 of 1903), sec. 3, is defined to include "any magistrate or justice of the peace, the sheriff, deputy-sheriff, and any officer, non-commissioned officer, constable or trooper of the town police or of the South African Constabulary or any member of any other police force established in this colony, the keeper and guards of any prison, inspector of natives, pass officer, and any person employed for the preservation and maintenance of the public peace, or for the service or execution of civil process and any person specially required by any warrant lawfully issued by any judge, magistrate or justice of the peace to perform any duty."

Peculium (from *pecus*, cattle) signifies property; the name given in Roman law to the property acquired by persons in the power of another, *i.e.* slaves and children in the power of their father. In the earlier Roman law such property, from whatever source it had been derived, belonged to him in whose power such persons were. An exception obtained in favour of the *peculium castrense*, which was the property given to a son when setting out on military service or acquired in the course of such service. This was the exclusive property of the son, and he could dispose of it either *inter vivos* or *mortis causa*, although, if he did not dispose of it by testament, the father was allowed to take it at his son's death, not as being entitled thereto *ab intestato*, but as the claimant of a *peculium*. The favour granted to the *peculium castrense* was afterwards by Constantine extended to the property acquired by a *filiusfamilias* as an officer of the palace, which was called the *quasi-castrense peculium*. The same emperor also introduced the *peculium adventitium*, which in the time of Justinian included all that came to a son from any other source than from his father, whether by his own labour or from his mother or other persons. Of this *peculium* the father had the usufruct, the ownership, however, being held by the son. Property which a son acquired from or through his father belonged to the father and was called *peculium profectitium*, because it came from (*profectum est*) the father. In the Roman-Dutch law property belonging to minors is classified as *profectitium* or *adventitium*. The former is such property as has been derived from the parents themselves either directly or indirectly, and includes baptismal gifts given by godparents, which are considered to be given more out of regard for the parents than the children, unless it has been otherwise expressly provided by the donor (Voet's *Comm.* 8, 1, 4). As in Roman law, such property belongs in full ownership to the father, although with regard to baptismal gifts the authorities are not unanimous. Schorer (*Note* 28) supports the view of Voet, but Van der Keessel (*Thes.* 104) quotes a decision of the Supreme Court to the effect that such gifts were regarded as belonging to the children, and not to the parents (see also Van Leeuwen's *Comm.* 3, 16, 7).

In profectitious property is also included whatever minors, who are supported by their parents, earn by their own labour, such earnings going to their parents as a set-off against their maintenance (Voet's *Comm.* 15, 1, 4; Grotius' *Introd.* 1, 6, 1; Van der Keessel *Thes.* 102–104; Van Leeuwen's *Comm.* 2, 7, 7). Where, however, a son who lives with his father carries on business separately from his father or as a partner with his father, the profits so acquired by the son will belong to himself and not to his father, and the more does this apply if the son lives separately from his father.

As regards adventitious property, or that which is not acquired from or through the parents, this belongs exclusively to the child, the parents not even being entitled to the usufruct of such property, although as natural guardian the father has the administration of it except where the property has been left to the child by others and placed under a different administration (Voet's *Comm.* 15, 1, 6; *Van Rooyen* v. *Werner*, 9 S.C. 425).

Pecuniary reward, a reward or compensation consisting of money. When this expression is used in connection with elections and illegal practices, the definition is usually extended to include any office, place or employment, or any valuable security or other equivalent for money or valuable consideration; see Act 26 of 1902 (C.C.), sec. 2.

Pedlar, in the Revenue Licenses Ordinance, 23 of 1905 (T.), sec. 2, means "any person who travels on foot and without a vehicle (other than a hand-barrow or hand-cart propelled by himself) or with a pack animal or carrier, and who carries goods for sale."

Peer, a person of equal rank; a nobleman; a member of the House of Lords.

Peerage, the dignity of the lords or peers of the Kingdom of Great Britain and Ireland.

Pegging, the act of demarcating an area of land, on a proclaimed digging, as a claim, water-right, stand, or the like. See Act 31 of 1898 (C.C.), secs. 32 and 78; Act 43 of 1899 (N.), sec. 97; Act 35 of 1908 (T.), pt. 1, ch. 5; Ordinance 3 of 1904 (O.R.C.), sec. 53; Ordinance 4 of 1904 (O.R.C.), secs. 69 *et seq.*; and *Berriman Syndicate* v. *Simpson*, 3 Off. Rep. 135.

Penal laws, laws which prohibit some act, and impose a penalty for their contravention.

Penal servitude. This form of punishment in Great Britain superseded transportation beyond the seas by an Act passed in 1853. It consists of imprisonment with hard labour for a long period of years, the minimum being three years.

Penalty. (1) A fine or punishment.

(2) A payment or forfeiture of money or some other thing for the non-performance of a condition of a contract, bond or similar obligation, or of a rule or regulation. *See* LIQUIDATED DAMAGES.

Pension, usually an annual payment made to a civil servant or some one in the military or naval service, in consideration of past services and in accordance with statute or regulation. *Pensions* may also be granted by private individuals to their employees. The recipient of a *pension* is called a pensioner.

As to assignment of a *pension* in Natal being valid, see *Hedges* v. *Bainbridge* (17 C.L.J. 200; 20 N.L.R. 205).

A pension may be attached in satisfaction of a judgment. As to effect of insolvency, see *In re Hansen* (21 S.C. 625) and *Ex parte Tom* ([1907] T.S. 31).

Pensionable officer, in the Transvaal Pensions Ordinance (30 of 1906), sec. 1, means "any officer in the public service who has, prior to the coming into operation of this Ordinance, been transferred to the public service from the civil or consular service of the United Kingdom or of a British possession with pensionable rights." See Transvaal Public Service and Pensions Act (19 of 1908), and Railway Service and Pensions Act, 20 of 1908 (T.). and 37 of 1908 (O.R.C.).

Peppercorn rent, a nominal rent.

Per aversionem, by bulk or in gross. Fungibles are said to be sold *per aversionem* when sold by the bulk without reference to exact quantity, as all the wine in a certain cellar or the grain in a certain store. In such a case the risk both as to quantity and quality passes to the purchaser as soon as the sale is completed by the consent of the parties, unless (as regards quality) the vendor knew that the goods would deteriorate before the time fixed for their removal, and failed to warn the purchaser; or unless he took upon himself the risk of deterioration for a certain period; or unless he gave an assurance that the goods would preserve their quality until the time for delivery and they became bad without any external accident; or unless he failed to take proper care of the goods during the time he was bound by law or agreement to take care of them. As regards his liability for the custody of goods sold *per aversionem,* the vendor must exercise the highest degree of diligence, loss caused by inevitable accident (*vis magna et fatale damnum*) alone being excused. This responsibility for the most exact diligence ceases when the time fixed for the removal of the goods has arrived, or, if no time has been fixed, after the expiration of a reasonable time from notice being given to the purchaser (Voet's *Comm.* 18, 6, 3 and 4).

Per capita, by or according to heads or individuals. The succession to a deceased person's estate may take place in one of three ways, viz., *per capita, per stirpes,* or *in lineas.* Where the estate is either in terms of the deceased's will or in accordance with the law of intestacy to be distributed *per capita,* it is divided into as many shares as there are individuals entitled to succeed, each taking one share. *See* PER STIRPES.

Per incuriam, by mistake or carelessness; antithetical to *de industria*, purposely or intentionally.

Per procuration, under procuration or agency; generally abbreviated "*per pro*" or "*p.p.*" These words do not necessarily mean that the person so signing is acting under a special written authority, but simply indicate that he signs on behalf of his principal in virtue of an authority which may be either implied or express (*Faure* v. *Louw*, 1 S.C. 3). "All that it really means is this: 'I am an agent, not having any authority of my own'" (*per* DE VILLIERS, C.J., *ibid.* at p. 11). By the Bills of Exchange Statutes (Act 19 of 1893 (C.C.), sec. 23; Law 8 of 1887 (N.), sec. 24; Proclamation 11 of 1902 (T.), sec. 23; Ordinance 28 of 1902 (O.R.C.), sec. 23; Bills of Exchange Regulations, 23 of 1895 (R.), sec. 23) it is provided that a signature by procuration operates as notice that the agent has but a limited authority to sign, and the principal is only bound by such signature if the agent in so signing was acting within the actual limits of his authority. Before the passing of the statute it was decided in the Cape Colony that where an agent so signs bills in carrying on the business of his principal, and these bills are always recognised by the latter, the signature by procuration does not throw upon those who take the bills the duty of inquiring in each particular case as to the authority of the agent if the bills are given or received in the ordinary course of business (*Faure* v. *Louw, ibid.*)

Per stirpes, by or according to stocks or parent heads, as distinguished from *per capita*. Where a succession takes place *per stirpes*, the estate is divisible not according to the number of persons entitled to succeed, but according to the number of parent heads whom the heirs represent, the share of each parent head being divided amongst his or her representatives. Thus, according to the law of intestate succession, children and their descendants succeed to their parents *per stirpes*. If, therefore, a man dies intestate leaving only grandchildren four of whom are by one son and two by another, the estate is divided into two equal shares, one going equally to the four grandchildren by the former son and the other to the two grandchildren by the latter. In this way a grandchild by one son gets one-eighth of the estate, while a grandchild by the other gets one-fourth. If, on the other hand, the deceased had left a will directing his grandchildren to succeed *per capita*, the estate would have been divisible into six parts, the number of grandchildren, each taking one part.

Peregrinus, a foreigner; a litigant who does not reside within the jurisdiction of the court. If a plaintiff he must give security for costs before he can be allowed to sue, but where he has immovable property within the jurisdiction, the value of which will suffice to pay the probable costs of the action, he is relieved from the necessity of giving such security (*Witham* v. *Venables*, 1 Menz. 291; *Lumsden* v. *Kaffrarian Bank*, 3 S.C. 366; *Schunke* v. *Taylor and Symonds*, 8 S.C. 104). If he is defendant in the action, or, being plaintiff, a claim in reconvention is made against him, any property he has within the jurisdiction may be arrested in order to found jurisdiction (*Schunke* v. *Taylor and Symonds, ibid.*). The property so arrested remains as satisfaction for any judgment that may be obtained, but can be released upon sufficient security being given to satisfy such judgment. If the non-resident defendant has no property within the jurisdiction he may be himself arrested if found within the jurisdiction and retained in custody until he gives security that he will satisfy the judgment.

Perennial stream. This term has been well defined in the Cape Irrigation Act (32 of 1906), sec. 3, which reads as follows: "*Perennial stream* means a natural stream which in ordinary seasons flows for the greater part of the year in a known and defined channel, and the water whereof is capable of being applied to the common use of the riparian proprietors. Provided that a stream which in part only of its course satisfies these conditions shall be deemed to be a *perennial stream* in so far only as regards such part."

"Broadly stated, our law recognises two classes of natural streams or water-courses—public and private. Under the designation of public streams are included all perennial rivers, whether navigable or not, and all streams which, although not large enough to be considered as rivers, are yet perennial, and are capable of being applied to the common use of the riparian proprietors. Under the designation of private streams are included rivers and streams which are not perennial, and streamlets which, although perennial, are so weak as to be incapable of being applied to common use" (*per* DE VILLIERS, C.J. in *Van Heerden* v. *Weise*, 1 A.C. 5).

Performance. In the Natal Play Rights Amendment Act (18 of 1899), *performance* is defined to mean "the representation or *performance* of any play right work in a public place."

Periculum rei venditae nondum traditae est emptoris, the risk of a thing sold, but not yet delivered, lies with the purchaser. Although the *dominium* in the thing sold passes to the buyer only when the price has been paid, unless credit has been given to him by the seller, yet the sale is considered as perfected from the moment when the parties are agreed as to the thing to be sold on the one hand and the price on the other. From that time, therefore, the thing, although not yet delivered to him, is at the risk of the purchaser, all fruits afterwards accruing and even alluvion in the case of land falling to his profit and the destruction or damage of the thing to his loss. "The commentators and jurists are not agreed as to the reason for this rule of the civil law, which is an exception to the principle *res perit domino*. . . . It seems to me a pure and baseless fiction to regard the purchaser, before delivery of the thing sold, as if he were its owner, for he has neither *dominium* nor possession" (*per* KOTZÉ, J.P., in *Grobbelaar* v. *Van Heerden*, [1906] E.D.C. at p. 232). The risk, however, will be upon the seller if when applied to for the purpose he fails to make delivery to the buyer. In the case of things which are capable of being weighed, measured or counted (*quae pondere numero mensurave constant*), the sale is not considered as completed, and the risk will not therefore pass to the purchaser, but will remain with the seller until the things have been appropriated to the contract by being weighed, measured or counted (*Poppe, Schunhoff & Guttery* v. *Mosenthal & Co.*, Buch. 1879, p. 91; *Taylor & Co.* v. *Mackie, Dunn & Co.*, Buch. 1879, p. 166). So, where anything is sold subject to a condition, the risk will be with the seller so long as the condition has not been fulfilled (Grotius' *Introd.* 3, 14, 34; Van Leeuwen's *Comm.* 4, 17, 2; Voet's *Comm.* 18, 6).

"**Perils of the seas,**" an expression used in marine policies, charter parties, &c. "The words obviously embrace all kinds of marine casualties, such as shipwreck, foundering, stranding, &c.; as also every species of damage done to the ship or goods at sea by the violent and immediate action of the winds and waves, as distinct from that included in the ordinary wear and tear of the voyage or directly referable to the acts and negligence of the assured as its proximate cause" (Arnould on *Marine Insurance,* 7th ed. sec. 812). See *Woodhead, Plant & Co.* v. *Gully* (14 S.C. at p. 112): "*Hillcrag*" v. *Beckett* (23 N.L.R. at p. 465).

"**Period of the war.**" In Ordinance 11 of 1902 (T.), sec. 1, the *period of the war*, referring to the Anglo-Boer War, is defined to mean "the period between the 11th October, 1899, and the 31st May, 1902, inclusive."

Perishable goods. "*Perishable goods* shall include fish, fruit, vegetables, plants, bread, meat, game, butter, eggs, milk, dogs, small animals, birds, poultry and any other thing which may hereafter be declared by the Governor by proclamation in the *Gazette* to be *perishable goods*" (Railways Regulation Act, 13 of 1908 (T.), sec. 2; Act 29 of 1908 (O.R.C.), sec. 2).

Perjury "is an assertion upon an oath [including an affirmation] duly administered in a judicial proceeding, before a competent court, of the truth of some matter of fact, material to the question depending in that proceeding, which assertion the assertor does not believe to be true when he makes it, or on which he knows himself to be ignorant" (Stephen's *Digest of Criminal Law,* 5th ed. p. 106). Van der Linden in his *Institutes* (2, 3, 3) says that the crime of *perjury* is committed "either when a person intentionally violates obligations which he had bound himself by an oath to fulfil, or when a person wilfully, and to the prejudice of a fellow-creature declares, under oath, that to be true which he knew to be false" (See *Rex* v. *Lalbhai,* 19 C.T.R. 751). "*Perjury* consists in wilfully and knowingly taking a false oath in a judicial proceeding, and to be proved must be established by witnesses" (*per* SMITH, Acting C.J., in *Queen* v. *Louw,* 7 S.C. 304; see also *Queen* v. *Lottering,* 9 S.C. 199).

It is thus defined in the Native Territories' Penal Code (Act 24 of 1886, sec. 106): "*Perjury* is an assertion as to a matter of fact, opinion, belief or knowledge made by a witness in a judicial proceeding as part of his evidence, either upon oath or in any form allowed by law to be substituted for an oath, whether such evidence is given in open court or by affidavit or otherwise, such assertion being known to such a witness to be false." As to a false statement on oath and a false declaration amounting to *perjury*, see secs. 108 and 109 of the same Code. As to Transvaal, see Law 4 of 1893.

To charge a person with *perjury* is highly defamatory, see *Kernick* v. *Fitzpatrick* ([1907] T.S. at p. 393).

Permanent forces. In the Cape Colonial Forces Act (32 of 1892), the expression *permanent forces* is defined to include "officers and men of the Cape Mounted Riflemen, and any other officers and men who by the terms of their commission, appointment or enrolment, and from the date thereof, are liable to render continuous military service under this Act."

Permissive power, authority conferred upon some public body or person by the legislature in terms simply enabling and not mandatory (see Maxwell's *Interpretation of Statutes*, 3rd ed. p. 334). "The omission to exercise a *permissive power* has been held not to constitute *culpa* in the legal sense" (*per* DE VILLIERS, C.J., in *Jordaan* v. *Worcester Municipality*, 10 S.C. at p. 163).

"Permit drunkenness." The words *permit drunkenness* in subsec. 1 of sec. 73 of Act 28 of 1883 (C.C.) "imply that there must be some actual, or at any rate constructive knowledge of the drunkenness on the part of the accused" (*per* BUCHANAN, Acting C.J., in *Queen* v. *Otto*, 13 S.C. at p. 253).

Perpetual acts "are those upon whose continuance no limitation of time is expressly named or necessarily to be understood. They are not perpetual in the sense of being irrevocable" (Craies' *Statute Law*, p. 64).

Perpetual silence. "The object of an action for *perpetual silence* is to prevent any alleged claim or demand from remaining in uncertainty, from a defendant losing any testimony or evidence he may then have wherewith to rebut the allegations of the other party, which he might lose if the action were indefinitely delayed; also, in the case of his death, to give less chance or proof for his executors or heirs to dispute the other party's claim; and also if he wishes to leave the country, though only on a visit, to prevent him being taken by surprise by an arrest for the pretended action" (Van Zyl's *Judicial Practice*, 2nd ed. p. 305).

Procedure by way of application approved; see *Ex parte Leyds* (1 Off. Rep. (Webber's trans.), p. 369). See *Brown* v. *Simon* ([1905] T.S. 311), where the law on the subject is fully discussed.

Perpetuity, an endless period of time; indefinite duration; the state of being perpetual.

Person. "In its primary signification the term *person* is confined to individual human beings, with reference to their capacity for having or being the subject of legal rights and duties; but by a more extended signification it has also been applied to various groups of men, who are spoken of in law as imaginary, fictitious or juristic persons, to distinguish them from human persons, who are called natural or real persons" (Maasdorp's *Institutes*, vol. 1, p. 1). "In a more extended sense, however, it is applied to various legal entities which are capable of possessing legal rights and of being subject to legal duties" (*ibid.* vol 1, p. 267).

The Interpretation Act, 1889 (Eng.), sec. 19, provides that "in this Act and in every Act passed after the commencement of this Act the expression *person* shall, unless the contrary intention appears, include any body of *persons*, corporate or unincorporate."

In the Native Territories Penal Code (Act 24 of 1886 (C.C.), sec. 5) the word *person* is defined to include "any person or association or body of persons, whether incorporated or not." In the Bills of Exchange Acts it is defined to include "a body of persons, whether incorporated or not." See Act 19 of 1903 (C.C.), sec. 1; Law 8 of 1887 (N.), sec. 1; Proclamation 11 of 1902 (T.), sec. 1; Ordinance 28 of 1902 (O.R.C.), sec. 1.

See also Act 26 of 1902 (C.C.), sec. 2; Act 37 of 1904 (C.C.), sec. 1; Act 40 of 1905 (C.C.), sec. 4; Act 23 of 1908 (C.C.), sec. 2; Proclamation 15 of 1902 (T.), sec. 2; Ordinance 3 of 1902 (O.R.C.), sec. 8.

In the Transvaal Criminal Procedure Code (1 of 1903), sec. 3, *person* "and 'owner' and other like terms, when used with reference to property or acts, include corporations of all kinds, and any other associations of *persons* capable of owning or holding property or doing acts; they also, when relating to property, include his Majesty."

As to "every *person*," see *Dely & De Kock* v. *Civil Commissioner* ([1906] T.S. at p. 96).

Personal actions, such actions as follow the person, and for that reason they are classed as movables.

Personal expenses. In the Cape Illegal Practices Prevention Act (26 of 1902), the expression *personal expenses* "as used with respect to the expenditure of any candidate in relation to any election, includes the reasonable travelling expenses of such candidate and his chief election agent, and the reasonable expenses of their living at hotels or elsewhere for the purposes of and in relation to such election."

Personal servitudes, "rights of enjoyment exercisable by a given individual, as such, over the property of another. . . They may be imposed upon movable as well as immovable property" (Holland's *Jurisprudence*, 10th ed. p. 218). The principal *personal servitudes* are usufruct; the right of use (*usus*); and the right of inhabiting a house (*habitatio*). Holland (*Jurisprudence*, 10th ed. p. 219) says, "The servitudes recognised by Roman law under the names *habitatio* and *operae servorum et animalium* were somewhat abnormal species of *usus*."

Personal statutes or laws, one of the three branches into which laws were divided by the civilians, the other two being real and mixed statutes or laws. By *personal statutes* are meant laws which are intended to define the condition or *status* of a person, such as the qualities of citizenship, legitimacy and illegitimacy, minority and majority, marriage and divorce, &c. Generally speaking, such laws, in contradistinction to real laws, which do not operate beyond the territory of the law-giver, follow and govern the person subject to them wherever he goes. *See* EXTRA TERRITORIUM JUS DICENTI IMPUNE NON PARETUR.

"**Personal supervision.**" As to work done under the *personal supervision* of a land surveyor in the Transvaal as contemplated by sec. 7 (*b*) of the Institute of Land Surveyors' Incorporation Ordinance, 1904, see *Institute of Land Surveyors* v. *Douglas* ([1908] T.S. at p. 33).

Personation, pretending to be some other particular person. In the Cape Colony, under Act 14 of 1874, sec. 43 (see also Act 9 of 1892, sec. 82), a person is guilty of *personation* who, knowing that he is not the person registered by or under a certain name upon any list of registered voters, shall nevertheless wilfully assume or pretend to be the person so registered, and shall vote or attempt to vote as being the person so registered. For *personation* in Natal, see Law 13 of 1893, sec. 18. For the Transvaal, see Ordinance 38 of 1903, sec. 73.

Pest. The term *pest* is found in the Cape Nurseries Inspection and Quarantine Act (29 of 1905), where it is defined to mean "any injurious insect or plant disease which the Governor may from time to time declare to be a *pest* within the meaning of this Act."

Pest remedy. "*Pest remedy* shall mean any substance manufactured, produced or prepared in any manner or imported into the colony and sold or intended for sale or distribution, for the prevention or destruction of any noxious plant or any parasitic pest of any plant whether of insect, fungoid or similar nature" (the Fertilisers, Farm Foods, Seeds and Pest Remedies Act, 20 of 1907 (C.C.), sec. 3).

Petitio principii, a begging of the question.

Petitioner, one who makes or presents a petition. See Act 6 of 1907 (T.), sec. 1.

Pettifogger, when applied to a lawyer means "a small man dealing with small cases in a not very reputable way. The expression when applied to a lawyer would convey to the ordinary man that the lawyer was a small man carrying on a shady and disreputable business" (*per* INNES, C.J., in *Pienaar* v. *Pretoria Printing Works, Ltd.*, [1906] T.S. at p. 813).

Picketing is a term employed in connection with strikes or other trade disputes: it has also been extended to political disputes. Generally speaking, it means the placing of men by a trades-union or other similar organisation in such a position as to intercept workmen (who are prepared to work for their employers) during a strike, and to induce or compel such workmen to cease work. See *Rex* v. *Jacob* ([1905] T.S. 88).

Pictura, painting; an artificial mode of accession which gives a person, who in good faith paints on another's canvas or tablet, the ownership of the picture, subject to the latter's right to compensation for the loss of his material. In the earlier Roman law the weight of authority seems to have been in favour of the opposite view, viz., that the painting acceded to the material, but Justinian, adopting the opinion of Gaius, laid it down that the material should become the property of the painter (*Institutes*, 2, 1, 34). According to Voet (*Comm.* 41, 1, 26) the canvas or tablet will accede to the painting, not invariably, but only when in the opinion of experts the artistic merit of the painting is such as to make it absurd to hold the contrary view.

Pignus judiciale, judicial mortgage. *See* PIGNUS PRAETORIUM.

Pignus legale, legal mortgage or hypothec, *i.e.* tacit hypothec, or hypothec arising by operation of law.

Pignus praetorium, judicial mortgage. When the goods of a judgment debtor have been attached in execution, a judicial mortgage is constituted in favour of the judgment creditor, which gives him the same rights as a person to whom movables have been pledged by delivery, or, where immovable property is the subject of the attachment, the same rights as a person having a special mortgage upon such property. The execution creditor may, however, have to share the proceeds of the sale of the property with other creditors, for if before the proceeds are paid over to him, such other creditors as have obtained judgment lodge writs of execution with the proper officer for executing writs, all will be entitled to rank concurrently on the proceeds of the sale (Voet's *Comm.* 20, 2, 32; *Roesch and Bruce* v. *Thomson, Watson & Co.*, 3 Menz. 114; see also Ordinance 3 of 1844 (C.C.)).

Further, by statute law in all the South African colonies a judicial mortgage is extinguished if, before the proceeds are paid over to the execution creditor, the debtor's estate is sequestrated as insolvent, the creditor's only preference in that case being for the costs of execution.

Pijnbank (D.), the rack; the torture; an instrument formerly employed in the Netherlands for the purpose of extracting from accused persons, by means of torture, a verbal confession concerning the commission of the crimes with which they were charged. See Kersteman's *Woordenboek*, vol. 1, p. 387.

Pilot, a person who, after examination, has been duly licensed by Government, or a harbour board, to navigate vessels in and out of harbour, or through channels or passages.

Place. As to a place used for the purpose of betting, see *Goldman and Others* v. *Rex* ([1908] T.S. 895).

As to *place* in the Transvaal Labour Importation Ordinance (17 of 1904), sec. 12, see *Rex* v. *Steil* ([1907] T.H. 31). *See* PUBLIC PLACE.

Place of entertainment, this expression is defined in Act 11 of 1905 (C.C), sec. 1, to mean "a building or erection of any description used for the performance of theatrical plays, operas, concerts and other entertainments." See also Act 25 of 1905 (C.C.), sec. 1.

"**Place of public resort,**" in the Transvaal Criminal Law Amendment Act (38 of 1909), sec. 1, is defined as "any place of entertainment, amusement, or refreshment to which the public have access, whether by payment for access or otherwise."

Place of worship. In Act 11 of 1905 (C.C.), sec. 1, the expression *places of worship* is defined to mean "any building used as a *place of worship*, or church and school combined." See also Act 25 of 1905 (C.C.), sec. 1.

Places of refuge were, amongst the ancients, places where those who, having without malice killed another, sought safety. They are not recognised under Roman-Dutch law.

Placita Generalia or **Communia,** an assembly held by the Carolingian monarchs for the hearing of civil and criminal complaints. This court was, prior to the twelfth century, the chief court of appeal (Wessels' *History*, p. 150). It is from the *Placita Generalia* that the English Court of Common Pleas derived its name (*ibid.* p. 150).

Plagium, man-stealing; the crime of carrying away or concealing a human being with a view to depriving him of his liberty. It is distinguished from abduction, which consists in carrying away a minor of either sex without the consent of parents or guardians for the purpose of marriage or from motives of lust (*Queen* v. *Motati*, *Queen* v. *Buchenroeder*, 13 S.C. 173).

Plaintiff. "The claimant or plaintiff is he who summons another before the judge, in order to plead in law against him" (Van Leeuwen's *Comm.* Kotzé's trans. vol. 2, p. 367).

Plan of contribution, an account framed by the trustee of an insolvent estate showing the amount the creditors who have proved upon the estate are liable to contribute *pro ratâ* towards the payment of the costs of sequestration, when the assets realised are insufficient for that purpose. As to the confirmation by the court of such a plan not being *res judicata* against the creditors who have proved, see *Steyn's Trustee* v. *Gous* (11 S.C. 348), and *Bell* v. *Bell's Trustee* ([1909] T.S. 51).

Plant, in the Natal Plants Diseases Act (45 of 1904), sec. 3, *plant* means "any tree, shrub or vegetation, and the fruit, leaves, cuttings, bark and any part or product thereof whatsoever, whether severed or attached."

Plantatio, planting. A species of accession, whereby that which is planted on another's land belongs to the owner of the land so soon as it has struck root and thus become attached to the soil (Grotius' *Introd.* 2, 10, 9; Van Leeuwen's *Comm.* 2, 5, 2; Voet's *Comm.* 41, 1, 25).

Platte land (D.), the country district in Holland.

Play right. In the Natal Play Rights Act (44 of 1898), sec. 2, the term *play right* is defined to mean "the sole and exclusive right to represent, perform, act, play, or exhibit any dramatic, operatic or musical work, being a tragedy, comedy, play, opera, farce, scene, pantomime (or its class), song, dance, or other scenic or musical or dramatic production or representation registered under this Act."

Plea. (1) The defendant's answer to the plaintiff's claim in an action.

(2) The answer of an accused person when called upon to say whether he is guilty or not guilty of the crime with the commission of which he is charged.

Plead, to present or file a plea; to answer a criminal charge or indictment by stating whether the accused person is guilty or not guilty; to urge a defence or excuse.

Pleader, one who pleads a cause or drafts pleadings.

Pleading, the statement of claim and defence, or the claim or defence, in an action.

Pleading over, the filing or presentation of a plea to the claim of the opponent, notwithstanding that an exception could be, or has been, taken to the declaration or plea of such opponent.

Pledge "is defined by Grotius to be a contract whereby a person places property in the hands of another as security for his debt. Anything which can be bought or sold is the subject of *pledge*, and incorporeal rights equally with corporeal things may be pledged (Voet, 20, 3, 1). To constitute a *pledge* which shall be valid against the creditors of, or subsequent purchasers from, the pledgor, there must be delivery or what is equivalent to delivery of the subject-matter of the *pledge* by the pledgor to the pledgee. Thus in a case of movables the goods must be placed in the possession of the pledgee, either by handing them over to him or by putting him in the position to exercise the sole control of them, as, for instance, by handing to him the key of the room or store in which the goods are locked up. In the case of immovable property delivery is effected or evidenced solely by registration of the mortgage bond, and no other proceeding is deemed to be equivalent to delivery. Thus the deposit of the title-deeds of the property, coupled with an agreement that the pledgee is to hold them as security, is insufficient. . . . An incorporeal right is by its nature not susceptible of physical delivery, but the pledgor must do some act to show that he divests himself of that right and vests it in the pledgee for the purpose of his holding it as security" (*per* SMITH, J., in *Smith* v. *Farrelly's Trustee* ([1904] T.S. at p. 954). In the Cape Pawnbrokers' Act (36 of 1889) a *pledge* is defined as meaning "an article pawned with a pawnbroker."

A *pledge* "confers no right of ownership on the pledgee, but only what is termed a *jus in re aliena;* the ownership still remaining with the pledgor" (*per* DE VILLIERS, C.J., in *Cape of Good Hope Bank* v. *Mellé*, 10 S.C. at p. 288).

Pledge, instrument of. *See* INSTRUMENT OF PLEDGE.

Pledgee, the person to whom some thing is pledged by another person, called the pledgor (*see* PLEDGE). "A pledgee cannot sell the goods deposited with him without going to the court and obtaining judgment" (*per* WESSELS, J., in *Stephens* v. *Whitford*, [1903] T.H. at p. 233). There is an exception to this rule in the case of certain pawnbrokers. "A pledgee only retains his real right in respect of the thing pledged so long as he remains in possession of it; this possession may be actual or constructive" (*per* DE VILLIERS, C.J., in *Heydenrych* v. *Fourie*, 13 S.C. at p. 373).

Pledgor, the person who pledges some thing to another person, who is called the pledgee (*see* PLEDGE).

Plena probatio, full proof, as distinguished from *semi-plena probatio* or half-proof.

Plenary, full; entire; complete.

Plene administravit, he has fully administered; the defence which an executor or administrator can effectually plead to any action raised against him after he has duly liquidated and distributed all the assets of the estate (*Brink* v. *Esterhuyzen*, 1 Menz. 473). If an executor has still funds in his hands belonging to the estate, he will be liable to a creditor even although the latter's claim has not been filed within the period fixed by law (*Moore's Executrix* v. *Le Sueur*, 2 Menz. 475).

Plenipotentiary, a person invested with full power. The term is chiefly applied to ambassadors and envoys.

Pleydoye (D.) [modern spelling *pleidooij*], the pleading of a legal practitioner before the court on behalf of his client.

Pluimgraaf (D.), an officer appointed over fowling, &c. *See* GRAAF.

Plus valet quod agitur quam quod simulate concipitur, that which is done is of more avail than that which is pretended to be done. In accordance with this maxim, if two parties pretend to enter into one kind of contract whilst their real intention was to enter into a contract of another kind, the contract made by them will be held to be that which they really intended, and not that which they called it. Thus, where A wished to purchase a portion of a piece of land, and B would only sell the entire land, and in order to avoid payment of transfer duty on the whole of the land the parties entered into an agreement, which they called a guarantee, for the sale by A of the entire land in whole or in lots to one or more purchasers, it was held that as the agreement had all the practical effects of a sale, the word "guarantee" could not disguise its real nature, and that transfer duty was accordingly payable (*Treasurer-General* v. *Lippert*, 2 S.C. 172). So a transaction which was in form a sale, but which was intended to be a pledge, has been held to be a pledge (*Hofmeyer* v. *Gous*, 10 S.C. 115; *Cholwich* v. *Penny*, 5 E.D.C. 270).

Police, a body of men constituting a civil force in any country, town or village for the maintenance of good order; the prevention and detection of crime; the enforcement of the law; and the apprehension of criminals or persons suspected of crime or breach of municipal regulations. The various police forces of the South African colonies and territories are regulated by statute. The earliest unrepealed statute (though considerably amended) is Ordinance 2 of 1840 (C.C.).

Policy. "The usual instrument containing a contract of insurance is called a *policy*, a term borrowed from the Italian merchants who introduced the practice of insurance into this country" [England] (Porter's *Laws of Insurance*, 5th ed. p. 22). See also various kinds of policy or insurance under their respective titles. In the Cape Life Assurance Act (13 of 1891), the term *policy* is defined to include "a contract for securing a life assurance, endowment or annuity."

Poll, the voting and registering votes at an election.

Pollicitatio, a mere offer or promise which has not yet been accepted by the person to whom it is addressed. This constitutes no binding obligation, and may be receded from at any time before acceptance (*Hossack* v. *Lippert*, 3 S.C. at p. 276).

Polling booth, a place temporarily used by lawful authority at an election for the purpose of receiving the votes of those entitled to vote. Also called a "polling station."

Polling officer, a person duly appointed to take a poll in a district, municipality or ward. See Act 14 of 1874 (C.C.), secs. 33 *et seq.*; Act 9 of 1892 (C.C.), secs. 2 and 40; as to *polling officer* in divisional council elections in Cape Colony, see Act 40 of 1889 (C.C.), sec. 4.

Polling place, a place duly appointed where the voting and registration of votes takes place at an election.

Polling station. *See* POLLING BOOTH.

Polygamy, having more than one wife or husband at the same time. Under Roman-Dutch law polygamy is forbidden.

Poort (D.), anciently denoted a town. Hence *poortier* means a burgher or citizen. *Poortierschap*, burghership, citizenship. *Poortghraaf*, governor of a city.

Poortghraaf (D.), a governor of a city. *See* POORT.

Poortierschap (D.), burghership, citizenship. *See* POORT.

Poortmeester (D.), burgomaster.

Portio falcidia. Falcidian portion. *See* LEX FALCIDIA.

Portio legitima, legitimate portion. Under the common law a person was obliged to leave a certain portion of his estate, called the legitimate portion, to his children and also to his parents and brothers and sisters. In the case of children, including their descendants by representation, the legitimate portion, if they were four or less in number, was one-third, and if more than four, one-half of what they would have inherited *ab intestato.* As regards parents and brothers and sisters, the portion was always one-third part, but brothers and sisters could claim it only where disreputable persons had been instituted under the will. (See Grotius' *Introd.* 2, 18, 5 *et seq.*, and Schorer *in notis;* Van Leeuwen's *Comm.* 2, 5; Voet's *Comm.* 5, 2, 46 *et seq.*, and 37, 6, 13). The legitimate portions have been abolished throughout the South African colonies, a testator being now at perfect liberty to dispose of his property without restriction.

Portio Trebellianica, the Trebellian portion. *See* SENATUS CONSULTUM TREBELLIANUM.

Possessio bona fide et possessio mala fide, possession in good faith and possession in bad faith; *i.e.* possession by one who is not, but believes himself to be the owner, and possession by one as owner who knows that he is not the owner. The rights of a *bonâ fide* possessor and *malâ fide* possessor naturally differ in important respects. First, with regard to improvements made upon the property, a *bonâ fide* possessor retains the ownership of the improvements until he parts with possession; when the owner demands possession, the *bonâ fide* possessor may retain possession of the property until he is compensated for the useful expenses incurred by him, *i.e.* the extent to which the value of the land has been enhanced by the improvements; and failing payment of such compensation he may remove the improvements in so far as he can do so without injury to the property, or he may claim compensation (*De Beers Consolidated Mines* v. *London and South African Exploration Co.*, 10 S.C. 359). A *malâ fide* possessor, on the other hand, may indeed remove improvements before the owner demands possession, but after demand made he loses his right to do so, and although he is, like the *bonâ fide* possessor, entitled to his useful expenses (*Bellingham* v. *Bloometje*, Buch. 1874, p. 39; *Colonial Government* v. *Smith & Co.*, 18 S.C 392), he has no right of retention. If, however, the owner stood by and allowed the *malâ fide* possessor to proceed with the improvements without objecting, such *malâ fide* possessor will have the same right of retention as a *bonâ fide* possessor. Where the right to compensation exists it lies not only against the owner, but also against a mortgagee whose bond was executed prior to the date of the improvements (*South African Association* v. *Van Staden*, 9 S.C. 95). With regard to the fruits of the thing possessed, a *bonâ fide* possessor acquires all the fruits gathered by him before *litis contestatio*, but such fruits may be set off against any claim he may have to compensation for improvements. A *malâ fide* possessor has no right to any of the fruits, but must return those gathered by him and pay compensation for those consumed.

Possessio justa et injusta, lawful and unlawful possession; one of the civil law divisions of possession. These terms simply mean a possession to which one has, or has not, a legal title. Thus a person is said to have lawful possession who possesses either in the character of owner or under legal or judicial authority. In this way those who hold a thing in pledge or by the leave and license (*precario*) of the owner are said to have lawful possession (Voet's *Comm.* 41, 2, 4). In relation, however, to certain interdicts, *unde vi, de precario, uti possidetis*, &c., *justa possessio* was a possession which had not been obtained *vi* (by force) *aut clam* (or by stealth) *aut precario* (or by leave and license) from the other party (*Digest*, 43, 17, 2, 3).

Possession "is a compound of a physical situation and of a mental state, that is, of the physical holding or detention of a corporeal thing by a person and of the mental state of that person towards the thing. In other words, it is the physical detention of a corporeal thing by a person, whether with or without any claim or right, with the intention of holding it as his own, to which the law has given its sanction by interposing certain legal remedies or interdicts for its protection, in case of its being interfered with by other persons. But it is essential to the existence of *possession* that there should at one time or another have been both such detention or occupation and such intention present together at one and the same time" (Maasdorp's *Institutes*, vol. 2, p. 13). Nathan in his *Common Law* (sec. 562) defines it thus: "*Possession* is defined as the detention of a corporeal thing, with the intention of holding it for oneself. It is the detention of a thing certain, whether it be of a thing in common between two possessors held indivisibly (when a thing has been transferred by way of sale or legacy to two persons jointly) or of an undefined share in a defined thing. There can clearly be no *possession* of an uncertain thing." Grotius (*Introd.* 2, 2, 2) says: "*Possession* is the physical occupation of a thing with the intention of keeping it for oneself, and not for another." The definition given by Van Leeuwen in his *Comm.* (Kotzé's trans. vol. 1, p. 198) is as follows: "*Possession* is only a bare and naked apprehension and detention of a thing with the intention of using it as one's own." "The right of the owner to possess is technically called the *jus possidendi;* the right of the possessor to continue to possess is called the *jus possessionis*" (Holland's *Jurisprudence*, 10th ed. p. 185, *q.v.*). The distinction between *possession* in English law and in Roman-Dutch law is discussed by Morice in his *English and Roman-Dutch Law*, 2nd ed. p. 70. *See* ACTUAL POSSESSION.

Possessor, a person who holds possession of a thing. *See* POSSESSION.

Possessory rights, such rights as arise from possession. *See* POSSESSION.

Post mortem examination, the examination of a corpse, by a medical man, for the purpose of ascertaining the cause of death. See statutes cited under heading INQUEST.

Posthumous work, a book, within the meaning of the Copyright Act, published after the death of its author. In the Cape Colony the copyright in every *posthumous work* endures for thirty years from the date of its first publication, and is the property of the proprietor of the author's manuscript from which such book shall be first published and his assigns (Act 2 of 1873, sec. 2). In Natal the period of protection is forty-two years from the date of the first publication (Act 17 of 1897, sec. 7).

Postliminium, postliminy or reverter. *See* JUS POSTLIMINII.

Postliminy. *See* JUS POSTLIMINII.

Post-nuptial contract, a contract made between husband and wife after marriage, embodying some or all of the conditions of an antenuptial contract. This class of contract is not recognised in South Africa except in Natal, where there is special legislation on the subject (Law 22 of 1863, sec. 7; and see *Doran* v. *Doran*, 13 N.L.R. 29). Where, however, spouses have entered into an antenuptial contract or agreement, but failed to have it reduced to writing or registered, the Court may upon proof that there was such an agreement before marriage allow it to be executed and registered after marriage without prejudice to the rights of creditors whose claims existed prior to such registration (*Re Abt and Wife*, 3 C.T.R. 480; *Ex parte Taylor*, 12 S.C. 348; *Ex parte Fricker*, 2 C.T.R. 312; *Ex parte Steyn*, [1905] O.R.C. 48; *Ex parte Stone*, [1906] E.D.C. 156; *Ex parte Weight and Weight*, [1906] T.S. 707; *Ex parte South*, 19 C.T.R. 760; *Ex parte Doxey*, [1909] T.H. 88). But in the absence of clear evidence of such antenuptial agreement, no alteration can be made in the common law position of the spouses (*Ex parte Cloete*, [1907] O.R.C. 11); see also *Re Levi* (6 C.T.R. 227), and *Ex parte Peters* (9 C.T.R. 468), for grounds upon which the court has refused to grant an order for allowing the registration of a contract after marriage.

Potash. In the Fertilisers, Farm Foods, Seeds and Pest Remedies Act, 20 of 1907 (C.C.), sec. 3, *potash* is defined to mean "anhydrous oxide of potassium."

Potestative conditions, an expression employed in connection with the institution of an heir. *Potestative conditions* are such as are dependent upon the will or ability of the person upon whom they are imposed. "A *potestative condition* must, as a general rule, be fulfilled by the person upon whom it is imposed, and that specifically in accordance with the testator's directions, though such fulfilment may be of no use to anybody. As to the time of fulfilment, the directions of the testator, if there are any, are to be observed" (Maasdorp's *Institutes*, vol. 1, p. 139).

Power of attorney, a written authority from one person (called the principal) in favour of another (called the agent) whereby the principal delegates to the agent the right and power to perform certain acts or deeds. Such a power may be special or general; and it may be revocable or irrevocable. *See* GENERAL POWER OF ATTORNEY; NECESSARY POWER; SPECIAL POWER OF ATTORNEY.

Praedial servitude. Servitudes which attach to immovable property are called *praedial servitudes*, and are divided into urban and rural. They are distinguished from personal servitudes in that, while the latter are given to and enjoyed by a person simply as a person, the former are not separable from the dominant tenement, but are exercised by the owner in virtue of his ownership. To them applies the maxim *praedium servit praedio*, *i.e.* immovables serve (or are under a servitude to) immovable property.

Praedium, immovable property, whether lands or houses. *See* PRAEDIAL SERVITUDE.

Praedium dominans, the dominant tenement; the landed property in favour of which a servitude exists.

Praedium rusticum, a rural tenement, as distinguished from *praedium urbanum,* an urban tenement. By these terms is not meant land situated in the country and the town respectively. *Praedium rusticum* signifies the soil itself, whereas *praedium urbanum* signifies any *superficies* or building on the soil, without regard in either case to whether the *praedium* is in the town or the country. In the same way *praedial* servitudes are called rural or urban accordingly as they affect the soil or anything raised upon the soil. For example, the servitudes *iter, actus; via, aquaehaustus,* being connected with the use of land, are called rural servitudes, while the servitudes *stillicidium, oneris ferendi* and *tigni immittendi,* being attached to buildings, are called urban servitudes.

Praedium serviens, the servient tenement; the landed property over which a servitude exists.

Praedium servit praedio, land is under a servitude to land. *See* PRAEDIAL SERVITUDE.

Praedium urbanum, an urban tenement. *See* PRAEDIUM RUSTICUM.

Praeferentie (D.), the right of preference; a preference among several pledges or mortgages.

Praelegacy, a precedent bequest; "a legacy left to one of the heirs, and which has to be paid out to him before any division of the estate. In such a case it will be open to the heir to repudiate the inheritance and yet claim the praelegacy" (Maasdorp's *Institutes,* vol. 1, p. 190).

Praeponens, a person who has appointed another (called *institor* or *exercitor*) to manage a business or undertaking on his behalf. *See* ACTIO EXERCITORIA and ACTIO INSTITORIA.

Praescriptie or **Verjaring** (D.), prescription. *See* PRESCRIPTION.

Praescriptio longissimi temporis, prescription of the longest time. In the Roman law this prescription was a period of thirty years, or forty years in the case of property belonging to the Church or the State or property hypothecated and in the possession of the debtor, and it protected the possession of the occupier without requiring *bona fides* or *justus titulus.* Between the *bonâ fide* and the *malâ fide* possessor, however, there was this difference, that the possession of the former for the requisite period made him the owner of the property, even although it had originally been stolen, whereas the latter by the prescription was merely protected in his possession, for if he lost possession he had no right to recover it, the action for that purpose lying with the true owner. Under the Roman-Dutch law the period of this prescription is one-third of a century for immovables and thirty years for movables. By statute law in the Cape Colony (Act 7 of 1865, sec. 106) and the Transvaal (Act 26 of 1908, sec. 15) the period of prescription for immovable property has been made the same as that for movables, viz., thirty years. As in the Roman, so in the Roman-Dutch law, neither *bona fides* nor *justus titulus* is required for this prescription (Van der Keessel, *Thes.* 207), it being sufficient that the possessor should hold the property neither by force nor by clandestine means nor upon the mere sufferance of the owner (*nec vi, nec clam, nec precario*) (Voet's *Comm.* 44, 3, 9; *see* USUCAPIO).

Praescriptis verbis, in the words before written. *See* ACTIO PRAESCRIPTIS VERBIS.

Pratique, a permission granted by a health officer to a vessel on arrival at a port or harbour, whereby she is permitted to enter such port or harbour and discharge cargo and those on board are authorised to land, so far as health laws and regulations are concerned. See the Cape Public Health Amendment Act (23 of 1897), secs. 46 and 47.

Preamble, an introductory statement in a statute or contract reciting briefly the reasons or object for which it was enacted or made.

Prebend, a fixed portion of the revenues of a cathedral church set apart for the maintenance or payment of certain persons called prebendaries.

Prebendal, relating to a prebend. *See* PREBEND. Van Leeuwen in his *Comm.* (Kotzé's trans. vol. 2, p. 174) says: "In *prebendal* or vicarial property, if the possessor has leased any lands belonging to the prebend and happens to die, it is considered that the lease is at an end, for no one can cede to another a greater right than he himself possesses."

Precario, by entreaty or request; by leave or license. Where an owner of property allows another to possess it until such time as he may redemand it, the property is said to remain with the possessor *precario*. *See* PRECARIUM.

Precarium, a species of the contract of *commodatum*. It differs from *commodatum* in that the subject of the latter contract is lent for a certain purpose or for a certain time, and cannot be reclaimed until the purpose has been fulfilled or the time has expired, whereas in *precarium* the subject is lent only during the pleasure of the lender, and can be redemanded at any time.

Precedents, decisions of the courts which serve as a guide in future cases. "All that we need note is that the adhesion by our judges to *precedent*, that is, their habit of deciding one case in accordance with the principle, or supposed principle, which governed a former case, leads inevitably to the gradual formation by the courts of fixed rules for decision, which are in effect laws" (Dicey's *Law of the Constitution*, 6th ed. p. 58). *See* LEADING CASES.

Precincts, the boundaries enclosing a place or the enclosed place itself. For *precincts* of a gaol see *Anson* v. *Rex* ([1906] E.D.C. 160).

Precious metals. *See* MINERAL.

Precious stones is defined in the Natal Mines and Collieries Act (43 of 1899), sec. 4, to "mean and include diamonds, rubies, sapphires and emeralds."

In the Transvaal Precious Stones Ordinance (66 of 1903) *precious stones* includes diamonds and any other gems or stones proclaimed such by the Lieutenant-Governor."

Predecease, to die before another person; the death of one person prior to the death of another, as, for instance, the predecease of one of two spouses.

Predecessor, one who has preceded another in some position or office; one who previously occupied a position or office, such as a predecessor in title.

Prefer. (1) To present or bring forward, as to prefer a claim or a complaint, charge or accusation against a person.

(2) To give or grant a preference to a person before another or others; for instance, to *prefer* one creditor before the other creditors. The question of intention to *prefer* is a question entirely of fact (*Du Plooy's Trustee* v. *Plewman*, 7 S.C. 336).

Preference. (1) The right of a creditor to be paid his claim in full before any payment is made by the debtor or his estate to concurrent creditors.

(2) A payment made by a debtor to one creditor before his other creditors. *See* UNDUE PREFERENCE.

Pregnancy. (1) The state of a female who has conceived or is pregnant.

(2) The quality of being full of important contents, issue or significance.

Preliminary examination (also called "preparatory examination"), a preparatory examination held by magistrates relating to crimes or offences which are alleged to have been committed within their districts, and which crimes or offences do not plainly appear to be proper for the cognisance of a court of summary jurisdiction. See Ordinance 40 of 1828 (C.C.), secs. 27 *et seq.*; Ordinance 1 of 1903 (T.), sec. 54; Ordinance 12 of 1902 (O.R.C.), sec. 35.

Premie van assurantie (D.), premium of assurance.

Premises. (1) A term used in drafting leases in England. There a lease is divided into several parts, *i.e.* (*a*) the *premises* (which contain a statement of the date, the names, addresses, &c., of the parties; the recitals; the operative words; and the description of the property leased; (*b*) the *habendum* (the part fixing the term); (*c*) the *reddendum* (reservation of rent); (*d*) the covenants, &c. That portion of the lease which precedes the *habendum* is called the *premises* (Woodfall's *Landlord and Tenant,* 17th ed. p. 156). In South Africa the term *premises* is frequently applied to the whole contents of a deed or document.

(2) Certain land with the buildings and erections thereon.

In the Cape Excise Spirits Act (18 of 1884), sec. 2, and in the Cape Additional Taxation Act (36 of 1904), sec. 2, the term *premises,* when used with reference to an excise trader, is defined to mean "any building or place used by him in the course of his business, and includes all buildings or places owned or occupied by or on behalf, or for the use of, such excise trader." For definition of the term *premises* in the Cape Scab Act (20 of 1894), see sec. 4 of that Act.

In the Transvaal Crimes Ordinance (26 of 1904), sec. 3, *premises* means "any building or structure or part thereof (not being a dwelling) habitually used as a shop, warehouse, storehouse, bank, office, school, or for divine worship, or any outbuilding occupied in connection with a dwelling or *premises* as herein defined." See also Ordinance 4 of 1905 (T.), sec. 2.

In the Public Health Ordinance, 31 of 1907 (O.R.C.), sec. 1, *premises* is defined to include "lands, buildings, vehicles, tents, vans, structures of any kind, streams, spruits, lakes, pans, dams, sluits, drains, ditches, or places open, covered or enclosed, whether built on or not, and whether public or private, and whether natural or artificial, and whether maintained or not under statutory authority."

See *Randall* v. *Town Council of Grahamstown* (11 S.C. 27; 4 C.T.R. 39); DWELLING.

Preparatory examination, equivalent to preliminary examination. *See* PRELIMINARY EXAMINATION.

Prerogative. "The *prerogative* is the name for the remaining portion of the Crown's original authority, and is therefore, as already pointed out, the name for the residue of discretionary power left at any moment in the hands of the Crown, whether such power be in fact exercised by the king himself or by his ministers. Every act which the executive government can lawfully do without the authority of the Act of Parliament is done by virtue of this *prerogative"* (Dicey's *Law of the Constitution*, 6th ed. p. 369). Also called the "Royal prerogative."

Prescribed. (1) The past tense of *prescribe;* rendered invalid by reason of adverse prescription.

(2) Laid down in some law, rules or regulations. See Act 36 of 1904 (C.C.), sec. 42.

Prescription. *Prescription* is of two kinds, acquisitive and extinctive. Acquisitive prescription or prescription as a mode of acquiring property has already been dealt with under *prescriptio longissimi temporis (q.v.).* By extinctive prescription or limitation of actions no property is acquired, but an action can be repelled on the ground that the time fixed by law as that within which it should have been raised has expired.

The period which is required for the *prescription* of a right of action varies according to the nature of the action. At common law the prescriptive period of all personal actions, where no other period has been fixed with regard to a particular action, is variously stated to be thirty years and a third of a century (see Maasdorp's *Institutes*, vol. 4, p. 149). By Act 26 of 1908 (T.), sec. 8, the Transvaal has adopted the period of thirty years.

Hypothecary actions, however, are at common law prescribed in forty years; by hypothecary actions being meant, not actions on a general bond which are subject to the above thirty years' *prescription* (*Peach & Co.* v. *Simon's Trustee,* 13 S.C. 56), but actions on a special mortgage of immovable property (*Schomberg's Executors* v. *De Vos's Executors,* 1 S.C. 325; Grotius' *Introd.* 2, 48, 44; Van der Keessel's *Thes.* 443). In the Transvaal, however, such hypothecary actions seem by the above Act to be subject to the thirty years' *prescription.*

At common law judgments of a court become prescribed in thirty years (Voet's *Comm.* 42, 1, 47); but in the Transvaal it is provided by Act 36 of 1908, sec. 9, that there shall be no *prescription* in respect of a judgment of a court of law.

Actions on a bill of exchange or other liquid document of debt, or in respect of a written acknowledgment of debt other than a mortgage bond, prescribe in eight years in Cape Colony (Act 6 of 1861, sec. 2). In the Transvaal the period of *prescription* with regard to such documents of debt is six years (Act 26 of 1908, sec. 8). Promissory notes are in Cape Colony subject to the same *prescription* of eight years, but by the Transvaal Act (sec. 8) a promissory note not negotiated is excepted from the six years' *prescription,* and presumably falls within the period "in respect of matters for which a period is not hereinbefore fixed," viz., thirty years (see sec. 9 of the Act).

The above eight years' *prescription* is also applied by the Cape statute (sec. 3) to actions "for money due for goods sold and delivered for money lent by the plaintiff to the defendant, for money paid by the plaintiff for the use of the defendant, for money had and received by the defendant for the use of the plaintiff (including the *condictio indebiti*), for rent upon any lease or contract for hire, for money claimed upon or by virtue of an admission of an account due upon an account stated and settled, for money due upon an award of arbitrators, for money due as the purchase money of fixed property, for money claimed for work and labour done and materials for the same provided, and for money claimed upon or by virtue of any policy of assurance." After repealing the 16th art. of the Placaat of the Emperor Charles V of 1540, the Cape statute (sec. 5) provides a three years' *prescription* for actions for fees and disbursements of advocates, attorneys, notaries, conveyancers, land surveyors or persons practising any branch of the medical profession, or for the amount of any baker's or butcher's or tailor's or dressmaker's or boot or shoemaker's bill or account or for the salary or wages of any merchant's clerk or other persons employed in any merchant's or dealer's store, counting-house or shop, or for the wages as a servant of any person coming under the definition of the term "servant" given in the Masters and Servants Act (15 of 1856).

The Transvaal Act also repeals the Placaat of 1540, and in introducing a three years' *prescription* (sec. 6) applies the same to some of the actions which fall within the eight years' *prescription* in the Cape Act. The section comprises: (*a*) the fees, disbursements, salary, wages or any other remuneration whatever due to any person for services rendered, labour done or work performed by him in his profession, trade, occupation or calling; (*b*) the price of movables sold and delivered, or of labour done, and materials provided, or board or lodging supplied; (*c*) any oral contract; (*d*) rent due upon an agreement in writing or interest due upon a mortgage bond; (*e*) all actions for damages; other than those for which another period of prescription is laid down in this Act; (*f*) *condictiones indebiti* and *condictiones sine causa.*

The *actio redhibitoria* and the *actio quanti minoris*, prescribed at common law by a period of six months and a year respectively, are by the Transvaal Act made both subject to a prescriptive period of one year.

Actions for *restitutio in integrum*, which at common law must be brought within four years, although relief may be granted at any time within thirty years (Voet's *Comm.* 4. 1, 20; Van Leeuwen's *Comm.* 4, 42, 3), are in the Transvaal Act definitely stated to prescribe in four years.

Actions of damages for defamation prescribe at common law by the lapse of the *annus utilis* (Voet's *Comm.* 47, 10, 21), and this period is retained by sec. 4 of the Transvaal Act. In the case of libel, however, the period of prescription at the Cape is by sec. 10 of Act 46 of 1882 six months.

"Present at the meeting." "An act which simply left the determination of a matter to a majority of vestrymen *present at the meeting* would not affect the common law right of the minority to demand a poll; and the 'meeting' would therefore be understood as continuing until the end of the poll" (Maxwell's *Interpretation of Statutes*, 4th ed. p. 126).

Presumptio hominis or **judicis** or **facti**, the presumption of the man or of the judge or of fact. This is the presumption which arises in the mind of the judge from the nature and circumstances of the case itself, as distinguished from a *presumptio juris*, which arises from the law, either statutory or customary.

Presumptio juris, a presumption of law; a presumption fixed by statutory or customary law, but which may be rebutted by evidence to the contrary. For example, it is a *presumptio juris* that a husband is the father of his wife's children, that a man is not supposed to make a donation of his property, that a legacy is revoked by the testator subsequently making a voluntary alienation of the thing bequeathed, or that a child between seven and fourteen years of age is incapable of wrong-doing (*incapax doli*) so as to be criminally punishable.

Presumptio juris et de jure, a legal presumption which amounts to a rule of law, and is so strong that it does not admit of evidence to the contrary. Thus an alienation of property made by a minor without the assistance of his guardians is null and void, as he is presumed to be incompetent to act for himself, and this presumption cannot be rebutted by contrary evidence. So also the expiry of the period of limitation of a right of action raises a conclusive presumption of satisfaction or abandonment of the claim. A child, again, who is under seven years of age is absolutely free from criminal responsibility, as he is presumed incapable of wrong-doing, and such presumption does not admit of rebutting evidence.

Presumption, "a *presumption* means a rule of law that courts and judges shall draw a particular inference from a particular fact, or from particular evidence, unless and until the truth of such inference is disproved" (Stephen's *Digest of the Criminal Law*, 5th ed. p. 2).

Prevent, to hinder or obstruct. "Where an adult person, who is a minor, is in any person's house and desires to stay there, and comes and states that he or she is not detained, but that it is of his or her free will that he or she stays there, it is difficult to hold that there is any prevention of that child being removed by the person legally entitled to the custody for the time being; but where we deal with small children ranging in age from six to ten or twelve, the case is very different, and we consider ourselves that the word *prevent* is not confined to cases of physical restraint or physical violence. We consider that where small children of this age are concerned, pressure put upon them is quite a sufficient prevention to give a magistrate jurisdiction, and that is the distinction we draw between this case and other cases where this question of prevention has come in" (*per* Mason, A.C.J., in *Puskan* v. *Veerasamy*, 22 N.L.R. at p. 159).

Previous conviction, the conviction and sentence of a prisoner on a former occasion.

The words *previous conviction* as used in sec. 42 of Act 20 of 1856 (C.C.) "mean, in my opinion, a conviction followed by a sentence entailing some punishment, however slight that punishment may be, and not a mere admonition or reprimand" (*per* SHEIL, J., in *Rex* v. *Bibby*, [1906] E.D.C. at p. 81).

As to proof of *previous convictions* in other countries, see *Jones* v. *Rex* ([1904] T.S. 890).

Primage, a payment for loading, &c., made by the consignor of goods to the master of the vessel in which the goods are shipped.

Primary school. In the Transvaal Education Act (25 of 1907) *primary school* means "a public school at which all children in attendance follow the course of primary instruction prescribed by regulation."

Principal. (1) One who is chiefly concerned; a person for whom an agent is acting or employed.

The term *principal* is defined in the Cape Workman's Compensation Act (40 of 1905), sec. 4, to mean "any person whose trade, business, contract or public function it being wholly or in part to do, perform or undertake a work to which this Act applies, employs a contractor to do it for him wholly or in part, and whether such contractor employs a sub-contractor or not, and shall include the legal personal representative of a deceased *principal* and the trustee of the estate of a *principal* when such estate has been sequestrated." See also Transvaal Workmen's Compensation Act (36 of 1907), sec. 1.

(2) The capital sum of money upon which interest is usually chargeable.

Principal in first degree. "Whoever actually commits or takes part in the actual commission of a crime is a *principal in the first degree*, whether he is on the spot when the crime is committed or not; and if a crime is committed partly in one place and partly in another, every one who commits any part of it at any place is a *principal in the first degree*" (Stephen's *Digest of the Criminal Law*, 5th ed. p. 30; see also *R.* v. *Abrams* (1 S.C. 393), where the subject is fully discussed).

Principal in second degree. "Whoever aids or abets the actual commission of a crime, either at the place where it is committed, or elsewhere, is a *principal in the second degree* in that crime" (Stephen's *Digest of the Criminal Law*, 5th ed. p. 31; see also *R.* v. *Abrams*, 1 S.C. 393).

Printer. *See* SERVANT.

Prior in sorte prior est in usuris, he who is first as regards principal is first as regards interest. In the Roman law a creditor could sue for any amount of interest not exceeding the principal sum, and for the whole of such interest he would in a competition with other creditors be entitled to a preference if his claim as regards the capital was preferent. This rule, which was adopted by the law of Holland, was early departed from, and the principle came to be that the interest for which a preference could be claimed should be limited to a certain number of years. Different places enacted different periods, but the rule at Amsterdam, where preference was allowed for one year's interest together with the current year's, has by custom been adopted in this country (*In re Meiring*, 2 Menz. 318). A mortgagee accordingly receives a preference for the stipulated interest for a year and the current year preceding the date of issue of the writ of execution or order of sequestration where no writ has been issued, and also for the further period from the issue of the writ or order until the date of payment (*Brink, N.O.*, v. *High Sheriff*, 12 S.C. 414; *Rooth & Wessels* v. *Benjamin's Trustee and the Natal Bank*, [1905] T.S. p. 630). In Natal, however, it has been held, following the Roman law, that there is no limit to the preference for interest, in so far as such interest does not exceed the principal sum (*Natal Investment Co.* v. *Natal Bank*, 1878–79, N.L.R. 10).

Prior tempore potior jure. *See* QUI PRIOR EST TEMPORE POTIOR EST JURE.

Prison, a place or building authorised by Government for the confinement or detention of criminals, persons charged with offences or crimes, witnesses specially detained, or civil debtors. "*Prison* shall mean any gaol, house of correction or lock-up now used or provided or hereafter to be appointed by the Minister as a place for the detention or confinement of persons liable to detention in custody, and shall include all yards and buildings in connection with such gaol or house of correction" (Act 23 of 1888 (C.C.), sec. 2). See Act 1 of 1897 (C.C.), sec. 2; Proclamation 36 of 1902 (T.), sec. 2; Ordinance 2 of 1904 (T.), sec. 1; Ordinance 3 of 1903 (O.R.C.), sec. 1; Ordinance 13 of 1906 (O.R.C.), sec. 2. See also *Anson* v. *Rex* ([1906] E.D.C. 160).

Prisoner. "*Prisoner* shall mean any person whether convicted or not under detention in any prison or lock-up" (Act 23 of 1888 (C.C.), sec. 2). For similar definition, see Ordinance 6 of 1906 (T.), sec. 3; Ordinance 3 of 1903 (O.R.C.), sec. 1.

The word *prisoner*, as used in sec. 14 of Law 14 of 1880 (T.), means one who has actually been in lawful custody in a gaol; therefore a person who escaped while under arrest, but before being committed to gaol, cannot be charged with a contravention of that section (*Rex* v. *Quarry*, [1903] T.S. 837).

Privaat water (D.), private water or private stream. "Broadly speaking, the common law divides rivers, streams, &c., into two classes—public streams and private streams. . . . Private streams are streams which do not fall within the definition of public streams" (Juta's *Waterrights*, p. 2). *See* PUBLIC STREAM. "Under the term "private streams" are included rivers and streams which are not perennial, and streams which, although perennial, are so weak as to be incapable of being applied to the common use of the riparian proprietors" (Maasdorp's *Institutes*, vol. 2, p. 104).

Private Bills. "Parliament now understands by *private Bills* all those projects of law which affect the interests of particular localities, and are not of a public general character, and are introduced by petition. Every Bill for the particular interest or benefit of any person or persons, whether it is brought in upon petition or motion, or report from a committee, or brought from the Lords, is a *private Bill* within the meaning of the table of fees established by the Standing Orders of the House of Commons" (Craies' *Statute Law*, p. 447). See Act 6 of 1887 (C.C.), providing for the taxation of costs relating to *private Bills* in the Cape Parliament; Act 6 of 1907 (T.), sec. 1; Act 41 of 1908 (O.R.C.), sec. 1.

Private company, in the Transvaal Companies Act (31 of 1909), sec. 2, means "a company which by its articles (*a*) restricts the right to transfer its shares; and (*b*) limits the number of its members (exclusive of persons who are in the employ of the company) to a number not exceeding fifty; and (*c*) prohibits any invitation to the public to subscribe for any of its shares or debentures."

Private forest. "*Private forest* shall include all land owned by any body or private person on which trees exist in such quantity that wood and arboreal products constitute the principal production of the soil" (the Cape Forest Act, 28 of 1888, sec. 2).

Private land. In the Transvaal Precious Stones Ordinance (66 of 1903) *private land* means "any area of ground of which the ownership is vested in an individual or company as shown by title or deed of transfer, and in the title of which there is no reservation by the Crown of precious stones and minerals;" and in the Transvaal Precious and Base Metals Act (35 of 1908), "any farm or piece of land (whether held in divided or undivided shares) which is not Crown land." See also Ordinance 3 of 1904 (O.R.C.), sec. 5; and Ordinance 4 of 1904 (O.R.C.), sec. 5.

Private location. In the Cape Native Locations Amendment Act (30 of 1899) the expression *private location* is defined to mean "any number of huts or dwellings on any private property occupied by one or more native male adults, such occupants not being in the *bonâ fide* and continuous employment of the owner or occupier of such land either as his domestic servants or in or about the farming operations, trade, business, or handicraft by him carried on upon such land."

Private nuisance. "A *private nuisance* is some unauthorised act which causes injury to property, or interferes with a person's rights over the property of others, or materially interferes with the ordinary physical enjoyment of property, by causing injury to health or sensible personal discomfort" (Stephen's *Comm.* 15th ed. vol. 3, p. 406). See Garrett on *Nuisances*, 3rd. ed. p. 2.

Private property. In the Cape Establishment of Native Townships Act (44 of 1908), sec. 1, "*private property* shall mean any landed property, not being landed property situate within the limits of any municipality or village management board area, at any time held under deed of grant, transfer or lease, and shall be deemed to include any erf or erven originally forming a portion thereof held either under separate deed or deeds of transfer or under lease."

Private railway. A term used in the Cape Railway Regulation Amendment Act (36 of 1895), where it is defined to mean "any railway, other than the Cape Government Railways, used for public purposes, and shall include any tramway, whether the method of traction be by means of horses, steam-power, electricity or other motive power."

"Private residences and grounds." An expression used in Act 11 of 1905 (C.C.), sec. 1, where it is defined to mean "any private residence or dwelling-house with any ground attached thereto." See also Act 25 of 1905 (C.C.), sec. 1.

Private stream. *See* PRIVAAT WATER; PRIVATE WATER.

Private water, an expression employed in Law 11 of 1894 (T.), sec. 2, where it is "applicable only to cases where the fountain or stream is not permanent, or not capable cf subdivision, or does not run in any defined course on to the farms of other persons." *See* PRIVAAT WATER.

Privatorum conventio juri publico non derogat, an agreement between individuals does not derogate from public law. Laws which have been passed, not for the prevention of public loss, but with reference to the affairs of private individuals, may be abrogated by the agreement of such individuals. . It is otherwise where the law concerns the public utility, or where, owing to weakness of sex or instability of youth or because they labour under some other defect, those for whose benefit the law has been enacted are forbidden to injure themselves by their own consent or to act contrary to their own interests, as where a dotal estate is alienated with the wife's consent or where minors, prodigals and other like persons contract to their own injury (Voet's *Comm.* 1, 3, 16). In accordance with this principle, a husband and wife, even if married by antenuptial contract, cannot infringe upon the rule of law which prohibits the one from making a donation to the other. The law having been introduced not for the benefit of the parties, but on grounds of public policy, a donation in violation of it is null and void (*Hall* v. *Hall's Trustee and Mitchell*, 3 S.C. 3). Again, under the Workmen's Compensation Acts (40 of 1905 (C.C.), sec. 37 and 36 of 1907 (T.), sec. 31), a workman is not allowed to contract himself out of the benefits of the Act, which was passed not for the benefit of private persons, but as a matter of public policy.

Privilege, an exclusive right granted by law in favour of a particular class of persons or in respect of a particular thing. *See* PRIVILEGIUM.

Privileged communications. (1) Such communications as a person is not compelled to disclose in an action or other legal proceeding, as, for instance, correspondence between an attorney and his client.

(2) Communications which in ordinary circumstances would be defamatory, but which in the special circumstances are protected against actions or prosecutions for defamation; such as the statements made in a House of Parliament by a member thereof, or in a court of law by judge, counsel, or witnesses.

Privileged will, a testament which is recognised as valid although not executed with the usual formalities; *e.g.* holograph wills, and wills made by soldiers while on active service. See *Re McCalgan* (10 S.C. 279; 3 C.T.R. 395); *Re Leedham* (18 S.C. 450).

"The law relating to *privileged wills* is in an unsatisfactory state" (*per* DE VILLIERS, C.J., in *Re Sluiter*, 17 S.C. at p. 382).

Privileges. *See* PRIVILEGIEN; PRIVILEGIUM.

Privilegien (D.), privileges, benefices or rights granted by a supreme power, but only within the scope of such power. *See* Van Leeuwen's *Comm.* 1, 3, 9. They "were special benefits accorded to an individual or to a particular district or town. These privileges were extremely important during the sixteenth and seventeenth centuries, for special advantages in the way of tolls, jurisdiction, succession, &c., had been granted to nearly all the large towns and important villages. As they differed materially from one another, the laws within a very small radius might be in hopeless conflict with one another" (Wessels' *History*, p. 209).

Privilegium, a privilege. Privileges are of two kinds, viz., (1) those which are granted in favour of any one of a particular class of persons (*privilegia personae*); and (2) those which are granted in respect of a particular thing, viz., the debt or cause of action (*privilegia causae*). Of the former kind is the preference accorded to certain parties in competition among creditors, such as that to a minor over the goods of his tutor, or to a wife for the recovery of her dowry. As examples of *privilegia causae* we have the preferences for funeral expenses and for fees for medical attendance during last illness. (See Voet's *Comm.* 1, 4, 1, 12–26.)

Privy Council, the principal council of state in Great Britain, consisting of a number of persons whom the sovereign appoints. The number of councillors is not limited. *See* JUDICIAL COMMITTEE OF THE PRIVY COUNCIL.

Prize. This term is defined in the Cape Lotteries Prohibition Act (9 of 1889) as follows: "*Prize* means money or any other matter, article or thing, including lands, houses, goods, wares, merchandise or other property, movable or immovable, and including any right to claim money, and any right of ownership, possession, use, usufruct or occupation of lands, houses, goods, wares, merchandise or other property" (sec. 3). See also Law 7 of 1890 (T.), sec. 6; O.R.C. Law Book, chap. 143, sec. 2 (2).

Prize fight, a contest with fists for prizes. That the fists may be covered with gloves seems to be immaterial; see *Couper and Others* v. *The State* (1 Off. Rep. (Webber's trans.), 186); *Clarke* v. *Bruning* ([1905] T.S. at p. 297). See *Austin* v. *Morrall and Others* (22 S.C. at p. 70).

Pro bono publico, for the public good.

Pro Deo, for God. Advocates and attorneys who have been appointed by the court to conduct the causes of those who, by reason of their poverty, have obtained leave to sue *in formâ pauperis,* are said to act for such suitors *pro Deo* or *gratis.* *See* PROBABILIS CAUSA.

Pro forma, as a matter of form.

Pro parte virili, for a man's share; for one's own proportion. *See* PRO RATÂ.

Pro rata, for a proportion. When two or more persons undertake an obligation, their liability, in the absence of any express agreement to the contrary, is merely joint, and not both joint and several. In other words, each of the co-obligors is bound only *pro ratâ* or for his proportionate share. The case of partners, however, also that of joint wrong-doers and tutors who undertake the same tutelage, are exceptions to this rule, each being liable severally for the whole debt or *singuli in solidum.* Another exception exists where the liability is founded on a bill of exchange or promissory note, joint drawers, acceptors or indorsers being liable jointly and severally for the whole amount of the bill or note unless the contrary appears on the face of the document (*Kidson* v. *Campbell and Jooste,* 2 Menz. 279; *Jacobson* v. *Nitch,* 7 S.C. 174).

Probabilis causa (litigandi), a probable ground of litigation. Before a person is allowed to institute or defend an action as a pauper, counsel must have certified that in his opinion there is a good cause of action or defence. Counsel's certificate, however, is not necessarily conclusive, because the opposite party may show cause to the contrary, and where it appears to the court there is no cause of action or defence, leave to sue or defend *in formâ pauperis* will not be granted (*Ex parte du Plooy*, 10 S.C. 7; *Brink* v. *Nederduitsche Gereformeerde Kerk in de Transvaal*, ([1907] T.S. 183).

Probate, an English term signifying the proof of the will of a deceased person in a competent court as required by law. Formerly wills were in England proved before the ecclesiastical judge; later in the Court of Probate: and, since the Judicature Act, in the Probate, Divorce and Admiralty Division of the High Court of Justice. The functions of the English Court of Probate are, in South Africa, performed by the Masters of the Supreme or High Courts of the various colonies; the only exception being Natal, where the duties of the Master, as, for instance, performed in the Cape Colony, are divided between the Master of the Supreme Court of Natal and the Registrar of Deeds. *See* LETTERS OF ADMINISTRATION; MASTER (2). The term *probate* is uncommon in South African statute law and legal phraseology, with the exception of Natal, where it is in common use; see Law 5 of 1898 (N.), "to provide for the registration and *probate* of wills in the Colony of Natal"; also Law 13 of 1869 (N.); Law 26 of 1880 (N.); and Act 19 of 1894 (N.), in all of which the word *probate* is frequently employed.

Process in aid. (1) An order of a colonial court granting aid to a trustee of a bankrupt estate situate in England. This *process in aid* is usually granted upon production by the representative of such trustee of an order of an English court, having jurisdiction, directing the trustee to seek the aid of such colonial court, and requesting the colonial court to act in aid under the provisions of sec. 118 of the English Bankruptcy Act of 1883 (formerly under sec. 74 of the English Bankruptcy Act of 1869). See *Howse, Sons & Co.'s Trustee* v. *Howse, Sons & Co.'s Trustees; Jocelyne* v. *Shearer and Hine* (3 S.C. 14); *Re N. Howse & Co.'s Estate* (3 E.D.C. 367); *Leslie's Trustee* v. *Leslie* ([1903] T.S. 839); *Ex parte Link's Trustee* ([1904] T.S. 251); *Donaldson* v. *B.S.A. Asphalte and Manufacturing Co.* ([1905] T.S. 753), and an article on the subject in 1 C.L.J. 21. This is sometimes called a request in aid.

(2) An order granted by the Supreme Court of the Transvaal Colony under sec. 14 of Proclamation 21 of 1902 (establishing courts of resident magistrate), whereby authority is given to the applicant, on an *ex parte* application, to sell certain immovable property of the respondent in satisfaction of a judgment of a court of resident magistrate; such property must be sold only through the Sheriff, and cannot be so sold without this *process in aid.* (See also *Gunningham* v. *James,* [1903] T.H. 491). This form of *process in aid* is not provided for in the Magistrate's Court Acts of the Cape Colony.

Proclaimed field, an area of land duly proclaimed according to law as a public diggings upon which the public may peg out claims and conduct mining operations. *See* PUBLIC DIGGINGS. The expression *proclaimed field* in sec. 92 of Law 15 of 1898 (Transvaal Gold Law) denotes an area under the jurisdiction of a mining commissioner, and includes ground held under *mijnpacht brieven* within that area (*Klippoortje Estates and Tramway Co., Ltd.*, v. *The Government*, [1905] T.S. 542). In the new Transvaal Gold Law (Act 35 of 1908), which repeals Law 15 of 1898, *proclaimed field* is defined as including "all proclaimed land, and so much of any unproclaimed land as may be declared portion of a *proclaimed field* under this Act or is at the commencement thereof a *proclaimed field*." "*Proclaimed land*" is then defined as "land proclaimed a Public Digging under this Act or Law No. 15 of 1898 or a prior law, provided it has not been lawfully deproclaimed." In the Transvaal Townships Amendment Act (34 of 1908), sec. 1, the term is defined as including, in addition to the meaning given to it in the above Act, "land proclaimed an alluvial digging under the Precious Stones Ordinance, 1903, or any amendment thereof."

Proclamation, an act of the High Commissioner, Governor or the Government duly published directing or allowing something to be done or prohibiting the doing of something.

As to withdrawal of a proclamation, see *Louw* v. *Mining Commissioner of Johannesburg* (14 C.L.J. 73).

Proctor, the name given to those who at one time in England were admitted and enrolled specially to practise and conduct suits before ecclesiastical and admiralty courts. By the Solicitors Act, 1887, 40 & 41 Vict. cap. 25, sec. 17, solicitors were allowed to practise as *proctors*, and by the Judicature Act, 1873, sec. 87, they are now called solicitors of the Supreme Court. In the Cape Colony the Supreme Court was empowered to approve, admit and enrol *proctors* by sec. 19 of the Charter of Justice of 1832.

Procuration. *See* PER PROCURATION.

Procurator, a person whom another has entrusted to carry out something for him; an agent.

Procurator ad causas, an attorney employed to assist a litigant in the conduct of his lawsuit (Wessels' *History*, p. 195). *See* ATTURNATUS JUDICIALIS.

Procurator ad negotia, an attorney who assisted his client in the transaction of business, as distinguished from a *procurator ad causas*. See Wessels' *History*, p. 195. *See* also ATTURNATUS EXTRAJUDICIALIS.

Procurator in rem suam, an agent in his own interest, *i.e.* an agent who has been appointed with regard to a matter which it is his interest or advantage to carry out, as distinguished from other agents, who act solely in the interest of their principals and are sometimes called *procuratores in rem alienam*. *See* IN REM SUAM.

Procureur (D.), an attorney of the court. *See* ATTORNEY.

Prodigal, a person who spends money extravagantly and wastefully, or who wastefully disposes of property without apparent necessity. "An important point on which Roman-Dutch law differs from English is, that under the former the Supreme Court can declare incapable of managing his affairs and appoint curators for a person who is not insane, but is recklessly extravagant in his habits. Such persons are known as prodigals or spendthrifts (*kwistgoeds*). By being made subject to curators they lose the civil capacity for dealing with their property, while their personal liberty need not otherwise be disturbed" (Morice's *English and Roman-Dutch Law*, 2nd ed. p. 30). By Roman law spendthrifts could be interdicted from the management of their property by the praetor. "The power of the Court to appoint curators over the property of *prodigals* is undoubted" (*per* DE VILLIERS, C.J., in *Re Chism*, 9 S.C. 61).

Produce. In Cape Colony, under Act 35 of 1893, *produce* is defined to include "all skins, hides, horns, wool, mohair and ostrich feathers." For definition in Transvaal, see Ordinance 6 of 1904, sec. 2.

Produced. In the Natal Copyright Act (17 of 1897), sec. 3, "*produced* means, in the case of a book, published; and in the case of a work of art, made."

Profectitious property, certain property of minor children. "*Profectitious property* is such as has been derived from the parents themselves either directly or indirectly, such as gifts given to infants by their godparents, which are considered as given out of regard for the parents rather than the children" (Maasdorp's *Institutes*, vol. 1, p. 233). *See* ADVENTITIOUS PROPERTY; PECULIUM.

Profert and oyer, an obsolete English practice which was abolished by the Common Law Procedure Act. "Where a party relied upon an instrument under seal in his pleading, and it was in his possession, he was bound to make *profert* of it, that is to say, he must have averred that he brought it into court; the other party could then demand *oyer* of it, that is to say, have it read to him. As a matter of fact the deed was not brought by the party into court or read to the other party, but a copy was given to him" (Bray's *Discovery*, p. 264).

Profits, the pecuniary value which is or may be derived from the occupation, exercise or enjoyment of the thing (Jenks' *Digest of English Civil Law*, bk. 1, sec. 45).

Prohibited immigrant, a person who is by statute prohibited from immigrating either by land or sea into a South African colony. See Act 47 of 1902 (C.C.), sec. 1; Act 30 of 1903 (N.); and Act 15 of 1907 (T.). See also chap. 33 of the Law Book (O.R.C.).

"I understand *prohibited immigrant* to mean a person who wishes to come into the colony, and who, by reason of the prohibitions of the law, is not at liberty to do so" (*per* BRISTOWE, J., in *Lalloo* v. *Rex,* [1908] T.S. at p. 633). See also *Ismail and Others* v. *Rex,* [1908] T.S. at p. 1091).

Promise. "By our law, differing in this respect from that of England, an action may be brought on a *promise* to answer for the debt of another, even although the agreement containing such *promise* be not in writing. But, as in actions to enforce contracts for the sale of land, clear and conclusive evidence of the *promise* is required" (*per* DE VILLIERS, C.J., in *Koster* v. *Blake*, 10 S.C. at p. 31). *See* CAUSA.

Promise to the public. "A promise to the public may, under certain circumstances, entitle any one of the public who has given the consideration upon which the promise was founded, to a fulfilment of the promise. But the promise must be in such a simple form that the mere acceptance of it would constitute a contract" (*per* DE VILLIERS, C.J., in *Fraser* v. *Frank Johnson & Co.*, 11 S.C. at p. 66). See *Carlill* v. *Carbolic Smoke Ball Co.* ([1893] 1 Q.B. 256; 62 L.J. Q.B. 257; 67 L.T. 837).

Promise upon request (*toezegging*) "is where a person for some reasonable cause, that is, in return for what has been given or done to him, promises and acknowledges himself bound to another in something upon the latter's request" (Van Leeuwen's *Comm.* Kotzé's trans. vol. 2, p. 4).

Promissory note is an unconditional promise in writing made by one person to another, signed by the maker, engaging to pay on demand or at a fixed or determinable future time, a sum certain in money to or to the order of a specified person or to bearer; a note is not invalid by reason only that it contains also a pledge of collateral security with authority to sell or dispose thereof; a note is inchoate and incomplete until delivery thereof to the payee or bearer; a note may be made by two or more makers, and they may be liable thereon jointly, or jointly and severally according to its tenor (see secs. 83–85 of the English Bills of Exchange Act, 1882; secs. 82–84 of Cape Bills of Exchange Act, 1893; secs. 82–84 of Natal Bills of Exchange Law, 1887; secs. 82–84 of Transvaal Bills of Exchange Proclamation, 1902; secs. 82–84 of O.R.C. Bills of Exchange Ordinance, 28 of 1902; secs. 82–84 of Rhodesian Bills of Exchange Regulations, 1895). Where nothing to the contrary appears on the face of it, joint makers of a promissory note are liable jointly and severally thereon (*Kidson* v. *Campbell and Jooste*, 2 Menz. 279; *Jacobson* v. *Nitch*, 7 S.C. 174).

In Natal there are certain restrictions on contracts of natives founded on promissory notes, bills of exchange and the like (Law 44 of 1877, sec. 8); also in respect of similar obligations executed by Indians (Act 48 of 1904).

For further definitions of *promissory note*, see Proclamation 12 of 1902 (T.), sec. 21; Ordinance 40 of 1904 (T.), sec. 9.

Promoter. In the Cape Colony the term *promoter* as used in secs. 90 and 91 of the Companies Act (25 of 1892) is defined in sec. 92 of that Act to mean "a *promoter* who was a party to the preparation of the prospectus or notice, or of the portion thereof containing such untrue statement, but shall not include any person by reason of his acting in a professional capacity for persons engaged in procuring the formaton of the company." This definition is taken verbatim from the English Directors' Liability Act of 1890, sec. 2. On this subject consult Palmer's *Company Precedents*, part 1, chap. 2. A somewhat similar definition is found in Act 31 of 1909 (T.), sec. 82 (5). See also Act 41 of 1908 (O.R.C.), sec. 1; and *Re Rosemount G. M. Syndicate in liqn.*, [1905] T.H. at p. 196).

Promulgation, the act of making known by public declaration. "By the Roman-Dutch law, as indeed by any civilised system of jurisprudence, a law before it can take effect requires to be promulgated. The expression of the will of the legislative authority does not acquire the force of law unless and until it has been promulgated in due form for the information of those whom it is to affect" (*per* Innes, C.J., in *Ismail Amod* v. *Pietersburg Municipality*, [1904] T.S. at p. 323). "All Acts of Parliament shall commence and take effect from and after their *promulgation* in the *Gazette*" (Act 5 of 1883 (C.C.), sec. 9).

Proof. (1) This term is defined in the Cape Excise Spirits Act (18 of 1884), sec. 2, and in the Cape Additional Taxation Act (36 of 1904), sec. 2, as follows: "*Proof* means the strength of *proof* as ascertained by Sykes's hydrometer;" see also Cape Sale of Food and Drugs and Seeds Act (5 of 1890), sec. 2; Act 33 of 1901 (N.), sec. 3.

(2) "The word *proof* seems properly to mean anything which serves, either immediately or mediately, to convince the mind of the truth or falsehood of a fact or proposition; and as truths differ, the *proofs* adapted to them differ also. Thus the *proofs* of a mathematical problem or theorem are the intermediate ideas which form the links in the chain of demonstration; the *proofs* of anything established by induction are the facts from which it is inferred, &c.; and the *proofs* of matters of fact in general are our senses, the testimony of witnesses, documents, and the like. *Proof* is also applied to the conviction generated in the mind by *proof* properly so called" (Best on *Evidence*, 10th ed. sec. 10).

Proof of debt, a term used in insolvency law signifying a statement of claim against the insolvent made upon oath by a creditor.

A creditor must prove his debt to the satisfaction of the Master or resident magistrate, by affidavit, which must be duly sworn, setting forth the nature of the debt; when it originally accrued to the creditor; that it is a just, true and lawful debt; what other persons, if any, are besides the insolvent liable for the payment of the debt or any part thereof, or that there are no such persons so liable; all pledges or securities held by the creditor from the insolvent for the debt or any part thereof, together with the value of such pledges or security; and, lastly, the creditor in such affidavit shall depose to the genuineness of all vouchers or evidence of debt which he shall produce with the affidavit. These vouchers, &c., are usually annexed to the affidavit. *Proofs of debt* are filed at a meeting of creditors of the insolvent. See Ordinance 6 of 1843 (C.C.), sec. 27; Law 13 of 1895 (T.), sec. 57; Law Book (O.R.C.), chap. 104, secs. 27 *et seq.* The method of proving debts in Natal is slightly different, inasmuch as there a debt may be proved by delivering or sending through the post in a prepaid letter to the Master or resident magistrate, or, if a trustee has been appointed, to the trustee, an affidavit verifying the debt; the trustee then files the proof at the first meeting of creditors held after the receipt by him of the affidavit (see sch. 2 to Law 47 of 1887).

Proof spirits. This expression is defined in the Cape Excise Spirits Act (18 of 1884), sec. 2, and in the Cape Additional Taxation Act (36 of 1904), sec. 2, as follows: "*Proof spirits* means such spirits as at a temperature of fifty-one degrees by Fahrenheit's thermometer shall weigh twelve-thirteenth parts of an equal measure of distilled water."

In Ordinance 32 of 1906 (O.R.C.), sec. 1, *proof spirits* means "a mixture of alcohol and water of such a density that the weight of 13 volumes at 51° Fahrenheit shall be equal to 12 volumes of water of the same temperature."

"Property and effects." An hotel company by its debentures charged "all its lands, buildings, property, stock-in-trade, furniture, chattels, and effects whatsoever, both present and future." Upon motion by a receiver and manager in a debenture-holder's action to enforce this security, it was held that the words *property and effects* were sufficient to include the goodwill and business of the company in the security, and that consequently a manager could be appointed for the purpose of realisation (*In re Lea's Hotel Co.; Salter* v. *Lea's Hotel Co.*, 9 Manson, 168; 18 T.L.R. 236).

Proprietor, a person who holds the exclusive right or title to some thing or property. In the Cape Registration of Designs Act (28 of 1894) the term *proprietor* is defined to mean "the author of any new or original design, unless he executed the work on behalf of another person for a good or valuable consideration, in which case such person shall be considered the *proprietor;* and every person acquiring for a good or valuable consideration a new and original design or the right to apply the same to any such article or substance as aforesaid, either exclusively of any other person or otherwise; and also every person on whom the property in such design or such right to the application thereof shall devolve shall be considered the *proprietor* of the design in the respect in which the same may have been so acquired and to that extent, but not otherwise." A similar definition is to be found in the Natal Registration of Designs Act (19 of 1899).

Proprio vigore, by its own force.

Prorogation of jurisdiction, extension of the jurisdiction of a court by consent of parties.

"There are no doubt cases in which *prorogation of jurisdiction* by consent is permitted in law, but that permission is not extended to causes which an inferior court is given no power whatever to entertain; see Voet (2, 1, 33, 36 and 48); Vromans, *de Foro Competente* (1, 1, 15 and 16); *Divisional Council of Riversdale* v. *Pienaar* (3 S.C. 252). The English reports contain many decisions upholding the principle that consent can give no jurisdiction to inferior courts in causes in which the legislature has not conferred the power to adjudicate, or to superior courts in causes in which they are forbidden to exercise jurisdiction (*Knowles* v. *Holden*, 24 L.J. Ex. 223; *Foster* v. *Underwood*, 47 L.J. Ex. 30; *Oulton* v. *Radcliffe*, 9 L.R. C.P. 189; *Queen* v. *Judge County Court of Shropshire*, 20 L.R. Q.B. 268; *British Wagon Co.* v. *Gray*, [1896] 1 Q.B. 35). And these cases show that jurisdiction is no more conferred by acquiescence than by prior consent to its exercise. To use the words of Lord Davey in the case of *Farquharson* v. *Morgan* ([1894] 1 Q.B. 552): 'Parties cannot by agreement confer upon any court or judge a coercive jurisdiction which the court or judge does not by law possess'" (*per* Mason, J., in *Ellis* v. *Morgan; Ellis* v. *Dessai*, [1909] T.S. at p. 582). See *per curiam Weatherley* v. *Weatherley* (1 Kotzé, 66).

Prorogation of Parliament, the putting off of a sitting of Parliament until the next session. It is distinguished from an adjournment, which is of either or both Houses and may be from day to day, whereas *prorogation* affects both Houses; and while in the case of an adjournment matters continue from the point at which they were left when adjournment took place, after *prorogation* Bills introduced, but not passed, are regarded as if they had never been before Parliament at all.

Prosecute, to pursue or follow after a person by means of legal proceedings with the object of obtaining a conviction or judgment; to continue legal proceedings, as to *prosecute* an appeal. See *Queen* v. *Bruyns* (16 S.C. 378).

Prosecution, the institution and conduct of criminal proceedings with the object of securing a conviction. The expression is also applied to the conduct of a civil action or appeal. Criminal *prosecutions* are usually instituted at the instance of the Crown, though where the Attorney-General refuses to prosecute a *prosecution* may be commenced and pursued by a private party having some substantial and peculiar interest in the issue of the trial (see Ordinance 40 of 1828 (C.C.), sec. 13; Ordinance 1 of 1903 (T.), sec. 12). See *Smith* v. *Desai* (24 N.L.R. at p. 332).

See "STOPPING THE PROSECUTION."

Prospect, in mining, to search or explore for precious or base minerals or precious stones.

The words "to develop" may sometimes mean "to *prospect*": see *Douglas* v. *Baynes* ([1907] T.S. at p. 513). *See* PROSPECTING.

Prospecting, in the Transvaal Gold Law (15 of 1898, sec. 3), means "the doing of all work which is necessary for the express search of the precious metals mentioned in art. 2 [of the Law] or which has in view the testing of the nature of the precious metals and mineral deposits, and the minerals present therein, which have been found." The above Law is now repealed by Act 35 of 1908 (T.), which in sec. 3 defines *prospecting* as including all work which is necessary for or incidental to the search for precious or base metals." The definition in the Precious Stones Ordinance, 66 of 1903 (T.), sec. 2, is very similar to that in Law 15 of 1898, as above.

In the Orange River Colony: "*Prospecting* shall mean the performance of all work and the carrying on of all operations which may appear necessary or desirable in the search for the precious metals mentioned in sec. 4 [of the Ordinance], or which have in view the testing of the permanency or payability of reefs or deposits containing any of such precious metals" (Ordinance 3 of 1904 (O.R.C.), sec. 5); see also Ordinance 4 of 1904 (O.R.C.), sec. 5.

Prospecting area. In sec. 7 of the Cape Precious Minerals Act (31 of 1898) it is provided as follows: "A duly licensed prospector shall have the exclusive right of prospecting on Crown land within a rectangular area, hereinafter called a *prospecting area*, 7500 feet long and 800 feet broad, at each corner of which it shall be his duty to put in pegs not less than two feet in height above the ground. Any such prospector shall during the currency of his license be at liberty to move such pegs to any other spot on Crown lands lawfully open to him, provided such spot or area does not interfere with the prospecting area of any other duly licensed prospector."

Prospecting claim. In Natal under the Mines and Collieries Act (43 of 1899, sec. 4) the term *prospecting claim* is defined to mean "a portion of ground of a size fixed by this Act assigned for the purpose of searching for minerals in accordance with the provisions of this Act." For sizes of claims fixed by the Act see respectively ALLUVIAL CLAIMS; METAL CLAIMS; and MINERAL CLAIMS. As to the issue of prospecting claim licenses, see sec. 11 of the Act.

Prospecting contract, in the Transvaal Registration of Deeds and Titles Act (25 of 1909), sec. 2, is defined as "a notarial deed by which the owner of land or the registered holder of mineral rights thereon grants the right to prospect and seek for any metal, mineral, mineral oil, or precious stones, together with the right to purchase either the freehold of or any right to metals, minerals, mineral oils or precious stones on that land or the right to lease any such right." See *Re Fourie and Others* (27 N.L.R. 342).

Prospecting license. A license issued by Government authorising the holder to prospect for minerals or precious stones or to peg claims; a license under which a prospecting claim is pegged off or occupied. In the Transvaal such a license issued under the Gold Law amounts neither to a lease nor an emphyteusis, and is not a tenure to which the doctrine of remission of rent in case of non-beneficial occupation is applicable; it is *sui generis*, and is governed entirely by the provisions of the Gold Law (*Neebe* v. *Registrar of Mining Rights*, [1902] T.S. 65); see Act 35 of 1908 (T.); Act 29 of 1908 (T.); Act 31 of 1898 (C.C.); Act 43 of 1899 (N.); Ordinance 3 of 1904 (O.R.C.); Ordinance 4 of 1904 (O.R.C.); Ordinance 8 of 1904 (O.R C.).

Prospector, one who examines and searches the land for minerals or precious stones. In the Precious Stones Ordinance, 66 of 1903 (T.), sec. 2, *prospector* means "a person who holds a license to prospect for precious stones."

In the Precious and Base Metals Act, 35 of 1908 (T.), sec. 3, *prospector* means "the person or persons by whom or on whose behalf a prospecting permit is held under this Act, and shall include the holder of mineral rights prospecting on land over which he holds such rights."

In the Mining of Precious Stones Ordinance, 4 of 1904 (O.R.C.), sec. 5, *prospector* means in accordance with the context (*a*) any person who holds a license to prospect for precious stones; (*b*) any owner who has given notice to the magistrate of his intention to prospect.

Prospectus. In company law a *prospectus* is a written or printed appeal or invitation to the public or to persons to whom it is addressed for subscriptions towards the capital or the debentures of a company; sometimes when the capital or debentures are fully guaranteed or subscribed it merely recites the particulars of capital and objects of a company with a view to giving publicity thereto and not for subscriptions. A *prospectus* is usually issued by the directors or promoters of a company. See Palmer's *Company Precedents*, 8th ed. part 1, p. 134. Act 25 of 1892 (C.C.), sec. 90, specifies particulars to be inserted in a *prospectus*; see also Act 31 of 1909 (T.), sec. 79; and Ordinance 2 of 1895 (R.).

As to liability of persons issuing a *prospectus*, for false statements therein, see Act 25 of 1892 (C.C.), sec. 91; Act 31 of 1909 (T.), sec. 82, and Ordinance 2 of 1895 (R.), sec. 45.

See SERVITUS PROSPECTUS.

Prothocol (D.), a protocol; a book wherein a notary gathers together and registers the minutes of all deeds and instruments passed before him in their order of date. On the death of a notary in the Netherlands his *prothocol* was handed over to the secretary of the town in which he resided for safe custody; in South Africa it is called a "protocol," and is handed over to the registrar of the Supreme Court of the colony in which he resided and practised.

Protonotarius, a term applied to the chief letter-writer to the king of the Franks in the middle ages (Wessels' *History*, p. 198).

Provisie in cas van reformatie (D.), a form of appeal in Dutch procedure in the sixteenth century. "In this case the losing party could, within a year after judgment was given, come to the superior court and ask that court to review the decision of the lower court. If the court thought fit to grant *provisie*, the respondent had to give security that he would restore what he had obtained by virtue of the judgment of the lower court" (Wessels' *History*, p. 188).

Provisie van namptissement (D.). *See* NAMPTISSEMENT; PROVISIONAL SENTENCE.

Provisional order of sequestration, a preliminary order granted by a judge or superior court placing the estate of a debtor under sequestration, provisionally, in the hands of the Master of the Supreme Court for the benefit of his creditors. *See* COMPULSORY SEQUESTRATION.

Provisional sentence, originally *namptissement* or *handvulling*. "*Provisional sentence* is a decree of the court in favour of a creditor on a written undertaking or acknowledgment of debt, signed by the debtor—the terms of which undertaking must be clear and definite, evidencing a liquid liability. After due summons of the defendant to acknowledge or deny his signature (a copy of the instrument being served with the summons), if he does not appear on the return day, or if appearing he does not deny his signature, this decree is granted on the mere production by the plaintiff of the document on which *provisional sentence* is claimed, the genuineness of the document being presumed, and the signature held to be acknowledged in default of denial" (1 Menz. 5). Payment by defendant is made "under security *de restituendo*, that is, when the defendant, having been condemned to pay the provisional judgment, pays only on the security being given by the plaintiff to refund the principal and interest if afterwards at the trial it should appear on the merits (or to use the technical expression, 'in the principal case') that the debt was not legally due" (Van Zyl's *Judicial Practice*, 2nd ed. p. 67). *Provisional sentence* was introduced into Holland in the sixteenth century.

Provisional trustee, a person provisionally appointed by the court on motion, to act as the trustee of an insolvent estate, generally with limited powers, pending the appointment by the creditors of a permanent trustee at the second meeting of creditors (see Ordinance 6 of 1843 (C.C.), sec. 43; Law 47 of 1887 (N.), sec. 47; Law 13 of 1895 (T.), secs. 71 and 72; chap. 104 of the Law Book (O.R.C.), sec. 43).

Proviso, a stipulation introduced into a section of a statute, or into a clause of an agreement, providing that the preceding part of the section or clause is subject to the provisions of such stipulation.

Proximate cause. "The plaintiff's want of ordinary care must, we have seen, be a *proximate cause* of his injury or it will not be contributory negligence. What then precisely is a *proximate cause?* It is a general rule of law that a man is responsible for the natural and probable consequences of his acts, and for these consequences only so far as they are natural and proximate, and such as may on this account be foreseen by ordinary forecast or, as it is sometimes expressed, a man is presumed to intend the natural and probable consequences of his acts. An act is the *proximate cause* of an event when in the natural order of things, and under the circumstances, it would necessarily produce that event, when it is the first and direct power producing the result, the *causa causans* of the schoolmen. . From the nature of the matter there can be no fixed and immediate rule upon this subject that can be applied to all cases; much must depend upon circumstances, and what is, or what is not, a *proximate cause* will very often have to be determined upon considerations of sound judgment and enlightened common sense without the aid of any certain rule or infallible precedent" (Beach on *Contributory Negligence*, 3rd ed. sec. 31).

Proxy. (1) A person acting as a deputy or substitute for another.

(2) A written authority authorising one person to act for another. Especially and commonly a written authority empowering a person to appear for another at a meeting of shareholders or debenture-holders and to vote thereat. So long as a *proxy* is properly stamped at the time of execution, its operative parts such as the name of the *proxy* or the date of the meeting at which it is to be used, may be filled in afterwards by any person properly authorised to do so (*Sadgrove* v. *Bryden*, 76 L.J. Ch. 184; [1907] 1 Ch. 318; 96 L.T. 361; 14 Manson, 47; 23 T.L.R. 255).

As to stamping *proxies* in England when intended for use in South Africa, see *Stockham and Others* v. *Colonial Building Corporation, Ltd.* (19 S.C. at p. 402).

Puberty, the age of fourteen for males, and twelve for females. Under Roman law persons reached a marriageable age when they had attained the age of *puberty*.

Public. In the Native Territories Penal Code (Act 24 of 1886 (C.C.), sec. 5) the word *public* is defined to include "any class of the *public* or any community." *See* PROMISE TO THE PUBLIC.

Public accountant. In the Audit Act, 14 of 1906 (C.C.), sec. 3, *public accountant* means "every person who by any law, regulation or appointment is charged with the duty of collecting or receiving, or who does actually collect or receive, any public moneys, or who is charged with the duty of disbursing or who does actually disburse any public moneys."

Public building. The term *public building* is defined in the Cape Public Health Amendment Act (23 of 1897), sec. 2, to mean and include "theatres, opera houses, halls, rooms, exhibitions, churches, chapels, meeting-houses, and all buildings used for purposes of public resort or assembly; also hotels, boarding-houses, and similar establishments in which twenty-five or more persons, besides the servants and family of the occupier, may be accommodated; and schools, factories, lodging houses, hospitals and benevolent or other asylums, in which above twenty-five persons in number are gathered or employed, or intended to be gathered or employed at one time." In Act 11 of 1905 (C.C.), sec. 1, "*public buildings* or places" is given a more restricted definition. See also Act 25 of 1905 (C.C.), sec. 1; and Ordinance 31 of 1907 (O.R.C.), sec. 1.

Public diggings, an expression employed in statutes relating to mines and minerals.

In the Transvaal, in Law 15 of 1898, sec. 3, *public diggings* signified "a proclaimed area, thrown open by lawful authority for prospecting, digging and mining." This Law is now repealed by the Precious and Base Metals Act, 35 of 1908 (T.), which in pt. i, ch. iv, makes provision regarding the proclamation of *public diggings*. In the Liquor Licensing Laws Further Amendment Act, 33 of 1909 (T.), sec. 2, *public digging* is defined as "land which is proclaimed land within the meaning of the Precious and Base Metals Act, 1908, or any amendment thereof, or land which is an alluvial digging under the Precious Stones Ordinance, 1903, or any amendment thereof."

As to the manner in which land is proclaimed a *public digging* in the Orange River Colony, see Ordinance 3 of 1904, sec. 5.

Public document. The question whether a document is a *public document* or not is frequently of importance in matters of evidence, as a *public document* proves itself when produced from the proper custody and is in itself evidence of the correctness of its contents. As to what constitutes a *public document*, the definition given by Lord BLACKBURN in *Sturla* v. *Freccia* (5 App. Cas. at p. 643) was accepted in *Northern Mounted Rifles* v. *O'Callaghan* ([1909] T.S. at p. 176) as correctly laying down the law on the subject. Lord BLACKBURN there said: "Now, my lords, taking that decision" (*i.e.* the decision in the case of the *Irish Society* v. *Bishop of Derry* (2 Cl. & F. 641)), "the principle upon which it goes is that it should be a public inquiry, a *public document*, and made by a public officer. I do not think that 'public' there is to be taken in the sense of meaning the whole world. I think an entry in the books of a manor is public in the sense that it concerns all the world interested in the manor. And an entry probably in a corporation book concerning a corporate matter, or something in which all the corporation is concerned, would be 'public' within that sense. But it must be a *public document*, and it must be made by a public officer. I understand a *public document* there to mean a document that is made for the purpose of the public making use of it and being able to refer to it. It is meant to be where there is a judicial, or quasi-judicial, duty to inquire, as might be said to be the case with the bishop acting under the writs issued by the Crown. That may be said to be quasi-judicial. He is acting for the public when that is done; but I think the very object of it must be that it should be made for the purpose of being kept public, so that the persons concerned in it may have access to it afterwards." In the above case of the *Northern Mounted Rifles* v. *O'Callaghan* it was held that the musketry register of a volunteer corps, although kept by virtue of statutory regulations, did not satisfy the requirements of this definition, and was therefore not a *public document*.

Public holiday. *See* BUSINESS DAY.

Public moneys. In the Audit Act, 14 of 1906 (C.C.), sec. 3, *public moneys* means "all moneys received or paid on behalf of the Consolidated Revenue Account, any loan account, any deposit account, or any other account which the Auditor shall be required by this Act or by any other Act, or by the Governor, to examine and audit."

"*Public moneys* shall include all public revenues, and in addition the proceeds of all loans raised, and all other moneys whatsoever received or held by, for or on account of the colony" (Audit and Exchequer Act, 14 of 1907 (T.), sec. 1; Audit and Exchequer Act, 17 of 1908 (O.R.C.), sec. 1).

Public notice, an expression defined in the Cape Additional Taxation Act (36 of 1904), sec. 42, as meaning "a notice inserted in the *Gazette* and published in English and Dutch in any newspaper circulating in a town or district." See Act 26 of 1902 (C.C.), sec. 2; and NOTICE.

Public nuisance. "A *public nuisance* is an unlawful act or omission to discharge a legal duty which causes inconvenience or annoyance to the inhabitants of or travellers through a particular locality, or interferes with the exercise or enjoyment by them of a right common to all" (Stephen's *Comm.* 15th ed. vol. 3, p. 405). See Garrett on *Nuisances*, 3rd. ed. p. 1.

Public office. The expression *public office* is in the Cape Illegal Practices Prevention Act (26 of 1902), sec. 2, defined to mean "any office under the Crown, or under any municipal or divisional council."

Public place. In the Licensing Act, 1902 (Eng.), sec. 8, *public place* is defined to include "any place to which the public have access whether on payment or otherwise." In the Street Betting Act, 1906 (Eng.), sec. 1 (4), *public place* "shall include any public park, garden or sea beach, and any unenclosed lane to which the public have unrestricted access, and shall also include other enclosed places (not being a park or garden) to which the public have a restricted right of access, whether on payment or otherwise, if at or near either public entrance there is conspicuously exhibited a notice prohibiting betting therein."

In the Transvaal Criminal Law Amendment Act (38 of 1909), sec. 1, *public place* is defined to mean "any place to which the public have access, but shall not include a 'place of public resort' as herein described." The definition given in the Act of a "place of public resort" is "any place of entertainment, amusement or refreshment to which the public have access whether by payment for access or otherwise." In *Rex* v. *Manderson* (Supreme Court, Transvaal, 17th December, 1909—not yet reported), it was held that a private lane to which the public had access without legal right was a *public place* within the above definition.

In the Cape Colony the term *public place*, as occurring in the Police Offences Act (27 of 1882), has been the subject of frequent judicial interpretation. Sec. 10 of the Act deals with the use of threatening, abusive or insulting words or behaviour with intent to provoke a breach of the peace or whereby a breach of the peace may be occasioned "in any street, road, *public place* or licensed house." In *Queen* v. *Brown* (7 S.C. 101) a person standing in the garden in front of his house was held to have contravened the above section by using abusive language to another person passing by on the public road on the ground that the language had been addressed to a person in a *public place* and was audible in that place. So the use of abusive language by one person to another, both standing on their respective stoeps, which adjoined each other and abutted on the public road, was held to be a contravention of the above section (*Rex* v. *Scharff*, 17 C.T.R. 1127). But the use of abusive language in a private dwelling-house to a person also within the house, although audible outside in a public square, does not constitute a contravention of the Act (*Queen* v. *Muller*, 16 S.C. 534). Nor is a shop a *public place* within the meaning of that section (*Rex* v. *Crozier*, 15 C.T.R. 274).

Under the Transkeian Penal Code (Act 24 of 1886) (C.C.), sec. 94, which deals with two or more persons disturbing the public peace "by fighting at any gathering at any kraal or after such gathering away from any kraal or any *public place*," it has been held that an ordinary fight between two natives in a police camp, without evidence to prove that the camp was a *public place*, was not necessarily an offence (*Rex* v. *Lethlaka*, 19 C.T.R. 467).

Public policy, see *South African Breweries, Ltd.*, v. *Muriel* (26 N.L.R. at p. 367); *Eastwood* v. *Shepstone* ([1902] T.S. at p. 302). *See* PRIVATORUM CONVENTIO JURE PUBLICO NON DEROGAT.

Public prosecutor, an officer duly appointed to conduct prosecutions on behalf of the Crown in the inferior courts.

"At the establishment of the Supreme Court [of the Cape Colony] it was intended by the Home Government that the office of *public prosecutor* should be established as in Scotland, for the purpose of criminal judicature; letters of instruction to that effect were sent out, and Mr. Justice MENZIES, who had already accepted another office, was specially appointed a judge of the Supreme Court for the purpose of preparing the introduction of the system. All criminal proceedings must be conducted on the principle that they are brought by the *public prosecutor*, that there is no power except through him. Private prosecutions could not be brought under Ordinance No. 40 [C.C.] until the *public prosecutor* had declined to prosecute and had given a certificate to that effect. Although this certificate is no longer required under Ordinance No. 73 [C.C.], yet the principle of all proceedings through the *public prosecutor* remains" (*per* WYLDE, C.J., in *Enslin* v. *Truter*, 1 Searle, at p. 213; the judgment was delivered in August, 1852).

Public purposes. In the Cape Electric Lighting and Power Act (42 of 1895) it is defined to mean "lighting any street or any place belonging to or subject to the control of the local authority, or any church or place of worship, or any hall or building belonging to or subject to the control of Government or of any local authority, or any public theatre, or the supply of an electric current for lighting purposes to consumers generally, and shall also mean the application of electricity as a motive power for tramways or any other like purpose."

See Proclamation 5 of 1902 (T.), sec. 2.

In Ordinance 11 of 1905 (O.R.C.) the expression *public purposes* includes (*a*) the construction and maintenance of works for the defence of this [O.R.C.] Colony, and the erection of buildings for the use of any police or defence force therein; (*b*) the construction and maintenance of tramways, electric power stations and conduits, telegraphs, telephones, public roads, streets, squares, cemeteries, markets, irrigation works, water courses, reservoirs and pipe lines, public buildings, schools and school grounds and native locations.

The expression *public purposes* was discussed by DE VILLIERS, C.J., in *Colonial Government* v. *Stephan Bros.* (17 S.C. at p. 515), when, in the course of his judgment, he said: "The only question, therefore, to be determined is whether the purposes for which the plaintiff requires the land are *public purposes*. The first is the landing and shipping of goods imported and exported by the Government or by the public. The defendants do not deny that this is in every respect a legitimate *public purpose*. . . . If the port should prosper it might, for instance, become necessary to provide a building for a periodical court, which would clearly be a purpose of public utility. . . . As to the erection of bathing houses for the use of the public, it would be going too far to hold that it is a *public purpose*, but the erection of stables for the housing of animals used in the conveyance of goods and of persons doing business at the port appears to be a *public purpose*. The erection of buildings for a public market and for the accommodation of persons having business to transact at Lambert's Bay would also be a legitimate *public purpose*, so long, at all events, as the place is recognised by the Government as a port for the landing and shipping of goods."

In England the expression *public purposes* has frequently been discussed in connection with the rateability of property; see, for instance, *Showers* v. *Assessment Committee of Chelmsford Union* ([1891] Q.B. 339), where the definition appears to be more restricted than in *Colonial Government* v. *Stephan Bros.* (*supra*).

Public revenues. In the Transvaal Audit and Exchequer Act (14 of 1907) *public revenues* means "all taxes, imposts, rates and duties and all territorial, casual and other revenues of the Crown (including royalties) from whatever source arising within the colony over which the Parliament of The Transvaal has power of appropriation." A similar definition is to be found in the Orange River Colony Act 17 of 1908.

Public right of way. "A *public right of way* is more onerous than an ordinary servitude in favour of individuals" (*per* KOTZÉ, J.P., in *Uitenhage Divisional Council* v. *Bowen*, [1907] E.D.C. at p. 80).

Public river, a term employed in the Mineral Law Amendment Act, 16 of 1907 (C.C.), sec. 24, where it is defined to mean "a stream whose bed within the limits of the dredging lease is not vested in any private person." *See* PUBLIC STREAM.

Public road, in the Roads Ordinance, 17 of 1905 (O.R.C.), sec. 1, means: "(*a*) Any road which the public had a right to use or of which the public had undisturbed and continuous use for a period of not less than two years immediately preceding the 12th day of October, 1899; (*b*) any road which shall have been in undisturbed and continuous use by the public for a period of not less than fifteen years subsequent to the 31st day of May, 1902; (*c*) any new main, district or farm roads proclaimed under the powers conferred by this Ordinance."

Public servant. In the Native Territories Penal Code (Act 24 of 1886 (C.C.), sec. 5 (*b*)), the expression *public servant* is defined to denote "a person falling under any one of the following descriptions, namely: (1) Every servant of the Queen; (2) every commissioned officer of the military or naval force of the Queen; (3) every judge; (4) every officer of a court of justice whose duty it is to investigate or report on any matter of law or fact, or to make, authenticate or keep any document or take charge or dispose of any property or to execute any judicial process, or to administer any oath, or interpret or preserve order in court; (5) every juryman or assessor assisting a court of justice; (6) every person who holds any office by virtue of which he is empowered to place or keep any person in confinement; (7) every officer of Government whose duty it is as such officer to prevent offences, to give information of offences, to bring offenders to justice, or to protect the public health, safety or convenience; (8) every officer in the service or pay of the Government, or remunerated by fees or commission for performance of any public duty."

In the Transvaal Criminal Procedure Code (1 of 1903), sec. 3, provides that "a person employed in the public service includes any person who is by law authorised or required to execute a particular duty towards the public, whether he acts gratuitously or not, whether he is paid by salary or fees, and whether he exercises any other profession or follows any other calling besides the performance of his public duties." In the Transvaal Public Service and Pensions Act (19 of 1908), sec. 1, the term is defined to mean "the system of employment of persons of European descent by the Government of this colony in the discharge of public duties in a department or office of such Government."

Public service. *See* PUBLIC SERVANT.

Public slaughter-house. *See* SLAUGHTER-HOUSE.

Public square, discussed in *Hanau and Others* v. *The State* (1 Off. Rep. (Webber's trans.), p. 87); *Town Council, Johannesburg,* v. *The Government* ([1902] T.H. 263).

Public streams. "Under the term *public streams* are included all perennial rivers, whether navigable or not, and all streams which, although not large enough to be regarded as rivers, are yet perennial and are capable of being applied to the common use of the riparian proprietors" (Maasdorp's *Institutes,* vol. 2, p. 103).

In the Transvaal *public stream* is defined in Law 11 of 1894 as "water flowing down in a defined channel, whether such channel shall contain water throughout the whole year or shall be dry during any period;" and in the Irrigation Act (27 of 1908) (which repealed Law 11 of 1894) as "a natural stream of water (*a*) which in ordinary seasons flows for the greater part of the year in a known and defined channel (whether or not such channel is dry during any period of the year); and (*b*) which is capable of being applied to the common use of riparian proprietors. A stream of water which fulfils these conditions as to part of its course only shall be deemed to be a *public stream* as regards such part."

Public things, such property as belongs to the public or to the State, and the use of which is common to all.

Publicani, the name given by the Romans to persons to whom tolls and customs, mines and other similar sources of revenue belonging to the State were farmed out.

Publication. (1) A printed and issued book, magazine, pamphlet, newspaper or the like. For the purposes of the Cape Obscene Publications Act (31 of 1892), the word *publication* includes "any book, newspaper, pamphlet, magazine, periodical, letter-press, writing, print, picture, engraving, lithograph, photograph, drawing or other similar representation."

(2) *Publication* of a slander "is the communication of the defamatory words to some third person or persons. . . . The *publication* of a slander involves only one act by the defendant; he must speak the words so that some third person hears and understands them. But the *publication* of a libel is a more composite act. First, the defendant must compose and write the libel; next, he must hand what he has written, or cause it to be delivered, to some third person; then that third person must read and understand its contents; or, it may be that, after composing and writing it, the defendant reads it aloud to some third person, who listens to the words and understands them; in this case the same act may be both the uttering of a slander and the *publication* of a libel. And even when the defendant is not himself the author, writer or printer of a libel, or in any way connected with or responsible for its being composed or written or printed, still he may be liable as its *publisher*" (Odgers' *Libel and Slander*, 3rd ed. p. 170; see also De Villiers' *Roman and Roman-Dutch Law of Injuries*).

(3) *Publication* of banns of marriage. In Cape Colony, Natal and Rhodesia (under sec. 2 of the Order in Council of the 7th September, 1838), banns of marriage may be *published* by ministers of the Christian religion between persons desirous of being joined together in matrimony. Such *publication* must be made in an audible manner some time during divine service, on a Sunday, in face of the congregation before whom such minister shall officiate in the parish in which one or both of the parties to be married shall dwell, for three Sundays preceding the solemnisation of the marriage, during the morning service, if there be service in the morning, or if there shall be no morning service then during the evening service. Sec. 2 provides that if the parties to be married dwell in different parishes the banns shall be *published* in like manner in both such parishes; and if the parties shall be of different persuasions the banns shall be *published* in like manner before each of the congregations to which the parties may respectively belong, whether both such congregations shall assemble in such parish or not. See also the following sections of the same Order in Council. The *publication* of banns in the Orange River Colony is regulated by sec. 3 of Law 26 of 1899, which is very similar to the Cape Colony law. In the Transvaal it is regulated by sec. 1 of Law 3 of 1871.

Publieke aanklager (D.), public prosecutor. See Proclamation 15 of 1902 (T.), sec. 17.

Publieke delverijen (D.), public diggings duly proclaimed as such. *See* PUBLIC DIGGINGS.

Publieke stroom (D.), a public stream. In Law 11 of 1894 (T.), sec. 1, *publieke stroom* is defined as meaning "water flowing down in a defined channel, whether such channel shall contain water throughout the whole year or shall be dry during any period [*of gedurende eenigen tijd droog ligt*]." Law 11 of 1894 (T.) has been repealed by Act 27 of 1908 (T.). *See* PUBLIC STREAM.

Puisne, of lower rank. All the judges who rank below a Chief Justice or a Judge President are *puisne* judges.

Purcnase, the acquisition of some thing or property under or by means of an agreement whereby some money consideration is given for such acquisition. *See* SALE.

Pure grape brandy. "*Pure grape brandy* or *grape brandy* means the unrectified distillate resulting from the distillation solely of wine or must with grape husks; the volatile constituents of which distillate (except water, as provided for in sec. 15 [of the Act]) are derived entirely from the above-named materials; provided that the alcoholic strength of such *pure grape brandy* be not lower than 25 degrees under proof, and not higher than 12 degrees over proof" (the Wine, Brandy, Whisky and Spirits Act, 42 of 1906 (C.C.), sec. 14).

Pure wine brandy. "*Pure wine brandy* means the unrectified distillate resulting from the distillation solely of pure wine or must; the volatile constituents of which distillate (except water, as provided for in sec. 15 [of the Act], are derived entirely from the above-named materials; provided that the alcoholic strength of such *pure wine brandy* be not lower than 25 degrees under proof, and not higher than 22 degrees over proof" (the Wine, Brandy, Whisky and Spirits Act, 42 of 1906 (C.C.), sec. 14).

Pure wine spirit. "*Pure wine spirit* means the rectified distillate resulting from the distillation solely of wine or must" (the Wine, Brandy, Whisky and Spirits Act, 42 of 1906 (C.C.), sec. 5).

Purge, to clear away or remove by some process of atonement; as, for instance, to *purge contempt, i.e.* to atone for a contempt of court; to *purge default, i.e.* to remove the bar, probably on payment of wasted costs, or on some condition, so that the party in default may again appear before the court.

Qadi, a native term. *See* IQADI.

Q.Q. *See* QUALITATE QUA.

Qua, as or in the character of. Thus where a trustee or executor sues on behalf of the estate which he is administering, he is said to sue *qua* executor or trustee.

Quacunque via data, in whatever way conceded; in whatever way taken.

Quadruplatores, public informers, among the Romans, who received a fourth part of the accused's confiscated property if their information resulted in a conviction.

Quae ab initio non valent ex post facto convalescere non possunt, things which are invalid from the beginning cannot become valid by subsequent act. *See* QUOD AB INITIO VITIOSUM EST, &c.

Quae pondere numero mensurave constant, things which may be weighed, numbered or measured. Such things are called "fungibles," because they are consumed in the using, as corn, wine, money, &c. They therefore properly form the subject of *mutuum,* or loan for consumption, as there the obligation of the borrower is to return, not the identical corn, wine, money, &c., but the equivalent of the thing borrowed in weight, number or measure. As, however, they perish in the use, fungibles cannot be given in commodate, or loan for use, which deals only with non-fungibles, such as a house or a piece of land. For the rules as to the passing of the risk in a sale of fungibles see Voet's *Comm.* 18, 6, 3 and 4.

Quaestio, a commission in Roman law appointed to try criminal offences.

Quaestor, the name of a class of Roman magistrates.

Qualification. (1) That which renders a person eligible to a certain office or profession, or to do a certain act.
(2) A restriction or limitation.

Qualified acceptance. In regard to bills of exchange, an acceptance may be either general or qualified. "A *qualified acceptance* in express terms varies the effect of the bill as drawn. In particular an acceptance is qualified which is—(*a*) conditional, that is to say, which makes payment by the acceptor dependent on the fulfilment of a condition therein stated; (*b*) partial, that is to say, an acceptance to pay part only of the amount for which the bill is drawn; (*c*) local, that is to say, an acceptance to pay only at a particular specified place: an acceptance to pay at a particular place is a general acceptance, unless it expressly states that the bill is to be paid there only, and not elsewhere; (*d*) qualified as to time; (*e*) the acceptance of some one or more of the drawees, but not of all" (Bills of Exchange Act, 1882 (Eng.), sec. 19; Act 19 of 1893 (C.C.), sec. 17; Law 8 of 1887 (N.), sec. 18; Proclamation 11 of 1902 (T.), sec. 17; Ordinance 28 of 1902 (O.R.C.), sec. 17.

Qualified indorsement, an indorsement of a bill of exchange which negatives or limits the liability of the indorser. See Bills of

Exchange Act, 1882 (Eng.), sec. 16; Act 19 of 1893 (C.C.), sec. 14; Law 8 of 1887 (N.), sec. 15; Proclamation 11 of 1902 (T.), sec. 14; Ordinance 28 of 1902 (O.R.C.), sec. 14.

Qualitate qua, a term used in Dutch practice and also in South African practice and commerce. It signifies that the person who has signed his name with the addition of the letters *q.q.* is acting not for himself, but on behalf of another person. It is usually abbreviated by the use of the letters *q.q.*

Quanti minoris. *See* ACTIO QUANTI MINORIS.

Quantum libet, as much as you like.

Quantum meruit, as much as he has earned. If a person engages another to do certain services, but no remuneration is fixed, the latter on the completion of the services will be entitled to a *quantum meruit*, or what is a fair remuneration for them in all the circumstances. Sometimes also a person who has contracted to do a piece of work, but has not completed it, is held to be entitled to a *quantum meruit* for the work which he has actually performed, *i.e.* where such work is of use or advantage to the employer (Voet's *Comm.* 19, 2, 40). Thus in *Alexander* v. *De Villiers* (3 C.T.R. 280), an architect employed in connection with the building of a church, although shown to have been negligent in the performance of his work and to have put an end to his contract without justifiable cause, was found entitled to a *quantum meruit* for the services actually rendered by him. (But see *Kyte* v. *McLeod*, 6 E.D.C. 43); also *Muller* v. *Crawley*, [1907] O.R.C. 12).

Quantum valebat, as much as it was worth.

Quarantine. "The term *quarantine* shall include in its meaning the interdiction of free communication with persons on land infected with disease or suspected of being so infected." This is the definition given in the Cape Public Health Act (4 of 1883), sec. 2; see also secs. 10 *et seq.* of the same Act; and Act 23 of 1897 (C.C.).

As to Natal, see Law 3 of 1858; Law 10 of 1859; Law 4 of 1882; Law 11 of 1883; Law 2 of 1884; Law 43 of 1884; Act 2 of 1897; Act 14 of 1899; Act 26 of 1899.

Quarta falcidia, Falcidian fourth. *See* LEX FALCIDIA.

Quarta trebellianica, Trebellian fourth. *See* SENATUSCONSULTUM TREBELLIANUM.

Quasi ex contractu, [arising] as if from a contract. An obligation which exists between persons, not by virtue of express agreement, but on account of the special relation of the one to the other, is said to be based on implied contract or to arise *quasi ex contractu*, *e.g.*

the obligation between a guardian and his ward, or that between a *negotiorum gestor* and the person whose affairs he has managed.

Quasi ex delicto, [arising] as if from a delict, or [arising] from a *quasi* delict. A *quasi* delict in Roman law was an act which did not amount to a delict, but which, owing to the default or negligence involved in it, rendered the doer liable to pay compensation for the damage caused. See Sandars' *Institutes*, 1, 16, 6. The classification of wrongs as delicts or *quasi* delicts is now obsolete in our law (Maasdorp's *Institutes*, vol. 4, p. 6).

Quasi-contract, an implied contract. "*Quasi-contracts* are obligations which give rise to contractual rights, including rights of action, although no special agreements have been entered into by the parties" (Nathan's *Common Law*, sec. 734). Van der Linden (*Institutes*, Juta's trans. p. 148) speaks of *quasi-contracts* as being "transactions which by their similarity to contracts cause similar obligations and actions to arise." The Dutch equivalent is *quasi contracten*. *See* QUASI EX CONTRACTU.

Quasi-delivery, a fictitious or symbolical form of delivery, usually having the same effect as an actual delivery; thus a man sells goods lying in a warehouse and transfers the ownership in such goods to the purchaser by delivery to the latter of the keys of the warehouse. *See* BREVI MANU.

Quasi-misdaaden (D.), "quasi-criminal acts, as when some damage is caused to a person by an act of ours of such a nature that, although it does not constitute a punishable offence, it nevertheless makes us liable for damages on account of the accompanying negligence or inadvertence" (Van der Linden's *Institutes*, Juta's trans. p. 154). *See* QUASI EX DELICTO.

Queen's warehouse or **King's warehouse.** Under the Customs Management Act, 10 of 1872 (C.C.), the term *Queen's warehouse* signifies "any place provided by the Crown for lodging goods therein for security of the customs."

For definition in Natal, see Act 13 of 1899, sec. 4, which is very similar to that of the Cape.

Qui approbat non reprobat, he who approves or accepts does not reprobate or reject. An heir or legatee cannot accept the benefits conferred upon him by the will of the deceased and at the same time repudiate the obligations which have been attached to such benefits (*Theunissen* v. *Theunissen*, 1 Roscoe, 107).

Qui facit per alium facit per se, he who does a thing through another does it himself. In accordance with this maxim a principal is held liable for the acts of his servants or agents acting in the course of their employment. The *ratio* of the rule is that as the principal has the choice of his servants or agents he is liable if he selects an unfit or improper person, and they are considered unfit or improper if they display incompetence or negligence in carrying out the work for which they were engaged. The exception to this principle, which obtains in English and also in American common law, where a servant sustains injury through the negligence of a servant in the same employment, *i.e.* the case of "common employment," has been the subject of conflicting decisions in South Africa. In *Hilpert* v. *Castle Mail Packets Co.* (12 E.D.C. 36) the doctrine of common employment was adopted by the court; but in *Lewis* v. *Salisbury G. M. Co.* (1 Off. Rep. 1) it was held to be unsound in principle and contrary to the Roman-Dutch law (see the judgment of KOTZÉ, C.J., for a review of the Roman-Dutch authorities upon the responsibility of a master for the negligent acts of his servants). Another exception to the principle expressed in the maxim is that which holds good where the performance of work has been entrusted to an independent contractor, who has immediate control of those employed to do the work; the contractor, and not his employer, being in that case responsible for the negligence of the workmen (*Kotzé* v. *Ohlsson's Cape Breweries*, 9 S.C. 319; *Chatwin* v. *C.S.A.R.*, [1909] T.H. 33, and authorities there cited). Although a principal is not responsible for the criminal acts of his servant or agent which he has not commanded or authorised (*R.* v. *Chabaud*, Buch. 1877, p. 149), he is equally punishable with the agent for such acts where he has directed or procured them to be done (*Aaron* v. *Rex*, [1909] T.S. 937).

Qui haeret in litera, haeret in cortice, he who holds by the letter, holds by the bark. In interpreting deeds and statutes, if it is clear from the deed or statute itself what the parties or the legislature intended, the court will give effect to such intention rather than to the precise signification of the words in which it is expressed. Where, however, it is not clear that the language is to be read and applied according to another than its ordinary sense, then the ordinary sense of the words must be adhered to. *See* NON QUOD DICTUM, &c., and QUOTIES IN VERBIS, &c.

Qui nimium probat nihil probat, he who proves too much proves nothing.

Qui prior est in sorte prior est in usuris. *See* PRIOR IN SORTE PRIOR EST IN USURIS.

Qui prior est tempore potior est jure, he who is prior in time is stronger or preferable in right. This is the principle according to which questions as to the preference of competing rights are frequently decided. Thus, as regards title to property, he who first seizes and reduces into possession a *res nullius* is to be preferred to one whose occupancy is of a later date. So the rule applies to mortgages, to the effect of making an earlier tacit or special mortgage preferent to a later tacit or special mortgage, and an earlier general mortgage preferent to a later general mortgage. The same principle also underlies the law relative to patents and to copyright.

Quick pursuit. Where a tenant removes movable property from the leased premises in order to defeat the landlord's lien for arrear rent, the landlord may, in Natal, follow and attach such movable property, provided he does so without delay. This following is called *quick pursuit.*

"The word 'quick' is not capable of accurate definition. What is *quick pursuit* will depend upon the circumstances of the particular case. What might be called quick in one case might not be quick in another. For instance, in the case of the removal from a farm, the time allowed would be longer than in the case of a removal from a town house" (*per* BALE, C.J., in *Houghting* v. *Lloyd,* 27 N.L.R. at p. 97).

Quicquid acquiritur servo, acquiritur domino, whatever is acquired for a slave or servant is acquired for his master. In accordance with this maxim of the Roman law a principal is entitled to sue upon a contract made by his agent, even although *ex facie* the contract the obligation appears to be incurred by the agent himself (*Cook* v. *Aldred,* [1909] T.S. 150).

Quicquid inaedificatur solo, solo cedit, whatever is built upon the soil accedes to the soil. *See* AEDIFICIUM SOLO CEDIT.

Quicquid plantatur solo, solo cedit, whatever is planted in the soil accedes to the soil. The owner of the soil, in other words, is the owner of everything planted in it. This does not apply, however, to crops sown by a lessee of land, which belong to the lessee, and not to the owner of the land; nor does it apply to trees which fall under the category of *silva caedua,* as these may be cut down by a lessee during the currency of the lease (*Houghton Estate Co.* v. *McHattie and Barrat,* 1 Off. Rep. 92; *Brice* v. *Zurcher,* [1908] T.S. at p. 1084).

Quid juris, what is the law?

Quid pro quo, something for something, *i.e.* something given in return for something else. Thus in the contract of sale the price paid and the thing sold are with respect to each other the *quid pro quo.*

Quilibet juri pro se introducto renunciare potest, any one may renounce a right which has been introduced for his own benefit. (Cf. *Privatorum conventio juri publico non derogat.*) Renunciation may be express or inferred from conduct. It is, for example, express where a person, who has been damnified by a contract made by him during minority, binds himself upon attaining majority not to seek *restitutio in integrum*, or where a plaintiff reduces his claim and sues for less than the actual amount which is due (*Van der Walt* v. *Hawkins*, 3 E.D.C. at p. 31). Renunciation is inferred from conduct, as where an act is done wholly and directly contrary to a privilege which consists in not doing something. As, however, no one is in case of doubt presumed to make a gift, renunciation which is inferred from conduct is very strictly interpreted. Accordingly the fact that a person has done a single act contrary to a privilege by virtue of which he could have declined to do it, will not deprive him of his privilege (Voet's *Comm.* 1, 4, 1, 22).

Quitantie (D.), a receipt; a written discharge of a debtor from the obligation due by him to his creditor.

Quit-rent tenure. (1) Quit-rent grants of land were first introduced in the Cape Colony in 1732, the grants being for a period of fifteen years, subject to a small annual payment to Government. The Government retained the ownership in the land and the right of resumption at the expiration of the term, but subject to payment of compensation to the extent of the value of the buildings and plantations: the grantee had the use of the land for the period of the grant. This system ceased in 1811, and all the grants which were then current have since been converted either into freehold or perpetual quit-rent, on the same terms as grants made under Sir John Cradock's Proclamation of 4th August, 1813. By this proclamation an entirely new tenure was introduced into the Cape Colony, namely, the perpetual *quit-rent tenure;* by this tenure the grantee or lessee obtained a perpetual right to the land described in the grant, subject to the annual payment of a small sum of money each year, called a "quit-rent"; and subject, further, to certain conditions and reservations in favour of the Crown. *See* LOAN PLACE.

As to quit-rent in Natal, see Law 17 of 1861; Law 21 of 1863; Law 17 of 1865; Law 23 of 1868; Law 16 of 1876; Law 17 of 1876; Law 33 of 1887; Act 31 of 1907.

Quo animo, with what intention.

Quo jure, by what right.

Quo nomine, in what name; on what account.

Quo warranto, a writ issued in England out of the King's Bench Division of the High Court of Judicature for the purpose of determining by what authority the person named in the writ claims some specified office or franchise. Prior to 1872 it was employed in connection with municipal elections; since then the Municipal Corporations Act, 1882, sec. 87 (45 & 46 Vict. c. 50, sec. 87) makes provision for election petitions, which replace to some extent the writ *quo* *warranto;* but the *quo warranto* still lies in cases of disqualification of municipal officers *after* election, and in this sense the expression is probably employed in Law 19 of 1872 (N.), sec. 130. It is uncommon in South Africa.

Quoad hoc, as regards this; to this extent.

Quocunque modo, in whatever way; in any way.

Quocunque nomine, under whatever name.

Quod bene notandum, which is to be especially noted.

Quod constat curiae, opere testium non indiget, what is clear to the court does not need the aid of witnesses.

Quod erat demonstrandum, which was to be proved, frequently abbreviated *Q.E.D.*

Quod initio vitiosum est non potest tractu temporis convalescere, that which is invalid from the beginning cannot become valid by lapse of time. Some acts or deeds. although owing to some defect they are of no avail so long as the defect remains, may be validated by subsequent act, as where an agent does something which is beyond the scope of his authority, but which is afterwards ratified by his principal. The above maxim refers to those acts or deeds which are invalid in themselves, and cannot become valid under any change of circumstances. For example, a will which is originally invalid owing to incapacity on the part of the testator or the witnesses, or to the omission of some necessary formality in its execution cannot become valid through change of circumstances or by lapse of time (Voet's *Comm.* 34, 7, 1). The same principle applies to contracts which are void *ab initio* as being illegal or immoral or contrary to public policy; no subsequent fact or deed can alter their original defect so as to make them binding between the parties (see *Asbestos Co.'s Trustees* v. *Hirsche and Others—Hirsche and Others* v. *Trustees of Asbestos Co.,* 10 S.C. at p. 96).

Quod non apparet, non est, that which does not appear, does not exist; things which do not appear or are not proved are presumed to be non-existent. This maxim is of important application in the law of evidence. Thus if a document upon which a litigant relies is not produced by him, the court must decide the question against him as if the document were non-existent, unless he proves his claim or defence *aliunde.* So where a contract has been reduced to writing, neither of the parties can afterwards set up previous negotiations as qualifying its terms, for the writing is regarded as the final agreement, and anything which does not appear there as non-existent. In like manner, the fact that a charge has been previously brought against a person, but has been withdrawn, no conclusion being reached, is not sufficient ground for refusing to enrol him as a law agent, as not being a person of good fame and character within the meaning of sec. 36 of Act 20 of 1856 (C.C.) (*Wilmot* v. *Resident Magistrate of Alexandria*, [1907] E.D.C. 286).

Quod quis ex culpa sua damnum sentit, non intelligitur damnum sentire, where one suffers loss through his own fault he is not considered to suffer loss, *i.e.* actionable loss. The doctrine of contributory negligence was expressed by the Roman law in this maxim (*Digest*, 50, 17, 203). Several examples of its application are to be found in the *Digest*. Thus if a slave were killed by persons throwing a javelin for sport, an action lay against them under the *Lex Aquilia;* but if the slave crossed the place where the javelin was being thrown, and was struck, no action lay, as the slave was to blame for crossing at an unseasonable time (*Digest*, 9, 2, 9, sec. 4). In the same way, if cattle were injured by falling into pits dug in places which people had a right to pass, the owner of the cattle had no action against the maker of the pits if he had had notice of their existence, and but for his own carelessness might have avoided the danger (*Digest*, 9, 2, 88).

Quorum, the number of members of a body fixed by law or constitution as necessary to be present in order to make the acts of the body valid, *e.g.* the *quorum* of two judges of the Supreme Courts under Charter of Justice (C.C.), sec. 33, Act 38 of 1904 (N.), sec 3, and Proclamation 14 of 1902 (T.), sec. 20, and the *quorum* of directors fixed by the articles of association of a company.

Quoties in verbis nulla est ambiguitas, ibi nulla expositio contra verba fienda est, where there is no ambiguity in the words, no construction contrary to the words should be made. This is a maxim of universal application in the construction of deeds and statutes. Words which are plain and unambiguous must be read and applied according to their popular or ordinary meaning, and not according to what the court might conceive to have been the real intention of the legislature (see *Van der Merwe* v. *Jumpers Deep, Ltd.*, [1902] T.S. at pp. 207 and 210; *Venter* v. *Rex*, [1907] T.S. at p. 918). Where the words have acquired a different technical meaning in legal nomenclature, or where the context or subject-matter clearly shows that they were intended to be used in a different sense, they will be applied according to that sense. Apart, however, from such cases it is not the province of the court to read words contrary to their ordinary meaning save where they are ambiguous or uncertain. Thus under the 8th section of Act 43 of 1885 (C.C.), which provides that no person shall be enrolled as an agent in any district where not less than two attorneys are in practice, it was held that the section could not be read as if the words "independent practice" had been used, and a magistrate could not therefore be compelled to enrol an agent in a district where three attorneys were in practice, even although they were all in partnership together

(*De Kock* v. *Resident Magistrate of Caledon*, 13 S.C. 386). See also *Robinson* v. *Roper*, *N.O.*, 3 H.C.G. at p. 205; *Beedle & Co. in liquidation* v. *Bowley*, 12 S.C. 401; see also A VERBIS LEGIS NON EST RECEDENDUM.

Q.V., abbreviation for *quod vide* (which see), being preceded by the reference to which attention is directed.

Raadpensionaris (D.), an official whose office dates back to the time of the Burgundian rule. "He was paid by the town, and was usually a lawyer of high attainments. His duties were to act as the spokesman of the town's representatives. He also advised the municipal body in difficult matters and conducted their lawsuits" (Wessels' *History*, p. 76).

Raaroof, Reeroof (D.), the robbing of a grave or of the dead.

Rachimburgii or **Rachineburgii**, certain counsellors who, during the Frankish monarchy, were selected for the hearing of causes tried according to the Salic law (Wessels' *History*, p. 158). It is doubtful whether they ever existed in the Netherlands (*ibid.*).

Railway. In the Transvaal and the Orange River Colony the Railways Regulation Act (13 of 1908 (T.) and 29 of 1908 (O.R.C.)), sec. 2, defines *railway* to mean "the whole or any portion of the railways," and *railways* to mean and include "all lines of railway within this colony over which the Governor or the Administration has control or rights, and all lands, stations, sidings, buildings, plant, machinery, rolling-stock and all other movable and immovable property and servitudes used in connection therewith." See also Ordinance 20 of 1903 (T.), sec. 2, and Ordinance 46 of 1903 (O.R.C.), sec. 2. It has been held in the Cape Supreme Court that although the building of a railway station is a work in connection with the *railway*, the station is not part of the *railway* (*Heathcote* v. *Colonial Government*, 23 S.C. at p. 56); see also *Slabber* v. *Bell*, (4 Searle, 3). It is, however, to be observed that while *railways* is defined by the Transvaal and Orange River Colony Acts (*supra*) as including *inter alia* stations, the Cape Regulation of Railways Act (20 of 1861) contains no definition of *railway*.

In the Regulation of Railways Act, 1871 (34 & 35 Vict. cap. 78) (E.), *railway* is defined to mean "the whole or any portion of a railway or tramway, whether worked by steam or otherwise, which has been authorised by any Act of Parliament or by any certificate under Act of Parliament."

In the Regulation of Railways Act, 1873 (36 & 37 Vict. cap. 48) (E.), *railway* includes "every station, siding, wharf or dock of or belonging to such railway and used for the purposes of public traffic," and in the Railway and Canal Traffic Act, 1854 (17 & 18 Vict. cap. 31) (E.), *rail-*

way includes "every station of or belonging to such *railway* used for the purposes of public traffic." See also sec. 2 (*s*) of the Canadian Railway Act (3 Ed. VII, cap. 58), where *railway* is defined to mean "any *railway* which the company has authority to construct or operate, and includes all branches, sidings, stations, depots, wharfs, rolling stock, equipment, stores, property, real or personal, and works connected therewith, and also any railway bridge, tunnel or other structure which the company is authorised to construct."

Railway buildings, see *Claremont Municipality* v. *Colonial Government* (22 S.C. at p. 104).

Railway station, as to whether a *railway station* is part of a railway, see *Slabber* v. *Bell* (4 Searle, 3).

"The building of a *railway station* is a work in connection with the railway, but the station is not part of the railway" (*per* DE VILLIERS, C.J., in *Heathcote* v. *Colonial Government*, 23 S.C. at p. 56). *See* RAILWAY.

Ranking of debts, an expression used in insolvency law, meaning the classification of proofs of debt or claims upon an insolvent estate in their proper order of preference, as prescribed or allowed in law.

Rape "is the act of having carnal knowledge of a woman without her conscious permission, such permission not being extorted by force or fear of immediate bodily harm" (Stephen's *Digest of Criminal Law*, 5th ed. p. 207).

"After all, *rape* is only the most aggravated form of indecent assault; and I can see no ground of principle upon which we should draw any distinction, so far as the consent of a child under the age of twelve years is concerned, between a charge of *rape* and a charge of indecent assault" (*per* INNES, C.J., in *Socout Ally* v. *Rex*, [1907] T.S. at p. 338).

Rapina, robbery; theft accompanied by violence.

Raptus, a crime in Roman law which included both of the distinct offences known to our law as abduction and rape. The former crime consists in the carrying away of a minor of either sex without the knowledge or consent of parents or guardians for the purpose of marriage or from motives of lust (*Queen* v. *Motati*; *Queen* v. *Buchenroeder*, 13 S.C. 173). Consent on the part of the minor, while it is no defence to a charge of abduction, affords a ground for mitigating the sentence to be imposed (*Barnard* v. *Rex*, [1907] T.S. 270; *Marais* v. *The State*, 6 C.L.J. 110).

Rate, a tax assessed upon property by some public authority having the legal power to do so.

Rateable property, such property as is capable of being rated or in respect of which a rate or tax may be levied by the municipality or other public authority within whose jurisdiction such property is situate. For a comprehensive, and not altogether clear, definition of *rateable property*, see the Transvaal Local Authorities Rating Ordinance, 43 of 1903 (T.), sec. 3; *Johannesburg Municipality* v. *Klipriversberg Estate G. M. Co.* ([1905] T.H. at p. 292). See also Proclamation 38 of 1902 (T.), sec. 2.

Ratepayer. The term *ratepayer* is defined in the Cape Public Bodies Private Bills Act (35 of 1885) to mean "every person liable to the payment of rates to or qualified to vote in the election of members of such public body;" and in the Cape Divisional Councils Act (40 of 1889), sec. 4, as meaning "a person liable to the payment of rates in any division."

In the Municipal Corporations Ordinance, 6 of 1904 (O.R.C.), sec. 2, as amended by Ordinance 14 of 1905 (O.R.C.), sec. 2, it means and comprises "every person who is the registered owner of rateable property valued in the municipal assessment roll at not less than £200 within any municipality, or who, being a lessee of such immovable property, has by terms of his lease taken upon himself the payment of the town rate, or who is the occupier of any immovable property within the municipality valued as aforesaid at not less than £300."

"Rates last due." This expression, occurring in sec. 275 of the Divisional Councils Act, 40 of 1889 (C.C.), refers only to the last yearly rate, and not to all arrear rates. See *Smuts* v. *Divisional Council of Cathcart* (13 S.C. 359; 6 C.T.R. 384); *Wood's Estate* v. *Bathurst Divisional Council* ([1906] E.D.C. 63). Accordingly where a person had bought land from an insolvent estate, but had not obtained transfer, and during the period of his occupation a road rate became payable to the divisional council, it was held that the council could not refuse to accept such rate when tendered by the purchaser, and so prevent transfer of the land to him until all arrear rates due by the insolvent estate had been paid (*Smuts* v. *Divisional Council of Cathcart, ibid.*).

Ratificatie (D.), ratification. *See* RATIFICATION.

Ratification, the act of ratifying; the state of being ratified (*see* RATIFY). As to presumption of *ratification*, see *Faure, Neethling & Co.* v. *Beyers* (12 S.C. 438). *See* OMNIS RATIHABITIO RETROTRAHITUR ET MANDATO PRIORI AEQUIPARATUR.

Ratify, to accept, confirm, sanction, or make valid some act or thing done by an agent or third party. *See* RATIFICATION.

Ratio decidendi, the ground of deciding a case.

Ratione domicilii, by reason of one's domicile; on account of domicile. Domicile is now the basis upon which jurisdiction is most commonly exercised. *See* RATIONE ORIGINIS.

Ratione originis, by reason of one's origin or birth. According to Voet (*Comm.* 5, 1, 91) a person may be sued in the place of his domicile by birth as well as in the place where he is actually domiciled. This was the principle of the Roman law, but even there it is probable that a plaintiff could sue in the *forum originis* only when the defendant was actually domiciled there (Westlake's *International Law*, 4th ed. p. 221). At any rate jurisdiction is no longer exercised *ratione originis*, but is now founded either upon the person being within the territory (jurisdiction *ratione domicilii*) or the thing being within the territory (jurisdiction *ratione rei sitae*) (Story's *Conflict of Laws*, sec. 539; Piggott on *Foreign Judgments*, cap. iii, secs. 3 and 8).

Ratione rei sitae, by reason of the position of the property. Jurisdiction may be exercised not only against persons domiciled within the territory, but also against those who are domiciled elsewhere by reason of the presence within the territory of property belonging to them, whether movable or immovable, such property being attached previous to the commencement of the action.

Rauwactie (D.), "an action in the first instance, whether in a principal case or by way of provisional sentence" (Van Leeuwen's *Comm.* Kotzé's trans. vol. 2, p. 466, translator's note). See *Commissioner of Mines* v. *Solomon and Others* ([1907] T.S. at p. 54).

Re et verbis, by the thing and the words; one of the three ways of joining co-legatees together in a bequest, viz., where they are conjoined both with regard to the subject of the legacy and by the words used, as where the testator says, "I leave my house to A and B." *See* JUS ACCRESCENDI.

Re tantum, by the thing only. One of the three ways in which co-legatees may be joined together in a bequest, viz., where the same thing is bequeathed to each, but in different parts of the will. *See* JUS ACCRESCENDI.

Real actions, actions available for the enforcement of a right to a thing, whether the right of ownership itself or some other right by which the right of ownership is affected, *e.g.* the right of possession, a right of servitude, &c. They are distinguished from personal actions, which are brought to enforce an obligation to do or to give something.

Real servitude, a servitude attached to land; a praedial servitude. *See* PRAEDIAL SERVITUDE.

Real statutes or laws, one of the three branches into which laws were divided by the civilians, the other two being personal and mixed statutes or laws. *Real statutes* are laws in which, although mention may be made of the person also, the intention is to make provision concerning things. *See* EXTRA TERRITORIUM JUS DICENTI IMPUNE NON PARETUR.

Reasonable notice. "Reasonable notice in the case of a monthly lease should be so given as to expire at the end of a month, unless there is custom or agreement to the contrary" (*per* INNES, C.J., in *Fulton* v. *Nunn*, [1904] T.S. at p. 126). See also *Paruk* v. *Hayne & Co.* (27 N.L.R. at p. 383).

Reassumption, a taking back again. See *Colonial Government* v. *Stephan Bros.* (17 S.C. at p. 396), where *reassumption* of land by the Crown is discussed.

Rebate, an allowance or deduction.

Rebut, to answer or oppose by plea or argument; to disprove.

Receipt, a written acknowledgment that something has been received; such, for instance, as a written acknowledgment of the payment of money in discharge of a debt. "I take the rule of our law to be that a debtor is not bound to pay his debt unless the creditor is ready and willing to give a *receipt* for the amount" (*per* DE VILLIERS, C.J., in *Van Noorden* v. *De Jongh and Hofmeyer*, 9 S.C. at p. 298).

As to stamping a *receipt* in Cape Colony, see *Rex* v. *Standen* (21 S.C. at p. 257).

See Stamp Duty Proclamation, 12 of 1902 (T.), sec. 31.

Receptum nautarum, cauponum, stabulariorum, the obligation of shipowners, innkeepers and stablekeepers; one of the kinds of quasi-contract in Roman law. In the Roman law, which is followed by the Roman-Dutch law, carriers by water, innkeepers and stablekeepers are responsible for the slightest degree of negligence with regard to property entrusted to them just as if they had concluded an express agreement to that effect, and are exempted from liability only where the loss has been caused by unavoidable accident (*damnum fatale*) or irresistible force (*vis major*). In our law this extraordinary liability has been held to apply equally to carriers by land (*Tregida* v. *Sivewright, N.O.*, 14 S.C. 82).

Recht (D.), right; claim; title; law; justice. *See* LAW. Decker, in a note to Van Leeuwen's *Comm.* (Kotzé's trans. vol. 1, p. 1) says: "The term *recht* is in our language used in a variety of senses: 1st, to denote judges (*rechters*), *e.g.* to come before the court; 2nd, for the citation, as to bring another into court; 3rd, for an action or claim, *e.g.* to cede one's claim. *Recht* is also used to denote the laws; the quality or capacity of a person, and, lastly, to denote the goodness of an act." Its two principal meanings, like the Roman *jus*, are (1) law and (2) a right. *See* JUS.

Recht der natuur (D.), natural law, or law of nature. *See* LAW OF NATURE.

Recht der volken (D.), the law of nations. *See* LAW OF NATIONS.

Rechtbank (D.), a court of justice; the bench on which the judges sit. See Wessels' *History*, p. 147.

Rechter (D.), a judge. Equivalent to the Latin *judex*.

Rechtsgebied (D.), jurisdiction.

Rechtsgebruik (D.), form of law; judicial custom.

Rechtsgeleerde (D.), a jurisconsult; a lawyer.

Rechtsgeleerdheid (D.), jurisprudence.

Rechtspleging (D.), administration of justice.

Rechtswetenschap (D.), the science of law.

Recognisance, a written obligation executed before a magistrate or some other proper official, whereby a person binds himself, under some specified penalty, to perform some particular act or appear at some particular court or place, within a time or on a day named in the obligation. *See* BAIL.

Reconciliatio, reconciliation; condonation (*q.v.*).

Reconstruction is not a legal, but a commercial expression, and bears no exact definite meaning. It involves the carrying on of substantially the same business by substantially the same persons; but it does not necessarily involve that *all* the assets or the liabilities shall pass over to the new or resuscitated company or that *all* the old shareholders shall be shareholders therein (*South African Supply and Cold Storage Co.; In re Wild* v. *South African Supply and Cold Storage Co.*, [1904], 2 Ch. 268; 73 L.J. Ch. 657; 91 L.T. 447).

Reconventie (D.), reconvention; a technical term in Dutch judicial practice signifying a counter-claim by the defendant against the claim of the plaintiff. See Van der Linden's *Institutes*, 3, 1, 2, 18; also CLAIM IN RECONVENTION.

Reconventio forum competens efficit, reconvention confers upon a court jurisdiction. In other words, reconvention or counter-claim may render a plaintiff subject to the jurisdiction of a court which would otherwise have no jurisdiction over him. Thus, if a *peregrinus* institutes an action against an *incola*, and the latter makes a claim in reconvention, the former cannot object that the court has no jurisdiction over him to try the claim in reconvention, nor can he by abandoning his action prevent the defendant from proceeding with his counter-claim (Voet's *Comm.* 5, 1, 78; *Schunke* v. *Taylor & Symonds*, 8 S.C. at p. 107).

Reconvention. *See* CLAIM IN RECONVENTION.

Record. (1) To take down in writing; to make a note of.
(2) The proceedings and documents in an action as kept by the registrar or other official of a court; documents relating to a matter and preserved for future reference.

Recoverable, see *Langford* v. *Moore and Others* (17 S.C. at p. 21).

Rectifier. The term *rectifier* is defined in the Cape Excise Spirits Act (18 of 1884) to mean "a person other than a licensed distiller who rectifies or compounds spirits." The same definition is given in the Additional Taxation Act, 36 of 1904 (C.C.), sec. 2. See Act 25 of 1905 (N.).

Redemptor, otherwise called the lessee in the contract of *locatio operis faciendi, i.e.* one who undertakes to perform a piece of work given to him by another; a contractor.

Reductie (D.) is a species of provocation or appeal against the decision of arbitrators. The Roman-Dutch law was not quite so strict as the English law in going behind the finding of arbitrators. Thus it allowed an appeal if it could be shown that the finding was not in accordance with what was fair and equitable, as well as upon the ground of irregularity or illegality (Kersteman's *Woordenboek, sub voce "Reductie"*). "The procedure of *reductie*" (says DE VILLIERS, C.J.) "was still in full use in Holland at the time of the cession of this [Cape] Colony to Great Britain, and is mentioned by Van der Linden (*Institutes*, 3, 1, 7) as one of the different kinds of appeal to the higher courts. It is a remarkable instance of the great, but silent influence of English procedure upon the practice of this court that no case can be found in which the Dutch process of *reductie* has been resorted to in this colony. Certainly since the appointment of English and Scotch judges in 1828 the principle of the finality of awards became firmly established in our courts" (*Dutch Reformed Church* v. *Town Council of Capetown*, 12 S.C. at p. 21). In South Africa an award of arbitrators will be set aside on the ground of irregularity or illegality (*Dietz* v. *Pohl*, 1 Menz. 397; *Wood* v. *Gilmour*, 3 Menz. 159; *Fryer* v. *King*, *ibid.* 160; *McDonald & Co.* v. *Gordon & Co.*, 1 Roscoe, 251; *Hampson* v. *Dixon*, 6 H.C.G. 159; *Engelbrecht* v. *Roos*, 4 S.A.R. 286).

Reef. (1) A vein or lode containing or supposed to contain minerals. In the Cape Precious Minerals Act (31 of 1898), sec. 3, the term *reef* is understood to include "all forms of ore deposits containing gold, silver or platinum occurring in the earth's crust that have been deposited subsequently to the formation of the enclosing country rocks. It shall include 'metalliferous bankets.'"

(2) The rock or shale surrounding a diamondiferous pipe or a diamond mine. In the Cape Precious Stones Act (11 of 1899), sec. 3, the words *reef or shaly ground* are taken to "apply to the shale, rock or soil outside and around diamondiferous claims, and shall not include what is commonly known as 'floating shale,' or shale and rock in or covering the actual claims."

Reef claim. "A claim acquired for the purpose of mining for gold or other precious metals found in a reef" (Ordinance 3 of 1904 (O.R.C.), sec. 5).

Reeroof (D.). *See* RAAROOF.

Re-examination, the further examination of a witness after he has been cross-examined.

Referee, a person to whom some dispute has been referred for investigation and report, or for his decision. A *referee* may be appointed either by the parties to the dispute or by the court.

Reformatory, an institution established by Government for the reception and custody of juvenile offenders. See Ordinance 6 of 1906 (T.), secs. 3 and 45; Act 38 of 1909 (T.), sec. 15.

Reformatory institution, a place set apart by law for the detention of youthful criminals (see Act 7 of 1879 (C.C.) and amending Acts).

Refresher, a fee paid to counsel, in addition to his fee on brief, for attendance in court on each day of the trial or hearing of a case, in which he is engaged, subsequent to the day on which it was set down for trial or hearing. This would also apply to an arbitration or other similar proceeding.

Refreshments. The term *refreshments* is defined in the Cape Railway Refreshment Catering Act (44 of 1902), sec. 1, to include "all articles of food, beverages and mineral waters commonly sold in restaurants and refreshment bars, dinners, suppers, tea, breakfasts, lunches, &c., tobacco, cigars, pipes, &c."

Register of Deaths. *See* DEATH REGISTER.

Register of Wills, a register kept in the office of the Master of the Supreme Court for the enregisterment by him of wills, codicils and other testamentary instruments after the death of the testators (see sec. 7 of Ordinance 104 of 1833 (C.C.)).

Registrar of Deeds, an official appointed by Government to take charge of and preserve the records of the Deeds Office and Land Register of the colony, as also to register deeds of transfer, mortgage bonds, antenuptial contracts, notarial bonds, *kinderbewyzen*, deeds of donation, deeds of servitude, &c. In the different colonies various other duties are imposed upon the *Registrar of Deeds;* for instance, in the Cape Colony the *Registrar of Deeds* controls the registration of trade-marks, designs, copyright in books, &c. Statutory provision is made in each colony regulating the office of the *Registrar of Deeds.*

The *Registrar of Deeds* took the place of the Judicial Commissioners under the old Dutch settlement at the Cape in 1829.

See LAND REGISTER. As to the duties and liabilities of the *Registrar of Deeds*, see *Cape of Good Hope Bank* v. *Fischer* (4 S.C. at pp. 374 *et seq.*).

Regula Catoniana, the rule of Cato. According to this rule a testament or testamentary provision which would have been invalid if the testator had died at the time of executing the testament cannot become valid by lapse of time or change of circumstances. Thus a will made by a person under the age of puberty is invalid, and will not be validated by the testator having before his death reached the age of puberty without revoking the will.

"**Regulating drainage.**" As to statutes empowering municipalities to make bye-laws *regulating drainage*, see *Oliff* v. *Worcester Municipality* (15 S.C. 203).

Regulation, a rule or order framed and promulgated under proper authority by a superior or governing body for the conduct and management of those under its control. See Cape Interpretation of Statutes Act (5 of 1883), sec. 7; Act 43 of 1895 (C.C.), sec. 1.

Rehabilitatie (D.), rehabilitation of an insolvent. *See* REHABILITATION.

Rehabilitation is a discharge from sequestration. Van Zyl in his *Judicial Practice* (2nd ed. p. 668) points out: "We are so used to the word *rehabilitation* that it is difficult to believe it is to be found in the Insolvent Ordinance [Ordinance 6 of 1843 (C.C.)] only once;" he adds that "discharge" is the legal term for what is popularly called *rehabilitation*. At p. 682 he gives the effect of discharge or *rehabilitation* under sec. 117 of the Cape Ordinance: (*a*) The insolvent is freed from all debts due at the time of sequestration; (*b*) "the insolvent is not reinvested with any part of his estate, nor is he liable for any debts existing at the date of sequestration;" and he points out that "unless the certificate of the creditors to the discharge be obtained within four years from the insolvency, the *rehabilitation* is entirely in the discretion of the court." See *Valenski & Lipschitz* v. *Lategan and Wife* (22 S.C. at p. 99).

Rei interitus, the destruction of a thing.

Rei vindicatio. *See* VINDICATIO REI.

Rejoinder, in pleading, is the defendant's reply to the plaintiff's replication.

Relation, a person connected with another by affinity or consanguinity; a relative.

Relative, a person connected by consanguinity or affinity; a relation. As to the use of the word *relatives* in a will, see *Re Mutery's Will* (5 S.C. 39).

Release "is of two kinds. The one takes place actually, and consists in a promise not to claim, as if the obligation had in reality been performed. The other takes place by implication of law" (Van Leeuwen's *Comm.* Kotzé's trans. vol. 2, p. 333), such as by prescription.

Release from sequestration, by a release from insolvency under Ordinance 6 of 1843 (C.C.), the insolvent is not freed from any of his debts, but "he is reinvested with the whole of his estate, assets and liabilities as they were at the date of sequestration, as if there had been no surrender" (Van Zyl's *Judicial Practice*, 2nd ed. p. 682).

Relevant "means that any two facts to which it [the word *relevant*] is applied are so related to each other that according to the common course of events one either taken by itself or in connection with other facts proves or renders probable the past, present or future existence or non-existence of the other" (Stephen's *Digest of the Law of Evidence*, 5th ed. p. 2).

Relictio haereditatis, the leaving of the inheritance to an heir; "an institution whereby a person entrusts the administration of his estate to another after his death" (Van Leeuwen's *Comm.* Kotzé's trans. vol. 1, p. 361; see also *ibid.* p. 343). The Dutch equivalent is *erflating*.

Reliction of inheritance. *See* RELICTIO HAERIDITATIS.

Rem pupilli salvam fore, that the pupil's estate will be safe or be kept secure. All tutors dative before entering on the administration of their ward's property are required to find security, to the satisfaction of the Master of the Supreme Court for the due and faithful administration and management of such property. Tutors testamentary are exempted from this, but on the application of the Master or any person interested they also may in certain cases be ordered by the court to find security.

Remaining extent, an expression used in conveyancing, signifying that portion of land which remains registered in the name of the original owner after certain other portion or portions have been deducted therefrom and registered in the Deeds Office in the name or names of other parties. See *Worcester Municipality* v. *Colonial Government* (8 S.C. 195), where these words, as appearing in a contract of sale, were discussed; see also *Hirsch* v. *Gill* (10 S.C. 156).

Remand, to send back an accused person to prison; to recommit a person to prison.

Remanet, an action which has been set down for one term and has been postponed to another.

Remedial statutes "are such as supply some defect in the existing law, or redress some abuse with which it is attended" (Stephen's *Comm.* 15th ed. vol. 1, p. 39; see also Craies' *Statute Law*, p. 60).

Remissie (D.), a form of pardon granted in the case of homicide or manslaughter; usually with the infliction of a fine to the Crown as compensation for the act (Van der Linden's *Institutes*, Juta's trans. p. 242).

Remove. Under Rule of Court 8 (C.C.) and 16 (*c*) (T.), an affidavit upon which a writ for personal arrest is obtained must *inter alia* contain an allegation that the deponent believes the defendant is about to *remove* or is making preparations to *remove* from the colony, and stating the reasons and grounds for such belief. It has been held that *remove* here means leaving with intent to evade payment of one's debt (*African Realty Trust, Ltd.*, v. *Goodwin and Wilson*, [1908] T.H. 202). An affidavit, therefore, upon which a writ of arrest is sought, must allege belief in removal in that sense and the reasons or grounds thereof. And where belief is based on information, though the source thereof need not invariably be stated, sufficient must be alleged to enable the court to verify independently the accuracy of such belief. Thus where an affidavit simply set out that deponent "was informed and verily believed that the respondent was about, or was making preparations to *remove*, and that he this morning embarked on a train *en route* for Bulawayo, where deponent is informed and verily believes he is bound for with the intention of remaining," it was held that the rule was not complied with, and the arrest founded thereon was set aside (*ibid.*).

Remuneratory donations. "I have not referred to *remuneratory donations*, which, being founded upon the principle of 'consideration,' stand upon a different footing from donations in the proper sense of the term, and do not, according to Voet (39,.5, 17), require registration at all. It was this class of donations which was dealt with in the case of *Brink* v. *Van der Byl* (1 Menz. 552), and *Melck* v. *David* (3 Menz. 684)" (*per* DE VILLIERS, C.J., in *Slabber's Trustee* v. *Neezer's Executor*, 12 S.C. at p. 168). *See* DONATIO REMUNERATORIA.

Renascentia, things that grow again. A usufructuary of land is entitled to the ownership of such fruits as grow again yearly. If they do not so increase again, as in the case generally of minerals and metals, he may indeed gather the fruits, but he is entitled only to the interest on their proceeds, for the fruits in such cases being part of the land itself, the capital belongs to the *dominus* (Voet's *Comm.* 7, 1, 24; Van Leeuwen's *Comm.* 2, 9, 4; Schorer, *Note* 226).

"Renew and extend." "You do not *renew and extend* a lease when you change its terms. True, a new lease in the sense of a new document was necessary, but the words *renew and extend* mean, it seems to me, that the new lease was to be in the same terms as the existing one; otherwise it would not be a renewal, but a fresh contract on new and different conditions" (*per* INNES, C.J., in *Strand Wood Co.* v. *Alexander and Friedman*, [1906] T.S. at p. 492).

Renewal. (1) Of a lease is a privilege granted in the lease to the lessee, whereby he has the right of extending the period of the lease for a further term. It is also the state of being renewed.

The rule that "hire goes before sale" will not apply to a mere right of *renewal* (*per* DE VILLIERS, C.J., in *Hite's Executor* v. *Jones*, 19 S.C. at p. 244).

(2) *Renewal* of a promissory note or bill of exchange "operates as an extension of the time for paying it" (Chalmer's *Bills of Exchange*, 5th ed. p. 224).

Renounce, to disclaim, abandon or disown.

Renovatie (D.), a writ of execution which, in Dutch practice, was equivalent to an alias writ of modern practice. *See* SOMMATIE. If the judgment was not satisfied within twenty-four hours of the issue of the *sommatie*, the *sommatie* was repeated, and in its repeated form was called a *renovatie*. Van der Linden's *Institutes*, 3, 1, 9, 6.

Renovatie-placaat (D.), a statute or placaat re-enacting the provisions of a prior statute or placaat.

Rent, the compensation payable, usually at stated periods, by a tenant to his landlord, for the use and occupation of the land, or premises hired by the tenant. *Rent* may in like manner be payable to the owner of movable property for the use of such movable property by a person hiring the same.

Rental, the gross amount of rents accruing from certain property.

Renunciation, the act of renouncing. *See* RENOUNCE.

Repair. In the Transvaal Fencing Act (12 of 1908) "*repair* shall, in relation to a fence or ditch or part thereof, include trimming, cutting and maintaining in good order."

Reparable, that which can be remedied. A term of the Roman-Dutch law denoting that a matter can be remedied or redressed by a definitive or final decision of a competent court—*ten definitive reparabel* (Van Leeuwen's *Comm.* Kotzé's trans. 5, 25, 13; *Donoghue and Others* v. *Executor of Van der Merwe*, 4 Off. Rep. 1).

Repatriation, the restoration of a person to his own country.

Repeal, to revoke or abrogate one law or statute by another. As to effect of *repeal* see Maxwell's *Interpretation of Statutes*, 4th ed. p. 622. The Cape Interpretation of Statutes Act (5 of 1883, sec. 10) provides that "the *repeal* of any law shall not have the effect of extinguishing any penalty, forfeiture or liability incurred under such law unless the repealing Act shall so expressly provide, and such law shall be treated as still remaining in force for the purpose of sustaining any proper action or prosecution for the enforcement or recovery of such penalty, forfeiture or liability;" and in sec. 11 of the same Act: "The *repeal* of any law whereby any former law was repealed shall not have the effect of reviving such last-mentioned law." See also *Colonial Government* v. *Standard Bank* (9 S.C. 253).

In the Transvaal Interpretation of Laws Proclamation (15 of 1902), sec. 7 (2), it is provided that "where any law *repeals* any other law, then, unless the contrary intention appears, the *repeal* shall not—(*a*) revive anything not in force or existing at the time at which the *repeal* takes effect; or (*b*) affect the previous operation of any law so repealed or anything duly done or suffered under the law so repealed; or (*c*) affect any right, privilege, obligation or liability acquired, accrued or incurred under any law so repealed; or (*d*) affect any penalty, forfeiture or punishment incurred in respect of any offence committed against any law so repealed; or (*e*) affect any investigation, legal proceedings or remedy in respect of any such right, privilege, obligation, liability, penalty, forfeiture or punishment as aforesaid; and any such investigation, legal proceeding or remedy may be instituted, contained * or enforced, and any such penalty, forfeiture or punishment may be imposed as if the repealing law had not been passed." This definition is taken over, with slight verbal alterations, from the Interpretation Act, 1889 (E.), sec. 38 (2).

Replication, the plaintiff's reply, in pleading, to the defendant's plea.

---

* This word "contained" is here given as printed in the official publication of the Transvaal Proclamations. Clearly it is an error, and should read "continued," as it does in the English Interpretation Act, 1889, sec. 38.

Reports generally means the Law Reports, which contain a statement of important legal proceedings in the superior courts, together with the judgments delivered therein. These *Reports*, unless subsequently overruled, are regarded as precedents. The South African Reports and the principal current English Reports are as follows:—

REPORTS.	ABBREVIATIONS.
Menzies' Reports	Menz.
Watermeyer's Reports	W.
Buchanan's Reports	Buch.
Searle's Reports	Searle or S.
Roscoe's Reports	Roscoe or R.
Foord's Reports	Foord or F.
Cape Supreme Court Reports from 1880	S.C.
Cape Times Reports	C.T.R.
Appeal Court Reports (Cape Colony)	A.C.
Eastern Districts' Court Reports from 1880–1905	1–19 E.D.C.
Eastern Districts' Court Reports for 1906 (and onwards).	[1906] E.D.C.
High Court of Griqualand Reports	H.C.G.
Natal Law Reports	N.L.R.
Reports of the High Court of the South African Republic.	Sth. Afr. Rep.
Official Reports of the South African Republic	Off. Rep.
Kotzé's Transvaal Reports	Kotzé.
Transvaal Reports, Supreme Court, for 1902 (and onwards)	[1902] T.S.
Transvaal Reports, Witwatersrand High Court, for 1902 (and onwards).	[1902] T.H.
Transvaal Leader Law Reports for 1909 (and onwards)	[1909] L.L.R.
Reports of the High Court of the Orange River Colony for 1903 (and onwards)	[1903] O.R.C.
Times' Law Reports	T.L.R.
Law Times' Reports	L.T.
Law Reports, Appeal Cases, 1891 (and onwards)	[1891] A.C.
Law Reports, Queen's Bench, 1891 (and onwards)	[1891] Q.B.
Law Reports, Chancery, 1891 (and onwards)	[1891] Ch.
Law Journal Reports, Privy Council	L.J., P.C.
Law Journal Reports, Queen's Bench	L.J., Q.B.
Law Journal Reports, Chancery	L.J., Ch.
Manson's Bankruptcy and Company Cases	Manson.

Representation. In the Natal Play Rights Amendment Act (18 of 1899), *representation* means "the *representation* or performance of any play right work in a public place."

Representative, one who stands in the position of, and acts for or on behalf of another; an agent duly authorised to act for his principal; a deputy.

Reprieve, to set free; to suspend execution of a criminal sentence. See Law 9 of 1876 (N.), where provision is made for the granting of conditional pardons in Natal, as also the issue of licenses to convicts to be at large upon certain conditions. See also Act 38 of 1909 (T.), pt. 2.

Repudiate, to disclaim; to refuse to acknowledge or to pay.

Repugnant, inconsistent with, or opposed to; as, for instance, where one part of a document or one section of a statute is inconsistent with, or opposed to, another part of the document, or another section of the same statute.

Request (D.), a petition to the court. See Van der Linden's *Institutes*, 3, 1, 2, 7.

Request, Courts of. *See* COURTS OF REQUEST.

Request in aid. *See* "PROCESS IN AID."

Required. *See* "THEREUNTO REQUIRED." See also *Teubes and Another* v. *Lourens* (24 S.C. at p. 692).

Rerum universitas, a collection of things, *e.g.* a flock of sheep, as opposed to *res singulares* or particular things, such as a sheep.

Res alicujus, things which belong to some one, as opposed to *res nullius*, things which belong to no one.

Res aliena, a thing belonging to another. The sale of a thing belonging to another is not illegal if made *boná fide*, but the buyer will be entitled to claim indemnity against eviction. Where the purchaser in such a case is aware of all the facts, and has not claimed to be indemnified against eviction, and the circumstances are such as to debar the true owner from recovering the thing or its value from the purchaser, the vendor will be entitled to recover the price from the purchaser (*Theron and Du Plessis* v. *Schoombie*, 14 S.C. 192). As regards stolen property, a sale of such property is void if both parties know that it is stolen. If they were not aware of the fact, but the purchaser ascertains it after the sale, and without being judicially evicted gives up the property to the true owner, he will be entitled to a refund of the price from the vendor upon proving that the latter had no right as against the true owner (*Nunan* v. *Meyer*, 22 S.C. 203). If the purchaser was aware that the property was stolen, while the vendor was not, the vendor will not be liable in case of eviction. If only the vendor knew, he is bound, if he has received the price, to deliver the property free from the taint (*vitium*) of theft or to pay damages (Voet's *Comm.* 18, 1, 16).

Res communes, common things; things the ownership of which belongs to no one, but the use and enjoyment to all, such as the air, running water, the sea and the shores of the sea (Justinian's *Institutes*, 2, 1, 1; Voet's *Comm.* 1, 8, 3; Van Leeuwen's *Comm.* 2, 1, 11; Grotius' *Introd.* 2, 1, 17 and 21).

Res extra commercium, things outside of commerce: things incapable of being owned or appropriated by any one. Such things are *res communes*, *e.g.* the air, the sea, the sea-shore, and the running water of public streams, which do not belong to any particular individual, but the use and enjoyment of which are common to all. Besides *res communes* the Romans also recognised as *res extra commercium* things which were devoted to religious or quasi-religious purposes, *i.e. res divini juris*. *See* DIVINI JURIS.

Res gestae, things done. This term is used to signify not only the particular matter or act in issue before the court, but everything said or done in connection with it, and being so inseparably a part of it as to be incapable of exclusion from any account that professes to be a full explanation of the transaction. On this ground statements which would otherwise be rejected as hearsay are often accepted as relevant evidence. In *Queen* v. *Le Roux* (14 S.C. 831) DE VILLIERS, C.J., said: "In the case of *R.* v. *Foster* (6 C. & P. 325) it was held on an indictment for manslaughter, that a statement made by the deceased immediately after he was knocked down by a vehicle, as to the cause of the accident, was admissible. That case, which was decided by three judges (PARK and PATTERSON, JJ., and GURNEY, B.), has sometimes been disregarded by single judges presiding at criminal trials, but it has never been distinctly overruled. In this colony the principle embodied in that case is well established, and the real difficulty lies in its practical application. The statement of the injured person is clearly not admissible if made after such a lapse of time or under such circumstances as might have enabled him to devise a story inconsistent with the truth. The fact that others had come up to the injured person before the witness to whom the statement was made is not conclusive against the reception of the evidence. In a street accident, for instance, a crowd might instantly assemble, and an exclamation or statement might be addressed to one of the later comers which could not well be excluded merely because he was not the first to arrive. The judge presiding at the trial is in the best position to decide as to the degree of relationship between the question under investigation and the making of the statement, and a wide discretion must, therefore, be left to him." See Taylor on *Evidence*, secs. 583 *et seq.* See also *Pinney* v. *Jones*, (1894) 42 Amer. State Rep. 209, where *res gestae* is defined as consisting of "the circumstances, facts and declarations which grow out of the main fact and are contemporaneous with it and serve to illustrate its character;" also *Milne* v. *Leisler*, 7 H. & N. 786; *Rosson* v. *Haigh*, (1824) 2 Bing. 99; *Wright* v. *Tatham*, (1837) 7 A. & E. 313.

Res in commercio, things capable of being owned or appropriated by private individuals, as distinguished from *res extra commercium*, things incapable of being so owned or appropriated.

Res integra, a matter which is complete or entire, *i.e.* upon which nothing has been done. The use of this phrase may be illustrated from the contract of mandate or agency. The principal may revoke the authority after its acceptance by the agent, provided the work under it has not yet been commenced. So, also, after the work has been entered upon he may revoke the authority as to the part which is still unexecuted if that part is severable from the part which has already been executed, but he cannot with impunity revoke the agency as to the executed part, that being no longer *res integra* (Story on *Agency* sec. 466). In the same way an agent may renounce his agency before commencing the work under it, but afterwards he is allowed to do so only upon indemnifying the principal for any damage caused to the latter through the non-performance of the unexecuted part (Story, *ibid.* 478). In Roman law the principle of *res integra* was of considerable importance in the case of innominate contracts, such as barter or exchange (*do ut des*), for either party had a *locus poenitentiae* or right to withdraw, even after there had been a *datio* on one side, so long as the other party had not moved to the execution of his part of the contract and the matter was in this sense still entire. In Roman-Dutch law, however, there is no *locus poenitentiae* in the case of such contracts, which, like other contracts, such as purchase and sale, become binding immediately upon the agreement of the parties (Voet's *Comm.* 19, 5, 2).

Res inter alios acta alteri nocere non debet, a thing done between certain parties ought not to prejudice a third party. Thus, subject to the ordinary rule that one decision may govern another as a precedent in respect of an identical legal point which arises in both cases, a judgment, although conclusive as between the particular parties to the action, cannot affect a person who was not a party to it. For the application of the rule to judgments and its qualifications see Broom's *Legal Maxims*, 7th ed. p. 731. Nor can the pleas or admissions of a person who is sued affect another, *e.g.* a co-debtor who was not a party to the action. In the law of evidence the maxim has a most important application (see Best on *Evidence*, 10th ed. secs. 506 *et seq.*).

Res ipsa loquitur, the thing speaks for itself. In accordance with the rule that the onus of proving an allegation lies upon him who makes, and not upon him who denies it, he who alleges negligence on the part of another must adduce evidence of it. In some cases, however, the circumstances are such as to raise a presumption of negligence, throwing upon the person charged with it the burden of proving the contrary. Thus, where a horse, having been hired in a sound condition, is returned with both knees broken and other injuries of so serious a nature as to make it necessary to destroy it, it will be inferred that the horse was negligently used by the hirer, for *res ipsa loquitur* (*Fick* v. *De Klerk*, [1907] E.D.C. 294).

Res judicata, a case or matter decided. The plea of *res judicata*, if substantiated, prevents a matter which has already been finally adjudicated upon being again made the subject of legal decision between the same parties or their representatives upon the same ground. The essentials of this defence are thus (1) that the subject-matter of the two actions is the same, (2) that they are between the same parties or their representatives, and (3) that they are based on the same grounds. (See Maasdorp's *Institutes*, vol. 4, p. 218.)

Res litigiosa, property in litigation. Such property may be validly sold, subject to the right of the seller's opponent in litigation to recover the property from the purchaser in the event of his being successful in the action (Grotius, *Introd.* 3, 14, 10; Van der Keessel, *Thes.* 630).

Res merae facultatis, a matter of mere power; a matter which is merely optional. Of this nature is the right to use a road or to build on one's own land. As such rights may or may not be exercised at the pleasure of those who are entitled to them, they cannot be lost simply by non-exercise for the period of prescription (Voet's *Comm.* 44, 3, 11). It is possible, however, that they may be lost by adverse user on the part of another for the prescriptive period, as where a person for that period uses a public road as his own private property by building upon it, putting a fence across it or in any other way so as to exclude the public from it (Voet's *Comm.* 13, 7, 7).

Res nova, a new matter; a matter which has not yet been the subject of legal decision.

Res nullius, a thing which belongs to no one, as distinguished from *res alicujus*, a thing which belongs to some one. Of *res nullius* some are capable of being the subject of private property (*res in commercio*), such as birds, fishes and wild animals, while others can never be owned by any individual person (*res extra commercium*), such as the air, the sea and the sea-shore. In the former sense a *res nullius* may either be a thing which has never been appropriated by any one, or a thing which, having been appropriated, has been abandoned by its owner with the intention of no longer owning it. In either case the thing becomes the property of the first occupier, *i.e.* of the person who first seizes and reduces it into possession.

Res publicae, public things; things belonging to the public as a whole, and which may be used by any member of the public, such as public highways, harbours and rivers (Justinian's *Institutes*, 2, 1, 2 *et seq.*; Voet's *Comm.* 1, 8, 8; Van Leeuwen's *Comm.* 2, 1, 12).

Res religiosae, religious things. *See* DIVINI JURIS.

Res sacrae, sacred things. *See* DIVINI JURIS.

Res sanctae, hallowed things. *See* DIVINI JURIS.

Res singulares, individual or particular things, such as a sheep, as distinguished from *rerum universitas*, a collection of things under some head, such as a flock of sheep.

Res singulorum, the property of private individuals, as opposed to things the use of which is common to all men (*res communes*), and things which belong to the public of a country as a whole (*res publicae*), or to a corporate body (*res universitatis*).

Res sua, one's own property.

Res sua nemini servit, no one has a servitude over his own property. If, therefore, the servient and the dominant tenement should be acquired by the same person, the previously existing servitude becomes extinguished by merger or confusion. Where the two properties are afterwards sold separately the question whether the servitude will revive depends upon whether the acquisition of the ownership of the two tenements by the one person was only temporary and revocable, as is the case where a husband, being the owner of the dominant tenement, acquires the servient tenement by way of dowry subject to a condition of restoration upon the dissolution of the marriage, or whether the tenements were merged without any intention of subsequent separation. In the former case only will the servitude revive (Voet's *Comm.* 8, 14, 4; 8, 6, 3). See *per* KOTZÉ, J.P., in *Salmon* v. *Lamb's Executor and Naidoo* ([1906] E.D.C. 351).

Res universitatis, things belonging to a corporate body created by the State (Justinian's *Institutes,* 2, 1, 6; Grotius' *Introd.* 2, 1, 24 and 31 *et seq.*; Van Leeuwen's *Comm.* 2, 1, 14).

Rescission, the act of abrogating or annulling.

Rescission of sale, the annulling or making void of a contract of sale either by mutual consent or upon some other ground allowed in law.

Rescripta, rescripts. These were answers given by the emperor under the civil law to magistrates who had referred doubtful points to him for instructions. *See* DECRETA.

Reservatoir. *See* CLAUSULE RESERVATOIR; RESERVATORY CLAUSE.

Reservatory clause, a clause inserted in a will by which the testator reserves to himself the right from time to time of making all such alterations in or additions to his will as he may think fit, either by a separate act or at the foot of the will, and desiring that all such alterations or additions so made may be considered as valid and effectual as if they had been inserted in the original will.

"A *reservatory clause* . . . is a clause by which the testator reserves the right, either by writing on the will itself or by a separate document, to make informal unattested dispositions varying the terms of the will. It is obvious that this privilege which the testator could reserve to himself, under our law, is one which must be narrowly regarded, and the exercise of which must be confined strictly within the limits allowed by the law; because if that were not done it might be difficult to safeguard against fraud the testamentary bequests of deceased persons. . . . Now it is clear that the principle of the efficacy of a *reservatory clause* in rendering valid unattested dispositions is one which, if extensively interpreted, would strike a blow at the usefulness of the safeguards to which I have referred. At the same time there can be no doubt whatever that the law of Holland did allow unattested codicils to be validated under such a clause. That doctrine was much commented upon by some Roman-Dutch writers, notably Voet (*ad Pand.* 28, 1, 29). He did not favour it, although he was bound to admit that it did exist; but he wished to see its operations confined to small bequests for charitable uses, and to other comparatively unimportant matters. The majority of Roman-Dutch writers, however, do recognise the use of codicils, valid under a *reservatory clause*, for purposes of great moment. They approve of legacies being given or taken away, and *fideicommissa* being established by such codicils. At the same time it appears to me clear, from the very nature of the doctrine, that the *reservatory clause* can only validate what the testator meant that it should. It is a power reserved by him, and it must be clear in respect of any particular informal document that he desired to exercise it. That appears to lie at the root of the doctrine. In the Cape it has been held, in the case of *Nelson* v. *Currey*, reported in 4 S.C. 355, that 'a *reservatory clause* in a will cannot confer validity upon a subsequent unwitnessed instrument unless such instrument is incontestably proved to have been executed by the testator, and unless it purports to be, and has been, exercised under and by virtue of such *reservatory clause*.' In giving judgment the Chief Justice said: 'All the writers whom I have consulted are agreed that a *reservatory clause* in a will cannot confer validity on a subsequent testamentary instrument unless that instrument is incontestably proved to have been executed by the testator, and unless it purported to be, and was, executed under and by virtue of the *reservatory clause* in the will.' That principle has been recognised in later decisions, notably in the case of *Van der Wall* v. *Executors of Van der Wall*, and it may now be regarded as established law in the Cape. Speaking with the greatest deference, my own view is that the judgment in *Nelson's* case is, upon the face of it, somewhat widely stated, because there are authorities which do not mention as a *sine qua non* that a codicil sought to be validated by the *reservatory clause* should expressly purport to have been made under that clause. Voet and Schorer (*Note* 181) are authorities which occur to one as not going quite so far. It appears to me, however, that what Sir Henry de Villiers meant was that all the authorities assume, from their language, that the codicil must be made by virtue of the *reservatory clause*, and that, speaking generally, the only satisfactory proof of the testator's intention would be a declaration to that effect in the codicil itself. But, however that may be, there is certainly direct, if not unanimous, authority in support of the proposition which the Chief Justice is reported to have broadly laid down. . . . The question is not entirely free from doubt, but there is strong authority in favour of the rule which has been adopted at the Cape, and in my opinion, in the absence of any local decision to the contrary—and none has been brought to our notice—it would be right to take the same view here. In the first place it ensures uniformity, and in the second place it does limit to some extent a principle which is very liable to be abused" (*per* INNES, C.J., in *Erasmus* v. *Erasmus' Guardians and Executors*, [1903] T.S. at p. 851).

Reserve, that which is held back from present disposal. The term is frequently applied to land held back from disposal by the Crown or by a municipality when the surrounding portions are being alienated. "The words '*reserve*' and 'grant' as applied to commonage lands are frequently used as synonymous terms" (*per* SOLOMON, J., in *East London Municipality* v. *Colonial Government*, 17 S.C. at p. 223).

As to the statutory *reserve* round a diamond mine in Cape Colony, see *Bultfontein Mining Board* v. *Armstrong and Another* (8 S.C. 236); *De Beers Mines* v. *McCarthy* (19 S.C. at p. 266).

Money being the property of a bank or company and held by it as a special fund wherewith to meet losses or other contingencies or to equalise dividends is also called a *reserve*.

Reside, to remain in a place as an inhabitant permanently or for a considerable time. *See* RESIDENCE; RESIDING. In Act 44 of 1904 (N.), sec. 3, *reside* is defined to mean "to have one's ordinary habitation on and to live upon the land not less than nine months in each year."

As to where a company *resides*, see *Portuguese Wine Depôt, Ltd.*, v. *Schenk and Others* ([1906] T.S. 174).

Residence. In the Transvaal Great Stock Brands Ordinance (15 of 1904), sec. 1, *residence* means "the *residence*, house, homestead or dwelling of the owner of any brand or great stock."

"The word *residence* is one which is capable of bearing more than one meaning, and the construction to place upon it in a particular statute must depend upon the object and intention of the Act. As was said by ERLE, C.J., in *Naef* v. *Mutler* (31 L.J. C.P. p. 359), '*Residence* has a variety of meanings according to the statute in which it is used.' And again in the case of *Re Bowie* (16 Ch. Div. p. 486) JAMES, L.J., says: 'There are cases in which it has been judicially decided, and I think rightly, that the words *residence* and 'business' have no actual definite technical meaning, but that you must construe them in accordance with the object and intent of the Act in which they occur.' Accordingly we find that the word has been variously interpreted in different cases. In the case of *In re Bowie*, already referred to, JAMES, L.J., says: 'Having regard to the object and intent of the rule, . . . I am of opinion that a man may fairly be said to reside where he is to be found daily.' Again, in the case of *Beedle & Co.* v. *Bowley* (12 S.C. p. 403), DE VILLIERS, C.J., says: 'When it is said of an individual that he resides at a place it is obviously meant that it is his home, his place of abode, the place where he generally sleeps after the work of the day is done'" (*per* SOLOMON, J., in *Buck* v. *Parker*, [1908] T.S. at p. 1104).

See *Hooper & Hansfield* v. *Barker* (27 N.L.R. 347); RESIDENT.

Resident, dwelling or residing in a place permanently or for a considerable time. See *Solomon* v. *Wolff* (15 S.C. 152).

"A *resident* in a country is a man who has his home in that country" (*per* INNES, C.J., in *Ismail and Others* v. *Rex*, [1908] T.S. at p. 1096).

See RESIDENCE.

"**Resident elsewhere.**" The jurisdiction conferred on magistrates in the Transvaal by sec. 12, sub-sec. *a* (2), of Proclamation 21 of 1902, over persons *resident elsewhere* must be restricted to persons *resident elsewhere* in the Transvaal (*Hajaree* v. *Ismail*, [1905] T.S. 451).

Resident householder, in the Municipal Corporations Ordinance, 6 of 1904 (O.R.C.), sec. 2, means and comprises "every person of full age who, being resident within any municipality, is the occupier of any house or other building within the municipality valued in the municipal assessment roll at not less than £200, or is the owner of immovable property within the municipality valued in the municipal assessment roll at not less than £100."

Resident magistrate. *See* MAGISTRATE.

Residing. "It is not alleged that the term *residing* has acquired the general technical meaning of 'having a place of business.' When applied to a corporation or a company the word would no doubt have this technical meaning, for the simple reason that the ordinary and popular meaning would be wholly inapplicable. When it is said of an individual that he resides at a place it is obviously meant that it is his home, his place of abode, the place where he generally sleeps after the work of the day is done. This is clearly the meaning which in the vast majority of cases the word, as used in the Act [Magistrate's Court Act, C.C.], must necessarily have" (*per* DE VILLIERS, C.J., in *Beedle & Co.* v. *Bowley*, 12 S.C. at p. 402). See *Oosthuizen* v. *Pienaar* (14 S.C. 373); RESIDE; RESIDENCE.

Residuary legatee, the person to whom the testator has left the balance or residue of his estate.

Residue, the remainder; that portion of a testator's estate that remains over after payment of his debts, and the legacies under his will.

Resignation, the giving up, or relinquishment from, an office, claim or possession.

Resolutien or **Besluiten** (D.). (1) Resolutions.

(2) Resolutions of the State; when these were passed and published they had the effect of law. This was also a form of legislation in the South African Republics, although in the Transvaal in *Brown* v. *Leyds, N.O.* (14 C.L.J. 71 and 94; 4 Off. Rep. 17), it was held that a *resolutie* (resolution) of the Volksraad had not, according to the Grondwet, the force of law. See *Blake* v. *Goldman and Others* ([1903] T.S. at p. 769).

Resolution, the formal decision of a deliberative body upon a proposition or matter brought up before it for discussion. *See* RESOLUTIEN.

Resolutive condition "is one according to which it is agreed that the property in the thing sold shall pass to the buyer, and it does so pass; and it is furthermore agreed that it shall only revert to the seller under certain conditions, for instance, if the price is not paid on a certain date" (Nathan's *Common Law*, sec. 861).

Respeyt (D.). *See* BRIEVEN VAN RESPEYT. Also spelt *Respyt* or *Respijt.*

Respondeat superior, let the principal answer or be responsible. The principal is liable for the acts or omissions of his servant or agent done in the course of his employment. The ground of this liability is that the principal has the selection of his servant or agent, and if the person he selects proves incompetent or untrustworthy in the employment for which he is engaged, any damage that results is due to the principal's own want of care (*Gifford* v. *Table Bay Dock and Breakwater Management Commission,* Buch. 1874, at p. 114; Story on *Agency,* secs. 308, 309, and 452–56). *See* QUI FACIT PER ALIUM FACIT PER SE.

Respondent, one who, in an application before the court, is called upon to answer to the claim of the applicant or the prayer of the petitioner; or the party who defends or opposes an appeal.

Respondentia, money borrowed upon the cargo in a vessel, and which is payable only on the safe arrival of the cargo at its destination. For the security of such advances a *respondentia* bond is usually passed in favour of the lender.

Restitutio in integrum, restitution in full, by which the parties to a contract are restored to the same position as they occupied before the contract was entered into. The grounds in Roman-Dutch law upon which the remedy may be granted to a contracting party are force or fear, fraud, damage to the extent of more than the half (*laesio enormis, q.v.*), minority, absence and justifiable error (*justus* *error, q.v.*). (Voet's *Comm.* 4, 1, 9–10; Van der Linden's *Institutes,* 1, 18, 10; Van Leeuwen's *Comm.* 4, 42; *McLeod & Co.* v. *Dunell, Ebden & Co.*, Buch. 1868, at p. 201; *Gous* v. *De Kock; Combrinck* v. *De Kock,* 5 S.C. 405; *Heatlie* v. *Colonial Government,* 5 S.C. 353; *Logan* v. *Beit,* 7 S.C. 197; *Vlotman* v. *Landsberg,* 7 S.C. 301.) At common law the period of prescription of the action for *restitutio in integrum* is, according to the better and prevailing opinion among the Dutch jurists, thirty years, except on the ground of minority, where it is limited to four years (*Umhlebi* v. *Estate Umhlebi and Another,* 19 E.D.C. 237). In the Transvaal, however, this action is now by Act 26 of 1908, sec. 7, subject in all cases to a four years' prescription.

Restitution. *See* RESTITUTIO IN INTEGRUM.

Restitution of conjugal rights. The action for *restitution of conjugal rights* is a preliminary suit between spouses, in a competent court, wherein the plaintiff claims an order upon the defendant to return to the plaintiff and to restore to plaintiff the marital privileges to which he or she is entitled; in such a suit it is necessary for the plaintiff to obtain a judgment before a decree of divorce *à vinculo matrimonii* on the ground of malicious desertion will be granted. This action is usually brought by one spouse, who has been wilfully deserted by the other, but in *Brown* v. *Brown* ([1905] T.S. 415) a wife deliberately and finally and without good reason denied her husband marital privileges, though she continued to reside in his house; the husband sought a decree for *restitution of conjugal rights* or in default divorce on the ground of malicious desertion; and the court held that he was entitled to such decree.

Restrictive indorsement. "An indorsement is restrictive which prohibits the further negotiation of the bill, or which expresses that it is a mere authority to deal with the bill as thereby directed, and not a transfer of the ownership thereof" (Act 19 of 1893 (C.C.), sec. 33 (1); Law 8 of 1887 (N.), sec. 34 (1); Proclamation 11 of 1902 (T.), sec. 33 (1); Ordinance 28 of 1902 (O.R.C.), sec. 33).

Retail, in small quantities; for instance, to sell by *retail* is to sell in small quantities.

In *Bowles* v. *Stott* ([1909] T.S. 412), where a sale of fourteen bags of seed potatoes to a farmer for planting purposes was held not to be a *retail* sale, and therefore not within the operation of the Placaat of the 4th October, 1540, BRISTOWE, J., dealing with the grounds for distinguishing between a sale by *retail* and a sale by wholesale, said: "Now 'quantity' is a relative term. What would be a large quantity for a bachelor, keeping up a bachelor establishment, is a small quantity for a man with a large number of children and dependents. So that quantity, taken by itself, is not a conclusive criterion. There may be cases in which mere considerations of quantity would govern the decision; but it is not in itself decisive. It must be looked at in conjunction with all the other circumstances of the case. That was the whole decision in *Spiller* v. *Mostert* ([1904] T.S. 634). That case may have gone a little far; but the principle on which it was decided, namely, that quantity is not in itself conclusive, seems to me to be correct. Again, the fact that the goods are resold is not conclusive. That was decided in *Loteryman & Co.* v. *Cowie* ([1904] T.S. 599). It was there held (and, in my opinion, correctly) that if the sale is *retail* in the first instance the fact that the goods are afterwards resold does not alter its character; it still remains a *retail* sale. On the other hand, a purchase by a *retail* dealer, in considerable quantities, of goods intended to be used in his business would clearly not be within the statute. . . . It seems to me that if goods are bought for the purposes of a business, that is, with a view to making profit out of them, the presumption, at all events, is that they are bought wholesale, and not *retail;* for persons who buy for their business usually buy wholesale, and the profit of the business frequently depends upon the difference between the wholesale and the *retail* prices."

Retail dealer. *See* RETAIL. The expression *retail dealer* is defined in the Cape Additional Taxation Act (36 of 1904), sec. 2, to include every holder of a bottle, club, or regimental canteen license, and any person holding a license falling within the definition as laid down in sec. 2, sub-sec. 7, Act 28 of 1883 [C.C.]." *See* Act 18 of 1897 (N.), sec. 2; Act 25 of 1905 (N.), sec. 4.

Retainer, the recognised arrangement by which, for a consideration by way of fee, a counsel's services are engaged by an attorney for his client; the term is also applicable to the engagement of the services of the attorney by his client.

Retentie (D.), the lawful withholding of some thing, belonging to another person, which we have in our possession, until such time as the owner of the thing has paid us that which he owes us in respect of the same thing. *See* JUS RETENTIONIS.

Retorsio injuriarum, retaliation of *injuria, i.e. injuria* by way of retaliation or defence. In an action for defamation it is necessary that the words complained of should have been used maliciously or *animo injuriandi,* and they are presumed to have been so used if the natural effect of the words when used in their ordinary sense is defamatory. There are cases, however, where such malicious intention is presumed to have been absent, and one of these is where a person, for the sake of defending himself against an accusation made by another, makes an imputation against his accuser (Voet's *Comm.* 47, 10, 20; Van Leeuwen's *Comm.* 4, 37, 1; *Norden* v. *Oppenheim,* 3 Menz. at p. 61). See also *African Life Assurance Co.* v. *South African Mutual Life Assurance Society* (18 C.T.R. 1056).

Retreat. In the Cape Inebriates Act (32 of 1896) the term *retreat* is defined to mean "a house licensed by the licensing authority named in this Act for the reception, control, care and curative treatment of inebriates."

Retrospective, affecting past matters or things. As to *retrospective* effect of statutes, see *Curtis* v. *Johannesburg Municipality* ([1906] T.S. 308).

Return. (1) "Sheriff's *return*" is an indorsement made by the sheriff or his deputy on all process issued out of a superior court and entrusted to him for service, showing the manner in which such process has been served. The *return* must be delivered (with the process) to the registrar of the court on or before the return day thereof, and must be signed by the sheriff or his deputy.

(2) "Messenger's *return*" relates to process issued out of a magistrate's court. The messenger indorses and signs his *return* on the process entrusted to him for service, and delivers the same to the clerk of the court on or before the return day.

(3) ' *Return* day," the day on which process issued out of a court is returnable. The sheriff has no authority to alter the *return* day in the summons even on defendant's request and with the consent of plaintiff (*Hansen & Schrader* v. *Pauling*, 4 S.C. 92).

(4) In the sense of going back to a place, or ceasing to be absent, see *Garlicke & Holdcroft* v. *Currie*, 27 N.L.R. at pp. 262 *et seq.* and cases there cited. In this case the word *return*, in this sense, was fully discussed, and it was held (at p. 168) that *return* as it appears in the Prescription Law, 14 of 1861 (N.), means "ceasing to be domiciled, or residing out of, or not within the colony."

Revenue, the income of a State derived from taxation and all other sources.

In the Cape Audit Act (14 of 1906), sec. 3 (*i*), *revenue* is defined to mean "all moneys collected or received for or on account of the Consolidated Revenue Account."

See PUBLIC REVENUES.

Review. "*Review* is capable of three distinct and separate meanings: (*a*) *Review* by summons: denotes the process by which, apart from appeal, the proceedings of inferior courts of justice, both civil and criminal, are brought before the Supreme Court, in respect of grave irregularities or illegalities occurring during the course of such proceedings; (*b*) *review* by motion: the process by which, where a public body has a duty imposed upon it by statute, or is guilty of gross irregularity or clear illegality in the performance of that duty, its proceedings may be set aside or corrected; and (*c*) a wider power specially given under particular statutes (*e.g.* Insolvency Law, Administration of Estates Law; Transfer Duty Laws) to the court or a judge, and enabling such court or judge, in respect of the matter referred to them, to exercise the powers of a court of appeal or review, or even of a court of first instance" (*per* INNES, C.J., in *Johannesburg Consolidated Investment Co.* v. *Johannesburg Town Council*, [1903]

T.S. 111). It is under this head that the most frequent instances of *review* occur, such as cases sent up daily by resident magistrates for review by a judge, and review from the ruling of the taxing-officer on taxation of bills of costs.

Revindicate, to reclaim. *See* VINDICATIO REI.

Revise, to examine carefully for the purpose of correction and amendment.

Revivor, a judgment reviving a superannuated judgment of an inferior court. See *De Beer* v. *Rose* (10 S.C. 48).

Revocable, capable of being revoked or made void.

Revocation, the act of making void some act, deed or authority previously granted or made by the person revoking: the state of being annulled or made void.

Revoke, to annul; to cancel; to make void.

Rifle. In the Transvaal Arms and Ammunition Act (10 of 1907), sec. 2, *rifle* means "any arm with one or more rifled barrels which is capable of being fired from the shoulder, save and except such *rifles* (commonly called rook rifles or saloon rifles) as the minister may by notice in the *Gazette* exclude from the scope of this definition." See also Act 23 of 1908 (O.R.C.), sec. 2.

"Right of free approach to the river," see *Boss* v. *Whyte* ([1906] E.D.C. at p. 318).

Right of way. *See* PUBLIC RIGHT OF WAY. Where it was agreed to give a *right of way* without any limitation as to width being specified, the court held that it was usual to give a width of 8 ft.; see *Pietersen* v. *Gabrielse's Estate* (21 S.C. at p. 204).

Riot "is an unlawful assembly which has actually begun to execute the purpose for which it assembled, by a breach of the peace, and to the terror of the public; or a lawful assembly may become a *riot* if the persons assembled form and proceed to execute an unlawful purpose to the terror of the people, although they had not that purpose when they assembled" (Stephen's *Digest of the Criminal Law*, 5th ed. p. 56).

Riparian farm. *See* RIPARIAN LAND.

Riparian land. In the Cape Irrigation Act (32 of 1906), sec. 3 (*f*), *riparian land* or riparian property "with reference to a stream, means land held under an original grant or under a deed of transfer of such grant, through which land or on and along the boundary of at least part of which land the stream passes, or a subdivision of such land even if the stream does not pass through or on and along any part of the boundary of the subdivision; and 'riparian owner' means the owner of such land."

In the Transvaal Irrigation Act (27 of 1908), sec. 2, "riparian farm" is defined as follows: "A farm held under an original grant or a deed of transfer of such grant through which, or along the boundary of any portion of which, a public stream flows. A subdivision of a riparian farm, even if a public stream does not flow through or along the boundary of the subdivision shall derive its riparian rights from the riparian farm of which it originally formed a portion, unless, in respect of the subdivision, no right to water from a public stream has been acquired by deed of transfer, agreement, order of a competent court, or other mode of acquisition. A farm which is Crown land and the situation of which in relation to a public stream would render it riparian, shall not be deemed to be non-riparian by reason that no original grant thereof has been made."

Riparian proprietor, the owner of riparian land, or of a riparian farm. *See* RIPARIAN LAND.

Risk, under this term is included every disadvantage which happens in respect of the thing sold (Voet's *Comm.* 18, 6, 1–7). *See* "AT MERCHANT'S RISK"; OWNER'S RISK; PERICULUM REI VENDITAE NONDUM TRADITAE EST EMPTORIS.

Road magistrate, a fit and proper person appointed by the Governor of the Cape Colony under Ordinance 9 of 1846, sec. 7, to act as such, with jurisdiction to try and determine in a summary manner certain offences under, or contraventions of, said Ordinance (for the Better Preservation of the Public Roads and the Prevention of Accidents and Injuries thereon). A *road magistrate* may exercise his jurisdiction in a purely summary manner wherever he may be at the time of complaint made; he must record his judgment in a record book as soon as possible after the determination of the case; he may issue a warrant to enforce his judgment. Such judgment is final and conclusive, without right of review or appeal.

Road of necessity, a necessary road. "As to the road being one of necessity to the plaintiff, the Court has never laid down any definite rule as to what circumstances would constitute such a necessity, nor is it advisable that such a rule should now be laid down. It is not necessary for the purpose of the present case to go so far as to hold that there can be no *road of necessity* over a neighbour's land unless the only possible approach to a public road is over such land. There may, perhaps, be cases in which the alternative route would be so difficult and inconvenient as to be practically impossible, and in such cases the Court might be justified in affording relief subject to compensation and the other restrictions mentioned by Voet (8, 3, 4)" (*per* DE VILLIERS, C.J., in *Van Schalkwijk* v. *Du Plessis and Others*, 17 S.C. at p. 464). See *Lloyd* v. *Oates* (27 N.L.R. 60). *See* SERVITUDE OF NECESSITY.

Robbery is an act of theft where the thing taken and carried away is on the body or in the immediate presence of the person from whom it is taken, and the taking is by actual violence intentionally used to overcome or to prevent resistance, or by threats of injury to the person, property or reputation of the person robbed (Stephen's *Digest of the Criminal Law*, 5th ed. p. 256).

"*Robbery* is open theft accompanied by violence" (Van Leeuwen's *Comm.* Kotzé's trans. vol. 2, p. 315; see also Decker's *Note*).

In the Native Territories Penal Code (Act 24 of 1886 (C.C.)), sec. 211, the crime of *robbery* is thus defined: "*Robbery* is theft accompanied by actual violence or threats of violence to any person or property, intentionally used to extort the property stolen, or to prevent or overcome resistance to its being stolen."

Rolling stock, a technical term employed in connection with railways, signifying locomotives, carriages, trucks and the like. In the Transvaal Railway Ordinance (60 of 1903), sec. 3, *rolling stock* includes "locomotive engines, tenders, carriages, wagons, trucks and trollies of all kinds." For similar definition, see Ordinance 45 of 1903 (O.R.C.), sec. 3. Both these Ordinances have been repealed by the Railways Regulation Act, 13 of 1908 (T.), and Act 29 of 1908 (O.R.C.), in which the same definition is given, with the exception that "motors" are added.

Romeinsche recht (D.), Roman law.

Royal game, in Act 11 of 1908 (C.C.), sec. 1, means the following animals: "Elephant, rhinoceros, hippopotamus, giraffe or camelopard, buffalo, eland, koodoo, hartebeest, bontebok, blesbok, gemsbok, rietbok, klipspringer, zebra, quagga, Burchell zebra or any gnu or wildebeest of either variety."

Royal prerogative. *See* PREROGATIVE.

Ruilen (D.), exchange or barter. An innominate form of contract (see Van Leeuwen's *Comm.* 4, 14). Grotius in his *Introd.* (Maasdorp's trans. p. 309) says: "Giving in return for giving, when it consists in single things, is called *barter*, which includes exchange in money, that is, when money is given for money as one commodity for another, which is called *exchange*. Since then *barter* is not purchase and sale, the peculiarities of purchase and sale, which include the right of *naasting*, do not apply to it; but if what is given turns out to be defective, restitution or compensation takes place in the same way as in the case of purchase and sale."

Rule. (1) An order of court, such as a *rule nisi*.

(2) A guiding principle, order or formula for the regulation of conduct or business. See Cape Interpretation of Statutes Act (5 of 1883), sec. 7.

Rules of Court, such rules as are framed and published by proper authority for the regulation of the practice and procedure of courts of law.

In the Transvaal Interpretation of Laws Proclamation (15 of 1902), sec. 11, *Rules of Court*, when used in relation to any court, means "rules made by the authority having for the time being power to make rules or orders regulating the practice and procedure of such court."

Rural lands, an expression used in Act 44 of 1904 (N.), sec. 3, where it means "lands outside the limits of a borough or statutory township or of any township or village under any Law or Act relating to such, or of any village or any group of houses which, in the opinion of the minister, is of an urban and not of a rural character."

Rural servitudes are "those which properly appertain to agriculture. Of these, some consist in doing something upon or over the land of another, or of suffering or not doing something in or upon our own land. *Rural servitudes* which consist in something done by one and suffered by another are a footpath, a road for driving, a drift-way, a way or passage, a passage to water, a water-leading, a passage by water and the like" (Van Leeuwen's *Comm.* Kotze's trans. vol. 1, p. 293).

Rural tenement (*praedium rusticum*), land used for agricultural or farming purposes. Correlative to "urban tenement." The test whether a tenement is rural or urban is not the place where the property is situated, but the use to which it is devoted (*per* DE VILLIERS, C.J., in *Nieuwoudt* v. *Slavin*, 13 S.C. 62). *See* PRAEDIUM RUSTICUM; also note of KOTZÉ, C.J., Van Leeuwen's *Comm.* vol. 1, pp. 305 *et seq.*

Saal (D.), the place of meeting for the purpose of discussing the affairs of the country. Some derive the *Leges Salicae* from the term (Meyer's *Woordenschat*).

Salary, the remuneration periodically paid or agreed to be paid by an employer to an employé for his service.

Sale. "The word *sale* is used with various meanings. To lawyers discussing it from an academic point of view it means the time when the parties have arrived at a valid and binding agreement, apart from any question whether the purchase-price has been paid or whether there has been delivery of the article sold. But it is also clear that in ordinary parlance the word *sale* is used in a somewhat wider sense than the mere agreement. In a cash transaction it means delivery of the property and payment of the purchase-price, and a *sale* is said to fall through when the seller or the purchaser fails to complete his part of the contract" (*per* WESSELS, J., in *Nimmo* v. *Klinkenberg Estates Co., Ltd.*, [1904] T.H. at p. 314).

In the Fertilisers, Farm Foods, Seeds and Pest Remedies Act, 20 of 1907 (C.C.), sec. 3, *sale* includes "exposing for *sale* and consigning or forwarding to an agent for the purpose of *sale*."

Sale on approval is a sale dependent on a condition precedent, *i.e.* there is no sale until the approval is given, either expressly or by implication. *See* SALE ON TRIAL, which is much the same kind of contract.

Sale on trial is a sale dependent on a condition precedent, for "there is no sale till the approval is given, either expressly or by implication resulting from keeping the goods beyond the time allowed for trial. . . . Failure to return the goods within the time specified for trial, makes the sale absolute" (Benjamin on *Sales*, 4th ed. p. 592).

Salting, the placing or depositing of any mineral or precious stone in or amongst rock, quartz or soil in such a manner as to lead a person finding such mineral or precious stone to believe that it was indigenous. See Act 16 of 1907 (C.C.), secs. 45 and 46; Act 43 of 1899 (N.), secs. 111 and 112; Ordinance 3 of 1904 (O.R.C.), sec. 27; Ordinance 4 of 1904 (O.R.C.), sec. 17; Ordinance 8 of 1904 (O.R.C.), sec. 9.

Salvage. (1) An allowance or compensation to which a person becomes entitled when, by means of his voluntary assistance or exertions, he has saved a vessel or goods from the perils of the seas, fire, pirates or enemies.

(2) The property saved through extraordinary and voluntary exertion of the salvors from the dangers of the seas, fire, pirates or enemies.

(3) The goods or property saved after shipwreck or fire.

Salvor. (1) One who renders assistance to a vessel in distress, and thereby saves or assists in saving such vessel; for such service he becomes entitled to a reward or compensation, called "salvage."

(2) One who renders assistance in an emergency, such as shipwreck or fire, and thereby saves some thing from destruction.

Sample, a small part taken promiscuously from a large quantity of any merchandise, produce, mineral, or the like, as a fair specimen or indication of the quality of the whole.

Sanitary board, a council having charge of the sanitary and municipal affairs of a town subject to Government control. There was a *sanitary board* in Johannesburg (T.) prior to 1897, as also in some other towns of the Transvaal.

Sanitary fees, certain fees or charges payable by the householders in some South African towns, such as in Johannesburg, for certain services rendered by the municipal or other local authority in connection with sanitation.

Sanity, soundness of mind.

Satio, sowing; the name given to the species of accession which arises from sowing on another man's land, that which is sown belonging to the owner of the land so soon as it has taken root and thus become attached to the soil (Grotius' *Introd.* 2, 10, 9; Van Leeuwen's *Comm.* 2, 5, 2; Voet's *Comm.* 41, 1, 25). *See* QUICQUID PLANTATUR SOLO, &c.

Satisfactory evidence. "By *satisfactory evidence,* sometimes called sufficient evidence, is intended that amount of proof which ordinarily satisfies an unprejudiced mind beyond reasonable doubt. The circumstances which will amount to this degree of proof can never be previously defined; the only legal test of which they are susceptible is their sufficiency to satisfy the mind and conscience of an ordinary man: and so to convince him that he would venture to act upon that conviction in matters of important personal interest" (Taylor on *Evidence*, 10th ed. sec. 2).

Scab Acts being very stringent in their operation, it is necessary that they should be strictly observed, and that the Court should place a strict interpretation upon the different clauses (*per* DE VILLIERS, C.J., in *Queen* v. *Holder*, 13 S.C. at p. 95).

Schaade (D.) [modern spelling, *schade*], damage, loss, injury. The Latin equivalent is *damnum.*

Schadevergoeding (D.), damages; indemnification.

Schalk (D.), a slave, a servant.

Schedule, a written or printed list or details attached to a statute, contract or other document; as, for instance, the *schedule* of repealed or amended statutes annexed to an Act of Parliament. Giving the particulars in a *schedule* is frequently more convenient than detailing them in the body of the document.

Schelte (D.). *See* SCHOUDT.

Schenking (D.), a gift or donation; in Latin *donatio;* also called *donatie.*

Schepenen (D.), the magistrates in Holland. *See* SCHOUT. "The *schepenen* were appointed for a certain fixed period, generally a year, and could be dismissed if they did not do their duties properly. No one could be appointed to the office unless he was a free and well-born citizen of certain means. He had to belong to a class known as *schepenbare mannen*. . . . In time, however, persons came to be appointed as *schepenen* who did not possess the above qualifications" (Wessels' *History*, pp. 159, 160). As to the court of *schout* and *schepenen*, see Wessels' *History*, p. 163. "*Schepenen* date back to the reign of Charlemagne" (Wessels' *History*, p. 158).

Schepenkennis (D.), a mortgage bond passed before the schepenen. See Van Leeuwen's *Comm.* Kotzé's trans. vol. 2, p. 123; Grotius' *Introd.* 3, 5, 1.

Schermschrift (D.), an apology.

Scholt (D.). *See* SCHOUDT.

Schot (D.), money. Hence *schot* and *lot*, that is, an assessment which every one had to pay.

Schotschrift (D.), a satire, pasquil.

Schoudt (D.), debt (*schuldt*).

Schoudt; Scholt; Schelte; (D.), in mediæval Latin *villicus*, he who assembled the court in civil matters and regulated the proceedings. The word is also synonymous with *At* or *Aesga*.

Schout (D.) was in Holland the sheriff. The term *schout* is derived from *schuld* (debt). See Van Leeuwen's *Comm.* Kotzé's trans. vol. 2, p. 357; and Grotius' *Introd.* 2, 28, 9. As to jurisdiction of the court of the *schout* as well as that of *schout* and *schepenen*, see Wessels' *History*, pp. 157, 161, 163. "The *schout* was appointed by the count, and his duties appear to have been both judicial and administrative. In this respect he resembled our resident magistrate, though, unlike our magistrate, he could not act judicially without the assistance of the schepenen. In the towns the *schout* and schepenen looked after the well-being of the citizens, saw that the city was properly policed, and made such regulations as are usually made with us by municipal councillors" (*ibid.* p. 163).

Schuldt or **Schuld** (D.), debt. *See* SCHOUDT.

Schuld-vereffening. *See* COMPENSATIE.

Scienter, knowingly. In the case of injury caused by animals the rule of English law is, that if the animal is of a tame and domesticated nature the owner is liable only if he knew the animal was dangerous. The owner of a dog, which is classed as a domesticated animal, is according to this rule held liable for injury caused by its biting some one only where previous knowledge (*scienter*) on his part of its vicious propensities is proved. Such proof, however, is by the Dogs Act, 1865 (28 & 29 Vict. c. 60), dispensed with in the case of injury to cattle or sheep. Although in our law there is, generally speaking, no action for injury done by animals without negligence on the part of the owner, it has been held that dogs are to be classed with animals *ferae naturae*, which are kept by the owners at their risk, and that proof of the owner's knowledge of their ferocity is unnecessary (*Graham* v. *Viljoen*, 8 Buch. p. 126; *Drummond* v. *Searle*, 9 Buch. p. 8).

Scientia utrinque par pares contrahentes facit, equal knowledge on both sides makes the contracting parties equal. One party to a contract cannot bind the other if by concealing what he privately knew he induced the other from his ignorance of the fact concealed to enter into the bargain. There is no obligation, however, on the one party to mention anything that the other actually knows or that is equally open to both to exercise their judgment upon. Thus where the proposal for a policy of fire insurance having been prepared by the agent of the insurance company after a full inspection by him of the premises, was signed by the insured in reliance upon the agent's correctness and without any intentional concealment, and the proposal stated that the walls were of brick and iron, a policy was issued which provided that it would be vitiated by material misdescription. Some of the walls in fact were of wood, brick and iron and two internal partitions were of canvas. It was held that the plaintiff's silence as to the nature of the walls did not amount to such a concealment as would deprive her of her right to recover the amount of her loss (*Drysdale* v. *Union Fire Insurance Co.*, 8 A.C. 63). So in the case of purchase and sale, a buyer has generally no remedy against the seller for patent and visible defects in the thing sold. He is presumed to have been aware of them, and both parties by their equal knowledge are regarded as on an equality. Accordingly where sheep affected with scab were selected and bought out of a flock by the purchaser himself, such a defect being perceptible to the naked eye and not latent, the purchaser was held not entitled to the *actio quanti minoris* for refund of part of the price (*Muller* v. *Hobbs*, 21 S.C. 669).

Scrip, a certificate or certificates issued by a company in accordance with its articles of association cert'fying that the person named therein is entitled to a specified number of shares in such company. When on a sale of shares the term *scrip* is used in the broker's note evidencing such sale, it means that the *scrip* shall be in proper form and in order (*Stewart* v. *Sichel and Others*, 4 S.C. at p. 438; *Wiarda* v. *Standard Bank*, 6 S.C. at p. 334).

Scriptura, writing; an artificial mode of accession by which a person who in good faith writes on another's paper, becomes the owner of the writing, subject to the right of the owner of the paper to compensation for its value (Grotius' *Introd.* 2, 8, 3; Van Leeuwen's

Comm. 2, 5, 4; Voet's *Comm.* 41, 1, 26). In the Roman law, on the other hand, the writing was held to accede to the paper, but if the writer had in good faith obtained possession of the paper he might defend himself against the owner of the paper by an exception of *dolus malus* should the latter refuse to pay the cost of the writing (*Institutes*, 2, 1, 33).

Sea-insurance. *See* MARINE INSURANCE.

Sealed will, synonymous with closed will. *See* CLOSED WILL.

Search warrant, a warrant issued by a magistrate, or other proper official, upon an information taken on oath that there is reason to suspect that stolen goods are concealed in any specified place, and authorising such place to be searched during the day time (Ordinance 40 of 1828 (C.C.), sec. 43). See Ordinance 1 of 1903 (T.), sec. 45, where the definition is more extended.

Sea-shore. "By the *sea-shore* is meant that portion of the shore which lies between high and low water mark, the use of which is common to all and can be prohibited by none, though the regulation of such use, in the interests of all who are entitled to it, is vested in the Government" (Maasdorp's *Institutes*, vol. 2, p. 8). See also *Anderson and Murison* v. *Colonial Government* (8 S.C. 393); *Milnerton Estates, Ltd.*, v. *Colonial Government* (16 S.C. 177); *Struben* v. *Colonial Government* (17 S.C. 242); *Horne and Another* v. *Struben and Another* (19 S.C. 317).

Seaworthy. A ship that is staunch and strong and in every way fitted for a voyage is described as *seaworthy*.

Second-hand goods. The expression *second-hand goods* is defined in the Cape Second-hand Goods Act (10 of 1895) to mean "old or second-hand clothes or goods, including defaced gold, silver-plated or steel-wrought goods, bought or obtained from any person other than a person licensed to sell or deal in the same."

Secondary department. *See* SECONDARY SCHOOL.

Secondary education. In the Transvaal Education Act (25 of 1907) *secondary education* means "education given in a secondary school or secondary department of a school."

Secondary school. "*Secondary school* and 'secondary department' shall mean a public school or department of such school at which the pupils in attendance follow a course of instruction extending beyond the course prescribed by regulation for a primary school" (Education Act, 25 of 1907 (T.), sec. 2).

Secretarii, a term sometimes applied to notaries in the middle ages; see Wessels' *History*, p. 198.

Security. In *National Bank of Wales, Ltd.; Cory's Case* (5 Manson, 373), it was held that the word *security* included everything that a banker would ordinarily accept as *security* for a loan, and *semble* (in the case of a company) would include the lien given to a company by the articles of association on its own shares. *See* VALUABLE SECURITY.

See, the diocese or jurisdiction of a bishop.

Seignorial fief is a fief that is given out by a king or prince, and possesses besides the privilege of jurisdiction, the titles of honour and dignities of kingdom, duchy, county, barony and the like (Van Leeuwen's *Comm.* Kotzé's trans. vol. 1, p. 256).

Self-defence. The Native Territories Penal Code (Act 24 of 1886 (C.C.)), sec. 62, provides that "every one unlawfully assaulted, not having provoked such assault, is justified in repelling force by force if the force he uses is not meant to cause death or grievous bodily harm, and is no more than is necessary for the purpose of *self-defence.*" See also sec. 63 of the same Act on *self-defence* against provoked assault; and Stephen's *Digest of the Criminal Law*, 5th ed. art. 221.

Sell. In the Transvaal Game Preservation Ordinance (6 of 1905), *sell* means "selling, hawking, offering or exposing for sale." *See* SALE; "SELL, DEAL OR DISPOSE OF."

"**Sell, deal or dispose of.**" This expression appears in Proclamation 104 of 1903 (Cape Native Territories), sec. 26, as also in the previous Proclamation 154 of 1885 (C.C.), sec. 10. The words "dispose of" following the words "sell" and "deal" must be restricted to transactions similar in character to those of sale and dealing; in other words, they must be taken to mean a disposal for some form of consideration. See *Regina* v. *Gontshe* (6 E.D.C. 280); *Rex* v. *Swartbooi* ([1906] E.D.C. 86).

Semble (Fr.), it seems; a word frequently used in the headnotes of reported cases to indicate the opinion of the court upon a point not directly decided.

Semi-plena probatio, semi-full proof; half proof; evidence from which some knowledge of the case may be obtained, but not sufficient to found a judgment upon (Van Leeuwen's *Comm.* 5, 22, 1 *et seq.*). Such in Roman law was the evidence of one person, which was not accepted as proof unless supplemented by other credible evidence. So the production of a merchant's books regularly and properly kept was deemed *semi-plena probatio* of his claim, and if confirmed by the oath of the merchant constituted full proof. This rule in favour of commerce was adopted by the law of Holland (Voet's *Comm.* 22. 4, 12), but as the difference between *plena* and *semi-plena probatio* has become obsolete in South Africa, the rule is no longer observed. It has, on the contrary, been held that as every party who is bound to prove any fact must produce the best evidence of which the fact is capable, a merchant's books verified by his oath are not sufficient proof of his claim; that the person who made the entries, if alive, must be brought to testify to their correctness; or the merchant himself must be able to swear that he read the entries while the transactions were fresh in his memory and that when he read them he knew them to be correct (*Van Niekerk* v. *Fagan*, 14 S.C. 49).

Semper necessitas probandi incumbit illi qui agit, the necessity of proof always lies upon him who takes action. *See* ACTORI INCUMBIT ONUS PROBANDI.

Semper qui non prohibit pro se intervenire, mandare creditur, in every case he who does not prohibit another from intervening on his behalf is presumed to have given a mandate. That is to say, if a person knows that another is doing certain acts in his name and raises no opposition or objection he will be regarded as having authorised these acts, and will be precluded from denying that the doer was his agent (*Faure* v. *Louw*, 1 S.C. at p. 8; Van Leeuwen's *Comm.* 4, 26, 5).

Senate. In ancient Rome the *Senate* was a permanent non-representative Council of Elders, composed mainly of ex-officials (Bryce's *History and Jurisprudence*, vol. 1, p. 181); it had originally considerable legislative and judicial power, but later it became the mere instrument of the emperor; "it died out in the disorder of the seventh century" (Bryce's *History and Jurisprudence*, vol. 2, p. 305).

The *Senate* of the United States consists of senators elected by the legislatures of the several States (Bryce's *History and Jurisprudence*, vol. 1, p. 505).

The *Senate* of the Australian Commonwealth is composed of senators elected by the people of the State (*ibid.*).

The *Senate* or Upper House of the Union Parliament of South Africa shall for ten years after the establishment of Union consist of eight senators nominated by the Governor-General in Council and eight senators from each of the provinces, *i.e.* Cape of Good Hope, Natal, Transvaal and Orange Free State, elected in the manner provided in the Act, or in all forty senators (see South Africa Act, 1909, sec. 24).

Senatus consultum, the name given to decrees or ordinances of the Roman Senate. "When the Roman people was so increased that it was difficult to assemble it together to pass laws, it seemed right that the Senate should be consulted in place of the people" (Justinian's *Institutes*, 1, 2, 5). During the time of the republic *senatus consulta* had in some few cases the force of law, but in the time of the emperors they were, with the exception of the emperor's enactments, the sole source of law.

Senatus consultum Macedonianum, said to have derived its name from a parricide called *Macedo,* provided that no one should lend money to a son under the power of his father without the father's consent. If the *filiusfamilias* were sued on such a loan he was allowed by the praetor to plead the *senatus consultum.* The exception, however, could not be raised if the *filiusfamilias* had a *peculium castrense* or *quasi-castrense* or if he had ratified the loan after becoming *sui juris* or had represented to the lender that he was *sui juris.* The *senatus consultum* is obsolete in the Roman-Dutch law, a minor being sufficiently protected by his right to restitution (Grotius' *Introd.* 3, 30, 3).

Senatus consultum Trebellianum. This law extended the principle of the *lex Falcidia*, which applied to legacies, to the case of *fideicommissa*, by enacting that an heir who was burdened with a *fideicommissum*, if nothing or less than a fourth of the estate was left to him, might deduct as much as would give him a clear fourth of the whole inheritance before handing the inheritance over to the fideicommissary heir. This enactment, which had the same object as the *lex Falcidia*, viz., to induce the instituted heir to accept an inheritance from which he derived no benefit, and so prevent the testament becoming invalid through his failure to adiate, has with the *lex Falcidia* been abolished in the South African colonies. *See* LEX FALCIDIA.

Senatus consultum Velleianum, which was passed in the consulship of Marcus Silanus and Velleius Tutor, A.D. 46, prohibited women from taking upon themselves the debt of a third party, although it did not declare any such suretyship void, but merely directed the magistrate to give effect to the prohibition in the exercise of his jurisdiction. The praetor carried out the direction by granting to a woman who was sued on the suretyship the *exceptio senatus consulti Velleiani* (Sohm's *Institutes*, p. 292).

"After the Senate had passed the *Senatus consultum Velleianum* considerable divergence arose among lawyers as to its operation. Doubts at first arose as to whether the suretyship of a woman was not absolutely void, but it was finally decided that, although prohibited by law, a woman could only take the benefit of the *senatus consultum* by pleading it" (DE VILLIERS, C.J., in *Oak* v. *Lumsden*, 3 S.C. 144. But see *Stainbank* v. *National Bank of South Africa*, 27 N.L.R. at p. 474, and the authorities there cited, according to which the benefit of the *senatus consultum* is not lost unless expressly waived, and may be taken advantage of although it be not pleaded. See also *Mahadi* v. *De Kock*, 1 H.C.G. 344).

The Roman-Dutch law adopted the Roman law, and women in order to be liable upon their contracts of suretyship have, "after being duly instructed" (Grotius' *Introd.* Maasdorp's trans. p. 210), to renounce this privilege of the *senatus consultum Velleianum* (*Oak* v. *Lumsden*, 3 S.C. 144). Similarly, by the *authentica si qua mulier* married women are prohibited from being surety for their husbands, except in so far as the debt in respect of which they became surety may be found to be for their benefit (Grotius' *Introd.* Maasdorp's trans. p. 210); but they may renounce this privilege. A notarial instrument is not essential to the validity of the renunciation (*Oak* v. *Lumsden*, 3 S.C. 144), but the very highest degree of proof is necessary, not only to establish the renunciation of the benefit, but also to show that a woman was aware of the effect of such a renunciation (*Marico Board of Executors* v. *Auret*, 14 S.C. 453). See appendix to vol. 2 of Van Leeuwen's *Comm.* pp. 618 *et seq.* on the *Senatus consultum Velleianum.*

Where a woman binds herself as surety for her husband it is not sufficient that she should renounce the *senatus consultum Velleianum:* in addition she must renounce the benefit of the *authentica si qua mulier* (Grotius' *Introd.* 3, 3, 19; Schorer, *Note* 2, 9, 9; Voet's *Comm.* 16, 1, 10; *Whitnall* v. *Goldschmidt*, 3 E.D.C. 314; *Stainbank* v. *National Bank of South Africa*, 27 N.L.R. at p. 476). If, however, the latter benefit is renounced, it is not necessary that a woman so binding herself for her husband should also renounce the *senatus consultum* (*Stainbank* v. *National Bank of South Africa, ibid.*). "In process of time the practice grew up that all women, whether married or not, could renounce the benefits introduced for their protection (Glück, sec. 925), and this practice also became a rule of the Roman-Dutch law. The only difference between the commentators is whether or not this renunciation of the *beneficia Senatus consulti Velleiani* and *Authentica si qua mulier* must take place in a public instrument, or can be effected in some other satisfactory way. All are, however, agreed that the renunciation is only binding on the woman where she has full knowledge of her legal rights. In other words, the renunciation must take place deliberately and advisedly. Consequently, where a married woman has renounced the *beneficia* in question, and has even stated in writing that she is aware of the nature of the benefits, if it be satisfactorily established that she was in reality ignorant of her rights at the time, she will still be entitled to rely on the benefits, which the law extends to women who have bound themselves as surety for another" (*per* KOTZÉ, J.P., in *Graaff-Reinet Board of Executors* v. *Maasdorp*, [1908] E.D.C. at p. 437).

Senile dementia, the dementia of old age; the mental failure that occurs in old age. See *Natal Land and Colonisation Co.* v. *Molyneux* (24 N.L.R. at p. 286).

Sentence, a judgment pronounced by a court of law upon a criminal after trial.

Separatio bonorum, separation of goods. Where a wife finds during marriage that her husband is squandering her property she may apply to the court for a separation of goods (Grotius' *Introd.* 1, 6, 24; Van Leeuwen's *Comm.* 1, 6, 7; *Sture* v. *Sture*, 1 Roscoe, 51; *Hayward* v. *Hayward*, 6 E.D.C. 192; *Ex parte Malagasi*, 9 E.D.C. 149).

The effect of a decree is that the husband cannot validly alienate the wife's property, and if he does alienate it she may reclaim it by a real action.

Separation. Spouses sometimes enter into an agreement, without the intervention of the court, called a "deed of separation," by which they agree to live apart, not to molest each other, and that the one shall not be responsible for the debts or engagements of the other. Such agreements for separation "will be effectual as between the spouses themselves or their representatives, but will not bind creditors or other third parties who are not representatives of either of the spouses, unless such third parties had special notice before their claims arose of the existence of the separation and of its terms" (Maasdorp's *Institutes of Cape Law*, vol. 1, p. 76). *See* JUDICIAL SEPARATION.

Separatistae, persons who are entitled to claim a separation of goods from the estate of an insolvent, viz.: (1) Creditors of a deceased person to whom an insolvent is heir may claim that the property belonging to the deceased's estate shall be separated from the heir's estate and applied to the payment of their claims; (2) legatees of such a deceased person and fideicommissaries of whose interests the insolvent is the fiduciary have a similar right (Van Leeuwen's *Comm.* 4, 13, 23; Voet's *Comm.* 42, 6).

Sequestration, the taking possession of the estate of an insolvent person. In practice the insolvent is divested of his estate by order of a competent court, and simultaneously it is vested in the Master of the Supreme Court for the benefit of the insolvent's creditors; it is then said that the insolvent's estate has been placed under *sequestration* in the hands of the Master of the Supreme Court. *See* COMPULSORY SEQUESTRATION; VOLUNTARY SURRENDER.

Serial work. In the Natal Copyright Act (17 of 1897), sec. 3, *serial work* includes encyclopædia, review, magazine, periodical work, or work published in a series of books or parts.

Serious and wilful misconduct, in the Transvaal Workmen's Compensation Act (36 of 1907), sec. 1, is defined to include "(*a*) drunkenness; (*b*) a wilful contravention of any law or statutory regulation made for the purpose of ensuring the safety of or preventing accidents to workmen; (*c*) any other act or omission which a court of law, having regard to all the circumstances of an accident causing injury, may declare to be serious and wilful misconduct."

Serjeant-at-law, a barrister in England or Ireland of high rank and appointed as a *serjeant* by the king's writ. Prior to the passing of the Judicature Act, 1873, the judges of the superior courts of common law were required to be *serjeants.* No *serjeants* have been appointed since 1868, their Inn has been broken up and the office will probably die out, but it has not been actually abolished. *Serjeants-at-law* formerly took precedence of other counsel, and even before the Attorney-General, except where the latter appeared "to move for the Crown." But in more recent times the order of precedence became changed, and King's Counsel now enjoy prior rank, although it is said that "in private society a *serjeant* takes precedence of a Queen's Counsel." The *serjeant* took a more comprehensive oath than a King's Counsel, by which he bound himself to truly serve the King and all his people (see Woolrych, *Eminent Serjeants-at-Law, Introduction*).

Servant, one who serves another, either for a consideration or voluntarily.

In the Cape Master and Servants Act (15 of 1856), sec. 2, *servant* is defined as "any person employed for hire, wages or other remuneration to perform any handicraft or other bodily labour in agriculture or manufactures or in domestic service, or as a boatman, porter or other occupation of a like nature." In the Cape Servants Registry Offices Act (20 of 1906) the term *servants* is given a somewhat wider meaning. See also Ordinance 8 of 1909 (R.), sec. 2.

Similar provision is made in the Natal Ordinance 2 of 1850, sec. 2; see also Law 17 of 1882, sec. 1; but in the Natal (Native) Master and Servants Act (49 of 1901), sec. 2, the words "miner, driver, herd" are added to the above definition.

The Transvaal definition of *servant* in Law 13 of 1880, sec. 2, is practically identical with that of the Cape definition.

See the Masters and Servants Ordinance, 7 of 1904 (O.R.C.), sec. 2.

As to a lithographic artist, see *Roper* v. *Argus Printing and Publishing Co.* (7 S.C. 3); a mason, *Rex* v. *Sango* (14 C.T.R. 117); navvy, *Clay* v. *Rex* ([1903] T.S. 482); foreman of steam laundry, *Pietersburg Steam Laundry Co.* v. *Sinclair* ([1904] T.S. 529); mason's assistant, *Rex* v. *Sango* (21 S.C. 35); printer, *Dugall* v. *Riches* (23 N.L.R. 94); a salesman, *Robertson & Co.* v. *Heathorn* (21 S.C. 427) and *Levey* v. *Bayes* (19 E.D.C. 167); a general clerk, *Miles* v. *Jagger & Co.* (21 S.C. 513). *See* FARM SERVANT.

Servants registry office. In the Cape Servants Registry Offices Act (20 of 1906), sec. 2, *servants registry office* is defined to mean "any premises or office at which is carried on the business of procuring the engagements of servants for employers, or employment for servants, but does not include any association or institution not carried on for the purpose of profit or gain."

Service. (1) Labour or duty performed for another.

(2) The delivery in the prescribed manner of a summons, writ or other process of the court upon a defendant or other person to whom it is directed. Such *service* is usually performed by the sheriff or messenger or his deputy. *See* SHERIFF.

Service by post. The Transvaal Interpretation of Laws Proclamation (15 of 1902), sec. 12, provides that "where any law authorises or requires any document to be served by post, whether the expression *serve* or the expression *give* or *send*, or any other expression is used, then, unless the contrary intention appears, the *service* shall be deemed to be effected by properly addressing, prepaying and posting a registered letter containing the document, and, unless the contrary is proved, to have been effected at the time at which the letter would be delivered in the ordinary course of post."

Servient tenement. *See* PRAEDIUM SERVIENS.

Servile persons "were those who were under servitude to a lord, and this seems to have been their origin. They were either the remnants of the Cimbri, who, when these countries [the Netherlands] were lying waste and unoccupied, first took possession of them; or, as some think, they are derived from the Hessi or Catti (called Nether Saxons), whose nobles and chief men took possession of the country, and were followed by their slaves and bondsmen and women, to whom they *allotted* the full right and property over the soil and lands portioned out; but subject to certain base or servile tributes and contributions and other subordinate duties, although not after the manner and severity of the Roman and heathen system of slavery, which was never in force amongst us" (Van Leeuwen's *Comm.* Kotzé's trans. vol. 1, p. 67).

Servitude "is a permanent limitation to, or derogation from, the right of enjoyment, owing to a right to a share in the use and enjoyment vested in some one other than the owner" (Maasdorp's *Institutes*, vol. 2, p. 32). Austin defines *servitus* as "a right to use or enjoy, in a given or definite manner, a subject owned by another" (*Jurisprudence*, vol. 2, p. 966, Campbell's edition).

Servitude of abutment is defined in the Transvaal Irrigation Act (27 of 1908), sec. 64, sub-sec. 1, as "the right to occupy, by means of a dam or weir, the bed or banks of a public stream or land adjacent thereto, belonging to another."

Sub-sec. 2 provides that "the proprietor, on whose ground a *servitude of abutment* exists, may, before the construction of the dam or weir is commenced, demand and thereafter shall be entitled to lead water therefrom, on paying to the holder of the servitude such proportionate cost of the dam or weir as may be agreed, or, failing agreement, as may be determined by arbitration." *See* SERVITUDE OF STORAGE; and for Cape Colony see Irrigation Act (32 of 1906), sec. 90.

Servitude of cutting wood, the right to cut wood. See *Queen* v. *Schulz* (13 S.C. 197), where such a servitude was recognised; also *Federal Timber Co.* v. *Celliers* ([1909] T.S. 909). See also Act 28 of 1888 (C.C.), sec. 8.

Servitude of necessity. "The court has more than once decided that a *servitude of necessity* cannot be claimed beyond what absolute necessity requires" (*per* De Villiers, C.J., in *London and South African Exploration Co.* v. *Bultfontein Mining Board*, 8 S.C. at p. 60). *See* Road of Necessity.

Servitude of passage of water is defined in the Transvaal Irrigation Act (27 of 1908), sec. 63, sub-sec. 1, as "the right to occupy so much of the land of another as may be necessary for or incidental to the passage of water, and shall include a right to construct on such land irrigation works necessary for such passage over, under or alongside another irrigation work, or to enlarge an existing irrigation work."

"The servitude shall include the right of access to any piece of land (after giving notice to the proprietor thereof) for the purpose of constructing, inspecting, maintaining and repairing such works" (*ibid.* sub-sec. 2).

"The servitude shall be subject to the duty of passage of water along such works by any proprietor on or over whose land the servitude exists, on payment of such proportion of the cost of constructing and maintaining such works as may be agreed, or, failing agreement, as may be determined by arbitration" (*ibid.* sub-sec. 3).

"In exercising such servitude across a public road, the holder thereof shall construct such works as will prevent danger or inconvenience to the public, and shall keep the same in repair, the manner of construction and repair being prescribed by the Minister for Public Works or the local authority (according as such road is under the control of the Government or a local authority)" (*ibid.* sub-sec. 4).

As regards Cape Colony, see Irrigation Act (32 of 1906), sec. 87, where it is termed the servitude of aqueduct.

Servitude of storage is defined in the Transvaal Irrigation Act (27 of 1908), sec. 62, sub-sec. 1, as "the right to occupy the land of another by submerging it with water by means of a dam or weir or other works, and shall include a right of passage over the land and along the boundary of and throughout the particular area subject to the servitude, for the purpose of maintaining and cleansing such works, or for any other purpose necessary for the effective enjoyment of the servitude."

"A *servitude of storage* shall not, subject to the terms of any award or agreement establishing it, deprive the proprietor of the area subject to the servitude of the use of that part of the area which is not submerged; provided such use is not detrimental to the enjoyment of the servitude" (*ibid.* sub-sec. 2).

"A *servitude of storage* shall give the holder thereof a prior claim to surplus water over servitudes subsequently acquired" (*ibid.* sub-sec. 3).

"When a permanent *servitude of storage* has been acquired by a proprietor over the land of another proprietor, the latter-named proprietor may, before the commencement of the storage-work and on payment of his proportion of the cost thereof (to be determined in case of dispute by arbitration), demand, and thereafter shall be entitled to receive, the benefit of the storage-work in the proportion which the capacity of that part of the reservoir, which is on the land subject to servitude, bears to the total capacity of the reservoir" (*ibid.* sub-sec. 4).

This servitude, together with the servitudes of abutment and passage of water (see *supra*), include a right to take materials from the land over which the servitude exists for the purpose of constructing, maintaining or repairing any irrigation works thereon (*ibid.* sec. 65).

Any person who has a proprietary interest in or the right to use water, or is entitled to supervise the use of water, may, subject to the payment of the compensation provided in the Act, claim temporarily or in perpetuity any of these servitudes, provided that—

(*a*) the period of a temporary servitude shall not exceed three years;

(*b*) no proceedings shall be taken for the acquisition of any such servitude while legal proceedings are pending as to the right to the water in respect of which the servitude is claimed;

(*c*) no such servitude shall give the person acquiring it a proprietary interest in the land on, over or through which it is exercised, and the proprietor of any such land shall remain subject to any encumbrance attaching to it (*ibid.* sec. 61).

See also Cape Irrigation Act (32 of 1906), secs. 88 and 89.

Servitus actus, the right of trek-path or cattle road; the right to drive beasts. In its full sense *actus* includes the right of walking, riding or being carried in a chair or litter, and, further, the right of driving a vehicle and cattle across the land of another. "There may be *actus* without the right of driving vehicles; if the road in respect to which the *actus* was granted is wide enough to admit of vehicles passing over, in such cases the right to drive vehicles was also presumed to be granted" (De Villiers, C.J., in *Breda's Executors and Another* v. *Mills*, 2 S.C. 195). The width of a cattle road will depend upon the number of cattle for which it is required, *e.g.* a track of one hundred and fifty yards in width is sufficient for four hundred head of cattle (*Laubscher* v. *Reeve and Others*, 1 Roscoe, 409, and 5 Searle, 195).

Servitus altius non tollendi, servitude of not building higher. This servitude prevents the owner of the servient tenement from raising his buildings higher, or from building beyond a certain height, for the sake of light to the dominant tenement or any other purpose (Voet's *Comm.* 8, 2, 8).

Servitus altius tollendi, servitude of building higher. Some writers on the civil law hold that this cannot properly be considered a servitude, and regard the term as inferring an extinction of the servitude *altius non tollendi* and the restoration to the owner of the servient tenement of his right to build as he pleases on his land. (See Sandars' *Institutes of Justinian*, 10th ed. p. 120.) This, however, is not the view of Voet, who regards the *servitus altius tollendi* as conferring a right on the dominant owner to build a wall on the servient tenement or to raise one already there higher, for the benefit of the light reflected therefrom or for the purposes of shelter, or to compel the servient owner to keep a wall on his ground standing or to raise it higher with the same objects in view (Voet's *Comm.* 8, 26).

Servitus aquae ducendae, servitude of water-leading. *See* AQUAEDUCTUS.

Servitus aquae hauriendae, servitude of drawing water. *See* AQUAEHAUSTUS.

Servitus cloacae, servitude of sewer or drain; the right to discharge filthy water through a sewer or drain running across another's land, as distinguished from the *servitus fluminis recipiendi*, which applies to clean and unpolluted water. If the sewer becomes stopped it must be repaired at the expense of the dominant owner, or, where it is a common sewer, at the expense of all those who make use of it (Voet's *Comm.* 8, 2, 14; Van Leeuwen's *Comm.* 2, 20, 11).

Servitus fluminis, the servitude of flowing rainwater (*flumen*). This servitude is of two kinds, being either the right to lead one's rainwater, collected in a spout, on to a neighbour's land (*servitus fluminis recipiendi*), or the right to claim that a neighbour's rainwater, so collected, shall be led on to one's own land (*servitus fluminis non recipiendi*) (Voet's *Comm.* 8, 2, 13; Grotius' *Introd.* 2, 34, 15 and 24; Van Leeuwen's *Comm.* 2, 20, 10). When the rainwater is not collected in a spout, but simply drips from the roof of the house on to the neighbour's ground, the servitude is called that of stillicide (*stillicidium*), in Dutch *dropvang*. Both these servitudes (*flumen* and *stillicidium*) apply only to clean water, unless it is otherwise provided in the deed of grant. In the case, therefore, of *flumen*, he who has the right to conduct his rainwater on to his neighbour's ground must provide by means of a grating that no filth will escape into the water-course (Grotius' *Introd.* 2, 34, 17; Schorer's *Note* 212; Van Leeuwen's *Comm.* 2, 20, 10). As no alteration can be made by the dominant owner whereby a servitude may be rendered more burdensome, he may not here either raise or lower the spout so as to be a greater burden to the servient tenement (Voet's *Comm. ibid.*; Grotius' *Introd.* 2, 34, 26).

Servitus itineris. A rural servitude giving the owner of the dominant tenement a right of going (*jus eundi*) on foot or on horseback, or of being carried in a chair or litter over the servient land (Voet's *Comm.* 8, 3, 1).

Servitus lapidis caedendi, servitude of cutting stone; a rural servitude entitling the dominant owner to cut as much stone from the servient tenement as may be required for the dominant tenement (Voet's *Comm.* 8, 3, 11).

Servitus luminis aperiendi, an urban servitude entitling the owner of the dominant tenement to have a window projecting over the servient tenement. This is also called window-right, and includes the right of free light or *servitus luminis non officiendi.*

Servitus luminis non aperiendi, a negative urban servitude which deprives the owner of the servient tenement of the right to have a window in his wall (Voet's *Comm.* 8, 2, 10).

Servitus luminis non officiendi or **ne luminibus officiatur,** servitude of not obstructing the light, or that lights shall not be obstructed; a negative urban servitude which requires the owner of the servient tenement to do nothing on his ground, whether by building or planting trees, whereby his neighbour's light or windows will be obstructed (Grotius' *Introd.* 2, 34, 20: Van Leeuwen's *Comm.* 2, 20, 13; Voet's *Comm.* 8, 2, 10 and 11; *St. Leger* v. *Town Council of Capetown,* 12 S.C. 249).

Servitus luminum seu luminis immittendi, the urban servitude which gives the dominant owner the right to have a window in his neighbour's wall (Voet's *Comm.* 8, 2, 9).

Servitus non prospiciendi, a negative urban servitude which prevents a person from looking on to his neighbour's property from his own land (Grotius' *Introd.* 2, 34, 27; Van Leeuwen's *Comm.* 2, 20, 17; Voet's *Comm.* 8, 2, 12).

Servitus oneris ferendi, servitude of bearing a weight or burden; an urban servitude in virtue of which the owner of the dominant tenement has the right to build or to rest the weight of his building upon the wall or property of the servient owner. This servitude differs from other servitudes (which consist *in patiendo*) in that the owner of the servient tenement is not only bound to suffer the burden, but in addition he is obliged to do something, viz., to maintain his wall or building so as to be fit to support his neighbour's building. For an explanation of this distinction see Van Leeuwen's *Comm.* Kotzé's trans. vol. 1, translator's note at pp. 307 *et seq.* The servient owner may, however, free himself from this obligation to keep in repair by giving up the supporting wall or building to the dominant owner. While the work of repair is being executed the dominant owner has to undertake the support of his own building (Voet's *Comm.* 8, 2, 1; Van Leeuwen's *Comm.* 2, 20, 2 *et seq.*).

Servitus operarum servorum et animalium, servitude of the labour of slaves and animals; a personal servitude of Roman law which gave the person who was entitled to it the right to the services of a slave or a beast of burden belonging to another. As in the case of *usus*, of which this servitude is an abnormal species, he who had the use of the services of the slave or animal could not transfer his right to another (*Institutes*, 2, 5, 3 and 4).

Servitus pecoris ad aquam appulsus, the servitude of driving cattle to water upon a neighbour's land (Voet's *Comm.* 8, 3, 11; Grotius' *Introd.* 2, 35, 19; *Laubscher* v. *Reeve and Others*, 1 Roscoe, 408; *Landman* v. *Daverin*, 2 E.D.C. 1).

Servitus pecoris pascendi, the servitude of pasturing or grazing cattle. *See* JUS PASCENDI PECORIS.

Servitus projiciendi, an urban servitude giving the dominant owner the right to project a portion of his building, such as a balcony or bow-window, over the servient tenement without actually resting on such tenement (Voet's *Comm.* 8, 2, 4; Mackeldey, sec. 317, n. 3).

Servitus prospectus or **ne prospectus officiatur,** servitude of prospect or view, or that the prospect or view shall not be obstructed. A negative urban servitude preventing a person from erecting buildings or planting trees on his ground whereby the view from his neighbour's property may be obstructed or interfered with (Grotius' *Introd.* 2, 34, 20; Van Leeuwen's *Comm.* 2, 20, 13; Voet's *Comm.* 8, 2, 12). As, however, all restrictions on the free use of one's own property are strictly interpreted, it has been held that the servient owner is not prevented from obstructing his neighbour's view by planting trees where the grant of the servitude is not in general terms, but simply provides that no buildings shall be erected whereby the view from the dominant tenement may be obstructed (*Myburgh* v. *Jamison*, 4 Searle, 8).

Servitus protegendi, a species of the *servitus projiciendi*, consisting in the right to project the eaves or roof of one's house over a neighbour's land (Voet's *Comm.* 8, 2, 4; Mackeldey, sec. 317, n. 3).

Servitus stillicidii, the servitude of dripping rainwater; a servitude respecting rainwater dripping from the eaves of the roof of a house on to a neighbour's ground, as distinguished from the servitude of *flumen*, in which the rainwater is collected from the roof in a spout, and so discharged on to the ground. Like *flumen*, this servitude is of two kinds, affirmative and negative, viz., the right to allow one's rainwater to drip from the roof of one's house on to a neighbour's ground, and the right to claim that a neighbour's rainwater shall be allowed to drip on to one's own land (Mackeldey, sec. 317, n. 4).

Servitus tigni immittendi, an urban servitude giving the dominant owner the right to insert a beam or beams into the wall of the servient owner for the purpose of supporting his own wall (Voet's *Comm.* 8, 2, 2; Grotius' *Introd.* 2, 34, 7–9; Schorer's *Note* 210).

Servitus viae, the chief rural servitude, which entitled the dominant owner to a right of way over the land of the servient owner, including the right to go on foot or on horseback over the land, to drive cattle or vehicles across it, and to drag stones, trees, &c., over it (Mackeldey, sec. 318 (*c*)).

Servituut (D.), a servitude. *See* SERVITUDE.

Session, the sitting of a legislature, court or other assembly for the transaction of its business.

"*Session* shall mean an ordinary or an extraordinary *session* of Parliament" (Act 12 of 1907 (T.), sec. 2).

Set-off, the extinguishment of debts which two persons mutually owe each other, by means of the claims which they mutually have against each other (Van der Linden's *Institutes,* Juta's trans. p. 168). "Compensation by our law is really equivalent to payment; it operates *ipso facto* as a discharge. So soon as there are two debts in existence between which there is mutuality, so that the one can be compensated against the other, then by operation of law the one debt extinguishes the other *pro tanto*" (*per* INNES, C.J., in *Symon* v. *Brecker*, [1904] T.S. at p. 747). "The French Code lays down broadly that *la compensation s'opère de plein droit,* even without the knowledge of the debtors, and that the two debts cancel each other rateably, from the moment that they co-exist—a view which was only very gradually approached by the Roman lawyers. The applicability of *set-off* has always been limited to debts of a readily calculable kind, and between the parties in the same rights. The doctrine was unknown to the English common law, upon which it was grafted for the first time by 2 Geo. II, c. 22" (Holland's *Jurisprudence*, 10th ed. p. 309).

Settlement. (1) The transference of property to a beneficiary or to trustees for the benefit of a beneficiary, usually upon specific conditions set out in a deed of settlement. *See* ANTENUPTIAL CONTRACT.

(2) The final adjustment of an action, dispute or controversy; the complete payment of a debt.

Several, separate and capable of being treated as such.

Sewage-works. The term *sewage-works* is defined in the Cape Public Health Amendment Act (23 of 1897), sec. 2, to mean and include "reservoirs, tanks, strainers, filter-beds, engines, pumps, and all machinery, buildings, things, lands, and cultivated lands, for dealing with and disposing of sewage or night-soil, except drains and sewers to which the words *drain* and *sewer* defined as aforesaid [in said Act] apply."

Sewer, a conduit or drain specially constructed for the purpose of carrying off surplus water or other liquids. See Act 32 of 1893 (C.C.), sec. 1. In the Cape Public Health Amendment Act (23 of

1897) the term *sewer* is defined to mean and include "*sewers*, drains, pipes, culverts, manholes, chambers, ventilating shafts, ejectors, sluices, and all things for and in connection with the conveyance of sewage or sewage effluent, except drains to which the word *drain* interpreted as aforesaid [in said Act] applies." For further statutory definition of the term *sewer*, see Act 25 of 1897 (C.C.), sec. 1.

Shall. As to whether this word is permissive or obligatory when used in statutes, see Maxwell's *Interpretation of Statutes*, 4th ed. pp. 360 *et seq.*; Craies' *Statute Law*, p. 252; Bishop on the *Written Laws*, sec. 112.

"The legislature has chosen to say that the petition *shall* be signed by the petitioner, and this is equivalent to providing that it *must* be so signed" (*per* KOTZÉ, J., in *Orpen* v. *Celliers*, 20 S.C. at p. 265).

"Shall and may." Where by a statute in England it was provided that a solicitor committing certain offences set out in a section of the statute "*shall and may* be struck off the roll," the court held that on such offences being proved the court had no discretion but to strike the solicitor off the roll (*Re Burton and Blinkhorn*, [1903] 2 K.B. 300; 72 L.J. K.B. 752; 89 L.T. 549; 19 T.L.R. 581).

"Shall be lawful." For interpretation of this expression in statutes, see Maxwell on *Interpretation of Statutes*, 4th ed. pp. 365 *et seq.*; Craies' *Statute Law*, p. 251; and Sutherland on *Statutory Construction*, secs. 460–62.

Share. "A *share* is the interest of the shareholder in the company measured by a sum of money for the purpose (*inter alia*) of dividend, but also qualified by the contract entered into by all the shareholders *inter se*" (*per* FARWELL, J., in *Borland's Trustee* v. *Steel Bros. & Co., Ltd.*, [1901] 1 Ch. 279; 70 L.J. Ch. 51; 17 T.L.R. 45).

In the Natal Share Pledge Act (33 of 1899) "the word *share* means any share or interest in the capital stock of any joint-stock company with limited liability, represented by a certificate signed and issued by the directors or other proper officers of such company, and whether the property of such company be movable or immovable, or both." In the same Act it is provided that the word *share* includes any form of stock issued by any such company.

Shareholder, one who is the registered holder of shares in a corporation, company or syndicate.

Sheriff, an officer appointed by the Governor of a colony to execute all the sentences, decrees, judgments, writs, summonses, rules, orders, commands and processes of any superior court, and to make a return thereof to the Registrar of the Court; he also receives and detains in prison all persons arrested by any order, writ or judgment of any superior court. In the Cape Colony the *Sheriff* is called the

High Sheriff; his office was created by Ordinance 37 of 1828; he has his office in Capetown, and formerly his appointment was made annually on the first Monday in January, but this is now altered, and his appointment is made in the same manner as that of other civil servants. The duties of *Sheriff* are very similar in all the South African colonies. The *Sheriff* appoints his own deputies, who are called deputy-sheriffs (see *Legal Handbook of British South Africa*, 1905 ed. pp. 222 *et seq.*). See Act 39 of 1896 (N.), sec. 65; Proclamation 17 of 1902 (T.); Ordinance 9 of 1902 (O.R.C.).

Ship, under the Merchant Shipping Act of 1894 (E.)—57 & 58 Vict. c. 60—sec. 742, the term *ship* includes "every description of vessel used in navigation not propelled by oars." This definition was taken over in the Cape Colony by the Local Merchant Seaman's Act, 1855 (Act 13 of 1855 (C.C.)), sec. 20. Under the Cape Customs Management Act (10 of 1872), sec. 2, the term *ship* signifies any *ship* or vessel, howsoever built or rigged. See also Act 47 of 1902 (C.C.), sec. 1; Act 37 of 1904 (C.C.), sec. 1; Act 26 of 1906 (N.), sec. 30; Ordinance 1 of 1906 (T.), sec. 30 of sch.

See "MANAGEMENT OF THE VESSEL"; SHIP.

Shop. The term *shop* in the Cape Medical and Pharmacy Act Amendment Act (7 of 1899) is, for the purposes of the Act, defined to mean and include "any place whereat drugs or chemicals other than those mentioned in the 54th section of the said Act are sold in the ordinary course of business, but shall not be taken to include any surgery, dispensary or other place whereat a medical practitioner compounds and dispenses medicines" under sec. 7 of the Act. In the Cape Shop Assistants Act (20 of 1899) the term *shop* is defined to mean "any building or portion of a building, or place in which goods are offered or exposed for sale by retail." See also Act 11 of 1905 (C.C.), sec. 1; Act 34 of 1905 (C.C.), sec. 1.

In the Natal Shop Hours Act (36 of 1905), sec. 4, *shop* includes "any building, room, market stall, tent, booth, or other place in or upon which goods are offered or exposed for sale to the public by wholesale or retail." As to whether a club is a *shop*, see *Ladysmith Corporation* v. *Cheeseman* (27 N.L.R. at p. 496).

In the Transvaal Shop Hours Act (32 of 1908), sec. 3, *shop* means "any building, structure, room, market stall, tent, booth, vehicle or any place whatever, if such building, structure, room, market stall, tent, booth, vehicle or other place be used for the sale therein, thereon, or therefrom of merchandise or goods or as a hairdressing saloon, but shall not include any premises licensed for the sale of intoxicating liquors under the provisions of the Liquor Licensing Ordinance, 1902, or any amendment thereof."

In the Orange River Colony, see Ordinance 1 of 1904, sec. 1; Ordinance 5 of 1906, sec. 1 (2).

Shop assistant. The term *shop assistant* is defined in the Cape Shop Assistants Act (20 of 1899) to mean "any person who works in a shop for hire or maintenance."

In the Natal Shop Hours Act (36 of 1905), sec. 4, *shop assistant* includes "salesmen and saleswomen, shop walkers, and others engaged in or about the selling of goods in a shop."

In the Transvaal Shop Hours Act (32 of 1908), sec. 3, it includes "a salesman and saleswoman, shopwalker and any other person engaged in any shop in or about the selling or supplying to customers of merchandise or goods or engaged in or about the preparation of the same for sale or supply in such shop."

Shopkeeper. The term *shopkeeper* is defined in the Cape Shop Assistants Act (20 of 1899) to mean "the person, company or association employing any person in any shop for hire or maintenance, and shall include any agent, manager, foreman or other person acting in the general management or control of such shop."

In Natal *shopkeeper* in the Shop Hours Act (Act 36 of 1905, sec. 4) means "the owner or the representative in Natal of the owner of the business carried on in any shop."

In the Transvaal Shop Hours Act (32 of 1908), sec. 3, the term *shopkeeper* "in relation to a shop shall mean its owner or the representative for the time being of such owner in the business carried on in the shop."

Si sine liberis decesserit, if he shall have died without children. Where a testator leaves property to a descendant who has no children, burdened with a *fideicommissum* in favour of a stranger or another descendant, the *fideicommissum* is subject to the implied condition if the fiduciary dies without children, and will fail if he leaves lawful issue surviving him (*Galliers and Others* v. *Rycroft,* 21 N.L.R. 148; 17 S.C. 569; 18 S.A.L.J. 177). Such a condition, however, is not implied in the case of an ordinary or direct substitution (*ibid.*).

Sic passim, so in various places.

Sic utere tuo ut alienum non laedas. Literally translated this maxim reads, So use your own property as not to injure another. But a person may by the use of his property cause loss to another without any action arising in favour of the latter As it is only where the legal rights of others are infringed by such use that an action lies, the maxim in order accurately to explain a principle of law should read, as suggested by Sir Frederick Pollock, *sic utere tuo ut aliena jura non infringas, i.e.* So use your own property as not to invade the rights of another. See *Le Roux* v. *Fick* (Buch. 1879, p. 33).

Sicut ante, as before.

Side-bar, a term applied to the attorneys of the superior courts of South Africa, as a body. Its origin in South Africa is obscure; it was probably created for convenient and euphonic reasons in contradistinction to "bar."

In Scotland *side-bar* is a term applied to the bar in the outer Parliament House in the Court of Session.

Side-bar rules, rules obtained without the aid of counsel. Such rules were generally obtained by means of a motion made by an attorney at the side-bar of the court, and were consequently known as side-bar rules.

"Signing their names," discussed in *Van Vuuren* v. *Van Vuuren* (2 Searle, at p. 120). *See* SIGN.

Silva caedua, wood fit for cutting, *i.e.* trees which after being cut renew their branches and roots so as to be fit for another cutting. A usufructuary may not only cut such trees provided he does so at the proper seasons, but he may also sell them as being properly the fruit of the soil (Voet's *Comm.* 7, 1, 22). In the case of *Houghton Estate* v. *McHattie and Barrat,* 1 Off. Rep. 92, it was held that a lessee was entitled to cut down gum trees planted by himself, as such trees belonged to the category of *silva caedua* (see judgment of KOTZÉ, C.J., at pp. 104 *et seq.*). This decision was followed in *Brice* v. *Zurcher* ([1908] T.S. 1082), where WESSELS, J., said: "I am not prepared to say that a gum tree, even though it belongs to the category of *silva caedua,* which has been manifestly planted near a house for ornamental purposes, as an ornamental tree, can be cut down. But if a lessee plants gums on the property leased, and those gums are not clearly for the æsthetic purpose of ornamenting the house or homestead, then I think that, in accordance with the decision in *Houghton Estate* v. *McHattie and Barrat* (1 Off. Rep. 92), the lessee is entitled to cut them down, just as in England a lessee can cut down pollards."

Simple contract, an English legal term signifying a contract that is not under seal.

Simul et semel, at one and the same time.

Sine animo furandi furtum non committitur, theft is not committed without the intention of stealing. *See* ANIMUS FURANDI.

Sine die, without a day. A matter is said to be postponed or adjourned *sine die* when it is postponed or adjourned without any day being appointed for its resumption.

Sign. The original meaning of the term *sign* is a "mark," from the Latin *signum.* "To *sign* one's name, as distinguished from writing one's name in full, is to make such a mark as will represent the name of the person signing the document. For that purpose it is no more necessary to write one's surname in full than it is to write one's Christian names in full" (*per* DE VILLIERS, C.J., in *Re Trollip,* 12 S.C. at p. 246).

See *Van Vuuren* v. *Van Vuuren* (2 Searle, at p. 122).

Signature, a person's name written on a paper, parchment or other material, by such person or his authorised deputy. *See* SIGN. The

Bills of Exchange Acts provide that "where, by this Act, any instrument or writing is required to be signed by any person, it is not necessary that he should sign it with his own hand, but it is sufficient if his *signature* is written thereon by some other person by or under his authority" (Act 19 of 1893 (C.C.), sec. 90; Law 8 of 1887 (N., sec. 90; Proclamation 11 of 1902 (T.), sec. 90; Ordinance 28 of 1902 (O.R.C.), sec. 90).

Single patient, an expression used in the Lunacy Acts. In the Cape Lunacy Act (1 of 1897), sec. 2, it is defined to mean "any person detained as a lunatic by order under this Act in any place other than an asylum or prison as defined in this section." See also Proclamation 36 of 1902 (T.), sec. 2; and Ordinance 13 of 1906 (O.R.C.), sec. 2.

Singular thing (*res singularis*), "contains no more or nought else than is indicated by itself, as this man, that field, that money" (Van Leeuwen's *Comm.* Kotzé's trans. vol. 1, p. 144).

Sinking fund, a fund formed by a Government, corporation or individual for the purpose of gradually redeeming the debt owing by such Government, corporation or individual.

Sisa, a native term used in the Natal Code of Native Law (19 of 1891, sec. 29 of sch.) to denote "a custom by which A deposits cattle or other live-stock with B; the property and increase remain in A, the use being enjoyed by B."

Sitting. As to the *sitting* of a superior court, see *Kirby* v. *Rex* ([1907] T.S. at p. 132).

Slaughter-house. The expression *slaughter-house* is defined in the Cape Public Health Amendment Act (23 of 1897), sec. 2, to mean and include "the buildings and places commonly called *slaughter-houses* or abattoirs, and also knacker's yards, and any building or place used for slaughtering or for dressing or preparing the carcases of cattle, horses or animals of any description."

See Public Health (Slaughter-houses) Act, 27 of 1906 (C.C.), sec. 1, where a definition of public *slaughter-house* is given.

Slip. "The broker, when requested to effect an insurance, prepares a brief memorandum of the leading particulars of the proposed risk, such as convey at a glance to those who are skilled in the business a sufficient notion of the intended policy to enable them to say whether, and at what premium, they will underwrite it. This memorandum, called the *slip*, is presented, if the insurance is effected at Lloyd's, successively to the underwriters there, who, if they think well of the risk and the premium at which it is offered, initial the *slip*, each for the sum he thinks proper to underwrite, and so on until the whole amount is subscribed" (Arnould's *Marine Insurance*, 7th ed. sec. 33).

Smalheeren (D.), lords subject to a superior.

Smart-money, excessive damages; money paid by a person to enable him to escape from an awkward or painful situation.

As to where the consideration for a promissory note was alleged to be *smart-money*, see *Van Dyk* v. *Udwin* (17 S.C. 56).

Smuggling, "importing or exporting prohibited goods, or without paying the duties on goods not prohibited; which practice is a fraud on the revenue, and is accordingly restrained by the statutes relating to the customs" (Stephen's *Comm.* 15th ed. vol. 4, p. 156).

Societas, the contract of partnership.

Societas leonina, a leonine partnership, that is, a partnership in which one of the partners is entirely excluded from all profit. *See* LEONINA SOCIETAS.

Society, a body or association of persons united together for some common object, such as literary, building, friendly, &c., *societies.* As to actions against unincorporated *societies* or clubs, see 23 S.A.L.J. 430. In Natal, under Law 35 of 1874, literary and other *societies* may acquire and hold immovable property, and may be registered in the Deeds Office.

See Law 4 of 1892 (O.R.C.), sec. 1 (*b*).

See BUILDING SOCIETY.

Socius criminis, a partner or accomplice in the commission of a crime. *See* PARTICEPS CRIMINIS.

Solatium. (1) Comfort. Thus by the strict Roman law women could not adopt children, but the emperor allowed them this privilege by way of comfort for the loss of their own children (*ad solatium liberorum amissorum* (*Inst.* 1, 11, 10).

(2) Payment or compensation made either voluntarily or upon judicial decree for loss sustained or injury suffered.

Sole heir "implies the exclusion of every one else" (*per* FINNEMORE, A.C.J., in *Spencer and Brandon* v. *Wilson*, 25 N.L.R. at p. 235). *See* HEIR.

Solicit, to incite another to commit a crime; to ask earnestly; "to *solicit*" is an offence under the immorality statutes (see *Guttenberg* v. *Rex*, [1905] T.S. at pp. 209 and 213).

Solicitor, an English term synonymous with "attorney" in South Africa (*see* ATTORNEY). Formerly in England *solicitors* were officers of, and practised in, the Court of Chancery, while attorneys were officers of, and practised in, the Common Law Courts, but by the

Judicature Act of 1873, sec. 87, the title of *solicitor* was given to all attorneys, *solicitors* and proctors. The title *solicitor* is frequently used in South Africa, but, strictly speaking, it has no legal recognition.

Solitary confinement, a form of punishment for criminals. This is now obsolete in England, as the Prison Act, 1865 (E.), prohibits prisoners from communicating with each other. It is, however, still operative in South Africa. The period of such confinement must be limited. It is regulated by statute and regulations.

Solutio indebiti, the payment of what is not due. *See* CONDICTIO INDEBITI.

Sommatie (D.), a writ of execution in Dutch practice. "The first step in every execution is the *sommatie*, which consists of a document to be delivered by the process-server or messenger to the execution debtor, by which he is called upon to satisfy the judgment within twenty-four hours, and to pay the costs, on pain of further execution" (Van der Linden's *Institutes*, Juta's trans. p. 331). *See* RENOVATIE.

Sovereign. (1) A ruler who exercises supreme power. *See* CROWN.

(2) A golden British coin representing in value twenty shillings.

Sparkling wine. "*Sparkling wine* means wine surcharged with carbonic acid gas, and to which cane sugar and pure wine spirit may or may not have been added, and includes champagne" (the Wine, Brandy, Whisky and Spirits Act, 42 of 1906 (C.C.), sec. 5).

Speaker, the officer who presides over a House of Parliament. "Each House of Parliament [in England] has its *Speaker*. The *Speaker* of the House of Lords—whose office it is to preside there, and to manage the formalities of business—is, by prescription, the Lord Chancellor, or Keeper of the Great Seal, or any other appointed by royal commission; and he need not necessarily be a peer. If none be so appointed, the House of Lords may, it is said, elect. The *Speaker* of the House of Commons is one of its members chosen by the House; but he must be approved by the Crown. And herein the usage of the two Houses differs, that the *Speaker* of the House of Commons cannot give his opinion or argue any question in the House except when the House has resolved itself into committee; but the *Speaker* of the House of Lords, if a Lord of Parliament, may do so" (Stephen's *Comm.* 15th ed. vol. 2, p. 483). The lower Houses of Parliament in the South African colonies are presided over by a *Speaker* and the upper by a *President*. See Act 13 of 1883 (C.C.), sec. 2 (2); Law 14 of 1893 (N.), secs. 28 and 29); Transvaal Con. Letters Patent, 1906, sec. 19; O.R.C. Con. Letters Patent, 1907, sec. 21. See also Act 3 of 1907 (T.), sec. 2. As to *Speaker* of the House of Assembly under Union, see the South Africa Act, 1909, sec. 46.

Special agent, a person appointed to do or perform certain particular business specified in the authority under which he acts. *See* SPECIAL POWER OF ATTORNEY.

Special justice of the peace, an official appointed by Government with limited jurisdiction to facilitate the trial of certain offences committed at places distant from the seat of a resident magistrate. See Act 10 of 1876 (C.C.); Act 40 of 1882 (C.C.); Act 13 of 1895 (C.C.); Ordinance 6 of 1902 (O.R.C.), sec. 16.

In the Transvaal provision is made by Ordinance 19 of 1904 for the appointment of resident justices of the peace to try the offences enumerated in the third schedule of the Ordinance; from a conviction by a resident justice of the peace an appeal lies to the resident magistrate of the district.

Special mortgage. (1) A mortgage bond passed before the Registrar of Deeds and duly registered in the Deeds Office, whereby the mortgagor specially hypothecates or mortgages his land, specifically described, in favour of the mortgagee as a security for a debt.

(2) A mortgage specially hypothecating certain movables. It must be registered as above, and delivery of the mortgaged things is necessary to its validity as against other creditors. But on this question of delivery see *Francis* v. *Savage & Hill* (1 S.A.R. 33).

Special power of attorney, a power of attorney authorising the person appointed to do or perform some special business on behalf of the grantor. A power of attorney in Natal authorising the collection of rents from natives on a specified farm, with authority to the grantees to sue for the recovery thereof, was held to be a *special power of attorney,* liable to one shilling stamp only, under sec. 26, schedule 3, Act 43 of 1898 (*In re Chadwick and Miller*, 29 N.L.R. 147).

Special referee, a person appointed to act as referee in some particular matter in dispute. *See* OFFICIAL REFEREE. See Act 29 of 1898 (C.C.), sec. 2; Act 24 of 1898 (N.), sec. 3.

Special resolution. In the Cape Colony under the Companies Act (25 of 1892) *special resolution* is defined as follows: "A resolution passed by a company under this Act shall be deemed to be special whenever a resolution has been passed by a majority of not less than three-fourths of such members of the company for the time being entitled, according to the regulations of the company, to vote, as may be present in person or by proxy (in cases where, by the regulations of the company, proxies are allowed), at any general meeting of which notice specifying the intention to propose such resolution has been duly given, and such resolution has been confirmed by a majority of such members for the time being entitled, according to the regulations of the company, to vote, as may be present, in person or by proxy, at a subsequent general meeting, of which notice has been duly given, and held at an interval of not less than fourteen days, nor more than two months, from the date of the meeting at which such resolution was first passed."

In the Transvaal a *special resolution* is described in sec. 67 of the Companies Act (31 of 1909). It provides for two meetings; at the first the resolution is passed in the manner required for the passing of an extraordinary resolution, and at the second meeting, to be held not earlier than fourteen days or more than one month after the first meeting, it is confirmed by the majority present or represented.

Specific performance. "The *specific performance* of a contract is its actual execution according to its stipulations and terms, and is contrasted with damages or compensation for the non-execution of the contract. Such actual execution is enforced under the equitable jurisdiction vested in the courts of this country by directing the party in default to do the very thing which he contracted to do, and, in the event of his disobedience, by treating such disobedience as a contempt of court and visiting it with all the consequences of such contempt, including imprisonment; and in some cases by doing in one way the thing which the defaulter was directed to do in another way, as, *e.g.* by vesting by an order of the court an estate which ought to have been vested by conveyance of the party. To say, as is above said, that the courts enforce actual execution according to the stipulations and terms of the contract is not quite exact; for the court rarely, if ever, interferes until the time for performance has passed and default been made; consequently the performance enforced by the court is almost always behind time as compared with due performance voluntarily yielded" (Fry on *Specific Performance*, 4th ed. p. 2). The doctrine of *specific performance* is fully recognised in the Roman-Dutch law, and prevails in South Africa (see Maasdorp's *Institutes*, vol. 3, p. 152, and Nathan's *Common Law*, vol. 2, p. 674).

Specificatio, one of the modes of artificial or industrial accession. It takes place when a person produces a new *species* by working up materials belonging to another or belonging partly to another and partly to himself in such a way as to give them a new form or character. Where the maker (*specificator*) has produced the new *species* partly out of his own materials and partly out of materials belonging to another, the article will belong to him whether it can be reduced to the original materials or not. If, however, the article has been made wholly out of the materials of another without his consent, the question of ownership will depend upon whether the article can be reduced to the original materials. If it can be so reduced, as where a vessel made of silver or gold can be again converted into rough silver or gold, the article will belong to the owner of the materials. If it cannot, as where beer is made from the corn and malt of another or wine from his grapes, the article will belong to the maker. According to Voet (*Comm.* 41, 1, 21) *bona fides* is not required of the maker in order that the new *species* may become his property, although *mala fides* on his part will render him criminally liable for theft by conversion. Grotius (*Introd.* 2, 8, 2) and Van Leeuwen (*Comm.* 2, 5, 6), however, maintain a contrary view, viz., that where the maker has acted *malâ fide*, the owner of the materials is to be preferred, the maker losing his labour and his own materials, if any; and Schorer (*Note* 87) quotes other writers in support of the same opinion.

Specification. (1) A *specification* of an invention in patent law is a description of the invention in respect of which the inventor seeks a patent. A *specification* may be either provisional or complete.

(2) A *specification* relating to a building contract is a description of the work and material provided for under the contract and the manner in which the work is to be performed.

(3) The making of a new *species* from materials belonging to another (*see* SPECIFICATIO).

Speelkinderen (D.) are bastard children born of unmarried persons; they are considered as having no father; natural born children. See Van Leeuwen's *Comm.* Kotzé's trans. vol. 1, pp. 47 and 338. *See* MATER NON HABET NOTHOS.

Spes, hope or expectation, *e.g.* the *spes* in favour of an insolvent with respect to any residue of his estate that may remain after his debts have been paid in full, or a *spes successionis* or expectation of succeeding to the estate of a deceased person. "All we have to decide is whether a mere expectation, or a *spes*, can be attached. In my opinion it cannot. Were it otherwise, we might find it difficult to know where to stop. A man's right to future inheritances might be attached. Let me suppose that to-morrow the applicant in this case obtained a large legacy sufficient to pay all his debts and leave a handsome surplus. He would get nothing of it; it would all go to the person who had bought his *spes*. If the law allows that, I do not know why any debtor's chance of an inheritance or of future gain, by industry or otherwise, should not be attached. If one *spes* can be attached, so can another. And important considerations of public policy would in such cases support what I think are the ordinary rules of law" (*per* INNES, C.J., in *Mears* v. *Pretoria Estate and Market Co.*, [1906] T.S. at p. 668). But the law recognises a *spei emptio*, as "so much for the chance of all the fish I catch to-day" (Sandars' note to Justinian's *Institutes*, 3, 23, pr.).

Spes matrimonii, the hope or expectation of marriage.

Spes successionis, the hope or expectation of succeeding to an inheritance. As contracts with respect to the succession to a person who is still alive are illegal, save where they form part of an antenuptial contract, a *spes successionis* cannot be the subject of a sale (Voet's *Comm.* 2, 14, 6); Grotius' *Introd.* 3, 1, 41; *Jones* v. *Goldschmidt*, 1 S.C. 116). But an inheritance coming from a person who is already dead may lawfully be sold (Schorer, *Note* 355).

Spillemaaghe (D.), a relation on the side of the mother; and *zwaardmaaghe* (D.), a relation on the side of the father, for it was the province of a man to handle a sword, and of a woman to handle the spindle.

Spirit vinegar. In the Cape Wine, Brandy, Whisky and Spirits Act (19 of 1908), sec. 16, "*spirit vinegar* or 'distilled vinegar' means the colourless product made by the acetous fermentation of dilute distilled alcohol, or by the distillation of one of the forms of vinegar hereinbefore defined." *See* VINEGAR.

Spirits. The term *spirits* is defined in the Cape Excise Spirits Act (18 of 1884) as follows: "*Spirits* means *spirits* of any description, and includes all liquors mixed with *spirits;* and all mixtures, compounds or preparations made with *spirits* and wood *spirits.*" The same definition is to be found in the Cape Additional Taxation Act (36 of 1904), sec. 2. See also Act 33 of 1901 (N.), sec. 3; Ordinance 29 of 1906 (O.R.C.), sec. 1.

Spirits of wine. This expression is defined in the Cape Excise Spirits Act (18 of 1884), sec. 2; and in the Cape Additional Taxation Act (36 of 1904), sec. 2, as follows: "*Spirits of wine* means spirits of the strength of not less than forty-three degrees above proof."

In Natal *spirits of wine* is defined in Act 33 of 1901, sec. 3, as "spirits of any strength exceeding fifty degrees over proof."

Spirituous liquor. In the Transvaal in Ordinance 32 of 1902, sec. 3, *spirituous liquor* means "intoxicating liquor manufactured by any process of distillation." See also Ordinance 8 of 1903 (O.R.C.), sec. 3.

Spoliation, writ of. The writ or mandament of spoliation "applies to cases in which a person has been deprived of the possession of property, whether movable or immovable, by force or violence, its object being to set aside the forcible dispossession with all its effects, and to replace everything in the state in which it was before the act of spoliation was committed" (Maasdorp's *Institutes*, vol. 2, p. 25). Restitution is granted where the maxim *spoliatus ante omnia restituendus est* applies (*White & Tucker* v. *Rudolph*, 1 Kotzé, 115; *Reynolds* v. *Orson*, 3 H.C.G. 145). *See* SPOLIATUS ANTE OMNIA, &c.

Spoliator, one who ousts another from possession by means of violence. *See* SPOLIATUS ANTE OMNIA, &c.; SPOLIATION, WRIT OF.

Spoliatus ante omnia restituendus est, a person despoiled must be restored to his possession first of all. This maxim refers to the protection which is accorded in law to mere possession. A person who has been forcibly deprived of the possession of property, movable or immovable, may upon an *ex parte* application obtain a rule *nisi* calling upon the respondent to show cause why he shall not be ordered to restore possession, the rule to act as an interdict preventing the respondent from parting with the possession until further order. If upon the return day the applicant proves his previous possession and his forcible dispossession by the respondent, the rule will be made absolute. The remedy is called in the Roman-Dutch law *mandament van spolie.* It is sufficient to entitle the applicant to the remedy that he should have been previously in possession, apart altogether from the grounds of his possession, whether just or unjust, provided that the possession was actual control coupled with the intention of the possessor to hold in his own right. Thus it will be no answer to an application for the remedy that the respondent is the owner of the property of which he forcibly took possession, for until the subject is restored to the applicant and the parties placed in the same position as they were previously to the act of spoliation, the question of their respective rights cannot be discussed and settled (*Loots* v. *Van Wyk*, 16 S.C. 419; *Crause* v. *Ryersbach*, 1 S.A.R. 50; *O'Connor & Co.* v. *Knight & Co.*, 16 C.T.R. 1066; *Wolff & Elias* v. *Collector of Customs*, [1906] T.H. 81). But where the applicant's possession has been unjust, he will not be entitled to the remedy as against the person from whom he took the unjust possession. Thus where he has obtained the property from the owner by theft or fraud, he cannot obtain an order of restitution against the owner merely because he was in physical possession at the time of the alleged spoliation (*Minitzer* v. *Kriel*, 19 C.T.R. 284).

Spolie (D.), spoliation. *See* SPOLIATION and SPOLIATUS ANTE OMNIA, &c. A possessory remedy borrowed from the common law, whereby the person who is forcibly dispossessed of a thing may obtain restitution. See Van der Linden's *Institutes*, 3, 1, 5, 4; Maasdorp's *Institutes*, vol. 2, p. 24.

Spondet peritiam artis et imperitia culpae adnumeratur, he warrants skill in his profession, and want of skill is regarded as a fault. If a person undertakes work requiring skill, and thereby professes to possess the skill which is usual in the business, he is bound to exercise such ordinary skill. If he has not the proper skill, or if having it he neglects to use it, then he will be liable for any damage arising from such inefficiency or negligence (*Gifford* v. *Table Bay Dock and Breakwater Management Commission*, Buch. 1874, at p. 116; Grotius' *Introd.* 3, 19, 11; Story on *Bailments*, sec. 431).

Sponsalia, espousal; betrothal. *See* BETROTHAL.

Sponte sua, of one's own free will; spontaneously.

Spoor. In the interpretation clause of the Native Territories Penal Code (Act 24 of 1886 (C.C.), sec. 5 (*l*)) "the word *spoor* denotes any mark or impression on, or disturbance of, the surface of any ground, or any mark or impression on, or disturbance of any grass, herbage or wood on such ground, or any matter or substance left or found upon such ground, grass, herbage or wood, indicating that any person or persons or any cattle have passed along in any particular direction." It may be added that in the same Act the word "cattle" is defined to comprise "horses, mules, asses, horned cattle, sheep, goats or ostriches." A similar definition of the word *spoor* is to be found in the Natal Cattle Stealing Act, 1898* (Act 1 of 1899).

Spoorweg (D.), railway.

Squatter is defined in the Cape Act 27 of 1889 (to amend the law for the prevention of vagrancy and squatting) as follows: "*Squatter* means any person who, not being a servant or apprentice of the owner of any farm, and not being himself the owner or lawful occupier of such farm, is notwithstanding permitted by such owner or lawful occupier to possess or occupy any hut, house or other building in or upon such farm." See also Act 23 of 1879 (C.C.); Act 20 of 1891 (C.C.); and Act 34 of 1895 (C.C.); and *Queen* v. *Jones* (9 S.C. 210).

As to *squatting* in Natal, see Ordinance 2 of 1855 (N.); Law 41 of 1884 (N.).

Staats President (D.), the State President. See Proclamation 15 of 1902 (T.), sec. 17.

Staats Procureur (D.), the principal legal officer of a state, and as such the head of the law department of the Government. The English equivalent is "Attorney-General." See Proclamation 15 of 1902 (T.), sec. 17.

Staats Secretaris (D.), the State Secretary. See Proclamation 15 of 1902 (T.), sec. 17.

Staatscourant (D.), an official gazette; the *Government Gazette* of the late South African Republic and Orange Free State respectively, wherein all government notices, proclamations, draft bills and the like were published.

Stad (D.), a town.

Stadhouder (D.), "the title of *stadhouder* has nothing to do with the word *stad*, meaning a town. It is derived from the word *steede*, and means the *steede* or *plaats houder*, *i.e.* the person who holds the place of another, a representative. . . . The Counts of Holland had from early days been accustomed during their absence to appoint *stedehouders* in the provinces to act as their representatives. The *stadhouder* had no legislative functions. He was an executive and administrative officer" (Wessels' *History*, pp. 89, 90).

---

* This Act is so described in Hitchins' *Statutes of Natal*, although it was promulgated on the 12th June, 1899.

Stadhouder en Leenmannen (D.), a feudal court of stadholder and vassals established in Holland in 1469 for the purpose of deciding all feudal cases and questions concerning fiefs (Van Leeuwen's *Comm.* Kotzé's trans. vol. 1, p. 20).

Stadsraad (D.), a town or municipal council. There was a *stadsraad* in Johannesburg prior to the Anglo-Boer war of 1899; it was established by Law 9 of 1899 (T.); it took over all the assets and liabilities of the former sanitary board (*gezondheids comite*). As to liquidation of debts of Johannesburg *stadsraad*, see Ordinance 27 of 1902 (T.); as to assets of *stadsraad* vested in the Johannesburg municipality, see Ordinance 62 of 1903 (T.).

Stamp duties, a popular form of imposing taxation, and of easily collecting revenue by means of stamps—either adhesive or embossed—upon documents, licenses, bills of exchange, and the like; it being usually provided by the statute imposing the stamp duty that the party who is under obligation to stamp the document will incur some penalty, or be at some disadvantage, if it is not duly stamped within a prescribed period.

Stand, a plot of ground. The term *stand* is in common use in the Transvaal on mining areas. For provisions in Transvaal Gold Law, 15 of 1898 (now repealed), see secs. 91 *et seq.*, and in new Gold Law (Act 35 of 1908) see secs. 77 *et seq.* The grant or lease of stands is subject to a monthly rental. See Act 25 of 1909 (T.), sec. 2; Ordinance 66 of 1903 (T.), sec. 2.

In the Orange River Colony, see Ordinance 3 of 1904 (O.R.C.), sec. 5; and Ordinance 4 of 1904 (O.R.C.), sec. 5.

Stand township is defined in the Transvaal Gold Law (15 of 1898, sec. 3) to mean "every area of land situated on a proclaimed diggings or on land proclaimed for the purpose of stands which has been either wholly or in part surveyed for stands by a Government land surveyor, and has been proclaimed as such or been approved by the Government." See *Bezuidenhout* v. *Transvaal Government* ([1904] T.S. at p. 667); Ordinance 66 of 1903 (T.), sec. 2; also First Schedule to Act 34 of 1908 (T.) for list of *stand townships* in the Transvaal.

Standard gold. *See* GOLD COINS.

Standholder, in the Transvaal Precious Stones Ordinance (66 of 1903), sec. 2, means "the registered holder of the title to a stand issued by the Crown."

Standplaats (D.), a term used in the Gold Law of the South African Republic signifying a stand; a piece of ground in respect of which stand license is paid to Government. *See* STAND.

Stante matrimonio, while the marriage exists; during the subsistence of the marriage. As a woman during marriage is under the guardianship of her husband, she cannot while the marriage subsists alienate her property without his consent, unless this power has been specially reserved to her by antenuptial contract, or bind herself by contract without his consent, save where she buys necessaries for the household, in which case she binds both herself and her husband, or where she carries on business as a public trader, all obligations undertaken by her in connection with such business being personally binding upon her. Neither can she as a rule appear in law either as a plaintiff or a defendant unless assisted by her husband.

Stare decisis, to stand or abide by cases already decided. "I think it is a sound rule to adhere to, that where once the court has laid down certain principles, if they are not found to be in direct opposition to the provisions of the law, for the court to abide by them" (*per* De Villiers, C.J., in *Queen* v. *Strydom,* 1 S.C. 60. See also *Jacobson* v. *Nitch,* 7 S.C. at p. 178). "Of course, in ordinary circumstances the court will abide by its decisions; *stare decisis* is a good rule to follow. But where a court is satisfied that its previous decision was wrong, and more particularly where the point was not argued, then I think it is not only competent for the court, but it is its duty in such a case not to abide by its previous decision, but to overrule it" (*per* Solomon, J., in *Rex* v. *Faithfull and Gray,* [1907] T.S. at p. 1081).

Stated account. *See* Account stated.

Status, state, condition or rank, defined by Savigny (*Private International Law,* sec. 362) as a person's "capacity to have rights and capacity to act," and by Story (*Conflict of Laws,* sec. 51) as "capacity, state and condition," such, *e.g.* as minority, emancipation, and power to administer one's own affairs. In Roman law "the technical term for the position of an individual regarded as a legal person was *status,* and the constitutive elements of his *status* were liberty, citizenship, and membership in a family" (Sandars' *Justinian,* 12th ed. p. xxxvi). "*Status* is the position which a *persona* occupies in the eye of the law" (*ibid.* p. 14). See *Mahludi* v. *Rex* (26 N.L.R. at p. 303). It is a general rule of private international law, subject to certain exceptions, that a person's *status* is determined by the law of his domicile (De Bruyn's *Opinions of Grotius,* pp. 72–76).

The maintenance of the *status* which is conferred by the contract of marriage on those who enter into it is considered so important by the law that the parties themselves cannot by agreement put an end to it (*per* De Villiers, C.J., in *King* v. *Gray,* 24 S.C. at p. 557).

Statute law is the written law; statutory enactments. See Dicey's *Law of the Constitution,* 6th ed. p. 27. *See* Law.

As to time when a statute becomes operative, *see* Time.

Stealing. *See* THEFT. "The fraudulent sale by a person of an article entrusted to him for safe-keeping amounts to an appropriation for his own use, and would be covered by the term *stealing* in its ordinary acceptation" (*per* DE VILLIERS, C.J., in *Queen* v. *Mattroos Jan*, 16 S.C. at p. 362).

Stedehouder (D.). *See* STADHOUDER.

Steede (D.). *See* STADHOUDER.

Stellionatus is defined by Voet as every deceit, dissimulation or imposture in fraud of another not coming under such specific classes of crime as obtaining money under false pretences, fraud, forgery and the other specific crimes included in the *crimen falsi*. Examples of this crime are: fraudulent alienation of things pledged, making away with or spoiling them, substituting other goods, fraudulently putting forward one creditor as having a preferent right over a thing pledged with the object of defrauding another creditor, pledging brass for gold, fraudulently giving a receipt as a creditor for money which has not been paid or demanding payment of money which has already been paid, &c. (Voet's *Comm.* 47, 20, 2; *Terrington* v. *Simpson*, 2 Menz. 115).

Stem (D.), a vote. *Stemballetje* is a ballot; *stembiljet*, a voting ticket; *stembus* is the ballot-box; *stemlijst* is the voters' list; and *stemrecht* is the right of voting.

Still, an apparatus used in the distillation of spirits, whereby the volatile matters are separated by means of heat from the substances in which they are contained, and are then recondensed into liquid form.

In the Cape Excise Spirits Act (18 of 1884), sec. 2, the word *still* is defined to include "any part of a *still*, and any distilling apparatus whatever for distilling or making spirits." A similar definition is given in the Additional Taxation Act (36 of 1904), sec. 2.

In Natal, in Act 33 of 1901, sec. 3, *still* means and includes "any *still* and apparatus for distilling or making spirits, or any part of such apparatus."

Still maker. The expression *still maker* is defined in the Cape Excise Spirits Act (18 of 1884), sec. 2, to mean "a person who makes or repairs any still or any distilling apparatus for distilling or making spirits, and includes the importer of any still or distilling apparatus." A similar definition is given in the Additional Taxation Act, 36 of 1904 (C.C.), sec. 2. *See* STILL.

Stille waarheden (D.), courts held once a year in various cities in the Netherlands by a judge appointed by the count. "Inasmuch as these courts were not open to the public, and as the accused were charged not openly by the complainant, but by an officer of the court, they were called *stille waarheden*" (Wessels' *History*, p. 156). These courts were hated by the citizens of the free towns, and they gradually disappeared during the fifteenth century (*ibid.*).

Stillicidium, stillicide; an urban servitude by which the owner of the servient tenement is bound to receive on to his property the rainwater which drips from the roof of the dominant owner's house. *See* SERVITUS STILLICIDII.

Stipulation. A condition imposed by one party upon the other in a contract; something agreed upon.

Stirps (pl. *stirpes*), the lineal descendants of a common ancestor. Under Roman-Dutch law children and their descendants succeed their parents, and this succession is described as being *per stirpes*. *See* PER STIRPES; SUCCESSION BY REPRESENTATION.

Stock-in-trade, the goods kept by a merchant or dealer for sale.

As to whether fixtures are included in the term *stock-in-trade*, see *Mahomed* v. *Sahib* (27 N.L.R. at p. 692), where, in the circumstances, it was held that they were not so included.

Stok (D.), fetters, imprisonment.

Stokdraager, Stokkeknecht (D.), a judicial officer or messenger.

Stokkeknecht (D.). *See* STOKDRAAGER.

Stooren (D.), to deny and traverse in court what the opposite party asserts and is prepared to confirm on oath (Meyer's *Woordenschat*).

Stop. "To *stop* anything is to arrest or impede its progress or to discontinue it. To *stop* an indictment is the same as to withdraw it" (*per* KOTZÉ, J.P., in *Kerr* v. *Rex*, [1907] E.D.C. at p. 339).

Stoppage in transitu. "Under English law *stoppage in transitu* is a right of the unpaid seller, who has delivered possession to a carrier or other bailee for conveyance to the purchaser, to resume possession of the goods, notwithstanding that the property may have passed to the buyer, and to retain them until payment or tender of the price. The effect of exercising the right is to revive the seller's lien. The right is exercised either by taking actual possession of the goods or giving notice to the carrier or other bailee in whose possession the goods are. In [Roman-] Dutch law *stoppage in transitu* is unknown. It has, however, been provided by legislation in Cape Colony that the principle of *stoppage in transitu* is to apply in that colony (General Law Amendment Act, 7 of 1879, sec. 1)" (Morice's *English and Roman-Dutch Law*, p. 137).

"**Stopping the prosecution,**" discussed, *Kerr* v. *Rex* ([1907] E.D.C. at pp. 338 *et seq.*).

Strafbare insolventie (D.), culpable insolvency. *See* CULPABLE INSOLVENCY; INSOLVENTIE.

Strandroof (D.), the crime of wrecking or plundering wrecks. See Van der Linden's *Institutes*, 4, 2, 8.

Stream. "*Stream* shall include all natural water-courses and artificial channels in which water flows, or has usually flowed" (the Cape Forest Act, 28 of 1888, sec. 2).

See the Irrigation Act, 32 of 1906 (C.C.), sec. 3.

Street, a roadway for public vehicular traffic with buildings, or plots of land intended for buildings, on either side, in a city, town or village.

"In the natural and popular sense of the word *street*, or the words 'new street,' I should certainly understand a roadway with buildings on each side (it is not necessary to say how far they must, or may be continuous or discontinuous); and by 'new street,' a place which before had not that character, but which, by the construction of buildings on each side, or possibly on one side, has acquired it" (*per* Lord SELBORNE in *Robinson* v. *Local Board of Barton-Eccles,* L.R. 8 App. Cas. at p. 801: 53 L.J. Ch. 231).

A *cul-de-sac* is as much a public highway or public *street* as any other *street* which is a thoroughfare (*Souch* v. *East London Railway Co.*, L.R. 16 Eq. 108; 42 L.J. Ch. 447).

As to the area of user of a *street* by a local authority, see *Finchley Electric Light Co., Ltd.*, v. *Finchley Urban District Council* ([1903] 1 Ch. 437: 72 L.J. Ch. 297; 88 L.T. 215).

The term *street* is defined in the Cape Public Health Amendment Act (23 of 1897), sec. 2, to include "any highway, public bridge, road, lane, footway, square, court, alley, passage, or public place, whether a thoroughfare or not." See also Act 11 of 1905 (C.C.), sec. 1; Act 25 of 1905 (C.C.), sec. 1. For a similar definition see Ordinance 31 of 1907 (O.R.C.), sec. 1.

For *new street* and *private street*, see Act 25 of 1897 (C.C.). sec. 1; for *old street, existing street* and *new street*, see Act 41 of 1899 (C.C.), sec. 1.

In Natal statute law see Law 23 of 1891, sec. 1; Act 31 of 1897, sec. 2.

Strike, in the Transvaal Industrial Disputes Prevention Act (20 of 1909), sec. 2, is defined as "the cessation of work by a body of employés acting in combination, or a concerted refusal, under a common understanding, of any number of employés, to continue to work for an employer in consequence of a dispute, when such cessation or refusal is for the purpose of compelling their employer, or of aiding other employés in compelling their employer, to accept specific terms of employment."

Stuprum, immorality; unchastity; antenuptial incontinence on the part of a wife. Where a woman prior to her marriage has had illicit intercourse with another man, as a result of which she has become pregnant, her husband, if he married her in ignorance of these facts, and after discovery has not condoned them, will be entitled to have the marriage set aside as null and void *ab initio* (Voet's *Comm.* 24, 2, 15; *Horak* v. *Horak,* 3 Searle, 389; *Seyelecho* v. *Seyelecho,* 14 C.L.J. 298; *Kotze* v. *Kotze,* 7 C.T.R. 314; *Shaw* v. *Shaw,* 26 N.L.R. 392; *Kilian* v. *Kilian,* [1908] E.D.C. 377; Van Leeuwen's *Comm.* Kotzé's trans. vol. 1, p. 122 and note (*h*)).

Sub voce, under such and such a word.

Subject. *See* BRITISH SUBJECT.

Sublease. An under-lease; a lease granted by a lessee to a sub-tenant.

"There is no doubt that a juridical difference exists between a *sublease* and a cession of a lease. In the former case the lessee still retains some portion of the rights and obligations of the lease, and only parts with a fragment of his rights, whilst in the latter he parts with all his rights under the lease" (*per* INNES, C.J., in *Rolfes Nebel & Co.* v. *Zweigenhaft,* [1903] T.S. at p. 190). A *sublease* does not create any contractual obligation between landlord and sub-lessee (*per* DE VILLIERS, C.J., in *Green* v. *Griffiths,* 4 S.C. 346). "The original lessor cannot claim rent from the sublessee, for unless there has been a complete assignment of the lease no privity of contract arises between them by virtue of the assignability of the lease" (*per* DE VILLIERS, C.J., in *Parkin* v. *Lippert,* 12 S.C. at p. 187). "The effect of a *sublease* is to create a new contract of letting and hiring between the lessee and sublessee, but not to transfer to the sublessee all the lessee's rights under the lease" (*per* DE VILLIERS, C.J., in *Nieuwoudt* v. *Slavin and Jowell,* 13 S.C. at p. 63).

Submission. In reference to arbitrations *submission* usually means a written agreement to submit differences between two or more parties to arbitration. In the Cape Arbitrations Act (29 of 1898), sec. 2, we find, "*Submission* means a written agreement to submit present or future differences to arbitration, whether an arbitrator is named therein or not." See also Act 24 of 1898 (N.), sec. 3; Ordinance 24 of 1904 (T.), sec. 2.

Subornation of perjury "is procuring a person to commit a perjury, which he actually commits in consequence of such procurement" (Stephen's *Digest of the Criminal Law,* 5th ed. p. 108). "*Subornation of perjury* is counselling any person to commit any perjury which is actually committed" (Native Territories Penal Code, Act 24 of 1886 (C.C.), sec. 106).

Subpœna, a summons issued by a court calling upon a person to attend before the court on a certain day, at a time specified, for the purpose of giving evidence in a certain cause, under a penalty in the event of failure to do so.

Subpœna duces tecum is a subpœna embodying a command to the witness to bring with him certain books or documents.

Subreptijf (D.). *See* OBREPTIJF.

Subscribe. (1) To contribute some money or thing towards a specified object or thing or for a particular purpose. "To *subscribe* means to pay over or deliver, with or without the intervention of an agent, to any person whatsoever, any sum of money or any article, matter or thing, movable or immovable, whether or not such article or thing be in itself of any pecuniary value, for and in consideration of and with a view to receiving from any person or persons whatsoever any right, or the recognition of any right, to participate in or any chance of securing, gaining or winning any prize in any lottery" (Cape Lotteries Prohibition Act, 9 of 1889, sec. 3). See also Law 7 of 1890 (T.), sec. 6; O.R.C. Law Book, chap. 143, sec. 2 (3).

(2) To sign, as, for instance, a testator subscribes to his testament.

Subscribed capital, that portion of the capital of a company which has been subscribed for by shareholders. See *Treasurer-General* v. *South African Association* (3 S.C. 306).

Subscription. *See* SUBSCRIBE. "*Subscription* means the money, article, matter or thing subscribed, including the proceeds of such article, matter or thing if sold or disposed of for money, and including any other article, matter or thing received therefor by way of exchange or otherwise" (Cape Lotteries Prohibition Act, 9 of 1889, sec. 3). See also Law 7 of 1890 (T.), sec. 6; O.R.C. Law Book, chap. 143, sec. 2 (4).

Substituted executor, an executor nominated and appointed (subject to proper official recognition) by an executor testamentary, by virtue of a special power of substitution contained in the will of a deceased person; the *substituted executor* acts in place of the executor testamentary during the lifetime of the latter. The power of substitution (and therefore the *substituted executor*) has been abolished in all the South African colonies except Natal (*In re Titterton,* 12 S.C. 1; Proclamation 28 of 1902 (T.), sec. 133: Ordinance 18 of 1905 (O.R.C.), sec. 113). As to Natal, see Act 19 of 1894, sec. 8.

Substituted service, "service on the defendant's agent, or by advertisement, or by sending the defendant notice of the writ in a registered letter, or by some mode of bringing the issue of the writ to the defendant's knowledge otherwise than by personal service" (Stephen's *Comm.* 15th ed. vol. 3, p. 530).

Substitution. (1) The institution of an heir in more than one degree; that is to say, the nomination of another heir in case the instituted heir should fail (Grotius' *Introd.* 2, 19, 1–9). "Grotius states that *substitution* may properly be made *ad infinitum*, and this is quite true by the common law; but by the Perpetual Edict, art. 16, *substitution* beyond the third person, including the first instituted heir, is prohibited" (Schorer's *Notes to Grotius*, n. 138). See also Van Leeuwen's *Comm.* Kotzé's trans. vol. 1, pp. 372 *et seq.*

(2) The appointment by an agent of another person to act in his stead as representing the principal, in virtue of a power to do so contained in his authority as agent. Such a *substitute* may not, however, appoint a further *substitute* without express authority. *See* DELEGATA POTESTAS NON POTEST DELEGARI.

Succession, a real right passed from a deceased person to a living person. Van der Linden in writing on the subject of "*Succession* in General" (*Institutes*, Juta's trans. 3rd ed. p. 52) says: "The second kind of real rights, or *jura in rem*, is the right of *succession*. A person who is entitled to an inheritance or a part thereof, as heir, or has acquired a title as legatee to any property, succeeds to all the rights of the deceased, so that the ownership acquired by the heirs or legatees is deemed a new species of ownership. This ownership, however, is not acquired *ipso jure*, but by taking possession." The mode of acquiring a right of *succession* is either by last will or *ab intestato*.

In the Cape Succession Duty Act (5 of 1864), sec. 1, a *succession* is defined as follows: "Every past or future disposition of property by reason whereof any person has or shall become entitled to any property, not being immovable property out of this colony or the income thereof, upon the death of any person dying after the taking effect of this Act, either immediately or after any interval, either certainly or contingently, and either directly or by way of substitutive limitation, and every devolution by law of any beneficial interest in property or the income thereof upon the death of any person dying after the time appointed for the taking effect of this Act, to any other person, in possession or expectancy, shall be deemed to have conferred or to confer on the person entitled, by reason of any such disposition or devolution, a *succession*."

Succession ab intestato, equivalent to "Intestate Succession" (*q.v.*). *See* AB INTESTATO.

Succession by representation, otherwise known as *per stirpes*, "is a legal fiction whereby a person remoter in degree of relationship steps into the place of a parent who was nearer in degree to the deceased, but has died before him, and takes that portion of the inheritance of such deceased person which the predeceased parent, if he had survived, would have been entitled to" (Maasdorp's *Institutes*, vol. 1, p. 110). *See* PER STIRPES.

Succession duty, a tax imposed in some of the South African colonies on the succession (*see* SUCCESSION) by a person to the estate, or some portion of the estate, of a deceased person.

Sue. "To *sue* is to bring an action, to demand something—either a declaration of rights, or an order that the opposing party shall do something or give something to the plaintiff" (*per* INNES, C.J., in *Gillingham* v. *Transvaalsche Koelkamers, Beperkt,* [1908] T.S. at p. 966).

Sufferance road, a form of rural servitude. "*Sufferance roads* (*bywegen*), otherwise called neighbourhood roads (*buurwegen*), are those which belong to some community, and are suitable for common use; and as they remain unenclosed for the convenience of such community, and accordingly suffer the passing to and fro of other people also, they are called *sufferance roads*" (Van Leeuwen's *Comm.* Kotzé's trans. vol. 1, p. 296).

"**Suffers.**" "A person *suffers* gaming to go on in his house who purposely abstains from ascertaining, or purposely goes out of reach of seeing or hearing it" (Maxwell's *Interpretation of Statutes,* 4th ed. p. 417).

"**Sufficient cause,**" fully discussed in *Silverthorne* v *Simon* ([1907] T.S. 123).

Sufficient evidence. *See* SATISFACTORY EVIDENCE.

Sufficient fence. In the Cape Stock and Produce Theft Repression Consolidation Act (35 of 1893), sec. 2, the expression *sufficient fence* when applied to wire fences is defined to mean "a fence of not fewer than four wires and not less than 3 ft. 6 ins. high; in other cases any fence, wall or hedge through which no stock could pass without breaking, or any natural boundary through or across which no sheep would ordinarily pass." For similar definition, see Ordinance 6 of 1904 (T.), sec. 2.

Sugar is defined in the Cape Excise Beer Duty Act (11 of 1884), sec. 2, as follows: "*Sugar* means any saccharine substance, extract or syrup, and includes any material capable of being used in brewing, except malt or corn." A further definition of the same word is given in the Cape Additional Taxation Act (36 of 1904), sec. 2, as follows: "*Sugar* includes any saccharine substance or syrup manufactured from any material from which *sugar* can be manufactured."

Sugar vinegar. In the Cape Wine, Brandy, Whisky and Spirits Act (19 of 1908), sec. 16, "*sugar vinegar* means the product made by the alcoholic and subsequent acetous fermentation, without distillation, of solutions of sugar or molasses with or without addition of an infusion of cereal grain." *See* VINEGAR.

Suggestio falsi, a representation of something false; one of the forms of fraud.

Sui generis, of its own kind or class; of a kind or class by itself.

Suicide, self-murder; the intentional killing of one's self. See Van Leeuwen's *Comm.* 4, 34, 11. Drunkenness is no excuse for the crime of attempting to commit *suicide* (*per* WESSELS, J., in *Fowlie* v. *Rex*, [1906] T.S. at p. 509).

Suit. "*Suit* seems to me to be synonymous, or nearly so, with action" (*per* INNES, C.J., in *Gillingham* v. *Transvaalsche Koelkamers, Beperkt*, [1908] T.S. at p. 966). *See* ACTION.

Summary conviction, in the Transvaal Criminal Procedure Code (1 of 1903), sec. 3, means "*summary conviction* before a court of resident magistrate or other inferior court exercising summary jurisdiction."

Summary jurisdiction, of a magistrate in the Transvaal under the Criminal Procedure Code, means "jurisdiction in all cases other than those where a preparatory examination is held" (*per* WESSELS, J., in *Rex* v. *Laa de Kuei and Another*, [1907] T.S. at p. 7).

Summary trial, in the Criminal Procedure Code of the Transvaal, means "any trial held before an inferior court in which no preliminary examination has been held" (*per* WESSELS, J., in *Rex* v. *Laa de Kuei and Another*, [1907] T.S. at p. 7).

Summons, a citation issued by a competent court commanding the person to whom it is directed (called the defendant) to appear before such court within a certain period or on a certain day to answer the claim of some other person (called the plaintiff).

Sunday. "Sundays are included in computation of time, except when the time is limited to twenty-four hours, in which case the following day is allowed" (Maxwell's *Interpretation of Statutes*, 4th ed. p. 522; see also *Rex* v. *Elvin*, [1904] T.S. 431).

See Ordinance 31 of 1905 (T.), sec. 3.

Superannuation. (1) "In the same way as prescription can be pleaded as a bar to certain actions, so can it be pleaded also as a bar to certain sentences of the court. But the difference between 'prescription to an action' and '*superannuation* of a sentence' is that the former, when once duly completed, is a perpetual bar to the action, whereas the latter may, at any time within the third of a century, be revived in the same or in a higher court. If not revived within that period the right to do so becomes prescribed for ever, and the judgment cannot be executed" (Van Zyl's *Judicial Practice*, 2nd ed. p. 308, *q.v.*). In the Transvaal it is provided by Act 26 of 1908, sec. 9, that there shall be no prescription in respect of a judgment of a court of law.

Rule 370 (C.C.) provides that no judgment shall become superannuated or require to be revived in the superior courts within a period of six years from the date thereof. The process of revival in the superior courts of Cape Colony is usually by means of summons (see *De Beer* v. *Rose*, 10 S.C. 48; 3 C.T.R. at p. 46; but see also *Re Petition of Cape of Good Hope Savings Bank* (1 C.T.R. 308), where revival was granted on motion).

The Transvaal Rule (Rule 63 of the Supreme Court) is much more explicit; it provides that "after the expiration of six years from the day whereon a judgment has been pronounced no writ of execution may be granted, unless the judgment be revived on a citation to the debtor issued for the purpose, but in such case no new proofs of the debt shall be required. Writs of execution of a judgment once issued remain in force, and may at any time be executed without being renewed until the judgment has been satisfied in full." The practice in the Transvaal in the superior courts is to apply for revival by motion; a summons is not necessary (*Mosenthal & Co.* v. *Hellman*, [1903] T.S. 556).

(2) In the magistrates' courts of the Cape Colony and Transvaal judgments require revival after twelve months from date of judgment, but in the Transvaal writs of execution once issued remain in force until such time as the judgment shall have been satisfied (sec. 14 of Proclamation 21 of 1902). The process in the magistrate's court for obtaining revival of judgment is by motion (*De Beer* v. *Rose*, 10 S.C. 48; 3 C.T.R. 45).

Superannuation fund, a fund established, usually by a Government or a corporation, for the purpose of making provision for the old age of its employés; the fund being usually created and kept on foot by means of annual subscriptions or contributions.

Superannuation pension, in Ordinance 30 of 1906 (T.), sec. 1, means "a pension payable to an officer retiring from the public service at the prescribed age applicable to such officer."

Superficies, otherwise called *jus superficiarium*, is the right in Roman law which one man has to the building on ground belonging to another, subject to the payment of a yearly rent: *i.e.* it is to things built on the ground what *emphyteusis* is to the ground itself. See Mackeldey, secs. 331 *et seq.*; Sandars' *Institutes of Justinian*, note to 2, 5, 6.

Superior courts are courts of record with extensive jurisdiction and presided over by judges. They are the Supreme Court, Eastern Districts' Court and High Court of Griqualand of Cape Colony; the Supreme Court of Natal; the Supreme Court and Witwatersrand

High Court of the Transvaal; the High Court of the Orange River Colony; and the High Court of Southern Rhodesia; together with circuit courts in all the colonies. By sec. 98 of the South Africa Act, 1909, the several Supreme Courts of Cape Colony, Natal and the Transvaal, and the High Court of the Orange River Colony are, on the establishment of the Union, to become provincial divisions of the Supreme Court of South Africa within their respective provinces, each to be presided over by a Judge-President; while the Eastern Districts' Court of Cape Colony, the High Court of Griqualand, the Witwatersrand High Court and the several circuit courts are to become local divisions of the Supreme Court of South Africa within the respective areas of their jurisdiction as existing at the establishment of the Union.

Support. (1) "The force of gravity causes the superincumbent land or building to press downward upon what is below it, whether artificial or natural; and it has also a tendency to thrust outwards, laterally, any loose or yielding substance, such as earth or clay, until it meets with adequate resistance. Using the language of the law of easements, in the case alike of vertical and of lateral *support*, both to land and to buildings, the dominant tenement imposes upon the servient a positive and a constant burden, the sustenance of which by the servient tenement is necessary for the safety and stability of the dominant. It is true that the benefit to the dominant tenement arises not from its own pressure upon the servient tenement, but from the power of the servient tenement to resist that pressure, and from its actual sustenance of the burden so imposed. But the burden and its sustenance are reciprocal, and inseparable from each other, and it can make no difference whether the dominant tenement is said to impose, or the servient to sustain, the weight. . . . Every owner has a right, *ex jure naturae*, that his own land shall not be disturbed by the removal of the *support* naturally rendered by the subjacent and adjacent soil" (Emden's *Law relating to Building*, 3rd ed. p. 259). It has been held in the Transvaal that owners of adjoining erven are mutually obliged to refrain from doing anything by which the necessary *support* for buildings on the neighbouring properties is removed (*Johannesburg Board of Executors and Trust Co., Ltd.*, v. *Victoria Buildings Co., Ltd.*, 1 Off. Rep. 43). As to lateral *support* in connection with adjoining diamond claims, see *London and South African Exploration Co.* v. *Rouliot* (8 S.C. 75).

(2) The maintenance due by parents to their children; by a husband to his wife; and by children to their indigent parents. *See* MAINTENANCE (1).

Supply. As to *supply* of liquor under liquor laws, see *Drew* v. *Rex* (24 N.L.R. 397); *Clegg* v. *Rex* (24 N.L.R. 402).

As to the *supply* of water by a water company in England, see *West Surrey Water Co.* v. *Guardians of Chertsey Union* ([1894] 3 Ch. 513); in the Transvaal, see *Witwatersrand Township, Estate and Finance Corporation, Ltd.*, v. *Rand Water Board* ([1907] T.S. 231).

Suppressio veri, a suppression of the truth; one of the forms of fraud.

Supreme chief, an expression employed in the Natal Code of Native Law (19 of 1891) to denote the officer for the time being administering the Government of the colony of Natal.

Supreme chief in council, an expression employed in the Natal Code of Native Law (19 of 1891) to denote the Governor and the Executive Council of the colony of Natal.

Supreme Court. (1) The *Supreme Court* of the Colony of the Cape of Good Hope was established by royal charter, granted by William IV in 1832, commonly called the Charter of Justice. The Charter provided that the *Supreme Court* should be a court of record, and should consist of one Chief Justice and two puisne judges. The number of puisne judges was increased to three in 1855; to four in 1864; to five in 1879; to six in 1880; and to eight in 1882, which is the present number (see Act 35 of 1896, sec. 3).

(2) The *Supreme Court* of Natal consists of one Chief Justice and three puisne judges (see Act 38 of 1904, sec. 2).

(3) The *Supreme Court* of the Transvaal was established under the name of the High Court of the Transvaal by Proclamation 14 of 1902. By sec. 1 of Ordinance 2 of 1902 the term Supreme Court was substituted for High Court, the court to consist of one Chief Justice and so many puisne judges as the Governor might from time to time appoint, not being less than three. The present number of puisne judges is six.

Under the South Africa Act, 1909, sec. 95, the *Supreme Court* of South Africa is to consist of a Chief Justice, the ordinary judges of appeal (being two in number) and the other judges of the Supreme Court of South Africa in the provinces (see secs. 95, 96 and 98 of Act).

Surete de corps. *See* BRIEVEN VAN SURETE DE CORPS.

Surety "is a person who for the greater security of debt binds himself by a promise for a principal debtor. All persons competent to make a promise may also become *sureties*" (Grotius' *Introd.* 3, 3, 12 and 13). "Very often other persons, called fidejussors or *sureties*, are bound for the promisor, being taken by promisees as additional security. Such *sureties* may accompany any obligation, whether real, verbal, literal or consensual; and it is immaterial even whether the principal obligation be civil or natural, so that a man may go *surety* for the obligation of a slave either to a stranger or to his master. A fidejussor is not only bound himself, but his obligation devolves also on his heir, and the contract of suretyship may be entered into before no less than after the creation of the principal obligation" (Justinian's *Institutes*, 3, 20, 1 to 3).

Suretyship "is the undertaking of an obligation, verbal or written, whereby one party pledges his credit for the fulfilment of an obligation by another, in such a manner, however, as not to release the person bound on the principal contract or obligation" (Nathan's *Common Law*, sec. 980). "*Suretyship* or guarantee, *intercessio*, in French *caution*, is a collateral engagement to answer for the debt, default or miscarriage of another. Although thus entirely subsidiary in its nature, it is sometimes legally binding when the obligation to which it is subsidiary is merely 'natural,' in other words, is incapable of being judicially enforced" (Holland's *Jurisprudence*, 10th ed. p. 299). *See* SURETY.

Surface rights, in the Transvaal Registration of Deeds and Titles Act (25 of 1909), sec. 2, means "all such rights as are described in Part II, Chapter IX, of the Precious and Base Metals Act, 1908, or any amendment thereof, whether the same depend upon a grant made under such Chapter or under Law No. 15 of 1898 or under a prior law, and shall include sites selected under section sixty-nine of the Precious Stones Ordinance, 1903, or any amendment of that section."

Surplus assets. The words *surplus assets* appearing in the articles of association of a company *primâ facie* mean what remains after all claims of creditors and the costs of winding up have been met (*Re Crichton's Oil Co.*, 9 Manson, 402; see also *Re New Transvaal Co., Ltd.*, 3 Manson, 264).

Surrejoinder, a pleading by plaintiff in reply to the defendant's rejoinder. As to necessity for obtaining the leave of the Court to file *surrejoinder*, see *Wilson* v. *Divisional Council of Komgha* ([1907] E.D.C. 277).

Surrender, to yield up or abandon some thing; to abandon one's estate as insolvent for the benefit of one's creditors.

Surrogated executor, an executor nominated and appointed (subject to proper official recognition) by an executor testamentary, by virtue of a special power of surrogation contained in the will of the deceased person; the *surrogated executor* acts in place of the executor testamentary after the death of the latter. The power of surrogation (and therefore the *surrogated executor*) has been abolished in all the South African colonies except Natal (*In re Titterton*, 12 S.C. 1; Proclamation 28 of 1902 (T.), sec. 133; Ordinance 18 of 1905 (O.R.C.), sec. 113). As to Natal, see Act 19 of 1894, sec. 8.

Survey. (1) The accurate representation of the position of defined areas of land on paper; the operation necessary for the purpose of showing the configuration of land on paper, and so bringing it into diagram.

See "BUYER TO PAY ALL EXPENSES IN CONNECTION WITH THE COMPLETING OF TRANSFER."

(2) The inspection and report by a duly appointed person of damaged goods or buildings for insurance purposes.

Suspensive condition occurs when the commencement of the operation of an act is made to depend upon its occurrence (Holland's *Jurisprudence*, 10th ed. p. 119). Thus in the case of sale it occurs when the parties to a sale "are considered as agreeing that the property in the goods which form the subject of the contract shall not pass to the buyer until and unless a certain condition—generally the payment of the purchase-price—is fulfilled" (Nathan's *Common Law*, sec. 861).

Suum cuique tribuere, to give to every man his due; one of the three leading maxims of the Roman law (*Institutes*, 1, 1, 3). *See* ALTERUM NON LAEDERE.

Sweet wine. "*Sweet wine* means wine containing sugar derived from the juice or must of the grapes, from which it is made, and not produced from imported raisins" (the Wine, Brandy, Whisky and Spirits Act, 42 of 1906 (C.C.), sec. 5).

Sweets. The word *sweets* is defined in the Cape Excise Beer Duty Act (11 of 1884), sec. 2, as follows: "*Sweets* means any home-made wine produced from the juice of fruit, and in which spirit is produced by fermentation."

Swing-gate, a gate placed by an owner or occupier of land across a road, path or track when he desires to fence in such land, so as to allow persons entitled to use such road, path or track as a free passage. The erection of a *swing-gate*, substantially constructed and properly hung, across a public road is compulsory in the Cape Colony, under Act 40 of 1889, sec. 153, where an owner or occupier desires to fence his land across which such a road runs. The *swing-gate* need not necessarily swing both ways; see *Queen* v. *Neethling* (11 S.C. 2). See also *Willemse and Others* v. *Lategan* (12 S.C. 335). As to *swing-gates* in Transvaal, see Law 9 of 1893, sec. 5.

Sworn appraisers. *See* APPRAISERS.

Symbolical delivery "is that which takes place by means of a symbol or external sign, which intervenes instead of actual transfer: by this means transfer of the keys of a granary, in front of the granary, constitutes a transfer of the goods or produce therein contained" (Nathan's *Common Law*, sec. 553). "No doubt a mere symbol is not sufficient to effect delivery; the goods must be subjected to the power of the person to whom delivery is intended to be made. That would be effectually done by giving him the key at the warehouse itself. A pledgee who is at the warehouse, and has the key in his hand, is in a position to exercise immediate power over the contents of the warehouse. The key is in one sense symbolical, but it is more than that, for it is the means by which the pledgee is enabled to have access to, and retain control of, the goods" (*per* DE VILLIERS, C.J., in *Heydenrych* v. *Saber and Others*, 10 C.T.R. 129).

Syndicate, an association of persons formed for the purpose of carrying out some joint venture. The liability of the members of a *syndicate* may be limited by registration as a joint-stock company with limited liability.

Synod, an assembly of ecclesiastical persons and delegates appointed to represent the Church in the various districts of a diocese or province, duly convened in accordance with the canons or laws of such Church, for the purpose of discussing and regulating the affairs thereof.

Taalman (D.), an interpreter; one who speaks for and on behalf of another; an attorney.

Tabellio, one who draws up written instruments; a notary.

Tacit hypothec. "In accordance with Dutch law, under certain circumstances a person's property is treated as being subject to a mortgage which enables it to be followed in the hands of third parties, and gives a preference as regards the proceeds of the sale of the property in the event of insolvency" (Morice's *English and Roman-Dutch Law*, p. 50).

In Law 13 of 1887 (N.) *tacit hypothec* is defined to mean "a legal as distinguished from a conventional claim or right of or to a hypothec, pledge, lien or the like, not being a claim for, of, or to retention, nor relating to maritime law in respect of any ship employed otherwise than chiefly for the purposes of any port of this [Natal] colony, or the precincts thereof, or for navigation in any river of this colony, nor being in respect of wages, material, necessaries or the like, connected with such first herein mentioned ship."

As to amendment of the law relating to *tacit hypothecations,* and the abolition of certain *tacit hypothecations,* in Cape Colony, see Act 5 of 1861. In Natal, see Law 20 of 1866, and Law 13 of 1887. In Transvaal, see Proclamation 28 of 1902, sec. 130 (see generally Van Zyl's *Judicial Practice,* chap. 33).

Tacit mortgage (also known as "legal mortgage" or "tacit hypothecation"), such mortgage as arises by operation of law. *See* TACIT HYPOTHEC.

Tacit obligation "arises by creation of law, in a manner analogous to contract; as where a person by some act binds himself to another just as if he had contracted with such other" (Van Leeuwen's *Comm.* Kotzé's trans. vol. 2, p. 6; see also Decker's *note, ibid.*). *See* QUASI EX CONTRACTU.

Tacit relocation, the implied renewal of a lease. "As has been justly remarked by Voet, a *tacit relocation* depends entirely upon the consent of the owner as inferred from his conduct, and therefore such consent cannot be extended beyond the necessary consequences to be deduced from his conduct" (*per* DE VILLIERS, C.J., in *Parkin* v. *Lippert*, 12 S.C. at p. 188; see also Voet, 19, 2, 9).

"**Taking.**" "The offence of *taking* game is complete when the game is snared, though neither killed nor removed" (Maxwell's *Interpretation of Statutes*, 4th ed. p. 419).

Tales, from *tales de circumstantibus* = such of the bystanders; an order made by a presiding judge at a criminal trial when there is a deficiency in the number of jurors present or able to serve, by which the sheriff or his deputy is commanded to summon and return so many qualified men, and liable to serve as jurors, from those persons present within the precincts of the court, or in the town or place where such trial is being held, as shall be necessary to make up the lawful number of jurors to serve on the jury. See Act 22 of 1891 (C.C.), sec. 43.

Talis qualis, such as it is.

Tausendschaft, a division of a tribe of the early Germans, consisting of 1000 men (Wessels' *History*, p. 19).

Taxation, the raising of revenue by competent authority by the imposition of taxes.

Taxing officer. "It was formerly the practice for the court, or one of the judges, to tax the costs in any case, but the court's functions in this respect are now performed by the *taxing officers* appointed by the respective high courts, or by the judge's registrar on circuit, all of whom have the power, without further or special reference from the court, to tax bills of costs of their respective courts of which due notice of taxation has been given" (Van Zyl's *Judicial Practice*, 2nd ed. p. 815). A *taxing officer* can only tax costs incurred in judicial proceedings (*Elliott* v. *Taylor*, 6 S.C. 18; *Burger* v. *Cape Central Railway Co.*, 6 S.C. 130).

As to *taxing officer* for taxing costs relating to Private Bills in Parliament, see Act 6 of 1887, sec. 1 (*b*); Act 6 of 1906 (T.), sec. 1: and Act 41 of 1908 (O.R.C.), sec. 1.

Taxpayer, a person who is liable for rates and taxes lawfully levied. See Act 36 of 1904 (C.C.), sec. 42.

Teelman (D.), an agriculturist, a husbandman.

Telegram. In Act 16 of 1901 (N.), sec. 3, *telegram* means "any message or other communication transmitted or intended for transmission by telegraph."

Temporalis actio, an action limited by some period of prescription; a term of the Roman law in contradistinction to perpetual actions (Mackeldey, sec. 213).

Temporary statutes "are those on the duration of which some limit is put by Parliament" (Craies' *Statute Law*, p. 63).

Tenancy, the occupation of lands or buildings by a tenant or lessee, with the consent of the owner or other person entitled to act as lessor. *See* EXPIRATION OF TENANCY.

Tenant, the occupier of lands or buildings under an agreement of hire made by him with the owner thereof. *See* LESSEE.

Tender. An absolute and unconditional offer made by a debtor to a creditor to pay a certain sum of money, which money the debtor must produce to the creditor at the time—unless actual production of money be waived by the creditor; a *tender* so made before action brought will protect the debtor against liability for costs if in such action no more than the amount tendered is awarded to the creditor by the court. A *tender* may in like manner be made of some thing. "Without adopting all the technicalities of the English rules regarding *tender* which prevailed before the passing of the Judicature Acts, I think we should adopt the principle that a *tender* to be valid must be unconditional. A conditional *tender* is really a contradiction in terms. A *tender*, in order to protect the defendant, must be a clear admission of liability and an offer to pay the amount thus unconditionally acknowledged to be due. For my own part, I think the rule might be more correctly expressed in this way, that no condition should be annexed to a *tender* to which the creditor has a right to object" (*per* INNES, C.J., in *African Agricultural and Finance Corporation* v. *Bouguenon*, [1904] T.S. at p. 537). *See* PAYMENT INTO COURT WITHOUT ADMITTING LIABILITY; Harris's *Law of Tender*.

Tents cannot "rightly be classed under the denomination of 'houses or other buildings,' because by no method of construction can a *tent* be regarded as a building" (*per* DE VILLIERS, C.J., in *Ex parte Greef and Others*, 24 S.C. at p. 524). *See* CANVAS HOUSES.

Tenure, the manner in or right by which immovable property is held by the person claiming ownership or possession thereof.

Terrier, a book or roll in which lands belonging to a person or corporation are fully described. The term *terrier* is uncommon in

South Africa; it is to be found in the canons of the diocese of Pretoria.

Testament, a will (*q.v.*).

Testamentary succession signifies the succession to the estate of a deceased person under, or by means of, a will or testament, and not *ab intestato*.

"Intestate is chronologically anterior to *testamentary succession*. Recent investigators, and especially Sir Henry Maine, have abundantly shown that there is in early times but little trace of individual ownership. Even grown-up children had only the most precarious interest during their lives in the property which they were allowed to handle, and on their deaths their father took possession of it as a matter of course. When the father himself died, his property passed of right to his surviving children, or if he left no children, then to certain precisely designated collateral members of his family, or in default, to that wider family which is known as a *gens* or clan. The idea that property really belongs to a family group, and that the right of an individual is merely to administer his share of it during his lifetime, may be said still to survive in those provisions against the total disinheriting of relations which modern systems have borrowed from Roman law, and less obviously in the rights given to next of kin under statutes of distribution" (Holland's *Jurisprudence*, 10th ed. p. 155). Some confirmation of Professor Holland's remarks in the foregoing quotation is to be found in the Natal Code of Native Law (Law 19 of 1891), where it is provided (sec. 97 of sch.) that *testamentary succession* is unknown; the heirship under native law being of two kinds (*a*) general to kraal property, and (*b*) special to house property. The heir is the eldest son of the chief house (*indhlunkulu*) or the person in law entitled to assume such position (secs. 99 and 100); the law then proceeds to enact the rules for the devolution of kraal property and for the succession to the status of a kraal head.

See WILLS.

Testate succession, otherwise called "testamentary succession," is a term employed to denote that the succession to the estate of the deceased person is under, or by means of, a will, and not *ab intestato*.

Testing right. The right or power of a court of justice to try or prove the validity of a bye-law or regulation by reference to the law conferring the authority to make such bye-law or regulation; or to try the validity of a given law by reference to the written constitution of the country, which is supreme. If, for instance, in any legal proceeding it becomes necessary to determine whether a corporation or other body has exceeded its powers, the court will examine the instrument creating and conferring such powers and test the given act or conduct of the corporation by reference to the instrument, just as the court will similarly examine whether an agent has exceeded his authority by referring to the terms of his mandate or power. In like manner the validity of a given law, or of any provision in the law, will be tested by the court by reference to the written constitution, and, if found to be in conflict therewith, will be declared to be null and void, for the constitution, as the supreme or permanent law of the land, must prevail. "In exercising this function the court does not by any means raise itself above the legislature, but remains within its province, by inquiring whether what has been submitted to it is in reality a law. The court does not take the initiative. It cannot act, and does not act, until a particular case is brought before it, and even then its action is confined to the particular case. If, with the view to a proper decision being arrived at, it becomes necessary, in the course of the judicial inquiry, to consider the validity of some law or other act of the legislature, it is the clear duty of the court to exercise that function. The court has to determine and decide upon both the facts and the law as applicable to those facts. This right and this duty belong exclusively to the court. The proposition in Story, 'No man can doubt or deny that the power to construe the constitution is a judicial power,' is irrefutable. Just as the court has, in the case of two conflicting statutes, to determine which is of force, so, in the event of a conflict between a statute and the constitution, the court must not only decide upon the matter, but hold that the fundamental law or constitution is supreme, and that any act or proceeding of the legislature contrary thereto is invalid, and cannot be enforced. The form or mode, therefore, prescribed by the constitution, in which the legislature is to declare its will and intention, and in which its commands must be expressed, in order to have the force of law and bind the people, must be strictly observed. There is nothing new or strange in this doctrine. It follows from the very nature of the case—from the existence of a popular Government under a *grondwet* like our own—and the general principles upon which it rests have been clearly set forth by the most approved jurists of Europe and America" (*per* KOTZÉ, C.J., in *Brown* v. *Leyds, N.O.*, 4 Off. Rep. 27).

So far as testing the validity of a given law by reference to the constitution is concerned, it is obvious that this can only arise in countries which possess a written constitution. It does not apply to a country like Great Britain. Thus Magna Charta and the Act of Union between England and Scotland can be altered or departed from by an Act of both Houses of Parliament assented to by the Crown. Where the written constitution is silent on the point the courts of justice will possess the *testing right*, for it is peculiarly the province of the judiciary of a country to decide upon all questions which arise out of the laws and the constitution (*Brown* v. *Leyds, N.O.*, *supra*, and authorities therein cited). It has been thought by some that the power possessed and exercised by the Supreme Court of the United States in declaring Acts of the legislature void, by reason of their being contrary to the constitution, is derived from an express provision in the constitution, and that without such provision the court would not possess this power. But this is an error. Art. 6 of the American constitution does indeed state, "This constitution and the laws made in pursuance thereof shall be the supreme law of the land;" but the most eminent American jurists have shown that the doctrine of the *testing right* is derived not from this article, but from sound and general principle. Thus Hamilton in the *Federalist*, No. 78, says, "There is no position which depends on clearer principles than that every act of a delegated authority, contrary to the tenor of the commission under which it is exercised, is void. No legislative act, therefore, contrary to the constitution, can be valid. To deny this would be to affirm that the deputy is greater than his principal; that the servant is above his master; that the representatives of the people are superior to the people themselves; that men acting by virtue of powers may do not only what their powers do not authorise, but what they forbid. The interpretation of the laws is the proper and peculiar province of the courts. A constitution is, in fact, and must be regarded by the judges as, a fundamental law. It therefore belongs to them to ascertain its meaning, as well as the meaning of any particular act proceeding from the legislative body. If there should happen to be an irreconcilable variance between the two, that which has the superior obligation and validity ought, of course, to be preferred; or, in other words, the constitution ought to be preferred to the statute, the intention of the people to the intention of their agents." In *Marbury* v. *Madison* (1 Cranch, 175 *et seq.*) MARSHALL, C.J., observed that an Act of the legislature repugnant to the constitution is void, and that this springs from the very nature of a written constitution. The particular phraseology of the constitution of the United States, art. 6, merely furnishes additional arguments in favour of the above general statement. Chancellor KENT in his *Comm.* (vol. 1, lect. 20) speaks of this judgment of MARSHALL, C.J., as possessing the precision and certainty of a mathematical demonstration, and, in discussing the doctrine that laws in conflict with the constitution are void, he treats the question as one of general principle. In like manner Story observes: "Hence we perceive that the above clause (art. 6) only declares a truth, *which flows immediately and necessarily from the institution of a national government.* It will be observed that the supremacy of the law is attached to those only which are made in pursuance of the constitution—a caution very proper in itself, *but in fact the limitation would have arisen by irresistible implication if it had not been expressed*" (Amer. Const. vol. 2, sec. 1837; *cf.* also sec. 1576).

In the Dominion of Canada the *testing right* and its application are clearly understood and universally adopted. "The federal union of Canada derives its existence from a constitution, known as the British North America Act, just as a municipal body or any incorporated company obtains its powers from the law bringing it into existence. Consequently every power—executive, legislative or judicial—exercised by the dominion or provincial governments, is subject to the constitution. This constitution comes under the conditions applied to all statutes or laws. Its meaning must be construed or explained by the judges who are its authorised interpreters. The judges of the courts of the provinces, from the lowest to the highest courts, can and do constantly decide on the constitutionality of statutes passed by the legislative authorities of the Dominion. They do so, in their capacity as judges and interpreters of the law, and not because they have any special commission to that effect, or are invested with any political duties or powers by the constitution" (Bourinot, *How Canada is governed*, ch. 6, p. 128). Similarly, the validity of the Acts of the newly created legislatures in the colonies of the Transvaal and the Orange River Colony will have to be controlled and tested by reference to the constitutions or instruments which have brought them into existence. By the South Africa Act, 1909, the provincial and local divisions of the Supreme Court of South Africa have jurisdiction to test the validity of any provincial ordinance (sec. 98 (3) (*b*)).

Theft. "*Theft* in Roman-Dutch law is the wrongful taking of any movable property without the consent of the owner, with the intention on the part of the taker to appropriate it. If the owner parts with the possession by reason of a false statement, he is not deemed to consent to its being either taken or appropriated by the taker. In this respect our law differs from the English law, which seems to hold that, although the owner has been deceived by a false statement, his parting with the goods shows his intention to part with his property in the goods. It is too late to inquire whether the distinction of the English law between larceny and obtaining goods by false pretences ought to be maintained in this [Cape] Colony. The latter offence has always been treated as *theft*, the charge in the indictment being sometimes *theft* only, and sometimes '*theft* by means of false pretences'" (*per* De Villiers, C.J., in *Queen* v. *Swart*, 12 S.C. at p. 422; see also sec. 7 of Act 3 of 1861 (C.C.)).

"By our law *theft* is defined as *contrectatio fraudulosa*, that is, a fraudulent handling of or dealing with the thing of another in such a way as to deprive an owner of his property. It is not necessary that the handling or dealing should be *lucri causa*. Both Matthaeus and Voet are very plain in their definitions of *theft*. While they include the words *lucri causa* as an element in their definition, Van Leeuwen does not. It is plain there may be *theft* without the essential of *lucri causa* being present. Such is the view of the law in South Africa, and there are English cases to the like effect" (*per* Kotzé, J.P., in *Maswana* v. *Rex*, [1909] E.D.C. at p. 355). See also *Reg.* v. *Fortuin* (1 A.C. 294–95) and Archbold's *Criminal Pleading*, 21st ed. pp. 379–80.

"*Theft* is a continuous crime so long as the property is in the physical possession of the thief" (*per* De Villiers, C.J., in *Queen* v. *Philander Jacobs*, Buch. 1876, at p. 175; see also *Regina* v. *Lepal*, 9 S.C. 263; *Queen* v. *Mattroos Jan*, 16 S.C. 361).

In the Cape Stock and Produce Theft Repression Consolidation Act (35 of 1893), sec. 2, the term *theft* is defined to "embrace, besides actual stealing: (1) receiving knowing to have been stolen; (2) attempting to steal; and (3) being or having been in unlawful possession, not being able to give a satisfactory account of such possession."

In the Cape Native Territories Penal Code (Act 24 of 1886), sec. 179, *theft* is defined as follows: "*Theft* or stealing is the act of fraudulently and without colour of right taking, or fraudulently and without colour of right converting to the use of any person anything or the use of anything capable of being stolen, with intent to deprive the owner thereof or to deprive any person having any special property or interest therein of such property or interest. It is immaterial whether the thing converted was taken by the thief for the purpose of the conversion, or whether it was at the time of the conversion in the lawful possession of the thief; provided that if any servant, contrary to the orders of his master, takes from his possession any food for the purpose of giving the same to any horse or other animal belonging to or in the possession of his master, the servant so offending shall not by reason thereof be deemed guilty of *theft*." See also secs. 180 to 186 of the same Code.

In the Transvaal Stock Theft Ordinance (6 of 1904), sec. 2, *theft* "embraces, besides actual stealing: (1) receiving stolen stock or produce knowing it to have been stolen; (2) attempting to steal stock or produce; (3) being or having been in unlawful possession of stock or produce, and not being able to give a satisfactory account of such possession; and (4) inciting to or counselling or procuring the *theft* of stock or produce."

As to whether it is defamatory to charge a person with *theft*, see *Steenberg* v. *Cooper* (21 S.C. at p. 494).

Theft by agent is defined in the Cape Native Territories Penal Code (Act 24 of 1886), sec. 183, as follows: "Every one commits theft who, having received any money, valuable security, or other thing whatsoever, on terms requiring him to account for or pay the same or the proceeds thereof to any other person, though not requiring him to deliver over in specie the identical money, valuable security, or other thing received, fraudulently converts to his own use or fraudulently omits to account for the same, or to account for or pay any part of the proceeds which he was required to account for or pay as aforesaid; provided that if it be part of the said terms that the money or other thing received, or the proceeds thereof, shall form an item in a debtor and creditor account between the person receiving the same and the person to whom he is to account for or pay the same, and that such last-mentioned person shall rely only on the personal liability of the other as his debtor in respect thereof, the proper entry of any part of such proceeds in such account shall be deemed a sufficient accounting for the part of the proceeds so entered."

"I have always regarded the 183rd section of the Native Territories Penal Code as fairly stating the law of the [Cape] Colony proper in regard to *thefts by agents*" (*per* DE VILLIERS, C.J., in *Queen* v. *Golding*, 13 S.C. at p. 215).

"Thereunto required." *See* "BEING THEREUNTO REQUIRED"; "REQUIRED."

Thesaurus inventus, treasure-trove (*q.v.*).

Thing. "A *thing* is the object of a right, *i.e.* is whatever is treated by the law as the object over which one person exercises a right, and with reference to which another person lies under a duty" (Holland's *Jurisprudence*, 10th ed. p. 95). It is thus defined by Grotius (*Introd.* 2, 1, 3 and 4): "By *things* we mean everything external to man, which can in any way be of use to man. They are distinguished either absolutely according to their natures or according to their relations to persons."

Through traffic, the traffic which passes from the one terminus of a railway system to the other, or from a station on one railway system to that of another; usually for long distances.

In the Transvaal Railways Regulation Act (13 of 1908), sec. 2, *through traffic* means "traffic which is carried over any railway, whether administered and controlled by the Administration or not." For similar definition see Act 29 of 1908 (O.R.C.), sec. 2.

Tichte (D.), crime, accusation. Hence *betichten* means to accuse, to inform against.

Ticket, a piece of cardboard or paper with something written or printed thereon, giving notice of some fact or price; or issued as an authority for doing some thing, with or without conditions. In the Cape Lotteries Prohibition Act (9 of 1889), sec. 3, the term is thus defined: "*Ticket* means any symbol, sign, token, warrant or list, or any other means or device of whatsoever nature or kind purporting or intended to confer upon or recognise in any person whatsoever any right or claim to compete for or receive any prize or to have any interest in any lottery."

In the Transvaal Railways Regulation Act (13 of 1908), sec. 2, *ticket* includes "a single ticket, a return ticket, a season ticket, a trip bearer ticket, and a mile coupon and any other written authority (not being a free pass) for a person to travel as a passenger on its railways." For the same definition see Act 29 of 1908 (O.R.C.), sec. 2.

Ticket-of-leave, a written permit or license granted sometimes in Great Britain to a convict, after a period of penal probation, authorising him to be at large before the expiration of his sentence upon certain conditions: it is revocable at any time for misconduct, or on breach of the conditions upon which it was issued, before the expiration of the original sentence. The term *ticket-of-leave* is to be found in the Cape statute book in Act 1 of 1860. In Natal licenses may be granted to certain convicts to be at large upon certain conditions (see Law 9 of 1876, sec. 2). For the Transvaal see Act 38 of 1909, sec. 10.

Ticket-of-leave man, a convict to whom a *ticket-of-leave* has been granted. *See* TICKET-OF-LEAVE.

Tick-infested. In the Cape Cattle Cleansing Act (31 of 1908), sec. 2, "*tick-infested* shall mean any animal visibly infested with ticks, and which it is shown has not been cleansed within the number of days required by this Act."

"**Tidal water**" is defined in the Cape Wrecks Removal Amendment Act (46 of 1885) to mean "any part of the sea and any part of a river within the ebb and flow of the tide at ordinary spring tides, and not being a harbour." See Cape Explosives Act (4 of 1887), sec. 36 (2).

Tigni immittendi. *See* SERVITUS TIGNI IMMITTENDI.

Tignum junctum, (lit.) beam joined. *See* ACTIO DE TIGNO JUNCTO.

Timber. "*Timber* shall include trees when they have fallen or have been felled, and all wood, whether sawn, split, hewn or otherwise fashioned" (the Cape Forest Act, 28 of 1888, sec. 2).

Time. As to computation of time according to Roman-Dutch law, see *Cock* v. *Cape of Good Hope Marine Assurance Co.* (3 Searle, at p. 117), and *Crego* v. *Bezuidenhout and Lark Syndicate* (4 Off. Rep. 95).

In construing a restriction in a liquor license in regard to *time*, the court held that the *time* referred to in the license was local *time*, and not railway or telegraph *time*, which differed from local *time* by about twenty minutes (see *Queen* v. *Rubenstein,* 7 S.C. 115). See also *Regina* v. *Pearson* (9 S.C. 261).

As to computation of *time* in connection with bills of exchange, see Act 19 of 1893 (C.C.), sec. 91; Law 8 of 1887 (N.), sec. 91; Proclamation 11 of 1902 (T.), sec. 91; Ordinance 28 of 1902 (O.R.C.), sec. 91.

The Transvaal Interpretation of Laws Proclamation, 15 of 1902, sec. 15, provides that "where any law, or any order, warrant, scheme, letters patent, rules, regulations or bye-laws, made, granted or issued under a power granted by any such law is expressed to come into operation on a particular day, the same shall be construed as coming into operation immediately on the expiration of the previous day." Sec. 16 of the same Proclamation provides for the exercise of certain statutory powers between the *time* of the passing of a law and the time of its coming into operation. *See* COMPUTATIO CIVILIS ET NATURALIS.

Time-bargain, a contract, usually made by a broker, for the sale of shares or stock at a certain price, but with the condition that delivery and payment shall be made on some specified future date.

"Time immemorial." On proof that a custom has existed for thirty years and upwards, and in the absence of any evidence as to when the custom originated, the Court will be justified in holding that it had existed immemorially (*Ludolph and Others* v. *Wegner and Others*, 6 S.C. at p. 199). In English law the time of legal memory originally ran from the reign of Richard I, but by the Prescription Act (2 & 3 William IV, cap. 71) this length of time has, as regards real rights and incorporeal hereditaments, been much shortened, and varies, with the nature of the right, from twenty and thirty years to forty and sixty years.

Time policy. "Most policies of insurance, other than marine, and many marine policies, are *time policies,* taken out for a fixed and certain period of time. Under such policies the assurance expires the latest moment of the last day therein named, unless a special time is named in the policy. And even if the days of grace are passed, many insurers will, if no loss has happened and no increase of risk has occurred, allow the policy to be rehabilitated on payment of the arrears with or without a fine for delay" (Porter's *Laws of Insurance,* 3rd ed. p. 107; see May on *Insurance,* 4th ed. sec. 34; Arnould's *Marine Insurance,* 7th ed. sec. 9). But *see* COMPUTATIO CIVILIS ET NATURALIS.

Timeously, in good time.

Timmeragie (D.), a term signifying a building. It "was used in the extended sense in which the term *tignum* had been used in the Roman law" (*per* DE VILLIERS, C.J., in *De Beers Consolidated Mines* v. *London and South African Exploration Co.*, 10 S.C. at p. 368). See also Placaat of 26th September, 1658, sec. 11 (2 *G.P.B.* at p. 2518).

Tithe. "The right to *tithes* is a right annually to enjoy a certain proportion of the fruits, whether this be a tenth, an eighth, eleventh, fifteenth, twentieth, thirtieth, or fortieth portion; and derives its name from the largest of these which is most in use" (Van Leeuwen's *Comm.* Kotzé's trans. vol. 1, p. 227); see also Decker's *note* on the subject of *Tithes, ibid.* p. 228).

Title-deed, the instrument or document which constitutes the evidence of ownership of land, such as the deed of grant or deed of transfer.

Titulo oneroso, by an onerous title; for valuable consideration; as distinguished from *titulo lucrativo,* by a lucrative or gratuitous title. *See* EX CAUSA LUCRATIVA.

"To be read as one with." *See* "AS ONE WITH."

To dip. The expression *to dip* is defined in the Cape Scab Act (20 of 1894), sec. 4, to mean "to plunge or immerse in a dipping tank containing such effective scab-destroying preparation as may from time to time be prescribed by regulation."

To note. In the Bills of Exchange Acts the expression *to note* means "to make a notarial minute in accustomed form of the circumstances of dishonour and at the time of dishonour of a bill or note" (see Act 19 of 1893 (C.C.), secs. 1 and 49; Law 8 of 1887 (N.), sec. 50; Proclamation 11 of 1902 (T.), sec. 1; Ordinance 28 of 1902 (O.R.C.), sec. 1).

"To repair," in the Transvaal Fencing Ordinance (7 of 1904), sec. 1, includes "to trim, cut and maintain a fence or ditch or part thereof."

Toezegging (D.), according to Van Leeuwen (*Comm.* Kotzé's trans. vol. 2, p. 4) *toezegging* is a promise upon request, as where a person for some reasonable cause, that is, in return for what has been given or done to him, promises and acknowledges himself bound to another in something upon the latter's request. It is opposed to *belofte* (a gratuitous promise). Grotius gives a somewhat wider meaning to the term. According to him *toezegging* includes any and every promise seriously made and accepted by the person to whom it is made (*Introd.* 3, 1, 10).

Toght (D.), usufruct.

Toghtenaar (D.), usufructuary.

Togt man (D.), an expresssion used in the Natal Act 28 of 1902, being an Act "to make better provision in regard to the *togt* labour system in boroughs." In that Act a *togt man* is defined as being "a day labourer or a person employed in service otherwise than under monthly or longer engagement, or a jobber, and applies only to natives."

Ton. "A ton is only a multiple of a hundredweight; it consists of 20 cwt., and as the hundredweight varies, so the *ton* must vary. In England the hundredweight is 112 lb., and therefore a *ton* consists of 2240 lb.; in this [Cape] Colony the hundredweight consists of 100 lb., and therefore the *ton* must consist of 2000 lb." (*per* DE VILLIERS, C.J., in *Cape Central Railway Co.* v. *The Government*, 4 S.C. at p. 362). In Dutch a *ton* or *tonne gelds* denotes one hundred thousand florins or guilders. The word also bears the same meaning as in English.

Tonnage, the weight of goods a ship or train carries; the estimated carrying capacity of a ship.

Tortious, having the character of a tort; wrongful. *See* TORT.

Totalisator or **Totalizator** (also rarely called *totaliser* or *totalizer*), a mechanical contrivance for enabling persons willing to bet on the event of any horse-race, to ascertain the state of the bets already made on the different horses about to run, and to calculate the chances of winning, according as they may bet on any particular horse (*Tollett* v. *Thomas*, L.R. 6 Q.B. 514). A ticket in the *totalisator* may be taken for a place or a win. The delivery of tickets at a fixed price continues until the race commences, after which no tickets for that race can be issued, and after the race has been decided the entire money taken by the *totalisator*, after deduction of a certain percentage (say 10 per cent.), is equally divided among the backers of the winning horse in the proportion to which he has been backed (*Brady* v. *S. A. Turf Club*, 16 C.T.R. at p. 609). In the Cape Colony a *totalisator* was in 1887 held to be an instrument of gaming within the meaning of Act 27 of 1882 (C.C.), sec. 7, sub-sec. 13* (*Day* v. *Cloete*, 5 S.C. 139); and again in 1906 it was held that a *totalisator*, as carried on by the defendant's club, besides being a means of betting, is a means of gaming, and is, therefore, illegal under Act 36 of 1902, part 2 (the Betting Houses, Gaming Houses and Brothels Suppression Act); this part of the Act deals with gaming, wagering and gaming houses (see *Brady* v. *S. A. Turf Club*, 16 C.T.R. 603; 23 S.C. 385).

Totidem verbis, in so many words.

Toties quoties, as often as.

Tout. (1) When applied to advocates, attorneys or professional men—to solicit employment in an unprofessional manner. As to touting by attorneys, see *Incorporated Law Society* v. *Dagg* ([1903] T.S. at p. 589); *Stanley* v. *Central News Agency* ([1909] T.S. 488).

(2) One who makes it his business to secure native labourers for a third party. The agents who secured native labour for the mines in the Transvaal were known as *touts*. The practice of touting was stopped in the Transvaal by Proclamation 37 of 1901, which enacted that it was unlawful for a person to act as a labour agent without a proper license. For definition of *tout* in Transvaal, *see* LABOUR AGENT.

In Natal (Act 36 of 1896, sec. 2, since repealed by Act 46 of 1901) *tout* or *labour tout* was defined to mean and include "any person who shall in his own name or otherwise, for the purpose of work or labour beyond the borders of this colony [Natal], procure or attempt to procure, ply, seek for, or engage natives in this colony, or shall supply or contract, or undertake to supply

---

* Sub-sec. 13 of sec. 7 of Act 27 of 1882 (C.C.) was repealed by sec. 37 of Act 36 of 1902 (C.C.), by which the following was substituted: "Betting in any street or open place, or playing therein at any game for a wager or stake, or playing at or with any table or instrument of gaming."

natives to be employed or engaged in work or labour of any kind beyond the borders of the colony; provided that hunters, travellers, and others taking native servants out of the colony under special permission of the Governor, under such rules and regulations as may be made for that purpose . . . shall not, nor shall the persons supplying such servants, be regarded by reason thereof as being touts within the intent and meaning of this Act." Act 46 of 1906, sec. 4, defines *tout* for the purpose of the Act to mean "any person who shall by himself or by any persons employed by him, and whether in his own name or otherwise, procure, or attempt to procure, seek for or engage natives in this [Natal] colony for service to be rendered to another person, or shall supply or contract to supply, natives to be employed in work of any kind."

Town lands. In the Transvaal Town Lands Disposal Ordinance (14 of 1904), sec. 2, *town lands* means "the lands referred to in the laws mentioned in the preceding section [being certain Volksraad Besluiten and Laws which are repealed partially or as a whole by the preceding section] as 'public *town lands* of towns,' or as 'common village or *town land*,' and vested by the said laws in the State."

Township is defined in Proclamation 35 of 1902 (T.), sec. 1, as meaning "a piece of land divided into stands or lots, described and shown on one general plan or diagram."

"*Township* shall mean any area of land which has been divided into lots exceeding fifteen in number, arranged so as to be intersected or connected by, or to abut on streets, thoroughfares, squares or open spaces within such area" (Townships Act, 33 of 1907 (T.), sec. 2).

"*Township* shall mean a *township* approved under the Townships Act, 1907, or any amendment thereof, or proclaimed under that Act or any amendment thereof, or otherwise established by lawful authority, or any area of land registered in the Deeds Office as a *township* at the commencement of this Act (Registration of Deeds and Titles Act, 25 of 1909 (T.), sec. 2)."

Trade, a handicraft; an occupation or a business carried on by a person for profit. In the Cape Additional Taxation Act (36 of 1904), sec. 42, the definition is extended and includes "every profession, vocation, trade, business, calling, employment and occupation, and includes the business of mining and quarrying."

"In my opinion, the mere making of bricks for the purpose of building a house on a man's property is not carrying on a *trade*. By the word *trade* I consider is meant any occupation from which a man derives profit or subsistence" (*per* DE VILLIERS, C.J., in *Green and Sea Point Municipality* v. *Egnal & Co.*, 19 S.C. at p. 381).

Trade description. "*Trade description* means any description, statement or other indication, direct or indirect, (*a*) as to the number, quantity, measure, gauge or weight of any goods; or (*b*) as to the place or country in which any goods were made or produced; or (*c*) as to the mode of manufacturing or producing any goods; or (*d*) as to the material of which any goods are composed; or (*e*) as to any goods being the subject of an existing patent, privilege or copyright; and the use of any figure, word or mark which, according to the custom of the trade, is commonly taken to be an indication of any of the above matters, shall be deemed to be a *trade description* within the meaning of this Act" (Act 12 of 1888 (C.C.), sec. 2). See *Colonial Government* v. *Spence & Drury* (11 S.C. 264; 4 C.T.R. 254).

For Natal definition of *trade description*, see Law 22 of 1888, sec. 3.

For that in the Transvaal, see Ordinance 47 of 1903, sec. 2 (1); and see *Collector of Customs* v. *Wolff & Elias* ([1906] T.H. at p. 91).

Trade-mark. "A *trade-mark* is a symbol which is applied or attached to goods offered for sale in the market, so as to distinguish them from similar goods, and to identify them with a particular trader or with his successors as the owners of a particular business, as being made, worked upon, imported, selected, certified or sold by him or them, or which has been properly registered under the Acts as the trade-mark of a particular trader" (Kerly on *Trade-Marks*, 2nd ed. p. 24).

For definition in Cape Colony, see Act 12 of 1888, sec. 2 (1), and Act 12 of 1895, sec. 2. In Natal, see Law 22 of 1888, sec. 3. In Transvaal, see Proclamation 23 of 1902, sec. 3; Ordinance 47 of 1903, sec. 2 (1). In the Orange River Colony, see Law 13 of 1893, sec. 1.

Trade-name, the name by which a certain business or article of commerce is known.

As to the right of exclusive use of a *trade-name*, see *Mitchell* v. *Hill* (25 N.L.R. 301); *James Humphris Co., Ltd.*, v. *Jacklin, Jenkinson & Co.* (27 N.L.R. 771).

Trade-union, in the Industrial Disputes Prevention Act, 20 of 1909 (T.), sec. 2, is defined as "any lawful organisation of employés formed for the purpose of regulating the relations between employers and employés."

Trader, a person who is engaged in commerce. See Law 16 of 1862 (N.), sec. 9.

Traditio, delivery. This term includes both the handing over of the possession of movables and the registration of the transfer of immovables. *See* DELIVERY.

Traditio brevi manu (sometimes written *traditio brevis manus*), short hand delivery; the name applied to a kind of constructive delivery in both the Roman and the Roman-Dutch law (Voet's *Comm.* 41, 1, 34). *See* BREVI MANU.

Traditio longa manu (sometimes written *traditio longae manus*), long hand delivery, as distinguished from *traditio brevi manu* or short hand delivery. This was a kind of constructive delivery in the Roman law, which took place by putting the thing to be delivered in sight so that the transferee could take it without hindrance (*Digest*, 46, 3, 79; Voet's *Comm.* 41, 1, 34).

Traditio symbolica, symbolical or constructive delivery. An example of this kind of delivery is where a person, having purchased a quantity of wheat stored in a warehouse, is given possession of the keys of the warehouse. By that symbol he is considered to have obtained delivery of the wheat (Voet's *Comm.* 41, 1, 34).

Tradition, transfer. *See* TRANSFER.

Traffic, the interchange or conveyance of passengers, goods, produce, live-stock, and other commerce upon or over a railway or road.

In the Transvaal Railways Regulation Act (13 of 1908), sec. 2, *traffic* is defined to include "not only passengers and their luggage and goods conveyed by the Administration, but also rolling stock." For similar definition see Act 29 of 1908 (O.R.C.), sec. 2.

Train. In the Transvaal Railways Regulation Act (13 of 1908), sec. 2, *train* is defined to mean "a locomotive engine or motor by itself, or any rolling stock that is drawn or propelled along a railway or is in course of being drawn or propelled along a railway by a locomotive engine or motor." For a similar definition see Act 29 of 1908 (O.R.C.), sec. 2.

Trajecticia pecunia, the term applied in Roman law to money lent on bottomry. *See* BOTTOMRY.

Transactie (D.), compromise; an agreement between litigants for the settlement of a matter in dispute (Grotius' *Introd.* 3, 4).

Transactio, transaction; compromise. *See* TRANSACTIE.

Transaction, (1) a matter of business that is completed between the parties or is in course of completion.

"The persons who enter into a *transaction* do so voluntarily" (*per* INNES, C.J., in *Colonial Treasurer* v. *Rand Water Board,* [1907] T.S. at p. 482). "A sale, strictly speaking, is a voluntary *transaction*, a lease is a voluntary *transaction*, and I should say an alienation is a *transaction* of a voluntary character" (*per* BRISTOWE, J., *ibid.* at p. 485).

(2) Compromise. *See* TRANSACTIE.

Transfer, the alienation, conveyance or cession of the ownership of some corporeal thing from one person to another, accompanied by delivery or something equivalent to delivery.

Transfer duty. A tax or duty payable to the Government on the alienation of land or other real rights, such as leases *in longum tempus*, mining rights, &c. The tax originated in the feudal times: "By the feudal law the vassal could not alienate without the consent of his superior, who generally extorted a fine or composition for granting it. This fine, which was at first arbitrary, came in many countries to be regulated at a certain portion of the price of land. In some countries, where the greater part of the other feudal customs have gone into disuse, this tax upon the alienation of land still continues to make a very considerable branch of the revenue of the sovereign" (Adam Smith's *Wealth of Nations*, bk. 5, c. 2). In Holland the duty amounted to a fortieth part of the price (Grotius' *Introd.* 2, 5, 13; Van der Keessel *Thes.* 202). It was known in Holland as *Heerenrecht*. Transfer duty is payable in all British South African colonies under special statutes; in the Cape Colony it is 4 per cent. on the purchase-price or value of the property alienated (Act 5 of 1884; Act 12 of 1908): in the Transvaal it is $1\frac{1}{4}$ per cent. (Proclamation 8 of 1902; and Ordinance 14 of 1905); in Natal it is 3 per cent. (Act 23 of 1907); in the Orange River Colony, except in the case of mining leases, it is 4 per cent. (Ordinance 12 of 1906); and in Rhodesia it is 4 per cent.

Transfer of land, the conveyance of land from the transferor to the transferee by means of a deed of transfer duly registered in the office of the Registrar of Deeds. *See* LAND REGISTER.

"The registration is a judicial act by virtue of which the full ownership passes from the transferor to the transferee. No servitude, encumbrance or other restriction upon the full ownership can be imposed without registration thereof in the Deeds Office and indorsement upon the registered deed. So long as a clean transfer stands registered the transferee enjoys the full rights of ownership, subject only to such exceptional rights as might be acquired by a lessee on a short lease, or by prescription, and to such tacit hypothecations as are recognised by law. But no prior agreement between the transferor and transferee can be set up to control the effect of the transfer, for the deed, when completed by the judicial act of registration, is regarded as embodying the final agreement between the parties. If the transfer has been induced by the fraud of one of the parties the court may, by way of *restitutio in integrum*, set it aside altogether. So the court may under certain circumstances set it aside, or, if need be, vary it on the ground of *justus error*. If the transferor or his agent has made a mistake by omitting to insert the terms of the original agreement, the transferee, if he has not accepted the deed under circumstances showing consent to a departure from such agreement, is entitled to claim a rectification of the deed" (*per* DE VILLIERS, C.J., in *Clayton, N.O.*, v. *Metropolitan and Suburban Railway Co. and Walker*, 10 S.C. at p. 302).

Transferee, the person to whom transfer, conveyance or cession of the ownership of some corporeal thing is given by a transferor or person transferring.

Transferor, the person who gives or grants transfer, conveyance or cession of the ownership of some corporeal thing.

Tranship (also sometimes written trans-ship) the transfer of goods from one vessel, train or truck to another.

Transire, means in England a permit from the customs house to let goods pass. In Natal in Act 13 of 1899 (Law relating to Customs and Shipping), sec. 4, *transire* is defined to mean "the account of coasting cargo and coasting ship's clearance."

Translative fact, a fact through which a right passes from one person to another. "*Translative facts* may be regarded from several points of view, and may be classified with reference to their voluntary or involuntary character, to the persons between whom the right passes, and to the extent of the right passed" (Holland's *Jurisprudence,* 10th ed. p. 153).

Transportuitmaker (D.), a conveyancer. In the late Republics in South Africa a conveyancer was called a *transport en verbanduitmaker.*

Traveller, one who makes or is making a journey from one place to another. As to interpretation of the term *traveller,* in a law under which a person is punishable who on Sundays sells or exposes for sale goods, merchandise, &c., excepting the supplying on Sunday of necessary food and drink to *travellers* and inmates by licensed hotel or boarding-house keepers, see *Levy* v. *Rex,* [1903] T.S. 603, where the court held that the widest interpretation must be given to the term *traveller,* there being nothing in the Law to define the word.

Travelling. In the Orange River Colony Scab Ordinance (14 of 1903), sec. 1, *travelling,* "where used in respect of animals, means driven or having within one month previous been driven for removal from one place to another upon or along any road or upon, over or across any land not being the property or in the occupation of the owner of such animals or of which the said owner does not *bonâ fide* hold the grazing rights."

"**Travelling trader,**" discussed in *Solomon* v. *Rex* ([1905] T.S. 216).

Traverse, to deny; as to deny an allegation in a pleading.

Treason. "Every one commits high treason who forms and displays by any overt act, or by publishing any printing or writing, an intention to kill or destroy the Queen, or to do her any bodily harm tending to death or destruction, maim or wounding, imprisonment or restraint" (Stephen's *Digest of the Criminal Law,* 5th ed. p. 42). "In every case in which any person shall be prosecuted within this colony [Cape Colony] for the crime of *treason* or misprision of treason, no witness shall be competent nor any evidence admissible or sufficient to convict the person so prosecuted, who would not be competent or which would not be admissible or sufficient to convict such person if prosecuted for any such crime in any of his Majesty's Courts of Record at Westminster; and that in every such case every witness shall be competent, and any evidence shall be admissible and sufficient to convict any person so prosecuted as aforesaid, who would be competent or which would be admissible and sufficient to convict if such person were prosecuted as aforesaid in any of his Majesty's Courts of Record at Westminster" (sec. 49 of Ordinance 72 of 1830 (C.C.)). As to the effect of this enactment, see *Queen* v. *Botha* (1 Searle, 149). See also "Notes on the Law of Treason, 18 S.A.L.J. 142, where the writer (F. G. Gardiner) shows that the difference between English and Roman-Dutch law of *treason* is not great.

Treasure-trove (*thesaurus inventus*), "a deposit of money, bullion, precious stones, &c., hidden in the earth or elsewhere, at a period beyond the memory of man, and the ownership of which has therefore become lost in obscurity, and the treasure therefore becomes *res nullius* once more" (Maasdorp's *Institutes*, vol. 2, p. 40). If the treasure is found on one's own property it belongs to the finder; if found on the property of another person, one-half belongs to the finder and the other half to the owner (Van der Linden's *Institutes*, Juta's trans. p. 47). Under English law *treasure-trove* is any money, coin, gold, plate or bullion—the owner of which is unknown—found hidden in the earth or other private place; such *treasure-trove* belongs to the Crown by virtue of the prerogative, but the claim of the Crown depends upon the hiding of the treasure (the owner being unknown) and not upon the abandonment (see *Attorney-General* v. *Trustees of the British Museum*, 19 T.L.R. 555).

Treating, the receiving or contracting for, by any voter either directly or indirectly during any election, any money, gift, loan or valuable consideration, office, place or employment, for himself or for any other person for voting or agreeing to vote, or for refraining or agreeing to refrain from voting at any election; or the receiving by any person, either directly or indirectly, of any money or valuable consideration on account of any person having voted or refrained from voting, or having induced any other person to vote or to refrain from voting at any election. For definition of *treating* at parliamentary elections in Cape Colony see sec. 3 of Act 21 of 1859. For *treating* in Natal, see Law 13 of 1893, sec. 20; in Transvaal, see Ordinance 38 of 1903, sec. 70.

Trebellian portion, introduced into Roman law by the *Senatus consultum Trebellianum*, provided that the direct heir who voluntarily accepted the inheritance was entitled to deduct a fourth share, in which case he became liable for his proportion of the debts, but not for the legacies, and if he had paid more than his share he could demand it back from the fideicommissary heir (Grotius' *Introd.* 2, 20, 6).

The Trebellian portion was abolished in the Cape Colony by sec. 1 of Act 26 of 1873, which is also operative in Rhodesia; it was abolished in the Transvaal by sec. 126 of Proclamation 28 of 1902; in the Orange River Colony by chap. 92 of Law Book, sec. 2, and Ordinance 18 of 1905; and in Natal by Law 7 of 1885, sec. 2.

Tree. "*Tree* shall include not only timber trees, but trees, shrubs and bushes of all kinds, seedlings, saplings and re-shoots of all ages" (Act 28 of 1888 (C.C.), sec. 2).

Trekker. (1) A colloquial Dutch expression signifying a person moving from one place to another with his cattle and goods. It occurs in Law 1 of 1893 (T.), secs. 7 *et seq.* See Act 43 of 1908 (C.C.), sec. 14.

(2) (D.), the drawer of a promissory note or bill of exchange.

Trekpad (D.), a rough track or path; a road which is not a public or proclaimed transport road. The term occurs in Law 1 of 1893 (T.), secs. 7 *et seq.* See Act 43 of 1908 (C.C.). (Cf. *per curiam* in *Niekerk* v. *Wakefield*, 13 C.T.R. 490.)

Trekpath. *See* TREKPAD.

Trespass. "A person commits a *trespass* by entering without lawful authority on land or premises in the possession of another" (Stephen's *Comm.* 15th ed. vol. 3, p. 401; see also Maasdorp's *Institutes*, vol. 2, p. 89).

Trial. (1) In civil proceedings, the judicial investigation of the claim and defence of litigants as disclosed in the declaration and other pleadings in a superior court, and in the summons and plea (verbal or written) in an inferior court; and for that purpose the hearing of such evidence as may be brought forward by the parties; after which the parties or their legal representatives (if they so desire) are heard, and judgment of the court is given. The term *trial* is not necessarily confined to cases in which evidence is heard; see *Saunders* v. *Butt*, ([1906] E.D.C. 17).

(2) In criminal cases, the judicial investigation of a complaint preferred by the Crown (in some cases by a private prosecutor) against an accused person, as disclosed in an indictment or summons, after he has pleaded not guilty, and the hearing of such evidence as may be brought forward by the prosecutor, with the object of ascertaining the guilt or innocence of the accused in respect of the crime or offence wherewith he stands charged.

"A *trial* of an accused person takes place when there is an issue raised between the accused and the Crown by a plea of not guilty. Then he is put upon his *trial*, evidence is called, and the case is investigated with a view of determining whether he is guilty or not.

But when a prisoner pleads guilty it is unnecessary to try him. There is no necessity for a finding of guilty; he is sentenced upon his own plea, upon his own admission of guilt" (*per* SOLOMON, J., in *Rotestrick* v. *Rex,* [1908] T.S. at p. 621). The practice that has been laid down that magistrates must take some evidence to prove that a crime has been committed, where a prisoner pleads guilty, is to satisfy the judges who review the cases, and does not constitute a *trial* (*ibid.*).

Tribe, a division of a native race under a more or less independent chief. In the Natal Code of Native Law (Law 19 of 1891, sch., sec. 8) the word *tribe* is defined to signify "a number, or collection, or body of natives forming a political organisation or community, and composed of not less than twenty kraals, under the government, control, or leadership of a chief, and which organisation or community has been recognised or established by the Supreme Chief. The communities existing now, or hereafter to be formed in connection with mission stations may be regarded as *tribes.*"

Tribunal, a court of justice.

Tributor for the working of a mine, an expression employed in the Transvaal Mines, Works and Machinery Regulations Ordinance (54 of 1903). *See* OWNER OF A MINE.

Tripartite, divided into three parts. A *tripartite* contract is a contract to which there are three parties.

Trouwbeloften (D.), espousals; a mutual agreement and promise of a future marriage. See Van Leeuwen's *Comm.* 4, 25; and Kersteman's *Woordenboek,* vol. 1, p. 553.

Trust. "A *trust* is an equitable obligation, either expressly undertaken or constructively imposed by the court, whereby the obligor (who is called a trustee) is bound to deal with property over which he has control (which is called the trust property), for the benefit of persons (who are called the beneficiaries or *cestuis que trust*), of whom he may or may not himself be one, and any one of whom may enforce the obligation. Any act or neglect on the part of a trustee which is not authorised or excused by the terms of the *trust* instrument or by law is called a breach of *trust*" (Underhill's *Trusts and Trustees,* 5th ed. p. 1).

Trustee. (1) "The *trustee* is the party who holds the trust property, but who, as *trustee,* cannot derive any benefit from it" (Stephen's *Comm.* 15th ed. vol. 3, p. 453). *See* TRUST; also Act 3 of 1873 (C.C.), sec. 1 (4); Act 36 of 1904 (C.C.), sec. 42; Law 4 of 1892 (O.R.C.), sec. 1 (*d*).

(2) The person in whom the estate of an insolvent person is vested

for the uses and purposes of the sequestration; see Ordinance 6 of 1843 (C.C.), sec. 48; Law 13 of 1895 (T.), sec. 84; Law 47 of 1887 (N.), sec. 53; Law Book, ch. 104 (O.R.C.), sec. 48.

"From the moment that his appointment takes place the *trustee* is the *dominus* of the entire estate possessed by the insolvent at the date of the sequestration" (*per* INNES, C.J., in *Collison, Ltd.*, v. *Castle Wine and Brandy Co.*, [1907] T.S. at p. 592).

(3) Directors of a company are in some sense *trustees;* see Palmer's *Company Precedents*, 8th ed. part i, p. 603.

Turba, a crowd. By a crowd or number of witnesses is the mode in which a custom is proved (Voet's *Comm.* 1, 3, 34; Van der Linden's *Institutes*, 1, 1, 7; Van Leeuwen's *Comm.* 1, 3, 11, and Decker, *ibid. in notis*).

Turnkey, the officer in a prison who has charge of the keys, and whose duty it is to lock and unlock the prison doors.

Turpis causa, an immoral or dishonourable motive or consideration. *See* EX TURPI CAUSA NON ORITUR ACTIO.

Tutelae administratio, administration of a guardianship. Guardianship gives rise to one of the quasi-contracts of Roman law, viz., quasi-mandate. Although the ward by reason of his minority is unable to give his guardian a mandate, the guardian is bound to the ward and the ward to the guardian just as if an actual mandate existed between them (Grotius' *Introd.* 3, 26, 4 *et seq.*).

Tutor dative, a person appointed by the Master of the Supreme Court, after observance of the prescribed formalities, to administer and manage any estate or property which may have devolved on, or come to belong to any minor, within a colony, and not at the time being under natural guardianship, or the guardianship of a duly confirmed tutor testamentary.

Tutor suspectus, suspected tutor. *See* ACCUSATIO SUSPECTI TUTORIS.

Tutors testamentary, persons appointed by the father of a minor, or by the mother of a minor whose father is dead, in any will or other deed, to administer or manage the estate, or take care of the person and property of such minor. A *tutor testamentary* may not assume or enter upon the management of the estate or property of the minor, except for the purposes of preservation and safe custody, until letters of confirmation have been granted to him by the Master of the Supreme Court in the prescribed form. "A tutor looks after the person as well as the property of the minors, whereas the curator nominate superintends their property alone" (*per* De Villiers, C.J., in *Eksteen* v. *Eksteen's Executors*, 4 S.C. at pp. 374 *et seq.*).

Tweetbroeder; Tweitbroeder (D.), a half-brother.

Tweitbroeder (D.). *See* Tweetbroeder.

Uberrima fides, the utmost good faith. This is essential to the validity of certain contracts which necessitate the reposing of confidence in one party by the other, *e.g.* the contract between principal and agent or insurer and insured. In such contracts any departure by means of misrepresentation, concealment or otherwise from the highest standard of good faith will have the effect of entirely avoiding the contract (*Matabele Syndicate* v. *Lippert and Others*, 4 Off. Rep. 372; *Transvaal Cold Storage Co., Ltd.*, v. *Palmer*, [1904] T.S. 4; *Richards* v. *Guardian Assurance Co.*, [1907] T.H. 24).

Ubi jus ibi remedium, where there is a right there is a remedy. That is to say, for every right the law provides a remedy either by way of an interdict to protect it or by way of an action to enforce it or to recover damages for its invasion.

Ubi uxor ibi domus, where the wife is, there is the domicile. This maxim is of frequent application in matrimonial suits, where a husband has left his wife in a country in which he himself was domiciled and his acquisition of a new domicile is doubtful. Thus in *Adams* v. *Adams* (2 S.C. 24) leave was granted to a wife to sue her husband by edict for divorce on the ground of malicious desertion, the husband having left her some years previously and gone to the Transvaal, where he was living in adultery. De Villiers, C.J., said, "The ordinary maxim is *ubi uxor ibi domus*—that is, the supposition is that if a man leaves his wife behind he does not intend to change his domicile. Of course, it is competent for the defendant to come into this court and set up the defence that his domicile is not in this country; but the court is not bound to presume that he has changed his domicile" (see also *Hawkes* v. *Hawkes*, 2 S.C. 109, and *Mason* v. *Mason*, 4 E.D.C. 330).

In order that the presumption may arise it is necessary that the husband should have had a domicile in the country where he has left his wife. This is illustrated by the case of *Walker* v. *Walker* (13 S.C. 363). There the parties were married in Cape Colony in May, 1881, the husband (respondent) being an itinerant lecturer and having at the time of the marriage no fixed domicile. In November, 1881, they left for Australia, where they lived together until 1893. In the latter year the wife, with the consent of her husband, returned to Cape Colony, the husband promising to follow her, but having failed afterwards to keep his promise. DE VILLIERS, C.J., said, "There is no proof that the respondent ever acquired a domicile in this colony. He was no sooner married than he went to Australia, where he has remained ever since. The fact that he promised his wife he would follow her does not prove a change of domicile. If he had brought his wife here and lived with her here for some time, there might have been some ground for granting this application" (see also *Ex parte Rosenwax*, 11 C.T.R. 10, and *Linley* v. *Linley*, 15 C.T.R. 564).

As *ubi uxor ibi domus* is a presumption that arises only in case of doubt, it may be rebutted by evidence of the husband's domicile being actually elsewhere. Thus it does not apply where the husband changes his domicile, but his wife refuses to join him (*Abrams* v. *Abrams*, 17 S.C. 418), or where the wife, whom the husband married in another country, does not accompany him to the country of his domicile (*Sklaar* v. *Sklaar*, 9 S.C. 336).

Uitgheraadt (D.), emancipated.

Uitheemsch (D.), foreign.

Uit-heymen (D.). *See* ALIENS.

Uitschuldenaar (D.), a creditor.

Uitval grond (D.), small pieces of land remaining over between surveyed or unsurveyed farms. See *Aaron* v. *Johannesburg Municipality* ([1904] T.S. at p. 710).

Ukungena, a native term used in the Natal Code of Native Law (Law 19 of 1891, sec. 24 of sch.) to denote "a special legal union with a widow by a full or half brother of her deceased husband, with the express purpose of raising up seed on behalf, and in the name of, the deceased husband." See also *Gobeyana* v. *Maranna* (21 N.L.R. 19).

Ukwetula or **Etula,** a native term employed in the Natal Code of Native Law (Law 19 of 1891, sec. 25 of sch.) in connection with the kraal family system, and denoting "a custom arising out of a marriage, and implies the transfer, in the discretion of the kraal head. of cattle from a lower to an upper house."

Ultimatum, the last offer, an offer setting out the conditions of a treaty or agreement, which, if not accepted (usually within a specified period) may result in negotiations being finally broken off.

Ultimus dies inceptus pro completo habetur, the last day is held to be completed at its commencement. *See* COMPUTATIO CIVILIS ET NATURALIS.

Ultra vires, beyond the power. This phrase is used of acts which purport to be done in virtue of a certain authority, but which are really in excess of such authority. Thus the act of an agent is *ultra vires* when it is beyond the scope of the authority conferred upon the agent by his principal; and a municipal bye-law is said to be *ultra vires* when it exceeds the authority conferred by law upon the municipality.

Umhlubulo, a native term used in the Natal Code of Native Law (Law 19 of 1891, sec. 28 of sch.) to denote "that portion of a slaughtered animal which is the perquisite of an inferior person or house from a superior person or house in a kraal."

Umninimzi, a native term signifying the recognised head of a native kraal. *See* KRAAL; see also the Native Territories Penal Code (Act 24 of 1886), sec. 5 (*k*).

Umpire, a person appointed to decide in arbitration proceedings where the arbitrators are unable to agree. See Act 29 of 1898 (C.C.); Act 24 of 1898 (N.); Ordinance 24 of 1904 (T.).

Umtakati, a native term signifying a witch or wizard who by means of witchcraft causes, or who by such means is reputed to be able to cause, injury to the lives and property of others. As to penalty in Cape Colony for naming or imputing any other person as being a wizard or witch, see Act 2 of 1895 (C.C.), sec. 1.

Unbroken case. *See* "ONE UNBROKEN CASE."

Unde vi, one of the possessory interdicts of Roman law, granted for the purpose of recovering lost possession of immovable property, but afterwards extended to movables, and deriving its name from the introductory words of the interdict, which ran: *Unde in hoc anno tu illum vi dejecisti aut familia tua dejecit, cum ille possideret quod nec vi nec clam nec precario a te possideret, eo illum quaeque ille tunc ibi habuit restituas.* To entitle a person to the interdict forcible dispossession was requisite, also actual possession at the time of dispossession. The interdict was available even against the true owner, in accordance with the maxim, *Spoliatus ante omnia restituendus est.*

Undemarcated forest. "*Undemarcated forest* shall include commonages or native locations, or any other land on which the Crown retains a right to the timber growing therein or thereon, and all vacant Crown land on which trees are growing or have grown" (the Cape Forest Act, 28 of 1888, sec. 2).

Underhand contract, a term applied to contracts leases or agreements executed by the parties themselves other than in the presence of a notary public; those executed before a notary public are described as "notarial contracts."

Underhand will, a will made in writing by a testator and signed at the foot or end thereof by him or by some other person in his presence and by his direction; and such signature must be made or acknowledged by the testator in the presence of two or more competent witnesses, present at the same time, and such witnesses must attest and subscribe the will in the presence of the person executing it. Where the instrument is written upon more than one leaf [in the Transvaal and O.R.C. Ordinances the word "sheet" is used in place of "leaf"] it must be signed by the testator and witnesses on at least one side of every leaf. A mark formally made by the testator when he is unable to write is equivalent to his signature. The execution of wills is regulated in the Cape Colony and Rhodesia by Ordinance 15 of 1845; in Natal by Law 2 of 1868; in the Transvaal by Ordinance 14 of 1903; and in the Orange River Colony by Ordinance 11 of 1904.

Undertaking. In the Natal Telegraph Act (16 of 1901), sec. 3, *undertaking,* in reference to a telegraph, includes "all the rights, powers, privileges, works and other property of the person owning the telegraph, for the transmission of telegrams in this [Natal] Colony, for money or other consideration."

Underwriter, a person who undertakes insurance by underwriting policies. "Every person capable of making a contract may be an insurer, and may authorise any person capable of being an agent to underwrite policies in his name and on his behalf. The practice of insuring with individuals was the earliest in use anywhere, and long continued to be followed in this country [England]" (Arnould's *Marine Insurance,* 7th ed. sec. 76).

"**Undistributed assets,**" when referring to a company, mean the undistributed assets of a company capable of distribution in the winding-up (*In re Land Mortgage Bank of Florida, Ltd.,* 5 Manson, 178).

Undue influence. (1) At elections: The making use, or threatening to make use, by any person either directly or indirectly, of any force, violence or restraint; or the infliction or threatening the infliction by himself or by or through any other person, of any injury, damage, harm or loss; or the practising in any other manner of intimidation upon or against any person, in order to induce or compel such person to vote or refrain from voting, or on account of such person having voted or refrained from voting at any election; or the impeding, prevention of, or interference with, by means of abduction, duress or any fraudulent device or contrivance, the free exercise of the franchise of any voter either to give or refrain from giving his vote (see sec. 4 of Act 21 of 1859 (C.C.)).

For *undue influence* in Natal, see Law 13 of 1893, sec. 20. In Transvaal, see Ordinance 38 of 1903, sec. 71.

(2) In regard to wills: See *Govu* v. *Stuart* (24 N.L.R. at p. 445).

(3) In regard to contracts, see Story's *Equity Jurisprudence*, vol. 1, sec. 239, and as regards

(4) Marriage, *ibid.* secs. 264 and 266.

Unilateral, relating to one side only; one sided.

Unilateral contract, a contract by which only one party is bound.

Universal heir, "means heir to everything" (*per* FINNEMORE, A.C.J., in *Spencer and Brandon* v. *Wilson*, 25 N.L.R. at p. 235). *See* HEIR.

Universal thing (*res universalis*), "contains more than is indicated by itself; and consists either of a whole including many parts, as an inheritance, or of a genus embracing several species, as, for instance, under the term *animal* both man and beast are included; under the term *beast*, horse, ox, ass; under *man*, John, Peter, Paul; and under *inheritance* is included all the property of the deceased, as house, garden, chattels, and so on" (Van Leeuwen's *Comm.* Kotzé's trans. vol. 1, p. 144).

Universitas, the whole. The *universitas* of an estate is the sum total of the rights and obligations of the estate. In the Roman law the term is more frequently used to denote a corporate body created by the State, *e.g.* a municipality or a trade guild. Such a *universitas* is a juristic *persona* quite distinct from the members composing it, having rights and liabilities apart from those of its members, and suing and being sued as a whole.

University. (1) An association or corporation established for the advancement of sound learning, and for conferring degrees. The University of the Cape of Good Hope was the first *university* to be established in South Africa. It was established and incorporated by Act 16 of 1873—subsequently amended by Act 6 of 1896. It consists of a chancellor, a vice-chancellor, a council of thirty members, and graduates; and is a body politic and corporate with perpetual succession and power to buy, hold, sell and lease property. The council appoints examiners for the examination of persons desiring to matriculate in the *university* or to obtain any degree, certificate or distinction from the *university*.

(2) The expression "*university* of things" is employed by Kotzé, C.J., in his translation of Van Leeuwen's *Comm.* vol. 1, p. 311, where, after treating of single things, it is said: "It now remains to consider a *university* of things, which consists in the right to an estate or inheritance and its administration." The learned translator in a footnote to this passage says that "things are divided into *res singulares*, *e.g.* a book, a sheep; and a *universitas rerum*, *i.e.* a collection of things, *e.g.* a flock, an inheritance with all its rights and duties attached." This no doubt explains the word *university* as used in the above quotation.

Unlawful assembly. The Cape Native Territories Penal Code (Act 24 of 1886, sec. 91) provides that "an assembly of five or more persons is designated an *unlawful assembly* if the common object of the persons comprising that assembly is: (1) To overawe by criminal force, or show of criminal force, any officer of the Government, or any public servant in the exercise of the lawful power of such public servant; or (2) to resist the execution of any law or any legal process." See also Stephen's *Digest of the Criminal Law*, 5th ed. art. 75.

"**Unless,**" see *Liebman* v. *Rex* ([1906] T.S. at p. 475).

Unlimited company is defined in the Cape Companies Act (25 of 1902) as "a company formed on the principle of having no limit placed on the liability of its members," and in the Transvaal Companies Act (31 of 1909), sec. 2, as "a company which has no limit on the liability of its members."

Unliquidated damages, damages that have not been exactly ascertained. In insolvency a claim for *unliquidated damages* should not be admitted until the amount due has been fixed by judgment of a competent court (*per* DE VILLIERS, C.J., in *De Klerk* v. *Zeeman*, 13 S.C. at p. 183). *See* LIQUIDATED DAMAGES.

Unqoliso, or **Ingqutu,** or **Mumba,** a native term used in the Natal Code of Native Law (Law 19 of 1891, sec. 26 of sch.) to denote "the cow or other head of cattle which is invariably gifted by the son-in-law elect to the mother-in-law elect on every marriage of a girl."

Unreasonable verdict. The *unreasonable verdict* of a jury may be set aside by the court, see *Lawrence and Others* v. *Executors of Lawrence* (25 N.L.R. 293).

"**Until fully paid for.**" Where certain machinery was purchased upon the condition that the price should be paid partly in cash and partly in promissory notes, and that the machinery should remain the property of the seller until the purchase-price had been paid in full; and the cash and notes were handed over to the seller, but before any of the notes had been paid the purchaser became insolvent; it was held that the sale was made upon a suspensive condition to be fulfilled on payment of the notes. DE VILLIERS, C.J., in giving judgment in this action, said: "I think that *until fully paid for* does not mean 'until promissory notes are given,' but 'until the promissory notes are paid.' These notes were to be given at the same time as the *balance* of cash was to be paid, and, as the cash was to be paid immediately on delivery, there would have been no sense in the condition that the property in the machinery should not pass until paid for, unless the payment required was a payment of the notes" (*Harcombe & Rylands* v. *Indelsohn's Trustee*, 4 S.C. 225).

Unwrought gold, in the Transvaal Gold Law (15 of 1898, sec. 3, now repealed), signifies "gold or precious metal in any form or connection whatsoever, which, although smelted, is not manufactured or made up into any article of commerce. It shall include also unrefined precious metal, under which, therefore, shall also be comprised amalgam, slimes and scrapings." *See* NATIVE GOLD; UNWROUGHT PRECIOUS METAL.

Unwrought precious metal. In the Transvaal Precious and Base Metals Act (35 of 1908), sec. 104, *unwrought precious metal* "shall include precious metal in any form whatever, which though smelted is not manufactured or made up into any article of commerce, and shall include amalgam, slimes, slags, black sands, pots, battery chips, sweeping of reduction works and scrapings and bye-products of unrefined precious metal."

In the Orange River Colony Mining of Precious Metals Ordinance (3 of 1904), sec. 124, *unwrought precious metal* means "any precious metal to which this Ordinance shall apply in any form or condition whatsoever, which although smelted is not manufactured or made up into any article of commerce, and shall comprise all such precious metals when unrefined, including amalgam and scrapings." *See* UNWROUGHT GOLD.

Urban district, an area or district surrounding a town; a defined district having an urban centre; see Act 8 of 1905 (C.C.), sec. 1: also 18 of 1909 (T.), sec. 2.

Urban servitudes "are those which properly relate to the enjoyment of a dwelling-house, or other occupied premises. Some of these consist in doing or suffering something; and others in forbearing or not doing something in favour of the neighbouring tenement. Servitudes of doing or suffering are the supporting of another's building, or suffering the insertion of an anchor or beam, receiving his rainwater, and leading water on or off, and the like" (Van Leeuwen's *Comm.* Kotzé's trans. vol. 1, p. 286). *See* PRAEDIUM RUSTICUM.

Urban tenement, land used for the erection of a house, or on which a house is built and required for the purpose of such house; land used for urban purposes. Correlative to "rural tenement." *See* PRAEDIUM RUSTICUM. The test whether a tenement is rural or urban is not the place where the property is situated, but the use to which it is devoted (*per* DE VILLIERS, C.J., in *Nieuwoudt* v. *Slavin*, 13 S.C. 62).

As to lessor's consent being necessary to the validity of an assignment of a lease, see *Parkin* v. *Lippert* (12 S.C. at p. 187).

Usage, long-continued practice or custom. "*Usage*, or rather the spontaneous evolution by the popular mind of rules the existence and general acceptation of which is proved by their customary observance, is no doubt the oldest form of law making. It marks the transition between morality and law" (Holland's *Jurisprudence*, 10th ed. p. 54). *See* CUSTOM.

Use. *See* USUS, which is its Latin equivalent.

"Usual common form." Where the articles of association of a company provide that all transfers of shares are to be in the *usual common form*, a transfer will not be deemed to have failed to comply with that requirement merely because it omits matters which would be contained in a common form, but are wholly immaterial—for example, the address of the transferor and the denoting number of the share, where both of these are well known to the directors (*In re Letheby and Christopher, Ltd.; Jones's Case*, 11 Manson, 209).

Usuarius, the person entitled to the right of *usus*.

Usucapio, usucapion or acquisition by use; a method of acquiring the ownership of property in Roman law. To convert possession into ownership a period of one year was sufficient in the case of movables and two years in the case of immovables situated in Italy. There was no usucapion of provincial lands, as these belonged to the emperor or the people, and could not be owned by private individuals. The peregrine praetors, however, protected the possession of the actual occupier of such lands against any claimant by allowing him, after possession for ten years, if he and the claimant lived in the same province (*inter praesentes*), and for twenty years if they resided in different provinces (*inter absentes*), to repel an action, by an exception which was called a *praescriptio*, from being placed at the beginning of the *intentio* or statement of claim. Finding these two systems, the *usucapio* of the *Jus Civile* and the *praescriptio longi temporis*, as it was called, of the *Jus honorarium*, subsisting side by side, Justinian by fusing them together devised a new *usucapio*, according to which ownership was acquired by three years' possession in the case of movables, and in the case of immovables wherever situated by "possession of long time," *i.e.* possession of ten years *inter praesentes* and twenty years *inter absentes*. In order that *usucapio* might operate it was necessary that the possession should be *bonâ fide* and *ex justa causa*, *i.e.* that the possessor should believe his possession rightful and have acquired it by some legal mode of acquisition. By *Novel* 117, however, Justinian adopted from the Theodosian Code a prescription called *longissimi temporis*, according to which possession for thirty years, or for forty years in the case of property belonging to the Church or the State or property hypothecated and in the possession of the debtor, cured any fault attaching to its acquisition or possession to the extent that such possession transferred the property where there was *bona fides*, and where there was *mala fides* enabled the possessor to repel actions for recovery of the property so long as he retained possession. Usucapion is no longer known in the Roman-Dutch law, the only prescription recognised as a mode of acquiring property being the prescription *longissimi temporis*, the period of which at common law is one-third of a century for immovables and thirty years for movables, but under Cape and Transvaal statute law thirty years alike for both kinds of property. *See* PRAESCRIPTIO LONGISSIMI TEMPORIS.

Usufruct "is the privilege of drawing the fruits of the property of another, without diminishing the property itself" (Grotius' *Introd.* Maasdorp's trans. p. 155).

Usufructuary, the person who holds or enjoys a usufruct. "The *usufructuary* is entitled to the 'fruits' of the property; whether 'natural,' as brushwood and the young of animals, 'industrial,' as crops and vintages, or 'civil,' as rent of land and interest of money. He has, in general, to exercise the right *en bon père de famille.* The right may be left by will or granted *inter vivos.* It is sometimes implied by law. So in France parents have the usufruct of the property of their children till they attain the age of eighteen. It may be let or alienated. It comes to an end with the death of the *usufructuary*, or other termination of the period for which it was granted, with the destruction of the property over which it is enjoyable, and with a *consolidatio* of the title of the proprietor with that of the *usufructuary*. It may also be forfeited by wrongful user, or by non-user" (Holland's *Jurisprudence*, 10th ed. p. 220). The *usufructuary* of a house is not bound to maintain an existing insurance upon it (*Meyer's Executor* v. *Meyer*, 1 S.C. 377). *See* USUFRUCT.

Usufructus, usufruct (*q.v.*).

Usurpatio, the technical name in Roman law for the interruption of prescription.

Usury. Formerly under Roman-Dutch law it was *usury* and a crime to charge a higher rate of interest than 6 per cent. per annum. In South Africa, "while excessive interest is still unlawful and cannot be recovered by action, the exacting of it is no crime" (Morice's *English and Roman-Dutch Law*, p. 347). See also *Dyason* v. *Ruthven* (3 Searle, 282); *Taylor* v. *Holland* (2 S.A.R. 78); *Roberts* v. *Booi* (4 E.D.C. 20); *Reuter* v. *Yates* ([1904] T.S. 855).

For the Cape Colony, see the Usury Act (23 of 1908).

Usus, one of the personal servitudes of Roman law, entitling the person in right of it (called the *usuarius* or usuary) to use the subject, but not to take any of the fruits which it produced. The right was thus less than that of usufruct, which included both the *jus utendi* (the right to use the property) and the *jus fruendi* (the right to enjoy its fruits). Unlike the usufructuary, too, the usuary could not let, sell or give the exercise of his right to another. The rigour of this principle was afterwards abated, and the usuary was permitted, where he would otherwise have derived little or no benefit from the right, to take as much of the fruits as was sufficient for his daily wants

(Sandars' *Institutes of Justinian,* 12th ed. p. 131). In the Roman-Dutch law the right is defined by Grotius (*Introd.* 2, 44, 6) as consisting "in reference to land in the occupation of the same without hindrance from the owner or his workmen, and in the right to take fruit, vegetables, flowers, hay and wood for daily consumption, but not to transfer the enjoyment of the same to others either gratuitously or for value; in reference to a house, in the right to inhabit the same with one's family and visiting friends, but not to let the same, unless indeed the house be too large for one family; and in reference to animals, in the right to use them for draught purposes, to take their manure and also milk for consumption, but not to appropriate their wool or increase."

Ut res magis valeat quam pereat, that the thing may avail (or be valid) rather than perish. This maxim expresses a rule to be followed in the construction of both statutes and private deeds. "Where the meaning of a section in a law is uncertain or ambiguous, it is the duty of the court to consider the law as a whole, and compare the various sections with each other and with the preamble, and give such meaning to the particular section under consideration that it may, if possible, have force and effect according to the well-known rule *ut res magis valeat quam pereat*" (*per* KOTZÉ, C.J., in *Hess* v. *The State,* 2 Off. Rep. at p. 117). So in the case of contracts or other private deeds, as the deed has presumably been written with the object of having some effect, that construction will be preferred which will give it some effect rather than that which will give it no effect at all. The rule only applies where the meaning of the words is ambiguous, and so open to construction. Where their meaning is clear and certain the maxim *a verbis legis non est recedendum* applies (*Hess* v. *The State, ibid. per* KOTZÉ, C.J., at pp. 117 *et seq.*).

Uti possidetis, the interdict used in Roman law for securing or protecting a person in possession of immovable property. The other possessory interdicts were *utrubi,* granted for the purpose of defending possession of movables, and *unde vi,* given to recover possession of immovables, but afterwards extended to movables. The interdict *uti possidetis* derives its name from the first words of the interdict, which was addressed to both parties as being equally plaintiffs and defendants, and was in the following form: *Uti eas aedes, quibus de agitur, nec vi nec clam nec precario alter ab altero possidetis, quominus ita possideatis vim fieri veto.* That party obtained the interdict who showed that at the time of its issue he possessed neither by force nor secretly nor by request from the other party (*nec vi, nec clam, nec precario*).

Utiles impensae, expenses which, although they are not necessary to preserve the property, nevertheless improve its market value. See *United Building Society* v. *Smookler's Trustees* ([1906] T.S. at p. 627).

Utrubi, one of the possessory interdicts of Roman law, being given for the purpose of protecting the possession of movable property. It was, like the interdict *uti possidetis,* addressed to both parties as being equally plaintiffs and defendants, and was in the following form: *Utrubi hic homo quo de agitur majore parte hujusce anni fuit, quominus is eum ducat, vim fieri veto.* The interdict was given to him who had possessed the subject for a greater part than his opponent of the year ending with the issue of the interdict, each party being, however, allowed to reckon as his own the possession of his predecessor in title as well. *See* UTI POSSIDETIS.

Utter barristers, barristers in Great Britain who are not King's Counsel, and who plead outside the bar; junior barristers. *Utter barristers* are said to have been so called because they sat or occupied the *uttermost* seats reserved for the bar.

Vacation, the period during which the courts are not regularly sitting; between the terms of the courts; holidays.

Vacua possessio, vacant or undisturbed possession. As in the Roman law, the obligation of a seller in the Roman-Dutch law is not to make the purchaser the owner of the thing sold, but only to give him vacant possession, *i.e.* he warrants the purchaser against eviction by any one having a better title (Voet's *Comm.* 19, 1, 10). If the seller is the owner he will, of course, make the purchaser the owner, but if he is not the owner he only guarantees the purchaser against being legally dispossessed by a third party (Voet's *Comm.* 19, 1, 11; Grotius' *Introd.* 3, 14, 6). The seller is not bound, however, to give security against eviction, unless that has been expressly stipulated for, or unless the purchaser's right to the thing is challenged before the price is paid in full (Grotius' *Introd.* 3, 14, 7; Van Leeuwen's *Comm.* 4, 18, 3).

Vaderin (D.), a mother.

Vagrant. The definition given in the Cape Act (23 of 1879) for the prevention of vagrancy and squatting is as follows: "Any person found wandering abroad and having no visible lawful means, or insufficient lawful means of support, who, being thereunto required by any resident magistrate, justice of the peace, field-cornet, police officer, police constable, inspector of native locations, or owner or occupier of land, or who having been duly summoned for such purpose, or brought before a resident magistrate or special justice of the peace in pursuance of this Act, shall not give a good and satisfactory account of himself, shall be deemed and taken to be an idle and disorderly person" (sec. 2); and "Every person found without the permission of the owner (the proof of which permission shall lie on such person) wandering over any farm, in or loitering near any dwelling-house, shop, store, stable, outhouse, garden, vineyard, kraal, or other enclosed place, shall be deemed and taken to be an idle and disorderly person" (*ibid.* sec. 4, as amended by Act 27 of 1889, sec. 2); and "Every person found wandering or being in any street or road ordinarily used by the public, or in any place of public resort, or in view thereof respectively, without sufficient clothing for the purposes of decency, shall be deemed and taken to be a disorderly person." See also Act 27 of 1889; Act 20 of 1891; and Act 34 of 1895; also *Queen* v. *Jones* (9 S.C. 210).

In Natal law see Law 15 of 1869, sec. 1; *Vinden* v. *Ladysmith Local Board* (17 N.L.R. 78); Law 16 of 1887; Law 39 of 1884, sec. 9; Law 22 of 1894, sec. 39.

In the Transvaal *vagrancy* is an offence, and is defined in Law 1 of 1881 as follows: "*Vagrants* or rascals are persons who have neither a fixed place of residence nor means of subsistence, and who are not in the habit of carrying on any trade or exercising any calling." See *Leigh and McDonald* v. *Rex* ([1904] T.S. 892).

Valuable consideration, *see* CONSIDERATION. As to *valuable consideration* in connection with Bribery and Corrupt Practices Acts, see *Burton* v. *Rhodes and Hill* (16 S.C. 3).

Valuable security, in the Transvaal Criminal Procedure Code, (1 of 1903), sec. 3, includes "any document which is the property of any person, and which is the evidence of the ownership of any property or of the right to recover or receive any property." See also Ordinance 26 of 1904 (T.), sec. 3—the Crimes Ordinance—where a similar definition is given, except that the last two lines read "of the right to recover, receive, *or be in possession* of any property" (the additional words are italicised).

Value. In the Bills of Exchange Acts *value* means valuable consideration. See Act 19 of 1893 (C.C.), sec. 1; Law 8 of 1887 (N.) sec. 1; Proclamation 11 of 1902 (T.), sec. 1; Ordinance 28 of 1902 (O.R.C.), sec. 1.

Value received. These words are sometimes inserted in a bill of exchange accepted for value and not by way of accommodation. "This has long been held not to be essential, for the law raises a *primâ facie* presumption of consideration. In the case of an accepted bill payable to drawer's order, the words "value received" mean value received by the acceptor; while in a bill payable to a third party they mean *primâ facie* value received by the drawer. Whether a bill expresses that value has been given or not, extrinsic evidence is admissible between immediate parties and those in privity with them to impeach the consideration, and show its absence, failure or illegality. . . Under some of the foreign codes it is essential that the nature of the consideration should in general terms be stated in the bill: see Netherlands Code, art. 100. The German Exchange Law, art. 4, and Italian Code, art. 251, do not require the consideration to be stated. By the French Code, art. 110, the nature of the consideration must be stated. A false statement of value constitutes a *supposition de valeur*, and avoids the bill in the hands of parties with notice; *Nouguier*, secs. 282, 283" (Chalmers' *Bills of Exchange*, 6th ed. p. 14).

Valued policy "is one in which the sum to be paid as an indemnity in case of loss is fixed by the terms of the contract" (May on *Insurance*, 4th ed. sec. 30). As to difference between a *valued* policy and an *open* policy, see OPEN POLICY. See also Arnould's *Marine Insurance*, 7th ed. secs. 9 and 336 *et seq*.

Valvassor (D.). *See* WALDVESTER.

Vassal, a tenant holding lands under obligation to render military service to his lord. *See* FEUD.

Vastgoed (D.), immovable property.

Veem, veim (D.), originally denoted a secret sentence, where the offender was put to death without the reason being proclaimed. Those who pronounced such a sentence were called *veemscheepenen*. This mode of procedure and punishment were introduced by Charlemagne among the Westphalians on account of their excessive stubbornness. At the present day *veem* denotes a company or society of persons of the same kind; a heap (Meyer's *Woordenschat*).

Veemgericht (D.), a secret tribunal or court of justice existing in the middle ages. *See* VEEM.

Veim (D.). *See* VEEM.

Veinout, Vennoot, Veingnoot (D.), a companion, a partner.

Vendor, a seller. See Natal Lung-sickness Prevention Act (30 of 1897), sec. 3.

Vendu-afslager (D.), an auctioneer.

Venia aetatis, dispensation of years; a privilege whereby minors were allowed under special circumstances to become majors before the age fixed for the attainment of majority. According to Grotius (*Introd.* 1, 10, 3) and Van der Keessel (*Thes.* 110, but cf. *Thes.* 161) *venia aetatis* could be obtained from the court, but the weight of authority favours the view that only the supreme power could grant it (Schorer, *Notes* 37 and 44; Voet's *Comm.* 4, 4, secs. 3 and 4; Van Leeuwen's *Comm.* 1, 13, 5; Decker, *ibid. in notis*). In the case of *Cachet* (15 S.C. 5; 8 C.T.R. 9) the court held that in the absence of clear legal authority that it had power to grant *venia aetatis* it was not prepared to exercise such a power.

As, however, it was clearly for the benefit of the minor, he having a good opportunity of commencing business for himself, the court, to enable him to do so, released him from tutelage and authorised the payment to him of an inheritance from the Guardian's Fund. In the Transvaal *venia aetatis* has been granted by the court (*Ex parte J. J. Botha*, 10 C.L.J. 174; *Ex parte C. H. M. Kisch*, 1 Off. Rep. 160); but it has now been held that the court has no such power (*Ex parte Moolman*, [1903] T.S. 159).

Vennoot (D.). *See* VEINOUT.

Vennootschap (D.), partnership.

Ventris inspectio, inspection of the womb. *See* DE VENTRE INSPICIENDO.

Venue, the place for trial of a cause or prosecution.

Verba generalia restringuntur ad habilitatem rei vel personae, general words are restricted to the fitness of the thing or person. That is, general words must be construed according to their aptitude to the matter or the person with whom they deal. Thus while an agent's authority is always construed to include all the necessary and usual means of executing it with effect (Story on *Agency*, sec. 58), language, however general in form, when used with reference to a particular subject-matter will be presumed to be used in subordination to that subject-matter (*ibid.* sec. 63). Accordingly where a power of attorney authorised an agent to ask, demand and receive from the East India Company . . all money that might become due to the principal on any account whatever, and to transact all business and on non-payment to use all lawful means for recovery, &c., it was held that the words "to transact all business" did not authorise the agent to indorse an East India bill, received under the power of attorney, in the name of the principal and to procure a discount thereon on such indorsement; for the words "all business" must be construed to be limited to all business necessary for the receipt of the money (*Hay* v. *Goldsmidt*, 2 Smith, 79; 1 Taunt, 349). So a power of attorney giving the agent full powers as to the management of a certain property, with general words extending these powers to all the property of the principal of every description, and in conclusion authorising the agent to do all lawful acts concerning all the principal's business and affairs of what nature or kind soever, does not authorise the agent to indorse bills of exchange in the name of the principal (*Esdaile* v. *La Nauze*, 4 L.J. Ex. Eq. 46); for where "in general mandates some things are specially expressed, the generality is not extended to cases of greater importance than those expressed" (Stair's *Institutes of the Law of Scotland*, 1, 12, 15).

For the application of the rule in the construction of statutes, see Maxwell's *Interpretation of Statutes*, 4th ed. pp. 89 *et seq.*, and Craie's *Statute Law*, 4th ed. pp. 167 *et seq.*

Verba ita sunt intelligenda ut res magis valeat quam pereat, words are to be so construed that the matter may be effectual rather than be of no avail. *See* UT RES MAGIS, &c.

Verbanduitmaker (D.), a conveyancer who prepares and registers bonds. In the late republics in South Africa a conveyancer was called a *transport en verbanduitmaker*.

Verbeteringen (D.), improvements to houses or immovable property.

Verbis tantum, by the words only; one of the three ways in which co-legatees may be joined together in a bequest, *i.e.* where the conjunction is only by the words used, but not with regard to the entire thing itself, as where the testator says, "I bequeath my farm to A and B in equal shares." *See* JUS ACCRESCENDI.

Verbruik-leen (D.), loan for consumption. Latin equivalent, *mutuum.* See Van Leeuwen's *Comm.* Kotzé's trans. vol. 1, p. 212, *in notis;* Grotius' *Introd.* 3, 10, 1.

Verdeeling (D.), division; distribution. See Kersteman's *Woordenboek*, vol. 1, p. 569.

Verdict is defined in the Cape Jury Trials Act (Civil Cases), 23 of 1891, to mean "the finding or findings of the jury upon any issue or issues tried by such jury, and includes any statement of facts as found by the jury to have been proved."

"*Verdict* and acquittal" discussed, *Kerr* v. *Rex* ([1907] E.D.C. at pp. 332 *et seq*).

As to setting aside an unreasonable verdict, see *Lawrence and Others* v. *Lawrence's Executors* (25 N.L.R. 293).

Vergunning (D.) [pl. *vergunningen*], a written permission granted by the owner of a farm or land in the Transvaal to a person, authorising such person under sec. 43 of the Transvaal Gold Law (15 of 1898, now repealed) to peg out claims on the owner's farm or land prior to its proclamation as a public diggings. Such right had to be exercised in a *bonâ fide* manner, and could not be granted by the owner to himself directly or through the medium of a dummy (*Gauf* v. *Modderfontein G.M. Co. and Another*, 12 C.L.J. 217; *Frische* v. *Modderfontein G.M. Co. and Another*, 13 C.L.J. 76). The number of *vergunning* claims that might be granted upon a farm were restricted according to a sliding scale based upon the area of the farm, as set out in sec. 43 above referred to.

Veritas convicii, the truth of the accusation. In an action for defamation it is not sufficient for the defendant to prove that the statements made by him are true: if he adopts this defence he must also prove that the statements were made for the public benefit (Voet's *Comm.* 47, 10, 9; Grotius' *Introd.* 3, 36, 2; Schorer, *Note* 479;

Van Leeuwen's *Comm.* 4, 37, 7, and Kotzé, *ibid. in notis; Mackay* v. *Philip*, 1 Menz. 455; *Sparks* v. *Hart*, 3 Menz. 5; *Botha* v. *Brink*, Buch. 1878, p. 118; *Michaelis* v. *Braun*, 4 S.C. 208).

Verjaring or **Praescriptie** (D.), prescription. *See* PRESCRIPTION.

Verley, Verlyd (D.), confession, acknowledgment.

Verlyd (D.). *See* VERLEY. *Verlyd* or *overlyd* also means death, decease.

Verlyden (D.), (1) to grant, give, cede.
(2) The same as *overlyden*, to pass along, to die.

Verplogenschout (D.), "or debt, is that which is contracted by bond executed before the magistrates (*schepenen*) under special hypothecation of any immovable property or other thing under that judge, which was anciently called *plogen*, or *plegen*, *plogte*, and *pleyte*" (Van Leeuwen's *Comm.* Kotzé's trans. vol. 2, p. 400).

Versterfrecht (D.), law of succession.

Vertical support. *See* SUPPORT.

Vessel, a ship. See Act 4 of 1902 (N.); *see* also "MANAGEMENT OF THE VESSEL"; SHIP.

Veto, the right to negative some act, or to forbid some thing. Bryce in his *History and Jurisprudence* (vol. 2, p. 302) points out that "to-day the so-called royal *veto*, which ought rather to be called the right of the Crown to take further time to consider the resolutions of the two Houses, subsists in theory unimpaired, though it has not been exercised since 1707." This, of course, refers to the British Houses of Parliament. The exercise of the right of *veto* in regard to colonial legislation is not uncommon.

Vi, aut clam, aut precario, by force, or by stealth, or by request. *See* NEC VI, NEC CLAM, NEC PRECARIO.

Via. *See* SERVITUS VIAE.

Via necessaria, necessary way or way of necessity. The owner of a piece of land which has no outlet to the public road is entitled to claim a right of approach over intervening land to the nearest public road (Grotius' *Introd.* 2, 35, 7, 8 and 11; Van Leeuwen's *Comm.* 2, 21, 7; Voet's *Comm.* 8, 3, 4). This approach is called a way of necessity, and must be of a sufficient width to allow a person to go not only on foot, but also with a vehicle (Van Leeuwen's *Comm. ibid.* 2, 21, 11; Schorer, *Note* 216). It differs from the servitudes *iter, actus* and *via* in that the owner of the servient property may enclose his land or even break or dig it up, provided that he allows the way of necessity whenever the use of it is required, or affords another convenient access to the public road (Schorer *ibid.*; Van Leeuwen's *Comm.* 2, 21, 8; *Peacock* v. *Hodges*, Buch. 1876, p. 69). The owner of the dominant tenement may, however, claim to have such a way of necessity converted into a full right of way upon payment of reasonable compensation to the owner of the servient tenement (Schorer, *ibid.*; Voet's *Comm.* 8, 3, 4). *See* ROAD OF NECESSITY.

Via publica, a high road; a road which has been declared a public road by the authorities. *See* VIA VICINALIS.

Via vicinalis, neighbour's road; one of the two kinds of public roads, the other being the *via publica.* A *via vicinalis* is "either a road in a village or a road leading to a town or village, which has been used by the public from time immemorial (*i.e.* for the period required for prescription) without any objection or hindrance from the neighbours over whose land it runs" (*Peacock* v. *Hodges*, Buch. 1876, p. 65; see also Voet's *Comm.* 43, 7, 1; Grotius' *Introd.* 2, 35, 10; Van Leeuwen's *Comm.* 2, 21, 9). Between the *via vicinalis* and the *via publica* there is this difference, that in the case of the former, which belongs to the various owners from whose land it is made up, the rights of the public are a matter of servitude exercised by each member of the public in his own right, whereas in the case of the latter the rights of the public are a matter of ownership exercised through the authorities (Maasdorp's *Institutes*, 2nd ed. vol. 1, p. 197).

Viam publicam populus non utendo amittere non potest, the public cannot by non-user lose its right to a public road. See *Jones* v. *Capetown Town Council* (12 S.C. at p. 25); also RES MERAE FACULTATIS.

Vicarial, pertaining to a vicar or substitute in office. Van Leeuwen in his *Comm.* (Kotzé's trans. vol. 2, p. 174) says: "In prebendal or *vicarial* property, if the possessor thereof has leased any lands belonging to the prebend and happens to die, it is considered that the lease is at an end, for no one can cede to another a greater right than he himself possesses."

Vierschaar (D.) was a government or town-house in which justice was publicly administered in Holland on certain days or at certain times; it was so called because anciently it consisted of a fourfold office—a judge, plaintiff, defendant, and the sheriff who demanded justice (Van Leeuwen's *Comm.* Kotzé's trans. vol. 2, p. 357). See also an instructive *note* by Decker (*ibid.* p. 360).

Vierschaarspannen (D.), to assemble or hold the court.

Vigilant creditor, a creditor who keeps his eyes open, and uses such means as the law allows him to obtain payment of money justly due to him (see *Horwitch's Trustee* v. *Twentyman & Co.,* 12 S.C. at p. 325).

Vigilantibus non dormientibus jura subveniunt, the laws come to the aid of the vigilant, not of the indolent; a maxim of general jurisprudence indicating that courts of justice do not encourage stale demands, and are not disposed to aid parties who have slept upon their rights. Upon the principle expressed in this maxim, error, in order to be a ground for restitution in contract, must be reasonable error; if it is the result of mere carelessness relief will not be granted. So, in the case of a landlord's hypothec, an attachment of the tenant's goods will not be granted if the landlord allows them to be removed before he applies for an order of court (*In re Price,* 3 S.C. 139); but if he applies for the order before the removal of the goods, then, although the tenant proceeds to remove while the order is being granted, the attachment may be made during the course of removal or even after the removal is completed and the goods are in the other premises (*Board of Executors* v. *Stigling,* Buch. 1868, p. 25); as to the Natal practice on this point, *see* QUICK PURSUIT. Again, after judgment and before there has been time to sue out civil imprisonment, the judgment debtor may be arrested if it can be shown that he contemplates leaving with intent to evade payment of the debt; but if since judgment the creditor has had sufficient time to issue execution, or if, having issued execution, he has had time to sue for civil imprisonment, and has not done so, the court will not grant an order of arrest.

Vindicatio rei, the general term applied in the Roman law to actions *in rem,* by which the owner of a thing claims the thing itself, as opposed to *condictio,* the term applied to actions *in personam,* or actions by which personal claims are enforced.

"The true owner of property, movable as well as immovable, which has been alienated without his consent, not only by one who has stolen it, but even by one to whom it has been lent, or let, or given in deposit, or by any other person not having a mandate to sell, may legally claim it from any one who is in possession of it, without making restitution of the price paid by him" (Van der Keessel, *Thes.* 183). See also Grotius' *Introd.* 2, 3 3; Schorer, *Notes* 66 and 334; Van der Linden's *Institutes,* Juta's trans. p. 50; *Beyers* v. *McKenzie* (Foord, 125); *Thima* v. *Kumarasamy* (23 N.L.R. 414); *Vorster* v. *Hodgson* (19 S.C. 493; 12 C.T.R. 893). The owner, therefore, of property which has been stolen may recover it not only from the thief himself, but also from any person, *bonâ fide* or *malâ fide,* into whose hands the property has come (Grotius, *ibid.* 2, 3, 5; Schorer, *ibid.*; Van Leeuwen's *Comm.* Kotzé's trans. 2, 7, 4; Voet's *Comm.* 6, 1, 7). "The remedy our law gives to the owner of stolen property is this: he may follow his property and vindicate it anywhere, provided it is still *in esse.* And he may bring an action *ad exhibendum* to recover the property or its value (should it have been sold or consumed) against the thief or his heirs, or against any person who has received it with knowledge of the taint" (*per* INNES, C.J., in *Leal & Co.* v. *Williams,* [1906]

T.S. at p. 558). See also *Ex parte Steytler, N.O.* (12 C.T.R. 10); *McKillop* v. *Zuckerman* (22 S.C. 448; 15 C.T.R. 655).

To this rule as regards stolen property there were several exceptions in the law of Holland, viz., with regard to goods sold in market overt, goods given in pledge to public pawnbrokers, or sold to old-clothes men and by them publicly exposed, and gold or silver sold to a goldsmith or silversmith and likewise exposed (Grotius' *Introd.* 2, 3, 6; Van der Keessel, *Thes.* 184; Groenewegen, *de Legibus*, C. 6, 2, 2); in which cases the owner was entitled to recover the property on tendering the price paid for it or, in the case of pawnbrokers, the amount advanced upon it. The case of goods sold in market-overt has been the subject of conflicting decisions in South Africa. *See* MOBILIA NON HABENT SEQUELAM and MARKET OVERT, and also the Dutch translation of Ant. Matthaeus, *Paroemia*, under the maxim *meublen hebben geen gevolg*, and the *Naareede* thereon. In *Muller* v. *Chadwick & Co.* ([1906] T.S. 30) it was held that the privilege in favour of pawnbrokers was of so local a nature as not to have been transferred to South Africa, and that pawnbrokers accordingly were not entitled as against the owner to retain stolen property upon which they had *bonâ fide* advanced money until they had been refunded the amount advanced. It is probable that the same view would be taken of the exceptions in favour of old-clothes men and gold or silver-smiths, viz., that they are obsolete and of no force in this country. (See Nathan's *Common Law*, vol. 1, pp. 363 *et seq.*).

In the case of stolen money, the owner is not entitled to recover it from another who has *bonâ fide* received it for value; and the same applies to bank-notes and other negotiable instruments "which have been placed in such a state that the maker can be sued thereon by any *bonâ fide* holder, and which are by commercial usage treated as cash" (*Woodhead, Plunt & Co.* v. *Gunn*, 11 S.C. 4; 4 C.T.R. 20; *York* v. *Van der Lingen*, [1866] 1 Roscoe, 337; *United South African Association, Ltd.*, v. *Cohn*, [1904] T.S. 733).

As regards the vindication of immovable property by legatees or fideicommissaries, see *Lange and Others* v. *Liesching and Others* (Foord, 55); *Booysen* v. *Colonial Orphan Chamber and Others* (Foord, 48); and *Lange* v. *Scheepers* (Buch. 1878, p. 92).

Vindication, in Roman law, a real action

Vindictive damages, exemplary damages; damages awarded as punishment in addition to compensation.

Vinegar. "All the definitions . . . quoted . . . agree in this that the substance must have a vegetable source. The word itself means 'sour wine,' and originally, no doubt, was confined to wines which had become sour by acetous fermentation. In course of time the word was used for other products of acetous fermentation, but in every authoritative description of the substance the infusion or concoction thus subjected to fermentation is assumed to be of vegetable origin, such as sugar, honey, and the like" (*per* DE VILLIERS, C.J., in

Queen v. *Eichorn*, 17 S.C. at p. 388). See *Rex* v. *Fish* (21 S.C. at p. 186).

In Act 19 of 1908 (C.C.), sec. 16, "*vinegar* means the product made by the alcoholic and subsequent acetous fermentation, without distillation, of a vegetable juice, infusion or decoction." *See* CIDER VINEGAR; GLUCOSE VINEGAR; MALT VINEGAR; SPIRIT VINEGAR; SUGAR VINEGAR; WINE VINEGAR.

Vinegar maker. The expression *vinegar maker* is defined in the Cape Excise Spirits Act (18 of 1884), sec. 2, to mean "a person who shall make, prepare, extract, distil, rectify, purify or sell any liquors prepared or capable of being used or applied for the purpose of making vinegar or acetous acid for sale." The same definition is given in the Additional Taxation Act, 36 of 1904 (C.C.), sec. 2.

Virtute officio, by virtue of one's office.

Vis divina, divine force; act of God; included in the term *vis major* (*q.v.*).

Vis major, greater or superior force; irresistible force. Generally speaking, no one is liable for damage caused by *vis major*. Thus, although carriers, innkeepers and stable-keepers, and the borrower in the contract of *commodatum* or gratuitous loan for use are liable for the slightest degree of negligence (*culpa levissima*), they are not bound to make good damage which is the result of *vis major*, as where the ship is wrecked or captured by pirates or the inn or stable or other place where the goods are kept is forcibly broken into and the goods are stolen (Voet's *Comm.* 4, 9, 2; 13, 6, 5). If, however, those persons have been guilty of negligence or have expressly undertaken liability in such cases, *vis major* will not avail to free them from responsibility. So in the case of letting and hiring, the Roman-Dutch law, following the Roman law (*Digest*, 19, 2), allows the lessee to claim a remission or abatement of rent in respect of loss or damage caused to him by *vis major*, as where he has been deprived of the beneficial enjoyment by the invasion of a foreign enemy or where agricultural land has been rendered unusually unproductive owing to tempests, inundation, and such like causes (*Rubidge* v. *Hadley*, 2 Menz. 174; *Rex* v. *Stamp*, 1 Kotzé, 1877–81, p. 63; *Partridge* v. *Adams*, [1904] T.S. 472; *Hansen, Schrader & Co.* v. *Kopelowitz*, [1903] T.S. 707; Voet's *Comm.* 19, 2, 23–24; Grotius' *Introd.* 3, 19, 2; Schorer, *Note* 394). As regards Cape Colony, such grounds of remission of rent have been abolished by Act 8 of 1879, sec. 7, which provides that "in the absence of any special stipulations to the contrary contained in any contract of lease, no lease of land shall become void or voidable, nor shall the rent accruing under such lease be incapable of being recovered on the ground that the property leased has through inundation, tempest, or such like unavoidable misfortune produced nothing." In *United Mines of Bultfontein* v. *De Beers Consolidated Mines* (17 S.C. 419) it was held that the words "such like unavoidable misfortune" include war.

Viva voce, orally.

Voetgangers (D.), in Ordinance 27 of 1907 (O.R.C.), sec. 1, is defined to mean "such locusts [as therein defined] while in their earlier stages, before they are able to fly, otherwise known as 'hoppers.'" The ordinary meaning of *voetganger* is a person who proceeds on foot. *See* LOCUSTS.

Voetstoots (D.), a term applied to sales of property without any warranty. *See* MET DEN VOET TE STOOTEN. See *Wilcken and Ackermann* v. *Klomfass* ([1904] T.H. at p. 96); also Van Leeuwen's *Comm.* Kotzé's trans. 4, 18, 7.

Void, having no legal force; wholly ineffectual.

Voidable, that which is capable of being made void.

Volenti non fit injuria, to one consenting no wrong is done. In other words, no one can complain of an act by which he is injured if he himself has consented to it. Thus an action will not lie where two persons enter into a boxing contest in the course of which one injures the other, provided the injury be inflicted in accordance with the rules of the game (Voet's *Comm.* 5, 1, 2). So, where the lessor of a house, wishing to repair the roof, which was becoming dangerous, gave due notice to the tenant to leave, and the tenant, having refused to do so, was injured by a portion of the roof falling during the work of repair, it was held that the tenant could not succeed in a claim for damages (*Davids* v. *Mendelsohn*, 15 S.C. 367; 8 C.T.R. 410). Upon the same principle, if a person entraps another into communicating the contents of a libel to a third party, he cannot be heard to complain of the communication (*Bennett* v. *Morris*, 10 S.C. 227).

The maxim is frequently urged as a defence to actions for damages for personal injuries sustained by servants in the course of their employment. In *Waring & Gillow, Ltd.*, v. *Sherborne* ([1904] T.S. at p. 344), INNES, C.J., said: "The maxim embodies a principle which, when confined within right limits, is both just and equitable. A man who consents to suffer an injury can as a general rule have no right to complain. He who, knowing and realising a danger, voluntarily undertakes to undergo it, has only himself to blame for the consequences. But like so many other maxims, the one under consideration needs to be employed cautiously and with circumspection. The principle is clear; the difficulty lies in the application of it—in deciding, in other words, under the circumstances of each particular case whether the injured man was *volens* to undertake the risk. A consideration of the grounds upon which the doctrine rests, and of the cases in which its scope has been discussed, leads to the conclusion that in order to render the maxim applicable it must be clearly shown that the risk was known, that it was realised, and that it was voluntarily undertaken. Knowledge, appreciation, consent—these are the essential elements; but knowledge does not invariably imply appreciation, and both together are not necessarily equivalent to consent."

Volksraad Besluit (D.), a resolution of the Volksraad. *See* RESOLUTIEN.

Volopbetaalde aandeelen (D.), fully paid up shares. *See* AANDEEL.

Voluntary confession. "It has always been considered by the court that this means that there must be no inducement or holding out of any hope of obtaining an advantage through the confession. Under such circumstances the court has always regarded as improper any expression which may operate as an encouragement to the accused to say something in the hope or under the impression that his position would be better than if he kept silence, and has refused confessions made in this way" (*per* KOTZÉ, C.J., in *The State* v. *Adam*, 1 Off. Rep. at p. 358).

Voluntary escape. In *Queen* v. *Loftus* (12 S.C. 434), where a prisoner—an assistant matron of a gaol—was charged with wrongfully, unlawfully, voluntarily and contemptuously permitting a prisoner to escape and go at large, DE VILLIERS, C.J., said: "*Voluntary escape*, with which the prisoner is charged, is not an offence known to the law of the [Cape] Colony. . . . For offences described by a single word in the Dutch law it is not difficult to find an exact English equivalent, such as 'theft' for *diefstal*, but where the Dutch law only furnishes a more or less lengthy definition, the nearest English equivalent must be found. 'Voluntarily allowing an escape' would be a very clumsy appellation, and instead of it the expression *voluntary escape* has been borrowed from the English law and used in the indictment. It is a somewhat ungrammatical expression applied to a person who allows another to escape, but it is sufficiently intelligible, more especially when read in connection with the detailed description of the offence contained in the indictment. . . . In the Roman law and earlier Dutch law a gaoler who allowed a prisoner to escape was liable, under certain circumstances, to the same punishment as the prisoner himself, but we have the authority of Groenewegen (*ad Cod.* 9, 4, 4) and Voet (*Comm.* 48, 3, 8) that in their time the punishment was discretionary." See also *Queen* v. *McDonald* (13 S.C. 397).

Voluntary surrender, the application to the Chief Justice or a judge of the Supreme or other competent court of a person, whose liabilities exceed his assets, for the acceptance of the surrender of his estate as insolvent. Such application is made upon petition in writing setting forth that such person is insolvent and is desirous of surrendering his estate for the benefit of his creditors. The judge to whom such petition is presented may direct that such person shall appear before him to be examined touching his insolvency or to require such proof thereof by affidavit of the insolvent and others, as to the judge may seem fit, or to direct the insolvent to appear before a commissioner to be examined concerning his affairs. Upon being satisfied as to the insolvency, the judge may accept the surrender of the estate, and by order under his hand direct that it should be placed under sequestration in the hands of the Master of the Supreme Court. In practice the debtor gives notice of his intention to surrender, frames a petition to the court and annexes thereto certain schedules in the prescribed form; these schedules comprise a balance-sheet with other statements showing the assets, movable and immovable, and the liabilities, secured and unsecured, all being verified by affidavit. After the lapse of a certain period the petition and schedules are presented to the court or a judge for acceptance, and are then dealt with in manner described above. The court will refuse acceptance if it appears that the surrender would not benefit creditors. A voluntary surrender may be made (1) by the insolvent himself; (2) by an authorised attorney of the insolvent if the insolvent himself is absent from the colony; (3) by the executors or curators of an estate; (4) by a partnership firm. As to *voluntary surrenders*, see Ordinance 6 of 1843 (C.C.), secs. 2 and 3; Law 47 of 1887 (N.), secs. 7–9; Law 13 of 1895 (T.), secs. 2 *et seq.*; O.R.C. Law Book, chap. 104, sec. 2.

Voluntary winding-up. A voluntary winding-up of a company takes place (*a*) whenever the period, if any, fixed for its duration in its articles has expired; or whenever according to the articles the period has arrived for its dissolution, and the shareholders in general meeting have resolved that it shall be wound-up voluntarily; (*b*) whenever the company has passed a resolution requiring the company to be wound-up voluntarily or otherwise agreeing to such winding-up. In some of the South African colonies such a resolution must be a "special resolution." See the Cape Companies Act (25 of 1892), sec. 178; and the Transvaal Companies Act (31 of 1909), sec. 156; Ordinance 2 of 1895 (R.), sec. 128.

Volunteer, in Ordinance 37 of 1904 (T.), sec. 1, means "any officer, warrant officer, non-commissioned officer or man belonging to a volunteer corps and enrolled under this Ordinance;" and so, too, in Ordinance 35 of 1905 (O.R.C.), sec. 1.

Voluptuariae impensae, expenses which neither preserve the property nor increase its market value, but merely gratify the caprice or fancy of a particular individual. See *United Building Society* v. *Smookler's Trustees* ([1906] T.S. at p. 627).

Vonnis (D.), sentence; judgment. See Wessels' *History*, p. 183.

Voogd (D.) [pl. *voogden*], guardian.

Voorkeurrecht (D.), a preferent right.

Voter, a person who is legally entitled to vote at a parliamentary, divisional council, municipal or some other election. See Act 40 of 1889 (C.C.), sec. 4; Act 48 of 1899 (C.C.); Act 26 of 1902 (C.C.), sec. 2.

As to voting at Natal Parliamentary elections, see Charter of Natal of the 15th July, 1856; Law 11 of 1865 relating to natives; Law 2 of 1883; Law 28 of 1887; Law 29 of 1887 especially; Law 5 of 1889; Law 18 of 1892; Act 8 of 1896.

As to *voter* in Transvaal, see Ordinance 32 of 1902, sec. 3.

As to the Orange River Colony, see Ordinance 6 of 1904, secs. 29 *et seq.*; Ordinance 12 of 1904, sec. 5; Ordinance 29 of 1905, sec. 10.

Voucher, any paper, document or receipt which furnishes evidence of the correctness of accounts, or evidence of the payment of money.

Voyage policy "is one in which the limits of the voyage are designated in the policy by specifying a certain place at which it is to begin (called the *terminus a quo*); and another at which it is to end (called the *terminus ad quem*); as, for instance, where a ship is insured 'at and from London to Buenos Ayres'" (Arnould's *Marine Insurance*, 7th ed. sec. 9).

Vremdeling (D.). Decker in a note to Van Leeuwen's *Comm.* (Kotzé's trans. vol. 1, p. 69) says: "What requires most consideration is the precise meaning of the term *vremdeling* (stranger), which, in truth, seems to denote nothing else than a person who is subject to some other sovereign, and therefore those persons are not *vremdelingen* (strangers), who, although by birth foreigners, have nevertheless come to reside under our jurisdiction; nor are they strangers who were born in Dutch India; nor, again, are they who were procreated abroad in a foreign country by their parents who are in the service of the Republic. From this every one can readily perceive of what great utility it is to have a correct idea of the above term (*vremdeling*)."

Vroedschappen (D.), the municipal council; the burgomaster and aldermen. In the Netherlands the government and guardianship of the towns were vested in the council and court of each town. The members of the council, who also were called *vroedschappen*, remained in office permanently, and the members of the court were chosen annually (Van Leeuwen's *Comm.* Kotzé's trans. vol. 1, p. 15). See also Wessels' *History*, p. 74.

Vroon, Frone, Frana (D.), exemption from all burdens, taxes and assessments, &c. As the Dutch Counts were exempt from all land taxes, their lands and waters were also called *vroonen* (Meyer's *Woordenschat*).

Vroondiensten (D.), services for which no salary or recompense was given.

Waaterleiding (D.), the right of leading off water from another's water. *See* AQUAEDUCTUS.

Water-brief (D.). *See* BYL-BRIEF.

Water court, a special court appointed by the Governor under the Cape Water Act (40 of 1899), and the Transvaal Irrigation Act (27 of 1908), sec. 53, to try disputes in connection with the diversion, use and appropriation of public water. Under the former Act the court consists of a resident magistrate having jurisdiction over the whole or some portion of the water district of the court and two landowners selected from a list of water court assessors not less than ten or more than twenty-five in number appointed for any water district by the Governor (sec. 3); under the latter Act it consists of three persons appointed by the Governor, one of whom, the president, must be a judge of the Supreme Court, a resident magistrate, or an advocate or attorney. From the decision of either water court an appeal lies to the Supreme Court.

Watergang (D.). *See* APPROACH TO WATER.

Waterhaling (D.), the right of drawing water from another's well or cistern. *See* AQUAEHAUSTUS.

Waterloozing (D.), a rural servitude conferring the right of drainage, "that is, the right to drain or discharge the water from one's own land on to that of another" (Grotius' *Introd.*, Maasdorp's trans. p. 152).

Waterrecht (D.), a waterright. A term used in the Transvaal Gold Law (15 of 1898, now repealed) signifying certain rights granted by the Government to a claimholder for the use of water within certain boundaries for the purpose of winning gold from his claims. *See* WATERRIGHT.

Waterright, a right or permission granted by Government to the holder of a prospecting or digger's license, or some other form of mining license, entitling such holder to collect, store, convey and use water upon and from his *waterright* for the purpose of treating ore or minerals upon his claims or other approved place. For *waterrights* in Natal, see Act 43 of 1899, secs. 70–80. For those in the Transvaal, see Act 35 of 1908, secs. 56 *et seq.*, and third schedule, secs. 14 *et seq.*; in the Orange River Colony, see Ordinance 3 of 1904, secs. 98 *et seq.*; Ordinance 4 of 1904, secs. 87 *et seq.*

Waterworks. The term *waterworks* is defined in the Cape Public Health Amendment Act (23 of 1897), sec. 2, to mean and include "streams, springs, wells, pumps, reservoirs, cisterns, tanks, aqueducts, cuts, sluices, mains, pipes, culverts, engines, and all machinery, lands, buildings and things for supplying, or used for supplying water." See also definition in Kingwilliamstown Additional Water

Supply Act, 6 of 1906 (C.C.), sec. 1; in East London Additional Water Supply Act, 26 of 1906 (C.C.), sec. 1; in Orange River Colony Public Health Ordinance, 31 of 1907, sec. 1.

Wager policy. "A *wager policy* is one in which it appears by its terms that the insured has no interest, or, in other words, runs no risk. It is a mere bet, and is known by the insertion of certain clauses—such as, 'without further proof of interest than the policy,' 'interest or no interest,' and their equivalents—having for their object to relieve the insured from the necessity of proving his interest in case of loss. In England such policies are prohibited, and such clauses are proof conclusive that the contract is a wager. In this country [America], however, they are only *primâ facie* evidence, and may be explained" (May on *Insurance*, 4th ed. sec. 33; see also Arnould's *Marine Insurance*, 7th ed. secs. 311 *et seq.* where the *wager policy* is fully discussed from the point of view of English law).

Wages. (1) The compensation or remuneration agreed upon between a master and his servant as being payable to the servant, generally at stated periods, or sometimes according to the amount of work performed; the latter is usually called "piece work." Servants are to some extent protected in the payment of their *wages* by Cape Act 18 of 1873, and the Cape Companies Act 25 of 1892, sec. 224; in the latter the liquidators of a company are authorised to pay in full arrears of salary and *wages* due to any servant of the company for a period not exceeding six months preceding its winding up; also by the Transvaal Law 13 of 1880.

In the Transvaal case *Edwards* v. *Rex* ([1903] T.S. 449), which was an appeal, the master had been charged with having wrongfully withheld his servant's *wages*; he was acquitted, but the magistrate gave judgment in favour of the servant, under sec. 21 of Law 13 of 1880, for one month's *wages* and one month's board in lieu of notice; the court, on appeal, held that the section applied only to cases where *wages* had actually been earned, and not to prospective *wages*.

(2) Under the Workmen's Compensation Act, 40 of 1905 (C.C.), *wages* is by sec. 4 defined as follows: "*Wages* means the average weekly earnings of the workman at the time of injury. If the *wages* are paid at the time of the injury at a rate per hour, the average weekly *wages* are to be taken as forty-eight times the rate per hour. If the *wages* are so paid at a rate per day, the average weekly *wages* are to be taken as six times the rate per day. If the *wages* are so paid at a rate per week, the average weekly *wages* are to be taken as that rate. If the *wages* are so paid at a rate per month, the average weekly *wages* are to be taken as one-fifty-second of twelve times the rate per month. No overtime payments are to be taken into account." The Transvaal Workmen's Compensation Act (36 of 1907), sec. 1, contains a similar definition, but adds, "If the *wages* are so paid at a rate calculated on work done, the average weekly earnings shall be computed in such manner as is best calculated to give the rate per week at which the workman was being remunerated; provided that where

by reason of the shortness of time during which the workman has been at work for the employer it is impracticable at the date of the injury to compute the rate of remuneration, regard may be had to the average weekly amount which during the six months immediately previous to the injury was earned by a person employed at similar work on the same terms of remuneration; and the average weekly earnings shall for the purpose of calculating *wages* mean the net sums paid to a workman by an employer after deduction of the value of any labour or material supplied by the employer and of overtime payments and of any sums usually paid by the employer to the workman to cover any special expenses entailed on him by the nature of his work."

Waiver, the passing by or declining to take advantage of a legal right, whereby such legal right becomes lost. "The performance of conditions precedent may of course be waived by the persons entitled to their performance; but any *waiver* to be binding must be made intentionally and with a knowledge of the circumstances of the case" (Fry's *Specific Performance*, 4th ed. sec. 987). "A *waiver* of a condition precedent amounts to a renunciation of a right, and such a renunciation cannot be inferred except from clear evidence" (*per* DE VILLIERS, C.J., in *Stewart* v. *Ryall*, 5 S.C. 153). "Objections grounded on the lapse of time are waived by a course of conduct inconsistent with the intention of insisting on such an objection: and in this respect it is immaterial whether time was originally of the essence or was subsequently engrafted on the contract" (Fry's *Specific Performance*, 4th ed. sec. 1120).

Waldvester, Houtvester (D.), a forester, called in the middle ages and under the feudal system *valvassor*, whose duty it was to protect forests and wastes.

Wandelbaar (D.), that which can be alienated.

Ward. (1) A person under the care of a guardian.
(2) A division of a municipality or borough. See Act 34 of 1907 (T.), sec. 2.

Wards' Book, a book kept in the office of the Master of the Supreme Court of the Cape Colony under sec. 27 of Ordinance 105 of 1833, containing a debit and credit account of moneys paid out or received by the Master on behalf of absent persons or of persons or estates under guardianship.

Warden, "any officer, male or female, appointed to manage and be in charge of a reformatory or portion thereof, and any person lawfully acting for such officer" (Ordinance 6 of 1906 (T.), sec. 3).

Warehouse. "It is a little difficult to draw the line of distinction between a building which is and a building which is not a *warehouse*. Some decisions have been given by which certain lines of definition have been excluded. It is no longer possible to argue that a *warehouse* is something limited to a building for the storage of goods in connection with a dock, wharf or quay, nor that it can only be a building with water contiguous. Nor can it be limited so as to apply only to a building where the public can send their goods to be stored for them, as in the case of the large furniture repositories. The word is applicable to a building used by the owner for the storage of his goods, though it has no connection of any sort with water transit" (*per* Collins, M.R., in *Green* v. *Britten and Another*, 89 L.T. at p. 714; [1904] 1 K.B. 350; 20 T.L.R. 116).

Under the Customs Management Act, 10 of 1872 (C.C.), the term *warehouse* signifies "any place, whether house, shed, yard or other place in which goods entered to be warehoused upon importations may be lodged, kept and secured without payment of duty." See also Queen's Warehouse; Act 13 of 1899 (N.), secs. 4 and 80.

In the Cape Excise Spirits Act (18 of 1884), sec. 2, the term *warehouse* is defined to mean "an excise *warehouse* approved as a general *warehouse* for the deposit of spirits, and includes an approved *warehouse* on the premises of a distiller, and a customs *warehouse*." The definition given in the Additional Taxation Act, 26 of 1904 (C.C.), sec. 2, differs slightly from this, and reads as follows: "*Warehouse* means an excise *warehouse* approved as a general or as a bonded *warehouse* for the deposit of spirits, and includes an approved *warehouse* on the premises of a distiller, an agricultural distiller, and a customs *warehouse*." See also Act 11 of 1905 (C.C.), sec. 1; Act 25 of 1905 (C.C.), sec. 1. See Act 33 of 1901 (N.), sec. 3.

In the Transvaal Railways Regulation Act (13 of 1908), sec. 2, *warehouse* is defined to mean "any building or place provided or used by the Administration, or by any railway servant in charge of a station, for the purpose of storing or depositing goods. Where it is more convenient to the Administration that the goods to be warehoused shall remain in trucks, those trucks when placed in a siding, shall for the purposes of this Act be deemed a *warehouse*." For similar definition see Act 29 of 1908 (O.R.C.), sec. 2.

"**Warned off,**" by a turf club, see *Sutton* v. *Livingstone and Secker* (27 N.L.R. at p. 55).

Warranty, a guarantee or undertaking express or implied.

Waste land. "The word 'waste' has different meanings, according to the context in which it is employed. As employed in the 111th section [of Act 26 of 1893 (C.C.)] the term *waste land* appears to me to mean land which is not registered in any one's name, and to the occupation of which no one has a *bonâ fide* claim" (*per* De Villiers, C.J., in *Colonial Government* v. *Town Council, Capetown*, 19 S.C. at p. 98).

Wasted expenditure. *See* Actual Cost.

Way of necessity. *See* Road of Necessity; Via necessaria.

Wedlock, matrimony; the wedded state.

Weederzaak, Weederzaaker (D.), an adversary, opponent.

Weener (D.). *See* WEWENAAR.

Weeskamer (D.), the Orphan Chamber; now replaced by the office of the Master of the Supreme Court (or, in some colonies, the High Court).

Well-born men "were originally those descended from free and respectable parents and ancestors" (Van Leeuwen's *Comm.* Kotzé's trans. vol. 1, p. 66).

Werf (D.), an empty space about houses or buildings. *Gemeene werf* denotes the place where the neighbours assembled in order to discuss and dispose of matters relating to their district or town. *Werf* also formerly denoted a shop, country house or place. It also signifies a wharf.

In South Africa the *werf* is the open space round about the homestead on a farm. Under the Gold Law (15 of 1898, now repealed) of the late South African Republic, the owner of a farm could retain and reserve the *werf* for himself upon the proclamation of such farm as a public digging.

Wet (D.) [pl. *wetten*], law; statutory enactment.

Wewenaar, Weener (D.), a widower, one who mourns (*weener*) for his deceased wife.

Wharfage, accommodation for vessels at a wharf; the charge made for such accommodation.

"Whenever required to do so." "An Act which enacted that a pilot was to deliver up his license to the pilotage authorities *whenever required to do so.* would call for implicit obedience to the letter, however arbitrarily the power which it conferred might be misused, and although the withdrawal of the license would in effect amount to a dismissal of the pilot from his employment" (Maxwell's *Interpretation of Statutes*, 4th ed. p. 11).

Whipping. Under the Native Territories Penal Code (Act 24 of 1886), sec. 10, "*whipping* shall consist of the infliction on a male person, who shall not have attained the age of sixteen years, of a number of strokes or cuts, not exceeding at any one time twenty-five, with a cane or rod, which last correction shall be administered by such person in such private place as the court shall appoint; and in case the father or reputed father shall in person express a desire to correct such offender himself in the manner adjudged by the court, it shall be lawful for the court to permit him to do so in the presence of any suitable person selected by the court to witness the infliction of such correction. . . . No female shall be liable to be flogged or whipped." See also Proclamation 21 of 1902 (T.), sec. 36; and Ordinance 1 of 1903 (T.), secs. 256–60.

Whisky. "*Whisky* means a spirituous liquor derived from grain by fermentation and distillation, the volatile constituents of which (except water, as provided for in sec. 15 [of the Act]) are derived solely from the above material" (the Wine, Brandy, Whisky and Spirits Act, 42 of 1906 (C.C.), sec. 14). *See* BLENDED WHISKY; MALT WHISKY.

White. The word *white* as used in sec. 11 of the Municipal Elections Ordinance, 1903 (T.), is substantially equivalent to "of European descent" (*Swarts and Appel* v. *Pretoria Town Council*, [1905] T.S. 621).

Wholesale, in large quantities, as distinguished from retail. The term *wholesale* was discussed in *Queen* v. *Strangman* (5 S.C. 82), where it was held that a miller who buys colonial grain and grinds it into flour is not a *wholesale* dealer, merely because he sells it in quantities of more than 100 lbs. in the absence of any evidence to show what is meant in the trade by *wholesale* dealing. In this case DE VILLIERS, C.J., remarked: "The common law affords no definition of the term *wholesale*, and the only enactment which bears upon the point is contained in the 22nd section of Act 3 of 1864;" the latter, he held, did not apply to the case then under discussion. Sec. 22 of Act 3 of 1864 (C.C.) was repealed by Act 38 of 1887 (C.C.).

See *Rex* v. *Reece* (21 S.C. at p. 199). *See* also RETAIL.

Wholesale dealer. *See* WHOLESALE. The term *wholesale dealer* is defined in the Cape Additional Taxation Act (36 of 1904) to include "any person who carries on the business of a retailer or bottle-store keeper on the same premises where he conducts his wholesale business."

See *Rex* v. *Reece* (21 S.C. at p. 199).

Widow, a married woman whose husband is dead.

Widower, a married man whose wife is dead.

Wijk (D.), a ward; a portion of a district.

Wilful misconduct. *See* SERIOUS AND WILFUL MISCONDUCT.

Wills. "A *will* is a declaration made by any person during his lifetime as to what he wishes to become of his property after his death. It is either a testament or a codicil" (Maasdorp's *Institutes*, vol. 1, p. 115). The proper form of execution of *wills* is prescribed by statute law. Morice in his *English and Roman-Dutch Law* (2nd ed. p. 277) defines a *will* as follows: "In Roman-Dutch law a *will* is properly a general expression meaning any declaration made by a person as to what he wishes to become of his property after his death, *voluntatis nostrae sententia de eo quod quis post mortem suam fieri velit* (the declaration of our wishes as to what is to be done after death) (Voet, 28, 1, 3). It includes a 'testament' or *will* solemnly executed with the necessary formalities and a 'codicil,' which originally required fewer formalities and contained a less complete disposition."

There are various classes of *wills*, viz.: (1) Notarial *wills;* (2) mutual *wills;* (3) closed or sealed *wills;* (4) underhand *wills;* and (5) privileged *wills.* Under privileged *wills* are included holograph *wills*, nuncupative *wills* and *wills* made by soldiers or sailors while on active service.

Winding-up, a term applied to the liquidation of a company.

Window-right, an urban servitude. It "is the right of having a window hanging or opening over another's land, which includes within itself a right to free light, which otherwise no one is obliged to permit" (Van Leeuwen's *Comm.* Kotzé's trans. vol. 1, p. 291).

Wine. In the Cape Colony *wine* is defined by the Compounded Spirits Regulation Act (20 of 1890), sec. 2, to mean "fermented liquor produced from grapes, the husks or stalks of grapes, and raisins, the produce of this [Cape] Colony, without the addition of any foreign substance other than water." In the Additional Taxation Act, 36 of 1904 (C.C.), sec. 2, it is defined to mean "*wine* of any description produced within the [Cape] Colony, and includes grape juice, grapes, husks, and stalks of grapes and raisins." See Act 42 of 1906 (C.C.), sec. 5.

In Natal, in Act 33 of 1901, sec. 3, *wine* means "any alcoholic liquor produced from the juice of fruits by fermentation."

Wine farmer is defined in the Cape Excise Spirits Act (18 of 1884), sec. 2, to mean "a farmer who cultivates vines on land in his own occupation, and who produces wine from grapes grown on such vines." The same definition is given in the Additional Taxation Act, 36 of 1904 (C.C.), sec. 2.

Wine vinegar. In the Cape Wine, Brandy, Whisky and Spirits Act (19 of 1908), sec. 16, "*wine vinegar* means the product made by the alcoholic and subsequent acetous fermentation, without distillation, of the juice of the grapes, or by the acetous fermentation, without distillation, of pure natural wine." *See* VINEGAR.

Wisselbrief (D.), bill of exchange.

Wisselrecht (D.), the law of bills of exchange.

Witchcraft, sorcery. See an article on this subject in 8 C.L.J. 210; see also Native Territories Penal Code (Act 24 of 1886, secs. 171–75). As to suppression of imputation or practice of pretended *witchcraft* in Cape Colony, see the Witchcraft Suppression Act, 2 of 1895 (C.C.). See also ISANUSI; UMTAKATI.

See Transvaal Crimes Ordinance (26 of 1904), sec. 29.

Witevrouwe, Witikewyf (D.), a soothsayer, magician, witch. *Witvrouwe* also denotes a widow, for women who were in mourning for their deceased husbands used to wear white, just as the Romans used to do.

"Without any deduction or abatement whatever." "It appears to me . . that these words should be confined to such deduction or abatement as might reasonably have been in the contemplation of the parties at the time when the lease was executed" (*per* DE VILLIERS, C.J., in *United Mines of Bultfontein* v. *De Beers Consolidated Mines, Ltd.*, 17 S.C. at p. 425).

Witikewyf (D.). *See* WITEVROUWE.

Witvrouwe (D.) *See* WITEVROUWE.

Woman. In the Cape Native Territories Penal Code (24 of 1886), sec. 5, the word *woman* is used to denote a female human being of any age.

A *woman* may be admitted as a sworn translator of the Supreme Court of the Cape Colony (*Ex parte Van Pelt*, 13 S.C. 476).

Woodreeve (D.). The *woodreve* and master companions constituted a special court in the Netherlands for the trial of matters concerning the chase and wildernesses. "All cases connected with the downs and the chase cannot be decided by any judge except the *woodreeve* and master companions. The *woodreeve* is the complainant and the master companions are the judges, selected by the county of Holland from among the principal of the nobility. They are three in number, and do justice and give sentence upon the complaint and demand of the *woodreeve* or his deputy, summarily without any set form of proceeding; and by virtue of the Ordinance of 26th December, 1517, they used to sit four times in the year" (Van Leeuwen's *Comm.* Kotzé's trans. vol. 2, p. 595).

Work. (1) This term is defined in the Cape Workmen's Compensation Act (40 of 1905), sec. 4, to mean "any employment in any trade, business or public undertaking in the [Cape] Colony on land or upon or within the territorial waters of the colony, but shall not mean or include domestic, messenger or errand service, or employment in agriculture." In the Transvaal Workmen's Compensation Act (36 of 1907), sec. 1, *work* shall mean "employment at or about any trade, industry, business or public undertaking in this colony, including employment in agriculture, but shall not include domestic service; and 'employment in agriculture' shall mean the employment of a workman in agriculture by an employer who habitually and regularly has in his employ one or more workmen not being members of his family engaged in agriculture; and 'agriculture' shall mean any work connected with or incidental to the tilling of the soil, stock rearing, or farming operations."

(2) In its sense as a *work* of art it is defined in the Cape Copyright in Works of Art Act (46 of 1905) to mean "a painting or drawing and the design thereof, a photograph and the negative thereof, and any positives or copies made therefrom, an engraving or a piece of sculpture."

In the Natal Copyright Act (17 of 1897), sec. 3, *work* includes book and work of art. *See* SERIAL WORK.

Work of art. This term is defined in the Cape Copyright in Works of Art Act (46 of 1905), to mean "a painting or drawing and the design thereof, a photograph and the negative thereof, and any positives or copies made therefrom, an engraving or a piece of sculpture." The definition in the Natal Copyright Act (17 of 1897), sec. 3, is as follows: "*Work of art* means a painting or drawing and the design thereof, or a photograph and the negative thereof, or an engraving."

Workable. In the Mineral Law Amendment Act, 16 of 1907 (C.C.), sec. 33, *workable* is defined to mean "the occurrence of minerals in such quantities as to indicate a probable profitable result in working."

Working capital, an expression signifying that portion of the capital of a company which is to be specially applied to its development, equipment and working.

In the Cape Colony in the Precious Stones Act Amendment Act, 1907, sec. 19, "the term *working capital* shall be taken to mean the actual capital expended on the equipment and development of the mine after the date of proclamation, but shall not include the purchase-price, if any, paid by the mineholder for the mine or any mining rights, or any costs of prospecting previous to proclamation."

In the Orange River Colony Mining of Precious Stones Ordinance (4 of 1904), sec. 47, as amended by Ordinance 16 of 1906, sec. 2, *working capital* means "the actual capital expended on the equipment and development of the mine after the date of proclamation, together with a sum to be decided upon by the Board prescribed in sec. 52 [of the Ordinance] as necessary for the purpose of carrying on mining operations, and shall include any sum paid by the mineholder in respect of land or any right over land acquired by him under the provisions of secs. 87 and 89, but shall not include the purchase-price, if any, paid by him for the mine or any mining rights or any costs of prospecting previous to proclamation: provided that whenever it shall be shown to the satisfaction of the Lieutenant-Governor that prior to the said date of proclamation capital has been expended by the mineholder on the acquisition or erection of plant or machinery for the said mine, which plant or machinery is in existence and necessary for the working of the mine, subsequent to such proclamation, the whole or such part of the cost of such plant or machinery and of the erection thereof as may be shown to the satisfaction of the Lieutenant-Governor to be the fair value of the same at the said date of proclamation may be included in the amount of the said *working capital;* provided always that no moneys expended or applied by the said mineholder or other person, whether before or after such proclamation, for the flotation of any syndicate or company or the raising of capital in connection with the said mine shall be included in such *working capital.*" It must be added that this definition has special application to mines in which, under the Ordinance, the Crown holds an undivided share; the owner being entitled to work the mine and to provide the *working capital* (see secs. 40–42 of the Ordinance).

Workman. The term *workman* is defined in the Cape Workman's Compensation Act (40 of 1905) to mean "any one employed in the [Cape] Colony or the territorial waters thereof by any person on, in or about a work to which this Act applies, whether in manual labour or otherwise, and whether the agreement is one of service or apprenticeship or otherwise and is expressed or implied, is oral or in writing, but shall not include a contractor or subcontractor. Any reference to a *workman* who has been injured shall, where the *workman* is dead, include a reference to his legal personal representative or to his dependents or other person to whom compensation is payable under this Act." In the Transvaal Workmen's Compensation Act (36 of 1907), *workman* is defined as being any white person engaged by an employer to perform work under agreement of service or of apprenticeship or otherwise, whether such agreement be expressed or implied, be oral or in writing and whether payment be made by time or calculated on work done; provided that the term *workman* shall not include (*a*) a person whose wages in respect of his work exceed five hundred pounds a year; or (*b*) a person whose work is of a casual nature, and who is employed to do work for an employer other than in such employer's trade, business or industry; or (*c*) an outworker: that is to say, a person to whom articles or materials are given out by an employer to be made up, cleaned, washed, altered, ornamented, finished or repaired or adapted for sale on premises not under the control and management of the employer; or (*d*) a person who contracts or subcontracts for the carrying out of work, and himself engages other persons (white or coloured) independently of his employer to perform such work.

Wort, in the Natal Act 33 of 1901, sec. 3, means "any liquid or substance containing saccharine matter before any fermentation has commenced."

Writers to the Signet, a body of law practitioners of ancient origin in Scotland; they had many important privileges, few of which remain; they practise before the Court of Session or Supreme Court of Scotland; and their duties correspond with those of a solicitor in England. Sec. 19 of the Cape Charter of Justice of 1832 authorised the admission of *Writers to the Signet* in Scotland as attorneys of the Supreme Court, and a similar provision has since been made in the other South African colonies. They are frequently known by the abbreviation "W.S."

Writing. "In every law expressions relating to writing shall, unless the contrary intention appears, be construed as including references to typewriting, printing, lithography, photography, and other modes of representing or reproducing words in a visible form" (Interpretation of Laws Proclamation, 15 of 1902 (T.), sec. 2). "When anything is directed to be done in *writing*, such direction shall, unless the contrary intention appears, be construed so as to include printing, lithography, and other modes of representing and reproducing words in a visible form" (the Laws Settlement and Interpretation Ordinance, 3 of 1902 (O.R.C.). sec. 10. See also Ordinance 10 of 1903 (O.R.C.), sec. 2).

Writing includes typewriting; see *Lawrence and Others* v. *Executors of Lawrence* (25 N.L.R. 80).

Year. In Natal, in Law 3 of 1887, schedule, a *year* is defined to mean "twelve successive calendar months, or from one part in a month in one year to the corresponding part in the month of the same name in another year, as the case may be."

Zaakweldig (D.), accessory, guilty of a crime.

Zegelrecht (D.), stamp duty.

Zeinde, zenne, zend, zeinte (D.), a meeting, a church-meeting or synod. The term is derived from *zenden*, to send, because those who attend the meeting are sent from all parts.

Zeinte (D.). *See* ZEINDE.

Zend (D.). *See* ZEINDE.

Zenne (D.). *See* ZEINDE.

Zwaardmaaghe or **Zwaertmaaghe** (D.), a relation on the side of the father. *See* SPILLEMAAGHE.

Zwazeling (D.), a brother-in-law.

Zwazeneede (D.), a sister-in-law.

Zweeghel (D.), a brother-in-law.

THE END.

Spotted something that isn't quite right?

Let us know and we'll fix it for future reprints.
And as a thank you for your diligence, we'll
send you a free Sothis book of your choice.

publisher@sothis.press

This page intentionally left blank

Made in the USA
Monee, IL
06 November 2026

68105236R00377